A Story of the Southern Synod
of the
Evangelical and Reformed Church

by

THE REV. BANKS J. PEELER, D.D.

PUBLISHED UNDER THE SUPERVISION OF
THE BOARD OF EDITORS, AND
AUTHORIZED BY THE SYNOD

REV. FRANK W. SNIDER, CHAIRMAN
REV. LONNIE A. CARPENTER, D.D.
MR. FRANK L. CLAPP
REV. AUBREY W. HEDRICK
MR. A. HOWARD WHITE

1740 - 1968

Dedication

This volume is dedicated to the Glory of God and in memory of devoted ministers and lay people of the Faith, who have by their labors established a rich and an abiding Christian heritage, and in honor of living sons and daughters of the Evangelical and Reformed Church who continue to emulate their example.

THE EDITOR

Rev. Banks J. Peeler, D.D.

THE BOARD OF EDITORS

Mr. Frank L. Clapp

Rev. Lonnie A. Carpenter, D.D.

Rev. Frank W. Snider

Mr. A. Howard White

Rev. Aubrey W. Hedrick

Preface

THIS IS THE FOURTH EFFORT at compiling the history of the former German Reformed Church in North Carolina. The first was "A Historical Sketch of the Classis of North Carolina" by George W. Welker printed in 1895, with Dr. Joseph L. Murphy as editor. The next was that of Dr. Jacob C. Clapp, editor entitled "Historic Sketch of the Reformed Church in North Carolina," published in 1908. In 1940, just after the Classis of North Carolina of the Reformed Church became Southern Synod of the Evangelical and Reformed Church, the "History of Southern Synod" by Dr. Jacob C. Leonard was published. Dr. Welker's first work was the basis for both of the later works on the history of the German Reformed Church in North Carolina. Both of the later histories have elaborated and brought up to the publishing date the history as it could be gathered and written.

History continues to be made. Twenty-eight years have passed since the History of Southern Synod was published. In that time World War II was fought. The merger of the Evangelical Synod of North America and the Reformed Church in the United States was consummated. And, now, the union of Congregational Christian churches and the Evangelical and Reformed Church is well in effect, and the former Reformed churches in North Carolina are a part of the United Church of Christ.

More than 100 ministers have come and gone among the congregations. Many congregations have completed new building programs. Most former charge alignments have been dissolved and some of them formed into new ones. Fifteen new congregations have been organized, fourteen of which continue to flourish. The history compiled by Dr. Leonard in 1940 has been long since sold out and is unavailable.

All of these factors, and others, led members of Southern Synod to see the need for a new and up-to-date history. This will be the last history written of the Southern Synod and the former German Reformed Church in North Carolina as an organized group. The Synod is now part of new geographical associations, having different boundaries than those of the original Classis and Synod.

The Synodical Council of Southern Synod invited its historian, the Rev. Frank W. Snider, to meet with it on November 7, 1963 for the purpose of discussing the possibility of writing a history of Southern Synod. As a result of this discussion, the president of Southern Synod appointed Rev. J. L. Levens, chairman, Rev. Frank

W. Snider and Mr. Henry Kennedy, Jr., a committee to study the subject and report its findings. On December 5, 1963, the committee reported to the Synodical Council. This report was referred to the Synod and presented to that body on April 30, 1964. It recommended that a history of Southern Synod be written. The report provided for a finance committee to be appointed by the president of Synod and an editorial board of five members to be named by the Synodical Council. One thousand dollars was appropriated to be used in writing the history. At a meeting of the Synodical Council held September 10, 1964, the president of Synod appointed a finance committee and the Board of Editors was named.

The Board of Editors began its work by asking each congregation and institution of the Synod to send in an up-to-date history. Records of all the pastors of Synod were requested and these up-dated by the chairman. Congregations and pastors generously responded. An additional $1,000 was set aside by the Synod which met in 1965, with which to employ an editor for writing the history. The Board of Editors was delighted in the fall of 1965 when Dr. Banks J. Peeler, retiring president of Southern Synod, accepted the appointment as editor and writer of this history.

With the efforts of Dr. Peeler added to those of the board, congregational histories were gathered and institutional histories were compiled, and the actual work was started. The burden of this effort has fallen upon Dr. Peeler. It has been a labor of love. He has spent two years reading, gathering material and writing the manuscript. Many miles have been traveled. A vast amount of correspondence has been handled. Numerous meetings have been held. All of this effort, plus love for and dedication to the Reformed heritage and people, have gone into the preparation of this work.

Resources are not available to adequately compensate for this invaluable contribution to the people of the Reformed Church in North Carolina. However, there are enduring intangible values—among them being the satisfaction of a "job well done," the joy and pride of knowing that readers will share this history for years to come, and the unalloyed pleasure of serving people whom one loves, and has served over a period of years.

It is the hope of the Board of Editors that this history will continue, and to some extent, complete the story of the Reformed Church and its successor the Evangelical and Reformed Church in the state of North Carolina. This volume is intended primarily as a readable story of the denomination. Thus, much valuable material could not be included. To have done so would have made the volume too large. Some oversights may also be apparent. These are unintentional. We have tried to choose wisely, including such factual information as we believe to be of greatest interest and significance.

We are grateful for the cooperation of pastors, congregational historians, committee members and others who have so graciously assisted us and responded to requests for material and information. Most of all we are grateful for the dedication of Dr. Banks J. Peeler and to God for his guidance in this important undertaking.

FRANK W. SNIDER, Chairman
The Board of Editors

Acknowledgements

READERS OF THIS VOLUME should be mindful of two important factors. The roots of Southern Synod and the churches represented by it, reach back to German settlements chiefly in North Carolina beginning about 1740. In order to make a consecutive record of these churches and their organized activities, the story must begin with that period, and end with the dissolution of the Synod in January 1968.

It is obvious, therefore, that no attempt could be made to be exhaustive. To do so would result in a much larger volume than could here be presented. However, every possible effort has been put forth to be thorough.

Material for this volume has been drawn from a multitude of sources. Appropriate reference has been made to those in the text as far as practical; also provided is a bibliography.

But these do not cover the very generous cooperation provided by pastors, congregational history committees and interested individuals, who have contributed valuable information by manuscript, anniversary brochures and pictures on file in the archives at Catawba College. Also, those who have read and criticized the text and offered helpful counsel, my wife, the board of editors, the finance committee and others.

For all of it I am deeply grateful.

THE EDITOR

Contents

CHAPTER I

Backgrounds

The Evangelical and Reformed Church

THE EVANGELICAL AND REFORMED CHURCH was established June 26, 1934 at Cleveland, Ohio. Meeting an appointment at 7 P.M. on that date official delegates of the Reformed Church in the United States assembled in Pilgrim Congregational Church, while those of the Evangelical Synod of North America awaited their arrival on the sidewalks outside Zion Evangelical Church. Forming a line two by two, one each of the uniting bodies, delegates marched to their pews inside the church where they heard official declarations and joined in partaking of the Sacrament of Holy Communion. Dr. Henry J. Christman, president of General Synod of the Reformed Church and Rev. Paul Press, president of the General Council of the Evangelical Synod, joined hands in the chancel. Dr. Christman remarked, "Blest be the tie that binds our hearts in Christian love," to which Mr. Press responded, "The fellowship of kindred minds is like to that above." With that symbolic gesture the spiritual union was consummated.

On the following morning the merger was implemented by the election of temporary officers, authorized by the plan of union to govern the United Church until a Constitution could be adopted. The Charter was granted under the laws of the State of New York. Dr. George W. Richards and Dr. Louis W. Goebel, chairmen of the two commissions on union, were elected president and vice president respectively of the Church. Six years later, in 1940, when General Synod convened at Lancaster, Pennsylvania, the Constitution was adopted.

At the time of the merger the Reformed Church in the United States consisted of six synods, fifty eight classes, 1,336 ministers, 1,697 congregations and 345,912 confirmed members. The Evangelical Synod of North America reported 21 districts, 1,300 ordained ministers, 1,243 congregations and 273,138 members. These figures obviously do not add up to one of the numerically major denominations in the Protestant family of churches, however, the Evangelical and Reformed Church was destined to be widely influencial in the area of inter-denominational cooperation during the years that have

1

followed. Dr. Samuel McCrea Calvert, General Secretary of the
Federal Council of the Churches of Christ, in an address delivered
on the occasion when the union was consummated, declared:

> This union . . . has far-reaching significance that transcends that of
> . . . other unions of the twentieth century, for the reason that, among
> other things, the two uniting churches . . . have entered upon it in such
> a spirit of complete mutual trust and respect that you have not had to
> define all the formal terms of agreement in advance. You have been
> willing to unite, and to work out the details of union afterwards in
> your united fellowship. You have become a single church without hav-
> ing drafted your constitution, without having set up a new doctrinal
> formula, without having decided how your various agencies are to be
> combined. You have not allowed any minor points of organization or of
> definition to obscure your unity of spirit and faith, or to become a bar-
> rier in your advance to a new expression of that unity. Your decision
> to unite and to trust to the future for the working out of the implica-
> tings of the union sets a new precedent in the history of American
> churches.[1]

There are factors in the cultures of these two communions which
made such a venture of faith not only possible but practical. Both
of them have roots in Germany and Switzerland dating back to the
Reformation. The Reformed lineage can be traced to the Palatinate
of Western Germany to the effort of Huldrich Zwingli in Zurich
and John Calvin in Geneva. Evangelicals stem from the predomi-
nantly Lutheran sections of Northern, Central and Eastern Germany. Recognizing that the Lutheran and Reformed churches
have a common heritage, the proposed Evangelical Union in 1817
in Prussia of the German states, opened the way for cooperation
without either body compromising any of their essential doctrines.
Therefore, both having the same national, racial, lingual and creedal
backgrounds, were destined to be confronted at some point in history with an opportunity for union.

Who are these people who have been so trustingly brought together into a new Communion? A very brief description of origins
will satisfy the purpose of this narrative. Dr. William Toth has
written the following lucid description of early German immigration to America.

> Our history begins with the German people who accepted the hospital-
> ity of these shores. Among them were Mennonies, German Baptists, Breth-
> ren, Dunkers, Amish and Moravian groups that belonged to the fringes of
> German Protestantism. The majority stemmed from a Reformed or Luth-
> eran background, which caused them to be designated as church people
> to distinguish them from the so called sects that did not enjoy any official
> status in the homeland. Germans could be found among the earliest set-
> tlers—humble artisans in Jamestown, more vigerous individuals like the
> astute soldier and statesman Peter Minuit in Amsterdam, adventurers and
> explorers like John Lederer in the Virginia colony, or scholars like Peter
> Fabian, a Swiss German who was a member of an expedition sent out in
> 1663 by the English Carolina Company to explore the Carolinas. Although
> a considerable sprinkling of Germans made their appearance early, the
> tide of immigration did not begin to flow until after the founding of Ger-

mantown in 1663 as a permanent settlement of Germans from the Palatinate.

From this time on, successive waves of German immigration touched our shores throughout the eighteenth century. A general idea of its force may be gained from the statistical picture in Pennsylvania. By 1727, when the migration became intensive, there were 20,000 Germans in Penn's colony; up to 1742 something like 18,000 were added. Six thousand more arrived by the end of 1748, and between 1749 and 1754 nearly 32,000 came through the port of Philadelphia alone. So numerous were the arrivals of these foreigners by 1727, that the Provincial Council deemed it necessary to require shipmasters to make lists of all immigrants and have them sign an oath of allegiance to the King of England. In testimony before the House of Commons in 1776, Benjamin Franklin declared that of the 160,000 white people in the Province of Pennsylvania, about one third were Germans. A conservative estimate of the German population of the thirteen colonies at the outbreak of the Revolution has been set at 225,000.

How many Reformed people came in this vast migration? No one will ever know. Concerning the most populous settlement in Pennsylvania, it was reported in 1730 that "the Reformed holding the old confession constituted more than one half of the whole number (of German), being about 15,000." In the middle of the eighteenth century, the estimate was 30,000 in Pennsylvania alone; at the end, the number of adherents in the organized church may have passed beyond 40,000. This much is known for certainty, that while numerically the left-wingers surpassed the church people in the beginning stages, the Reformed element forged ahead as long as migration was predominently from Swiss and Rhenish lands.[2]

From Pennsylvania these German immigrants moved West into Ohio, Indiana and other adjacent states. In 1740 many of them turned Southward into Virginia, North Carolina and South Carolina in search for land suitable for homesteading.

A century after the Reformed people arrive on American soil, came those of the Evangelical Synod of North America. Those people came from the Eastern, Northern and Central section of Germany, seeking relief from poverty and political pressures which followed the Napoleonic Wars. After the defeat of Napoleon in 1814, German citizens faced conditions somewhat similar to those in our own Southland at the close of the Civil War. Moved by exaggerated reports of riches and opportunities on the American frontier, they acted to take advantage of them. Some of those immigrants landed at Eastern Ports such as Philadelphia and Baltimore, and by stagecoach and other means of travel, moved to the interior around Pittsburgh and Cleveland. Others, in increasing numbers, landed at the mouth of the Mississippi River. From New Orleans they travelled up the Mississippi and Missouri rivers eventually settling in areas around St. Louis and Chicago. "Religiously, they represented not so much the Luthern and Reformed churches as that "Evangelical Union" of the two which had been effected in Germany in and after 1817."[3]

German immigrants, in collaboration with others, made a number of attempts to establish settlements in the Southeast, with discouraging results. Since those efforts do not essentially contribute to the story being developed here, the concern from this point will be with the migration of Palatinate Germans from Pennsylvania South which began about the year 1740. Crowded for good farm land in Pennsylvania, and enticed by moderate climate and the prospect of large acreage at reasonable prices, people who lived in Berks, Lancaster, Montgomery, York, Cumberland and Adams counties turned southward in large numbers. Following the mountain slopes through Maryland into Virginia by way of the Shenandoah Valley, through the Blue Ridge, across the Dan River, they came to the valleys of the Haw, Yadkin and Catawba rivers. Here they found good land and delightful climate, and began to select home sites, making satisfactory financial arrangements for same with agents of the Earl of Granville who had supervisory control over the land.

Those first settlers took up land in the area of what is now known to be Alamance, Orange, Guilford and Randolph counties in the valley of the Haw River. Usually meeting houses for educational and religious purposes were among the first buildings erected in the settlement. Near the center of this area stands Brick Reformed Church. Dr. George W. Welker has captured the spirit and sense of religious devotion which characterized these early settlers in the following statement.

> Late on Saturday evening in the summer of 1748, three emigrant families on their way from Oley, Berks County, Pennsylvania, to Western North Carolina, in quest of a new home, arrived near where stands St. Paul's or Grave's Church. They pitched tents for the night near a spring of living water, and soon each was busy in his or her appropriate work of preparation. They seemed to forget the fatigue of long travel, and had one looked in upon them he would have seen that they looked forward to the coming Sabbath as a day of rest. They conscientiously kept God's Holy Word, while journeying slowly to their distant homes in the wild woods.
>
> The fathers of "Brick Church" were Sabbath-keeping men. How many of the blessings which their children have since enjoyed may be traced to the keeping of God's commandment we cannot say; yet, no doubt, God has remembered children's children for this hallowed Sabbath, there kept by the brothers George Valentine and Ludwig Clapp or Klapp and Mr. Hunter, their brother-in-law.[4]

Others in the immigrant train took a slightly Southwest direction, arriving in the fertile and rolling valley of the Yadkin River, comprising Rowan, Cabarrus, and Davidson counties. On the North side of the river are found such names as Hedrick, Sowers, Leonard, Beck, Hinkle among others, in whose midst is the historic Pilgrim Church. On the South side scattered throughout the valley are names common to this day such as Holshouser, Brown, Peeler, Cline, Kluttz, Barrier, Lyerly, Barnhardt and Bost. On a knoll in Southeast Rowan County stands the ancient Grace (Lower Stone) Church. And, beyond the Catawba River, in the South Fork Settlement, two miles West of Newton, is the old St. Paul's Church. Pioneer Henry Weidner, who came to Sherrill's Ford as early as 1739, and established his home in Catawba County in 1740, was joined by others of his countrymen among them being the Abernathys, the Shufords, the Warlicks, the Carpenters, the Hunsuckers and the Rowes.

In each settlement, without fail, was a "house of worship." Usually congregations organized themselves into union churches, composed of Lutheran and Reformed neighbors, and others who chose to become a part of the fellowship. These were ministered to by available preachers, usually of the Reformed or Lutheran faiths, and managed by officers elected by the cooperating congregations. As those communities expanded and more ministers became available, the desire for denominational organizations and separate churches grew keener. One by one union churches disappeared. At the present time only one union church appears on the roll of Southern Synod, that being Salem Church, Lincoln County.

Old Brick Church Where
Classis Was Organized 1831

Over a period of eighty years these Reformed congregations operated virtually without benefit of organizational connection or ecclesiastical supervision. Ministers, with a few exceptions, were itinerate preachers or "missionaries" sent out by the German Reformed Synod whose seat of authority was located in Pennsylvania, some five hundred miles away. Considering the hazards of communication in those days and limited ministerial oversight available to them, it is remarkable how vigorous a group of churches in central North Carolina had become. By their own request they

were granted permission by the German Reformed Synod to effect
a supervisory organization of their own. The Classis of North
Carolina was, therefore, organized May 21, 1831. Sessions were
held in Brick (Klapp's) Church, Guilford County, with an official
attendance of four elders and four ministers. Ministers present
were: Revs. William Hauck, John G. Fritchey, Daniel B. Lerch,
John H. Crawford; elders: Col. Daniel Clapp, Esq. Adam Roseman,
Col. John Hoke and Col. Philip Hedrick. The Classis represented
six ministers and twenty four congregations. Rev. George Boger,
living in the State of North Carolina, and Rev. John Brown of Virginia were unable to attend the meeting. Seven of the twenty four
congregations were located in Rockingham and Augusta counties
of Virginia.[5]

The seventeen congregations in North Carolina were: Emanuel,
Grace, St. Paul's, St. John's and Daniel's, in Lincoln County; Grace,
Bear Creek, Savitz's (Mt. Zion) and Cold Water (Gilead), in
Rowan, Cabarrus and Montgomery Counties; Coble's, Clapp's, Shu-
maker's and Stoner's, in Guilford and Orange Counties; Beck's,
Emanuel, Leonard's (Pilgrim), and Sower's (Beulah), in David-
son.[6] These congregations actually became the nucleus for the
Classis.

The creation of this new ecclesiastical body provided administrative direction and precious fellowship for the scattered churches
in the area, generating incentive for church extension and a more
generous disposition to cooperate in denominational causes at home
and abroad. The report of the committee on The State of Religion,
submitted during the sessions of this historic first meeting of the
classis, reflects the outlook of church leadership at that time.

> That notwithstanding the German Reformed Congregations, in this por-
> tion of the Lord's vineyard, having been long destitute of stated ministers,
> and notwithstanding the peculiar situation of those congregations, and
> the many formidable difficulties which have presented themselves at dif-
> ferent times; yet, they have reason to be thankful to the great Head of
> the Church, that our brethren in the Lord have not altogether labored in
> vain. The preaching of the Word, together with the administration of the
> ordinances, is, in most of the congregations, well attended. . . .
>
> Most of the congregations which have been regularly supplied with
> preaching of the Word, and the administration of the ordinance, since they
> have been supplied with stated ministers, are increasing in numbers and
> we trust in vital piety and Godliness. It is true that the labors of our min-
> isters are too scattered at this time, . . . but we believe that, as they in-
> crease in numbers, this disadvantage will be removed by increasing the
> number and condensing the labors of their ministers.[7]

These are the people, who 103 years later, merged with their kins-
men, representing the Evangelical Synod of North America, to form
Southern Synod of the Evangelical and Reformed Church.

1. *Schaeffer,* Charles E., Historical Sketches of the Congregational Christian
   Churches and The Evangelical and Reformed Church, 1955, p. 23.
2. *Toth,* William, History of the Evangelical and Reformed Church, 1961,
   p. 4 ff.

3. *Dunn*, David, The American Church of the Protestant Heritage, 1953, p. 299.
4. *Clapp*, Jacob C., Editor, Historic Sketch of the Reformed Church in North Carolina, 1908, p. 118.
5. ———. Minutes. Classis of North Carolina, 1831, 1929, Supplement, p. 50.
6. *Clapp*, op. cit., p. 51.
7. ———. Minutes. op. cit., p. 13.

Organization of Southern Synod

First Church, Salisbury where Southern Synod was organized.

SOUTHERN SYNOD was one of thirty four judicatories in the governing system of the Evangelical and Reformed Church. Its geographical boundaries were those which outline the States of North Carolina, South Carolina, Georgia and Florida, commonly referred to as the Southeast area. On the roll in 1939, when the Synod was organized, were sixty two congregations; all of which were located in the Piedmont Sections of North Carolina, except St. John's, Atlanta, Georgia; St. John's, Homestead, Robertson Memorial, Miami, and United at Reddick in Florida. Those sixty two congregations represented a total confirmed membership of 11,171 people, and a Sunday School enrollment of 12,134 pupils. On the roll were fifty nine ministers; thirty two of whom were serving pastorates, twenty four either retired or active in other fields of service, and three licentiates.

When General Council of General Synod, Evangelical and Reformed Church, began setting up area judicatories, by administrative authority, a convening committee was appointed. The business of this committee was to prepare for and effect an organization in the Southeast. The personnel of that committee consisted of Dr. Jacob C. Leonard, Convener, Lexington, North Carolina; Dr. Harry D. Althouse, Hickory, North Carolina, and Rev. Henry A. DeWald, Atlanta, Georgia. In cooperation with Dr. Louis W. Goebel, president of the General Synod and chairman of General Council, plans were detailed to organize the churches of the area May 30, 1939 at 2 p.m. Sessions were held in the First Evangelical and Reformed Church, Salisbury, North Carolina, of which Dr. George T. Fitz was pastor.

A report of the roll secretary, Rev. Charles E. Hiatt, Lexington, North Carolina, showed the presence of thirty-five ministers, twenty-six laymen and three licentiates. These were:

> *Ministers:* Jacob C. Leonard, D.D., William H. McNairy, D.D., John H. Keller, D.D., John C. Peeler, D.D., Shuford Peeler, D.D., C. Columbus Wagoner, John A. Koons, Jacob A. Palmer, D.D., William C. Lyerly, Milton Whitener, Charles W. Warlick, D.D., A. Odell Leonard, D.D., Banks J. Peeler, D.D., Augustus C. Peeler, Hugo C. Kellermyer, Bruce A. Wentz, Ph.D., Hoy L. Fespeman, Charles E. Hiatt, William H. Causey, D.D., Roy C. Whisenhunt, Harry D. Althouse, D.D., William S. Gerhardt, Allen K. Faust, Ph.D., Huitt R. Carpenter, George T. Fitz, D.D., Carl H. Clapp, Joshua L. Levens, Walter W. Rowe, D.D., O. Bain Michael, S.T.D., Roy E. Leinbach, Jr., George E. Dillinger, S.T.D., Lonnie A. Carpenter, D.D., Aubrey W. Hedrick, Henry A. DeWald, Norman C. Zulauf and William P. Jenkins.
>
> *Laymen:* W. Clifton Pickett, Sr., First Church, Lexington; Crawford L. Swing, Lower Davidson; Sidney S. Rowe, Catawba; Odus C. Carpenter, Lincoln; William G. Hinkle, Heidelberg, Thomasville; John F. Troxler, First, Greensboro; Robert O. Burkhart, Second, Lexington; Ernest M. Cheek, First, Burlington; Edgar V. McGee, Waughtown; Charles T. Barrier, Trinity, Concord; James M. Hedrick, First, High Point; Jesse W. Warlick, Corinth, Hickory; Ray P. Lyerly, Rockwell; Hoy Moose, Bear Creek; James A. Shuford, Emanuel, Lincolnton; Kieffer A. Kluttz, First, Salisbury; Loomis F. Kluttz, Grace, Newton; Ernest E. Michael, Upper Davidson; Adolphus A. Blackwelder, Zion, Lenoir; David L. Linn, Landis; Lewis Carrigan, Mt. Zion, China Grove; Russell A. Robinson, First, Charlotte; Everett A. Sink, Memorial, Winston Salem; Paul B. Cline, Keller; C. A. Wilson, Bethany, Claremont; E. H. Wildberger, St. John's, Atlanta, Georgia.
>
> *Licentiates:* David E. Faust, Ph.D., A. Wilson Cheek and Terrell M. Shoffner.
>
> *Advisory:* Ministers—Dr. Louis W. Goebel and Dr. William E. Lampe, president and secretary of the General Synod; Dr. John Lantz, a member of the General Council; Felix B. Peck, S. T. D., Louisville, Kentucky; Harvey W. Black, D.D., Pittsburgh Synod; and Lee A. Peeler, D.D., Virginia Classis.
>
> Elders—George H. Moose, John W. Peeler, Herbert W. Coble, Samuel P. Whitt, M. Glenn Pickett, George H. Fowler, Dr. Howard R. Omwake, president of Catawba College, and George C. Fisher.

Dr. Harry D. Althouse was named temporary president and Dr. Jacob C. Leonard temporary secretary. Drs. Goebel and Lampe addressed the Synod and served as resource persons on matters pertaining to organization and procedure. A nominating committee composed of Dr. Walter W. Rowe, Dr. Banks J. Peeler and James R. Young submitted the following report.

Officers of the Synod: President, Dr. Harry D. Althouse; vice president, Rev. Henry A. Dewald; secretary, Dr. Jacob C. Leonard; treasurer, Rev. Milton Whitener.

Synodical Council: Dr. Harry D. Althouse, Rev. Henry A. DeWald, Dr. Jacob C. Leonard, Rev. Milton Whitener, and Elder John T. Fesperman.

Placement Committee: The members of the Synodical Council constitute the Placement Committee.

Committees:

1. Board of Examiners: Revs. C. Columbus Wagoner, George T. Fitz, John A. Koons, President Howard R. Omwake.

2. Kingdom Service: Rev. A. Odell Leonard and Adolphus A. Blackwelder, 1 year; Rev. Hoy L. Fesperman and C. E. DeChant, 2 years; Rev. Hugo C. Kellermeyer and Ernest M. Cheek, 3 years.

3. Evangelism: Rev. Joshua L. Levens and James R. Young, 1 year; Rev. Jacob A. Palmer and Ray P. Lyerly, 2 years; Rev. Carl H. Clapp and James A. Shuford, 3 years.

4. Christian Social Action: Rev. Roy C. Whisenhunt and Loomis F. Kluttz, 1 year; Rev. John C. Peeler and Otho L. Linn, 2 years; Rev. Roy E. Leinbach, Jr. and Edgar V. McGee, 3 years.

5. Christian Education and Publication: Rev. Huitt R. Carpenter and John F. Troxler, 1 year; Rev. Aubrey W. Hedrick and Hoy Moose, 2 years; Rev. George E. Dillinger and Jesse W. Warlick, 3 years.

6. National Missions: Rev. Norman C. Zulauf and W. Clifton Pickett, Sr., 1 year; Rev. Shuford Peeler and Herbert W. Coble, 2 years; Rev. William C. Lyerly and Chester Deal, 3 years.

This report was unanimously adopted. Officers were declared elected, and then properly inducted into their respective offices. President Louis W. Goebel conducted the simple but impressive ceremony. Thus, Southern Synod of the Evangelical and Reformed Church was officially organized, and began its work.[1] Only legal detail was yet to claim attention.

When the Southern Synod convened in its second annual sessions at Zion Church, Route 1, Thomasville, North Carolina, February 13, 1940, a document was presented and approved transferring all rights and privileges from the former Classis of North Carolina to the Southern Synod. The text of this document and the action on it appears below.

Whereas The Reformed Church in the United States and the Evangelical Synod of North America have united to form the Evangelical and Reformed Church.

And, whereas, the Classis of North Carolina was a part of the Reformed Church in the United States, and whereas, under the new Constitution of the Evangelical and Reformed Church, the Classis of North Carolina, together with certain other congregations, will hereafter be designated as the Southern Synod of the Evangelical and Reformed Church; and whereas, the Southern Synod is the successor of said Classis of North Carolina, and as such is entitled to succeed to all the rights, privileges, powers, duties and responsibilities of said Classis:

Now, therefore, be it resolved, That the Classis of North Carolina does hereby authorize the said Southern Synod of the Evangelical and Reformed Church; and whereas, the Southern Synod is the successor of

said Classis of North Carolina, and as such is entitled to succeed to all
the rights, privileges, powers, duties and responsibilities of said Classis:
    Now, therefore, be it resolved, That the Classis of North Carolina
does hereby authorize the said Southern Synod to the Evangelical and
Reformed Church to exercise all rights, privileges, powers, duties and
responsibilities heretofore exercised by the Classis of North Carolina in
its official capacity, and the said Classis of North Carolina does hereby
convey, assign, transfer and set over to the said Synod, its successor, all
of its property, real, personal and mixed, wherever situated, and the said
synod shall assume all the duties, liabilities, obligations and debts now
resting upon the said Classis of North Carolina.
    J. C. Leonard, Stated Clerk (Seal), February 13, A. D., 1940.
On the foregoing proposal of the Classis of North Carolina, the Southern
Synod of the Evangelical and Reformed Church took the following action:
    Whereas, the Classis of North Carolina has, by resolution adopted on
the 13th day of February, 1940, authorized the Southern Synod of the
Evangelical and Reformed Church to exercise all the rights, privileges,
powers, duties and responsibilities heretofore exercised by the Classis of
North Carolina in its official capacity, and the said Classis of North
Carolina has conveyed, assigned, transferred, and set over to the said
Synod, its successsor, all of its property, real, personal and mixed, where-
ever situated.
    Now, therefore, be it Resolved, That the Southern Synod of the Evan-
gelical and Reformed Church does hereby accept all of said rights, and
and does hereby assume all of the duties, obligations, liabilities and debts
heretofore resting upon the Classis of North Carolina.[2]

The purpose of this new organization is briefly summed up in
the Preamble to the Constitution of the Evangelical and Reformed
Church. It says:

    For the maintenance of truth and order in the proclamation of the
    Gospel of our Lord Jesus Christ and the advancement of the Kingdom
    of God in accordance with the Word of God, the Evangelical and Re-
    formed Church, formed by the union of the Evangelical Synod of North
    America and the Reformed Church in the United States, ordains this
    constitution to be its fundamental law and declares the same to have
    authority over its ministers, members, congregations and judicatories.[3]

The Constitution also makes a definite statement on doctrine:

    The Holy Scriptures of the Old and New Testaments are recognized as
    the Word of God and the ultimate rule of Christian faith and practice.
    The doctrinal standards of the Evangelical and Reformed Church are:
    the Heidelberg Catechism, Luther's Catechism and the Augsburg Con-
    fession. They are accepted as authoritative interpretation of the essential
    truth taught in the Holy Scriptures.
    Wherever these doctrinal standards differ, ministers, members and
    congregations, in accordance with the liberty of conscience inherent in
    the Gospel, are allowed to adhere to the interpretation of one of these
    confessions. However, in each case the final norm is the Word of God.
    In its relation to other Christian Communions, the Evangelical and
    Reformed Church shall constantly endeavor to promote the unity of the
    spirit in the bonds of peace.[4]

The Church recognizes two sacraments instituted by Christ.
These are Holy Baptism and the Lord's Supper. Accepted rites are:
confirmation, ordination, consecration, marriage and burial. Congregations are allowed freedom of worship. Forms of worship are
provided in the Book of Worship, approved by the General Synod,

Synod House, Salisbury, N. C.
Erected in 1956

but these are only accepted norms which may or may not be used according to the desires of the local congregation. Festival Seasons of the year are observed as a matter of choice.

The program of Christian Service as approved by the Executive Committee of the Evangelical and Reformed Church, was accepted by Southern Synod. Its motivation has been described as follows:

> We have a witness to give to Christendom and the world: That the Spirit of our Lord can not only bring us together, but keep us together; that we are facing the new day with the old faith strengthened in unity, with the old message made more appealing and emphatic by the great love that binds us together.
>
> We have a sacred heritage to leave to our children. Let us enlarge it by ever increasing diligence in the Master's work and increasing care in the administration of our stewardship.[5]

Annual Meeting of Southern Synod, First Church,
Greensboro, North Carolina, April 1964.

Southern Synod began in earnest to set its house in order antici-pating these aims. Ecclesiastical and lay organizations were tailored to fit into the pattern. Institutions and agencies within the bounds of Synod were geared to the program. The whole operation pre-sented a promising future, generating a spirit of optimism on all levels in the life of the Synod. Indeed, a fresh new spirit permeated the rank and file of the church membership, reflected in such prac-tical areas as evangelism, stewardship of life and possessions and church extension. During the twenty five years which ensued, six-teen new congregations were organized within the bounds of the Synod; fifteen large charges, composed of from two to four churches, involving forty three congregations, were reconstructed into thirty five charges.

In 1955 Southern Synod elected a full-time president in the per-son of Dr. Harvey A. Fesperman, and established central offices in Salisbury, North Carolina. There a building was erected suitable for executive offices and living space for the new official. During the major part of that time, Southern Synod paid its apportionment budget in full, involving commitments to General Synod and pro-gram obligations in the local area. This was accomplished in addi-tion to greatly expanding such church related institution and agen-cies as Catawba College, Nazareth Children's Home, Johns River Valley Camp and the Blowing Rock Assembly Grounds.

Southern Synod officially became a part of Southern Conference of the United Church of Christ, on September 30, 1965, when it met as a uniting body with the Convention of the South and the Southern Convention for that purpose. At that time the Synod was designated an Association in the new administrative arrangement, and began to phase out its activities, gearing them into the Western and the Eastern Areas of Southern Conference. Final action dis-solving the Synod occurred January 31, 1968, when The Council met delegating certain unfinished business to the Trustees of Synod and other instructed committees.

1. ———. Minutes. Southern Synod, 1939, p.1ff.
2. *Ibid.* p.10.
3. ———. Constitution and By-Laws, Evangelical and Reformed Church, p.5.
4. *Ibid.* p. 5 ff.
5. ———. The Executive Committee, Evangelical and Reformed Church, Our Church and Her Task, 1935, p.3.

CHAPTER II

Agencies and Organizations

The Reformed Church Standard

EARLY IN THE HISTORY of the Reformed Church in North Carolina, its leaders realized the practical necessity of publications as channels through which to educate and to promote. In 1833, shortly after the Classis of North Carolina had been consummated, that body went on record strongly supporting the denominational magazine. Ministers were enjoined to "make renewed efforts to increase the subscription list of the editor to the Messenger, in order to justify him in more frequent publication of that valuable periodical."[1] This journal, however, did not totally satisfy the need of frontier churchmanship. The need for a channel of communication between the churches was keenly felt during the days of separation caused by the Civil War. In 1864, a study committee was set up by the Classis empowered to purchase a printing press and recommend detail incident to publishing a paper within its bounds.[2] The venture did not prove feasible, therefore, it was dropped for the time being. In 1873, another effort was made to establish a newspaper for the Classis, but this also faltered due largely to lack of interest among the churches.[3]

Nothing further appears to have been done until 1887, when in January a monthly magazine, entitled The College Visitor, published under the auspices of the Philomathean Literary Society of Catawba College, appeared. Its primary aim was to serve alumni, students and friends of the college; however, from the beginning a section for church news and editorials was managed by a church news editor, therefore did much in keeping the Reformed Church constituency in North Carolina informed. The periodical was edited by Dr. John A. Foil, Rev. Joseph L. Murphy and students J. M. L. Lyerly and J. C. Leonard. Dr. Foil introduced the visitor with an appropriate editorial.

In sending out our tiny bark upon the stormy sea of Journalism, we trust the hope that it will be sustained, and may not be considered either presumptuous or ill advised. The claims of Catawba College on the commun-

ity and on the intelligence of the country are not in this introduction to be
considered, while her right to establish a monthly magazine to further her
interests, the cause of education and the good of humanity, can not be questioned. We need, therefore, to make no apology for the appearance of
this our first issue. . . .

 This magazine will, of course, be educational in character, but as it will
also be the organ of Catawba College, personals of those who have been,
and are now connected with the college, and articles written by some of
the many who were educated here, will appear from time to time. It is
hoped that they will be interesting to the community as well as to those
who have studied here, and they will reflect the mind and spirit of the
installation while the selected articles will be for the general improvement
of mind and morals. We will gladly welcome to our columns contributions
from any who feel an interest in the cause and are disposed to help us. . . .[4]

The College Visitor enjoyed an interesting and successful career,
but it did not totally meet the needs of the Reformed Church in
North Carolina. In 1893, Rev. Joseph L. Murphy, who had served
as church news editor for the College Visitor, then pastor of Corinth
Reformed Church, Hickory, North Carolina, started a parish publication entitled The Corinthian. Because of economic pressures it
was discontinued after a few months. In 1894, with approval by
the Classis of North Carolina, The Corinthian was enlarged and
published monthly "devoted to the interests of the Reformed
Church in North Carolina."[5] It was edited by Dr. Murphy and
supported through private subscriptions. The first issue appeared
March 1, 1894, and editorially commented:

 After a few month's suspension, it has been decided to begin again the
publication of The Corinthian. The crisis in the financial world made it
necessary for us to discontinue the paper for a short time, but the demand that the paper be continued has been great, and we have yielded
to the request of friends. It will be necessary to make a few changes.

 In the first place, the price of the paper has been increased. To this
we feel that no one will object, when it is known that the editors are
not trying to make money, but simply to pay expenses.

 In the second place it will be changed from a congregational paper
to a classical one. It will now be published in the interest of the entire
Classis. Every minister in the Classis is asked to become a contributor,
and every officer is asked to become an agent. It is desired that every
marriage, that every baptism and confirmation and death shall be published. In short, we wish to make The Corinthian the medium of exchange so that the church in the Eastern part of the Classis may know
each month what the church in the West is doing, and vice versa.

 In the next place, we have associated with us in the editorial work,
Rev. J. C. Leonard, D. D., of the Upper Davidson Charge. Brother
Leonard is young and full of energy and hope and the sunshine of life,
and will bring to the columns of The Corinthian the best efforts of his
facile pen. Now, we ask you, dear reader, to lend us your influence,
and by influence we mean send us your subscription and the names of
your neighbors for the paper.[6]

The Corinthian was well received, and the announced policies
were pursued until March 1, 1906. At that time a number of important changes were made in format and management. The
editor explained:

This is the fourteenth anniversary of this paper and the new year is entered by inaugurating several changes. The name is changed to The Reformed Church Standard. The reason is that the former name was too local. The paper was started as a parish paper of Corinth Reformed Church, Hickory, North Carolina, and the name was most appropriate, but the paper has outgrown the limited field of a parish paper and is now the organ of the Classis and we hope to make it the Standard of the entire church in the South. It is changed from a monthly to a semi-monthly. This is done in response to an imperative demand. The price however is to remain the same.

In order that the interests of the church may be served more faithfully, we have associated with us the Rev. C. E. Wehler as Business Manager. He has qualifications which fit him for this position, and he has had experience in newspaper work.

The paper is now published by a company. This company is composed of men noted for their business qualifications and devotion to the Reformed Church.

With faith in the South we give ourselves cheerfully to this work. We place our trust in God, but at the same time rely upon the support of the brethren throughout the entire Classis. We shall endeavor to serve the entire church in the South and any brother may feel perfectly free to use the columns of The Standard to present his work to the people. We solicit the news from every part of the Classis.[7]

The Standard was recognized as an official organ of the Classis of North Carolina, managed and edited by representatives of the Classis authorized to do so; but, published by private interests. Attempts were made in 1909, 1910 and 1916 to have Classis take over the enterprise, but on each occasion for good reasons, the effort did not succeed. In 1916, St. James Church, Mt. Pleasant, North Carolina addressed an overture to the Classis proposing three things: that the Classis secure control of the Reformed Church Standard; that the paper be published and sent free to the members of the Reformed Church in North Carolina; and that an apportionment be laid upon the different churches to pay expenses. This overture was referred by the Classis to a committee for study and report, the committee being composed of Revs. J. L. Murphy, W. H. McNairy and Elder J. L. Fisher.[8]

In 1917 the Classis heard their report and approved recommendations which appear below:

That the Classis of North Carolina agree to pay Rev. J. M. L. Lyerly, owner of the Reformed Church Standard, the sum of $150. for the paper, and that the Classis elect an Editor-in-Chief, a Business Manager and a Board of Associate Editors to be composed of a representative from each district of the Classis, of Catawba College and of Nazareth Orphans' Home.

The persons so elected shall formulate plans for running the paper, Classis being responsible for the financial support of the paper.[9]

An editorial staff, elected during the same sessions of the Classis, consisted of Dr. Joseph L. Murphy, Editor-in-Chief; District Editors: Revs. Harvey A. Fesperman, William C. Lyerly and G. Ermine Plott; Institutional Editors: the President of Catawba College and the Superintendent of Nazareth Orphans' Home. Rev. William

H. McNairy was elected Business Manager.[10] The Standard was published on subscriptions and gifts during the first year, but in 1918 a sum of $650 was apportioned to the churches through the benevolent budget for its support. In 1918 the business manager reported to the Classis:

> We issued The Standard twice each month since last Classis. The untimely death of the Editor-in-Chief was quite a blow to the paper. After consulting the editors, I secured the services of Brother Walter W. Rowe, who has done the work faithfully.

FINANCIAL REPORT

Money Received:
Borrowed from the Treasurer of Classis	$ 25.00
Collected on Subscriptions	277.36
Collected on Advertisements	20.90
	$ 323.26

Paid Out:
For Printing and Mailing	$ 298.00
For Postage and Paper	9.20
For General Expense	15.04
	$ 322.24
Balance on hand	1.02
Owe the Treasurer of Classis	25.00

After the first year, a policy of "no advertising" was adopted by the Classis for the paper, Catawba College being the exception, and that was gratis.[11]

In 1934 the Evangelical and Reformed Church was born, resulting from the merger of the Reformed Church in the United States and the Evangelical Synod of North America. In 1939 Southern Synod appeared on the scene as a unit in the administrative structure of the new Communion. The Standard adjusted to its new environment by making necessary format and name changes; otherwise its policy of reporting the news to the churches and promoting the program of the denomination remained the same.

Over a period of seventy two years The Standard has been managed and edited by elected ministers of the church with standing in the Classis. Theirs has been a labor of love without financial compensation, rewarded only by an appreciative constituency. In 1955, when Southern Synod elected its first full-time president, a part of his duties being promotion, editorial and publication responsibilities for The Standard were assigned to him. This arrangement continued until January 1, 1966, when The Standard was merged with other periodicals to form The Southern Conference News of the United Church of Christ. The final issue of The Standard, dated December 15, 1965, carries an authentic announcement.

> This is the final issue of The Standard. The next publication will appear sometime after the first of the year, and as an organ of The Southern Conference of the United Church of Christ. The new publication will represent the merging of three papers now being published in this section of the

United Church—The Newsletter by the Convention of the South, the Christian Sun by the Southern Convention, and The Standard by the Southern Synod.[12]

Of interest in this connection will be the names of the editors who have through the years produced this paper.

Rev. Joseph L. Murphy, D.D. 1894-1909
Rev. Jacob C. Clapp, D.D., Co-editor 1909
Rev. Walter W. Rowe, D.D., Co-editor 1909
Rev. J. M. L. Lyerly, Ph.D., Co-editor 1909
Rev. Walter W. Rowe, D.D., Co-editor 1910-1933
Rev. J. M. L. Lyerly, Ph.D., Co-editor 1910-1913
Rev. J. M. L. Lyerly, Ph.D., Co-editor 1914-1916
Rev. Walter W. Rowe, D.D., Co-editor 1914-1916
Rev. J. M. L. Lyerly, Ph.D., ...1916-1917
Rev. Joseph L. Murphy, D.D., ...1917-
Rev. Walter W. Rowe, D.D., ...1917-1923
Rev. C. Columbus Wagoner 1923-1938
Dev. Walter W. Rowe, D.D., ...1939-1950
Rev. William C. Lyerly 1950-1952
Rev. Terrell M. Shoffner 1952-1955
Rev. Harvey A. Fesperman, D.D. 1955-1963
Rev. Banks J. Peeler, D.D., ...1963-1966

1. ———. Minutes. Classis of North Carolina, 1833, p. 44.
2. ———. Minutes. *Op. cit.,* 1864, p.318.
3. ———. Minutes. *Op. ctt.,* 1873, p. 139.
4. Foil, John A., The College Visitor, Vol. 1, 1887, p.6.
5. ———. Minutes. *Op. cit.,* 1894, p.9.
6. Murphy, J. L., The Corinthian, Vol. II, March 1894, p.2.
7. Murphy, J. L., The Reformed Church Standard, Vol. XIV, March 1906, p.2.
8. ———. Minutes. *Op. cit.,* 1916, p.34.
9. ———. Minutes. *Op. cit.,* 1917, p.23.
10. *Ibid.* p.33.
11. ———. Minutes. *Op. cit.,* 1918, p. 35.
12. *Peeler,* Banks J., The Standard, Vol. LXXIII, December 15, 1965, p.1.

Missionary Agencies

MISSIONARY AGENCIES have played a major role in the life of the German Reformed Church in North Carolina, and its successor the Evangelical and Reformed Denomination. Among early missionary minded, venturesome spirits who served scattered German settlements prior to 1764 in the area were, Revs. Christian Theus, James Martin and Richard Dupert. In 1812 came Rev. James R. Riley and in 1817 Rev. John S. Ebaugh and others were agents of the German Reformed Synod sent into North Carolina as itinerate preachers. In 1832, one year after the Classis of North Carolina had been organized, that body took decisive action leading to fruitful missionary results.

> Resolved, that a committee be appointed to make early and earnest application to the Missionary Society of the German Reformed Church for a missionary to labor in the destitute places within the bounds of the Classis for one year, and that the members of the Classis assiduously endeavor to raise a fund to support him.[1]

In 1835 the Classis acted to effect its own Missionary Society, and named a committee to draw up rules by which to govern its conduct.[2] In 1836, that governing instrument was presented to the Classis and by it approved. Article I. states its name and object.

> This society shall be denominated the Home Missionary Society of the Classis of North Carolina. The object of the society shall be to raise pecuniary aid for those preachers who may be called to disseminate the Gospel of Jesus Christ among indigent and destitute brethren and friends in the Southern and Western Country.[3]

As a result of this effort, Rev. W. C. Bennet was sent by the Missionary Society of the Reformed Church to serve six churches in the Newberry District of South Carolina. On October 17, 1832, Rev. W. C. Rankin was commissioned to serve churches in Catawba and Burke counties, North Carolina. In 1895 Dr. George W. Welker wrote, "The work of home missions has been kept before the Classis at all times, but, so desultory has been the work, it is not much to show at this day. When this Classis was organized, the congregations in South Carolina were not extinct, and it was the custom to require each minister to visit these churches once a year. For reasons not now known this very irregular and ineffective work was intermitted entirely."[4] However, it is a matter of record that, beginning with about 1885, accepting such support as could be provided by the Board of Missions and other similar sources like the Missionary Society, ministers of the Classis assumed additional responsibilities in organizing new congregations at points of opportunity through out the Piedmont Region of North Carolina. Some progress was recorded. In 1813, there were thirty three congregations on the roll of the Classis; in 1900 there were forty four. This record is impressive only against a background of scarce money and scattered people, both of which were very much in evidence during this period.

It is important to remember that the missionary spirit was apparent in the life of the church at that time; that a new emphasis had been added. Church leadership was beginning to talk about missions abroad. In that atmosphere in 1897, the Woman's Missionary Society of the Classis of North Carolina was born, which set itself to the task of missionary study and promotion at home and abroad. On October 11, 1909 a Layman's Missionary Convention was held at First Church, Salisbury, North Carolina. In 1910 a study committee reported to the Classis of North Carolina:

> The hearts of the men of the Protestant Churches of America have been moved in the interest of missions in these latter years as never before. The laymen of the church, farmers, merchants, bankers, manufacturers—all classes of business men—have caught the larger vision which points to the giving of the Gospel to the world in this generation. The reflex influence of this great movement is touching, and will continue to affect, all lines of church work, at home and abroad.
> That the Classis of North Carolina may take advantage of this great layman's movement to our profit, we submit the following:

> Resolved, that a strong committee, consisting of one minister and one elder from each district of the Classis, be appointed to arrange a convention to be held at some central point within the year.
>
> Resolved, that we call upon all of our ministers and elders and people to work to secure a large attendance of men at this convention.
>
> Resolved, that, in harmony with the spirit of the Layman's Missionary Movement, we call upon all congregations to contribute liberally to the various causes of benevolence.
>
> Resolved, that we pledge ourselves to increase our offerings for the cause of Foreign Missions so as not only to meet the apportionment for this purpose, but to raise large sums over and above this amount.[5]

A laymen's convention, evidently with success, was held April 17-18, 1912 in Catawba County.[6] In 1915 a committee was named by the Classis consisting of Revs. W. W. Rowe, J. A. Koons, L. A. Peeler, with instructions to "make recommendations concerning a Missionary Conference."[7] That committee recommended that a Summer Missionary Conference be held within the bounds of Classis in July 1915 at Claremont College.[8] For lack of interest among the churches it did not occur.[9] That same year the Classis took further action:

> Resolved, that a committee consisting of three ministers and three laymen be appointed to consider the advisability of holding a Missionary Conference within the bounds of the Classis of North Carolina sometime during the year, and that the chairman of the committee be permitted to supplement the committee in case it is decided to hold the conference.

The committee consisted of Revs. A. D. Wolfinger, J. A. Koons, J. C. Peeler and Elders J. T. Hedrick, J. E. Holshouser and J. F. Herman.[10] This committee made a progress report in 1917:

> Your committee on Summer Conference would report, that several meetings of the committee were held during the year. Sub-committees were appointed and the program of education carried out. All the churches with the exception of a few in central district were visited by either laymen or ministers.
>
> Central conventions were held in all but the central district. The subjects discussed dealt with Scriptural principles of giving; practical methods of church finances; the place of lay service in the church, and the work of the Sunday Schools.
>
> Great interest was manifested by the people and various expressions given for a continuation of this work. Your committee believes that this has much to do with seven out of eight charges in the western district paying the apportionment in full; in developing tithers and making the Every-Member-Canvass a greater success.
>
> Your committee is of the conviction that this program of education should be continued during the year, and would so recommend. We would recommend the appointment of one minister and layman in each of the districts as the committee to whom the work shall be referred, and also, the work of the Stewardship Committee, the same to be known as the Missionary and Stewardship Committee.[11]

In the meantime the Classical Woman's Missionary Society had sent an overture to the Classis of North Carolina, asking that provision be made for a state-wide Summer Conference to be held in

1918.[12] That overture was approved and a committee was authorized consisting of Rev. Lee A. Peeler and Elders A. A. Blackwelder and A. L. Shuford, Sr., to meet with a similar committee from the Woman's Missionary Society to plan for and execute such a conference. The planning group met at the Startown parsonage, Newton, North Carolina, Route 1, on May 11, 1918. Present were: Mrs. Shuford Peeler and Mrs. Lee A. Peeler, representing the Woman's Missionary Society and Rev. Lee A. Peeler and Elder A. A. Blackwelder, representing the Classis. Dr. Jacob G. Rupp, representing the Board of Missions, was present for consultation. Plans were developed to conduct a conference on the campus at Catawba College July 18-23, 1918. Mrs. C. C. Bost, Rev. W. W. Rowe and A. L. Shuford joined planning sessions held at Corinth Church, Hickory, North Carolina, June 6th.

Because of its historical interest that first conference program has been included in this story.

PROGRAM SUMMER CONFERENCE, JULY 18-23, 1918
OF THE REFORMED CHURCH, CATAWBA COLLEGE,
NEWTON, NORTH CAROLINA.

Daily Program

Rising Bell, 7:00
Morning Watch, 7:30
Breakfast, 8:00
Intercession, 9:00-9:20
Bible Study, 9:30-10:05
Mission Study, 10:10-11:10
    Courses A. "Tokohu," The Scotland of Japan by Christopher Noss
          Led by Mrs. J. C. Rupp, Allentown, Pa.
        B. Our Home Mission Work by Dr. Charles E. Schaeffer
          Led by Mr. J. S. Wise, Philadelphia, Pa.
        C. Church Efficiency by Laymen's Missionary Movement
          Led by Dr. A. D. Wolfinger, Newton, North Carolina.
        D. Miss Wistaria at Home by Margaret String
          Led by Miss Ida Hedrick, Lexington, North Carolina.
Institute Hour, 11:15-12:15
    Led by Dr. Jacob G. Rupp, Allentown, Pa.
Dinner, 12:30
Rest Hour, 1:30-2:30
Recreation, 3:00 to 5:30
Supper, 6:00
Study Period, 7:00-7:40
        Course E—Class for Leaders, led by Rev. Lee A. Peeler.
        Course F—Life and Work Meetings, addressed by conference
          leaders.
Vesper Service, 7:45
Platform Meeting, 8:30

Vesper Meetings
Theme: The Church at Work.

Thursday, July 18—Jesse Warlick, leader; "The Church Praying."
    Address: Rev. Roy E. Leinbach, Sr., High Point, N. C.
Friday, July 19—A. A. Blackwelder, leader; "The Church Studying
    the Bible." Address: Rev. Shuford Peeler, Charlotte, N. C.

Saturday, July 20—J. W. Peeler, leader; "The Church Worshipping."
Address: Rev. J. H. Keller, China Grove, N. C.
Monday, July 22—Miss Ollie Cline, leader; "The Church Saving
Souls." Address: Rev. J. C. Peeler, Lexington, N. C.
Tuesday, July 23—Miss Ola Linn, leader; "The Church and Social
Service." Address: Rev. F. R. LeFevre, Greensboro, N. C.

Platform Meetings

Thursday—Rev. J. A. Palmer, presiding.
Illustrated Lecture, Dr. James I. Good, Philadelphia, Pa.
Friday—Rev. W. H. McNairy, presiding.
Illustrated Lecture, Dr. James I. Good.
Saturday—Rev. J. M. L. Lyerly, presiding.
Address: Dr. Charles E. Schaeffer, Philadelphia, Pa.
Monday—Rev. W. C. Lyerly, presiding.
Address: Mr. J. S. Wise, Philadelphia, Pa.
Stunt Night.
Tuesday—Open Conference.

Sunday Program

9:30—Sunday School, Charles H. A. Rupp, Superintendent, Charlotte, N. C.
11:00—Conference Sermon, Dr. Charles E. Schaeffer.
Presiding, Rev. D. E. Bowers.
7:30—Young Peoples' Rally
Address: Dr. J. C. Leonard, Lexington, N. C.
8:30—Mass Meeting. Rev. A. S. Peeler, presiding.
Address: Dr. Charles E. Schaeffer.

Summer Conference,
Catawba College, 1939

A meeting of the delegates took place during conference week,
when action was taken to create a "permanent organization" entitled, "The North Carolina Missionary Conference." This conference, directly related to the Classis of North Carolina, was to be
managed by a committee composed of two people from each of
the three districts in the Classis, elected annually by the conference. The first committee was named: Rev. Lee A. Peeler, chairman; Mrs. C. C. Bost and A. A. Blackwelder, Western District; Rev.
Harvey A. Welker and Mrs. G. T. Crowell, Central District; and

Mrs. J. T. Plott and J. T. Hedrick, Eastern District. This new venture in missionary education was declared successful, enrolling 104
delegates and presenting a wealth of diversified missionary information. It continued to prosper, and convened each summer on the
campus at Catawba College, Newton, North Carolina until 1924.
At that time the school was relocated at Salisbury, North Carolina,
and the annual summer conference program transferred to that
campus. In 1953 it was moved again. This time to the recently
acquired property at Blowing Rock, North Carolina, known as the
Assembly Grounds of Southern Synod.

Polio epidemics caused cancellation of program plans in 1935
and in 1944. The Summer Missionary Conference survived two
church mergers. In 1934, it became an agent of Southern Synod,
Evangelical and Reformed Church. In 1957, it began to adjust to
a new environment created by the appearance of the United Church
of Christ.

Concerned lest the conference become obsolete, its leadership
through the years was sensitive to the denomination's missionary
and promotion needs at home and abroad. It not only taught current literature and promoted approved projects, but made token
material gifts from time to time to such causes as Catawba College,
the Asheboro and Brightwood mission congregations, and to missionary interests in Japan. In 1947, in order to be a more useful
educational factor in the life of the denomination, by vote of the
delegates, the conference was made a part of the Christian Education Administration of Southern Synod. In more recent years, it
has served as a channel through which the Women's Guild has dis-
pensed much of its literature and program ideas. Currently it is
being adjusted to fit the promotion pattern conceived by the Department of Lay Life and Work in Southern Conference of the
United Church of Christ.

1. ———. Minutes. Classis of North Carolina, 1832, p. 19.
2. ———. Minutes. *Op. cit.*, 1835, p. 64.
3. ———. Minutes. *Op. cit.*, 1836, p. 72.
4. *Welker,* George W., A Historical Sketch of the Classis of North Carolina,
   1895, p. 32.
5. ———. Minutes. *Op. cit.*, 1910, p. 56.
6. ———. Minutes. *Op. cit.*, 1912, p. 23.
7. ———. Minutes. *Op. cit.*, 1915, p. 20.
8. *Ibid.* p. 30.
9. ———. Minutes. *Op. cit.*, 1916, p. 5.
10. *Ibid.* p. 26.
11. ———. Minutes. *Op. cit.*, 1917, p. 26.
12. ———. Minutes. *Op cit.*, 1918, p. 38.
13. ———. Minutes. North Carolina Summer Conference, 1918, p. 6ff.

The Women's Guild

ANTECEDENTS OF THE WOMEN'S GUILD of the Evangelical and Reformed Church in North Carolina are The Aid Societies followed

by the Woman's Missionary Society. Aid societies were primarily concerned with local needs, often instruments for stimulating action in favor of a new church building, an educational annex, new carpet for the sanctuary and parsonage improvements. Prior to 1897 societies were active at Grace Church, Newton, organized in 1885; Trinity Church, Concord, 1886; Memorial Church, Maiden, 1890; Corinth Church, Hickory, 1890; Bethany Church, Crescent, 1893; and Trinity Church, Conover, 1894.[1]

However, as the denomination became missionary conscious, these societies gradually expanded their interests to include missionary effort at home and abroad. Corinth Church, Hickory appears to have pioneered in this phase of Christian concern. Similar interest developed among the women of Trinity Church, Concord, under the leadership of Rev. and Mrs. B. F. Davis. On January 18, 1897 ten women of Trinity Church met in the home of Sarian Shuping, 35 West Corban Street and effected an organization which they named the Woman's Missionary Society. On the charter list were the names of Mrs. B. F. Davis, Mrs. J. C. Lippard, Miss Mollie Fetzer, Mrs. R. T. Lippard, Miss Fannie Lippard, Mrs. Sarian Shuping, Mrs. G. T. Crowell, Mrs. M. E. Barrier, Mrs. L. P. Davis and Miss Addie Barrier.[2]

These ladies, manifesting a decided interest in missionary education and promotion, encouraged Mrs. B. F. Davis to communicate with other churches in the Classis of North Carolina, suggesting a state-wide organization. The Classis of North Carolina was scheduled to convene at Mt. Hope Church, Guilford County, May 5-8, 1897. Dr. James D. Andrew, serving his first pastorate at that church, moved by her appeal, invited interested people to the meeting for discussion and possible organization in conjunction with those sessions of the Classis. At 1 p.m. May 6, 1897 fourteen women

delegates met in a classroom of Mt. Hope Church and effected The
Woman's Classical Missionary Society of the Reformed Church in
North Carolina. Enrolled delegates were: Mrs. G. T. Crowell and
Miss Frances Lippard, Concord; Mesdames Joseph L. Murphy and
Alice Ingold Murrill, Hickory; Miss Mary Ida Hedrick, Upper
Davidson; Mrs. William H. McNairy, East Rowan; Mrs. J. P. Linn,
West Rowan; Mrs. John Ingle, Mt. Bethel Mission, Blowing Rock;
Mrs. Jesse Welker Starr and Miss Mamie Clapp and Mannie Mont-
gomery and Mrs. Fanny Lowe, Guilford; Miss Jennie McNairy,
Central Rowan; and Mrs. Clarence Clapp, Thomasville. Miss Eulala
Darr was a visitor from the Lutheran Church.

Miss Mary Ida Hedrick was elected president; Mrs. Joseph L.
Murphy, vice president; Mrs. Alice Ingold Murrill, recording secretary; Miss Mamie Clapp, treasurer and Mrs. B. F. Davis, who was
prevented from attending the meeting because of illness in her
family, corresponding secretary.[3]

A series of delightful amenities followed between the newly
formed Woman's Classical Missionary Society and the Classis of
North Carolina. The Rev. W. H. Stubblebine was delegated to
"convey to the ladies, now assembled for the purpose of organizing
a Woman's Classical Missionary Society, the cordial greetings of
the Classis of North Carolina, and an expression of our hearty sympathy with the movement." The ladies responded in kind.

> Resolved, That we, the members of the Woman's Missionary Society of
> the Classis of North Carolina, thank you, the Classis of North Carolina for
> the kindly greeting and cordial endorsement extended to us this afternoon.
> We respectfully ask your reverend body to cooperate with us in organizing
> Missionary Societies and Mission Bands in charges where they do not exist.
> Also we ask for your prayers that God will enable us to serve Him in such
> a way as to bring honor to His name and souls into His kingdom.[4]

The answer to that communication was immediate:

> Resolved, that we hear with great pleasure of the organization of a
> Woman's Classical Missionary Society within the bounds of the Classis
> of North Carolina, believing that in this organization we will have a val-
> uable aid in our missionary operations.
> Resolved, that we extend to these women our warm appreciation of
> their devotion to the interests of the Reformed Church in the South, and
> assure them of our cordial sympathy and assistance.
> Resolved, that we invite the Woman's Classical Missionary Society
> to meet annually at the same time and place with us.[5]

Of historical importance is the Woman's Meeting arranged by
the program committee of the Classis, and scheduled for Wednesday at 8 p.m. It appears in full below:

PRESIDING, MISS MARY IDA HEDRICK

I.	Organ Voluntary	Miss Frances Lippard
II.	The Scriptures, Miss Hedrick; Prayer, Dr. Jacob C. Clapp	
III.	Music—"Send Out Thy Light."	The Choir
IV.	Address of Welcome	Mrs. Jesse Welker Starr
V.	Response	Mrs. Alice Ingold Murrill

VI.	Solo—"I Know That My Redeemer Liveth."
	.... Mrs. Joseph L. Murphy
VII.	Paper .... Mrs. B. F. Davis
VIII.	Paper .... Miss Hedrick
IX.	Music .... The Choir
X.	Recitation—"Sweet Messenger of Heaven." Mrs. J. P. Linn
XI.	Solo—"The Holy City." .... Mrs. Murphy
XII.	Reading .... Miss Lippard
XIII.	Paper .... Mrs. John Ingle
XIV.	Invitation to Brothers of Classis to speak
XV.	Collection .... Dr. Joseph L. Murphy
XVI.	Benediction .... Rev. A. H. Smith

The audience was large and interested; the offering amounted to $7.07.

Among significant actions taken during the organization meeting were: Authorizing that four dollars be sent from their limited treasury, two dollars each to Mt. Bethel Mission, Blowing Rock and the Mission at Salisbury. Also a request directed to the Classis asking for cooperation in "organizing Missionary Societies and Mission Bands in charges where they do not exist." The intent of this new organization and something of the scope of its program is described in a set of policy resolutions prepared by the Executive Committee and adopted by the society in session at its second annual meeting held at Grace Church, Newton in 1898:

> Whereas, the success which has thus far attended our efforts, and the encouragement which has been given us, confirms our beliefs that we are called in the providence of God in this work, and inspires in us the hope of enjoying His Blessing; therefore,
>
> Resolved, that we will lengthen our cords and strengthen our stakes by the following declarations:
>
> First, the aim and purpose of the Woman's Missionary Society of the North Carolina Classis, is to arouse our women to greater activity in religious and missionary work, and, by concentration of effort, to increase their usefulness in saving souls and extending God's kingdom on earth.
>
> Second, that we pledge ourselves for the present year to support the Girls' School at Sandai and to a Building Fund for Home Missions giving all funds above contingent expenses, three-fifths to the Girls' School and two-fifths to the Building Fund.
>
> Third, that in as much as it is the duty of Auxiliary Societies to sustain the Classical Society, we ask at least one-half of all membership dues be sent to the Classical Treasury.
>
> Fourth, that we urge the organization of Auxiliary Societies wherever and whenever practicable, and especially do we plead the importance of organizing the children into Mission Bands.
>
> Fifth, that we recommend our Church and Missionary Literature, especially the Corinthian, The Woman's Journal and the Mission Band Helper to the hearty support and earnest study of our women, and that they so inform themselves of the needs of our Church work at home and in foreign fields as that they may act intelligently and sympathetically in all matters pertaining to the Master's cause.
>
> Sixth, that in forming Women's Societies we have no desire to discourage mixed organizations, but that, on the contrary, we recognize the importance of enlisting Christians of all ages and both sexes in the active service of our Congregational Societies.[7]

These resolutions set the stage for missionary study and promotion in the local congregation on three age levels: among adults,
primarily women; among children, both sexes, organized in the
Mission Band; and among girls and young women of high school
and college age in the Girls' Missionary Guild. It also prepared the
way for developing the Summer Missionary Conference, which
served the constituency from 1918 to 1954, meeting annually at
Catawba College located at Newton, North Carolina, later at Salisbury, until 1952, thereafter at the Assembly Grounds, Blowing Rock,
North Carolina.

Thus, over a period of forty four years this unusual organization
served the Kingdom of God, effecting practically every phase of
life in the local congregation and the Classis. In 1941, in the process
of implementing the merger which had accrued in 1934 between
the Reformed Church in the United States and the Evangelical
Synod of North America, women's work in the Evangelical and
Reformed Church was consolidated. The official name adopted for
this new organization was "The Women's Guild of the Evangelical
and Reformed Church." Considerable detail, requiring patience
and generosity, were necessary in closing out the old organization
and fitting it into the new one. Cabinet personnel who successfully
prepared for this change were:

> Mrs. William H. Causey, president; Mrs. H. Smith Barrier, first vice
> president; Mrs. Harry D. Althouse, second vice president; Mrs. Augustus
> C. Peeler, recording secretary; Mrs. Daisy Fisher Patterson, correspond-
> ing and statistical secretary; Miss Mildred O. Suther, treasurer; Mrs.
> C. C. Bost, historian; Mrs. Howard R. Omwake, secretary of literature;
> Mrs. Banks J. Peeler, secretary of thankoffering; Mrs. J. H. Allen, secre-
> tary of life members and members in memoriam; Mrs. J. Thomas Leonard,
> secretary of Christian citizenship; Mrs. John W. Hedrick, secretary of
> organization and membership; Mrs. Roy C. Whisenhunt, secretary of
> stewardship; Mrs. Robert E. Leonard, secretary of orphan home projects;
> Mrs. R. A. Robinson, secretary of Girls' Missionary Guild; Mrs. John
> Causey, secretary of Mission Band; Mr. K. A. Link, editor of the women's
> column for the Standard.[8]

The Classical Woman's Missionary Society began in 1897 with
fourteen registered delegates and a financial balance of $8.00, four
dollars of which were contributed to two missionary projects within
the Classis of North Carolina. The books were closed in 1941 with
a membership of 1,355 women representing almost every congregation in the Classis. Receipts for that year were $7,324.

Roster of Presidents	
Mrs. H. J. Conrad	1897-1903
Mrs. A. W. George	1903-1904
Mrs. C. C. Bost	1904-1916
Mrs. Lee A. Peeler	1916-1929
Mrs. Edgar Whitener	1929-1931
Mrs. C. Columbus Wagoner	1931-1933
Mrs. Lee A. Peeler	1933-1935
Mrs. William H. Causey	1935-1941

Mrs. C. C. Bost, synodical historian, has written an appropriate valedictory, with which this section of the story of women's work in the Reformed Church ends.

> This meeting marks the closing of forty-four busy years,
> Years crowded with happiness mingled with tears;
> Each year brought new faces, there were new hands to clasp,
> As we met at new churches old friends' hands to grasp.
> To the W. M. S. N. C. Classis we bid a reluctant adieu;
> We have love you, we still love you, so faithful and true;
> Of this love and loyalty we are come here to tell
> To the Great Women's Guild we love equally well.
> There will be no sad ending a valedictory may bring,
> We will go on rejoicing with brave hearts that sing,
> And the love for each other will grow with the years;
> We will help one another through smiles and through tears.
> As the years pass before us, grown closer together,
> We will meet in the Guild in all sorts of weather.
> But whether the sun is shining or skies are overcast,
> We will all meet together in a Great Guild at last.
> In this day that is mingled with joy and with tears
> We are not overwhelmed by our sorrows or fears;
> With the future faced bravely we courageously tell
> To the Guild and the Society, Hail! and Farewell!
> 'Till we meet in that fair land of Peace and Love,
> The House of Our Father in Heaven above.

The completion of forty four years by the Woman's Missionary Society of the Classis of North Carolina, Reformed Church in the United States, marks the end of an era. That body met at Grace Reformed Church, Newton, North Carolina, April 9-10, 1940, and, for all practical purposes, except for precious memories, closed the doors to the past and faced a whole new future. This change had been initiated by the merger of the Reformed Church in the United States and the Evangelical Synod of North America. Drastic changes in organization and program were required.

The Executive Committee of National Women's Guild, appointed a committee composed of Mrs. Howard R. Omwake, Mrs. Banks J. Peeler, Mrs. Roy C. Whisenhunt, Mrs. Andrew M. Crowell, Miss Helen Abernethy and Mrs. H. A. DeWald, charging it with the responsibility for setting up the new organization in Southern Synod. Mrs. Omwake was asked to chair the committee, but due to illness in her home, declined the appointment. Mrs. Peeler accepted the chairmanship. Thus began a period of synodical leadership for Mrs. Peeler which ended seven years later, first as convening officer for the proposed organization, then as president of the Synodical for two years operating under the "Articles of Merger," and four years more governed by the regularly adopted Constitution and By-Laws.

These were pioneering days. The organization meeting took place at the First Evangelical and Reformed Church, Salisbury, North Carolina, October 3, 1940. Because of its historical value, the entire agenda is included in this story.

THE PROGRAM

9:30 a.m.—*Registration*

FIRST SESSION

10:30 a.m.—*Devotional Period*

Theme: Laborers Together With God. Mrs. H. A. DeWald, Atlanta, Georgia.

Music: Prof. Harold Dickensheets, Head of the Voice Department, Catawba College

Presentation of the Convening Committee by Mrs. Jesse Mengel, Reading, Pennsylvania.

Report of the Convening Comittee, Mrs. Banks J. Peeler, Lexington, North Carolina.

Articles of Merger Governing the Synod.

Declaration of the Organization of the Southern Synodical Women's Guild.

Announcement of Committees.

Report of the Chairman of the Registration Committee.

Presentation of the Literature Display.

Report of the Nominating Committee and the Election.

Hymn 326. Guide Me, O, Thou Great Jehovah.

Prayer of Dismissal.

12:30 p.m.—*Fellowship Luncheon*

Toastmistress, Miss Helen Abernethy, Lincolnton, North Carolina.

AFTERNOON SESSION

2:00 p.m.—*Devotional Period*

Hymn 419. I Love Thy Kingdom, Lord.

Prayer

Presentation of Graph and discussion.

Business

Report of the Tellers

Report of the Nominating Committee for Delegates.

Election of Delegates to the General Meeting of the Women's Guild.

Minutes, Read of the Day's Proceedings.

Installation of Officers in charge of Dr. H. D. Althouse, President of Southern Synod, Hickory, North Carolina.

Music: Mrs. David E. Faust, Instructor in music, Catawba College.

The Offering

Closing Meditation

Theme: Submission to God. Mrs. W. H. Causey, President, Classical Woman's Missionary Society of North Carolina, Winston Salem, N. C.

The Benediction

Hymn 48. (1st Stanza) "God Be With You 'Till We Meet Again."

Total number of delegates and visitors in attendance were 194. Mrs. Jesse Mengel, Reading, Pennsylvania, treasurer of the National Women's Guild, called the meeting to order and defined the bar of the house. Mrs. Banks J. Peeler, Lexington, North Carolina, the Convener, was then presented, who conducted the business of the sessions.

The Articles of Merger by which the Synodical Guild was to be governed until the Constitution and By-Laws could be prepared and approved, were adopted.[9] Mrs. Mengel read the "ceremony of the dedication of the organization of the Women's Guild of Southern Synod." The Synodical was, therefore, in business with endless detail and careful planning yet to be done. Elections resulted in naming Mrs. Banks J. Peeler, president; Mrs. V. Clifton Lanier, vice president; Mrs. George T. Fitz, secretary; and Miss Mildred O. Suther, treasurer. A constitution committee was authorized by the Executive Board, and immediately appointed in the persons of Mrs. Robert E. Patterson, chairman, Mrs. Andrew M. Crowell and Mrs. Howard R. Omwake.

Realizing that a strong Synodical Guild depended upon active local societies, the Board of Directors set up as one of its major objectives a well organized unit in each local congregation, and named December 4, 1941 as the date when local society units would make the switch to the Guild. Also, recognizing that an effective synodical program depended largely upon cooperation from the "top down," the denominational program for women's work was approved by the Executive Board which took immediate steps to implement it.

Commendable progress was made during the first biennium as is reflected in excerpts from the President's report to the Synodical September 29, 1942.[10]

> Almost two years ago, October 3, 1940, a delegated body of women, representing the entire Southern Synod, convened in First Church, Salisbury, North Carolina, having as their purpose to organize the Southern Synodical Women's Guild. In the two intervening years, the organization work has been completely effected. In April 1941, the second step was taken, when the Synodical Guild was divided into two smaller groups, the Catawba and the Piedmont Regional Women's Guilds. The final step in completing the organization was taken December 4, 1941, when local Women's Guilds were organized. A total of fifty three local Guilds, on or near that date, were completed; Catawba reporting 29, and Piedmont 24.
>
> At the spring Regional meeting this year, the two Regionals reported a total membership of 1,758; Catawba reporting 964, and Piedmont 794. . . . Most of the churches have women yet whom we have not reached . . . We are now reporting 25 Girls' Guilds, with a total membership of 307.
>
> Our two years of experiment and newness in Women's Guild work are finished. Much literature is available to acquaint us with the mechanics of our work. I challenge each member to so thoroughly familiarize herself with the full program, that we may definitely step out of this stage of newness and uncertainty into active, working Women's Guild members.

That same year, the historian, Mrs. C. Columbus Wagoner, recorded;

> The Executive Committee of Southern Synodical Guild . . . undertook the next step: that of organizing the Regional Guilds. It had been decided to form two Regionals, the Yadkin River being the dividing line; the Catawba, composed of churches west of the Yadkin (Including churches in Georgia and Florida) 33 in number; the Piedmont, embracing 25 churches east of the Yadkin. The dates for organization being April 24, 1941 at Mt. Zion Church, China Grove, North Carolina, for the Catawba Regional; and April 22, First Church, Greensboro, for the Piedmont Regional.[11]

Officers for each of these regionals were elected. For the Catawba group, Mrs. John T. Fesperman was elected president; Mrs. H. Smith Barrier, first vice president; Mrs. Walker Lyerly, second vice president; Mrs. Evans Bost, secretary; and Mrs. Roy C. Whisenhunt, treasurer. Succeeding Mrs. Fesperman in the office of president have been: Miss Verna Lentz, Mrs. Huitt R. Carpenter, Mrs. Hal Hoyle, Mrs. W. C. Lyerly, Mrs. Hoy L. Fisher, Mrs. T. F. Hart, Mrs. Lewis Everline, Mrs. J. J. Gminder, Mrs. George Fleming and Mrs. Robert E. Myers.

The first set of officers in the Piedmont Regional were: President, Mrs. George E. Dillinger; first vice president, Mrs. Andrew M. Crowell; second vice president, Mrs. Joshua L. Levens; secretary, Mrs. Coy E. Moose; treasurer, Mrs. J. Alexander Smith. Successors to Mrs. Dillinger in the office of president were: Mrs. Hoy L. Fesperman, Mrs. John Causey, Mrs. V. Clifton Lanier, Miss Jessie Leonard, Mrs. Aubrey W. Hedrick, Mrs. Henry Kennedy, Jr., and Mrs. William Hedrick.

Undoubtedly a major item on the agenda for consideration at the first biennial meeting was the report of the committee on Constitution and By-Laws. That this committee had done its work well is implied by the fact that the document was presented and read and adopted with a minimum of change.[12]

In 1942 a distinct pattern for program and promotion emerged. At that time ten departments with their chairmen were named for the Synodical.

The Departments

Spiritual Life	Mrs. K. A. Link, Lenoir
Missionary	Mrs. H. D. Althouse, Hickory
Stewardship	Mrs. A. O. Leonard, Lexington
Thanksoffering	Mrs. Rodney L. Coleman, Burlington
Christian Citizenship	Mrs. W. H. Causey, Winston Salem
Social Service	Mrs. H. Smith Barrier, Concord
Membership	Mrs. Ralph Long, Charlotte
Girls Guild	Mrs. Hoy L. Fesperman, High Point
Education	Mrs. Joshua L. Levens, Greensboro
Historian	Mrs. C. Columbus Wagoner, Lexington

The same pattern was followed in each of the regionals, being coordinated by the Synodical and Regional Boards. Beside being a tremendous missionary and promotional influence in the life of Southern Synod, the Guild has consistently carried out its program of stewardship and kingdom building, following a policy of lending a hand where help was most needed. Among these projects have been, current building needs at Nazareth Children's Home, Catawba College, the Blowing Rock Assembly Grounds and Johns River Valley Camp. In the department of church extension new mission starts have benefitted generously from Guild resources. Needy college students and missionary effort abroad have also found themselves to be beneficiaries of this unfailing source of benevolent concern.

Mrs. Peeler was succeeded in the office of president by Mrs. John T. Fesperman, Miss Verna Lentz, Mrs. V. Clifton Lanier, Mrs. Alvin R. Keppel, Mrs. Aubrey W. Hedrick and Mrs. Henry Kennedy, Jr.

As these lines are being written, the Synodical Women's Guild and its program of activities are in process of being channeled into the larger effort as described by the Council of Lay Life and Work of the United Church of Christ. President Sarah E. Hedrick, reporting to the Southern Synodical Women's Guild, April 1964 said;

> There will be a joint meeting of the women's executive boards of Southern Synod, Southern Convention, and those board members of the Convention of the South, who live in North Carolina and Eastern Virginia, to be held at Elon College on Monday afternoon, June 15, prior to the opening of Summer Conference. The purpose is to determine ways, in addition to the Summer Conference and Laity Workshops, in which our work may be merged. It is hoped that the Steering Committee, made up of three presidents and three other women will work on such plans which may be consummated at the Summer Conference a year hence, when it will meet at Catawba College. However, until such time as a Conference on C L L W is organized, no fixed pattern of women's work will be adopted.[13]

At a meeting of Southern Synod, acting as an Association of Southern Conference, which convened at Catawba College, Salisbury, North Carolina, October 25, 1966, the committee on Lay Life and Work reported:

> The Lay Life and Work movement on all levels of the United Church of Christ seems not yet to have crystalized, and perhaps has had to take some backward steps before launching out in a workable plan.
>
> In our own Conference the Board of Directors has approved plans for the organization of a conference-wide Women's Fellowship and a conference-wide Men's Fellowship. The women are to organize at a delegated meeting to be held at First Christian Church, Burlington, North Carolina, on Saturday, November 12, 1966, beginning at 10 a.m. The men are to organize at a similar type meeting at First Reformed United Church of Christ at Burlington, North Carolina, November 27, 1966, beginning at 2 p.m. Each of these meetings is to have one voting delegate from each local church of the conference, and it is proposed that they elect officers, adopt working rules, and make plans for future activities.
>
> Proposed working rules . . . . as developed for the women's group of the conference are as follows:
>
> 1. The name of this organization shall be The Church Women of the Southern Conference of the United Church of Christ.
>
> 2. Purpose: In cooperation with the committee on Lay Life and Work, the purpose of this organization shall be to increase, develop and coordinate the activities and participation of laywomen in the church as a means of witnessing effectively for Jesus Christ in all areas of life.
>
> 3. The officers shall be: President, First and Second Vice President, Secretary and Treasurer.
>
> 4. The Executive Committee shall be composed of the officers, the Area Convener and three representatives from each area. The Area Convener and three representatives shall serve until such time as permanent area officers are elected.

5. This organization shall meet at least annually, the time and place set by the Executive Committee.

6. Each church shall be entitled to one voting delegate to the annual meeting or special meetings of the organization. Churches may send additional non-voting representatives.

7. These working rules may be amended at any regular meeting by a two-thirds vote of delegates present and voting.[14]

1. *Patterson,* Mrs. H. J. etc., Facts, Faces, Memories, Woman's Missionary Society, 1941, p. 50.
2. *Peeler,* Banks J., Trinity Evangelical and Reformed Church, 75th Anniversary, 1956, p. 6.
3. *Patterson.* op. cit., p. 8.
4. ———. Minutes. Classis of North Carolina, 1897, p. 19.
5. *Ibid.* p. 20, 38.
6. *Patterson.* op. cit., p. 8.
7. ———. Minutes. op. cit., 1898, p. 79.
8. *Patterson.* op. cit., p. 45ff.
9. ———. Minutes. Southern Synodical Women's Guild, 1942, p. 5ff.
10. ———. Minutes. op. cit., p. 15.
11. *Ibid.* p. 19.
12. *Ibid.* p. 40.
13. ———. Minutes. op. cit., 1964, p.
14. ———. Minutes. Southern Synod, Acting Association, 1966, p. 17.

The Churchmen's Brotherhood

THE CHURCHMEN'S BROTHERHOOD of the Evangelical and Reformed Church stems from a number of factors, all of them aimed at enlisting and coordinating the man power of the church "for the cultivation of the Christian life through study, prayer, fellowship and service, and for the support and success of the whole program of the Church in the local congregation, the community, the denomination, and the world at large."[1] Among these early stimulating factors were the Brotherhood of St. Andrew and Philip, the Laymen's Missionary Movement and the Reformed Churchmen's League. With the approval of General Synod of the Reformed Church in the United States, the league was organized July 23, 1929 at a meeting of the Executive Committee of the Men's Missionary Movement which met at Wernersville, Pennsylvania. Subsequently the General Committee of the Laymen's Missionary Movement was reorganized to provide adequate representation from each of the Classes in the denomination.

Members of the committee present at Wernersville were: J. Q. Truxell, first vice president of General Synod; Dr. George L. Omwake, president of Ursinus College; Dr. Joseph Apple, president of Hood College; Professor E. M. Hartman, president of Franklin and Marshall Academy; Harry E. Paisley, treasurer of the Reading Railroad Company; L. F. Teel, Shippensburg, Pennsylvania; Judge D. J. Snyder, Greensburg, Pennsylvania; Emory L. Coblentz, Frederick, Maryland; William B. Haeussler, New York, N. Y.; and Dr. William E. Lampe, secretary of the Laymen's Missionary Movement.[2] J. Q. Truxell was named first full-time secretary of the Reformed Churchmen's League, and was asked to spend a large share of his time visiting local congregations to organize additional leagues. In 1930, as a result of effective field work, he reported that he was "persuaded more than ever that the men of the Reformed Church are anxious for larger service in Kingdom work.[3]

The first denomination-wide churchmen's convention was held November 10-12, 1931 at Harrisburg, Pennsylvania. Five hundred sixty-six delegates were registered, whose announced objective was the "consolidation of the men in a determined effort to make the denominational program of the Reformed Church effective."[4] Favorable reactions from that convention were voiced throughout the denomination, summed up by Dr. Charles D. Spotts:

> The convention at Harrisburg assured a continued existence of men's work in the Reformed Church. Therefore every congregation ought to step in line with the mind of General Synod when it authorized the organization of the Reformed Churchmen's League. There are at least four good reasons for the organization of a chapter in each local congregation: the men need it . . .; the pastor needs it . . .; the local congregation needs it . . .; and the denomination needs it.[5]

Slow but steady progress in men's work marked the next four years. Then, on August 18-20, 1936 occurred a history-making event. The Reformed Church in the United States and the Evangelical Synod of North America having merged in 1934, the two major men's organization of these communions, the Reformed Churchmen's League and the Evangelical Brotherhood, met in convention at Buffalo, New York. In 1937, the committee on Churchmen's Brotherhood of the Classis of North Carolina reported:

> The outstanding event in men's work of the denomination during the year, was the joint convention of the Reformed Churchmen's League and the Evangelical Brotherhood at Buffalo, New York on August 18-20, 1936. As a result of this meeting, these two organizations have merged into the Churchmen's Brotherhood. Beginning January 1, 1937, the brotherhood work will be under a unified administration with offices in Philadelphia, Pennsylvania and St. Louis, Missouri.[6]

This convention gave new impetus to men's work throughout the Evangelical and Reformed Church. In 1938, 648 chapters, enrolling 27,000 men were reported to the executive offices. The Classis of North Carolina, already supplied with organized Men's Bible Classes, sought to do brotherhood work through these classes. A standing committee on the Churchmen's Brotherhood was created, consisting of five people, instructed to channel program materials and administrative decisions to the local congregations. Where advisable, the committee was also directed to encourage the formation of new chapters of Brotherhood. In 1940, this committee in its report to Synod, noted with pleasure that in 1937 there were seven men's organizations with a membership of 204 in the Classis of North Carolina. In 1938, the number had increased to twelve chapters with 301 members.

In 1942, churches in Davidson County invited all men's organizations to send representatives to a meeting held at Pilgrim Church, whose purpose was to explore the possibility of setting up a district organization. Officers were elected, and a second meeting of similar nature was planned for all churches east of the Yadkin River. At that time the Eastern District of the Churchmen's Brotherhood was effected. Officers elected were: F. W. Gibhardt, president; H. D. Sink, first vice president; Robert T. Johnson, second vice president; Henry Kennedy, Jr., secretary; Fonzo Sink, treasurer; and Revs. Hoy L. Fesperman and A. Odell Leonard, advisors.

The Executive Committee of the Eastern District of Southern Synod met February 19, 1945 at the Sheraton Hotel, High Point, North Carolina, to outline plans for the creation of a Federation of Brotherhood Chapters in the Southern Synod. The federation meeting took place April 24-25, 1945 on the Catawba College campus. Fifty one delegates were registered, representing the following churches: First, High Point; First Burlington; Trinity, Conover; Faith, Brookford; First, Greensboro; Corinth, Hickory; St. John's, Kannapolis; Hedrick's Grove, Davidson County; First, Lexington; Second, Lexington; Grace, Newton; First, Salisbury; First, Winston Salem; Ursinus, Rockwell; First, Asheboro; Trinity, Concord; and St. James, Mt. Pleasant. Twenty two brotherhood chapters were reported in the synod.

Robert T. Johnson, who had effectively promoted the cause of brotherhoods in Southern Synod, presided over the opening session, and Dr. Banks J. Peeler, temporary chairman, stated the purpose of the gathering. Among speakers who were heard during the sessions were: Dr. Charles F. Freeman, Associate Executive Secretary of the Churchmen's Brotherhood in the Evangelical and Reformed Church; Dr. Alvin R. Keppel, president of Catawba College; and Dr. David E. Faust, professor of Bible at Catawba College.

A nominating committee recommended a set of officers, who were promptly elected. Robert T. Johnson was named president; Joseph L. Murphy, J. York Peeler and Garland Bright, vice presidents; Frederick W. Warlick, secretary; Willie F. Everhart, treasurer; Revs. A. Wilson Cheek, Roy C. Whisenhunt and Banks J. Peeler, ministerial advisors.[7]

Completing the synodical administrative picture the Western and Central sections of the church in North Carolina were urged as early as possible to effect District Organizations. When this had been accomplished, the president of each district became a vice president in the Synodical organization, therefore, a member of the Executive Committee. The Western District was organized November 2, 1944 at Trinity Church, Conover, North Carolina.

Adrian L. Shuford, Sr. was elected president; Dennis Rabb, vice president; William R. Weaver, secretary; and Murphy Wagoner, treasurer.

Central District was organized May 11, 1945 at Mt. Zion Church, China Grove, North Carolina. Dermont Weaver was elected president; Thomas L. Moose, vice president; Lewis Carrigan, secretary; and H. Smith, Barrier, treasurer.

With the administrative organization completed, two matters of major importance claimed the attention of the Executive Committee. An organization is ineffective without a program of study and service. President Robert T. Johnson, with the approval of the Executive Committee, met this need in asking the Synodical Brotherhood to cooperate in raising $25,000 with which to liquidate debts and make certain required improvements at the Blowing Rock Assembly Grounds; in promptly paying annual brotherhood dues, providing for administrative expenses and church extension; and in making contributions to the denominational heifer fund with which to aid depressed European countries. He also stressed the importance of regular monthly meetings of local chapters for worship, study and fellowship.[8]

Churchman's Brotherhood
Federation Meeting at
Catawba College, 1947

With the blessing of Southern Synod, an invitation was extended by the Synodical Brotherhood to the National Board to hold the national convention in 1948 within the bounds of Southern Synod on the campus at Catawba College. On this matter the committee on Auxiliary Organizations of Southern Synod in April 1948 remarked:

> The year 1948 finds all eyes of the men of General Synod turned toward Catawba College, Salisbury, North Carolina, where the National Convention is to be held September 1-5. An excellent program has been arranged, and there are good things in store for all who attend.[9]

In reporting on convention proceedings, the Rev. A. W. Meck-stroth, convention scribe, wrote:

> The days of September 1-5 will be treasured by the several hundred delegates who attended the Fourth Annual National Convention of the Churchmen's Brotherhood of the Evangelical and Reformed Church, held at Catawba College, Salisbury, North Carolina.
>
> The Brotherhoods of Southern Synod served as hosts and raised nearly $4,500. to entertain the delegates. A $1,000. check was presented to the convention by A. L. Shuford, Sr. in behalf of the men of Southern Synod.
>
> Leadership of the local convention committee was in the able hands of Thomas L. Moose, superintendent of Nazareth Orphans' Home of Rockwell, North Carolina, and Robert T. Johnson of First Church, Burlington, North Carolina and a member of the National Brotherhood Board. The beautiful city of Salisbury had a real share in the convention plans through its newspapers, radio stations and other facilities. Quite naturally North Carolina had the largest number of delegates in attendance, with Missouri, Pennsylvania, Ohio, Illinois and Wisconsin ranking next in number.[10]

Among churchmen who addressed the convention at appropriate times on the agenda were: Dr. Alvin R. Keppel, president of Catawba College; Mayor S. Holmes Plexico of Salisbury; Dr. John Lentz, vice president of the Evangelical and Reformed Church; Rev. Walter O. Wagner, St. Louis, Missouri; Dr. John Beigelisen, professor of New Testament Literature, Eden Theological Seminary; and executive secretaries of the various departments of denominational work, such as Evangelism, World Service, International Missions, Kingdom Service and Christian Social Action. Walter Graham, a Congregational Christian layman, addressed the convention in the interest of church union.

From its organization in 1945 until 1962 the Synodical Brotherhood made steady progress. Beginning with twenty two brotherhood chapters in as many congregations of Southern Synod, it reached a maximum enrollment of sixty-six chapters in 1961. For effective administrative purposes, these chapters were gradually subdivided into four districts: the Western, located west of the Catawba River; the Central, involving churches between the Catawba and Yadkin rivers; the Davidson, comprising chiefly churches in Davidson County; and the Eastern, including all churches east of Davidson County, reaching as far as Raleigh, North Carolina. Districts held semi-annual rallies, in the spring and fall, usually focusing attention upon some pertinent interest in the denominational program of study and service. These gatherings provided inspiration and fellowship so vital in maintaining desirable communication.

Over a period of years, the Easter Breakfast accepted as a synodical emphasis in 1952, proved to be a spiritual uplift. It projected the thought of Christian laymen holding fellowship around the table on Easter morning with the Risen Christ as the unseen guest.

As many as 2,000 men were served on a single Easter morning on a chapter basis in the churches throughout the Synod.

Almost every phase in the life of the church benefitted from the generous benevolence of these dedicated men. Among financial beneficiaries have been Nazareth Children's Home, Catawba College, John's River Valley Camp and the Blowing Rock Assembly Grounds. A revolving loan church building fund, starting with a few dollars, expanded into a sum of approximately $25,000. From it such mission churches as Edgewood, Burlington; St. Andrew's, Lexington; St. Matthew's, Charlotte; St. Peter's, Greensboro; and St. Thomas, Winston Salem, have benefitted. Scholarships on the college level have been provided for needy students. Each year generous support has been accorded benevolent projects agreed upon by the National Brotherhood Board.

Perhaps the most substantial contribution made by this organization to the life of the Southern Synod has been in the form of an alert and qualified leadership. From its ranks have come elders, deacons, Sunday School superintendents and teachers, youth counsellors, personal workers in evangelism and people generally who have given positive support to all worthy kingdom causes. Without becoming spectacular or dominating, the Churchmen's Brotherhood, along with the Women's Guild, have provided moral and spiritual muscle for the total life of the Synod.

Following the consummation of the United Church of Christ in 1957, as a result of a merger between the Evangelical and Reformed Church and the Congregational Christian churches, brotherhood activities, like other phases in the life of the denomination, faced drastic changes in habit and program. The nature of this adjustment is reflected in Article 82 of the Constitution of the United Church of Christ. It says:

> The General Synod shall establish a Council for Lay Life and Work as the instrumentality of the United Church of Christ responsible for increasing, developing and coordinating the activities and participation of laymen and laywomen in the Church as a means of witnessing effectively for Jesus Christ in all areas of life.

Since 1960 authorized officials, in consultation with study committees, conferences and workshops, have sought ways and means for translating this constitutional provision into a workable plan for the denomination. Obviously a satisfactory pattern has not been evolved. However, on November 12, 1966 men's work in Southern Conference was organized into a conference-wide Men's Fellowship.[11] In the meantime the Synodical Brotherhood continues to serve its chapters at points of need, including Spring and Fall rallies of district organizations. Current synodical officers are: Willie F. Everhart, president; R. E. Lassiter, John W. Sullivan, J. Richard Kirk, Sr., and Mike Abernethy, vice presidents; J. C. Corsbie, secretary; and Howard Regan, treasurer.

SYNODICAL BROTHERHOOD PRESIDENTS

Robert T. Johnson 1945-1946
Thomas L. Moose 1947-1949
Russell W. Whitener 1950-1951
James E. Swicegood 1952-1953
Thomas L. Moose 1954-1955
Frederick L. Barkley 1956-1957
Harold M. Lemons 1958-1959
Paul Shoaf 1960-1961
George D. Peeler 1962-1963
Frank L. Clapp 1964-1965
Marcus B. Crotts 1966-1967
Willie F. Everhart 1968-

1. *Darms*, John M. G., Handbook of the Churchmen's Brotherhood of the Evangelical and Reformed Church, ———, p. 5.
2. ———. Reformed Church Standard, September 1, 1929, p. 1.
3. ———. Standard Op. Cit., July 1, 1930, p. 4.
4. ———. Standard Op. cit., November 15, 1931, p. 1.
5. ———. Standard Op. cit., February 15, 1932, p. 2.
6. ———. Minutes. Classis of North Carolina, 1937, p. 18.
7. ———. Standard Op. cit., June 1, 1945, p. 1.
8. ———. Standard Op. cit., August 1, 1945, p. 1.
9. ———. Minutes. Southern Synod, 1948, p. 73.
10. ———. Standard Op. cit., November 1, 1948, p. 1.
11. ———. Minutes. Southern Synod, Acting Conference of the United Church of Christ, 1966, p. 17.

Young People's Societies

A SEPARATE REPORT on young people's activities of the Reformed Church in North Carolina appeared in the minutes of the Classis of North Carolina in 1908. At that time a report by the committee on Sunday Schools records an enrollment of eighty five young people in three societies.[1] In 1909 the statistical record carried six societies, junior and senior groups at Grace Church, Newton; one each at St. Mark's, Burlington; St. James, Mt. Pleasant; Shiloh, Faith; and First Church, Greensboro, totalling 169 members. Reports of this nature were received by the Classis each year through 1914. At that time thirteen societies had enrolled 337 members, who were collecting money and spending it almost totally for benevolent causes. These societies were listed under such titles as Young People's Society, Christian Endeavor, Mission Band and the Young People's Guild.

Because of these encouraging responses, the classical committee on young people's work asked that, wherever possible, similar youth groups be organized in all congregations, and the Classis appointed Rev. Clarence Woods as Superintendent of Young People's work, suggesting that if practicable a "Classical Convention" be arranged during the year for these societies.[2] The convention did not occur, but the wisdom of these plans is reflected in the report of the committee in 1915, when eighteen societies were recorded, with a total enrollment of 650 members.[3] The Rev. Jacob A. Palmer, serving as Superintendent of Young People's work in 1915, remarked.

> I can not but feel that we need many more such societies in our classis. If we as a church are to grow in efficiency and be able to meet the demands upon us, we need to give more attention to the training of young people. . . . . .
> I, therefore, recommend that this Classis instruct the Superintendent of Young People's Societies for the coming year to visit churches where young people's societies have been organized and where the prospects for such organization seem brightest, and speak in the interest of this work.[4]

From this point a pattern for young people's work in the Classis began to develop. By 1917 there were organized youth groups in one half of the congregations of the Classis.[5] The observance of Young People's Day began in 1918. War years of 1919 to 1922 had an adverse effect upon the movement, but expanded again after the Armistice, when young people returned to their families and homes. However, in 1928, realizing that young people's activities in the Classis, except for Mission Band and the Girl's Missionary Guild, were suffering from lack of supervisory control and overall organization, the committee on Young People's Societies of the Classis set up a pilot project conference at St. John's Church, Kannapolis, North Carolina April 27-28, 1928. The published program adequately explains the purpose and records its leadership.

> The Young People's Conference planned for the Central Section of our church in North Carolina is the first of its kind offered to our young folks. It is, therefore, an experiment. It covers the following charges: Faith, Rockwell, Bear Creek, Keller-Gilead, Concord, Charlotte, Kannapolis, Mt. Zion-Landis and Salisbury. Any young people of these charges may attend. Its sessions will be held in the Kannapolis church. The first meeting is at 7:45 Friday evening, and runs through Saturday, closing at 4:30.
> Leaders and helpers are: Miss Katherine A. Miller, Director of Young People's Activities of the Reformed Church; Rev. John W. Myers, newly elected professor of Religious Education at Catawba College; Rev. A. Odell Leonard, pastor of Second Reformed Church, Lexington; Professor E. N. Peeler, principal of Granite Quarry High School; Miss Josephine Safrit, teacher in Granite Quarry High School.[6]

The report of the committee on Young People's Societies to the Classis in May of that year is explicit.

> From a study of the reports of young people's work, we are glad to note a marked increase in every column except money raised for local societies. In many instances the increase over last year is double.
> On April 27-28, 1928, a young people's conference was held at St. John's Church, Kannapolis, North Carolina, with great success. Those responsible for the conference have rendered a valuable service to the cause of young people's work in the North Carolina Classis. In view of the success of said conference, and upon the request of this body of young people, we recommend:
> That, instead of appointing a committee on Young People's Societies as heretofore, that Classis appoint a permanent committee on Young People's Work consisting of five members (three ministers, one from each

district of the Classis), and two elders. The minister from each district
to be a pastoral advisor for the District Young People's organization that
is or will be formed.[7]

These plans set the stage for the first classis-wide youth conference, which occurred at First Reformed Church, Salisbury, North
Carolina May 2-3, 1929. Two hundred delegates were registered,
representing twenty-nine churches. A temporary organization was
effected for "the purpose of better enabling themselves to reach out
and aid their groups in other congregations."[8] Through Elder John
F. Carpenter of Maiden, North Carolina, a gift of ten acres of land
located on the Catawba River Northwest of Hickory, North Carolina was made available for a camp site. The Young People's Committee of Classis was authorized to investigate its feasibility.

A Second Annual Conference was held at Trinity Church, Concord, North Carolina, April 24-25, 1930, when a permanent organization was set up. Carl F. Herman was elected president; Miss
Lucille Lopp, vice president; Miss Bernice Lyerly, secretary; Miss
Gladys Love, treasurer; district vice presidents: Miss Roxie Wel-
born, Eastern; Frank K. Bostian, Central; Woodrow Coulter, Western. The Young People's Association of the Reformed Church in
North Carolina, was adopted as a name for the new organization.
The program of the World Christian Endeavor Union was approved
as a working basis, and local societies were encouraged to affiliate
with the Christian Endeavor Society. Recognized also as operating
in the area of youth interests were Boy Scouts of America and the
Girls' Missionary Guild. To promote interest among societies, three
district conferences, each under supervision of its district vice president, were scheduled for that fall.[9]

District conferences proved to be popular and effective in stimulating interest and unifying the concerns of young people throughout the Classis, reaching a total attendance of 252 people in 1936.
The Annual Conference registered 387 delegates in 1938. Young
people were on the move throughout the church in North Carolina.
The proposed camp site on the Catawba River did not materialize;
however, other plans did develop, and a first camp session was held
at a site on Johns River eighteen miles Northwest of Lenoir, North
Carolina in July 1936. There was an enrollment of thirty campers
plus staff. Considering local activities—conferences, weekly gatherings, camp and study groups—perhaps at no other time to date in
the history of the Classis did the church present a better, more effective teen-age training program. On occasion of its Tenth Anniversary, the Young People's Association of the Reformed Church in
North Carolina, reported sixty-one affiliated societies with an enrollment of 1,571 people and contributions totalling $1,014.

Young People's Activities, like other phases in the life of the
church, were effected by the merger which took place in 1934
between the Reformed Church in the United States and the Evan-

gelical Synod of North America, forming the Evangelical and Reformed Denomination. At the time of this merger, the Evangelical Synod had an effective youth organization with a well defined program of action, represented in the Evangelical League. No such denomination-wide youth organization existed in the Reformed Church. Nearest to a recognized organization was the Heidelberg League approved by the Synod of the Northwest. Youth Activities of the Reformed Church, in their varied forms, were administered through the Youth Department of the Board of Christian Education, with emphasis on the Christian Endeavor concept of program study and action.

Merger conversations had projected united youth activities in some form. Thus, in 1936, Dr. Fred D. Wentzel was made full-time director of youth work in the Evangelical and Reformed Church. In setting up the first National Conference on Christian Education at Lakeside, Ohio in 1937, a special study committee provided for a youth assembly. That assembly established a National Youth Cabinet and elected its members, which consisted of nine young people, five adults and two staff consultants. In February 1938, a statement of purpose was evolved, which, in 1940, was adopted and became the working standard by which denominational Youth Cabinet and elected its members, which consisted of lows:

> The Youth Fellowship of the Evangelical and Reformed Church unites all young people of the denomination in this eight-fold purpose:
> —To come to a more intimate knowledge of God, by practicing His presence, studying His word and doing His will.
> —To arrive at a clearer understanding of what is meant to be Christian, and to give ourselves more and more to the Christian way of life.
> —To develop an affection for the church, concern for its total program, here and abroad, and the will to make its spirit and its work increasingly Christian.
> —To unite all young people of our denomination in a fellowship committed to the Christian way of life, and a wider fellowship including all other young people of like convictions.
> —To use our time, whether at work or leisure, for the welfare of society and our own best selves.
> —To face the ethical and social problems of our day squarely, intelligently in the light of the teachings of Jesus.
> —To render service, in the spirit of Jesus, to people and to causes in our communities and beyond.
> —To work with all people of goodwill who strive for a world of righteousness and justice, racial, economic and political.[10]

When the Young People's Conference of Southern Synod met in the spring of 1940 at Shiloh Church, Faith, North Carolina, a Synodical Youth Cabinet was created. Its personnel consisted of Roy Kirk, president; Miss Violet Hoffman, vice president; Mrs. Charlotte Druery, secretary; Miss Lucille Warlick, treasurer; chairman of the Western District, Adrian L. Shuford, Jr.; Central District, Mrs. Charlotte Druery; Davidson-Forsyth District, Theodore Leonard;

Eastern District, Miss Violet Hoffman. The cabinet was composed of nine members; three elected by the young people, three by Southern Synod, and three by the first six. The cabinet proceeded to affiliate with the National Youth Fellowship Movement, and urged districts and local societies to do the same.[11] It follows, therefore, that the program for young people's work in Southern Synod was fashioned after the denominational pattern.

This is not to imply that young people of the area accepted in package form the program handed down by the National Youth Cabinet; on the contrary, using such ideas as were adaptable, they developed their own plans and procedures suited to local needs. Among the many interests that appeared on this program was camping. Johns River Valley Camp became a popular summer training grounds for several hundred Junior, Junior High and Senior Young people each year. The Annual Convocation, buttressed by four district conferences each year, and supported by sixty-eight local societies, kept a growing number of purposeful young people interested in matters of the Christian faith and practice. These young people supported projects and cooperated in carrying out assignments, ranging from personal evangelism on the local parish to church extension in the Synod and Japanese relocation centers on the national level.

When the question of inter-church cooperation appeared, this section of the church was usually in the limelight. As early as 1947, seventy-five young people of the denomination joined a like number from the Congregational Christian Churches, in exploring ways and means for voluntary fellowship and program cooperation.[12] Also, a joint meeting of Youth Fellowship of Southern Synod, Evangelical and Reformed Church with the Pilgrim Fellowship of Southern Convention of Congregational Christian Churches was proposed for July 3, 1948. It is interesting to note that in 1958, one year after the merger of the Evangelical and Reformed Church and the Congregational Christian Churches, young people of the merged church were working together in areas of program, fellowship and Campus Ministry.[13]

By 1951 youth work in Southern Synod had become so varied and extensive, that upon recommendation of a study committee, it was placed by the Synod under the supervision of the Committee on Christian Education and Publication. At that time the Synod discontinued the practice of electing members to the Synodical Youth Cabinet. The purpose of this move was to establish a closer relationship with the total educational program of the Synod, assuring coordination of and better implementation of all youth interests.[14] In 1953, student work as it was related to college and university campuses in North Carolina, became a primary concern of the committee on Christian Education and Publication. Nineteen sixty was typical of synodical youth activities. That year, the annual convocation was divided into two sections: Junior High young people who met at Shiloh Church, Faith, North Carolina, and Senior Young People who convened at Grace Church, Newton, North Carolina. The Junior High Group registered 280 delegates at their spring rally, while Seniors registered 250; also, in the same spring 600 young folks gathered at First Church, Salisbury, North Carolina for a "Heritage Heyday" program, dramatizing the denomination's rich cultural and religious heritage.

A recitation of these facts is important only as they relate to this segment of serious minded, purposeful youth in the Evangelical and Reformed Church, so typical of those who compose the reliable core of this generation. They were a wholesome, courageous lot. Sensing the hope for a more unified and just society latent in a united, but not necessarily a merged Christendom, the Youth Fellowship joined hands with their seniors in developing the union between the Evangelical and Reformed Church and the Congregational Christian Churches, creating the United Church of Christ. In order to more adequately express their concern about the role of the church in their generation, a new name "Youth Ministry" was coined. The nature of that ministry as they conceived it is described in the following statement:

> Driven by our vocation as Christians, and inspired by our hope in God, we enter into and take upon ourselves the Youth Ministry of the United Church of Christ.
>
> To minister is to serve. In this sense all of us in the church are called to minister and to be ministered unto. Christ's love makes us sensitive to the needs of others—young and old—and each of us responds according to his own compassion and talents.
>
> Through the United Church Youth, the United Church of Christ's ministry involving youth of the ages 14 to 18, we undertake to make the whole church sensitive to the special needs and concerns of high school young people, as well as to make the young people sensitive to the whole church, to other youth, and to the world.
>
> As persons, young people are passing through those unique years when they are sharpening their focus on life. These are days of preparation-apprenticeship. Youth face complex decisions and they look to the church for guidance. Youth need opportunities to test their life philosophy and their personal abilities in an understanding and compassionate fellowship. They have fresh ideas and varied talents for developing their own program. In the life of the church they can minister, but they also need to be ministered unto. Youth want to help, but they also need to be helped. Youth are churchmen today, not simply persons preparing for churchmanship tomorrow.
>
> All adults have an important role in the church's youth ministry. Their experience is in many ways greater than that of youth. They have the advantage of a longer perspective on life. But adults also experience rejection and doubt, and therefore feel the need of understanding and love and of being accepted as a person.
>
> In the fellowship of mutual trust, we, young people and adults, can grow and minister together as we seek to serve in Christ's name. Thus, in the church's youth ministry we strive toward mutuality of youth and adults at every level of United Church Youth.[15]

The Youth Fellowship of Southern Synod has also stated its covenant in lucid language. It reads:

> We, the youth of the United Church of Christ, affirm that God has made himself known to us in Jesus Christ and has called us into His Church. Believing that he seeks us in holy love, we would respond by joining together in covenant with Him.
>
> He gathers us into a living fellowship in which we encounter one another as unique persons who are created in His image. We seek to express the spirit of this fellowship in all our relationships.
>
> Our vocation is to witness to the message and mission of the church among all people, serving the world in the name of Christ, and striving toward the establishment of brotherhood, justice and peace. Our hope is in God who, in Jesus Christ, offers redemption to all men and gives promise of His kingdom of love.[16]

1. ———. Minutes. Classis of North Carolina, 1908, p. 24.
2. ———. Minutes. Op. Cit., 1914, p. 49.
3. ———. Minutes. Op. Cit., 1915, p. 64.
4. *Ibid.* Minutes. Op. Cit., p. 28.
5. ———. Minutes. Op. Cit., 1917, p. 50.
6. ———. Reformed Church Standard, April 15, 1928, p. 3.
7. ———. Minutes. Op. Cit., 1928, p. 18.
8. ———. Minutes. Op. Cit., 1930, p. 19.
9. ———. Minutes. Op. Cit., 1931, p. 22.
10. *Tani,* Henry, Manuscript. History of the Youth Fellowship, Evangelical and Reformed Church, 1958, p. 2.
11. ———. Minutes. Southern Synod, 1941, p. 37.
12. ———. Minutes. Op. Cit., 1947, p. 38.
13. ———. Minutes. Op. Cit., 1958, p. 47.
14. ———. Minutes. Op. Cit., 1951, p. 16.
15. ———. The Plan for the Youth Ministry, United Church of Christ, 1962, p. 2. (Department of Youth Ministry).
16. ———. Youth Fellowship Handbook of Southern Synod, 1961, p. 2. (Prepared by the Synodical Youth Cabinet).

The Historical Society

No official effort appears to have been made to conserve the historical record of the Reformed Church in North Carolina prior to 1879. At that time the Classis of North Carolina asked Dr. George W. Welker, its Stated Clerk, to prepare a "General Historical Essay" to be read at the 50th Annual Meeting of the Classis. This was done, but the manuscript evidently was not published.

Four years later the Classis made the following announcement:

> The Classis of North Carilina appointed the Rev. Dr. Welker and Rev. Professor J. C. Clapp to prepare a narrative of its proceedings, at its last annual meeting held in the Pilgrim Church and have it published in pamphlet form for the use of the churches under its care. As well as they are able, in the limited time afforded them, they have performed the work given them, and now send it forth to the churches, hoping it may prove satisfactory and also serve the interests of this member of the Church of our Lord Jesus Christ.[1]

In 1888, "Revs. Messrs. Clapp, Murphy and Welker were appointed to prepare a concise history of the Reformed Church, its doctrine and government with an account of its rise and history in North Carolina to be published with the Minutes of the Classis."[2] That brief historical sketch was published in the 1888 volume of the Minutes of the Classis.[3]

In 1895, a manuscript entitled "A Historical Sketch of the Classis of North Carolina," was discovered among the papers of the late Dr. George W. Welker. With permission of his widow, Mrs. Emily Jane Welker, Dr. Jacob C. Clapp added a paragraph on the "Mode of Travel," and Dr. Joseph L. Murphy wrote an introduction preparing it for publication. It was published that year in brochure form, printed by A. L. Crouse, Hickory, North Carolina.

During the following decade historical data accumulated in the office of the Stated Clerk of the Classis and as it did, sentiment crystalized favorable to publishing a history of the Reformed Church in North Carolina. Therefore, in May 1904, the Classis acted as follows:

> Whereas, It is desirable to have a history of the Classis which shall be as full and complete as possible, and
>
> Whereas, It is necessary in order to have this that a diligent research and careful investigation be made, and it is evident that this can be accomplished best by uniting all forces and resources at hand, therefore;
>
> Resolved, That this work be committed to the following committee: Rev. Jacob C. Clapp, D.D., Editor-in-Chief; Rev. Jacob C. Leonard, B.D., Assistant Editor-in-Chief; John A. Foil, Ph.D., Rev. Paul Barringer, Rev. Calvin B. Heller, and Rev. Joseph L. Murphy, D.D., Associate Editors.
>
> Resolved that Rev. William B. Duttera, B.D., Ph.D. be constituted Business Manager.
>
> Resolved, That the editor-in-chief and his assistant shall review all manuscript prepared for the book, and that they, in conjunction with the business manager, shall submit to the Classis, either in annual or special session, a report of their work, and the plan of their work, and that no contract for printing shall be made until the Classis shall have approved the report of the editor-in-chief, and his assistant, and the business manager.
>
> Resolved, That all money accruing from the sale of the book above the cost of publishing shall be placed in the hands of the Treasurer of Classis and shall be used to assist mission charges within the bounds of Classis.[4]

This volume was published four years later, in 1908, under the title "Historic Sketch of the Reformed Church in North Carolina."

In 1922, a permanent committee on the Historical Society appeared in the record. Its purpose as stated was to cooperate with the denominational society in conserving and transmitting documents such as books, tracts, phamplets, brochures of an historical nature to accepted repositories. The committee was composed of Rev. Jacob C. Leonard, Rev. Walter W. Rowe and Elder J. J. Correll.[5]

In 1929, by authority of the Classis, a unit of the Historical Society was established in North Carolina. Dr. O. Bain Michael was elected president; Rev. C. Columbus Wagoner, vice president; Dr. Jacob C. Leonard, secretary-treasurer; Rev. Milton Whitener, curator; and Mrs. Dora L. Kline, librarian. The organization began immediately collecting historical material and placing it in the vault at Catawba College.[6]

Resulting from the merger of the Reformed Church in the United States with the Evangelical Synod of North America and the establishment of Southern Synod, the Historical Society was transferred to that body in 1940.[7]

This was a transition period in the life of the Reformed Church in North Carolina, therefore, strongly invited a chronicle of its history to the present time. Dr. Jacob C. Leonard undertook the task on his own initiative, producing the "History of Southern Synod, Evangelical and Reformed Church," in 1940. An appreciative Synod adopted the following resolution:

> After many years of faithful research and the gathering of material, rich in historical interest to the former Reformed Church in the United States and the Evangelical Synod of North America, and especially materials related to the activities of the churches and institutions within the bounds of the Southern Synod, Dr. J. C. Leonard, for 48 years Stated Clerk of the North Carolina Classis and at present Secretary of the Southern Synod, has completed his "History of Southern Synod, Evangelical and Reformed Church."
>
> In recognition of this splendid contribution to the historical records and progress of the Evangelical and Reformed Church, be it resolved that:
>
> 1. That Southern Synod hereby express its appreciation to Dr. J. C. Leonard for his untiring labors.
>
> 2. That we commend this new publication, "History of Southern Synod, Evangelical and Reformed Church," to the members and friends of our congregations.

In 1944, by action of Southern Synod, composition of the Historical Society was changed to "be composed of three members, one of whom shall be on the Faculty or Administrative Staff of Catawba College; that they serve for a period of five years; that they report to the Synod only when they have something new.[8]

This policy continued until 1956, when Rev. Frank W. Snider was named by the Synodical Council as Historian. The Historical Committee of General Synod has established a set of rules by which the historian was to be governed. These appear below:

> 1. To solicit and collect historical materials.
>
> 2. To keep a record of all historical material received and to make a report on same each year to the Synod.
>
> 3. To secure the approval of the Synod to turn this material over to the archives of the Lancaster or Eden Seminaries.
>
> 4. To be responsible for fostering general inaerest in the history of local churches, church-related institutions and the Synod as well as the denomination.
>
> 5. To cultivate the spirit of research with the object of encouraging both amateur and trained historical students to write articles for publication.
>
> 6. To support all activities and aims of the Historical Committee by effective cooperation.
>
> 7. To cooperate with Synod President in all that concerns the Historian's office.

These guidelines were faithfully followed by the historian in developing a workable rapport with all phases in the life of Southern Synod. Valuable data was compiled, some cataloguing was done and a repository in the archives on the campus at Catawba College was arranged for.[9]

On November 30, 1958, forty-five persons assembled in the lecture room of the Catawba College library, when a southern chapter of the Historical Society was organized. Twenty-six people joined the chapter. Dr. Bruce A. Wentz was elected president; Mr. Frank L. Clapp, vice president; Mrs. Fred Kepley, secretary; and Dr. Jacob A. Palmer, treasurer.[10]

Realizing that another transition was taking place in the church, which would eventually involve the dissolution of Southern Synod, a committee was appointed in 1958 by the Synodical Council to investigate the cost and other circumstances involved in publishing an up-to-date history of the Synod. The committee consisted of Rev. Frank W. Snider, Rev. A. W. Hedrick and Mr. Farel W. Warlick. The results of that investigation were of necessity preliminary and inconclusive, but helpful.

On November 7, 1963, by invitation, the historian appeared before the Synodical Council and further discussed the advisability of publishing a history of the Synod. Out of this consultation grew a committee composed of Rev. Joshua L. Levens, chairman, Rev. Frank W. Snider and Mr. Henry Kennedy, Jr., instructed to make a thorough study of the subject and to report its findings.[11] That was done and the report of the committee follows:

The special committee appointed by the president of Southern Synod to study the possibility of writing a history of Southern Synod makes the following recommendations:

1. That a history of Southern Synod be prepared and written.

2. That 3000 copies be printed. That cost, as the committee has been able to determine, will be about $10,000.

3. That a Finance Committee of three be appointed by the president of Synod to promote the financing and sale of the history.

4. That we sell shares for this project at $10 per share and that we set a goal of 500 shares.

5. That the president of Synod and the members of the Finance Committee select ten captains to head up the sale of these shares and that these ten captains select their helpers from all parts of the Synod to assist in the work.

6. That receipts be given those buying shares and that the receipts be printed in triplicate.

7. That captains and helpers conduct a pre-printing sale of the history sometime near the printing date. The price is to be $5 per copy.

8. That an Editorial Board of five be appointed by the Synodical Council to gather materials and determine the policy of the history.

9. That Synod provide secretarial help, part-time help.

10. That, if possible, a professional writer be used in the actual writing and preparation of the history.

11. That Southern Synod appropriate $1,000 to be used in writing the history, and if a profit is realized from the sale of the history, that $1,000 be paid to the local Historical Chapter for its use.[12]

At a meeting of the Synodical Council, held September 10, 1964, to evaluate the findings of this study, a finance committee and a board of editors were set up. Mr. Henry Kennedy, Jr., chairman, Mr. Harry Corriher, Mr. James E. Swicegood, Mr. C. W. Starr and Mr. Claude S. Abernethy were named to the Finance Committee; and Rev. Frank W. Snider, chairman, Rev. A. W. Hedrick, Dr. Lonnie A. Carpenter, Mr. Frank L. Clapp and Mr. A. Howard White to the Board of Editors. In the fall of 1965 the board of editors appointed Dr. Banks J. Peeler to assemble the material and prepare the manuscript for publication.

The Southern Chapter of the Historical Society continues to collect documents of historical value. These are deposited in the Archives at Catawba College, where a wealth of unclassified material has been assembled. In time this material will be classified and properly catalogued. This chapter meets annually, usually in November. Current officers are: Rev. Frank K. Bostian, president; Rev. Banks D. Shepherd, vice president; Dr. Felix B. Peck, secretary; Rev. John D. Bonebrake, treasurer; and Dr. Banks J. Peeler, librarian. Rev. Frank W. Snider continues to serve as the authorized historian.

1. ———. Minutes. Classis of North Carolina, 1883, p. 1.
2. ———. Minutes. *op. cit.*, 1888, p. 16.
3. ———. *Ibid.* p. 17.
4. ———. Minutes. *op. cit.*, 1904, p. 344.
5. ———. Minutes. *op. cit.*, 1922, p. 12.
6. ———. Minutes. *op. cit.*, 1929, p. 13, 24.
7. ———. Minutes. *op. cit.*, 1944, p. 39.
8. ———. Minutes. *op. cit.*, 1944, p. 39.
9. ———. Minutes. *op. cit.* 1955, p. 39, 40.
10. ———. Minutes. *op. cit.*, 1959, p. 48.
11. ———. Minutes. *op. cit.*, 1964, p. 12.
12. ———. *Ibid.* 1964, p. 20.

CHAPTER III

Educational
Institutions

Education Prior to 1850

FORMAL EDUCATION, not always easily available for the rank and file in early German Settlements in North Carolina, was regarded by those industrious people as a mark of high attainment. Distance and economics usually created an impassable barrier for all except the favored few. By distance is implied that church schools were located four hundred miles away in Pennsylvania; by economics is meant small incomes and the lack of ready cash placed the coveted privilege of formal learning completely out of reach for most young people. To solve some of these difficulties, the church took a hand. Being tenaciously loyal to church related institutions, there should be no surprise when in 1834, three years after the Classis of North Carolina came into existence, that body became parent to an Education Society, whose announced purpose was to aid young folks in their pursuit of an education.

During its sessions, which began May 10th at Savits (Mt. Zion) Church, Rowan County, Rev. John H. Crawford, William C. Bennet and Elders John C. Barnhardt and John Coulter were instructed to draft a constitution suitable for governing such a venture. Later in the sessions of that same meeting of the Classis, the committee presented its report, which was adopted. It detailed plans for an organization destined to play a major role in the development of the German Reformed Church and its successor, the Evangelical and Reformed Church, in North Carolina. Because of its historical importance the complete text of that Constitution is included in this story.

CONSTITUTION OF THE EDUCATION SOCIETY

I. This society shall be called the Education Society of the North Carolina Classis of the German Reformed Church; the object of which shall be to aid in the education of indigent and pious young men, within the bounds of the classis, for the Gospel ministry.

II. The officers of the society shall be president, two vice presidents, a secretary, a treasurer, and five managers, who shall be elected annually;

49

and who shall constitute a Board of Education to carry its objectives into effect.

III. It shall be the duty of the president to preside, to keep order and to give the casting vote; and in case of his absence, the senior vice president, or in case of the absence of both, the junior vice president shall occupy the chair.

IV. It shall be the duty of the secretary to keep a faithful record of all proceedings; and to conduct all of the correspondence of the society.

V. It shall be the duty of the treasurer, safely to keep all funds of the society; and to make no remittances or payments, without an order from the Board of Education. He shall also give bond, with approved security, for all the society's money in his hands.

VI. Any person paying two dollars annually shall be a member of society; any person paying twenty dollars at one time, shall be a member for life.

VII. Local societies, within the bounds of the Classis, may become auxiliary by transferring their funds to the treasurer of this society, annually; unless they shall themselves, individually, be able to support at least one beneficiary. They shall in that case, only be required to report to the secretary, without paying anything into the treasury; and shall have power to appropriate their funds to the benefit of their own beneficiary as they deem most advisable.

VIII. The Board of Education shall from time to time, as they deem most practicable, select poor and pious young men, belonging to the churches within the bounds of the Classis; who feel themselves called to and are desirous of entering the Christian Ministry; and aid them in receiving an education preparatory to that sacred office.

IX. The beneficiaries of the society shall be under the complete direction and guardianship of the Board of Education, who shall make all contracts for their support. And, in no case, shall these young men receive money into their own hands to be disposed of at their own discretion.

X. No beneficiary shall receive pecuniary aid from the society, as an exclusive gift; but on the contrary, it shall be considered a loan with provisions as follows: 1. He shall pledge himself to enter the ministry in the German Reformed Church; 2. He shall give approved bonds for all the money applied to his use by the Board of Education; 3. He shall refund all money expended for his benefit, with interest from the date of its expenditure; if he at any time, during his studies, shall change his mind, and turn his attention to some other profession or pursuit, or attach himself to some other church; 4. If he shall enter the ministry of the German Reformed Church, he shall, if able, refund all money applied to his use by the Board of Education, without interest, within the term of four years from the date of his licensure; 5. If any, or the whole of the money shall remain unpaid at the expiration of the term of four years, he shall from that time be required to pay interest; 6. If, through the providence, of God, he shall be prevented from entering the ministry by disease or death, or if in the course of the same providence, he shall always remain poor after entering the ministry, he, or his friends, shall never be called upon, either for the principle or the interest.

XI. Five members of the Board of Education shall constitute a quorum to transact business, at any of the meetings of the society, or of the board regularly called.

XII. The annual meeting of the society shall be held on Saturday, previous to the second Sabbath in May, at the place where Classis meets; when a sermon appropriate to the occasion shall be preached.

XIII. This Constitution can only be altered at an annual meeting, by a majority of two-thirds of the members present.

The first board was constituted by the following persons: Revs. John G. Fritchey, president; John H. Crawford, senior vice president; William C. Bennet, junior vice president; William C. Rankin, secretary; Mr. Daniel Conrad, treasurer. Managers were: Daniel Conrad, Major Jacob Barrier, John C. Barnhardt, Jacob Leonard, Col. John Hoke and Col. Daniel Clapp.[1]

The obvious primary purpose of the Education Society was to aid worthy young men in preparing for the Christian Ministry in the German Reformed Church. However, there were other intangible benefits. In 1838 the Rev. George Boger wrote, "There is a great disposition manifested on the part of our churches to sustain our institutions, and to increase the spread of the Gospel, both at home and abroad."[2] In the same year Classis acted to express its pleasure and satisfaction with the progress being made throughout the church in the state, and declared its support of church literary and theological institutions, located at York, Carlisle and Mercersburg, Pennsylvania. These revealing resolutions state:

> That the Classis is deeply sensible, that the prosperity of our German Reformed Zion, under the blessing of God, chiefly depends upon our literary and benevolent institutions.
> That the present encouraging prospects of our institutions afford ample ground for greater and more efficient effort on the part of the members of this Classis and increase their obligations to secure the permanent endowment of our schools.
> That in the election of a professor of theology, at the approaching meeting of the Synod, we do unanimously agree in instructing our delegates to support the re-election of Dr. Mayer, knowing him to be the choice of the church in the South.[3]

Rev. David Crooks also wrote, with approving enthusiasm, about progress within the Classis in the year 1843:

> Of the German Reformed Church in North Carolina, the record of more than eighty years, is now entered upon the table-book of eternity. Of the men who then ministered to her in holy things not one remains. Much of their history, too, glimmering as it does through the lapse of eighty years, is but dimly seen and little known. On the 23rd day of May, 1831, our Classis drew the breath of organic life. Of the ministers whose prayers and efforts then warmed it into being, but two remain in its connection. From its organization up to the present time, it has passed through a variety of trials. True, however, in its devotion to the interests of the church, it has maintained its existence and bids fair to increase both in stature and wisdom.
> In regard to this acquisition, Classis owes an expression of gratitude for our colleges and Theological Seminary. Without the aid of such institutions, no efforts, however pious they might be, could secure to the Church that respect to which she is entitled, and to which she ought most certainly aspire. To take our proper stand among the sister churches with which we are surrounded, light is indispensably necessary. If other denominations prosper only in the soil of ignorance, it can never be so with us; if others glory in their shame and boast of their abilities without the aid of learning, it must not, it cannot be so with us. We owe our being as a branch of the Protestant Church to the triumphs of light over darkness, error and superstition. A knowledge of the Greek restored the

Scriptures in their purity in Germany. From that moment a struggle ensued between light and darkness. Our fathers resisted even unto blood, and finally succeeded in throwing from the bosom of the Church the spiritual encumberances of ignorance and crime with which she was oppressed.

The Protestant cause struck her roots deep, and still deeper, in the soil of truth and Scriptural intelligence, and spread her green branches far and wide, under covert of which the virtues, the wise and good, love to take shelter. Our institutions should, therefore, be regarded as a nucleus around which the Church should be disposed to concentrate her efforts. The sacred soil upon which they are erected should be kept constantly bedewed with the balmy influence of prayer. Nor will her zeal be unrewarded. Their reflex influence, conducted as they are by an able-and pious faculty, upon the Church must be of the happiest kind. From them streams must ever issue to water and make glad the garden of our God.

With regard to an enlightened ministry, we have always taken high ground, and thus far, by the grace of God, we have been able to maintain it. Indeed, so great and so rapid have been our advances within the last few years, that the greatest danger at the present juncture is that of being exalted above measure, of forgetting our dependence. We also, at this time enjoy the blessings of union. . . . a union which binds heart and hand and effort around truth and principle. . . . Our pulpits are now regularly filled. Our churches enjoy steadily the means of grace and the ordinances of the House of God. We are growing in numbers, as well as in moral and religious strength. . . . This to us will constitute a year of years. Its record will ever be regarded as a bright spot on the pages of the past, upon which memory will love to linger, and it may be from which it will turn in pain.[4]

Stimulated by such progress, progressive churchmen began to discuss the possibilities for establishing a church-related school in North Carolina. In 1849, when the Classis met at Newton, the problem of education was formally presented for discussion, which resulted in the following action: "Resolved, that a committee be appointed to report at the next meeting of the Classis, on the propriety of establishing a school of high order within the bounds of the Classis and under its control."[5] The committee consisted of Dr. George W. Welker, Dr. Jeremiah Ingold and Elder Henry Sechler.

After considerable investigation, land was acquired in the town of Newton, North Carolina, and on it certain buildings were erected in preparation for establishing a high school at that place.[6] A committee consisting of Rev. John H. Crawford, Rev. Robert Crooks, F. D. Reinhardt, Esq., M. L. McCorkle, Esq., and John Wilfong, Esq., was named to lay plans for the opening of the school.[7] The committee named Rev. C. H. Albert principal and teacher, who associated with himself Professor H. H. Smith. The school was begun December 3, 1851, enrolling "thirty-two pupils with encouraging prospects for the future."[8]

With this announcement an era in education among German Reformed Church people in North Carolina came to an end, and another began with good reasons for optimism. For the High

School, suffering some reverses during the Civil War, became Catawba College with recognized standing in educational circles of that day, to be followed in 1880 by the founding of Claremont Female College by Corinth Reformed Church, Hickory, North Carolina. During this period also sprang up a system of academies throughout the Classis not necessarily sponsored by the denomination, but inspired and directed by leaders of the Church, chiefly ministers. Typical among these being Bethany Academy founded in 1858, Pilgrim Academy in 1890, Arnold Academy in 1891 all in Davidson County; Crescent Academy in 1896 located in Rowan County; Catawba Academy established in 1851 and conducted in connection with Catawba College at Newton until 1923. There were others. These private schools eventually gave way to progress, as the State Department of Public Instruction provided for instruction on this level in its High School System.

1. ――――. Minutes. Classis of North Carolina, Reformed Church in the United States, 1834, p. 37 ff.
2. ――――. Op. cit., 1838, p. 99.
3. Ibid. p. 96.
4. ――――. Minutes. Op. cit., 1843, p. 159 ff.
5. ――――. Minutes. Op. cit., 1849, p. 96.
6. ――――. Minutes. Op. cit., 1851, p. 127 ff, p. 139 ff.
7. Ibid. p. 140.
8. ――――. Minutes. Op. cit., 1852, p. 141.

Catawba College, "A College of Our Own"

IN COLLABORATION with President Alvin R. Keppel and Dean of the College Donald C. Dearborn, Dean of the Faculty Raymond Jenkins in 1951 was requested to write a brief history of Catawba College entitled "A College of Our Own." The manuscript was prepared for publication in brochure form as a part the 100th Anniversary activities of the college.

In 1967, Dr. Jenkins was invited to bring the story up to date and prepare it for publication in this volume. His contribution will be found on the following pages under the above named title taken from the brochure.

Foreword

THIS STORY of the first century of Catawba College was written at the suggestion of The Centennial Committee as an expression of gratitude and affectionate appreciation to the countless men and women who have had a part in bringing Catawba to this, her hundredth year. It has become also a statement of faith in the future of the institution, founded upon the ideals and built by the toil of these men and women.

Material has been drawn from the college catalog, other official journals and student publications. Liberal use has been made of "The History of Catawba College" by Dr. J. C. Leonard. Correspondence of the Reverend Jeremiah Ingold was made available by the Rev. Robert V. Moss. Mrs. Carl Leonard has made a number of pictures available, as has Dr. W. Augusta Lantz. To these people we express our thanks. We hope that their contributions, and this story, may serve to renew in members of the Catawba family today the fervor for Christian education of the men of 1851.

CATAWBA COLLEGE, APRIL, 1951

The Founding, 1851-1865

No BOOK of fiction can today be written that reads as interestingly, that presents such high moments of suspense or that reflects so faithfully the mores of the various periods of the past century as the factual story of the conception and life of Catawba College during her first one hundred years of distinguished service. Woven into this most fascinating tapestry of the birth and life of a great Christian school are high moods and low, examples of great courage and of human frailty, years of prosperity and years of dire distress, successes and failures—but through them all an indomitable will and an unfaltering goal. Proof of these latter two is the milestone which she is this year celebrating— her one hundredth birthday.

On one of the granite pillars of the east gate of Harvard University there is insculped this interesting statement, which was orignially printed in a pamphlet published in 1643 by our Puritan forbears:

"After God had carried us safe to New England
   And we had builded our houses,
Provided necessaries for our livelihood,
Reared convenient places for God's worship
   And settled the civil government,
One of the next things we longed for
And looked after was to advance learning
   And perpetuate it to posterity,
Dreading to leave an illiterate ministry
To the Churches when our present ministers
   Shall lie in the Dust."

In this brief but revealing statement we find expressed the typical background philosophy responsible for bringing into being the first and many of today's greatest institutions of higher learning. And Catawba College, although established 215 years after Harvard, is no exception. Being motivated by this same desire "to aid in the education of indigent and pious young men—for the Gospel ministry," the North Carolina Classis of the Reformed Church in 1834 organized an "Education Society." For fifteen years this "Society" helped to send young men to certain northern schools of the denomination so that they might receive training

St. Matthew's Arbor

for Christian service. At an historic meetings of this Society, held at St. Matthew's Arbor, near Newton, North Carolina, in the year 1849, the following simple but profound suggestion was voiced: "Why not found a college of our own in our midst?" It was this simple seed thought which soon took root, because it was sowed at a time when faith and zeal and Christian fortitude ran high in the lives of that little company of Reformed churchmen. Within two years this casually expressed dream had already become a reality, and a new youngster, named Catawba College, was seeing her first light of day in a little North Carolina town called Newton.

To be sure, she was not a "blue baby," but she was nevertheless puny and, for a considerable period, her survival hung in the balance. Her early years were struggling ones, and she was not immune to the many juvenile diseases that beset infants of tender years. Nor was her life wholly normal and healthy even after she reached her teens, for as a matter of fact, it was just at that time that she was forced to face the same kind of harrowing experiences which she has since faced numerous times. For she was called to war. The war between the states perpetrated a crisis for all, and educational institutions were no exception. But again she came through—not only through one such major conflict but through three, and she stands today infinitely stronger and greater than ever before. No doubt the underlying reason for this can be likened unto that ascribed to Sir Galahad's stamina and fortitude when it was said of him, "His strength is as the strength of ten because his heart is pure."

But now let us focus our camera upon some close-ups of those memorable years of her early beginnings.

We have already mentioned the historic meeting of Classis in St. Matthews Arbor in 1849 and the casual suggestion that fired the imagination and faith of all present, but we have failed thus far to identify the speaker. He was a layman—a young attorney, himself the product of a Christian liberal arts college, a Mr. M. L. McCorkle, better known later as the distinguished and highly esteemed jurist, the Honorable Judge McCorkle. Although, as has been said, his original idea struck fire among many, yet it was he who followed through, and it was largely through his early efforts that this "dream" was transformed into the reality of "deed."

A minimum monetary goal of $15,000 was subsequently set and in June, 1851 Classis voted that when this goal was reached, the school should be established. On that first committee charged with raising these minimal finances, we observe in addition to Judge McCorkle, who headed the list, such names as Q. A. Shuford, John Coulter, David Crooks, Daniel Finger, Thornton Butler, John Swing, Jacob Berrier, G. W. Welker, Josiah Clapp, Levi Correll, John Lantz and George Barnhart. Many of these names are intimately woven throughout all of Catawba's rich history and many of these same surnames are still prominent in her current operation.

Fifteen thousand dollars is today a relatively small capital sum, especially when one compares it with Catawba's current annual operating budget which runs over six hundred thousand. But it was only $15,000 then that was to determine whether or not the school would be established. Of no particular consequence now are the experiences of that first committee in raising the necessary amount. It is, however, significant to observe that the sum was not fully raised before the school was founded. This fact *is* significant for it is this kind of faith that characterizes Catawba's entire history.

It is furthermore interesting to note that the welfare of the Reformed Church itself figured prominently into the choice of the school's first location. This is evidenced by a letter recently discovered, written by the Rev. J. H. Crawford to the Rev. J. Ingold in which this interesting comment appears: "I think we ought . . . to locate the school at Newton. It might do more to save this charge than anything else, and would be as favorable a location as we could get."

In another letter from the Rev. G. W. Welker to the Rev. J. Ingold, the following revealing information is reflected concerning the school's specific professional and vocational objectives. Three "orders of students" were comprehended: (1) "those intending to enter some college," (2) "those interested only in the courses 'in our school,'" and (3) "those intending to study their own language and mathematics and to prepare for public school teaching, for farming, for trades and for merchandising."

An interesting sidelight on monetary values at that time is reflected by this excerpt from a letter penned by the Rev. J. H.

Crawford in October, 1851, addressed to the Rev. J. Ingold. He says, "And now comes the tug of war about boarding. What can we afford to board at? Provisions are very high. How many students can we put into a room this winter? I would like to put four." (What would you think of charging) "$1.25 a week for board, room and furniture—not including washing, firewood and candles?" "Brother, it is a troublesome business from first to last, and I am getting my full share of the trouble if nothing more, but I will not complain."

The school opened on December 3, 1851, in a one-room weather-boarded house known as the "Old Academy Building." It had been a private ungraded school owned by the town. The Rev. C. H. Albert, a Pennsylvanian, was named the first principal and Mr. H. H. Smith, a New Hampshirite, his assistant. Thirty-two students were enrolled for the first session. In addition to his administrative duties as principal, the Rev. Mr. Albert was professor of Belles Lettres and Latin and Greek. Mr. Smith taught mathematics, natural science and modern languages.

By action of Classis on the following February (1852) the new school was formally placed in charge of a board of seven commissioners in the persons of the Rev. John H. Crawford, the Rev. C. H. Albert, Messrs. John Wilfong, M. L. McCorkle, F. D. Reinhardt, D. B. Gaither and Joseph Reinhardt. In May of that same year, Classis voted that the control of the school be vested in a Board of Trustees, consisting of eighteen members. The first board thus elected consisted of: John Coulter, Jonas Ramsour, Esq., G. P. Shuford, Joseph Reinhardt, F. D.

Old Academy Building, Newton, North Carolina

Reinhardt, Esq., Col. Philip Hedrick, John Wilfong, E. R. Shuford, George Setzer, T. W. Bradburn, Jacob Ramsour, Jacob Clapp, the Rev. J. H. Crawford, M. L. McCorkle, Esq., Jonas Bost, Dr. Q. A. Shuford, Col. George Barnhardt and Levi Correll.

In his "History of Catawba College," Dr. Jacob C. Leonard says, "Most of them (the trustees) were large farmers and probably all owned slaves. In this, their wealth was more *apparent* than real and (they) had little money to give the College."

Despite serious financial handicaps, the school nevertheless progressed, and a little over a year later it was incorporated under a Charter issued and ratified by the General Assembly of the State of North Carolina. (December 17, 1852). In 1859 the first amendment to this charter was ratified. This amendment read in part as follows:

"That an act, entitled 'an act to incorporate Catawba College' passed at the General Assembly of 1852-53, be so amended as to prohibit the sale or barter of spirituous liquors within two miles of Catawba College, in the County of Catawba." This original charter is still in force although in subsequent years a number of other amendments have been added, none of which, however, have in any way affected the original plan or intent of the founding fathers.

The name "Catawba," under which this charter was written, seemed to be a "natural" in view of the school's location in the county of Catawba near the Catawba River and in a section of the State where this old Indian tribal name had become almost a byword.

The Rev. Mr. Albert's administration covered but two years (1851-53), whereupon he was succeeded by his assistant, Professor H. H. Smith.

Because of Professor Smith's strong and affable personality, his sound scholarship and his breadth of culture, he, rather than the Rev. Mr. Albert, is oftentimes considered the College's first president. President Smith's tenure was likewise a short one of only three years for in 1856 he was called to the University of North Carolina where he taught for the next twelve years.

At the close of President Smith's administration, in 1856, the faculty resigned largely, it seems, because current operating funds were insufficient. The property was then leased to one of the professors, a Mr. Charles W. Smythe, who conducted a high school until 1859.

Soon after Professor Smythe's departure, in 1859, there came to Catawba College from Pennsylvania a minister by the name of the Rev. A. S. Vaughan. Although the school was not operative during the academic year 1859-60, Mr. Vaughan saw great possibilities for the future of the institution and therefore immediately set about raising $60,000 as an endowment fund. By the fall of 1860 he had secured about half that amount and the institution was reopened. He, therefore, became the fourth president, although at a most inauspicious time.

By the spring of 1861 the war situation had become increasingly acute and the majority of the relatively few students who had enrolled in the fall of that year had now enlisted in The Confederate Army. President Vaughan thereupon withdrew and returned to Pennsylvania. This left but one full-time faculty member in the person of Jacob C. Clapp. Professor Clapp finished the term with the few students who remained.

During the war years, with their accompanying dearth of young men in civilian life, the institution was kept open at the insistence of the community but operated solely on the level of an academy, with Mr. Clapp continuing as its directing head.

Although relatively little is recorded concerning the identity of all of the school's first students, the following are mentioned in one connection or another: Tom and Sam Lowe, J. C. Clapp, who later became the institution's president, Alphonso Clapp, J. W. Foust, Eli Warlick, Dan Wilfong, G. R. Rendleman, M. E. Lowrance, W. M. Abernethy, S. M. Finger, J. M. Johnson, P. R. Barringer, A. S. Fraley, G. W. Robinson and J. A. Moose. Record has it that only one student was graduated with the A.B. degree prior to the Civil War. He was Dan Wilfong and his diploma, written on home-tanned parchment, is still in the possession of some of his relatives.

Dr. J. C. Clapp
1861-1900

Reflecting something of the curriculum and the type of public performance that obtained in the first decade of the school's operation is a unique program for an "Exhibition" at Catawba College dated May 20, 1857. On it are listed nine individual presentations including five "English Declamations," one "Translation into French," and one "English Translation from Cicero." Commenting on this program, a commencement orator in 1897 said: "There were giants in those days." And that comment can no doubt be seconded in this Year of Our Lord nineteen hundred and fifty-one.

From that which has hitherto been written in this brief resumé, one may conclude that the so-called "early struggling years" were not as hazardous and as "struggling" as initially indicated. Lest this mistaken idea prevail, let us peruse a few direct quotations from personal letters exchanged between prominent Reformed clergymen of that day whose concern for the future of the College is thereby clearly reflected:

(March 2, 1852)
"It seems to me that the state of things in Newton is no better. There are strong indications that Brother ———— is about to make an entire failure in the village of Newton.'

(March 31, 1852)
"There is something behind the curtain pushing out the devil-up-ments. My heart bleeds—but I still hope good may come out of the evil."

(August 19, 1853)
"Surely you will say the Classis is in a fearful condition, yes, dying by its own suicidal acts; but yet I have some hope, but my hope is merged in the school. . . . And to the school I will cling."

(July 1, 1854)
"The crisis in the history of Catawba College seems to be developing itself much faster than could have been expected. . . . The original design of Catawba College was that it should be a Christian school. And the moment it ceases to be such, I shall have no more interest in it."

(October 20, 1954)
(Speaking of a new professor)
"In my humble opinion, . . . it will matter but little who suits or or who does not suit Catawba College, as it will soon be among the 'has beens'. Should there be any considerable falling off in the number of students next session, of which there is possibility, it will, without some new effort effectually made, seal the destiny of Catawba. As to my part, the institution has lain so close to my heart, I have had my thoughts on it day and nights, even since its existence, and I have spent my energies, my time, my money until I am well-nigh ruined." .

(January 11, 1855)
"If the College is to go down—and go it must without a new channel being opened, I will go in for selling it and dividing the proceeds equally among the contributors."

(March 3, 1855)
"But after all, is it not suicidal to talk of the dissolution of the College. It cannot die a natural death. It has too much vigor and life."

Trials? Tribulations? Juvenile diseases? Growing pains? There you have them, reflected in the actual words of some of the men who were right on the scene. But withal, Catawba College survived even the devastating war between the states.

Post-War Years, 1865-1885

Eighteen sixty-five! The fighting over, the young men of Catawba County, of Rowan, Cabarrus and Lincoln, came drifting back to the farms and towns of the Piedmont. The Bosts, the McCorkles, the Mooses, the Rowes, the Setzers, the Sherrills, the Shufords, the Wilfongs, and a dozen others, whose names a short while ago were the rosters of the Confederate companies, now sought to pick up and knit together the raveled ends of their lives. Boyish heroes that they were, those men came back to no G. I. Bill, no post-war boom of television, new cars, or housing projects. There remained in defeated and exhausted North Carolina only the courage of men and women, the soil, and the guiding hand of God.

These boys wanted education, and there was the little school in Newton to give it to them. The Reverend Jacob Clapp had kept classes in session throughout the War for a handful of boys and girls. Now he was joined by Major S. M. Finger; and by the Spring of eighteen sixty-six forty boys were studying Horace, Virgil, Cicero, Caesar, Xenophon, Demosthenes, Surveying and Navigation, Algebra, Geometry, University Arithmetic, English, Natural Philosophy; and, a few venturesome souls, French and German. The stated purposes of the school, now known as Catawba High School, were

(1) To prepare young men for the Freshman, Sophomore, or Junior Class in College.
(2) To give thorough instruction in the English branches and Sciences, with a view to making practical business men.

By eighteen seventy, eighty-five were in attendance. The Spring term lasted from January to May and the Fall term from July to November. Tuition ranged from three to five dollars per month, and room and board, including washing and fuel, was about twice this amount. Dr. Clapp was said to be a strict disciplinarian, and rules of conduct were rigid. Study hours were from eight to twelve, one-thirty to five, and seven-thirty to bedtime at nine. Students were expected to be in their rooms during these hours, unless they were in class. Students were "required not to have in their possession any deadly weapon, not to use indecent or profane language, not to play at cards or gamble, not to keep or drink intoxicating liquor, and not to be guilty of any improprieties which they know to be wrong." "Incorrigible offenders are punished, according to the nature of offence, by chastisement, reprimand, suspension, or expulsion." Frequently the offender was punished by being set to cutting down stumps on the campus.

Dr. Clapp and Major Finger had had as assistants several young men including, for short periods of time, M. L. Little and J. D. Rowe. In eighteen sixty-eight John A. Foil entered the school and, after three years, the Junior Class at Ursinus College. He was graduated there in eighteen seventy-three and in that same year returned to Catawba as assistant to Dr. Clapp. Major Finger withdrew from active participation, remaining on the Board of Trustees and serving Catawba for many years thereafter. Thus began the association between Dr. Clapp and Reverend Mr. Foil, which was to continue throughout their lifetime. Each of these men gave forty years to the school. Their abilities and personalities were so complementary that, under them, Catawba blossomed. The curriculum was expanded to include Chemistry, Physics, Biology, Mental and Moral Philosophy, and History. The number of students remained fairly constant, between eighty and one hundred. For the most part these boys came from Catawba, Lincoln, Gaston, Rowan, Cabarrus, Davidson, and Mecklenburg counties. Whether they came to prepare for further college work, for the classical education requisite for studying for a profession, or to prepare themselves for better citizenship in professions requiring less formal training, they gained by association with Clapp and Foil religious and moral training and inspiration of the finest kind.

During the decade of the 'eighties four developments took place which were to be significant in the future of the school. Dr. Foil had married Miss Sue Lantz, daughter of the Reverend John Lantz. Her younger sister, Augusta, had completed all the work offered to girls by the local schools, and was ambitious to continue preparation for college. At her father's request, Dr. Clapp permitted her and his own daughter, Emma, to attend classes with the boys during the year eighteen seventy-nine-eighteen eighty. The experience was a happy one, so much so, in fact, that the next year announcement was made of the addition of a Female Department. "They (the girls) study in separate rooms under the immediate control of a teacher, and are not allowed to meet the young men except in the recitation rooms; save that the young ladies may, once a week, receive calls according to strict parlor etiquette." In such casual fashion, Catawba became co-educational.

At frequent periods during and after the war the teachers of Catawba had held classes for younger boys and girls who had no other schools available to them. Now, about eighteen eighty, a Primary Department was established. This department was continued until the establishment of a public graded school in the town of Newton in nineteen five.

In the year eighteen eighty-one classes in the "Science and Art of Teaching" under the Reverend J. D. Gurley were begun. "Normal School" was added to the name of the institution, and Catawba began her considerable contribution to the forces of public education in the state. Major Finger was serving, about this time, as State Superintendent of Public Instruction, and the public schools were beginning to recover from the misgovernment of the Reconstruction period. Soon they were to take over the immense load of primary and secondary education carried for all these years by the private schools and academies.

Catawba had been chartered as a college, and before the War had granted at least one bachelor's degree. Now in eighteen eighty-five she resumed her collegiate work and again became in name and fact Catawba College.

A College Again, 1885-1900

THE RESUMPTION OF COLLEGE WORK came about as a result of the natural demand of students for work beyond that given in the academy. Many of the reasons for the original founding of the college continued, including the difficulty of financing the education of men who had to go to Northern colleges. The church wanted an educated ministry, and it was nearly impossible to persuade young men from the North to come to North Carolina as pastors. Further, the leaders of the church had long recognized the strength of an educated laity. Consequently, the leaders of the Classis, through their representation on the Board of Trustees, were the staunchest supporters of plans for expansion.

Dr. Foil was extremely anxious that work at the college level be undertaken and with some hesitation President Clapp agreed. Necessary increases in the faculty and considerable expenditures for new equipment would tax the resources of the college and make new support mandatory. Appeals to the church in the North were fruitless. At last, the people of North Carolina recognized that whatever aid Catawba was to receive must come from themselves. There seemed some hopes of increased support, and consequently the enlarged program was begun.

North View of Main Building and Student Body, Newton Campus

In eighteen eighty-nine the first class of three young men was
graduated. Two of them, J. C. Leonard and J. M. L. Lyerly,
became leaders among the ministers of the North Carolina Classis; the third, M. A. Foil, a respected and beloved physician.
From this time until nineteen twenty-three classes of from two
to 19 were graduated nearly every year. The first woman to graduate was Miss Helen Foil, in eighteen ninety-three. Her sister
Miriam followed in eighteen ninety-six and Miss Annie Clapp in
eighteen ninety-seven.

The college curriculum in the beginning was fixed for all students. It contained much Greek and Latin, Mathematics through
Calculus, Natural Science including Chemistry, Physiology, Bot-
any, Geology and Mineralogy, Astronomy and Physics, a year
each of English Rhetoric and Literature, two years of German,
Psychology, Logic, Philosophy and Aesthetics, Christian Evi-
dences, Moral Philosophy, and a one-semester course in Political
Science. Juniors and Seniors prepared and delivered original
orations as a part of their required work. Within a few years a
differentiation was made between the Classical and Scientific
Courses, the distinction being chiefly in the substitution of
French for Greek in the Scientific course. For a time after nineteen hundred a third course, the Literary course, was also permitted, particularly "for young ladies" who might study advanced
courses in literature and both French and German instead of
advanced Mathematics and Science. About this time, also,
courses in History, Sociology, Economics, and Education were
offered, and after nineteen ten Juniors and Seniors were permitted a limited number of elective courses, the choices being
rather strictly regulated. This pattern persisted until suspension
of college work in nineteen twenty-three.

Life for students in the little country town of Newton centered in informally organized activities much like those of today. Most of the students lived in the dormitories or houses
adjacent to the college. Meals were taken in homes or in boarding clubs. The latter were operated by a student manager on
a cost basis and provided meals for five or six dollars a month.
Chickens at fifteen cents each, butter at fifteen cents a pound,
apples and peaches at fifty cents a bushel, and steak at twenty
cents a pound appear in the account books of such a boarding-
club manager, as well as several entries for students who bar-
tered produce from the farms of their fathers for a month's
board. A few boys earned their room rent by building fires in
the stoves in each class-room.

Greatest student interest, perhaps, centered in the literary
societies, of which the Philomathean and Athenaean have the
longest history. Regular meetings were held at which visiting
speakers presented lectures, or students read their original compositions. Oratory and debate were in high favor, especially

among those who intended to study law, or for the ministry. Each society presented a public program at some time during the year, frequently at the close of the term before Christmas. Competition was keen as each society sought to outdo the others.

A joint venture of the literary societies began in eighteen eighty-seven in the publication of a college magazine. The first such journal was called "The College Visitor" and had as its editorial board two faculty members and three students. Subscriptions were sold not only to students, but throughout the Classis, at fifty cents a year. A stock company was organized among citizens of Newton to underwrite this venture, and some revenue was derived from advertisers. A consistent advertiser was the University of North Carolina, which boasted, in eighteen ninety, of its faculty of sixteen members. The perennial problem of censorship by faculty members of student materials must have arisen early, for in the second issue appears the statement, "Perfect harmony exists among the different members of the editorial staff of The Visitor, but, at the same time, the chief wants it distinctly understood that he is not responsible for all that finds a place in its columns, especially among the College Notes and Personals. It is only when occasion demands that he exercises special authority and says what may and what may not be inserted. After the graver part of the work has been completed, he is usually satisfied to let the rest be conducted in a way most congenial to his associates."

This magazine continued sporadically under its original title, then as the "Catawba College Educator" and later as "The Catawbian" for twenty years or more. Its contents were student and faculty essays, poems, short stories, articles on education, and a page or two of college and personal news. Church news of the North Carolina Classis was also included.

Each of the literary societies had its own hall, arranged for its regular meetings and containing its library. For some years these libraries appear to have been the only source of material for students. Later they were merged, and from them a college library grew. Librarians of that time, too, had troubles still familiar, for one editor of The Visitor writes: "It is a problem so far unsolved as to how we can get back the books that belong to the library. If you see anybody who has one of them, tell him kindly that the librarians want it."

Co-education necessitated social events which were occasionally sponsored by the literary societies, but perhaps more often by the college faculty. The Visitor again complains, "A sociable is now in the air but it is very doubtful about its being in the minds of the professors to grant one." The sociable was held, however, and a later report says, "The Matron's Hall was the recipient of a grand serenade on Friday night after the sociable, by the Newton Silver Cornet Band. While the band was sending forth its strains of sweet music, the young ladies and gentlemen were engaged in social conversation, concerning the music, of course. The band dispersed and the young men remained until one of the professors came around and announced that: 'The sociable and serenade are now over. I will say good-night and the young men will follow suit'—and they followed suit."

Again from The Visitor, "We know one young man who has been with his girl eleven nights in succession—we will not say that he is a student." It is needless to say that what appears to have been then a record has long since been surpassed.

The faculty were not entirely unaware, however, of the stimuli of co-education. One note reports, "The teachers say that they are going to send a delegation of young ladies around to inspect the young men's rooms. We do not doubt that all rooms will be kept in the best style after this." The inspection was carried out, and the only criticism was that apparently the "broom handles were too short to sweep under the beds."

Athletics and physical education played an important role in student life from the beginning. Professor Smith, one of the first teachers, was an expert boxer and fencer, and instructed the boys in these sports and in gymnastics. Jacob Clapp, in his student days, was one of the outstanding boxers.

Instruction in Hygiene was included in the Natural Science curriculum very early, and by eighteen eighty there was listed in the catalog each year an instructor in "calisthenics." Sports were on a more informal basis and official statements concerning them do not appear until after nineteen hundred, but The Visitor has several accounts of baseball games in eighteen eighty-eight. "Baseball is out of date with the students; a few broken fingers, several broken windows, and a lecture from headquarters has about closed the season." In eighteen ninety, "Athletic refreshment gives a new zeal in mental labor. The students have a new football and all seem to take great interest in the game." On October fourth, eighteen ninety, a football game was played between two teams from the college, the score being six to five. This was, perhaps, the first football game played at Catawba. The game did not catch on and inter-collegiate games were not played for some time. In nineteen five, the Catawbian reports, "A feeble effort was made early in the season to put a football team in the field, but the result was a failure. The students at Catawba have an unexplainable aversion to football, and it is unfortunate that such is the case, for we have the material at hand for the making of a strong, winning team."

The editorial urged provision of a gymnasium for indoor sports and commented on the enthusiasm for baseball and tennis. The baseball schedule in the Spring of nineteen six included games with Lenoir College, Davidson, Guilford, Oak Ridge, Charlotte University, St. Mary's College, Mt. Pleasant Institute, Salem

Boys School, Asheville School, and others. Prospects for the season were good, according to the student writer.

For several years prior to this the catalog had carried the following official statement on athletics: "The authorities of Catawba College believe in athletics. That there may be the best results in mental development and discipline, the student must have proper exercise. There is present in human nature, and especially in boy and girl nature, the desire to play. This is not assumed, but is natural, and must be taken into account. At the present time baseball is the feature of exercise at Catawba, and clearly has the right of way. Tennis, however, is quite popular with a number of students, and football is growing in favor. The purpose is to enlarge upon these, and to have a regular system requiring a certain period of time for systematic exercise. Athletics is, therefore, to receive more attention at Catawba than heretofore, and this is because of its great value in proper discipline. It will, however, always be given a subordinate place and will only be encouraged because of the splendid service it renders in the developing of college spirit and of healthful physical manhood and womanhood." The catalog of nineteen seven carries pictures of the football, baseball, and track teams, and the next year basketball was added to the schedule.

The Fine Arts, too, were emphasized and formal instruction in music, painting, and drawing was given after about eighteen eighty. Elocution and oratory were in high favor, particularly in the activities of the Literary Societies, and programs of Orations and Declamations featured every Commencement season. Original literary compositions were encouraged, and awards were given for meritorious performance.

Student life was a simple life, compared with present-day activities, but withal it must have been a good and happy life. Certainly there was no room for confusion of purpose, or misunderstanding of why the college existed, or why its students were there.

Years of Struggle, 1900-1923

FROM THE BEGINNING, Catawba's greatest problems had been financial. There was never enough money for buildings, equipment, or faculty salaries. In the earliest years of the college a rather substantial endowment was accumulated, but this was lost in bonds which became worthless during the Civil War. Following that struggle the small constituency of the Reformed Church in North Carolina, suffering all the depression of Southern economy of the period, could do little to help the college. Only the tremendous efforts of President Clapp and Dr. Foil served to keep up the standards of instruction. Debts were accumulating, expansion of facilities was mandatory, and, with the resignation of President Clapp in nineteen hundred, some action seemed necessary.

The story of the next twenty years is, from this point of view, a dreary one. Able and devoted men struggled heroically but hopelessly against the burden of debt and indifference. Sporadically, hope rose high with new promises, only to be dashed when the necessary help failed to be forthcoming. C. H. Mebane, a former State Superintendent of Public Instruction, served as president following Dr. Clapp. During his administration student enrollment reached an all-time high of about two hundred. This enrollment overtaxed the facilities of the college, but Mr. Mebane felt he could not command the support necessary for expansion, and consequently resigned after four years.

The Reverend George A. Snyder was then called from the pastorate of Christ Reformed Church in Hagerstown, Maryland, to bcome president. Encouraged by gifts from Northern friends, he began an expansion program. The faculty was substantially increased, a large addition to the main building was constructed, and some endowment funds were secured. But interest on the funds borrowed for construction ate up the income from endowment and the impetus was lost. Dr. Snyder resigned in nineteen eight, and for two years leadership was given by Dean William R. Weaver as acting president, assisted for a few months by Dr. Charles E. Wehler, pastor of Grace Church, Newton. Mr. Weaver, in recent years a prominent business man of Hickory, served the college faithfully and well for a period of ten years as teacher, dean, and acting president. Dr. Clapp and Dr. Foil also returned briefly in this period to do what could be done. In nineteen ten, John F. Buchheit was elected president, serving for three years. During this period the faculty was again built up, laboratories were newly equipped, and general repair and modernization of buildings effected. But the perennial problems of finance continued. Dr. Foil was forced to resign because of ill-health. Professor Weaver resigned the next year, and Buchheit withdrew in the following one.

When the Reverend J. D. Andrew accepted the presidency in nineteen thirteen, the situation was becoming almost hopeless. Buildings were in disrepair, it was hard to get and keep qualified teachers, and enrollment was dwindling. The esteem in which Reverend Mr. Andrew was held throughout the Classis prompted some parents to send their children to Catawba, but many of the Reformed families were going elsewhere so that their college work would be recognized. In nineteen fifteen the State Department withdrew its accreditation of Catawba as a four-year college, and in fact granted recognition to its graduates for only one year of college work. Income was so low that nothing could be done and finally, in nineteen eighteen, Dr. Andrew resigned.

FACULTY 1917: Seated: *Flossie Frazier, President J. D. Andrew, Pauline Holstein.* Standing: *Geo. C. Warlick, Mary Barringer, H. B. Overcash, Myrtle Gross, A. P. Whisenhunt, Mazie Schmidt, W. W. Rowe, A. C. Sherrill*

Dr. A. D. Wolfinger, pastor of First Reformed Church of Greensboro, accepted the presidency in May, nineteen eighteen. He had previously been associated with Central Seminary and with Ursinus College as Field Secretary, and consequently had a good understanding of the problems he faced. The Classis, meanwhile, was becoming aware of the imminent loss of its college, and beginning to do something about it. Such men as Dr. J. C. Leonard, Dr. J. L. Murphy, Mr. J. T. Hedrick, Mr. John W. Peeler, Mr. Edgar Whitener, and many others came forward with financial help, and, more important, with determination to rebuild a standard, fully accredited college. Such denomination-wide campaigns as the Forward Movement brought some help and a measure of interest and enthusiasm on the part of the Board of Home Missions. Dr. Wolfinger, with this support, was able to restore the college so that the State Department agreed to give its students credit for three years work instead of the one received earlier.

About this time the offer of a partially completed building and a large tract of land in Salisbury was made to the Board of Trustees. The Board, the North Carolina Classis, and denominational leaders felt that here was an opportunity for real growth. With the determination that nothing less than a fully accredited, four-year college would meet the needs of the constituency, it was decided to close the college at Newton in nineteen twenty-three, to reopen in Salisbury as soon as possible, and to secure, for once, the money necessary to do these things. New leaders arose, including Mr. J. P. Linn, Mr. L. A. Corriher, Rev. Mr.

J. H. Keller, Rev. Mr. Shuford Peeler, Mr. J. T. Plott, Mr. J. O. Moose, and Mr. H. A. Rouzer, the latter a Salisburian, not of the Reformed Church, but who was active in enlisting support among the citizenry of Salisbury. Here the work of the college was resumed in nineteen twenty-five.

The decision to move the college was not an easy one to make. For seventy-two years the college had served its people, and served them well. Many devoted men and women had made personal sacrifice, almost beyond our comprehension, to preserve it. But to them, as well as to future generations, the challenge was to go forward with new determination. The rise of Catawba College since nineteen twenty-five has fully vindicated the judgment of those who made the decision.

Maturity, 1925-1951

Beautiful and historic salisbury was chosen as the new home for Catawba. In the midst of the rich Piedmont section of North Carolina and readily accessible to the congregations of the Southern Synod, the location soon proved to be an inspired choice.

The J. T. Hedrick Administration Building, Salisbury Campus

Two miles from Salisbury was a large Tudor Gothic building originally costing $300,000. Designed for a preparatory school or college, it contained sufficient space to house an almost complete college plant. Encouraged by the financial support of the citizens of Salisbury and Spencer, the members of the Reformed Church, and the late J. T. Hedrick for whom the building was named, the Trustees of Catawba College purchased the building and grounds for $46,818.60.

Dr. Elmer R. Hoke, a prominent minister and professor at Hood and Lebanon Valley Colleges, was elected president of Catawba College on August 7, 1924. When Dr. Hoke arrived in Salisbury on April 1, 1925, a man of less faith and courage would have faltered. The campus was a field of barren clay. An herculean task confronted him. It was his responsibility to organize and establish an old college in a new location. Not only did Hedrick Hall need complete renovation, but a part of its roof had blown off; this had to be repaired. Dr. Hoke organized, in Salisbury and Rowan County, the North Carolina Classis, and the Church in the North, a drive for an endowment fund of $400,000. This task was made doubly difficult as the former sponsors of the building had twice solicited funds from local citizens and had twice failed to establish a going institution. It is small wonder that some donors declared that they would make their contribution when the college opened a second year.

President Hoke was also responsible for persuading a sufficient number of students to attend the new Catawba to warrant the employment of a faculty. To W. Augusta Lantz, Dean of Women, and the Reverend Shuford Peeler, Dean of Men, go the credit of interviewing students in the community and in the families of the church. After countless personal calls they succeeded in procuring 127 students, the largest class that had ever attended Catawba College. In the first sophomore class of seventeen were some men who have already received recognition of their talents; among them were Dr. Carey H. Bostian, Dean of Instruction at State College; T. H. Kenerly, a prominent merchant of Salisbury; Dr. G. G. Grubb of the Department of English at Wake Forest, and the Reverend Ray R. Fisher, pastor of the Augsburg Lutheran Church of Winston-Salem.

E. R. Hoke,
1924-1931

In the Spring of 1926 a committee of the North Carolina Conference of Colleges recommended that Catawba College be accredited; the College Rating Board of North Carolina forthwith placed Catawba among the four-year colleges of the state. In 1928 the college was admitted to membership in the Southern Association of Colleges and Secondary Schools; the minimum endowment necessary for admission was met by the giving by the N. C. Classis of a note for $50,000. This accreditation, due to the indefatigable efforts of Dr. Hoke and the ministers and laymen of the Classis, established the reputation of the college in the East and paved the way for the influx of students from the North, particularly Pennsylvania.

Particularly active at this time, and since, in support of the college was the Women's Missionary Society, through its organizations in the North Carolina Classis, the Potomac Synod, and the Church at large. Zartman Hall was a gift of this organization, together with much equipment and a sizeable scholarship fund.

During the presidency of Dr. Hoke eight essential buildings were erected: Zartman Hall—the first dormitory for women—in 1925, the Linn-Corriher Gymnasium in 1926, the Home Economics Building in 1927, two apartment houses for the faculty in 1927 and 1928, the Brodbeck Conservatory of Music in 1929, Claremont Hall and the residence of the president in 1930. The Shuford Athletic Field was completed in 1929 and a baseball field in 1932. Within five years Dr. Hoke, with the cooperation of the Board and the Church, raised the funds for and supervised the building of a complete college plant. In 1931 Dr. Hoke died of endocarditis. His death was a great blow to the college. But in the six years of his administration he had left as a monument to his courage and vision a well-established college.

As Dr. Hoke's successor the Trustees were very fortunate in securing Dr. Howard R. Omwake, Dean of Franklin and Marshall College. Educated at Princeton, Dr. Omwake was a scholar and a cultured gentleman. His genial personality together with the hospitality of his gracious wife soon won the hearts of the students, the faculty, and the citizens of Salisbury. A leader ripened by experience in higher education at Princeton, Beirut, and Lancaster, Dr. Omwake made the college a center of culture in the Piedmont and cemented the cordial relations of town and gown, students and faculty.

Under Dr. Omwake the campus was extended and a few needed buildings were erected. In 1934 the Newman Ball Park, given by citizens of Salisbury and named in honor of Dr. H. H. Newman, was enclosed and furnished with a grandstand. The Dr. M. A. Foil House, named to honor an esteemed benefactor of the college, was built in 1938. In this same year the erection of Rahauser Hall provided the college with a commodious, up-to-date dining hall.

During the thirties the colleges of America were intent upon revising their curricula with the aim of correcting the defects of the elective system, which had been popular in the first quarter of the century. With the purpose of making every student a well-rounded personality, Catawba set up a plan wherein every student chose a major and related minor from one of five fields of study: languages and literature; philosophy, education, and religion; the social sciences; mathematics and the physical sciences; and the fine arts. The minimum requirement for the major field was 42 semester-hours—24 in the major and 18 in the related minor. To make sure that every student was acquainted with fields other than his major, he was required before graduation to pass at least six semester hours in every other group of studies. Students who did excellent work in all their courses were graduated with honors: *cum laude, magna cum laude,* and *summa cum laude.* To date three students have received their degree *summa cum laude*: Harold J. Wolfinger '36, Donald L. Whitener '43, and Morris M. Galloway '48.

Dr. Howard R. Omwake
1931-1942

The departments of Business Administration, Home Economics, and Music, which had been set up under Dr. Hoke, were more thoroughly organized and improved under Dr. Omwake's administration. Sufficient courses were given in each department to prepare students not only to teach these subjects but also to pursue them as professions. The Department of Music showed phenomenal growth. The building and equipment of Brodbeck Conservatory of Music made it possible for instruction to be given in piano, organ, string and wind instruments, voice, and the appreciation and theory of music. Frequent recitals were given by students, and the College Choir made a tour of North Carolina, Virginia, Maryland, and Pennsylvania, singing to large and appreciative audiences.

The intention of Dr. Omwake in accepting the presidency was to do his utmost to make Catawba one of the best small colleges in the South. To this end, he felt it necessary that administration and faculty formulate the basic aims of the college. In the Aims the college predicated its function and acknowledged its responsibility for the complete development of its students. The kind of liberal education outlined in the Aims is well epitomized in the words of John Milton: "that which fits a man to perform justly, skillfully, and magnanimously all the offices, both private and public, of peace and war." The spirit of mutual helpfulness and friendliness, which has characterized Catawba since its inception, was especially exemplified in the daily life and work of Dr. Omwake. In the death of Dr. Omwake in the summer of 1942 the college suffered an immeasurable loss. In his ten years as president his influence was not written in visible brick and stone so much as it was engraved upon the hearts and lives of the whole Catawba family. His rich personality brought home to all the truth of Wordsworth's lines:

> There is
> One great society alone on earth
> The noble living and the noble dead.

All who knew Dr. Omwake felt that he was indeed a member of that "great society," that grand community.

Upon the death of Dr. Omwake, the Trustees selected as Catawba's new president, Dr. Alvin R. Keppel. Dr. Keppel with his talented wife and genial son, Bob, and daughter, Junia, joined the Catawba family in the fall of 1942. An able executive, an inspiring speaker, and a director of the educational work of the church, Dr. Keppel brought to the college a vigorous leadership. Through his energetic efforts Catawba was soon serving the nation by providing instruction, housing, and maintenance for an Air Force Unit of two hundred men. At the end of the Second World War a Veterans' Guidance Center was established at Catawba; for five years Catawba was one of the main centers in North Carolina for the counselling of veterans. In 1948 a World Government Institute was established at Catawba and Professor George W. Greene, a former Commander in the U. S. Navy, became its Director. Thus Catawba continues to serve the nation in war and peace.

Shortly after Dr. Keppel's inauguration, Dr. Edgar Whitener, who as President of the Board of Trustees had for twenty years served his Alma Mater with untiring devotion, resigned on account of illness. As his successor the Trustees chose Dr. Banks J. Peeler, the Vice-President of the Board. In this happy choice the college was again fortunate for Dr. Peeler, like his predecessor, wishes to make Catawba a great Christian college, and he holds that Catawba has a unique service to render to the community, state, and nation.

The president and the Trustees now went ahead on a comprehensive program to improve the physical facilities and increase

The Rahauser Dining Hall

the endowment of the college. All buildings were repainted and modernized. In the last nine years the endowment has been almost doubled and approximately a million dollars has been invested in buildings, a stadium, and a central heating plant. Throughout this period of expansion L. A. Corriher, J. W. Abernathy, and Adrian Shuford, Jr., Trustees of the College, have been very generous as well as untiring in raising the necessary funds. More than 100 acres were purchased, making the campus 190 acres in extent. Housing accommodations for the faculty were obtained by the purchase of the house now occupied by Dr. Dearborn and the beautiful Derendinger property, Hearth Hill. The wisdom of these purchases was shown within a few years when real estate and housing doubled in value. In 1946 the Salisbury-Rowan Residence Hall for Men was undertaken by the citizens of Salisbury and Rowan County to show their loyalty and high regard for Catawba. Completed in 1948, this impressive three-story building of Gothic architecture provides living quarters for 172 men, an apartment for the head resident, a recreation room, and a beautifully appointed social hall. The entire campus, with its magnificent trees, shrubs and flowers now has the atmosphere associated with "bright college years."

The President and Trustees also took measures to insure the health and well-being of the students. A resident graduate nurse was employed, and the infirmary was equipped with the most up-to-date facilities. For the last five years physical records of all students have been kept, and every student has been given a physical examination each year by competent physicians and surgeons.

To provide greater security for the faculty the Trustees in 1944 supplemented a plan of group-insurance, which had been in effect for some years, by their approval of Catawba's becoming a member of the Teachers' Insurance Annuity Association. The TIAA plan involves a contribution of 5% of salary per annum by both the college and the employee. All the administrative staff and faculty participate in this retirement and annuity plan.

With the challenge presented by the influx of veterans, the president and Dean Dearborn undertook to revise the curriculum and to extend the program of counselling. To make all students aware of our heritage of freedom and Christian idealism as well as to prepare them for a calling, the faculty set up a core-curriculum, adding a course in foreign language, speech, mathematics, social science, and religion or philosophy to the previously required subjects. Under the new counselling program most of the faculty were assigned students whom they were to advise throughout the four-year course. The Dean of Men and Dean of Women were also allotted more time for individual and periodic counselling.

Catawba's presidents have endeavored to make the college a cultural center of the community and of the Piedmont. The Blue Masque, the dramatic society of the college, was formed in 1925. Under Mrs. Loton A. Corriher, who was Director of Dramatics and Head of the Department of Speech for twenty-three years, the Blue Masque staged numerous plays which in the quality of interpretation and acting were not surpassed by any undergraduate group in North Carolina. To stimulate interest in dramatic art by the writing of one-act plays, Mrs. Corriher has since 1929 given annually to the winner of the Blue Masque Cup a replica of the large cup, upon which the name of the winner has each year been inscribed. Two Shakespearean productions of the Blue Masque, which its patrons will long remember, were *Romeo and Juliet* and *Julius Caesar*.

For more than twenty years Catawba has had a Department of Art. At first the offerings of the department were centered in the history of architecture, sculpture, and painting; by means of slides the study, interpretation, and appreciation of the great masterpieces were stressed. Several illustrated courses in extension, especially designed for teachers in the public schools, were also given in many cities of the Piedmont. In addition to these courses in the appreciation of art, the college in recent years has offered courses in the techniques of creative art, which are annually attracting students in increasing numbers. At Commencement for the last three years there has been an exhibit of original work of students in charcoal, pencil, pen and ink, pastel, water color, and oil. In 1949-50 there were three exhibits in the Great Hall of the Salisbury-Rowan Dormitory: Japanese Prints, Life in Eighteenth-Century England, and Water Colors of artists of the Carolinas exhibited under the auspices of the Mint Museum of Charlotte.

The importance of music in the cultural development of students has always been stressed at Catawba. To supplement the usual courses in theoretical and applied music, students and faculty in the department give many recitals each year. The college choir and band, both large and active, likewise give frequent concerts. Organized in 1945 by Professor Harry F. Taylor, the Catawba Octet is called upon constantly. The Octet has made two trips North, singing in churches and at alumni clubs. In 1948 the Octet sang in the Hollywood Bowl at the International Kiwanis Convention and in 1949 at the Music Educators' Convention in Tampa, Florida. The teachers of music in the public schools hold the annual competitions of the Central Carolina District at the college. To stimulate a lively interest in music among all students the college provides an Artist Course or Concert Series, which features some of the world's greatest artists. Last year Mrs. Winifred Macbride Thomas, Professor of Piano, was pianist in the London String Quartet in Cesar Franck's Piano Quintet; she has often appeared in the past with this distinguished group. Mrs. Thomas has also played the solo part in two piano concertos on the College-Community Artist Course: The Emperor Concerto of Beethoven with the Detroit Symphony, and the Tchaikovsky Concerto in B Flat Minor with the National Symphony. Fifty compositions, mostly choral, of Christopher Thomas, Head of the Department, have been published. Marian Anderson has often sung two of his songs, one of which, "O Men From The Fields," she has recorded on the Red Seal Series of the Victor Recording Company.

Athletics during the past twenty-five years at Catawba have been marked by steady progress both in the improvement of the physical plant and in the caliber of the teams. Shuford Football Stadium can now comfortably accommodate 6,000 people, Newman Baseball Field 4,000. Future building plans will soon provide ample seating in the Linn-Corriher Gymnasium. To round out a fine physical plant, there are also three intramural fields and several tennis courts.

The coaches of football in 1925 were two prominent physicians of Salisbury: Dr. Harold H. Newman and Dr. Graham Ramsay; they served the college without pay. The head coaches from 1926 to 1934 were Flake Laird, Carl Davis, and Charlie Moran. From 1934 till the present time Gordon A. Kirkland has been director of Catawba's entire athletic program. During these seventeen years he has, with the loyal cooperation of students, faculty, and alumni, developed teams noted for their fighting spirit and good sportsmanship. Inspired by his character and ability, many Catawba graduates are now coaching and teaching in the high schools of the Southeast.

Since 1925 the football teams have won 152, lost 68, and tied 10 games; basketball teams have won 277 and lost 241; and baseball teams have won 259 and lost 147. Though accurate records are not available, the athletic program during this period has also included intramural and inter-collegiate soccer, track, tennis, and golf.

Championships were won in football in 1934, 1938, 1940, 1942, 1944, 1945, 1946, and 1947; basketball in 1944 and 1945, and baseball in 1936, 1937, 1938, 1942, 1943, 1944, 1945, 1947, and 1948. The highlight of the past twenty-five years was the appearance of the Catawba football teams in the Tangerine Bowl at Orlando, Florida, on January 1, 1947, and January 1, 1948. Catawba won on both occasions, defeating Maryville College by 31-6 in 1947 and Marshall College 7-0 in 1948.

At all times the president and faculty have been cognizant of their civic responsibilities. They speak frequently in the pulpit and the civic clubs, and most of them have held responsible offices in organizations which serve the common good. In 1945 President Keppel was a delegate at the conference of educators who met to consider the problems of the United Nations; since that time he has given many addresses, stressing the need of implementing the UN. In 1947 Dr. Keppel was chairman of a committee of the North Carolina College Conference whose duty it was to analyze and evaluate the Report of the President's Commission on Higher Education. In 1947 and 1948, he was chairman of the Commission on Christian Education of the Association of American Colleges. In 1949 he was president of the Council of Church-Related Colleges of North Carolina. In 1941 Dr. David E. Faust was chaplain of the Department of North Carolina of the American Legion; and in 1945 and 1946 he was president of the Salisbury Interracial Council. For several years Dr. Raymond Jenkins has been a member of the State Panel of Arbitrators, and he and Dr. Donald Dearborn have arbitrated several labor disputes under the auspices of the American Arbitration Association. Dr. Dearborn has also been a member of the Advisory Committee of the State Recreation Commission and is on the Board of Trustees of the Salisbury Schools. For many years Dr. Bruce Wentz has shown his colored photographs of significant events at the college to local groups and alumni. In 1947, at the invitation of Dr. Milton L. Braun, the Southeastern Section of the American Physical Society met at the college; in 1948, when Dr. Braun was president, this society met at Oak Ridge. In the summer of 1949 Dr. Braun was Senior Research Physicist at the K-25 Laboratory at Oak Ridge. In the spring of 1950 the North Carolina Academy of Science was the guest of the college.

In his efforts to enlarge the services of Catawba Dr. Keppel has not overlooked the prime end of a small Christian college. It is expressed in the religious aim: "To build Christian character by the study of the Bible and Christian literature; to instill a conviction that all men, as sons of God, are brothers; and to make the personality of the Master Teacher the integrating force in daily living." Though all the faculty in their courses are conscious of this main purpose of the college, they in 1947 instituted two courses in the Department of Philosophy: Religious Values in Today's World and Christian Ethics. The aim of these courses, as well as those in the Department of Religion, is to familiarize students with Christian concepts which are eternally valid. Students are also helped to achieve the religious aim of the college through various groups. The Adelphians, young men who are preparing to enter the ministry, are a prominent and active group on the campus. The college likewise encourages all students to attend the church of their choice and to be active in their denominational groups. During the last five years, the college has brought to the campus for Religious Emphasis Week a minister who knows how to challenge young men and women to assert their better selves. His addresses and informal meetings, sponsored by the Y.W.C.A. and Y.M.C.A., have been very helpful and fruitful. In his second year, Dr. Keppel inaugurated a monthly vesper service which has enabled students to hear some of the best preachers in the nation. To make the college a dynamic force in the church in North Carolina, the president has invited a minister of the Evangelical and Reformed Church to address the students in the College Chapel on every Monday of this centennial year. In September of this year the faculty met for a three-day Retreat at Wildacres. Here, amid the majestic mountains of North Carolina, they evaluated their teaching in the light of the *Aims of the College* and rededicated themselves to create a better and greater Catawba.

Throughout this hundred years of progress the aim of the administration and faculty at Catawba has been to help the student achieve self-mastery that he might become a true Christian. Dr. Keppel epitomized this ideal in his Report to the Trustees on February 17, 1948: "Catawba's ultimate objective must be to help fashion not merely good doctors or good lawyers or good business executives or good breadwinners, but good men." Catawba's growth and service to the church, state, and nation have gone far beyond the dreams of her founders in 1851. With God's help the next hundred years will mark far greater achievement.

The Administration of President Keppel

THIS HISTORICAL SUMMARY has been written in capsule form by Dr. Alvin R. Keppel, of his tenure as president of Catawba College, at the request of Dr. Banks J. Peeler, who prepared it for publication.

Dr. A. R. Keppel, 1942-1963

The full and unabridged history of these twenty-one years is to be found in the Annual Report Volumes prepared by Dr. Keppel for the annual meetings of the Board of Trustees. The chronicle is made up of excerpts from these annual reports. Obviously only a few of the highlights can here be recorded.

1942-43. The College Community was saddened by the passing of its beloved president, Dr. Howard R. Omwake, who had served so well as Catawba's president for twelve years. A new president took office at the beginning of the 1942-43 academic year in the person of Dr. Alvin R. Keppel, who had previously served as the Executive Secretary of the Board of Christian Education and Publication of the Evangelical and Reformed Church, with offices in Philadelphia, Pennsylvania.

Before the new president had become even partially acclimated, the sad news reached the campus that the President of the Board of Trustees, Dr. Edgar Whitener, who had served so well and so long in that capacity, had been stricken with a heart attack and would therefore be unable to continue his services. Therefore, the Vice President of the Board, Rev. Banks J. Peeler, graciously agreed to serve as Acting President until the Trustees could take appropriate action.

World War II was still in progress which fact was sadly reflected by the dearth of civilian male students. Enrollment as of the beginning of 1942 fall term stood at 370. A civilian Pilot Training Unit of twenty men ran the total enrollment to 300. With so limited an enrollment, income from tuition covered far less than half of the College's operating costs and since the College had no reserve fund on which to draw and was currently operating in the red, Catawba College faced a critical financial emergency.

The first order of business, therefore, which confronted the new president was the financial crisis and the crisis brought about by a dearth of students. In the President's first report to the Board of Trustees, he therefore spoke to these two crises, expressing his philosophy with reference to their solution. He said,

> I believe in a balanced budget and in realistically and immediately tackling the task of such balancing. I furthermore believe that if this institution is to remain solvent and if academic standards are not to be sacrificed, one or more of the following courses must be pursued:
> 1. We must make a renewed and all-out effort to increase appreciably the College's "Gift Program," notwithstanding the current low level of the nation's economy.
> 2. We must borrow sufficient monies to meet emergency needs if a plan can be devised which will guarantee amortization of such a loan within a reasonable period of time.
> 3. As a last resort we must cut the number of our faculty and staff members if this can be done without violating contracts or jeopardizing academic standards or threatening the institution's future.
> 4. We must at once try to find a way to increase student personnel. In my judgment, the best and perhaps the only opportunity to achieve this goal at such a time as this is by securing some kind of a government program which would bring to the campus a detachment of trainees whose workday would be divided between courses in matters military and liberal arts; the latter under the tutelage of Catawba's regular teaching staff.

After most serious consideration by the Trustees of these various proposals, it was unanimously agreed to ask the President of the College to pursue immediately and aggressively proposals 4, 1, and 2 in that order. This was done, and in the process of exploring proposal 4, many days and even weeks were spent in Washington, pleading Catawba's case with top officials in the Army, Navy and Air Force. Early results of these negotiations proved quite discouraging. In fact, the first response was flat rejection. But persistence paid off, and on March 12, 1943, the Southeastern Training Command of the Army notified the College of its intent to send an Air

Force detachment to Catawba College at an early date. On April 4, 1943, such a detachment numbering 208 men arrived on the campus. These men were housed in two college dormitories, the Administration Building dormitory section and Zartman Hall, and so the program so persistently sought after and so desperately needed now became a reality.

This saved the day for Catawba College in terms of additional funds for operating, in terms of utilization of faculty who were operating on exceedingly lean work schedules, and in terms of pros· pective government subsidies, sufficient to underwrite the cost of major building renovations and repairs so urgently needed. Approximately $50,000 was spent on the Administration Building alone.

Among other significant achievements during the 1942-43 academic year were: a) the establishment of a new counselling system, and b) with other liberal arts colleges of the state, the organization of a new cooperative organization to be known as "The Council of Church-Related Colleges of North Carolina." It is interesting to note that this newly organized body proved to be the forerunner of "The North Carolina Foundation of Church-Related Colleges" which currently nets its member institutions over half a million dollars per year through cooperative gifts.

Among honorary degree recipients at Commencement time were: the New President of the Board of Trustees, the Rev. Banks J. Peeler; and Mr. Stahle Linn, a long-time and devoted Trustee.

1943-44. Civilian student enrollment as of the beginning of the fall term was 259; accumulated cash to that date amounted to $124,-754.19. Cash contributions to the Building Fund during the 1943-44 academic year totalled $39,317.42; total gifts to the school during the fiscal year of 1943-44 was $83,655.56. Subsidy from the Evangelical and Reformed Church increased during the year from $600 to $1,200. The Air Crew Program worked admirably. Extensive physical plant improvements were made, including such items as 190 window sash in the Administration Building, drastic revision of the heating plant and the inauguration of a Faculty Retirement System effective September 30, 1944.

In cooperation with Rowan Memorial Hospital, a Nurses Training Program was established, and an Adult Education Program was added to the curriculum. A weekly radio broadcast program on the general theme, "Catawba Educates for Life" was undertaken with good success.

1944-45. The civilian student enrollment at the beginning of the fall term was 297. That year total gifts to the school amounted to $50,278.21. To meet new and changing needs, the Constitution and By-Laws of the Board of Trustees were revised. The Air Crew Program was terminated, necessitating a complete reversion to an all-civilian student body, with the loss of government subsidy. In adjusting to new financial needs created by this loss of revenue, tuition was advanced from $185 to $210.

Facing equipment needs, the Board of Trustees gave serious consideration to a proposed program of expansion comprehended in the building of a library, a central heating plant, a chapel, a men's dormitory, a new gymnasium and swimming pool, a woman's dormitory and a science building. A first step in that direction was taken when the Board of Trustees authorized a contract with Architects Charles C. Benton and Sons, with instructions to develop a campus master plan for future building developments.

1945-46. By the beginning of the fall term in 1945 student enrollment had climbed to 397, advanced at the beginning of the winter semester to 477. Summary of all gifts from February 1945 to February 1946 amounted to $74,783.94.

During this year major plant improvements comprehended modernization of the business offices, establishment of a new infirmary in the southwest wing of the Administration Building, beautification of the entrance and installation of a retaining wall and sidewalk at the south end of Claremont Hall.

On July 1, 1945, a Veteran's Guidance Center was established on the campus. Income from this new project helped to offset the loss in revenue caused from the now terminated Air Crew project.

Through the Trustees' committee on Finance, a restudy was made of the college's present portfolio of investments for the purpose of selling such stocks and bonds which had sizable dividends and purchasing such other stocks as the current market and prospective earnings seemed to recommend. This study resulted in net earnings of $14,947.

A good portion of the college's long-range "Master Plan of Expansion" was completed by the architect and whereupon submitted to the Trustee for study, but the most concrete evidence of the progress which was made during 1945-46 in the province of plant expansion was the purchase by the college of two tracts of land adjacent to the present campus opposite and across the road from the Administration Building. This tract comprised 98.9 acres and holds tremendous promise for intelligent future college development.

A local campaign, under the caption of The Four Hundred Club, to secure funds for the erection of a men's dormitory, was successfully inaugurated. Admission of the largest mid-year group of students in the history of the institution, 114, and the acceptance of the college into membership of the American Council of Education constitute the highlights of 1945-46.

1946-47. The fall term in 1946 started off with an enrollment of 699. The summary of gifts earmarked for all purposes received from February 1946 to February 1947 was $253,968.40.

As a result of a comprehensive study by the administration and faculty of the college's curriculum, two far-reaching recommendations of the Curriculum Committee were approved by the Trustees, both to become immediately effective:

> Recommendation 1, That the establishment of a Core Curriculum which in effect will specify certain required courses to be taken by all students, the total of which will constitute about half of the courses needed for graduation.
>
> Recommendation 2, The Bachelor of Arts degree will be the only degree henceforth conferred by Catawba.

Both of these recommendations were adopted by the Trustees.

At the suggestion of the College Auditor and supported by the Finance Committee and the president of the college, the following recommendations were also approved by the Trustees and their 1947 Annual Meeting:

> 1. That all real estate and buildings which are used for instructional and solely college purposes and for which no use or occupancy charge is made, shall be carried in the plant fund.
>
> 2. That all dormitories and apartment houses from which rents are received, should be transferred to the Endowment Fund.

Catawba's athletic prowess was given national recognition in that its football team was invited to the Tangerine Bowl both in 1946 and 1947. It won both years.

Introduced by Catawba's President, and concurred in by the North Carolina Council of Church-Related Colleges, a request was made of the North Carolina General Assembly by Catawba's President that church-related and private non-profit educational institutions be declared exempt from paying North America State Sales tax, thus placing them in the same category as stated educational institutions. This tax-exempt bill was passed by the Legislature, and the new statute became immediately effective. With the unanimous approval of the Trustees, the corporate name of the college was changed from "The Trustees of Catawba College" to "Catawba College."

1947-48. Another increase in student enrollment was reported in the fall of 1947, it being 802. General gifts for all purposes February 1947 to February 1948 totalled $234,886.14. Operating profit for that year was $835.31, with a surplus at the end of the year of $16,685.31. A campaign for funds in the Southern Synod of the Evangelical and Reformed Church moved slowly but steadily, reporting cash to date of $18,172.50.

1948-49. The year 1948-49 can very well be termed a "Year of Culmination." For many of the physical expansion projects of the college culminated during those months. Among these being the Foil House which was enlarged and remodelled; the erection of a 125 foot brick garage which was adapted, by the installation of shower and toilet facilities, heat and light, to be temporary quarters for 100 men; the Salisbury-Rowan Men's Residence Hall, designed to accommodate 175 men, was completed; a 240 foot 13 tier steel grandstand was erected to accommodate attendance at games on the football stadium; and two first class concrete all-weather tennis courts for student use were constructed. Other important items in this category include, concrete roads and curbing in newly developed areas of the campus, brick entranceway at the intersection of Summit Avenue and College Road, extensive grading and landscaping, installation of a thermostatic control system in all campus buildings, and the establishment of a modern well-equipped infirmary.

1949-50. By 1949 enrollment began to level off, and gifts to the college for all purposes receded. Physical improvements included modernizing the Science laboratories, and the installation of a depreciation policy. The Endowment was reported to be $675,-239.36, and the plant fund stood at $1,237,869.53.

The president of the college called attention the disturbing fact that in all likelihood the next five years would be some of the most difficult ones for American institutions of private higher education. Giving as reasons the current decrease of birth rate and the steady increase in operational costs. However, according to statisticians, there will again be an upward swing in college enrollment beginning in 1955 and 1956. The president added, "There is no doubt about the fact that it will take real educational statesmanship to steer successfully through this predictive five-year "low."

1950-51. This is the year in which Catawba College celebrated her "Century of Progress." Appropriate activities called attention to one hundred years of outstanding service to her church, her community, her state, and through her graduates, to the far-flung nations of the world.

In an inspiring mountain-top setting at Wild Acres, North Carolina, free from distraction, the faculty and the administrative staff, spent three busy and highly profitable days thinking through together ways and means whereby they could more effectively achieve the school's objectives. The total experience proved to be most worthwhile for all who share in it.

1951-52. Dr. Banks J. Peeler, the efficient and genial president of the Board of Trustees for the past nine years, asked the board not to re-nominate him for that position for the ensuing year. Most reluctantly the Trustees acceded to his wishes. Deep appreciation was expressed to him for a task exceedingly well done. The Vice President, Mr. Adrian L. Shuford, Jr., was thereupon elected to succeed Dr. Peeler.

One of the brilliant highlights of 1951 was the very successful celebration of Catawba's Centennial. All of the events as planned by the Centennial Committee were carried through with a kind of artfulness and meaningfulness that would have done justice to any college or university in the land.

A Spiritual Convocation dedicated to the Southern Synod of the Evangelical and Reformed Church opened the celebration. An outdoor drama depicting the long rich history of the institution was skillfully presented at Commencement time to an audience of two thousand persons. A stimulating and challenging Academic Convocation, attended by official representatives of many of the country's leading colleges and universities, constituted a fitting close.

1952-53. The Centennial Celebration served as an inspiration for the whole college community, the church and alumni. By the end of the year 1953, the president of the college asserted, "That the current academic year has been the greatest and most rewarding which he has yet experienced in the eleven years of his administration." Supporting this conviction, he cited the increased number of financial donors during the year, the apparent high esteem with which the colleges of the state and neighboring states regard Catawba's principles, policies and achievements.

Over a period of three years, Catawba made a study of "What is a Christian College" with wholesome results. In a similar vein a committee of 117 students worked together ten weeks planning for the Annual Religious Emphasis Week. Construction on the new library was begun within the past twelve months, groundbreaking ceremonies occurring on May 31, 1952.

1953-54. At the February meeting of the Board of Trustees in 1954, President Keppel reported:

Corriher-Linn-Black Library

In 1942 the Catawba College campus consisted of 84 acres and 13 buildings. Today it comprises 184.7 acres and 20 buildings, including a central heating plant, the Salisbury-Rowan Men's Residence Hall, an infirmary and drama workshops the Corriher-Linn-Black Library, the Dean's residence, Heath Hill Faculty Apartment and Heath Hill Lodge. . . . .

Academic standards have been appreciably raised through policy changes such as the adoption of a Core Curriculum and a more rigid screening of students applying for admission. In the past twelve years, 1,394 students have graduated with bachelor degrees. This is 166 more than were graduated from Catawba College in the previous 90 years. The full-time teaching faculty consists of 42 people as against 28 in 1942. A retirement system was adopted in 1944. In 1951 the Federal Social security and group insurance plan were added to include college employees. In 1942 the total subsidy granted Catawba College by the Evangelical and Reformed Church was $4,569, in 1954 it should be $31,080 and the next year it will total $41,000. . . . Statisticians predict an upswing in enrollment due not only to the release of men now in the armed services but also from population increase as well.

1954-55. In this academic year student enrollment increased to 539, and gifts for all purposes to $102,607.86. It was necessary also to make considerable physical adjustments in order to provide for additional courses of study and administrative offices. Recital Hall was enlarged by remodelling the entire first floor of the music building; speech and drama rooms were created on the first floor of the old library quarters; and a Baroque organ, the gift of Mr. and Mrs. Adrian L. Shuford, Sr., was installed in Recital Hall. The highlight of the year was a Convocation celebrating the 20th Anniversary of the merger of the Reformed Church in the United States and the Evangelical Synod of North America, which attracted more than 2,000 people. The convocation speaker was Dr. G. W. Grauer.

1955-56. The college Registrar's report indicated a student enrollment increase of 27½ per cent over the previous year, and that 20 different religious denominations were represented in the student body. Capital indebtedness was liquidated and three sizable grants were received totalling $126,732. A lot at the corner of Lantz and Brenner Avenues was donated to Southern Synod on which to erect a combination president's home and executive offices. The site was an outright gift, but the deed contains a reversionary clause should the property cease to be used for synodical purposes.

This year also had its sad moments. On December 20, 1955 the college suffered a severe loss in the passing of Mr. Lotan A. Corriher, for many years an influential member of the Board of Trustees. Next to his family, and his business, Catawba was his primary interest. He worked for it; he prayed for it; he lived for it.

1956-57. A Capital Funds Campaign for $1,500,000 was initiated December 1, 1955. At a meeting of the Finance and Executive committees held December 14, 1956, Mr. Robert McBride, the Capital Fund Campaign Director, reported that cash and pledges received to date totalled $719,431.99. By February 1957 cash and pledges approximated $1,000,000.

An historical marker commemorating the founding of Catawba College at Newton, North Carolina in 1851, and its subsequent relocation at Salisbury in 1925; was unveiled in 1956 located on the Salisbury campus. The marker was placed there by the Department

of Archives and History of North Carolina, initiated by Honorable
Wilson W. Warlick, Federal Judge of the Western District of North
Carolina, who also made the presentation address.

1957-58. At the beginning of the fall-winter term enrollment was
787. Gifts to all funds from February 1957 to February 1958
amounted to $231,477.10. A 15-year study made by the school in
its operating fund, its plant fund and its endowment fund, reflects
the following interesting comparisons:

	1943	1958
Plant Valuation	$695,220	$3,000,000
Endowment	300,000	943,387
Operating Budget	162,637	730,147

Of interest also is the current faculty salary scale which reflects
a 13 per cent increase adopted by the Board in February 1957.

Instructors	$3,300-$4,000
Assistant Professors	3,600- 4,600
Associate Professors	4,200- 5,600
Professors	5,000- 6,500

National recognition was accorded two of Catawba's depart-
ments—Drama and Education. Of all the colleges in the nation,
Catawba was the one school chosen to represent this country at the
International Festival of Amateur Theatre held at Monte Carlo in
September 1957, and she was approved for a chapter of the na-
tional honorary education society—Kappa Delta Pi.

In a "surprise action" by the Board of Trustees and the Alumni
Association, a citation and plaque were presented to President Keppel in recognition of his fifteen years of dedicated service in the
office of president of the college.

1958-59. Heading the list of achievements for the current year is
unquestionably the completion of the new and functional science
building. This new facility was dedicated on October 11, 1958 and
named for Mr. Adrian L. Shuford, Sr., and his family, all of whom
have generously given of themselves for others.

A faculty handbook was published which represents several years
of work on the part of the administration and faculty. It should
members of the college community, both trustees of the institution,
passed to their eternal reward: Dr. John W. Peeler and Dr. W.
Augusta Lantz.

The community was saddened by the passing of Mr. E. L. Callo-
way who, for sixteen years, served the college well as superintendent of building and grounds. Two other devoted and beloved
members of the college community, both were trustees of the institution, passed to their eternal reward: Dr. John W. Peeler and Dr.
W. Augusta Lantz.

At its February 1959 meeting, the Board of Trustees gave hearty
approval and encouraged President Keppel to attend the meeting
of the General Council of the World Alliance of Reformed Churches

holding the Presbyterian Order which met the following summer in Sao Paulo, Brazil. He had been elected by the General Synod as one of the delegates representing the Evangelical and Reformed Church.

1959-60. In this academic year the following plant improvements and major equipment purchases were recorded: North wing of the Administration building was converted into classrooms, a language laboratory, faculty offices and a girls' lounge. The college placement office was drastically remodelled, and the secretarial department were refurnished with new equipment to provide for more efficient teaching. New furniture for the men's dormitory in the Administration building was installed at a cost of $9,000, and dormitory rooms on the first floor of the same building were converted into a faculty men's lounge. Also new bookkeeping equipment was purchased involving an expenditure $7,500, modernizing the college's accounting system.

Heaviness of heart prevailed among all trustees, faculty, students and friends of the college, in the passing of Dr. Russell W. Whitener, a member of the Board of Trustees and for many years its secretary; also, the beloved Professor George W. Greene, former Alumni Secretary and teacher extraordinary.

In a statement concerning his retirement, Dr. Keppel remarked that it has been his considered hope and purpose to retire at age 65. Since he was fast approaching that age, he respectfully requested the Board of Trustees to give serious consideration to the choice of his successor. However, the Trustees urgently requested him to reconsider his proposed intention, and took action to provide an administrative assistant. The matter was referred to the Executive Committee for action.

1960-61. As of this current year, 38% of the faculty have their Ph.D. degrees, and others are in process of receiving the same. The office of Registrar and Director of Admissions, which had been combined in a single position, was separated. The division was made because of a heavy work-load, and designed for administrative efficiency. A significant development in the curriculum was the establishment of a Department of Geology and a Department of Astronomy.

After years of consultation, presidents of the colleges which form the North State Intercollegiate Athletic Conference agreed to put into effect immediately a plan which solved many of the problems involving ever increasing athletic subsidy and financial competition on the part of member schools. The purpose of this agreement and the regulations thus subscribed to are as follows: a ceiling was placed on the number of athletic grants in each major sport; uniform procedure for recruiting potential athletes; inauguration of a new policy which gives the member school the right to award only single year grants; a system of internal supervision spearheaded by the presidents themselves. The plan was supported and approved by the Board of Trustees of Catawba College.

In view of the fast expanding economy involving higher operating costs, the Trustees at their Annual meeting held February 21, 1961, took favorable action on the following items: a new faculty salary scale: Instructors $4,500-$5,000, Assistant Professors $4,800-$6,000, Associate Professors $5,300-$6,800, and Professors $6,000-$8,000; that salaries of faculty members be increased next fall by an approximate average of 11%; that tuition fees be increased $100 to $450.

Approval was given the "Catawba March Forward" plan as described by President Keppel including plans to execute it. A committee was named to investigate the matter of putting on a campaign for funds with which to erect a chapel on the campus, and Mr. Albert Carpenter was employed to fill the newly created position of Business Manager.

1961-62. The fall-winter term began with an all-time high enrollment of 940 students. Gifts to all funds from February 1961 to February 1962 totalled $294,858.73. The institution was urgently in need of teaching and program activity space, therefore, the Trustees authorized the Building Committee to seek bids for the

College Community Building
Keppel Auditorium—Hedrick Little Theatre

proposed College-Community Building and to bring this project to an early completion. In May 1961 a campaign for funds was launched in the Salisbury Community for $600,000 with which to erect a facility to house an auditorium and a little theatre. The campaign was directed by President Keppel, and with the help of approximately 250 Salisbury and Rowan citizens, raised in cash and pledges a total of $615,699.85. In appreciation for his excellent leadership in this undertaking, the auditorium was named "The Alvin R. Keppel Auditorium," by the Board of Trustees.

An addition to North Hall dormitory for women was constructed during the summer and occupied in the fall of 1961. It was noted that the Endowment Fund had reached $1,606,388.65.

Two other items of interest occurred during that academic year. President Keppel was named by the United Church of Christ as a delegate to the Ninth Assembly of the International Congregational Council, scheduled to meet on July 4-12, 1962 at Rotterdam, Holland. As an encouragement to avail himself of this high privilege, the Board of Trustees voted to extend his leave from the college up to six weeks with a gift of $500 for additional expenses.

Piedmont University Center of North Carolina, a new development in the field of interinstitutional cooperation and one that promises revolutionary changes in higher education in this state, was about to be born. Catawba College was excited in being able to claim charter membership in the venture. This new organization became a reality March 1, 1963.

1962-63. Businesswise this year will be remembered. Enrollment went up to 956; gifts, dividends, interest and stock gains up to $423,125.13; pledges on the Chapel Fund reached $338,321.33 of which $115,000 had been received in cash; the Endowment Fund was nearing $2,000,000 and the institution was free of debt—current and capital. Construction of the new chapel was also approved.

Academically an institutional self-study, an operation usually occurring every ten years, was completed under the supervision of the Southern Association of Colleges and Schools As a result Catawba College received an exceptionally high rating. These and other factors contributed to campus morale of an unusual high quality.

At a special meeting of the Board of Trustees held in the fall of 1962, President Keppel informed the board of his invitation to become the first Executive Director of the Piedmont University Center of North Carolina, embracing sixteen liberal arts colleges of the State in an excitingly new program of interinstitutional cooperation. He said that, in view of the fact that he had already alerted the Board of Trustees, of his imminent retirement, and in view of the tremendous challenge which this cooperative program offers, he had decided to accept the offer of the Directors of Piedmont University Center, and, with the board's approval, terminate his active relationship with Catawba College, as its president, as of March 1, 1963.

Board of Trustees of Catawba College, 1963

This information, while presenting no real surprise, was received with hesitation. After serious attempts to dissuade President Keppel of his expressed intention, the resignation was reluctantly accepted. In Part III of his final report to the board, in discussing something of his hopes for the future of Catawba College, he said,

> I believe that the genius and worth of Catawba College must rest ever more securely upon its philosophy of remaining not only a good college of liberal arts eternally striving for academic pre-eminence, but primarily a laboratory for Christian living where faculty and students working together in oneness of spirit set as their primary objective that spiritual dimension which alone justifies the name *Christian* college and alone interprets *higher* education as a *higher way of life.*

Thus brought to a close an administration of twenty-one years, one of the great and meaningful periods in the history of Catawba College. Subsequently Dean Donald C. Dearborn, who had served the institution with distinction in a variety of positions over a period of twenty-eight years, was named to the presidency.

The Administration of President Dearborn

Dr. Donald Curtis Dearborn assumed the Presidency of Catawba College on March 1, 1963; he was inaugurated on February 20, 1964. President Dearborn was uniquely prepared for his office. His positions as Professor of Mathematics, Registrar, and Dean of the College gave him the background to realize what Catawba needed to become—an outstanding college of liberal arts, a well-planned curriculum, and a well-trained faculty. His service and

associations with the United
Church of Christ also made him
an ideal choice. For many years
he had served as treasurer on
the Council of the Southern
Synod, as a delegate to the General Synod, and as a member of
its Executive Council. He was
a delegate of the Church at the
Assembly of the World Council
of Churches which met in the
summer at Evanston, Illinois in
1954 and at New Delhi, India,
in 1961; and he was selected to
go to Upsala, Sweden, in 1968.

In all the offices in the College and in the Church Dr.
Dearborn had served with dignity and distinction, and he had
been very influential in advanc-
ing the reputation of Catawba.

Dr. Donald C. Dearborn
1963-1967

When he became President, friends of the College, as well as the
faculty and trustees, knew they had a man upon whom they could
entirely rely and of whom they might be justly proud.

Under the able leadership of President Dearborn Catawba's
growth and development continued. The influence of the school
in the community and throughout the Piedmont was greatly enhanced by the completion of four beautiful buildings: The Chapel,
the College-Community Centre, and two dormitories—Abernethy
Hall and Woodson Hall. The number of applications for admit-
tance doubled. The enrollment in the autumn of 1963 was 817 and
1,046 in 1967. During his administration an increasing proportion
of students lived on the campus and came from outside North Carolina. The number of students housed on the campus was 554 in
the first semester of 1963 and 776 in 1967. The total charges for
both day and boarding students almost doubled. Though expenditures increased by an average of $100,000 per year, the stability
of the College was fully assured by an increase of total assets from
two and a half million in 1963 to eight million in 1967. These improvements in living conditions ushered in a better morale and cultural atmosphere.

During Dr. Dearborn's administration many facilities to meet
the needs of students and faculty were added. These included ten
new classrooms and a bookstore, laboratories for the departments
of geology, education and language, an art studio, a speech therapy
center, and a number of offices for the faculty. Practically all of
these improvements were completed by the maintenance crew of

the College under the expert direction of Forest G. Pridgen, the Superintendent of Buildings and Grounds. Steam lines were also replaced and a new boiler and control system installed; and all the new buildings as well as many of the old were equipped with modern furniture. The Hedrick Administration Building was almost entirely converted into classrooms, laboratories, and offices for the faculty. Two additions to Rahauser Hall together with two additions to North Hall and the two new dormitories made it possible to serve and house 800 students.

The Southern Synod Chapel (*inside*)

Notable among the improvements on the campus was the completion of the Gothic Chapel. It was dedicated on February 2, 1964. The bronze plaque in the narthex bears this legend: "The Chapel of Catawba College, built by Southern Synod of the Evangelical and Reformed Church *To The Glory of God* and in honor of Julius Whitener Abernethy, Sr., trustee, advisor, and benefactor."

In the first semester of 1966-67 two well-planned dormitories, Abernethy Hall and Woodson Hall, housing 130 men and 170 women, were ready for students. The two buildings cost about a million dollars, but they greatly relieved congestion on the campus and provided the college with sufficient dormitory space for 360 men and 380 women.

In the spring of 1964 the College-Community Centre, which includes the Alvin Robert Keppel Auditorium, the Hedrick Little Theatre, and the beautiful exhibition hall, the Crystal Lounge, was completed. On March 2 the building was dedicated, and here on March 2-15 occurred the first Fine Arts Festival held at Catawba College. The festival began with a concert by the Detroit Symphony Orchestra. Designed by John Erwin Ramsay of Salisbury, the Centre has attracted the attention of architects throughout the Southeast. For carrying to completion this beautiful facility the thanks of the community are due the New Building Committee of the Trustees, and particularly its chairman, Dr. E. Alvin Goodman, Jr. Under its able Manager, Hoyt M. McCachren, the Centre has already become the preferred meeting place of many of the cultural organizations of Salisbury and the surrounding area. Some significant event occurs here almost daily. The completion of this Centre heralded a new peak of cooperation and cordial relations between the College and the community.

Throughout his administration Dr. Dearborn's prime interest was the enrichment of Catawba's program; like Dr. Keppel, he aimed

Outside of Chapel

to make Catawba a good, liberal arts college. All of the new buildings, of course, eliminated many problems and provided a more congenial atmosphere for serious study. The cultural opportunities of students were greatly enhanced by a federal grant to enrich the program in speech and art at Catawba and Livingston College, and by the establishment of the Piedmont University Center. In 1963-64 President S. E. Duncan of Livingstone and President Dearborn initiated a program whereby advanced students in either college could enroll in courses needed for a major at the neighbor institution.

In 1966-67 the facilities of both colleges were partly financed by a federal grant of $100,005. Under Title III of the Higher Education Act of 1965, Catawba and Livingstone, in cooperation with George Washington University, received this grant for equipment and salaries to improve the offerings in speech and art. Their curricula now include courses designed to identify and correct defects in speech, debating, and the history of art.

In 1963 the Piedmont University Center was established by the Mary Reynolds Babcock Foundation. Under the able leadership of Dr. A. R. Keppel, the executive director, its operations have greatly expanded. Committees of the eighteen member colleges cooperate in sharing the cultural advantages of traveling exhibits in arts, science, and industry. Every year several distinguished scholars and artists visit the campuses of the member colleges, hold conferences, and give lectures. To improve the quality of instruction at the eighteen colleges, the Center in 1963 inaugurated and subsidized a system of leaves of absence for advanced study for a few members of each faculty each year. Through a grant from the Fund for the Advancement of Education to the Piedmont University Center, Catawba arranged to send three members of its faculty for subsidized study each summer for five years.

In August, 1963, David E. Setzer was appointed Director of Public Relations. In the past five years his multifarious activities have been of untold value in making the image of Catawba attractive. In addition to sending out almost daily releases of news stories—general, feature, and sports, he has supervised virtually all the publications of the College: brochures, announcements, programs, calendars, and *Campus*.

In 1963 he made a colored motion picture of Catawba College. This picture has been updated and shown countless times in churches and schools from Connecticut to North Carolina. He has also handled all the correspondence and arranged for the Annual Banquet of the Indian Club, the college booster organization. The image of Catawba which he has created has markedly contributed to the success of the Catawba Challenge.

The first two sentences of President Dearborn's report to the Trustees in February, 1966 read: "Someone has said that a good college requires good students, a good faculty, and a good curriculum. The achievement of excellence in all these areas, however, seems to involve a fourth factor; namely, an adequate financial structure." In a denominational college the success of any administration is, of course, dependent upon adequate support from private sources. Fortunately, the number of "hilarious givers"—those who give joyfully thinking only of what their gifts may do to help others, mounted steadily from 1963 to 1967.

In 1963-64 gifts for current operations totaled over $90,150. These gifts included about $25,000 from the North Carolina Foundation of Church-Related Colleges and about $50,000 from the United Church of Christ. In 1964-65 the total was $100,213; in 1965-66 $154,702; in 1966-67 $166,714; in 1967-68 $172,420. The loyalty of Catawbans to their Alma Mater is attested by the fact that the number giving as well as the amounts given to the Alumni Fund has steadily increased. The number who gave in 1963 was 85; in 1967 it was 1,106. In 1966 Dr. Annie Shuford Rankin and Dr. and Mrs. Adrian L. Shuford, Jr. gave a splendid pipe organ for the College Chapel.

Notable among the bequests were gifts from the estates of Mary Eva Corriher, Florence Wehr, Dr. J. A. Smith of Lexington, and a gift of the entire estate of Dr. Lulu Ruth Reed, Librarian of the College from 1943 to 1965. The general endowment of the College was greatly increased by a bountiful bequest of Dr. Margaret C. Woodson. She bequeathed her residual estate to a trust fund, the Margaret Cunningham Woodson Foundation; one-fifth of the annual income was distributed by the Directors to Catawba in 1966; this first gift amounted to $29,500. The amount in 1967 was $30,-500; in 1968 $32,750.

The loyalty of all the Trustees is illustrated by their steadfast support and countless gifts during the administration of both Dr. Keppel and Dr. Dearborn. The success of the Catawba Challenge, an ambitious expansion program designed to raise $5,000,000 with which to provide urgently needed buildings and equipment and to enlarge the endowment, was fully assured when the gift of $675,-000 by the Trustees was announced.

In recent years the gifts of two families deserve special mention—those of the late Burl Hedrick and of the late Adrian L. Shuford, Sr. The son-in-law of Burl Hedrick, Dr. E. A. Goodman, Jr. '38, has given unstintedly of his time, talent, and resources to the construction and completion of the four beautiful buildings that have been erected on the campus in the last five years. The outstanding benefactor of Catawba during the administration of Dr. Dearborn was Dr. Julius W. Abernethy. His gifts of money, time, and financial counsel together with the assurance that he will match every dollar given to the Catawba Challenge assure a great future for Catawba.

This account of the administration of President Donald C. Dearborn would not be complete without a tribute to Dr. Adrian L. Shuford, Jr., the President of the Board of Trustees. His never-failing fidelity to Catawba College, together with the steadfast cooperation of Dr. Daniel E. Kirk, Dean of the College, has given both faculty and administration the confidence to carry on; a wheelhorse on a great team, he has ably directed the operations of the college when there was no President to preside. The quick selection of his committee of the economist and experienced administrator, Dr. Martin Luther Shotzberger as President of Catawba, gives all lovers of the college the assurance that she will continue to be a first-rate college of liberal arts.

After the death of their President, the faculty expressed their love of Dr. Dearborn and their loyalty to Catawba in this resolution:

> Deeply grieved over the death of our beloved friend and leader, President Donald C. Dearborn, the faculty of Catawba College extends its sympathy to his children and his beloved wife, Mary Omwake Dearborn.
>
> A man of pre-eminent talents, Doctor Donald Curtis Dearborn was, by virtue of his training and experience as Professor of Mathematics and Registrar, and Dean of the College, ideally qualified to be President of Catawba. For thirty-three years he labored without thought of self to make Catawba one of the foremost colleges of the Southeast. He knew her vital needs, and he also knew what makes a great college of liberal arts. Every year under his guidance at Catawba the cause of learning advanced.
>
> Doctor Dearborn was a man of high spiritual stature, great of heart and mind, keen in judgment, and moral insight. Modest and genial, he earned the love and esteem of us all; and we deeply mourn his untimely loss.
>
> Moved by the thought of his dedicated service to Catawba and to the advancement of learning, we here resolve to carry on in his spirit and to emulate his example in the cause for which he gave the last full measure of devotion.

At its meeting held on December 14, 1967, acting for the Board of Trustees, the Executive Committee, approved the following resolution:

> With profound sorrow, the Board of Trustees record the death of the beloved president of Catawba College, Dr. Donald Curtis Dearborn. Dr. Dearborn gave unstintingly of his time and talents to Catawba College over a span of thirty-three years as professor, dean and since 1964 as president. His individual personality, clarity of thought, sincere loyalty, enduring qualities of affection and friendship, dignified humility and profound Christian faith won for him the love and respect of all who had the privilege to know him and work with him.
>
> The members of the Board of Trustees recognize the loss that is felt in other fields of Dr. Dearborn's interests. As a dedicated leader, on all levels of the United Church of Christ—from the local congregation, through the Southern Conference and the General Synod. As an active worker in the local and State Civitan organization. As a concerned citizen in community affairs. In every activity, on and off the campus, to which he could devote his time for the betterment of his fellowman.
>
> Be it therefore resolved, That this expression of sorrow and apprecia-

tion be sent to the family of Dr. Dearborn and that the same be spread on the minutes of the Board of Trustees at its Annual Meeting on February 20, 1968.

ROSTER OF PRESIDENTS

Rev. Charles H. Albert	1851-1853
Mr. Hildreth H. Smith	1853-1856
Mr. Charles W. Smythe, on lease basis	1856-1859
Rev. A. S. Vaughn	1860-1861
Rev. Jacob Crawford Clapp, D.D.	1861-1900

The school operated during War years as an academy. From 1865 to 1885 it operated under the name of Catawba High School. In 1885 it resumed operations under its original charter again as Catawba College.

Mr. Charles H. Mebane	1900-1904
Rev. George A. Snider	1904-1908
Mr. William R. Weaver, Acting President	1908-1910
Mr. John Frederick Buchheit	1910-1913
Rev. James David Andrew, D.D.	1913-1918
Rev. Abram D. Wolfinger, D.D.	1918-1923
Rev. Elmer R. Hoke, Ph.D.	1924-1931
Mr. Howard R. Omwake, Litt.D.	1931-1942
Mr. Alvin R. Keppel, LL.D.	1942-1963
Mr. Donald C. Dearborn, Ph.D.	1963-1967
Mr. Martin Luther Shotzberger, Ph.D.	1968-

Claremont College

TWENTY YEARS before the establishment of Southern Synod, Claremont College had ceased to operate. However, a complete story of education in the German Reformed Church and its successor the Evangelical and Reformed Church in North Carolina will include at least a digest of events about that highly respected and widely influential institution of higher learning. The way was opened to close it on May 24, 1914 when the Classis of North Carolina took action suggesting the suspension of its academic work.[1]

Concerning early schools in Catawba County, and particularly in the village of Hickory, North Carolina, the Hickory Daily Record says:

> Although "free" schools had been established in Catawba County before the war between the states—and they were considered above the general average of those being operated in North Carolina—it seems that in the village of Hickory the private schools were forerunners of public schools by some years.
>
> Local writers, in tracing the history of the city's earlier schools, gave as the reason the private schools were not easily replaced by public schools was that a teacher recognized as a real master of his profession, could earn a great deal more by conducting his own school than he could by teaching in a free enterprise.
>
> In the past, judging from early accounts of Hickory's first schools and teachers, written by Hickory's older residents, the private schools conducted here, and their teachers, were among the finest available . . . Dr. R. W. Carver, for many years superintendent of the Hickory city schools . . . said that the first school at Hickory Tavern, as he had been told by some of the city's older residents, was a frame structure located

on what is now First Avenue S. E. in the vicinity of the "Old Log Cabin" next to the old abandoned cemetery.

After the building became more or less too dilapidated for use, the school for a time moved into the first floor of a two-story building erected by the Reformed Church, then known as the German Reformed Church, about 1868. The upper story was used as a chapel, or church, by the Reformed congregation, and the downstairs as a school room.[2]

Private schools continued in this building until the early years of 1880. Here, beginning in 1876, H. M. Blair and Professor Lacey established the Blair-Lacey High School, which in 1878 when W. P. Ivey replaced Professor Lacey, became the Blair-Ivey High School. It was with this school that promoters of Claremont College proposed to begin instruction for girls.

Evidently for some time interest was being stimulated among citizens of Hickory and vicinity favorable to a private school for girls and young women. A leader in this movement was Mrs. John Wilfong, who asked for a meeting of the Corinth Reformed Church consistory to consider the matter. The meeting was held April 24, 1880 in the home of Mr. and Mrs. John Wilfong. Present were Dr. Jeremiah Ingold, pastor of Corinth Reformed Church, W. R. Reinhardt and J. F. Murrill, elders in the congregation, and A. A. Shuford, A. C. Link and B. F. Ingold, deacons, Mrs. Wilfong was well prepared to present and support her cause. She had received from Mr. and Mrs. Henry W. Robinson the donation of a lot, forty feet front, which was a part of the Old Hickory Tavern lot, on which she proposed should be erected a new Reformed Church, thus releasing the old church building in which to begin the proposed school for girls. A. A. Shuford and A. C. Link supported the proposition, which was immediately and unanimously approved by the consistory. Various plans were proposed for founding the school, but that suggested by J. F. Murrill appears to have been accepted. It provided that a competent lady teacher be employed who would for the present, cooperate with the Blair-Ivey High School, then in operation on the first floor of the Reformed Church building, located on First Avenue S. E. The plan, however, was never executed.[3]

Circumstances altered those first plans. Dreams and hopes for a girls' school of distinction were discussed with Dr. Samuel R. Fisher, Philadelphia, Pennsylvania, editor of the Reformed Church Messenger, who wrote a series of articles in support of a school of this character in the South. These articles came to the attention of Rev. A. S. Vaughn, who had served as president of Catawba College briefly in 1860-1861. Mr. Vaughn immediately contacted Dr. Ingold concerning the venture. A special meeting of the Corinth Church consistory took place July 10, 1880, called by Dr. Ingold "to consider a proposition from Rev. A. S. Vaughn to return to North Carolina and build up a female school of high grade in or near Hickory." Mr. Vaughn was invited to come to Hickory August

5, 1880 and appear before the consistory to discuss his ideas for establishing such an institution. The record says,

> When Mr. Vaughn appeared before the consistory of Corinth Church in August, he was full of enthusiasm and zeal, perhaps visionary. He had great plans. He had a vision of a school—the greatest of the South; it was to be a Wellesley of the South. He seemed to be equally confident that he could secure money from the North to finance his scheme. He dreamed of great philanthropic souls in the North on charity bent.[4]

Mr. Vaughan proposed an independent non-denominational school. He wrote:

> What is called sectarianism, an evil with modern forms of Christian activity, is to be forever excluded. Christ and His precious Word, form the central principles of all nurture and instruction. Christ in the heart is the key that unlocks all the glories of the universe.[5]

His concept made no place for a fashionable, finishing, boarding school especially suited to the needs of young women, but an institution committed to prepare young people for an important mission and purpose in life. Reactions to these ideas were mixed. The liberal outlook and high cultural tone fitted perfectly into the catholic spirit of the Reformed Church people, but serious objection prevailed with reference to property rights and management. Compromising somewhat their own notions on these matters with the Vaughn plan, interested citizens of the community began to make pecuniary and property arrangements for opening a girl's school in Hickory. Mr. and Mrs. Henry W. Robinson deeded twenty two acres of land located in the Northeast section of the community to the cause, and an organization was effected to canvas the area for funds. The school was organized under a charter granted by the State of North Carolina, August 25, 1880. A committee of organization consisted of J. F. Murrill, J. G. Hall, A. A. Shuford, A. L. Shuford, R. B. Davis, and two other men whose names are not available.

The Charter, which was executed July 28, 1880 and probated by Judge M. O. Sherrill, was signed by J. F. Murrill, J. G. Hall, A. M. Peeler, R. B. Davis, A. A. Shuford, A. S. Abernethy, A. L. Shuford, W. P. Reinhardt, John W. Robinson, M. L. McCorkle, J. Ingold, R. W. McComb, A. C. Link, J. T. Johnson and S. T. Wilfong. The document, which follows, is self-explanatory:

> Claremont College, Catawba County, North Carolina.
> We, J. F. Murrill, J. G. Hall, A. M. Peeler, R. B. Davis, A. A. Shuford, A. S. Abernethy, W. P. Reinhardt, J. W. Robinson, M. L. McCorkle, S. T. Wilfong, R. W. McConb, Rev. Jeremiah Ingold, Dr. J. T. Johnson and A. C. Link, all of Catawba County and the State of North Carolina, being desirous of forming ourselves into a private corporation, for the purpose of promoting female education and establishing a female college in the town of Hickory, in the county and state aforesaid, of high grade by the name of Claremont Female College, and by that name shall have a perpetual succession and common seal and shall be able and capable to sue and be sued in law and equity and to plead and be impleaded

and shall take, demand and receive and possess all goods and chattles, lands and tenements which may be given to said corporation, or said trustees and their successors for the use and benefit of said corporation, and shall take and receive all donations made and appropriate them according to the wishes of the donors and to the purpose hereinafter declared, and by purchase or otherwise shall take, hold and possess to themselves and their successors in office for ever any lands and tenements which may be sufficient for said college and college purposes and may purchase and hold for the purpose of said institution such personal property as they may deem necessary, provided the said real and personal property shall not exceed in value at any one time the Sum of Two Hundred Thousand Dollars ($200,000.).

I. That said trustees of said corporation and their successors in office shall have power to elect such president, professors and tutors for said college as they may see fit and proper and have power to remove same for misbehaviour, inability or neglect of duty or any other sufficient cause as to them may seem expedient.

II. That upon the death or resignation or removal of any member of the Board out of the State of North Carolina, his place shall be filled by the congregation or church to which he belongs or is a member, provided, that in case of the failure of any church or congregation to appoint a trustee after reasonable notice of such vacancy, the Board of Trustees may elect, provided always that three-fifths of said trustees shall be members of the Reformed Church, formerly known as the German Reformed Church, and provided further that said trustees shall have power to remove any of their number for misconduct, neglect of duty, inability or other sufficient cause.

III. That said trustees shall have power of confering such degrees and marks Classical and literary distinction as is usual in colleges and universities.

IV. That said trustees may admit into said College, as pupils, boys under the age of ten years, in the Primary Department.

V. That said trustees, or a majority, may make such By-laws, Rules and Regulations for the government of said college as they may deem best for the same, not inconsistent with the constitution and laws of North Carolina and those of the United States.

VI. That when ever either of said trustees shall remove from the State of North Carolina or cease to be a member of the church or denomination to which he belongs at the time of appointment, or election or to be a member of the church from which he may have been selected by his respective congregation his place shall be vacated and filled as is heretofore provided in case of death or resignation.

VII. The officers of this corporation shall be president, secretary, and treasurer, to be elected by the board of trustees.

VIII. That the said trustees shall make such rules and regulations as to the duties and the manner of electing their offices as they may see fit.

IX. The individual corporators shall not be individually liable for the debts of said corporation.

X. No person of color shall be admitted a pupil in said institution.[6]

In view of constitutional requirements, a list of the first trustees with their church affiliation is valuable in this connection: J. F. Murrill, A. A. Shuford, A. L. Shuford, W. P. Reinhardt, J. Ingold, S. T. Wilfong, John W. Robinson, M. L. McCorkle and C. A. Link, were members of the Reformed Church; J. G. Hall and R. W. McComb,

Presbyterian; A. M. Peeler, Lutheran; R. B. Davis, Episcopal; A. S. Abernethy and J. T. Johnson, Methodist.

The school was formally opened in the fall of 1880, operating in the Reformed Church building, which was a two-story structure. The first floor was divided into three rooms, where teaching was done. Courses in music were taught in the home of Mrs. J. F. Murrill. The faculty was composed of Rev. A. S. Vaughn, Miss Edwina Shearn and a Miss More. There were three departments of instructions: the Primary, providing five years; the Preparatory, including four years; and college level courses consisting of four years of study. Claremont was modeled and its courses of study were fashioned after Wellesley College; its professors and instructors were to be Wellesley and Smith College graduates or their equivalent.

Claremont College, Main Building

While the school operated in the Reformed Church building, work on an appropriate structure on college property proceeded under the supervision of A. L. Shuford. This construction was financed by money pledges made in a canvass of the community for funds, and was later known as the south wing. Other additions to the faculty and staff were made as the school expanded. Among these first appointments being Miss Batchelor, Miss Ida Pettit, Miss Belle Haven, Miss Alive Eversten, Miss May Ramsaur, Miss Amelia McComb, librarian, and Sarah C. Perrin, superintendent of catering, cooking and housekeeping. Operations continued in the Reformed Church building until the fall of 1883. At that time the brick structure on the college campus, although unfinished, was occupied.

Claremont Female College appeared to be well on its way, when at the end of 1883, President Vaughn presented his resignation. He left the community at the beginning of 1884. His resignation was a compromising disappointment to the trustees and to a wide circle of supporters who had come to believe in the validity of their enterprise. It was the more serious because the institution was left without either a fixed administrative policy or plans for the future. Hopes for developing Claremont into a quality school of high academic standing and wide influence faded. However, leaders did not despair. Miss Florence L. Chase, a member of the faculty, was engaged to complete the school year as administrator. Lacking financial and moral support from the community, and finding themselves with an institutional orphan, the trustees adopted a policy of leasing the property for school purposes to qualified educators, for what could be financially realized from its operation. The new policy met with varying results, sometimes successful but always a struggle, and continued in effect until 1907. A list of administrators, with dates of their tenure in office, reflects something of the story.

CLAREMONT COLLEGE ADMINISTRATORS, 1880-1916

Rev. A. S. Vaughn	1880-1883
Miss Florence L. Chase	1884-
Mrs. Alice Thurston	1884-1886
Mrs. — Boney	1886-1887
Professor A. C. Hottenstein	1887-1888
Professor W. H. Sanborn	1888-1892
Dr. Joseph L. Murphy	1892-1896
Mr. S. D. Hatton	1896-1900
Mr. M. W. Hatton	1900-1902
Mr. A. J. Bolin	1902-1905
Professor D. W. Reed	1905-1907
Dr. Joseph L. Murphy	1907-1915
Dr. J. M. L. Lyerly	1915-1916

Thirteen different people managed the school during its life time. Only President Murphy served in that office more than four years, and nine of its Presidents served four years or less. In 1907 lease on the property was suddenly surrendered. "The trustees then turned the school over to Rev. J. L. Murphy, president of the board, to make the best possible arrangements." This act named Dr. Murphy a second time to head the institution in an emergency, a responsibility which he held until the close of the academic year 1915. The new president made required arrangements to continue the school, and at the same time posed with his board of trustees the advisability of establishing an administrative relationship with an ecclesiastical body. F. A. Clinard, therefore, submitted the following resolution which was approved by the board, instructing President Murphy to present it to the Classis of North Carolina:

Resolved, that the trustees of Claremont Female College tender to the Classis of North Carolina, Reformed Church in the United States, for a girl's school or young ladies school, Claremont Female College, free of rent, said Classis to make all necessary repairs and build any additional buildings they may deem proper and keep the property insured and said Classis to retain the College as long as they maintain a school for girls or young ladies.[7]

Upon receipt of the above communication, on February 12, 1907 at a called meeting of the Classis a commission was appointed to study the matter and report. The commission composed of Dr. Jacob C. Leonard, Dr. William B. Duttera and Dr. Walter W. Rowe made its report the following May which was approved. The text reads:

We have given the subject careful consideration. We find that the property consists of seventeen acres of land on a beautiful elevation within the corporate limits of the town of Hickory. Substantial brick buildings in a reasonably good state of preservation occupy a central position in a campus of native oaks. The buildings contain recitation rooms, a chapel, parlor, dining rooms, kitchen and dormitories sufficient to accomodate fifty girls. These buildings have water connections with the city mains, and a private sewerage system. A conservative estimate places the value of the property at $25,000.

The trustees of Claremont College propose the following terms of transfer:

"I. Articles III and VII of the charter shall be so amended as to lodge in the Classis of North Carolina, Reformed Church in the United States, the election of three-fifths of the said trustees of Claremont Female College, members of said Reformed Church. Successors to the remaining two-fifths of said trustees shall be elected by the said Board of Trustees, viz., the Board composed by those elected by the said Classis of North Carolina and the present two-fifths of the Trustees, and thereafter vacancies in the two-fifths number shall be filled by the said Board of Trustees. Provided, that should the Classis of North Carolina for two years fail to maintain a female college as provided by the charter, then the said property shall revert to the Board of Trustees created as the present board.

II. The officers of this Board of Trustees are hereby directed to take at once the steps necessary to carry the foregoing into legal effect.

III. This action shall go into effect immediately upon legal ratification, provided the Classis of North Carolina takes favorable action."

Your commission, after careful consideration of the facts in the case, recommend the following:

1. That the terms of transfer proposed by the Trustees be approved, and that Claremont College be accepted by the Classis of North Carolina.

2. That the trustees to be elected by the Classis be divided into three groups to be elected at this meeting as follows: Three to be elected for a term of one year, three for a term of two years and three for a term of three years; and that hereafter successors to those whose term expires be elected at each annual meeting of Classis.

3. That the Board of Trustees divide into three groups the six trustees to be chosen by the Board, two to be chosen at the first meeting for one year, two for two years and two for three years, and thereafter at each annual meeting of the Trustees successors to those whose term expires shall be chosen.

4. That the Trustees elected by Classis at this meeting be instructed to proceed as soon as practicable to carry out the terms of transfer.[8]

At a meeting of the Board of Trustees held January 5, 1909, a committee consisting of J. L. Murphy, C. C. Bost and A. C. Link was appointed to arrange for charter amendments required to place the school in proper relation to the church. This was done, and the document which appears below was ratified February 12, 1909.

Whereas on the 28th day of July 1880, J. F. Murrill, A. A. Shuford, J. G. Hall and others obtained a charter from the Superior Court of Catawba County incorporating an institution for the promotion of religion, morality and learning therein, named Claremont Female College, and have maintained a school and acquired valuable real and personal property at Hickory, North Carolina, held by them as trustees under said name; and whereas, in the promotion of the objects of said charter, desire to place the said school and its property under the control of the Classis of North Carolina, Reformed Church in the United States, and have reached a satisfactory agreement with said Classis to that end, and desire to obtain from the General Assembly of North Carolina ratification of its said Charter, with certain amendments thereto:

The General Assembly do enact: now, therefore,

Section 1. That the name of Claremont Female College, at Hickory, North Carolina, shall be and the same is hereby changed to "Claremont College."

Section 2. That articles three and seven of the original charter of Claremont Female College, obtained in 1880, be and the same are hereby stricken out and the following inserted in lieu thereof:

That the trustees of Claremont College shall be fifteen in number, the present board being Rev. J. L. Murphy, D.D., Rev. J. C. Leonard, D.D., A. A. Shuford, Rev. J. C. Clapp, D.D., C. C. Bost, L. A. Carpenter, F. A. Clinard, H. D. Warlick, E. L. Shuford, C. M. Shuford, G. H. Geitner,

Rev. W. H. McNairy, J. E. Wilfong, J. W. Robinson, and N. M. Seagle, and they and their successors in office shall constitute the board of trustees of Claremont College; that said trustees above named shall continue in office until the regular annual meeting for the year 1909 of the Classis of North Carolina, Reformed Church in the United States, and at which time said Classis shall elect three members of said board to serve one years, three to serve for two years and three to serve for three years, and annually thereafter three members for a term of three years; and the board of trustees of said college shall themselves elect six of their own successors in office, beginning with the next annual meeting in such way that the term of office of two members so elected by them shall expire annually: Provided, that in the event of the said Classis of North Carolina, Reformed Church in the United States shall fail for two years to maintain a female college, as provided by the charter of Claremont College, or shall fail to carry out the conditions of maintenance and preservation of property assumed by said Classis, then such failure shall vacate the offices of the nine trustees elected by said Classis, and they are thereby declared vacant, and Corinth Reformed Church, at Hickory, North Carolina, shall have full power and authority and it shall be the duty of the congregation of said church in meeting assembled for that purpose, to elect nine members of the board of trustees of Claremont College to take the place of those whose offices are vacated by this act, and thereafter said trustees shall be elected annually by said church, as hereinabove provided for by said Classis: and they, with other members of said board, shall take possession of all Real and Personal property belonging to Claremont College; and either the pastor, the Consistory or any three members of said Church may by proper notice call a meeting of the Congregation of said Corinth Reformed Church, and those present at said meeting shall have the power to elect nine Trustees under this act.

Section 3. That the said original charter of said College is in all respects wherein the same is not inconsistent herewith recognized, ratified and confirmed.

4. That this act shall be in force from and after its ratification.[9]

With the school's relation to the Classis of North Carolina established two additional major avenues of influence were available to the administration. The source of students extended throughout the Reformed Church in North Carolina, and from the same area reasonable financial support could be expected. Claremont College enjoyed encouraging returns from these sources during the next few years; however, a church constituency of less than five thousand people could scarcely enrich two campuses with either a multitude of students or overflowing treasuries. That competition developed between Claremont College and Catawba College, both under administrative control of the Classis of North Carolina, should not be considered unusual; but that the situation deteriorated to a harmful state did prove embarrassing to responsible people. Sensing that something should be done about the growing unpleasantness between the two institutions, President Murphy of Claremont, in his annual statement to the Classis of North Carolina in 1914, said,

> The time has come when the church in North Carolina should stop playing at running schools. The educational problem is one of the greatest confronting the Church in our State, today and while not offering any solution, I suggest that the Classis appoint a committee to act with like committees representing Claremont and Catawba Colleges with a view of adjusting our educational work.[10]

The committee on education, taking note of his suggestion, reported with specific recommendations during the same sessions of the Classis. The committee recommended:

> Whereas it seems practical, feasible and desirable that our educational work in these two institutions (Catawba and Claremont Colleges) should in some way be coordinated for the sake of harmony and efficiency, therefore,
>
> Resolved, that the Classis of North Carolina hereby appoints a committee of three, and request the Trustees of Catawba College and of Claremont College to appoint similar committees of the same number, the said nine men to constitute a joint commission charged with the duty of formulating a plan by which the important work of the two institutions may be coordinated.[11]

The commission was authorized and appointed, making its report to the Classis May 22, 1915. The report recommended:

> Resolved that the Classis of North Carolina hereby adopts the following as its policy to be pursued in the work of Catawba College, Newton, and Claremont College, Hickory:

> Catawba College, after the close of the present scholastic year, be
> our school for boys and young men. Girls may be admitted to the classes
> of the institution, but only as day pupils. The boarding department
> shall be maintained for boys and young men exclusively.
>
> From the same date, Claremont College shall be our school for girls
> and young women, providing home accommodations and an educational
> curriculum in harmony with the demands of the times in a college of
> the Classis to be called for its consideration.[12]

While the new policy was generously supported by the delegates,
its wisdom was seriously questioned by many people, a number
of whom were officials of the Classis who were especially concerned
about the future of coeducation. Other emotional factors entered
the picture—normal sentiment which had developed favorable to
each school, the financial inability of the Reformed Church in North
Carolina to maintain two separate schools, perhaps others—but the
central issue, stripped of its contributory factors, was coeducation.
In this respect forward looking leaders in the Church were several
generations ahead of their times. Since then education in the State
of North Carolina has moved slowly but surely toward the policy
of preparing young people together to live in a democratic society.

On the following Monday, May 24, 1915, the committee on overtures under pressure presented a request that the educational policy
adopted the previous Friday be rescinded. The overture was approved, and after extended and heart-searching discussion, the matter of policy was disposed of in the following historic statement,
supported by two-thirds of the voting delegates of the Classis:
"Resolved, That the Trustees of Claremont College be informed
that the Classis of North Carolina does not hold them bound to
conduct a Woman's College the next two years."[13]

This action implied two things: That the Classis, according to
provisions in the Charter, returned Claremont College to its original owner, Corinth Reformed Church; and that the educational
policy of the Reformed Church in North Carolina is coeducational.
The school's last years, 1915-1916, were under the supervision of
Dr. J. M. L. Lyerly and supported by a faculty composed Miss
May Lyerly, Miss Helen Troup, Miss Ethel Peeler and Miss Jose-
phine Pritchard. It was operated on an independent status, amenable to a board of trustees elected by Corinth Reformed Church.
Over a period of thirty six years, Claremont College had educated
hundreds of young ladies, preparing them for useful living, and
had numbered among its faculty some of the great educators of
the country.

At a meeting of the Board of Trustees July 24, 1919, a plan was
offered to the City of Hickory whereby the Clearmont College property, consisting of seven acres of land and a good brick school
building, could be deeded to the city for educational purposes.
Attending that meeting were: Dr. Walter W. Rowe, pastor of Corinth Reformed Church and president of the Board of Trustees, J.

W. Warlick, G. H. Geitner, B. B. Blackwelder, Charles H. Geitner, A. A. Shuford, L. F. Abernethy, E. L. Shuford, Dr. J. H. Shuford, Edgar Bolick, George F. Bost, C. C. Bost, John W. Robinson, W. H. Ingold and S. L. Whitener. Although the City Council and a wide circle of citizens in the local community were interested in the proposition, it was not until October 9, 1925 that the present impressive high school building which stands on that property, was finished and formally opened.[14]

At first glance the loss to the educational work of the Reformed Church in the State of this valuable property appears to be a major mistake; however, remembering the economic limitations of the church in those days and trends in modern education, an increasing number of informed churchmen agree with the decision made in 1914 in favor of coeducation. Claremont College had a record of exceptional service to young people. The hundreds of beneficiaries are no doubt grateful to the Hickory Community, Corinth United Church of Christ, her concerned people, and especially to Dr. Joseph L. Murphy who spent so much of himself in service to that institution.

The story of Claremont College is incomplete without at least a brief reference to this noble son of the Church. Dr. Walter W. Rowe has written feelingly concerning him:

Dr. Joseph Lorenz Murphy, son of Pleasant Murphy and Barbara Long Murphy, was born July 10, 1858, and departed this life October 11, 1917. . . . He was closely identified with every department of work in his denomination. Frequently he was a delegate to the Synod and General Synod. He was also closely allied with our educational interests. For years he had been a Trustee of Catawba College and for many years he was president of its Board. During his entire ministry in Hickory he was connected with Claremont College in the capacity of Trustee, teacher and President. He was also a member of the Board of Managers of Nazareth Orphans' Home, and always keenly interested in its welfare. He was largely instrumental in giving to the Classis the Reformed Church Standard as we have it today, and at the time of his death was editor of same. . . .

Dr. Joseph L. Murphy

How thankful we should be for his life! May his example be an inspiration to the young men of the Church and community, and his deeds be a cherished memory to us all. Those who knew him best loved him most, and those who knew him least loved him much. How appropriate his own words used in reference to another: "His soul has gone out where the darkness disappears and the shadows flee away. Comparing his entire life with the model laid down in God's Word, we can not hold from him the unbidden homage, "Of such is the Kingdom of Heaven."[15]

1. ———. Minutes. Classis of North Carolina, 1915, p. 30.
2. ———. Hickory Daily Record, 50th Anniversary Edition, September 11, 1965, p. 12-Eff.
3. *Murphy*, Joseph L., A Historical Sketch of Claremont College,———, p. 3.
4. *Ibid.* p. 6 ff.
5. *Ibid.* p. 6.
6. ———. Book of Deeds, Catawba County, 1889, p. 59.
7. *Murphy, op. cit.* p. 21.
8. ———. Minutes. *Op. cit.* 1907, p. 31.
9. *Murphy, op. cit.,* p. 24.
10. ———. Minutes. Op. cit., 1914, p. 37.
11. ———. Minutes. *Op. cit.,* 1914, p. 38.
12. ———. Minutes. *Op. cit.,* 1915, p. 29.
13. ———. Minutes. *Op. cit.,* 1915, p. 29.
14. ———. Hickory Daily Record, *op. cit.,* p. 6-E.
15. ———. Minutes. *Op. cit.,* 1918, p. 70.

CHAPTER IV

Benevolent Institutions

Nazareth Children's Home

NAZARETH CHILDREN'S HOME, Rockwell, North Carolina, Route 2, was founded by people who believed in the social application of the Christian Gospel. In writing an open letter to the churches of the first century A.D., James the brother of Jesus remarked, "Religion that is pure and undefiled before God and the Father is this: to visit the orphans and the widows in their affliction, and to keep oneself unstained from the world." In 1899 a group of concerned people submitted to the Classis of North Carolina, Reformed Church in the United States, a resolution asking that a study be made of the feasibility of establishing a home for orphaned children within the bounds of the Classis. The resolution was approved, and a committee composed of Revs. J. M. L. Lyerly, James D. Andrew and Harvey A. M. Holshouser was appointed with a request to investigate and report. Their findings were submitted to the Classis in April 1900, which stated:

> Up to this time nothing of practical turn has come to hand, but having recently learned that there is a possibility that something may be accomplished in connection with boards already established in the way of a branch home, your committee is of the opinion that, it is advisable to appoint a committee looking to the practical turn that may be made by conferring with such boards as may be of assistance in the accomplishment of our cherished object, and to report at some future special, or the next regular meeting of Classis.[1]

In 1901 a plan of promotion and education was inaugurated throughout the Reformed Church in the state, spearheaded by the committee, involving all active pastors. A descriptive article was published outlining objectives and asking for money with which to underwrite the cause. Pledges were valid when as much as $3,000 had been obligated. Encouraging results attended the effort, producing pledges totaling $2,341.40, mostly from congregations in Rowan and Cabarrus counties.[2] In order to speed up the effort, Dr. Lyerly was made special agent, and vested with authority to present the cause in churches through out the Classis during the year 1903. With only part time effort by the agent, twelve charges yielded a total of $3,824.40. When, therefore, the Classis convened in the spring of that year, it acted as follows:

> Resolved, that, in as much as conditions have been complied with in the securing of $3,000 in subscriptions, a committee be appointed with Rev. J. M. L. Lyerly as chairman, with instructions to formulate plans for the purpose of carrying out the action of last year to establish an orphan's home.[3]

Serious discussion ensued indicating that the Classis was about evenly divided on the project; however, the resolution was finally approved by a one-vote margin. The committee proceeded to carry out instructions, convening July 24, 1903 in the parsonage at Concord, North Carolina. Here details were worked out and agreed upon. A special meeting of the Classis occurred August 13, 1903 at First (Faith) Church, Salisbury, North Carolina, when the committee made its report. The report was approved, recommending,

> 1. That the proposed orphanage be located at Crescent, North Carolina.
> 2. That the name be "Nazareth Orphan's Home."
> 3. That the Board of Managers shall consist of twelve members to serve four years: three to be elected for one year, three for two years, three for three years, and three for four years, after which three shall be elected each year, beginning with the annual meeting of 1905. The power to elect to be vested in the Classis of North Carolina.
> 4. The Board of Managers shall have power to transact all business relative to the home and make an annual report to the Classis.
> 5. The following constituted the Board of Managers: one year, Rev. S. W. Beck, Dr. W. B. Duttera, J. C. Lippard; two years: Rev. W. H. Causey, Rev. W. H. McNairy, J. H. Moose; three years: Rev. H. A. M. Holshouser, Rev. C. B. Heller, T. W. S. Grimes; four years: Dr. J. M. L. Lyerly, Dr. J. L. Murphy, Rev. J. D. Andrew.[4]

An offer of at least three acres of land "in close proximity to an excellent grade school" in the city of Salisbury by representative citizens was made, provided the institution be established in that city. However, extenuating circumstances were unfavorable to such a move, therefore the offer was regretfully refused. When Classis met at First Church, High Point, North Carolina beginning May 4, 1904, the president of the Board of Managers of the proposed Nazareth Orphan's Home submitted his first report. He said:

> Immediately after the special meeting of Classis, the Board of Managers of Nazareth Orphan's Home organized and elected the following officers: Chairman, J. M. L. Lyerly; Secretary, W. B. Duttera, Treasurer, J. H. Moose. A charter which we herewith present, has been secured at a cost of $3.50.
> A tract of land containing sixteen and two-fifths acres has been purchased for the sum of four hundred and ten dollars. Of the purchase price, three hundred and sixty-two dollars and seventy five cents has been paid, leaving a balance due of forty seven dollars and twenty five cents.
> Since the organization of the board several applications for admission of children into the home have been made, but for lack of means, their admission could not be granted. In view of the fact, then, that the institution is needed, the board could do nothing more than has been done.
> The board asks your honorable body to urge upon the pastors and

people the collection of outstanding pledges, and that as far as possible, all the money be in the hands of the treasurer not later than January 1, 1905. It is the purpose of the board to get up plans and specifications for the buildings etc., as soon as the money in hand will warrant.[5]

This report was adopted. The two documents which appear below, The Certificate of Incorporation and the Constitution and Regulation of the Orphan's Home, were approved at the same time.

CERTIFICATE OF INCORPORATION

This is to certify that we, Revs. J. D. Andrew, Burlington; S. W. Beck, Conover; W. H. Causey, Lexington; W. B. Duttera, Salisbury; C. B. Heller, Maiden; H. A. M. Holshouser, Lexington; J. M. L. Lyerly, Crescent; W. H. McNairy, Lenoir; J. L. Murphy, Hickory; and T. W. S. Grimes, Thomasville; J. C. Lippard, Concord; and J. H. Moose, Gold Hill, (all of North Carolina), do hereby associate themselves into a corporation, under and by virtue of the provisions of act of the legislature of the state of North Carolina, Session 1901, entitled "An act to revise the Corporation Law of North Carolina," and the several supplements thereto and acts amendatory thereof.

1st. The name of the Corporation is Nazareth Orphan's Home (Incorporated).

2nd. The location of the principal office in this state is at Crescent, Rowan County, and the name of the agent there upon whom process against this corporation may be served is J. M. L. Lyerly.

3rd. The objects for which this corporation is formed are to establish at or near Crescent, North Carolina, in Rowan County, a Home or Orphanage for the care, control, maintenance and support of such indigent orphans as the Board of Managers may decide to provide for, which children shall be received only upon compliance with such rules as the Board of Managers may prescribe for their reception. That the Board of Managers may make by-laws for the government of the Home and for the preservation of good morals therein, and may discharge any child so received into the Home whenever, in their opinion, the good of the institution so requires. That any child or children when so received, shall be under the exclusive care and control of the Board of Managers, and shall not be removed without their consent.

4th. That the Board of Managers of the said Home shall not exceed twelve in number, all of whom shall be elected by the Classis of North Carolina, Reformed Church in the United States, and the Board of Managers shall at all times be amenable to the said Classis and may be removed by such Classis at any time for Cause. The Board of Managers shall be elected by the said Classis under such rules and regulations as the Classis may prescribe, and the term of office of each of the Board of Managers shall be fixed by the Classis.

5th. That all gifts, grants, purchase, devise, or bequests or the proceeds of such, made to said Board of Managers, shall be held by them in trust for the use and benefit of the Classis of North Carolina, Reformed Church in the United States, for the purpose of maintaining the Orphan's Home, when the conditions of the gift, grant, bequest, or devise does not otherwise forbid.

6th. That the Board of Managers shall elect one of their number Chairman, also a Secretary and a Treasurer. They may also elect a Superintendent for the Home and such other teachers and servants as they may deem necessary for the successful operation of the institution. They shall also fix the salary attached to each officer; but the Superintendent, by and with the consent of the Board of Managers, may fix the compensation of the servants of the Home.

7th. That the Board of Managers are authorized by and with the consent of the Classis of North Carolina, Reformed Church in the United States, to change the location of the Home at any time.

8th. That this corporation shall have no capital stock, and its period of existence is unlimited.

In witness thereof, we have hereunto set our hands and seals, the 23rd day of October, A. D. nineteen hundred three.

S. W. Beck, W. B. Duttera, C. B. Heller, H. A. M. Holshouser, J. M. L. Lyerly, J. L. Murphy, John H. Moose. Signed, sealed and delivered in the presence of O. D. Davis, Notary Public.

The above document was probated October 30, 1903, at Raleigh, North Carolina by J. Byron Grimes, Secretary of State.

CONSTITUTION AND REGULATION OF THE ORPHAN'S HOME

Article I. Of the Board of Managers.

Section 1. The Board of Managers shall consist of twelve members who shall hold office for four years, unless the Classis shall judge it expedient to remove them at an earlier period.

The members shall be so arranged that three of them shall go out of office at the meeting of Classis each year, but shall be eligible for re-election by the Classis.

Section 2. In case vacancies occur on the Board by death, removal, resignation or refusal to serve, the Board of Managers shall have the power to declare and fill vacancies until the next meeting of the Classis.

Section 3. The Board of Managers shall hold at least two regular meetings, one of which shall be at the annual meeting of the Classis and the other shall be at the Orphan's Home, and at such time as may be necessary. Five members, meeting after ten days' notice, shall constitute a quorum.

Section 4. The Board of Managers shall have the power to elect one of their number Chairman; also a Secretary and a Treasurer; and, to appoint and employ such superintendents, managers and teachers, and other help as the necessities of the Home may require. These officials shall all be elected annually.

Section 5. The Chairman of the Board of Managers shall call special meetings when requested to do so by three members of the Board, or when in his opinion the good of the institution requires it.

Section 6. The Board of Managers shall choose annually an Executive Committee of five members of whom the Chairman shall be ex-officio chairman, to hold office for one year, three of whom after due notice shall constitute a quorum. To this Executive Committee the management of the Home may be entrusted under the supervision of the Board of Managers, to whom they are responsible.

Section 7. The Board of Managers shall purchase such additional grounds convenient to the Home as may be needed for building and farming purposes and shall erect such buildings as the necessities of the institution shall require and their means shall justify.

Section 8. The Managers are authorized and directed to procure funds for the establishment and support of the Home by means of appeals to the churches, by circulars or by direct application of the Superintendent or other agents duly authorized and commissioned by them.

Section 9. The Board of Managers shall make a report each year to the Classis of North Carolina at its annual meeting of their transactions during the past year, including a complete statement of the condition of the Home, its finances, officials, helps, number of orphans and plans adopted for their education and training.

Article II. Of the Executive Committee

Section 1. To the Executive Committee shall be entrusted the general direction of the Home and the execution of the plans and orders of the Board of Managers.

Section 2. The Executive Committee shall meet at the call of the Chairman whenever the business of the institution requires it. Three members of the committee shall constitute a quorum.

Section 3. The Executive Committee shall have charge of the erection, repair and care of the grounds, furniture and implements and of the general management of the Home.

Section 4. The Executive Committee shall make an annual report of all their proceedings to the Board of Managers, to be incorporated by them in their annual report to Classis.

Article III. Of the Superintendent

Section 1. The Superintendent shall have immediate charge of the Home.

Section 2. He shall make provision for the support and clothing of the orphans, superintend their education and religious training and regulate the time for study, work and recreation.

Section 3. The Superintendent under the general direction of the Board of Managers or of the Executive Committee shall attend the meetings of our church bodies and visit the churches to present the claims of the Home, awaken interest in its objects and solicit funds, provisions and clothing for the inmates.

Section 4. With the approval or consent of the Executive Committee, the Superintendent shall have the power to employ matron, teachers and other helpers and laborers in case of vacancies, and to receive suitable orphans into the institution.

Article IV. General Objects of the Home

Section 1. The design of the Classical Orphans' Home is to furnish the advantages of a Christian home to the destitute children deprived of one or both of their parents.

Section 2. Indigent children between the ages of five and eighteen years of age, of sound mind, and free from loathsome, contagious or incurable diseases, of whom there is reasonable hope of future usefulness, may be received and maintained in the Home, upon certificate of a minister or church consistory and of a reputable physician in active practice.

Section 3. The children shall be supplied with sufficient wholesome, nutritious and well prepared food, decently clothed, and provided with comfortable rooms, bedding and furniture, and receive kind and parental treatment.

Section 4. They shall be assembled every morning and evening for family worship, which shall consist of reading the Word of God, singing and prayer, and such brief religious instruction by oral address, recitation or repeating the Catechism as may be deemed most suitable for them.

Section 5. The children shall also receive instruction in the Bible at other times, especially on the Lord's Day when they shall be instructed in the Catechism and shall be taken to church or chapel service at least once each Lord's Day, when practicable.

Section 6. They shall receive instruction in the rudiments of a good common school education during a proper number of hours five days in each week for at least six months in the year, from a competent and approved teacher.

Section 7. Special attention shall be given to the industrial feature in the training of the children, and all of them shall be required to work a suitable number of hours each day at the usual domestic employments of a well ordered household; shall be taught cooking, sewing, washing and housekeeping on the part of the girls, while the boys shall be taught gardening, farm labor, care of stock, or mechanical employments; by these means dispensing as far as practicable with hired help.

Section 8. The children of the Home shall not be sent out as hired servants into any families, but may be placed in suitable Christian homes at the direction of the Executive Committee, under such rules and regulations as they may prescribe. And it shall be the duty of the Superintendent, as far as practicable, to see that they are properly treated after they are sent out into families.

Section 9. At or near the close of the eighteenth year of age of the beneficiaries, it shall be the duty of the Superintendent, aided by the Executive Committee, to secure positions for them, in families, on farms, factories, machine shops, stores, or other suitable places, where they can earn an honest living, and be useful to society and the church.

Section 10. The Superintendent shall have the power to receive such children and upon such conditions as are enumerated in Article IV, Section 2.

Section 11. When the Superintendent shall discover any child to be incorrigible, or injurious to the other inmates, such child, with the approval or advice of the Executive Committee, shall be returned to his home or neighborhood.

Article V. General Regulations

Section 1. The salaries of the Superintendent, Matron, Teachers, Agents, and other employes of the Orphan's Home shall be fixed by the Board of Managers, and shall be paid by the Treasurer from the current funds of the institution.

Section 2. All necessary expenses of the Board of Managers and of the Executive Committee shall be paid by the Treasurer.

Section 3. All other matters not herein determined shall be arranged by the Executive Committee.

Section 4. These regulations may be changed by the Board of Managers at any regular meeting, as the suggestions of experience and necessities of the institution may demand.[6]

In 1905 the president of the Board of Managers reported cash and pledges amounting to $4,500, secured from twenty congregations within the Classis and that collection on pledges was progressing satisfactorily.[7] A central building located on the original 16-acre plat was proposed to satisfy beginning needs. It was to be a two-story structure, 84 by 64 feet in size, estimated to cost $5,000. This building project was interrupted by the acquisition of the adjacent McNairy farm consisting of eighty five acres of land, including a ten-room house, barn and other appropriate building suitable for institutional use. This property was purchased for the sum of $4,100, bringing land holdings of the orphanage to approximately 100 acres, and cleared the way for appointing a staff of workers and accepting applicants for inmates.

Nazareth Orphan's Home opened its doors December 2, 1906, when Miss Mary P. Abbott, serving as superintendent and four children moved into the "McNairy House." On October 12 Jeanette, Williams and Robert Carriker were admitted. Edward G. Cowan was received November 28. These constituted the first family of Nazareth Orphan's Home and reduced to reality a dream. Seven

McNairy Cottage, the Superintendent's Home

years before that a group of Christian leaders, led by Dr. J. M. L. Lyerly, submitted to the Classis a resolution proposing such an institution.[8]

First years in the life of an organization are usually difficult. Nazareth Orphan's Home proved the point, economics being the chief concern. In 1906 Dr. Paul Barringer was named financial agent, who worked closely with Superintendent Abbott in underwriting a budget. Early in 1907, however, the Board of Managers observed that the work was too varied and demanding for one person to manage, even with voluntary financial assistance, and proceeded to effect certain staff changes. Professor Harvey F. Frick was named Superintendent, and his wife, Mrs. Myrtle Frick, Matron. Miss Mary Abbott, because of her particular talents in such affairs, was made General Financial Secretary. However, Miss Abbott resigned within a month thereafter, and Miss Ethel S. Shaffner was named to succeed her, beginning June 1, 1908.[9]

In an effort to more dramatically present the claims of the institution to the Reformed Church constituency in North Carolina, Anniversary Day was begun September 12, 1907. Visitors came from all sections of the church in North Carolina, a few from Virginia and Pennsylvania, but especially from Rowan County and vicinity. Honorable W. W. Kitchen made an appropriate address during the morning, and the children performed with songs, recitations and pantomime during the afternoon. Refreshment stands and voluntary solicitors reported total earnings and collections during the day in the amount of $400. Anniversary Day became an institution, serving as a rallying occasion for church and community over a period of fifty three years. An estimated crowd of 15,000 people is reported to have been present on a single anniversary day. Not least among its many assets was a liberal source of income with which to bolster the current budget. Nearby churches such as Shiloh Faith, Ursinus and Lowerstone Rockwell, each year gave of their time and resources in the sale of food in advancing the cause. The Woman's Missionary Society of the Classis of North Carolina, prepared articles of clothing and "knick-knacks" which they sold at a generously patronized bazaar each Anniversary Day, adding the proceeds to the orphanage current fund. However, like many effective benevolent ventures, the anniversary observance served its day, and became a casualty of changing times. When, in 1959, the churches proposed to make budgetary provision for the home in lieu of special money-raising schemes, this phase of special emphasis largely financially motivated, was discontinued. The last Anniversary Day was held in August 1959.

At the end of 1908 Superintendent Frick reported farm yield in the following amounts: 250 bushels of corn, 1,000 quarts of canned food, two and a half bales of cotton, seventy five bushels of sweet potatoes and forty five bushels of irish potatoes. All work on the farm, in those days, was being done by the superintendent, matron and the children. In addition to a reasonable yield in produce, through the years the farm has been a practical training school for growing young people, teaching them the value of scheduled work habits, industry, and domestic routine. A qualified agriculturist was later employed to manage the farm and dairy, contributing appreciably to the home's program of training and table needs.

Superintendent and Mrs. Frick served until January 10, 1910. Rev. and Mrs. E. Garver Williams succeeded them, but responsibilities of a growing institution proved too demanding for people of their age. After a short administration of a little more than one year, Mr. and Mrs. Williams resigned. They were succeeded on April 1, 1911 by Rev. and Mrs. J. W. Bell. Mrs. Bell developed the singing class, which made its first appearance at St. Matthews Church, Lincoln County, May 2, 1912. Seventeen children composed the class. This and succeeding singing groups, made a lasting impression upon the churches of the Classis, and were successful in presenting the needs of the home to growing audiences. Offering receipts accruing from singing class programs in 1919 reached the healthy sum of $2,700.[10]

In 1915 the Board of Managers reported that "a large two-story granite building now under roof adorns the beautiful grove in front of the girls' building.[11] The structure was ready for dedication Anniversary Day 1917.[12] This new facility provided space for a chapel, school rooms and a dormitory for boys. With a grant of $96.75 from the Rowan County Department of Public Education, an eight months school was set up on the campus for the forty five children enrolled there, and conducted in that building. The venture did not prove advisable, and was continued only until 1922, when arrangements were made to enroll these children in the county public schools.

Completing a successful administration of six years, Rev. and Mrs. Bell resigned effective June 1, 1917. Rev. and Mrs. W. B.

Werner, who had already engratiated themselves with Reformed Church people in North Carolina, left a pastorate at Brunswick, Maryland, to fill the vacancy. With the aid of a farm manager, and their daughter, Helen, they ran the eight months school, trained the singing class, attended the welfare of the children now numbering fifty, and provided for them the physical and emotional care characterized by a Christian Home. Serving well, over a period of five years, the Werners resigned effective August 25, 1922, and returned to the pastorate.

Rev. A. Samuel Peeler was elected Superintendent October 1, 1922. During his brief administration, the policy of enrolling the children in the public schools was begun, hoping thereby to more adequately prepare them for public life in a free society. The new superintendent encountered unsettled conditions caused chiefly by "insufficient and transitory help," having had several temporary matrons over a period of eight months. The responsibility was too much for a bachelor, even one with an abiding compassion for parentless children. He resigned September 1, 1923.

The Board of Managers was fortunate in the selection of Dr. William H. McNairy, whose superintendency began September 1, 1923. He was a builder, and an excellent manager. Drastic changes in policy and property improvement were required. The State Health and Welfare Department was steadily adjusting upward its standards for institutions of this kind. These requirements rendered Nazareth Orphan's Home substandard, which condition had to be corrected. Plans and specifications for a state approved dairy barn were accepted by the board in 1924, and the dairy herd was improved. A dormitory for girls, the Payne Building, replacing the overcrowded "McNairy House" was authorized, erected in 1925, and occupied November 12 of that year.[13] McNairy Cottage, a home for the superintendent, was erected on a lot purchased from Dr. C. Banks McNairy, in 1929.[14] The Lyerly Building was enlarged and renovated the same year.[15] In 1930 the superintendent reported, "that the herd of dairy cattle furnished ample dairy supply for the home; that the garden and fields yield vegetables in season as are needed; that wheat enough was produced to feed all for the year."[16]

At the end of his 9th year Superintendent McNairy resigned, effective August 31, 1932.

Dr. J. M. L. Lyerly departed this life March 17, 1923. He died as he lived, active; being pastor of the Waughtown Charge, Reformed Church in the United States, Winston Salem, North Carolina at that time. At a meeting of the Board of Managers, which occurred May 2, 1923, appropriate resolutions were read and adopted. They state:

> Whereas, God in his allwise providence has seen fit to call from the Church Militant to the Church Triumphant, our beloved brother and co-worker, the Rev. J. M. L. Lyerly, Ph.D.;

Whereas it was largely through his influence, that the Classis of North Carolina undertook the great and important task of establishing our orphanage at Crescent, North Carolina, and that from its very beginning he was a member of the Board and also president of same;

Resolved, that we as members of said Board do recognize in the departure of Dr. Lyerly a very great loss to the Board and the institution. He was always willing to give of his time and means to the development of the Home and made sacrifices for the same for which we shall hold him in grateful rememberance. May those who are left behind be just as loyal and faithful as he was in the discharge of their duties as members of the Board. We commend his family to our Heavenly Father who always cares for those who belong to him.[17]

Dr. Lyerly, more than any other individual, was the moving spirit in the founding of Nazareth Orphan's Home, and over a period of twenty years was the inspiration for its development. During this time his voice was raised in public assembly and private conversation, his purse was opened and his home made available to parentless children. Nineteen of those years he effectively led the Board of Managers in administering the affairs of that institution. In partial recognition for devotion to cause beyond the call of duty, a grateful board of co-workers named the stone boys' dormitory and chapel "The Lyerly Building," and set aside funds with which to completely furnish a room in the Payne Building for girls.

It is significant that the eighth superintendent of this institution should be Ray P. Lyerly, third son of Dr. and Mrs. J. M. L. Lyerly. He was elected to that office September 1, 1932, and with full and generous support of Mrs. Lyerly, served successfully in it for eleven years. He possesses much of the compassion of his father for the poor, and especially indigent children. Before his election to that office, he had served as a teacher and administrator in the public schools and two terms as sheriff of Rowan County. He possesses natural ability to mingle freely among people of all ages. He is known as a builder of men and women prepared to cope with life in a free society. His administration, unlike some of his predecessors, was faced with no program of physical and material expansion, but was concerned with developing the inner life of the institution and personal graces of the individual.

Appropriate activities were planned and executed for the 30th Anniversary of the founding of Nazareth Orphan's Home, which was observed July 4, 1936. Dr. John C. Peeler, Promotional Director of Catawba College, delivered an inspirational address when a publication entitled, "Thirty Years of Service," compiled by Rev. William C. Lyerly, Secretary of the Board of Managers, was released.

When, in 1939, the Classis of North Carolina, Reformed Church in the United States, became the Southern Synod of the Evangelical and Reformed Church, the charter of the home was amended to bring it into proper relation with that body. Nazareth Orphan's Home thus became an institution under the control of Southern

Synod.[18] In the same year Elder Charles E. DeChant and Deacon James C. Penny of First Church, Charlotte, North Carolina, with the support of Superintendent Lyerly, visited the churches of Synod seeking consistent financial support from them for the current budget. Sixteen hundred members of the churches under wrote the annual budget of Nazareth Home to the extent of $7,500. This marked the beginning of a shift in method of support among the churches from free will offerings and special emphases to an annual budgeted item in local church financing.

Concerning the development of the institution, in 1940, the Secretary of the Board of Managers, wrote:

> It took two full years to solicit funds enough to warrant the founding of the home, and almost six years until the home was actually open to care for children. . . . During these years 198 children have been nurtured in the home; and of this number 152 have been sent out to take their place in life.
> This home had difficulty in raising $3,000. to open its doors Now Nazareth Orphan's Home has 270 acres of land, the Lyerly Building for boys, the Payne Building for girls, including Santee Hall, the Hood Cottage, the McNairy dairy barn, the Superintendent's Home, the Nellie Whitener Laundry, and equipment for all these. The total plant valuation is in excess of $100,000. This home has endowment and annuity funds invested at a cost of $66,200, and an actual value in excess of the original investment. During these years about $225,000 has been spent on the operation of the home.[19]

Superintendent Lyerly resigned September 1, 1943. With a sense of accomplishment, a regretful board accepted it.

Thomas L. Moose succeeded Mr. Lyerly on September 1, 1943, Mr. Moose was prepared for a career in animal husbandry at State College of the University of North Carolina. He had spent five years on a ranch near Lima, Peru, South America, and more recently had been associated with his father in business at Concord, North Carolina. He was asked by the Board of Managers to accept this increasingly responsible position. In his first annual report to the board he remarked: "I have known happiness and contentment here that I have never known before. I hereby dedicate all my efforts, all my meagre talents . . . to the welfare of the body, mind and soul of these children and to the glory of God."[20]

In outlining his program the new superintendent listed such fundamental factors as, spiritual nurture of the boys and girls as a foundation for the good life; enriching the soil on the 300-acre farm according to United States Farm Standards; expanding the dairy herd and live stock; increasing the output of milk, butter, eggs, pork and farm produce for home consumption; and keeping the church informed of home activities through accepted communication channels. He also reported income from garden, farm and dairy in excess of $6,734, and an enrollment of fifty four children.

In 1947 sixty nine children were served by the institution, the largest number to date in any one year. Those children gained weight ranging from one to twenty pounds, and all of them were identified with Bethany Evangelical and Reformed Church through its program of worship, Sunday School and various youth groups; also had opportunities to participate in the Synod's program of camps and conferences. The older young people were instructed in the Christian Faith, and those who chose to do so, were confirmed into membership with the Church. Campus life was supervised by a self-governing body composed of elected leaders and adult counsellors.

Children in Nazareth Home also grew physically and mentally. Recorded statistics in 1948 reflect that they grew physically an average of 1.7 inches in height, and an average of 9.5 pounds in weight. Twenty one of them had an average scholastic grade of A, twenty six a grade of B, and only ten a grade of C. The superintendent wrote:

> The end of 1948 left this institution the strongest, the most peaceful, and the most secure at any time in its history. We are able to provide high living standards and better opportunities for the children entrusted to us. As a result we seem to detect higher moral values and greater accomplishments on the part of the children. We have a most capable staff to direct and execute our program of child welfare.[21]

This concern for the orphanage family reached beyond the staff and campus. Bethany church made its contribution through the pastor and appointed church leadership, by means of stated periods of worship, week-day religious instruction, friendly relationships and pastoral oversight.[22] In reciprocal action, the Board of Managers each year contributed to the church budget, and in 1950, seeking to encourage the congregation in its effort to provide better facilities, contributed a lot on which to erect a parsonage and timber with which to construct it.[23]

The 50th Anniversary of the founding of the home was observed on Anniversary Day, the first Thursday in August 1956. An appropriate program was presented. A history entitled, "Nazareth Orphans' Home, Golden Anniversary," written by Superintendent Moose was released. Plant assets at that time were valued at $200,-996. The 295 acres of land were evaluated at $30,500; the buildings at $147,560; and equipment at $22,926. The report of the superintendent covering the first eleven months of 1956 records: 41 children enrolled, 18 girls and 23 boys. Their denominational backgrounds were: Evangelical and Reformed, 10; Baptist, 12; Friends, 1; Church of God, 3; and 15 claimed no church background. Twenty-two of them were placed in the home by Public Welfare Departments; 13 by parents and relatives; and six by pastors and members of the Evangelical and Reformed Church.[24]

With the assurance of an exceptionally satisfactory administration, covering a period of thirteen years, Mr. Moose resigned effective December 1, 1956.

The job cut out for Rev. Melvin T. Hamm who assumed duties as superintendent December 1, 1956, was by no means a relaxing position; on the contrary, campus facilities in general required immediate attention. The Church's program of Health and Welfare imposed standards requiring drastic changes, which neither the members of the Board of Managers nor the rank and file of church membership in Southern Synod were at the time prepared to approve. In order to financially provide for limited material improvements on the property, a campaign for $25,000 was inaugurated among the churches of synod. With this money improvements were effected to satisfy the State Health Department, but these fell short of the State Department of Public Welfare and Denominational Health and Welfare standards in living quarters. Work on these deficiencies continued as funds and leadership could be provided. The property committee was authorized by the Board of Managers to employ an architect and develop plans and specifications for two cottage-type dormitories for boys.[25] These cottages, completed at a cost of $130,000, were occupied in 1960. They were dedicated November 6 of that year, naming one in memory of Carl Lyerly, a son of Dr. and Mrs. J. M. L. Lyerly; the other in memory of Dr. and Mrs. J. Alexander Smith, devoted leaders in the First Evangelical and Reformed Church, Lexington, North Carolina.

Carl Lyerly Cottage—J. A. Smith Cottage

Meeting the pressure of changing times, Anniversary Day was discontinued in 1959. At the same time the Board of Managers took action, changing the name of the institution to Nazareth Children's Home.[26] Mr. Hamm resigned the superintendency after serving three difficult years.

Charles F. Beidler, with special training in welfare work, was made superintendent August 1, 1960. The administration of Superintendent Beidler is marked by adjustments suited to current standard welfare policies in managing benevolent institutions. In consultation with Dr. Lee W. Rockwell, General Secretary of the Division of Health and Welfare of the United Church of Christ, and the cooperation of a sympathetic Board of Managers, adjustments were made in staff, salaries, housing conditions, integration and other matters of primary social and cultural significance.[27] When, on September 30, 1965, Southern Conference of the United Church of Christ, with which Southern Synod of the Evangelical and Reformed Church had merged, was consummated, Nazareth Children's Home became an institution under the administrative authority of that body.[28] On March 16, 1966 the Board of Managers of the home took action recognizing such a relationship.

Mr. Beidler resigned the superintendency effective October 12, 1966. Rev. Aubrey W. Hedrick, an aggressive and reliable administrator, took office January 1, 1966, but returned to the pastorate January 1, 1968. He was succeeded in office by Mr. Howard Regan, a highly respected business man and lay leader in Beck's United Church of Christ, Lexington, North Carolina.

1. ———. Minutes. Classis of North Carolina, 1900, p. 132.
2. ———. Minutes. *Op. cit.*, 1902, p. 220.
3. ———. Minutes. *Op. cit.*, 1903, p. 278.
4. ———. Minutes. *Op. cit.*, 1904, p. 383.
5. *Ibid.* p. 367.
6. *Ibid.* p. 373.
7. ———. Minutes. *Op. cit.*, 1905, p. 434.
8. ———. Minutes. *Op. cit.*, 1907, p. 62.
9. ———. Minutes. *Op. cit.*, 1908, p. 64.
10. *Lyerly*, William C., Thirty Years Service, Nazareth Orphan's Home, 1936, p. 13.
11. ———. Minutes. *Op. cit.*, 1915, p. 59.
12. ———. Minutes. *Op. cit.*, 1917, p. 45.
13. ———. Minutes. *Op. cit.*, 1925, p. 54.
14. ———. Minutes. *Op. cit.*, 1929, p. 37.
15. ———. Minutes. *Op. cit.*, 1930, p. 38.
16. ———. Minutes. *Op. cit.*, 1931, p. 48.
17. *Moose*, Thomas L., Nazareth Orphans' Home, Golden Anniversary, 1956, p. 73.
18. ———. Minutes. Southern Synod, 1940, p. 37.
19. ———. Minutes. *Op. cit.*, 1941, p. 41.
20. ———. Minutes. *Op. cit.*, 1944, p. 52.
21. ———. Minutes. *Op. cit.*, 1949, p. 56.
22. ———. Minutes. *Op. cit.*, 1952, p. 44.
23. ———. Minutes. *Op. cit.*, 1950, p. 46.
24. ———. Minutes. *Op. cit.*, 1957, p. 50.
25. ———. Minutes. *Op. cit.*, 1959, p. 66.
26. ———. Minutes. *Op. cit.*, 1960, p. 54.
27. ———. Minutes. *Op. cit.*, 1961, p. 49.
28. ———. Minutes. Southern Conference, United Church of Christ, 1965, p. 4.

The United Church Retirement Home

THE UNITED CHURCH RETIREMENT HOME project grew out of informal discussion occurring over a period of years among Evangelical and Reformed Churchmen. It was brought to the attention of Southern Synod in 1954, when, in connection with the report of the committee on Benevolent Institutions, Elder J. Yorke Peeler spoke favorably concerning such an institution located in this section of the denomination, suggesting that it could possibly be developed on Nazareth Children's Home property and administered by the same staff. The Synod, responding to his appeal, took action approving the establishment of a home for the aged within the bounds of Synod, instructed the Nazareth Home Board of Managers to study its feasibility, and authorized the board to solicit and receive gifts of money, bonds and property in anticipation of such an event.[1]

J. Yorke Peeler, Treasurer of the Nazareth Children's Home Board was authorized by that board to be custodian of such receipts. His first report in 1955 showed collections amounting to $555.81. Encouraged by initial gifts, the Synod renewed its request in 1956 for further study of the project by the Nazareth Children's Home Board of Managers. Complying with this directive, a committee was named by the board consisting of Dr. Banks J. Peeler, Superintendent Thomas L. Moose and Treasurer J. Yorke Peeler, with instructions to interview representative people throughout the Synod, consider financial requirements, State Health and Welfare involvements and report. This was done. Findings clearly reflected the inadvisability of a financial campaign to underwrite necessary expenditures in starting a home for the aged. Catawba College Chapel and The Assembly Grounds improvement and expansion programs, requiring large sums of money, were before the churches at that time. The Synod, therefore, took action asking the churches to continue their offerings to the cause, and where advantageous to make the proposed home for the aged a subject for discussion in local official circles.

In 1957, Synod appointed a committee with instructions to further study ways and means of establishing a home for the aged, and to make proposals for advanceing the cause. The committee consisted of Revs. Lawrence A. Leonard, John W. Settlemyre, Roy E. Leinbach, Jr. and John Robinson, Sr. and Willie F. Everhart. In 1958, Southern Synod elected a twelve member board of trustees, composed of nine men and three women with a three years rotating term of office. In 1959, that number was increased to sixteen, the board to be composed of twelve men and four women, and the additional members were to be elected by the board itself. To these sixteen people were entrusted "the responsibility for administering the affairs of the proposed institution and to be invested with the control and care of all funds" . . . and directed to "work in con-

junction with any similar board or committee appointed by the
Southern Convention of the Congregational Christian Churches,
Homewood Church Home Board of Managers, Nazareth Children's
Home Board of Managers or any other benevolent institutions.[2]
The first twelve members were elected by Southern Synod, and
these met shortly thereafter and organized themselves: Rev. Law-
rence A. Leonard, Chairman; Willie F. Everhart, vice chairman;
Mrs. Hiram E. Davis, secretary; Dr. Verne Blackwelder, treasurer;
Rev. Edwin M. Alcorn, Rev. G. Melvin Palmer, Mrs. Henry Ken-
nedy, Jr., J. Yorke Peeler, Mrs. W. C. Lyerly, Rev. Joshua L. Levens,
Harold Lemons and Rev. John W. Settlemyre.[3]

In anticipation of requirements by the North Carolina Medical
Care Commission, Southern Synod Council on February 16, 1959,
approved a request from the Board of Trustees of the Home for the
Aged for a change of name to "The Evangelical and Reformed
Church Nursing Home."[4] But a request laid before Southern Synod
in April of that year, "Authorizing the board to make application
to the North Carolina Medical Care Commission for two-thirds of
the cost of construction of a 50-bed home to cost between $100,000
and $150,000," was turned down.[5] A conference did occur on May
14, 1959 between members of the Nursing Home Board and the
Executive Secretary of the North Carolina Medical Care Commission, seeking information and counsel concerning procedures, approval, and possible financial support. However because of unac-
ceptable commitments required of state supported institutions of
this sort, an application for enrollment and support was not issued.
The Nursing Home idea seemed no longer appropriate for the type
of service proposed by the church for its aged citizens. In the light
of merger commitments, Southern Synod authorized the name
changed to "The United Church Retirement Home," and invited
offers of land on which such a home within the bounds of the
Southern Church could be erected.[6]

Because of the particular needs of aging people, the original
scheme for establishing the home included a unit for each of the
three areas of church in North Carolina and Virginia. Accordingly,
offers of property were made from interested people at Lenoir,
Newton, Concord, Lexington, Thomasville and Burlington. Development of such properties was not anticipated simultaneously,
but in sequence as they could be managed, financially and otherwise. This concept has not been altered. It is evident that the
Board of Trustees was making commendable progress, the one
major deterent being money. The report of the Treasurer in 1963
reflected a balance of $6,929.58; by April 1964 net worth of the
project had reached $15,905.58. This income had accrued largely
from congregational offerings and budgeted items on the basis of
$1.00 per member. On April 7, 1964, Architect Vernon E. Lewis
presented for approval to the board preliminary floor sketches for
a building designed to accommodate twenty four guests.[7]

Articles of Incorporation were authorized by the Board May 2, and recorded in Rowan County November 13, 1961. The Text follows:

The State of North Carolina, Department of State

To whom these presents shall come, Greeting:

I, Thad Eure, Secretary of the State of North Carolina, do hereby certify the following and hereunto attach five sheets to be a true copy of Articles of Incorporation of The United Church Retirement Home and the probates thereon, the original of which was filed in this office of the 13th day of November 1961, after having been found to conform to law.

In witness whereof, I have hereunto set my hand and affixed my official seal.

Done in Office, at Raleigh, this 13th day of November in the year of our Lord, 1961.

Signed: Thad Eure, Secretary of State.

Articles of Incorporation of The United Church Retirement Home
A Non-Profit Organization

We, the undersigned natural persons of the age of twenty one years or more, acting as incorporators for the purpose of creating a non-profit corporation under the laws of the State of North Carolina, as contained in Chapter 55A of the General Statutes of North Carolina, entitled, "Non-Profit Corporation Act," and the several amendments thereto, do hereby set forth:

I.

The name of the Corporation is The United Church Retirement Home.

II.

The period of duration of the Corporation shall be perpetual.

III.

The purposes for which the Corporation is organized are:

A. The conducting and management of a home or homes for aged members of the Evangelical and Reformed Church and for such other persons as may be admitted in accordance with the rules and regulations adopted by the Board of Trustees of said corporation.

B. To provide for the care of those persons admitted to the home or homes by the acquisition or construction of suitable buildings equipped to meet present and future requirements for a home for the aged.

C. And, in connection with the purposes above set forth and in order to carry them out, to receive and acquire by gift or bequest or otherwise, and to hold real and personal property, to lease and sell its holdings, to make investments of its funds, to borrow money, secured by mortgage on its property or otherwise, to accept gifts and bequests and to apply the principal and interest as may be directed by the donor, or as the Board of Trustees may determine in the absence of such direction, and finally to take such other steps as the said Board of Trustees deems requisite to carry out its general purpose and as are permitted by law to non-profit corporations and to have all other power with which such corporations are endowed.

IV.

The Corporation shall have no members.

V.

The control and operation of the Corporation shall be vested in a Board of Trustees consisting of sixteen (16) members whose term of office and election shall be as set out in Article VI hereinafter; said Board of Trustees shall elect from its members the officers of the Corporation which shall consist of a President, Vice President, Secretary and a Treasurer, such officers are to be elected for a term of one year and shall hold office until their successor or successors are duly elected and qualified; all members of the Board of Trustees shall serve without remuneration. The duties of the officers and Trustees shall be prescribed by the By-Laws.

VI.

The Directors of the Corporation shall be designated as members of the Board of Trustees and shall be elected as follows:

A. Twelve members shall be elected by the Southern Synod of the Evangelical and Reformed Church or its successors at the next annual meeting of said body; four of the said members shall be elected for a one year term, one of whom shall be a woman; four for a two-year term, one of whom shall be a woman; and four for a three-year term, one of whom shall be a woman; thereafter, said body, at each annual meeting, shall elect four members for a term of three years each, one of whom shall be a woman.

B. Four additional members of the Board of Trustees, one of whom shall be a woman, shall be elected by the Board of Trustees at its organizational meeting, said members to serve for a term of one year.

VII.

No part of the income of the Corporation or no part of the property or assets of said Corporation upon dissolution of liquidation shall ever insure to the benefit of any of the Board of Trustees. Upon the dissolution or liquidation of the Corporation, all of its property and assets after the payment of claims and liabilities, shall belong to and be the property of the Southern Synod of the Evangelical and Reformed Church or its successors.

VIII.

The Board of Trustees shall have the general management of the affairs of the Corporation and may, from time to time, designate duties to committees or individuals, as it may see fit.

IX.

The Board of Trustees shall at its organizational meeting adopt By-Laws not inconsistent with the Articles of Incorporation and such By-Laws may be amended at any time by said Board of Trustees by a two-thirds majority of its members present and voting.

X.

These articles of Incorporation may be amended by the affirmative vote of two-thirds majority of the members of the Board of Trustees voting at either an annual meeting or at a special meeting called for such purpose, provided a written notice of the proposed resolution to amend such Articles be given each member at least ten days prior to the meeting.

XI.

The address of the initial Registered Office of the Corporation is as follows: 204 Lantz Avenue, P O Box 375, Catawba College, Salisbury, North Carolina, Rowan County. The name of the initial Registered Agent of the Corporation at the above address is Dr. H. A. Fesperman.

XII.

The number of Trustees constituting the initial Board of Trustees shall be sixteen (16), and the names and addresses of the persons who are to serve as Trustees until the first meeting of the Corporation or until their successors are elected and qualified are:

Rev. Lawrence Leonard, Route 1, Burlington, N. C.

Mr. Harold Lemons, 2410 Waughtown St., Winston Salem, N. C.

Rev. G. Melvin Palmer, P. O. Box 10021, Greensboro, N. C.

Rev. John Settlemyre, Route 1, Whitsett, N. C.

Mr. Dewey Drum, Radio Station WSOC, Charlotte, N. C.

Mr. J. Yorke Peeler, Rockwell, N. C.

Mrs. Hiram Davis, P. O. Box 30, Landis, N. C.

Rev. Edwin Alcorn, P. O. 274, Conover, N. C.

Mr. Willie Everhart, 1405 S. Main St., Lexington, N. C.

Rev. J. L. Levens, 3120 Robin Hood Road, Winston Salem, N. C.

Mr. Vernon Lewis, 100 N. Church St., Burlington, N. C.

Mr. Jack Faw, Conover, N. C.

Mrs. J. Lincoln Link, P. O. Box 155, Welcome, N. C.

Mr. J. Lewis Patterson, P. O. Box 1230, Concord, N. C.

Mrs. George Fleming, Route 1, China Grove, N. C.

Mr. Wade Shuford, Jr., care of Northwestern Bank, Hickory, N. C.

XIII.

The names and addresses of all the Incorporators are:

Mr. Willie Everhart, 1405 S. Main Street, Lexington, N. C.

Rev. A. Odell Leonord, N. Church Street, Lexington, N. C.

Mr. Elmer Nance, 510 Fairview Drive, Lexington, N. C.

In testimony whereof, we, the undersigned have hereto set our hands and seals, this the 9th day of November 1961.

Willie F. Everhardt (Seal)

A. Odell Leonard (Seal)

Elmer P. Nance (Seal)

The State of North Carolina, Davidson County.

This is to certify that on the 9th day of November 1961, before me, Mattie B. Myers, Assistant Clerk, Superior Court, personally appeared Willie F. Everhart, Rev. A. Odell Leonard, and Elmer Nance, who I am satisfied are the persons named in and who executed the foregoing Articles of Incorporation, and I, having first made known to them the contents thereof, they did each acknowledge that they signed and delivered the same as their voluntary act and deed for the uses and purposes therein expressed.

In testimony whereof, I have hereto set my hand and affixed my official seal, this the 9th day of November, A.D., 1961.

Signed: Mattie B. Myers, Assistant Clerk, Superior Court.[8]

In 1965 an unusual proposition was laid before the United Church Retirement Home Board of Trustees, boosting the morale of the church throughout the Synod and forcing immediate action on the part of the board. Dr. and Mrs. Julius W. Abernethy, Newton, North Carolina, proposed:

1. Mrs. Abernethy to donate their home place, known as the Morrison Farm, composed of near 100 acres of land and appropriate buildings, located two miles east of Newton, North Carolina, on the Charlotte Highway as a site for the United Church Retirement Home;

2. Dr. Abernethy to donate $200,000 over a period of three to five years;

3. Dr. Abernethy to raise and additional $100,000 in Catawba County;

4. Provided, the United Church Retirement Home Board of Trustees would match the gift of Dr. Abernethy by raising $200,000 by the end of 1966.[9]

Accepting this challenge, the board moved swiftly to lay plans for a financial campaign with which to meet it. Rev. Roy E. Leinbach, Jr. was asked to direct the campaign. Mr. Frank L. Clapp was elected Executive Secretary, on a free service basis, with instructions to visit the churches of Synod and interested individuals, providing information about the cause and seeking gifts to the campaign fund. A topographical survey was made of the "Morrison Farm," laying out streets, walks and appropriate garden areas; also, architectural drawings of the institution as it will appear when completed. Immediate plans called for the erection of a central building which provides rooms for forty residents, including administrative offices, chapel, kitchen, dining hall, nurses quarters, a game and hobby room and appropriate porches. As the need requires and money is available, six ten-room wings may be added to provide living quarters for sixty other people. Also, proposed are nine duplex cottages containing small apartments for eighteen couples, making a total resident capacity of one hundred thirty two people.

To make possible this ambitious project, Dr. and Mrs. Abernethy adjusted upward their first proposition, challenging members of the United Church of Christ to contribute $500,000, which they will match. In the meantime, the campaign moved steadily forward, anticipating that construction on the central building would begin in 1970.[10]

1. ———. Minutes. The Southern Synod, 1954, p. 53.
2. *Ibid.* p. 42.
3. *Ibid.* p. 98.
4. ———. Minutes. *Op. cit.,* 1959, p. 25.
5. *Ibid.* p. 44.
6. ———. Minutes. *Op. cit.,* 1960, p. 32.
7. ———. Minutes. *Op. cit.,* 1964, p. 51.
8. *Office of Clerk of Court,* Rowan County, Film 247, p. 1186.
9. ———. Minutes. *Op. cit.,* 1965, p. 58.
10. ———. Brochures. The United Church Retirement Home, Inc., 1966.

CHAPTER V

Camps and Conferences

Johns River Valley Camp

AGITATION IN FAVOR of a camping program for the Classis of North Carolina began as early as 1928. At that time activities of young people in the Reformed Church in the area were being organized. Youth and youth leaders were on the alert to discover the best possible program of service and education to meet their needs. Since other sections of the denomination were developing camps, it seemed appropriate that young people of the Classis of North Carolina should also have one. John F. Carpenter, an influential member of Memorial Church, Maiden, North Carolina, proposed to give a camp site located three miles Northwest of Hickory on the south bank of the Catawba River. The property consisted of ten acres of land beautifully located on an elevation in the bend of the river. His proposition came to the attention of Classis, which body referred it to the committee on Young People's Work for study and recommendation.[1]

But the Classis was not ready to take such an involved step forward. Organized youth work was just beginning to take form in 1928, and was not very well established. Its program was nebulous.[2] In order to equip the property and prepare it for acceptable camp and conference work, required a considerable financial outlay, which the Classis was in no position at that time to provide. Those were financial depression years, when the churches were struggling to meet ordinary budgets, especially apportionment asking. Then, too, there was considerable sentiment favoring a site for this kind of work located further West at same choice spot in the mountains in the vicinity of Blowing Rock. The committee, therefore, recommended that the inauguration of a camp program be postponed.

The decision to postpone establishing a camp did not end the discussion. Young people on the congregational level, fast becoming an impressive influence in area church councils, continued to promote the idea. Four years later, in 1936, an overture appeared

Administration Building,
Assembly Hall and Cabins

on the agenda of the Classis of North Carolina from the Young People's Conference, over the signature of its president, Miss Geneva Leonard, petitioning that body to consider "establishing a camp for the Classis." Their request was honored, and a committee composed of Revs. H. D. Althouse, George T. Fitz, and Mr. Herbert W. Coble, was named to consider the matter.[3]

The committee proceeded immediately to carry out the wishes of the Classis. The Kiwanis Club of Lenoir, North Carolina made available a Boy Scout Camp, rent free for one year, provided the Classis of North Carolina would share the expense of conditioning the property for use. It was located eighteen miles West of Lenoir along the Johns River on the Edgemont Road. In consultation with Dr. Fred D. Wentzel of the Youth Department of the Reformed Church and C. Dennis Rabb, representing the Kiwanis Club, preparations were made for a summer camp program scheduled for July 22 through August 5, 1936. The program was set up as a pilot project. The site was named "Johns River Valley Camp," a title which has stuck with the camp through the years. Mr. Althouse was named Camp Director. Teachers were: Revs: George T. Fitz, Roy C. Whisenhunt, Banks J. Peeler, and Professor W. Farel Warlick and Miss Frances Fields. Miss Ruth Leonard, Miss Margaret Rabb, Mrs. Roy C. Whisenhunt and Miss Margaret Warlick were chosen to be girls' counsellors. The boys were under the supervision of Revs. Huitt R. Carpenter and Joseph D. Andrews, the latter serving as Recreation Director. Mrs. Robert E. Leonard served in multiple capacity as Dietician, Kitchen Supervisor and Cook. A daily schedule was strictly followed. Prescribed courses of study, recreation periods, and nature observation hikes were pursued.[4]

Thirty young people enrolled in this interesting adventure, and the camp period actually began the afternoon of July 22. Camp property consisted of 125 acres of virgin wooded land, nestled between two mountain ranges, enhanced by the Johns River which flowed through the center of it. On the grounds were eight roughly constructed buildings: three log cabins, one of which was occupied by the caretaker, one by girl campers and one by boys; a large boy's shack; a small bunk house for girls; "Rocking Chair" cabin; "Corn Crib" cabin; and the assembly hall used for kitchen, dining hall and general program purposes. Bunk houses were equipped with hand made wooden double-decker beds, on which were large sacks filled with straw. In the assembly hall and kitchen were kerosene lamps and or lanterns, and each camper used a flashlight in sleeping quarters. Water was piped to the assembly hall from a spring located several hundred yards West up the gorge. And, do campers need to be reminded that there were plenty of black mud, rain, chiggers and reptiles of all sorts? In the stream was mountain trout, and scattered over the hills like a garden in spring were flowers, berries, scented shrubs and a wall of protective stone, such as Nature alone can provide.

Probably half of the campers were homesick during the first week, wondering what unholy Providence had led them to such a place; but as the second week drew to its close those same people began to wonder why they had to return to their respective homes. Considering all of the inconveniences imposed by such living, those two weeks must have deposited some abiding values with those first campers. One strongly suspects that among them were: some new and lasting friendships; wholesome instruction in an uninhibited Christian atmosphere; and an opportunity to see life good as the Creator made it. Camper statements are not available which reflect the multitude of vocal expressions appreciative of those meaningful days; however, the 1937 edition of "The Johns River Valley Camp Album" says, "This year two camps were held, a Junior and a Senior camp. There were more than twice as many campers, and more churches represented. Our stay there was one of . . . profit and pleasure, and we know we can never forget it."

"Uncle" Farel Warlick, as he was by the campers affectionately called, served as resident manager at Johns River Valley Camp during the years of 1936-1940, and usually served on the camp faculty during camp season. "Uncle Farel" has verbally described an anxious afternoon which occured in the summer of 1940. "The Caldwell County 4-H Club was in camp. It was during the "August Flood," which closed the camp for the rest of the summer. A landslide of many tons of dirt, water, potatoes etc. swept down vesper hill and carried away a large open building that had the week before housed two dozen girl campers, caused me many frightening dreams. This land-slide luckily for all of us occurred while the campers were eating supper in the large building used for cooking, eating and recreation." No one was hurt, but it is understandable when he writes, "Many weekends I stayed alone at camp, cleaning up after each camp period and waiting for the new camp to come in. Having then only lanterns to light up the grounds; only the birds and other creatures to keep me company; I admit that I often got quite lonesome and longed for my more comfortable home. But someone had to pioneer in this project if it was to succeed."[5] This devoted Educator and Elder of Trinity Church, Conover, North Carolina, like a host of others, did what was required to establish this important agency in the life of the Southern Church.

The credibility of these conclusion is substantiated by the fact that those thirty campers returned to their respective churches, told the story, which grew into a ground swell in favor of making the camp a part of the church's regular summer program of youth activities. A consultation committee drawn from the 1936 camp leaders, submitted the following set of recommendations for consideration to the Classis of North Carolina.

> That the Classis hold both a Junior and a Senior Young People's Camp during the summer of 1937, and that a committee composed of four ministers and three laymen, one of them is to be a woman, be appointed for the purpose of setting up the camps.
> The Kiwanis Club of Lenoir has offered to the Evangelical and Reformed Church, Classis of North Carolina, the property known as the Johns River Valley Camp, the purchase price being $1,500. without interest, to be paid at the convenience of the Classis:
> a) We recommend to the Classis the purchase of the property.
> b) That the money be raised by popular subscription, and a committee be appointed to raise the above sum.
> c) That a Board of Managers be appointed, whose duty shall be to care for the property, make necessary improvements, etc. That this committee serve two years.
> d) That the title of the property be vested in the Trustees of the Classis.

The Classis acted favorably on the above recommendations and appointed committees and the Board of Managers as follows:

> 1. Board of Managers: C. Dennis Rabb, chairman; John F. Carpenter, George H. Fowler, and Revs. C. Columbus Wagoner, Jacob A. Palmer and John H. Keller.
> 2. Subscription Committee: Revs. Walter W. Rowe, chairman; Banks J. Peeler, and Joseph L. Murphy, Ernest Fouts and J. Yorke Peeler.
> 3. Committee to Arrange for Junior and Senior Camps to be Conducted in the summer of 1937: Revs. H. D. Althouse, chairman; A. O. Leonard, J. L. Levens, George T. Fitz, and W. Farel Warlick, John T. Fesperman and Mrs. R. A. Robinson.[6]

Committees on arrangement made good progress in planning for two camps in 1937; collecting a total of $1,630 through free will offerings in the churches and individual gifts from interested people through out the Classis; and completing the transaction for the

purchase of the property from the Kiwanis Club of Lenoir. However, since the camp project now involved property, it should be
managed as a business establishment; therefore, the Classis approved resolutions providing for the same:

> Resolved that the Classis of North Carolina rescind its action of one
> year ago in regard to the appointment of committees for the Johns River
> Valley Camp.
> Be it further resolved that a Board of Managers of nine members be
> elected by the Classis. Three to be elected for one year; three to be
> elected for two years; three to be elected for three years. Each year
> thereafter three shall be elected for three years as their terms expire.
> The purpose of the board shall be to administer the affairs of the camp
> in the matter of its care, material improvements, etc. The board shall
> have the power to conduct campaigns, to raise funds for said camp and
> also to appoint a committee which shall arrange for camps to be con-
> ducted by the Reformed Church each year. All committees shall make
> their reports to the Board of Managers.
> We recommend that the nine members to be elected on the Board of
> Managers of the camp be referred to the committee on nominations.[7]

The Board of Managers which was subsequently elected by the
Classis was composed of Revs. C. Columbus Wagoner, H. D. Alt-
house, and J. Yorke Peeler, one year; Revs. Shuford Peeler, Jacob
A. Palmer, and J. W. Warlick, two years; Revs. A. O. Leonard,
Banks J. Peeler, and C. Dennis Rabb, three years.[8] Realizing that
the Reformed Church had, and intended to keep faith with the
original intent and purpose of those grounds, in 1941, the Kiwanis
Club of Lenoir cancelled its note of $1,000 held against the John's
River Valley Camp property. At that time Jesse W. Warlick, who
had so satisfactorily guided the camp enterprise as chairman of its
Board of Managers, issued a statement. It read:

> The deed of the land calls for 125 acres more or less. This has been
> surveyed out, and the bounds established by an engineer employed by the
> Camp Trustees. The deed is a warranty deed in fee simple, made to Jacob
> A. Palmer, L. O. Carbaugh and Walter S. Hunt, Trustees of the Classis
> of North Carolina of the Evangelical and Reformed Church or their
> successors in office.
> The approach from state highway No. 90 over the Johns River is
> across a combination dam and concrete bridge which was constructed
> in 1938 at a cost of a little in excess of $2,000.
> The present buildings on the camp site are: The caretaker's home on
> the East side of the river on the highway, built in 1940; the main as-
> sembly hall acquired with the land and now used also as a kitchen and
> dining hall; three other buildings which were acquired with the land,
> one of them used for girls' sleeping quarters, the two others as quarters
> for counsellors and directors four new buildings for girls' and boys' sleep-
> ing quarters, the gift of and known as the Peeler Cabin, the Herman
> Cabin, the Hedrick Cabin and the Barnhardt Cabin. These total build-
> ings accommodate comfortably eighty persons. All of the buildings of
> the camp are electrically wired for lights, and a few lights are on the
> grounds out of doors. We have $2,600 of insurance coverage.
>   . . . In addition to the buildings named above, we have two small
> buildings equipped with showers and toilets, and these are connected
> with a state approved sewer disposal plant.[9]

In 1944, an additional tract of 100 acres of land lying West of the property was acquired for the sum of $600,[10] and in 1953 Julius W. Abernethy donated another adjoining tract, bringing total acreage up to approximately three hundred. Each year property has been improved and equipment added. Buildings have been erected as needed and as resources provide.

In order to determine the proper use to be made of the recently acquired Hughes Estate, Blowing Rock, North Carolina, and its relation to the Johns River Valley Camp property and program, in 1946, Southern Synod took action placing the two properties under the same board, consisting of twelve people.[11] A study committee was set up composed of five ministers and five lay-people, with representation from Johns River Valley Camp, the Summer Conference, the Women's Guild, the Men's Brotherhood and the Youth Fellowship, charged with detailing "buildings and developments adequate to take care of the proposed program for five years, ten years and into the future."[12]

This venture served to clarify a number of things. Chief among them being that the two properties in their respective settings provide different opportunities for development. Each in its own way could fill a very definite need in the program of the Synod. Johns River Valley Camp was not suited for sizable conferences and week-end retreats; and in similar manner the Hughes Estate could not very well fit into the pattern of camping and over-night gatherings of young people. It was, therefore, clear that each property should be developed in its own setting, and governed by its own board of managers. Accordingly, in 1947, the Synod reversed its action of the previous year, authorizing that a board of nine members each be created with which to govern the two projects.[13] Provision was made by which six of the nine members of the Johns River Valley Board of Managers are to be elected by the Synod, and the six so elected will elect three additional members. These are to be staggered so that two will be elected for three years, two and one-year periods. Those elected by the six members shall also be one for three, two and one-year periods.[14]

Camp leaders had felt for sometime, for obvious reasons, that the summer education and promotion programs should be developed under the supervision of the Board of Christian Education and Publication of the Evangelical and Reformed Church. Therefore, on July 23, 1947, the Board of Managers voted to recommend the same to the Synodical Council of Southern Synod. That body agreed to try the arrangement through the summer of 1948, and referred it to the Synod's committee on Christian Education for execution.[15] This arrangement did much to clarify administrative responsibilities. The Board of Managers was responsible for property, equipment and housing; the Committee on Christian Education for program and program personnel. The formula was workable and has since that time proven to be satisfactory.

The camp grew in popularity. In addition to a full summer schedule of church related activities, groups outside the Evangelical and Reformed Church have usually filled in the gaps during the camping season, beginning the last of May and ending the middle of September. In 1942, three hundred Evangelical and Reformed young people were enrolled in supervised Christian Education activities at Johns River Valley Camp, plus a number of 4-H Clubs. In 1943, 831 were enrolled there. In 1950, the summer schedule was completely filled, and in 1952, 1,000 persons benefitted from its facilities. In 1959, which was perhaps the banner year to date, the camp ran solid for fifteen weeks, serving twenty five different groups and touching an aggregate of 1,400 people. Six weeks of that time was used by Evangelical and Reformed people.

Something of how the camp is managed is reflected in the annual report of the Board of Managers to Southern Synod in 1956. The report states:

> We believe that the camp is administered in the most efficient and economical manner that present circumstances will permit. Mr. George Rabb of Lenoir serves as Treasurer and Business Manager. During the camping season he visits the camp once each week to oversee the work and to pay bills. Working under him is a caretaker, Mr. Floyd Coffey, Mr. Coffey lives on the property the year round, and during the main camping season he is full-time employee, keeping the grass mowed, removing garbage, and attending to other things. Also, the kitchen staff is employed for the period during which we serve meals. These ladies are experienced cooks, operating a public school cafeteria during the winter season. They perform their work under the regular inspection service of the Public Health Department.[16]

Space will not permit an accounting of all gifts and sources of help that have gone into the development of Johns River Valley Camp; however, the list which appears below strongly indicates the gracious goodwill and generous cooperation received from the church and many friends through the years.

BUILDINGS AND EQUIPMENT

1938, Electric Lights paid for from the General Fund.
1939, Peeler Cabin given by Dr. & Mrs. Shuford Peeler, Charlotte.
1940, The Caretaker's House paid from the General Fund.
1941, Hedrick Cabin given by Mrs. J. T. Hedrick, Lexington.
1941, Barnhardt Cabin given by Mr. & Mrs. M. C. Barnhardt, Salisbury.
1942, Herman Cabin given by Winfield Herman, Conover.
1948, The Bell given by the Southern Railway.
1948, Toilet Facilities for boys paid from the General Fund.
1949, Toilet Facilities for girls paid from the General Fund.
1951, A Pavilion given by Jesse W. Warlick, Hickory.
1951, Two Pavilions given by Charles Turner, Newton.
1952, Corriher Cabin given by Fred J. Corriher and O. C. Corriher, Landis.
1952, Southern Synod Cabin paid from Southern Synod Appropriation.
1954, Administration Building paid for from gifts by the Churchman's Brotherhood, Women's Guild, Youth Societies of Synod, and lumber cut from camp property.

1956, Beck's Church Cabin given by Men of Beck's Church, Davidson County.

1957, Brotherhood Cabin given by the Synodical Brotherhood through the Districts.

1959, The Well and Equipment given by Jack Faw, Conover and Albert Leftland, Jr., Newton.

1963, New Kitchen paid from gifts by the Women's Guild, Churchman's Brotherhood and Sunday Schools of Southern Synod.

1963, Mt. Zion Church Cabin given by Mt. Zion Church, China Grove.

1964, Paved Playground Area paid from the General Fund.

1965, Caretaker's Storage House paid from the Central Fund.

1966, Paved Road to Camp and Parking Areas paid out of General Fund.

RECORD OF CASH GIFTS

1941, A. L. Shuford, Sr., Conover	$ 500.00
1941, Shuford Mills, Hickory	2,000.00
1943, Shuford Mills, Hickory	500.00
1943, A. L. Shuford, Sr., Conover	1,000.00
1943, A. L. Shuford, Jr., Conover	500.00
1944, A. A. Shuford, Jr.	500.00
1945, Shuford Mills, Hickory by J. W. Warlick	500.00
1946, J. W. Abernethy, Newton	500.00
1947, J. W. Warlick, Hickory	300.00
1947, Shuford Mills, Hickory	500.00
1947, A. L. Shuford, Sr., Conover	500.00
1947, Wade H. Shuford, Hickory	500.00
1948, Shuford Mills, Hickory	2,000.00
1949, A. L. Shuford, Sr., Conover	1,000.00
1949, A. L. Shuford, Jr., Conover	250.00

Property evaluation also makes an interesting story. A descriptive paragraph appears in the 1962 report of the Board of Managers. It reads:

> During the past year there have been requests by agencies of the United Church of Christ for evaluation and description of our Johns River Camp properties. The evaluation has been set at $60,000. Half of this amount is for the 300 acres of land, and the other half for the buildings. The land extends from the crest of the mountain range on the East to a point about two-thirds up the mountain range on the West, and for about three-quarters of a mile up the river to the North of the bridge, and for about a quarter of a mile down the river to the South.
>
> There are seventeen buildings on the grounds, and four open air pavilions. The buildings consist of an administration building with offices, a camp store, and a large fellowship hall; a dining hall; eleven cabins; a craft shop; two rest rooms with hot water showers; and a dwelling for the caretaker. There is a large playground area suitable for softball, volleyball, croquet and horseshoes. The Johns River is ideal for swimming; with the depth of water controlled by gates. On the mountain side, overlooking the valley, a lovely place of worship has been developed, and is called Vesper Hill. The surrounding woodlands provide abundant grounds for hikes and nature study.[17]

The spiritual value of this camp over the years in shaping young lives and in generating goodwill and wholesome cooperation among the churches in the Synod is beyond estimate. That it has been impressively effective can not be questioned. Except for the care of grounds, preparation and serving food, and travel, Johns River

Cabins, Administration Building, Dining Room

Valley Camp has been and continues to be a voluntary enterprise. This has been true with ministers and lay-people alike. Rev. Aubrey W. Hedrick began serving on the Board of Managers in 1948. Except for two years, 1951-1952, he has continuous tenure on it to the present time, since 1953 its capable chairman. In reporting to the Southern Synod in 1957, he remarked:

> We are this year marking the 20th Anniversary of our ownership of Johns River Camp. We believe that the camp has rendered an outstanding Christian service in the life and development of our beloved Synod. It has been there that some of our ministers first felt the call to become servants of the church; it has been there that many hundreds of our young people found their faith strengthened, and returned to their local churches with new enthusiasm and greater dedication to God; it has been there that countless new friendships developed which have brought enrichment to life, and have resulted in added interest between churches and people of our Synod.[18]

This valuable agency of the Southern Synod has been transferred and is now one of a number of camp and conference grounds of the Southern Conference of the United Church of Christ. It is destined to make an effective contribution to the cause of Christian Education and character building in the larger constituency.

1. ———. Minutes. Classis of North Carolina, 1930, p. 20.
2. ———. Minutes. *Op. cit.*, 1931, p. 32.
3. ———. Minutes. *Op. cit.*, 1936, p. 17.
4. ———. Minutes. *Op. cit.*, 1937, p. 20.
5. *Hedrick,* Aubrey W., A History of Johns River Valley Camp, 1965, p. 10.
6. ———. Minutes. *Op. cit.*, 1937, p. 20.
7. ———. Minutes. *Op. cit.*, 1938, p. 20.

8. *Ibid.* p. 21.
9. ————. Minutes. Southern Synod, 1941, p. 37.
10. ————. Minutes. *Op. cit.,* 1944, p. 41.
11. ————. Minutes. *Op. cit,.* 1946, p. 47.
12. *Ibid.* p. 49.
13. ————. Minutes. *Op. cit.,* 1947, p. 42.
14. *Ibid.* p. 42.
15. ————. Minutes. *Op. cit.,* 1948, p. 41 .
16. ————. Minutes. *Op. cit.,* 1956, p. 56.
17. ————. Minutes. *Op. cit.,* 1962, p. 63.
18. ————. Minutes. *Op. cit.,* 1957, p. 60.

Blowing Rock Assembly Grounds

A. A. Shuford Worship Centers

Blowing Rock, North Carolina at the eastern edge of the beautiful Blue Ridge resort area, is an ideal place for summer church conferences and retreat programs. Over a period of years, leaders of Southern Synod of the Evangelical and Reformed Church discussed possible locations for such an assembly site. On October 10, 1944, when the Fall Educational and Promotional Conference was in session at Grace Church, Newton, North Carolina,

> Rev. Dr. W. W. Rowe told the Conference of the opportunity for the Synod to purchase a very desirable real estate (The Hughes Estate) in Blowing Rock adjacent to our property, called "The Little White Church,"

the former Mt. Bethel, Blowing Rock. It is a tract of some 58 acres of land with a beautiful elevation, highest in that vicinity, and improved with a very large house and other buildings. This might prove to become a conference grounds. The Synod is not in session, as the Fall Conference is for education, inspiration. However, President Fitz asked for a vote on purchasing the property, the cost being $17,500. The vote was almost unanimous, probably a few did not vote, for interested parties to take over the property and hold same for the Synod.[1]

When Southern Synod met in legislative session in April 1945 at Trinity Church, Conover, North Carolina, it voted to purchase the Hughes Estate, authorized the deed to be drawn in favor of the trustees of Synod, approved a loan of $5,000 from the Trustees of John's River Valley Camp with which to close the transaction and directed the Synodical Council to appoint a committee "to complete the deal and raise the money and administer the property."[2] The committee consisted of Dr. Walter W. Rowe, chairman, Rev. Huitt R. Carpenter, Dr. A. Odell Leonard, and A. L. Shuford, Sr., Herbert W. Coble and Jesse W. Warlick.

Directives of the Synod were carried out. And in May 1946 the committee announced that Mrs. Mary Shuford Davis, a daughter; A. Alex Shuford, Jr., W. B. Shuford, Harley F. Shuford, Alex Menzies grandsons; Mrs. Kathrine Menzies Matthews, a granddaughter; Adrian L. Shuford, Sr., a nephew; and Jesse W. Warlick, a friend; had assumed the purchase price of the Hughes Estate of $16,500, with the understanding that it be made a memorial to the late Abel A. Shuford, Sr. Southern Synod approved the agreement and the property was named and dedicated to the memory of Mr. Shuford in a formal program which occurred on the grounds August 3, 1952. Dr. Walter W. Rowe, wrote:

> It is a worthy tribute to the memory of the late Abel A. Shuford, who was not only a friend of the church, but also a friend of man. He was a leader in the business, educational and religious life of his city, county and state. He was a pioneer banker and cotton mill industrialist in his immediate community. He also served on the board of several of our state institutions and was always a loyal and substantial supporter of Catawba College, serving on the board of this institution for many years. Many are the young men whom he helped in their early days by encouragement and also in a financial way. To them his memory is blessed.[3]

In the meantime the property had been improved and made usable for church conferences and small group retreats. In 1946, a Board of Trustees, consisting of twelve members, was elected by Southern Synod, "to supervise and control the property in conjunction with John's River Valley Camp. Nine members of this board are to be elected by the Synod and those elected to elect three additional members. The present board of John's River Valley Camp shall constitute the nine members to be elected by the Synod. It is suggested that the board divide itself into two divisions. Six members to be responsible for the John's River Valley Camp and six for the Blowing Rock Estate."[4] However the arrange-

ment to govern jointly the two projects proved unwise, and was
therefore changed in 1947. In its place two boards of trustees were
created and their personnel elected by the Synod, providing nine
members each. In each case six of the members were elected by
the Synod, and those elected named three additional members.
These were staggered so that three members were elected for three
years, two and one-year periods. To the Blowing Rock Assembly
Grounds Board were named Dr. H. D. Althouse, Dr. A. Odell
Leonard, Rev. Huitt R. Carpenter and G. Sam Rowe, A. L. Shuford,
Sr. and Herbert W. Coble; these named Dr. Walter W. Rowe, Rev.
Roy E. Leinbach, Jr. and Raymond Starr.[5]

In 1947 G. Sam Rowe was asked by the Board of Trustees to
make a survey of the property, laying out streets, proposed recreation areas and building lots. By action of Southern Synod in 1948
the property was named "The Blowing Rock Assembly Grounds,"

Assembly Hall and Dining Room

and in the same year Synod approved a financial campaign of $150,-
000 for essential buildings and permanent ground improvements.
Proposed improvements included: two cottage-type dormitories to
house thirty people each, two six-room cottages, a kitchen and dining room to serve 350 people, and an adequate water supply.[6] In
preparation for such expansion, a complete topographical survey
of the land was made, showing location of buildings, play areas,
roads and possible home building plots.

This proposed expansion of facilities anticipated an enlarged staff and an extended summer program of activities. Mr. and Mrs. Perry A. Carpenter were secured as manager and hostess for the summer of 1949, through whom reservations were made for the use of the property; who also served meals to an increasing number of guests, especially week-end visitors, mostly from churches of the Synod. At the end of the summer, Mr. Carpenter reported: 1390 registrations and 516 overnight guests. Because of his death, Mr. and Mrs. Carpenter served only one year. However, their effort reflected the wisdom of full-time management on the grounds during summer months. In 1950, Mrs. Homer O. Bonds was employed as manager and hostess, serving in that capacity with distinction each summer, June through September, until 1967.

Acting upon legal advice from Attorney Russell W. Whitener, Southern Synod directed the Synodical Council to incorporate the Blowing Rock Assembly Grounds, and transfer the deed to the property to the Trustees of that Corporation.[7] The text of those proceedings follows:

The State of North Carolina, Department of State

To whom these presents may come, Greeting:

I, Thad Eure, Secretary of State of the State of North Carolina, do hereby certify the following and hereto attached (five (5) sheets) to be a true copy of the Certificate of Incorporation of Blowing Rock Assembly Grounds, Inc., and the probates thereon, as the same taken from and compared with the original filed in this office on the 8th day of November A. D., 1950.

In witness whereof, I have hereunto set my hand and affixed my official seal.

Done in office, at Raleigh, this 8th day of November in the year of our Lord 1950.

Thad Eure (Seal), Secretary of State.

64058 Certificate of Incorporation of the
Blowing Rock Assembly Grounds, Inc.

This is to certify that we, the undersigned, do hereby associate ourselves into a non-stock, non-profit corporation, under and by virtue of the laws of the State of North Carolina, as shown in Chapter 55 of the General Statutes of North Carolina entitled "Corporations," and the several amendments thereto, and to that end do hereby set forth:

1. The name of this Corporation shall be the Blowing Rock Assembly Grounds, Inc.

2. The location of the principal office of the Corporation in this State shall be at Blowing Rock, Watauga County, North Carolina.

3. The objects and purposes for which this corporation is formed are:

a) To establish and maintain an Assembly Grounds or Meeting Place for the Southern Synod of the Evangelical and Reformed Church, its successors and assigns, in or near the town of Blowing Rock, North Carolina.

b) To erect, build, and provide structures, buildings facilities, machinery and appliances, recreation and playgrounds, as the Board of Trustees may deem advisable and necessary in the development and maintenance of the Assembly Grounds or other real estate belonging to said Corporation.

c) To receive, purchase, acquire, hold, rent, deal in, trade, encounter, develop, use, cultivate, sell, transfer, mortgage, dispose of and otherwise handle and improve all kinds of property, real, personal and mixed.

d) To receive, acquire, or obtain property, real, personal or mixed, by purchase, gift, will devise, bequest, donation, or in any other manner permitted by law, and to use, develop, manage, improve, lease, exchange or otherwise handle, deal in, and dispose of all properties or any rights or interest therein necessary for or incident to the conduct of the general business of the corporation.

e) To organize, conduct and carry on various plans, efforts and undertakings for the general moral, mental, physical, social and spiritual well being and improvement of members of the Evangelical and Reformed Church and all other people as the Board of Trustees may deem advisable.

f) To do and perform all other matters and things allowed by law and as may be performed by corporations and as may be required or deemed necessary to obtain the objects and ends for which this corporation is organized.

And in order to properly prosecute the objects and purposes above set forth, the corporation shall have the power and authority, with the consent of Southern Synod or its Synodical Council, to purchase, lease or otherwise acquire, hold, mortgage, convey or otherwise dispose of all kinds of property, both real and personal, both in this state and all other states, territories and dependencies of the United States and generally to perform all acts which may be deemed necessary or expedient for the purpose and successful prosecution of the objects and purposes for which this corporation is created.

4. The period of duration of this corporation shall be unlimited, but in the event of the dissolution thereof, for any reason whatsoever, all of the assets and property of the corporation shall be given, assigned and transferred over to the Southern Synod of the Evangelical and Reformed Church, or its successors, and said property shall be owned by said synod in fee simple.

5. This corporation shall have no capital stock, and it shall be operated solely for charitable and religious purposes.

6. The names and post office addresses of the incorporators are as follows:

A. L. Shuford, St., Conover, North Carolina
A. Odell Leonard, Lexington, North Carolina
Dr. A. R. Keppel, Salisbury, North Carolina
Mrs. Agnes A. Peeler, Lexington, North Carolina
Huitt R. Carpenter, Faith, North Carolina
Harvey A. Fesperman, Burlington, North Carolina
Mrs. Marie R. Hoyle, Lincolnton, North Carolina
Mrs. Annie W. Shuford, Conover, North Carolina
Joshua L. Levens, Salisbury, North Carolina
Arthur Detwiler, Lenoir, North Carolina
Herbert Coble, Burlington, North Carolina
Harland Deal, Lenoir, North Carolina.

7. The incorporators shall constitute the Board of Trustees of said corporation, and upon organization of the corporation, it shall proceed to divide the membership of the Board of Trustees into three parts; one-third shall hold office for one year; one-third for two years; and one-third for three years. All successors to said Board of Trustees shall be elected for three years, three-fourths from the Southern Synod, or in case of vacancy, by the Synodical Council of the said Southern Synod, at least three of whom shall be members of the Synodical Women's Guild, and the Trustees shall select and elect the other one-fourth of the members of

said Board. The Board of Trustees shall submit annually to the Southern Synod a complete report of its activities, and, in all matters, shall be subject to approval of the Southern Synod or the Synodical Council of said Synod. The Southern Synod may, at any time, decrease or increase the number of members of the Board of Trustees of this Corporation.

In Testimony Whereof, we, the said incorporators have hereunto set our hands and seals, this the 30th day of October, 1950.

A. L. Shuford (Seal)
A. Odell Leonard (Seal)
A. R. Keppel (Seal)
Mrs. Agnes A. Peeler (Seal)
Huitt R. Carpenter (Seal)
H. A. Fesperman (Seal)
Herbert Coble (Seal)
Mrs. Marie R. Hoyle (Seal)
Mrs. Annie W. Shuford (Seal)
Josh Levens (Seal)
Arthur R. Detwiler (Seal)
Harland Deal (Seal)

The State of North Carolina, County of Rowan

This is to certify that on the 30th day of October, 1950, before me, Mildred K. Peeler, A Notary Public, personally appeared A. L. Shuford, Sr., A. Odell Leonard, A. R. Keppel, Mrs. Agnes A. Peeler, Huitt R. Carpenter, Harvey A. Fesperman, Mrs. Marie R. Hoyle, Mrs. Annie W. Shuford, Joshua L. Levens, Herbert Coble, Harland Deal and Arthur Detwiler, who, I am satisfied are the same persons named in and who executed the foregoing Certificate of Incorporation of the Blowing Rock Assembly Grounds, Inc., and I, having made known to them the contents thereof, they did each acknowledge that they signed, sealed and delivered the same as their voluntary act and deed for the uses and purposes therein expressed.

In testimony whereof, I have hereto set my hand and affixed my notorial seal, this the 30th day of October, 1950.

Mildred K. Peeler, Notary Public

Commission Expires 7:23:51

Filed November 8, 1950
Thad Eure, Secretary of State.[8]

Legal detail having been satisfied, adequate facilities became the next order of business for the Board of Trustees. In 1952, the Walter W. Rowe Dormitory was erected at a cost of $40,000 and completely furnished through the efforts of the Women's Guild of Southern Synodical, under the supervision of Mrs. Marie R. Hoyle. The building was named for Dr. Walter W. Rowe, a widely influential minister of the church, credited with proposing the idea of acquiring the Blowing Rock Assembly Grounds property for a conference site and inspiring its early development. In the same year, an out-of-doors worship center was built and a water tank erected at a cost of approximately $15,000.[9] In 1953 a second well was drilled and a hard surfaced road constructed connecting conference areas with official state paved highways. This work was done through the influence of the Churchmen's Brotherhood by the North Carolina Highway Commission as a service to the public.

Before the season began in 1953, a dining hall, kitchen, and an assembly room, all under one roof, were erected costing approximately $30,000. Expenditures to that date on improvements, including new buildings, repairs on the "big house," and water supply approximated $101,000, the current debt being only $35,000.

Walter Rowe Dorm

It is evident that progress, though slow, was steady. The Assembly Grounds were becoming a center of summer activities for almost every phase of the educational and promotional program of the Synod. State-wide groups, district organizations and local congregations were making this delightful spot a converging place. In 1953, four thousand people visited the grounds and used the facilities. In order to financially undergird this important new development in the life of the Southern Church, in 1952 the Synod took action asking the churches to contribute the equivalent of the Apportionment in 1952-1954 to this agency. That practice continued longer than the designated period of three years, for in 1958 sixty eight congregations had contributed a total of $86,722.77.[10] In 1956, president of the Board of Trustees, Rev. Huitt R. Carpenter in making his annual report to Southern Synod, remarked,

> We are grateful for the cooperation and encouragement of the following: President of Synod and the Synodical Council; the pastors and members of our congregations; the Women's Guild and Churchmen's Brotherhood; the

Committee of Synod; and a host of individuals who have offered words of encouragement and prayers for our task.[11]

At that time the debt had been reduced to $33,000, of which $5,000 was a loan from Southern Synod. Assets were estimated at $200,000. Among listed needs of the establishment were: a new dormitory, class room space, reconditioning of roads, extension of water lines, and recreational facilities.[12] The $5,000 note to Synod was paid in 1959.

Housing facilities were greatly improved when, in 1960, two duplex family-type cottages were erected. One of these was named "The A. L. Shuford, Sr. Cottage," and dedicated to the memory of Elder A. L. Shuford, Sr. of Trinity Church, Conover, North Carolina. Mr. Shuford was instrumental in establishing the Blowing Rock Assembly Grounds. He was a successful industrialist, giving liberally of his time and resources to the local congregation. As a deacon, elder, Sunday School superintendent and teacher he was loyal and devoted. In wider circles of the denomination, he served on the Synodical Council, Nazareth Children's Home Board and a number of times as delegate to the General Synod. The other duplex cottage was made possible through the liberality of Herman Barringer, after whom it is named. He is a son of the late Dr. Paul Barringer, a member of St. James Church, Mt. Pleasant, North Carolina, and a devoted friend and supporter of the Assembly Grounds project.

Ten thousand five hundred persons visited the Assembly Grounds during the 1962 season: 1368 attended public worship either in the assembly room or at the "Little White Church;" 6,211 meals were served, and 2,227 overnight lodgings were provided. Contributions from the churches that year totalled $6,264.93.[13]

Over a period of twenty years this useful institution has made steady progress, providing reasonable equipment and a well defined inspirational and educational program of conference, retreats and congregational gatherings, representing all phases in the life of the Synod. However, with the advent of Southern Conference of the United Church of Christ when Southern Synod merged with that body on September 30, 1965, many of these retreats, conferences and some committee meetings of necessity were shared with other conference grounds in the area. Therefore, the Blowing Rock Assembly Grounds Board of Trustees was faced with the problem of adjusting its offerings to meet the needs of the new and larger constituency. Obviously drastic changes in program and management were required. Feeling its way ahead in 1966, the board elected Dr. George E. Dillinger full-time Executive Director and assigned to him the responsibility for leadership in developing a meaningful program and of managing its fiscal affairs.

On the property at the present time are eleven buildings and points of interest, established there by grateful benefactors. These occupy an elevation which rises above the town of Blowing Rock, lying under the shadow of Old Grandfather Mountain. The scene is breath-taking, and the atmosphere is invigorating. Henry Van Dyke has captured something of the atmosphere of this unusual place in his poem, "God of the Open Air." He wrote:

> By the breadth of the blue, that shines in silence o'er me,
> By the length of the mountain lanes that stretch before me,
> By the height, of the cloud that sails, with rest, in motion,
> Over the plains and the vales of the measureless ocean,
> Oh, how the sight of things that are great, enlarges the eyes
> Leads me out of the narrow life, to the peace of the hills and
>   the skies.[14]

To this place, fashioned by the Divine Hand, go hundreds of people each season just to breathe the air and catch the vision of larger things.

1. ———. Minutes. Southern Synod, 1945, p. 20.
2. *Ibid.* p. 68.
3. ———. Minutes. *Op. cit.*, 1946, p. 47.
4. *Ibid.* p. 47.
5. ———. Minutes. *Op. cit.*, 1947, p. 1.
6. ———. Minutes. *Op. cit.*, 1948, p. 45.
7. ———. Minutes. *Op. cit.*, 1950, p. 36.
8. ———. Office. Register of Deeds, Watauga County, Boone, North Carolina, Book B. Corporations, p. 325.
9. ———. Minutes. *Op. cit.*, 1952, p. 21.
10. ———. Minutes. *Op. cit.*, 1958, p. 71.
11. ———. Minutes. *Op. cit.*, 1956, p. 47.
12. *Ibid.* p. 48.
13. ———. Minutes. *Op. cit.*, 1963, p. 59.
14. ———. Brochure. Spiritual Horizons, ———, p. 3.

CHAPTER VI

Living Churches in North Carolina

Beck's Church, Davidson County

Beck's German Reformed Church, six miles Southeast of Lexington, North Carolina, was originally located on a tract of fifty three acres of land deeded November 5, 1787 by Dr. John Billings, Leonard Smith and others to Martin Frank, and Frederick Billings of the "Profession of the Church of England," and David Smith and Henry Lookinbee of the "Profession of the Church of the Dutch Settlement on Abbotts Creek," Trustees of the two congregations. The agreement, including a meeting house and burying grounds at nearby Abbotts Creek, was made to these Trustees and their successors in office forever.[1]

Language used in the deed requires some interpretation.

Martin Frank and Frederick Billings were Trustees of the Lutheran Church, called in the deed, "The Profession of the Church of England." David Smith and Henry Lookinbee were Trustees of the Reformed Church, called in the deed, "The Profession of the Church of the Dutch Settlement on Abbotts Creek." These peculiar titles arose from the fact that members of the Reformed and Lutheran Churches could not speak English. The officials gathered from their broken explanations that the first-named represented a denomination somewhat like the Church of England, and wrote the deed accordingly. The officials also understood that the latter trustees represented a denomination identical with the "Dutch Congregation on Abbotts Creek," already mentioned in the official records of 1783, and so wrote the title.[2]

Several facts are established by this record. The land was deeded to people of the Reformed and Lutheran faiths and their successors; also, a building existed there prior to 1787.

Itinerate missionaries of the Reformed faith, such as Rev. Samuel Suther, served this settlement periodically, providing the sacraments, religious instruction for young people, and public services for the community, before the congregation was established. Thus, on the local level, the Christian faith depended largely for its sustained stimulations upon dedicated laymen such as Captain Peter Hedrick and his sons. Mr. Hedrick was one of the first land barons of Davidson County, holding title at one time to as many as 1,400 acres. He was a widely influential citizen, thoroughly devoted to church and community. His body was laid to rest in Beck's Church cemetery. As a worthy tribute to his memory, a monument at his grave was unveiled on November 31, 1933, placed there by relatives and friends. On it is inscribed in part the following sentiment, translated from the German language:

Peter Hedrick was born December 17, 1733, and died January 24, 1798.
When we have scarce been born, it is from the first step of life to the cool grave of death only a short measured step. Alas, with each moment goes our strength backward; for we are with each year, all ripe for the bier of death. Who his house now well ordered, he goes with joy of the world, since scarcely on the contrary eternal death can come.

Of such people Beck's Reformed Church has been built.

The exact date of organization can not be established; however, it is thought that Rev. Jacob Schneider, who served Reformed Churches in Davidson County during that time, was its organizer in the year 1787. Dr. George W. Welker commented, "Members of the congregation are largely made up from families of the Swings, Hedricks, Smiths, Billings, Millers, Imblers, etc. No records exist to show by whom the congregation was organized, but it is probable that it was done by Rev. Schneider, whose ministry was coeval with the settlement of that region."[3]

The congregation worshipped with their Lutheran neighbors in the log meeting house until 1878, when the Lutheran segment withdrew and built a church of their own on a lot adjoining the original tract. The Reformed congregation proceeded to build a suitable frame church north of the log meeting house. This move was predicated by internal strife, evidently stimulated by the Tennessee Lutheran congregation. Later the question of land ownership was raised by the Reformed folks which was settled by the Courts favorable to the Reformed congregation, due primarily "to a lapse of time in filling vacancies on the list of Trustees for the Lutheran Synod."[4]

Beck's Church has thrived through the years. Its equipment was greatly enlarged in 1934, in the pastorate of Dr. James D. Andrew, by the addition of Sunday School rooms. In 1948, an adequately equipped hut was erected on the grounds for social and recreational purposes. However, within a few years, this antiquated church building could no longer satisfy the needs of a new church. A building committee was elected, which was instructed to investigate needs and submit recommendations. The committee consisted of Zeno Greer, Roy Burkhart, Elwood Younts, Crawford Swing, Grover Parks and J. E. Miller. The new edifice was completed in 1951, and formally occupied on Pentecost Sunday, May 13. It was dedicated debt free July 22, 1951 at 2:30 p.m. Addresses were delivered by Dr. John C. Peeler and Rev. Charles E. Hiatt, both former pastors. Rev. Aubrey W. Hedrick, president of Southern Synod, extended greetings. The pastor, Rev. C. Nevin Stamm, performed the act of dedication.

On March 9, 1953, Hedrick's Grove Church withdrew to become a self-supporting congregation, leaving Beck's and New Jerusalem churches to constitute the Lower Davidson Charge.[5] Since Hedrick's Grove had made satisfactory financial arrangements concerning the parsonage, Beck's Church proceeded immediately to erect a parsonage of their own, locating it on land immediately across the road in front of the new church. Plans were developed for the house, and its construction was supervised by Robert Swing, Zeno Greer, Crawford Swing, Elwood Younts and Grover Parks. Groundbreaking ceremonies occurred March 14, 1954. It was a rainy day, and the large crowd sloshed through mud to the top of the hill, taking part in history-making activities. The house was dedicated Sunday afternoon, November 21, 1954, when Dr. Aaron R. Tosh, president of Southern Synod, made appropriate remarks. Because of rain, dedication ceremonies were held in the sanctuary.

An event of historical interest was the observance by the congregation of its 175th Anniversary of Organization. It occurred September 9, 1962, when Rev. Richard N. Davis preached the sermon. At one forty five in the afternoon an impressive monument at the front entrance of the improved church cemetery was dedicated, in loving memory of Bessie Miller Parks, on which is inscribed:

> The congregation of Beck's Reformed Church was organized in the year of our Lord, 1787, under the leadership of Rev. Mr. Schneider. The first house of worship was a log structure, located in the proximity of this marker.

Fifty three acres of land were given November 5, 1787 by Dr. John Billings, L. Smith and others, to the Trustees of the Lutheran and Reformed Congregations. These two communions worshipped as a Union Church from that time until 1878.

In 1878 a large frame church was built some 200 yards North of this marker. This building was used until the present church, a brick structure, located some 300 yards South of this marker, was dedicated to the service of the Lord on July 22, 1951.

Thirty-six ministers have labored in the Beck's Reformed Congregation since its organization.

The act of dedication was performed by Dr. Harvey A. Fesperman, president of Southern Synod. Following this brief but impressive ceremony, the congregation reassembled in the sanctuary for a "Recognition Service." Among those who were recognized and spoke briefly were: Revs. Charles E. Hiatt, Horace S. Sills, Roy C. Whisenhunt, Rex O. Dobey, Donald J. Selby; also, Rev. D. B. Summers, minister of the Beck's Lutheran Church. Rev. Wade H. Curran, Jr. directed activities.

For the first time in its history of 177 years, on June 30, 1964, Beck's United Church of Christ became a self-supporting congregation.[6] Rev. Wade H. Curran, Jr., who had been serving as pastor of the Lower Davidson Charge, resigned that office. This act opened the way for him to accept the pastorate of Beck's Church, now constituted a separate Charge.

Under the pressure of growth, in 1966, the congregation took action to erect a two-story brick educational annex, containing 6,900 square feet of floor space, providing nine classrooms, assembly and conference rooms. Its construction was supervised by Coy Weaver, Elwood Younts, Bobbie Swing, Franklin Burkhart, Grover Parks, Victory Fouts and Fred Miller. The building was dedicated July 31, 1966, by the pastor, Rev. Ingle O. Cook. Chaplain Wade H. Curran, Jr. delivered the address.

ROSTER OF PASTORS

Rev. Jacob Schneider,
Organizer 1787-1792
Rev. Samuel Weyberg 1793-1798
Rev. Jacob Christman 1798-1803
Rev. George Boger,
Itinerate 1803-1812
Rev. Andrew Loretz,
Itinerate 1803-1812
Rev. J. R. Riley, Rev. William Weinel, Rev. H. B. Dieffenbach, Rev. Jacob Scholl, Rev. J. S. Ebaugh, Rev. George Leidy, Rev. John Rudy, Rev. George
Boger 1812-1827
Rev. William Hauck 1828-1832
Rev. W. C. Bennet 1832-1838
Rev. David Crooks 1838-1846
Rev. F. W. Plassman 1846-1848
Rev. Thornton Butler 1848-1851
Rev. William Sorbor 1853-1856
Rev. Thorton Butler 1856-1857
Rev. P. Allison Long 1858-1864
Rev. M. L. Hedrick, Dr. A. R. Holshouser, Dr. William H. McNairy, Rev. L. M. Kerschner,

Rev. H. E. Sechler, Dr. William H. Causey, Dr. Paul Barringer, Dr. P. M. Trexler 1862-1909
Rev. J. M. L. Lyerly, Ph.D. ..1909-1918
Rev. John C. Peeler, D.D. 1918-1923
Rev. A. Samuel Peeler 1923-1929
Mr. Roy C. Whisenhunt,
Student Summer Supply 1929-1930
Rev. James D. Andrew, D.D. 1931-1937
Rev. Charles E. Hiatt 1937-1950
Rev. Roy E. Leinbach, Jr.,
Supply 1950-1951
Rev. C. Nevin Stamm 1951-1952
Rev. Lionel A. Whiston, Ph.D.,
Supply 1952-1953
Rev. Horace S. Sills 1953-1960
Rev. Donald J. Selby, Ph.D.,
Supply 1961-1962
Mr. Wade H. Curran, Jr.,
Summer Student Supply 1961-
Rev. Wade H. Curran, Jr. 1962-1965
Rev. Raymond C. Craven,
Supply 1965-1966
Rev. Ingle O. Cook 1966-

1. ———. Book of Deeds, Rowan County, 1787, No. 12, 74.
2. *Clapp,* Jacob C., Editor, Historic Sketch of the Reformed Church in North Carolina, 1908, p. 170.
3. *Welker,* George W., Colonial Records, North Carolina, Volume III, p. 742.
4. *Morgan,* Jacob L., Editor, History of the Lutheran Church in North Carolina, 1953, p. 167.
5. ———. Minutes. Southern Synod, 1953, p. 14.
6. ———. Minutes. *Op. cit.,* 1964, p. 64.
7. *Sills,* Horace S., Beck's Evangelical and Reformed Church, 1955, p. 5.

Bethany Church, Catawba County

THE EARLY HISTORY of Bethany Church is obscure, chiefly because no one bothered to keep the records. However the oral story of the congregation's first activities is as follows. Preaching Services were held in the old Witherspoon school house, a log building located in the Fairgrove community, as early as 1903. No particular denomination sponsored these meetings. In fact, the first church building, a frame structure, appears to have been completed before a decision was reached to petition for affiliation with any denomination.

From the old school house the interested group moved to the site of the present church, where for sometime open air meetings were held under a brush arbor. During the early months of 1906, plans were completed to erect a church building which served the congregation until 1952. Among those first interested families were Mr. and Mrs. Logan Wilson, Mr. and Mrs. Charles Wilson, Mr. and Mrs. Pinkney Wilson, and Mr. and Mrs. Billy Witherspoon. Mr. Pinkney Wilson describes the beginnings of the church as follows, "Almost the entire congregation of this church belongs to one family, Wilson. We have chosen the name, Bethany, because of the family at Bethany, where Jesus often dwelt. On the fourth Sunday in March, 1909, the following petitioners asked the Classis of North Carolina to be organized: Alford Wilson and wife, Z. N. Jones and wife, E. G. Bost and wife, C. A. Wilson, A. L. Hicks, W. P. Sigmon, P. A. Wilson, L. P. Wilson and wife, Mrs. Sophia Wilson, Pinkney Rowe, W. P. Huffman, A. Sigmon, William Poovey, Ella Lee Wilson and Lester Wilson."

The petition was granted and Dr. Jacob C. Clapp was appointed to effect the organization under the name of "Bethany Reformed Church." On the fourth Sunday in May, 1909 the organization was completed. Logan Wilson, Pinkney Wilson, and Pinkney Rowe were named Elders; Alfred Wilson, William Poovey and A. L. Hicks were made Deacons.

In 1944, while Rev. A. Wilson Cheek was serving as supply pastor, plans were drawn for a brick veneered structure, by a committee composed of Edgar H. Witherspoon, Clarence Witherspoon and A. Wilson Cheek. During the summer of 1945, a charge composed of Bethany and Smyrna churches was created. Rev. Claude W. Kelly was called to be its first full-time pastor, and began his work there November 11, 1945. At the same time the charge was enrolled by the Board of National Missions in the Department of Town and Country with subsidy at the rate of one third of the pastor's salary. Land was purchased adjacent to the church property on the east side, from Mrs. Coley Cline on which a parsonage was built for the charge and by it jointly owned. The house was occupied by the pastor in the spring of 1946.

Because of the urgent need of additional Sunday School space, a building committee was appointed to study the problem, consisting of John O. Cline, Herbert Hartsoe, Vernon Yount, Fred Rowe, Edgar Witherspoon, Sr., and Earl Reinhardt. When in July 1951, the new pastor Rev. Nevin H. Feather arrived, plans had been drawn and the congregation was ready to proceed with construction of the building. The old church building and hut were later sold. The new house of worship was occupied the first Sunday in November 1952. A year later, on November 1, 1953, it was dedicated. The charge went to self-support January 1, 1957. Additional space in the parsonage, consisting of a pastor's study, a porch and a bedroom was completed as a joint project of the charge in 1958.

A memorable occasion was the observance of the congregation's Golden Anniversary held May 24, 1959. An anniversary sermon was delivered by the pastor, and during the afternoon, Dr. Lonnie A. Carpenter, pastor of Trinity Church, Conover delivered an appropriate address. Present membership of Bethany Church is 133 confirmed people. The church enjoys a healthy, aggressive outlook, and is concerned to accept its share of the denomination's program of Kingdom promotion.

ROSTER OF PASTORS

Rev. Jacob C. Clapp, D.D. 1909-1910
Rev. John H. Keller, D.D. 1911-1912
Rev. John C. Peeler, D.D. 1912-1918
Mr. Banks J. Peeler,
  Summer Student Supply 1918-
Rev. Oliver H. Sensenig 1919-1921
Mr. O. Bain Michael,
  Summer Student Supply 1922-
Rev. Harvey G. Kopenhaver 1922-1925
Rev. C. Columbus Wagoner 1925-1930
Rev. Clarence E. Whetstone 1931-1932
Rev. Carl H. Clapp 1933-1940

Rev. A. Wilson Cheek, D.D.,
  Supply 1940-
Rev. Roy E. Leinbach, Jr.,
  Supply 1941-
Rev. A. Wilson Cheek, D.D. 1941-1944
Rev. Lonnie A. Carpenter, D.D.,
  Supply 1945-
Rev. Claude W. Kelly 1945-1949
Rev. Shuford Peeler, D.D.,
  Stated Supply 1949-1951
Rev. Nevin H. Feather 1951-1966
Rev. Banks D. Shepherd 1966-

References:

> *Feather,* Nevin H., A History of Bethany United Church of Christ, 1964.
>
> *Clapp,* Jacob C., Editor, Historic Sketch of the Reformed Church in North Carolina, 1908.
>
> *Leonard,* Jacob C., History of the Southern Synod of the Evangelical and Reformed Church, 1940.

Bethany Church, Davidson County

BETHANY REFORMED CHURCH, Route 9, Winston Salem, North Carolina, began as a union effort with their Lutheran neighbors, dating back to the beginning of the German Settlement in that section of Davidson County. It was first known as the church at Fredericktown, in deference to Frederick Miller who signed the deed for the land on which the church was built and who played a leading role in the erection of the first building.

The text of that deed is revealing.

> This indenture was made the first day of August in the year of our Lord one thousand seven hundred and eighty nine between Frederick Miller of Rowan County in the State of North Carolina of the first part and the inhabitants of Brushy Fork belonging to the Societies of the Church and Presbyterian parties as the second part witnesseth, that the said Frederick Miller for and in consideration of the sum of one pound and thirteen shillings current money of North Carolina to him in hand paid before the ensealing and delivering thereof by the aforesaid parties of the second part, the receipt whereof the said Frederick Miller doth hereby acknowledge. . . . . to be for the use of building a meeting-house and other religious purposes.[1]

Certain terms in this deed are confusing, unless the reader understands that it was drawn when public officials knew very little about German culture, especially the German Reformed Church. They, therefore, used language common in religious circles of that day. "Societies of the Church" referred to those of the Lutheran persuasion; while "Presbyterian Parties" defined people of the Reformed faith.

Shortly after this deed was made Reformed and Lutheran neighbors, in keeping with their German custom, made plans to erect a meeting-house in the settlement. This house was a log structure 30 by 40 feet in size with galleries on three sides. The pulpit was of the usual European style, goblet shapped, supported by a poplar post, and large enough to accommodate only one person.[2] Known first as the church at Fredericktown, the community later was nicknamed "Possumtown" as a prank. Opossum hunters deposited two of these hapless animals in the home of Mr. Miller, while he with more conscientious brethren were attending a religious meeting at the church. The name appears to have clung to the community and the church until 1861, when the new frame structure was erected. At that time the name of the church was changed. Rev. P. Allison Long, reading the ritual of dedication, called it Bethany. The location being a delightful spot, it was a happy choice, denoting the congregation since that time.

When the first service was conducted in that community is not known, but certainly before 1789. True to the tradition of their fathers, among the first cooperative community activities provided in the new settlement, was a place for Divine services. There is no reason to believe that these pious German pioneers acted differently at this location. It is known, for instance, that itinerate ministers of the Reformed faith preached in that part of the State of North Carolina as early as 1768, perhaps as early as 1759. Rev. Samuel Suther preached at regular intervals in Pilgrim Reformed Church, twelve miles further south on Abbotts Creek from 1768 to 1786. Following him came Rev. Jacob Schneider. It is known that the Mr. Schneider organized Beck's Reformed Church in 1787, and it is more than likely that he not only preached for the Fredericktown folks prior to the founding of this church, but organized it. Rev. Andrew Loretz and Rev. George Boger followed him. This church prospered until 1812; then, until 1848 for lack of pastoral care, the congregation disintegrated.

Dr. George W. Welker has written concerning Bethany Church in this period.

> Bethany Church . . . was, in earlier records, known as Fredericktown. Here, at the distance of twelve miles East of Lexington, on the upper Abbotts Creek, the Longs, Oakleys, Beckerdites, Clodfelters, with other of their co-religionists, who now sleep in the populous graveyard hard by, and united with their Lutheran neighbors to put up their first place of worship. It is probable that it was organized about the same time, and under the same ministration, as the Pilgrim Church. For want of spiritual ministration, the Reformed people suffered their organization to fall into disuse, but under the ministry of Thornton Butler, 1848 to 1856, it was revived and grew to become a prosperous church.[3]

In 1848, Rev. Thornton Butler, then a young man recently ordained to the Christian ministry by the Classis of North Carolina, concerned about the Fredericktown congregation, counselled with John Long, Samuel Yokeley and Henry Clodfelter seeking ways and means of reviving it, reorganized the few remaining members. Proposed methods of promoting it were foreign to German church life, but after considerable discussion and some compromise, a plan was agreed upon. A camp-meeting was arranged which began Friday evening before the third Sunday in August 1851, continuing through Wednesday of the following week. Preachers for these meetings were: Rev. Thornton Butler, Dr. George W. Welker and Dr. Jeremiah Ingold. Similar meetings took place each year through 1858; however, the Reformed people discontinued their participation in them 1854.[4]

The Lutheran congregation did not prosper after the Civil War; hence, in 1902 the Lutheran people discontinued to hold services at that place, and arranged a satisfactory division of property.[5] "Three acres of land were reserved for the cemetery to be held in common; and the remaining land was divided into two parts, one part containing four acres and the other two acres. The Reformed received two acres, and went to work at once to build a new church."[6] Later the congregation bought the other four acres; hence, owns the whole of the original plot except the cemetery which is held in common.[7]

The cornerstone for the new church building was laid March 14, 1903, and the house was completed during the summer, being dedicated November 15 of that fall. Dr. Joseph L. Murphy preached the sermon. Dedication rites were conducted by the pastor, Dr. H. A. M. Holshouser.

In 1928, in the pastorate of Rev. Hoy L. Fesperman, Sunday School rooms were added and new heating equipment installed. In 1935, a social activities building was erected. On July 30, 1939,

Bethany Church observed its 150th Anniversary of Organization, scheduling activities which continued through the day. Dr. Jacob C. Leonard delivered an historical address at 11 a.m., and during the afternoon former pastors and others spoke briefly. Among those making addresses were: Dr. Jacob A. Palmer, Dr. Shuford Peeler, Rev. Joshua L. Levens and Rev. Hoy L. Fesperman.

Anticipating physical expansion, in 1958, a finance committee was authorized to suggest ways and means for accumulating funds. In 1959, a planning committee was appointed to study needs and make recommendations. The committee was composed of E. B. Mendenhall, Jr., Mrs. Paul Livengood, Mrs. LeRoy Bailey, Charles Everhart and Roy Barrier. Plans were developed, involving an educational annex and remodeling the sanctuary. The proposed plans for the educational annex provided space for fourteen classrooms, a kitchen, a fellowship hall and other necessary facilities. The remodeled sanctuary included a new choir and chancel arrangement, additional pews and a new vestibule. These plans were approved and a contract was awarded for an expenditure of $50,091. Construction began July 1960. The cornerstone was laid April 16, 1961. Dedication of the entire building occurred May 21, 1961, at 2:30 p.m. Rev. Joshua L. Levens, a former pastor, preached the sermon; Rev. Raymond C. Craven, a son of the congregation, made the dedicatory prayer. Dedication rites were in charge of the pastor.

For many years Bethany Church was associated with others neighboring congregations in the Upper Davidson area for pastoral oversight. On December 5, 1946 it was constituted with Hebron and Bethlehem churches as the North Davidson Charge. In 1950 Hebron withdrew to become a self-supporting church. This new arrangement of churches required the erection of a parsonage for the North Davidson Charge, now composed of Bethlehem and Bethany congregation. The house was built at Bethany in 1953, involving an expenditure of $14,000, each church sharing in the cost. The next ten years were marked by physical and material progress, especially during the ministry of Rev. Carl C. Kreps. When, therefore, on April 30, 1961 Bethlehem withdrew to become a self-supporting congregation, Bethany was ready to take a similar step forward.[8] An agreement was reached with reference to the parsonage, and Mr. Kreps was called to be the first full-time pastor of Bethany Church, which he served until January 1, 1963.

Rev. Carl R. Martin came to the parish March 1, 1964, and served until 1967. Bethany is one of the oldest Reformed churches in Davidson County, and has given a good account of its stewardship. Six sons have gone into the Christian Ministry: Rev. P. Allison Long, Rev. Thomas Long, who is also claimed by Hebron Church, Dr. Joseph L. Murphy, Rev. John A. Long, Dr. William H. Causey and Rev. Raymond C. Craven.

ROSTER OF PASTORS

Rev. Jacob Schneider	1789-1792	Rev. Jacob A. Palmer, D.D.	1912-1918
Rev. Andrew Loretz	1803-1812	Rev. James D. Andrew, D.D.	1918-1924
Rev. George Boger	1803-1812	Rev. A. Odell Leonard, D.D.,	
Vacant		Supply	1925-1927
Rev. Thornton Butler	1848-1851	Rev. Hoy L. Fesperman	1927-1929
Rev. William Sorber	1853-1856	Rev. A. Odell Leonard, D.D.,	
Rev. Thornton Butler	1856-1857	Supply	1929-1934
Rev. P. Allison Long	1858-1862	Mr. Huitt R. Carpenter,	
Rev. Thomas Long	1862-1887	Summer Student Supply	
Rev. G. Dickie Gurley,		Mr. Carl H. Clapp,	
Assistant	1885-1886	Summer Student Supply	
Rev. Julius H. Shuford	1887-1888	Mr. Joshua L. Levens,	
Rev. Jacob C. Leonard, D.D.	1889-1897	Summer Student Supply	
Rev. H. A. M. Holshouser,		Rev. Joshua L. Levens	1934-1937
Ph.D.	1897-1903	Rev. C. Columbus Wagoner	1938-1947
Rev. William H. Causey,		Rev. John W. Settlemyre	1949-1953
D.D.	1903-1907	Rev. Harvey H. Koonts, Jr.	1954-1955
Vacant	1907-1910	Rev. Carl C. Kreps	1956-1963
Rev. William H. McNairy,		Rev. Carl R. Martin	1964-1967
D.D.	1910-1911		

1. *Leonard*, Jacob C., Centennial History of Davidson County, North Carolina, 1927, 1927, p. 458.
2. *Ibid*. p. 458.
3. *Welker*, George W., Colonial Records of North Carolina, Volume VIII, p. 743.
4. *Clapp*, Jacob C., Editor. Historic Sketch of the Reformed Church in North Carolina, 1908, p. 172 ff.
5. *Morgan*, Jacob, L., Editor. History of the Lutheran Church in North Carolina, 1953, p. 169.
6. *Leonard, Op. cit.*, p. 461.
7. *Leonard*, Jacob C., History of Southern Synod, Evangelical and Reformed Church, 1940, p. 177.
8. ———. Minutes. Southern Synod, 1960, p. 70.

Bethel Church, Stanley County

THE "BEAR CREEK" COMMUNITY, located at the extreme West end of Stanley County, takes its name from a creek by that name which flows through the area. It was originally settled by German families of the Reformed and Lutheran faiths. From reliable sources it is known that the following families were represented: Henry Seitz, Zacharias Lyerly, John Barrier, William Heynsemann, Matthias Barnhardt, Henry Hahn, Henry Smith, Christopher Gregory, Jacob Hegler, John Reidenhour, William Lowder, Andrew Smith, Mrs. Rebecca Moose and Jacob Barrier.[1]

Occasional religious services were conducted in the area, mostly in the barns of Christopher Lyerly and Col. George Barnhardt, over a period of thirty or more years prior to the appearance of the Reformed and Lutheran Union Church.[2] Such services included the preaching of the Gospel, performing the rites and administering the sacraments of their faiths. The Rev. Samuel Suther, for instance, who was pastor of the nearest established Reformed congregation, Grace (Lower Stone) Church on nearby Second Creek, Rowan County from 1768 to 1786, and the Rev. Andrew Loretz

who followed him could have performed these services. Prior to
this time Rev. James Martin and Rev. Richard Dupert were in the
area, as were Rev. Samuel Weyberg and Rev. George Boger for a
time after 1886.[3]

The inference is that on or about the year 1806 a union congregation composed of Reformed and Lutheran families was formed.
For on March 21, 1806 the first church building was begun, which
served these families for a period of sixty nine years. The church
was constructed of pine logs and erected in two days by means of
a "house raising," a custom so prevalent among German folks in
those days.[4] The tract of land on which it was erected, consisting
of 110 acres, was given to the two congregations by Christopher
Lyerly and his son, Jacob Lyerly, and was deeded to Henry Smith
and his successors in office July 2, 1809. Due to economic pressures, considerable time, probably thirty years, lapsed before the
church was entirely finished.

An unfinished house, however, did not deter a devout people
from satisfying their longing for Divine Worship. On Pentecost,
May 25, 1806, the congregation assembled in the unfinished church
and heard a sermon delivered by Rev. George Boger, a native North
Carolinian, who had been ordained to the Christian ministry in
1803. Mr. Boger served the congregation as its first pastor, dating
from 1806 to 1830.[5] Evidently Mr. Boger served both Reformed
and Lutheran families, for in those days the congregation supported
the same pastor and was generally served by the same officers. In
1806 Christopher Lyerly, Lutheran, and Henry Seitz, Reformed,
were installed deacons of the congregation. In 1811, when the
above officials were elevated to the office of Elder, John Barrier,
Reformed, and William Heynsemann, Lutheran, were elected deacons.

This relationship continued for almost three fourths of a century, when the two congregations separated, effecting the division August 16, 1875. In making the adjustment, the Reformed congregation retained the old property, while the Lutheran congregation moved two miles east and built a new house of worship. Not all of the Lutherans were willing to leave the old church environment; hence a small group remained as a Lutheran congregation, but eventually most of them affiliated with the Reformed Church.[6]

The Reformed congregation worshipped in the old church building until 1878, when a new building was erected. Begun in January, the new sanctuary was finished and dedicated the fourth Sunday in October 1878. During these operations Rev. R. F. Crooks was pastor and Daniel M. Moose was a prominent layman, taking a leading part in the affairs of the congregation.

Activities leading to the new and third house of worship began in 1926. J. Wade Moose, J. A. Rowland and M. M. Palmer were named to the building committee with supervisory authority. The new church was constructed of stone, brick and wood. The cornerstone was laid on the second Sunday in October 1929, ceremonies being in charge of Dr. Charles W. Warlick, pastor of the church, under whose guiding hand the edifice was completed and dedicated free of debt. Dedication services took place the fourth Sunday in May 1930.

Bethel Church has been effective in the life of the denomination throughout its history. The One Hundredth Annual Sessions of the Classis of North Carolina convened at Bethel Church May 5 to 7, 1930.

On June 30, 1935 a monument was dedicated to the memory of Christopher Lyerly, influential churchman, architect of the first house of worship, charter member of Bethel Church, donor of the site on which the church stands and soldier in the Revolutionary War. The marker occupies a prominent place in the church cemetery.

This widely influential and effective rural church was cited as the "Rural Church of the Year," by the North Carolina Grange in 1960. The Rev. Charles E. Hiatt was its pastor.

Three sons have been ordained to the Christian Ministry, and have served faithfully and well in the United Church of Christ: Rev. C. Columbus Wagoner, Rev. Felix B. Peck, S. T. D., and Rev. Jacob C. Palmer, D.D.[7]

ROSTER OF PASTORS

Rev. George Boger 1806-1830	Rev. Anthony Shulenberger 1910-1911
Rev. Daniel B. Lerch 1830-1834	Rev. Border L. Stanley 1911-1913
Rev. John Lantz 1837-1853	Rev. William C. Lyerly 1914-1918
Rev. Thornton Butler 1853-1869	Rev. Aaron R. Tosh, D.D. 1919-1921
Rev. John C. Denny 1869-1874	Rev. Charles W. Warlick,
Rev. Robert F. Crooks 1876-1881	D.D. 1921-1929
Rev. G. Dickie Gurley,	Rev. William S. Gerhardt 1930-1941
Supply 1882-1884	Rev. Aubrey W. Hedrick 1942-1949
Rev. Calvin Boyd Heller 1884-1891	Rev. Thomas Hoffman 1950-1953
Rev. Paul Barriner, D.D. 1894-1900	Rev. Merle F. Sollinger 1954-1958
Rev. John H. Keller, D.D. 1901-1906	Rev. Charles E. Hiatt 1958-1967
Rev. E. Garver Williams 1907-1909	Rev. Harold Holste 1967-

1. *Clapp*, Jacob C., Editor. Historic Sketch of the Reformed Church in North Carolina, 1908, p. 216.
2. *Morgan*, Jacob L., Editor. History of the Lutheran Church in North Carolina, 1953, p. 257.
3. *Clapp. Op. cit.*, p. 217.
4. *Morgan. Op. cit.*, p. 257.
5. *Clapp. Op. cit.*, p. 217.
6. *Morgan. Op. cit.*, p. 258.
7. ———. Manuscript. Bethel (Bear Creek) Church, Stanley County.

Bethel Church, Catawba County

BETHEL REFORMED CHURCH, Catawba County, is located eight miles south of Hickory, North Carolina on the old "King's Mountain" road. It is a result of the desire to meet religious needs of St. Paul's Church and Grace Church families who lived in the forks of Henry Fork and Jacob Fork rivers.[1] This is the section of Catawba County into which Henry Weidner and Conrad Yoder with their families came in 1750 to make their homes.[2] As Henry Weidner was a moving spirit in the founding of "Old St. Paul's Church," so, with Jacob Shuford, he undoubtedly became influential in establishing Bethel Church.

Records in the early days of Bethel Church are scarce, for long periods, non-existent. However, from reasonably reliable sources a fairly satisfactory brief story of "early Bethel" can be pieced together. Later sources are more numerous and reliable.

Rev. John H. Crawford, then pastor of Grace Church, located some six miles south of the Bethel community on the King's Mountain road, met preaching appointments at Minerva School House, located near the home of Jacob Shuford at the cross roads. These appointments were scheduled for Sunday afternoons, as far back as 1847, perhaps earlier, stimulating the desire among neighbors for a church in their midst. A meeting of interested citizens, "for the purpose of considering the propriety of building a house of worship," took place in the winter of 1847-1848. This meeting was held in the woods, supposedly in the neighborhood of where the church now stands. As reported by an attendant at the gathering, snow began to fall fast before the assembly adjourned. A small house, 22 by 32 feet was built, evidently a rather crude structure, without such common necessary conveniences as a stove. Worshippers usually gathered about an open fire built in the church yard, around which they stood to warm themselves before entering the church for worship.

While no specific date can be established on which the congregation was organized, it is obvious that it was effected by Rev. John H. Crawford sometime during the year 1848. Lazarus Dietz made a deed September 2, 1848 for the land on which the church was built to Jacob Shuford and Henry Link. An old church record states that three children were baptized in 1848, the first receiving that sacrament in the new church. And the minutes of the Classis of North Carolina in 1849, report Bethel Church yoked in a charge with Grace Church.[3]

A charter membership list is not available; however, among officials who through the first sixty years of its existence served the Church, the following have been recorded: elders: Peter Finger, H. W. Link, Peter Rowe, Z. R. Whitener, John Robinson, J. S. Whitener and R. L. Whitener; deacons: J. E. Wilfong, A. Whitener, D. W. Whitener, Wm. Abernethy, William Dietz, David Setzer, R. L. Whitener and D. H. Whitener. Two joint consistory meetings of the Catawba Charge, of which Bethel was a part, were held in 1852 and 1854 respectively. The president of that body and presided at the meetings was Henry Link, a member of Bethel Church, and the secretary was John Coulter, a member of Grace Church.[4]

That first inadequate building served the congregation until 1886, when it was removed from the church grounds and converted into a "country store." On January 31 of that year, by unanimous vote of the Consistory, action was taken to erect a new church to be constructed of brick. The building committee consisted of Augustus Whitener, J. Sidney Whitener and James E. Wilfong. When the cornerstone was laid September 8, Rev. Calvin B. Heller made the address. The sanctuary was finished and occupied in 1887.

A parsonage of wood material, owned jointly by the South Fork Charge, consisting of Daniel's, Grace, Route 1, Newton, St. Paul's and Bethel congregations, was built at Startown, North Carolina in 1906. A modern brick house for the minister was erected along the west side of the old one in 1946. Bethel built a log hut located southwest near the church building in 1955, which was greatly improved and repaired in 1948, being stuccoed on the outside and completely refinished on the inside, suitable for educational and recreational purposes. A cemetery is maintained by the congregation on church grounds, which dates back as far as 1860. Here lie the bodies of two ministerial sons; Rev. Julius H. Shuford and Rev. Sterling W. Whitener.

The congregation voted to erect an educational annex January 10, 1965, and authorized a building committee composed of Howard Barger, Carroll Abernethy, Jr., Charles M. Cecil, Frank Whitener, Mabel Weaver and Rev. Roy E. Leinbach, Jr. to supervise its construction. Work on the building was begun April 1, 1965, completed the following September and occupied in November. Total cost amounted to $18,000.

The congregation maintains two well managed organizations. The Sunday School has been and is being led by such influential people as Gordon L. Whitener, Harry Whitener, Charles M. Cecil, Carroll Abernethy, Jr., and Miss Mary Belle Tate. The Lay Life Fellowship organized in 1963, successor to the Women's Guild and the Churchmen's Brotherhood, and designed to provide programs and study opportunities for men, women and young people, has been directed by such leaders, among others, as Mrs. Herbert Teague, Mrs. Ray Weaver, Mrs. Charles Dickenson, Charles M. Cecil, Frank Whitener and Harry Whitener.

The centennial of the organization of the church was observed the week of October 17, 1948. Major concerns in the life of the Church were emphasized in a well developed program of activities such as, the Women's Guild, Young People's Activities and Reformed-Lutheran relationships. Visiting speakers for the occasion were: three brothers who are sons of the congregation: Rev. Sterling W. Whitener, Missionary to China; Dr. Russell W. Whitener, Attorney of Newton; Dr. Daniel J. Whitener, Dean, Appalachian State College. Rev. Milton Whitener, Business Manager of Catawba College, also a son of the congregation, preached the Centennial Sermon. Dr. Harry D. Althouse delivered the "opening" sermon on the 17th.

From its founding in 1847 until 1903, Bethel Church was a part of the Catawba Charge, which included Grace, Route 1, Newton, and Corinth, Hickory. When, in 1903, Corinth Church became a self-supporting congregation and was declared a charge, Bethel and Grace were served three years by ministerial supply preachers. In 1906, Bethel, St. Paul's, Grace, Route 1, Newton and Daniel's were constituted the South Fork Charge. The South Fork Charge was dissolved in 1956, resulting from a study made of the area by the Department of Town and Country of the Board of National Missions. At that time Bethel and St. Paul's became the United Charge of Southern Synod, Evangelical and Reformed Church, of which Rev. Roy E. Leinbach, Jr. is currently the energetic and successful pastor.

Bethel Church has given four sons to the Christian ministry. They are Rev. Julius H. Shuford, 1849-1925; Rev. Sterling W. Whitener, 1894-1950; Rev. Macon A. Huffman, 1887-1958. Rev. Milton Whitener was baptized in Bethel Church but was not confirmed there, the family having moved out of the area before he was of confirmation age.[5] Pastors and known ministerial supplies of the church since its organization, appear below.

ROSTER OF PASTORS

Rev. John Hobert Crawford 1847-1853
Rev. Jeremiah Ingold, D.D. 1856-1873
Rev. Julius H. Shuford 1874-1876
Rev. Jacob C. Clapp, D.D.,
  Alternate Supply 1876-1877
Rev. John A. Foil, Ph.D.,
  Alternate Supply 1876-1877
Rev. Alexander Sidney
  Vaughn 1881-1883
Rev. Alfred Pierce Horn 1883-1884
Rev. George Dickie Gurley 1884-1885
Rev. George Ritter 1885-1890
Rev. Joseph Long Murphy,
  D.D. 1890-1903
Rev. Peter Melanthan Trexler,
  D.D. 1903-
Rev. Samuel Washington
  Beck 1903-1905
Mr. Milton Whitener,
  Student Supply 1905-
Rev. John A. Foil, Ph.D.,
  Supply 1905-1907
Rev. Samuel Washington
  Beck 1907-1909
Rev. Harvey Grant
  Kopenhaver 1910-1915

Mr. Harvey Augustus Fesperman,
  Supply 1915-1916
Rev. Harvey Augustus Fesperman,
  D.D. 1916-1921
Mr. Banks J. Peeler,
  Summer Student Supply 1921-
Rev. John B. Swartz 1922-1926
Rev. Ezra H. Ginther 1926-1927
Rev. William Clarence
  Lyerly 1928-1931
Mr. Carl H. Clapp,
  Student Supply 1931-1932
Rev. Huitt Rudisill
  Carpenter 1932-1935
Rev. Olin Bain Michael,
  S.T.D. 1935-1941
Rev. Harry Daniel Althouse, D.D.,
  Supply 1941-
Rev. Karl Roebuck Flocken 1942-1945
Rev. Arthur Wilson Cheek, D.D.,
  Supply 1945-1946
Rev. William Clarence
  Lyerly 1946-1953
Rev. Roy Ezra Leinbach,
  Jr. 1954-

1. *Presler*, Charles J., Editor. A History of Catawba County, 1954. p. 1.
2. *Clapp*, Jacob C., Editor. Historic Sketch of the Reformed Church in North Carolina, 1908, p. 244.
3. ———. Minutes. Classis of North Carolina, 1849, p. 115.
4. *Leinbach*, Roy E., Jr., Manuscript. Bethel Church, Catawba County, 1965, p. 2 ff.
5. *Ibid*. p. 7.

Bethlehem Church, Davidson County

BETHLEHEM REFORMED CHURCH, Route 10, Winston Salem, North Carolina, located near the Forsyth-Davidson County line, was born in a revival of religious interest. In the summer of 1913, citizens living in the vicinity of the "Old Gum Tree," a number of whom were members of Hebron Church, invited Rev. David E. Bowers to plan for and conduct a series of out-of-doors services for the community. Through his influence a brush arbor was erected on land belonging to Mrs. Katherine Stewart, and on September 9, 1913, Mr. Bowers conducted the first of those services at that place. More than three hundred people were in attendance. The service was a free, informal affair consisting of gospel songs, scripture reading, prayers and a sermon, but very effective.

The generous response of people living in the community stimulated discussion favorable to the establishment of a church. A committee was appointed to investigate its feasibility, and if results were
favorable, to solicit money and material with which to erect a building. The committee was composed of Misses Hassie Bodenheimer
and Bessie Stewart, Napoleon Beckerdite, Banks Beckerdite and Mr.
Bowers. M. C. Bodenheimer, T. H. Livengood and Alfred Stewart
were designated Trustees of a congregation yet to be organized.

On the 13th of October 1913, Mrs. Katherine Stewart and her
children, Bessie, Claudia, Moses, Joseph, Charles and Ollie Stewart
Gardner and her husband, Rufus Gardner, deeded one acre of land
to the Trustees upon which to build a church. The building committee consisted of Rev. David E. Bowers, chairman, Banks Beckerdite and Andrew Beckerdite. Miss Hassie Bodenheimer was named
treasurer. Construction on the church building began in the fall,
and by March 1914, it was ready to be used. The first service was
held in it on March 27. The cornerstone and dedication rites were
performed May 31, 1914, after the structure had been completed
and freed of debt. Rev. Jacob A. Palmer, pastor of the Upper
Davidson Charge, made the address at the cornerstone laying ceremony held at 11 A. M., and Dr. Jacob C. Leonard, pastor of the First
Reformed Church, Lexington, preached the dedicatory sermon at
2 o'clock in the afternoon.[1] Of interest is the fact that this place of
worship was built, paid for, and dedicated before the congregation
was organized.

The Sunday School was established June 28, 1914. Officers named
were: Charles E. Hiatt, who later became a minister in the Reformed Church, superintendent; Relie Charles, assistant super-

intendent; Hassie Bodenheimer, secretary-treasurer; Banks Becker-dite, assistant secretary-treasurer; Lessie Sink, organist and Madge Beckerdite, assistant.[2]

In May 1914, a request was presented to the Classis of North Carolina, "From members of the Reformed Church within the bonds of the Waughtown Charge, to be organized into a congregation known as Bethlehem Reformed Church."[3] That request was granted. Rev. David E. Bowers was instructed to organize the congregation which was incorporated in the Waughtown Charge. He reported to the Classis in the spring of 1915: "We beg leave to report that the Bethlehem Reformed Congregation was organized September 22, 1914, with 28 members."[4] The charter member list consisted of M. C. Bodenheimer, Louisa Jane Bodenheimer, Hasseline Bodenheimer, O. H. Bodenheimer, Agnes Reed, Christine Bodenheimer, Drucilla Jones, Sarah Gardner, Julius Gardner, Claudia Stewart, Ada Jones, Anna Stewart, Ada Stewart, Joseph Ray, Nancy Stewart, Hezekiah Jones, Esther Gardner, Nellie Johnson, Ellen Stewart, Cassie Jones, Bertha Stewart, Katherine Stewart, Rufus Gardner, Laura Willard, Lula Johnson, Bessie Stewart, C. F. Willard, August Jones and Ollie Gardner. M. C. Bodenheimer and Julius Gardner were elected elders; Joseph Ray and Rufus Gardner, deacons. Mr. Bowers served the congregation as a part of the Waughtown Charge until October 1921, when he died.

During the next forty five years, involving seven pastorates, the church made only nominal progress. Being always associated in a charge consisting of two or more congregations, only limited pastoral attention was available to the community. However, traditional services were held there during those years, and the property, including the cemetery, were kept in good condition. For instance, in 1936 the cemetery was enlarged; Sunday School classrooms were added twice; modern heating equipment was installed; and in more recent years, the sanctuary was remodeled and equipped with new pews, pulpit furniture and floor carpet.

In 1960 the congregation was large enough and resources were sufficient to justify a venture as a self-supporting church. The Southern Synod approved a request from Bethlehem Church and it was declared an independent, self-supported congregation as of April 30, 1961.[5] Rev. Joshua L. Levens, then pastor of the St. Thomas Mission, Winston Salem, was appointed by Southern Synod as Stated Supply. This service he rendered over a period of sixteen months. During that time a new and well equipped parsonage was built near the church and the membership was greatly numerically increased. Having received a call to become pastor of the church, Mr. Levens accepted it and began serving as its first full-time minister living on the parish as of September 1, 1962.

Realizing the need for better and more modern equipment, a building committee was elected composed of L. C. Beckerdite, Jr., chairman, Houser Reid, Roger Whitman, Howard Dorsett and C.

J. Miller, with instructions to develop long-ranged plans by which it could be secured. A two-acre tract of land along the east line of church property was purchased from the Stewart Estate, the parsonage was cleared of debt, and a building fund was started, which in 1966 had a cash balance in excess of $10,000.

The church has a confirmed membership of 160 people, a Sunday School enrollment of 200 pupils and is located in a steadily expanding edge of greater Winston Salem. Since 1966, Rev. Weldon T. Madren has been serving the parish.

ROSTER OF PASTORS

Rev. David E. Bowers,
Organizer 1914-1921
Rev. J. M. L. Lyerly, Ph.D. ..1922-1923
Rev. Augustus C. Peeler 1923-1937
Rev. Roy C. Whisenhunt 1937-1942
Rev. Hiram E. Davis 1942-1947
Rev. John W. Settlemyre 1947-1953
Rev. Harvey H. Koonts, Jr. 1954-1955

Rev. Carl C. Kreps 1956-1961
Rev. Joshua L. Levens,
Stated Supply 1961-1962
Rev. Joshua L. Levens 1962-1965
Rev. Banks J. Peeler, D.D.,
Stated Supply 1965-1966
Rev. Weldon T. Madren 1966-

1. *Leonard*, Jacob C., History of the Southern Synod, Evangelical and Reformed Church, 1940, p. 222.
2. *Levens*, Joshua L., Bethlehem United Church of Christ, 1965, p. 1 ff.
3. ————. Minutes. Classis of North Carolina, 1914, pp. 25, 26.
4. ————. *Op. cit.*, 1915, p. 25.
5. ————. Minutes. Southern Synod of the Evangelical and Reformed Church, 1960, p. 70.

Beulah Church, Davidson County

IT APPEARS THAT a layman inspired the founding of Beulah Reformed Church, Route 8, Lexington, North Carolina. Philip Sauer (Sowers), came to North Carolina in 1753, took up a large tract of land on "Swearing Creek," Davidson County, married shortly thereafter, and on that land established a home. He became ancestor to all the people in that section of the state known by the name of Sowers. Largely through his influence the first grant of land was made to the "Dutch Congregation on Abbott's Creek," later named Pilgrim Church. When the Reformed element in the congregation was organized, he became a charter member and served as one of its first elders. The first entry on the baptismal record of that church was Anna Catherine, the first-born child of Mr. and Mrs. Philip Sauer.[1]

In later years, when that area required additional church facilities, Elder Sauer donated eleven acres of land located northwest of Pilgrim Church, on which was erected the Sauer's Meeting House. The building was constructed of logs, and stood at the northeast corner of the present church cemetery. When that congregation was organized, he became a charter member and served as one of its first officials. Itinerate ministers preached there before the church was organized. Since people of the Reformed, Lutheran and Moravian faiths were represented in the community, it is reasonable to conclude that some of these preachers were Moravian. However, the Rev. Jacob Schneider, pastor of the Reformed Churches in Davidson County, effected the organization in 1788 and served as its first pastor.[2] Among family names prominent in the early history of this church were, Koontz, Everhart, Sauer (Sowers), Livengood, Hege, Berrier, Grimes, Wehrle (Whirlow), Schaaf (Shoaf). Most of these names are still found on the roll of members.

Little is known of the work that was done by the Sauer's Congregation from 1788 until the latter part of 1800. Virtually no congregational records are available for that period. It has been suggested that they were either lost or destroyed, if, indeed, records were kept at all. However it is known through other sources that Reformed, Lutheran and Moravian neighbors met there for religious services. The Records of the Moravians in North Carolina provide an interesting paragraph on activities at Sauer's Church in 1837.

> After preaching the pastor went with Br. Christian Rippel to the so-called Sauer's Church 8 or 9 miles from Friedberg in Davidson County at the head of the Reedy Creek. This church, or congregation, consists of German Reformed and Lutherans although served mostly by preachers of the former.
>
> For some years it seems there had been a joyous spirit of agreement among members of these affiliations, promoted especially by the services of two preachers, Jenkins and Bennet. Some weeks ago Communion was attended by 184 persons, Reformed, Lutheran, and Methodists, who communed in brotherly love. I preached first in English, and next in German by special request because this settlement is populated with many German descendents. So many hearers had assembled that the church could hardly hold them and they had to go out to stand in the woods. They were very attentive in both meetings. It seems that a so-called revival had been going on there for some time and the religious life shows itself in all kinds of

wild outbreaks after the fashion of the Methodists. Therefore I was pleas-
antly surprised by the spirit of brotherly love that was shown by so many.

Pastor Jacob Miller will no longer serve this church for he has thought
of moving to the state of Indiana, and for the time being neither Lutheran
nor Reformed preachers serve this congregation; so I was asked if meanwhile service might be provided by the Brethren, especially since in former
years preaching service had been supplied from Salem. After a cordial
farewell and repeated requests to come and preach again, we rode to the
home of Mr. Jacob Sauer, an esteemed member of this church, and ate
dinner. Then, happy and thankful for the support the Lord had given us
that day, we returned home.[3]

While many faiths were represented among brethren who worshipped at Sauer's Church in unity for many years, it was never
organized a union church. Mr. Sauer specifically designated that
the land should be used on which to erect a Reformed Church;
therefore no union organization was effected.[4]

The original log house served that community until 1851, when a
white frame structure was erected a few yards northeast of the
original site. This second building was remodeled and equipped
with new furniture in 1893, during the pastorate of Dr. Jacob C.
Leonard. Rededication services were conducted July 23 of that
year. Dr. James D. Andrew preached the sermon. Tradition says
that the name of the church was probably changed from Sauer's to
Beulah about that time. Many of the older deeds to the property
support this contention, in that these refer to the church as Sauer's
Meeting House; while later records use the name Beulah.

The Davidson Charge, which consisted of all the churches in
Davidson County, was divided into the Upper Davidson Charge
and the Lower Davidson Charge during the pastorate of Rev. P.
Allison Long. In 1864 a special committee on the division of this
charge, reporting to the Classis of North Carolina, recommended:

> That classis confirm the action of the consistory demanding the change
> —The Lower Davidson Charge to consist of Beck's, New Jerusalem,
> Emanuel and Mt. Carmel churches; the Upper Davidson Charge of
> Bethany, Pilgrim, Pleasant Retreat and Beulah churches. Also that the
> pastoral relations now existing between the Upper Charge and the Rev.
> P. A. Long and that between the present Lower Charge and the Rev.
> Thomas Long be and hereby dissolved.[5]

This action cleared the way for Rev. P. A. Long officially to become
pastor of the lower group of churches and Rev. Thomas Long to
become pastor of the upper group. Rev. Thomas Long had served
as assistant pastor of the Davidson Charge since his ordination in
1863. This charge arrangement continued until 1909, when Hebron,
(Pleasant Retreat), was detached from the Upper Davidson Charge.
In 1946 Bethany was detached, Beulah and Pilgrim continuing as a
two-point charge in the Upper Davidson group.

In 1888 the Upper Davidson Charge built a parsonage a short
distance northeast of Pilgrim Church near Pilgrim Academy on U.
S. Highway 29. The pastor, Dr. Jacob C. Leonard, being a bachelor

lived in the house with Sheriff and Mrs. A. T. DeLapp, who for a time provided board for boys attending the academy. A matter of interest in this connection is the erection of Arnold Academy in 1891 within the Beulah Church parish, by members of the Beulah congregation. The academy was located on what is now known as the Center Church Road, and provided excellent educational opportunities for boys and girls in the community of High School age, until the state made provision for such training in its school system.

In 1921, inspired by the energetic leadership of Dr. James D. Andrew, the third church building was erected, replacing the old one that had served the community over a period of seventy years. That new house provided adequate facilities for worship and education. During the pastorate of Rev. Joshua L. Levens, which began in 1934, a church hut was erected west of the sanctuary which housed a fellowship hall and kitchen and used for educational and recreational purposes. In 1937, the Upper Davidson Charge built a new parsonage on Beulah Church land, facing Arnold Road, a short distance west of the church. Rev. and Mrs. C. Columbus Wagoner were its first occupants.

In 1951 the share of Pilgrim Church in the parsonage was purchased by the congregation, when Beulah Church became a self-supporting charge. Student G. Melvin Palmer did supply work that summer, and upon graduation from Theological School and ordination to the Christian ministry in 1952, became its first full-time pastor. During his ministry a modern Educational building, of brick construction, was erected north of the sanctuary, involving an investment of $41,000. It provided for a pastor's study, a nursery, and class rooms arranged in departments for young people through the junior high school ages. Groundbreaking ceremonies were held October 11, 1959. The building was occupied January 1, 1961. Appropriate dedication services were held September 24, 1961, when Rev. G. Melvin Palmer made an appropriate address. The pastor, Rev. Henry J. Meier, read the ritual of dedication, who also remarked,

> The new building with its adequate facilities, is a big asset to the Children's Division of the Sunday School, and will mean much in the proper religious training of the children of our congregation and community. . . . .
> This new educational building, fully equipped and paid for, is an evidence of the fine Christian Spirit of the members of Beulah congregation.[6]

In 1963, the congregation prepared for and observed its 175th Anniversary of Organization. An elaborate program of activities was developed by a committee consisting of Graham Sowers, Wade Brinkley, Holland Tussey, Leonard Berrier, Jule Byerly and Wade Freedle. Services began August 18, and continued through the week, ending the 25th. Dr. Banks J. Peeler, president of Southern Synod, preached the sermon on the 18th at 11 a. m., when certain memorials were dedicated; Dr. Jacob A. Palmer delivered an address at 7:30 in the evening. Other visiting speakers during the week were, Rev. Joshua L. Levens, Rev. Carl T. Daye, Rev. Raymond C. Craven, Dr. A. Odell Leonard, Rev. Huitt R. Carpenter and Rev. Max L. Tussey. An anniversary booklet entitled, "175th Anniversary, Beulah United Church of Christ," was published by a committee composed of Mrs. Shelley Leonard, Elmer R. Everhart and Graham Sowers.

Beulah Church has been an effective force for good in the Arnold Community over a period of 180 years. It has shared membership with other churches of all faiths as they have been disbursed into areas of the nation's life. In 1946, when Paul's Chapel was organized in the Jakesville Community, its charter membership was drawn from a number of surrounding churches, but Beulah Church provided a majority of them. Dr. O. Bain Michael, a son of the congregation, gave the site on which Paul's Chapel and parsonage stand.

Two sons have become ministers of the United Church of Christ: Dr. O. Bain Michael and Rev. Max L. Tussey. Current confirmed membership of the church is 350 people. The present devoted pastor is Rev. Henry J. Meier.

ROSTER OF PASTORS

Rev. Jacob Schneider 1788-1792	Rev. Jacob C. Leonard, D.D. 1889-1897
Rev. Samuel Weyberg 1793-1798	Rev. H. A. M. Holshouser,
Rev. Jacob Christman 1798-1803	Pd.D. 1897-1903
Rev. George Boger 1803-1812	Rev. William H. Causey,
Rev. Andrew Loretz 1803-1812	D.D. 1903-1907
Rev. George Boger 1812-1827	Vacant 1907-1910
Rev. James Riley 1812-1827	Rev. William H. McNairy,
Rev. William Weinel 1812-1827	D.D. 1910-1911
Rev. H. B. Dieffenbach 1812-1827	Rev. Jacob A. Palmer, D.D. 1912-1918
Rev. Jacob Scholl 1812-1827	Rev. James D. Andrew, D.D. 1918-1924
Rev. J. S. Ebaugh 1812-1827	Rev. A. Odell Leonard, D.D.,
Rev. George Leidy 1812-1827	Supply 1925-1927
Rev. John Rudy 1812-1827	Rev. Hoy L. Fesperman 1927-1929
Rev. William Hauck 1828-1832	Rev. A. Odell Leonard, D.D.,
Rev. W. C. Bennet 1832-1838	Stated Supply 1929-1934
Rev. David Crooks 1838-1846	Summer Student Supplies; Mr.
Rev. F. W. Plassman 1846-1848	Huitt R. Carpenter, Mr. Carl H.
Rev. Thornton Butler 1848-1851	Clapp, Mr. Joshua L. Levens
Rev. William Sorbor 1853-1856	Rev. Joshua L. Levens 1934-1937
Rev. Thornton Butler 1856-1857	Rev. C. Columbus Wagoner 1938-1946
Rev. P. Allison Long 1858-1863	Rev. Carl T. Daye 1947-1950
Rev. Thomas Long 1863-1886	Summer Student Supply,
Rev. G. Dickie Gurley,	Mr. G. Melvin Palmer 1951-
Assistant 1885-1886	Rev. G. Melvin Palmer 1952-1960
Rev. J. H. Shuford 1887-1888	Rev. Henry J. Meier 1961-

1. *Clapp*, Jacob C., Editor. Historic Sketch of the Reformed Church in North Carolina, 1908, p. 176.
2. Meier, Henry J., 175th Anniversary. Beulah United Church of Christ, 1963, p. 3 ff.
3. *Rights*, Douglas LeTell, Records of the Moravians in North Carolina, 1837, p. 4302.
4. *Clapp. Op. cit.*, p. 177.
5. ————. Minutes. Classis of North Carolina, 1864, p. 315.
6. *Meier*, Henry J., Religious Education Building. Beulah United Church of Christ, 1961, p. 7.

Boger Church, Cabarrus County

THE EAST ROWAN CHARGE, extending over a wide area in Rowan, Cabarrus and Stanley Counties, covered too much territory for one minister to effectively administer as a parish. Therefore, in 1904, when Rev. Walter W. Rowe began serving on the Charge, he asked the Classis of North Carolina to investigate the possibility of establishing a church in the Watts Cross Roads Community.[1] During the following year, two services were held in the Cruse Schoolhouse, the first on July 31. Apparently other Reformed Church ministers,— Revs. Paul Barringer, Samuel W. Beck and John H. Keller—had previously held meetings at that place.

In 1905, Mr. Rowe reported to the Classis that the outlook for a growing congregation in the Watts Cross Roads Community was promising, and he was instructed to organize a church there if circumstances warranted it.[2] On the following June 25, a building committee was appointed, composed of G. H. Boger, J. A. Watts, E. C. Mesimer and J. W. Foil. Erection of a frame building which cost approximately $600 was begun in September. The cornerstone was laid November 17, and it was completed and occupied within a few months thereafter. Money and material with which to complete operations were collected from interested people who lived in the area.

The land on which the church stands was once owned by Rev. George Boger, who was ordained to the Christian ministry March 6, 1803 at Mt. Zion (Savit's) Church, Rowan County. Mr. Boger served his entire ministry or forty four years within the bounds of the Classis of North Carolina. The site was donated for the purpose by Mrs. Caroline Boger; thus the church gets its name "Boger Reformed Church," honoring this devoted minister of the Gospel. The new sanctuary was dedicated April 29, 1906. Dr. Jacob C. Clapp preached the dedicatory sermon.[3]

By authority of the Classis of North Carolina, the congregation was organized October 25, 1905, Rev. Walter W. Rowe being the presiding officer. There were seventeen charter members. On the roll were Caroline Boger, Susan E. Boger, Mary A. Boger, George A. Boger, G. H. Boger, Annie Bonds, Charlie Bonds, E. C. Mesimer, Isabelle Mesimer, Madalene Mesimer, Cora Mesimer, G. A. Moose, M. Alice Moose, J. A. Safrit, Lillian A. Safrit, J. A. Watts and Myrtle Watts. J. A. Watts and G. H. Boger were elected elders, and E. C. Mesimer and J. A. Safrit, deacons. G. H. Boger was elected trustee, and J. A. Watts was named secretary of the consistory and treasurer of the congregation. A constitution was also adopted at that meeting. In May 1906 the congregation was enrolled by the Classis, and Elder J. A. Watts took his seat as a member of that body.[4] Being attached to a charge composed of Bethel (Bear Creek) and St. James, Mt. Pleasant, Rev. E. Garver Williams served as its first regular pastor.[5]

In 1942, after thirty seven years, the congregation began to feel the need for new and modern equipment. Rev. Aubrey W. Hedrick who was serving as pastor of the congregation at the time, suggested that a building fund be started. The fund grew steadily. By 1951 a building committee was authorized, and the following people were appointed to membership on it: Rev. Thomas Hoffman, chairman, W. Herman Kluttz, Marvin C. Watts, Frank B. Goodman, Warran Manus, Carl Moss, Kenneth Manus, Ray Boger and Lonnie Bost.

Building plans were developed and approved. On March 2, 1952, construction on the new church building began. It was finished by the following November. The old church house was moved back several hundred feet to make room for the new, and conditioned for recreation and social purposes. On November 30, 1952, using an appropriate ritual, the old church was named "Memorial Hall," and rededicated. Following this ceremony the congregation moved en-masse to the new building, laid the corner stone, and entered the sanctuary where dedicatory services took place. Rev. Aubrey W. Hedrick, president of Southern Synod, who ten years earlier had inspired the congregation to make plans for just such an occasion, delivered an appropriate sermon.

Debt free, on October 30, 1955, this small but dedicated congregation observed its 50th Anniversary of Organization. Notes were burned to symbolize their economic and material accomplishment. The Rev. Carl T. Daye, a former pastor, returned to deliver the anniversary address.

Sunday School rooms were added later. When Dr. Felix B. Peck, then living in retirement, agreed to serve the St. James-Boger Charge as stated supply, it was with the understanding that they continue to contribute according to their standard of Christian Stewardship, and invest such gifts in benevolent projects in denominational causes at home and abroad. Thus, began a new venture in church expansion. All benevolent causes benefitted from this new policy, and two new units were added to their local church equipment.

A Sunday School annex was completed in 1964, and dedicated November 1 of that year. Two former pastors, Revs. Carl T. Daye and Banks D. Shepherd, assisted in the service. On November 8, 1964 a "Relinquishing Service" was performed in the old building before it was torn down to make way for the New Fellowship Hall. Dedicatory services were held November 15, 1964 for the new hall, which was named "Peck Fellowship Hall," honoring their supply pastor. The Rev. H. Wayne Peck, son of Dr. & Mrs. Felix B. Peck, delivered the dedicatory address.

With the shifting population from town to country, this church is in a position to render a real service to the Watts Cross Roads section of Cabarrus County.

ROSTER OF PASTORS

Rev. Walter W. Rowe, D.D.,
  Supply and Organizer 1904-1906
	Rev. Charles W. Warlick,
	  D.D. 1921-1930

Rev. Paul Barringer, D.D., Supply 1906-1907	Rev. William S. Gerhardt 1930-1941
Rev. E. Garver Williams 1907-1910	Rev. Aubrey W. Hedrick 1942-1949

Rev. Anthony Shulenberger,
  Supply 1910-
	Rev. Lionel A. Whiston, Ph. D.,
	  Supply 1949-1950

Rev. Anthony Shulenberger ..1910-1911	Rev. Thomas Hoffman 1950-1953
Rev. Dugan C. Cox, Supply 1911	Rev. Lionel A. Whiston, Pr.D.,
Rev. Border L. Stanley 1911-1913	1953-1954
Rev. Paul Barringer, D.D.,	Rev. Carl T. Daye 1954-1958
Supply 1914-	Rev. David E. Faust, Ph.D.,
Rev. William C. Lyerly 1914-1918	Supply 1958-

Mr. Frank L. Fesperman,
  Summer Student Supply 1918-
	Rev. Donald J. Selby, Ph.D.,
	  Supply 1958-

Rev. Aaron R. Tosh, D.D. 1919-1921	Rev. Banks D. Shepherd 1958-1962
	Rev. Felix B. Peck, S.T.D., Stated Supply 1963-

1. ———. Minutes. Classis of North Carolina, Reformed Church in the United States, 1904, p. 337.
2. *Ibid.* 1905, p. 408; 1906, p. 8.
3. *Clapp*, Jacob C., Editor. Historic Sketch of the Reformed Church in North Carolina, 1908, p. 241.
4. ———. Minutes. *Op. cit.*, 1906, p. 10.
5. *Ibid.* 1907, p. 70.
   Peck, Felix B., Manuscript. Boger United Church of Christ, 1964.

Brick Church, Alamance County

IT IS REMARKABLE how much a single family can shape the destiny of a community. The Clapp family of the Brick Church, Guilford County, sometimes referred to as the Beaver Creek Settlement, is an illustration. Rev. Jacob C. Clapp, D.D., one of the illustrious sons of the German Reformed Church in North Carolina, was a member of that clan.

George Valentine Clapp and his brother, John Ludwig Clapp, sailed from Rotterdam on a ship named "James Goodwill," landing in Philadelphia, Pennsylvania September 27, 1727.[1] These brothers were from the Palatinate section around the Rhine River. Their families were liberty-loving, God-fearing people through whose veins flowed blood of the best European strain, who came to America seeking civil and religious liberty.

A choice bit of romance is traditionally tied up with the early part of this story. During the 18 years which followed his arrival in this country, George Valentine Clapp courted and married Mary Albright. It is a well established tradition that, while living in Pennsylvania, Mrs. Clapp dreamed of their migration to North Carolina and the place where they would eventually make their home. She afterwards declared that the hillside east of Brick Church, now a part of the cemetery, was what she saw in her dream. In that cemetery her body was laid to rest.

During the migration which began about 1740, George Valentine and his family came to North Carolina from Berks County, Pennsylvania, landing there about the year 1745. John Ludwig Clapp did not arrive until sometime later, perhaps in 1748, when migration was at high tide.[2] The Clapp families chose land on Beaver Creek for their permanent home, purchasing it from the Colonial Government whose agent was Henry McCulloch.[3] These two families were the founders of the Reformed Church in Guilford and Alamance Counties. Others who joined them about the year 1748 include the Albrights, Courtners, Mays, Swings (Schwencks), Greasons, Ingolds, Hoffman, Fousts (Fausts), Ingles, Linebergers, Whitsells, Sharps (Scherbs), and the Sheperds (Schaeffers).[4]

When cabins had been constructed in which to live and to store supplies, these hardy "Reformed Pioneers" moved to erect a log schoolhouse on the Brick Church site. Here, for 16 of 17 years on each Lord's Day, religious services were conducted by itinerate preachers and appointed laymen. So strongly did the Clapp family figure in those early religious operations, that the congregation by common usage came to be known as Clapp's Church. Ministers known to have visited in the area were two of the "Reformed faith," Rev. James Martin, a Swiss who came in 1759 from South Carolina, and Rev. Richard Dupert, a Hugonot from Gaston County, North Carolina, who appeared in 1764.

About 1764 Reformed and Lutheran neighbors moved jointly to erect a log church on the Low's Lutheran Church site. This building was used by Reformed and Lutheran families until the separation which occurred during the distressing days of the Revolutionary War.[5]

There is no documented record that Clapp's Church was organized prior to 1770. Rev. Samuel Suther, who evidently organized the congregation, became its first regular pastor, conducting services for both the Reformed and Lutheran people in the log house at Low's Church. This relationship did not long continue, because early in the pastorate of Mr. Suther the Reformed congregation was locked out of the Low's Church building. Rather than cause further trouble among neighbors, the Reformed congregation withdrew and began holding services in the schoolhouse on the Clapp's Church grounds.

Dr. George W. Welker, in explaining Mr. Suther's leadership in that community wrote:

> He was an ardent and fearless patriot, and was very obnoxious to the Tories, and was in full sympathy with the men who signed the Mecklenburg Declaration, in whose midst he had lived.[6]
> . . . He was . . . strong in his belief of the doctrines he held and taught, he was ever ready to do battle with all gainsayers. It was his delight to sally forth on adventures as a polemical knight-errant, and it was quite probable that for one of his powerful and sarcastic attacks on the Lutheran peculiar Sacramental doctrines, and their Toryism, he was excluded from Low's Church.[7]

Thus, under the leadership of such men as Ludwig Clapp, Matthias Schwenck and George Gourtner, who were serving as elders in the church at the time, the congregation proceeded to build a house of worship of its own on the site of the old schoolhouse. The new and larger church was not completed until 1786, four years after Mr. Suther had resigned his pastorate and left the community.

Beginning in 1783, except for a brief period of two years when Rev. John Bithahn was pastor, the church was vacant 15 years. However the parish was not without ministerial oversight. Rev. Andrew Loretz made periodic visit to the congregation, baptizing and confirming their young, and performing other functions usually limited to ordained ministers. The consistory also named Elder Jacob Clapp and Schoolmaster Scherer official liturgists, who took care of Lord's Day Services, involving prayers, Scriptures and printed sermons which usually were read by them.

In 1801, Rev. Henry Dieffenbach began his ministry to the congregation, which continued until 1807. Then followed 14 years more when the church was without the services of a regular pastor. Rev. John Loretz resumed periodic visits, and at other times services were led by appointed laymen. As a result of a strong personal plea made by Captain William Albright before the Coetus in 1812 for more pastoral oversight in the Carolinas, the following year Rev. J. R. Riley, a young man of exceptional personal charm and piety, was sent to minister to the churches in Guilford County, Clapp's Parish included.

Mr. Riley's visit did two important things for Clapp's Church. It brought encouragement to discouraged parishioners. On October 16, 1813, fifty seven people who had been prepared for membership by the visiting minister, accepted the vows of the church. It was an experience about which the community talked for many years. Then, too, the log church building that had served the congregation since 1870 had fallen into decay. Under the inspiring leadership of Mr. Riley, instead of erecting a frame building which had already been determined, the members agreed to build one of brick. Since these were prosperous days for the congregation, when Captain Albright, Jacob Clapp and Daniel Albright were influential leaders, necessary funds were raised without difficulty. The brick church was partially built in 1814; however, because of a defect in the foundation which weakened the walls, it was used unfinished until 1841. The walls were then torn away, rebuilt, and the entire structure remodelled.

Because this was the only known brick church building in North Carolina at that time, citizens began to refer to it as "the brick church." Since then the congregation has come to be known as "Brick Church."

Ministers believed to have visited and served the Brick Church community during this period were Rev. John Jacob Larose, 1795; Rev. William Houck, 1818; Rev. Jacob Schell and Rev. John Ebaugh, 1819; and Rev. George Leidy, 1819-1820. From this point in history the fortunes of the Brick Church Parish appear to have changed for the better. Rev. John Rudy became pastor of the church in 1821 and continued to serve it through 1825. He was a man of piety and of unlimited energy, but because of a feud which developed between himself and the Clapp household, he returned to New York. From 1825 to 1828 Rev. William Paisley, a Presbyterian minister, agreed to supply the pulpit, and did so with satisfaction.

At Christmas 1828, Rev. John H. Crawford began a ministry to the congregation which continued almost 12 years. Circumstances required that he face a number of acute current problems, an immediate hazard being the language barrier. Until then the German language was used in all church gatherings and very largely in domestic and business circles. The German people being by nature freedom-loving, home-building and industrious folk, manifested little interest beyond the immediate neighborhood. They were inhibited by culture and language. These characteristics separated them from the main stream of civic, social, political and religious society. Instead of becoming a part of and adjusting to the inclusive environment with which they were surrounded, they became socially and culturally ingrown. Against these conditions the more progressive element and the new generation of young people revolted. The minister, sensing the need for adjustment, began by suggesting that church services be conducted at least in part in English instead of German. His effort met with serious opposition. But the struggle was worth the price which had to be paid. For this was the period in which the German Reformed Church in North Carolina marks the beginning of its emergence into the main stream of the social, political, civic and religious life of the state.

Still another history-making event occurred at Brick Church during this adjustment period. For many years, Southern churches had operated more or less as independent units. Their only ecclesiastical affiliation being the Synod of the German Reformed Church, whose authority, by virtue of numbers and prestige, was located 500 miles away in Pennsylvania. Therefore in May 21-23, 1831, by authority of the Synod, four ministers and four elders, representing the churches in North Carolina, met a Brick Church and officially organized the Classis of North Carolina, predecessor to the Southern Synod of the Evangelical and Reformed Church. Rev. J. G. Fritchey and Col. John Hoke, represented churches west of the Catawba River; Rev. D. B. Lerch and Esquire Milo Roseman, churches between the Catawba and Yadkin Rivers; Rev. William Houck and Col. Phillip Hedrick, churches in Davidson County; and Rev. J. H. Crawford and Col. Daniel Clapp, churches in Guilford and Alamance Counties.[8]

An outstandingly fruitful ministry was brought to a close on September 30, 1840, when Mr. Crawford departed to serve churches in Lincoln County. However, what turned out to be a new and even more eventful ministry was begun in November 1841 by Dr. George W. Welker, who served congregations in the area, Brick Church among them, until he retired in 1893. While serving Brick Church, he ministered to the Mt. Hope people in Guilford County. He also was a moving factor in recovering the scattered members of the Shoemaker's congregation, reorganizing and relocating it near Elon College as St. Mark's Church.

Dr. Welker was not only a great pastor and organizer. He was one of the leading theologians and pulpiteers of his generation in the state of North Carolina. He was a vigorous campaigner against the evils of liquor and the demoralizing social by-products of the Civil War. A reliable parliamentarian and fluid writer, he served the Classis of North Carolina in the office of Stated Clerk for 51 years. His entire ministry was spent in his adopted state on the Guilford Parish. The fruit of his ministry continues to be felt throughout the church in this area.

Dr. James D. Andrew, a protege of Dr. Welker, rounded out a century and a half for the Brick Church congregation. He ministered to the parish from 1893 until 1898. Arriving at this point provided an opportunity for pastor and people to assess their heritage and to think about the future. Dr. Andrew and his successor, Rev. George A. Stauffer who served until 1902, helped Brick Church to take stock of its contribution to the community, church and state, when the Commonwealth was emerging from colonialism into statehood. Nearby is the Alamance Battleground, a constant reminder that many of their husbands and sons died there in the cause of freedom. The old house, perhaps the first brick church erected in the state, stood like a silent sentinel, as a testimonial that the Christian Gospel had been declared there by faithful people for 150 years. The ecclesiastical body of their beloved church, the Classis of North Carolina, had been born in that old house. Many of the personal battles of moral and spiritual ethics had been resolved there by honorable men who sat on the consistory from generation to generation. What a heritage!

But to look back constituted only half of the picture. What of the future? The first 18 years of the 20th Century brought little relief in their search for trained ministerial leadership. During this time seven different pastors served the parish. These were: Rev. William S. Clapp, 1904; Rev. Paul Barringer, 1905; Rev. M. L. Klopfenstein, 1906; Rev. C. Columbus Wagoner, 1907; Rev. J. L. Bowers, 1907-1911; Rev. Dugan C. Cox, 1912-1914; and Rev. Albert Klinger, 1916-1920. Thus, the burden of leadership, not a new experience for the Brick Church people, was destined to again fall primarily upon the shoulders of laymen. Among those who played an active role in the drama of that period were Daniel Albright, William Albright, Abram Shepherd, George W. Clapp, B. Frank Low, Joel W. Clapp and Simon L. Shepherd.

After this came another period of ministerial supplies, when neighboring pastors, because of the press of their own parish responsibilities, could provide only preaching on Sundays and emergency services involving the rites and sacraments. Among those who "went the second mile" were Dr. J. M. L. Lyerly, 1920-1922; Rev. William C. Shaw, 1922-1923; Rev. William H. Groff, 1924; Student Hoy L. Fesperman, during the summers of 1925-1926; Dr. Harvey A. Fesperman, 1926; and Rev. Harvey A. Welker, 1926-1927.

With the arrival of Rev. Charles E. Hiatt, May 27, 1927, began the longest pastorate since the turn of the century and was considered to be a most happy and productive one. In 1931, the congregation was host to the Classis of North Carolina for its Centennial Observation,[9] and in 1934 the old German Reformed Church joined other congregations of like faith in becoming a part of the newly-merged Evangelical and Reformed denomination.

Brick Church appeared to be on its way again when, on May 15, 1938, Rev. Aubrey W. Hedrick appeared and admirably took up where Mr. Hiatt left off, expanding all parts in the life of the church. Rev. Sterling W. Whitener, missionary on leave from China, served the congregation for four years beginning in 1942. Rev. Arthur R. Detwiler, serving as supply for a time, became pastor in 1946. Certain physical improvements which had been started were finished. This was a period of renewed activity and numerical growth. The congregation voted to become a one-point charge on February 13, 1948.

Ministerial supplies again appeared in the persons of Student Richard A. Cheek, Student John Lackey, of the Congregational Christian denomination, Dr. John C. Peeler and Rev. Hoy L. Fesperman. In 1949 a new parsonage was erected on land donated to the church by Otis M. Noah. Rev. John C. Chatlos became the first full-time pastor on January 6, 1950, serving until October 30, 1953.

During the following two years Dr. John C. Peeler served as supply pastor. Under his leadership, the congregation made preparations for some badly needed educational equipment. A building committee was authorized, which developed plans and presented them for approval on February 20, 1955. Construction on the building began the following spring and was completed at a total cost of $50,000 and occupied in 1956.

Due to personal illness, Dr. Peeler was forced to relinquish pastoral duties to the congregation in 1955. Ministerial functions then were provided by Student Bobby R. Bonds, Rev. J. Wayne Fouts, John W. Settlemyre, Rev. C. Donald Lyerly and Dr. Jacob C. Palmer. When, on June 17, 1956, Rev. James R. Cress came to the parish, it was the occasion of his installation as well as the dedication of the new educational facility. In June 1957, once more the old German Church, giving expression to its innate sense of Christian fraternalism, became a member of the United Church of Christ, the most recent venture of the denomination in inter-church cooperation.

Rev. Carroll Eugene Bartholomew began a pastorate here in July, 1963, but resigned in 1965 to enter the chaplaincy of the United States Armed Service. Dr. John G. Truitt is currently serving the congregation as State Supply.

ROSTER OF PASTORS

Rev. Samuel Suther 1770-1781
Rev. John Bithahn 1786-1788
Rev. Andrew Loretz, Supply 1788-1800
Rev. Henry Dieffenbach 1801-1807
Rev. James R. Riley, Supply 1813-1814
Rev. John Rudy 1821-1825
Rev. John H. Crawford 1828-1840
Rev. George W. Welker,
    D.D. 1841-1893
Rev. James D. Andrew, D.D. 1893-1898
Rev. George A. Stauffer 1898-1902
Rev. William S. Clapp,
    Supply 1904-
Rev. Paul Barringer, Supply 1904-1905
Rev. M. L. Lopfenstein,
    Supply 1905-1906
Mr. C. Columbus Wagoner,
    Student Supply 1907-
Rev. Joshua L. Bowers 1907-1911
Rev. Dugan C. Cox 1912-1914
Rev. Albert Klinger 1916-1920
Rev. J. M. L. Lyerly, Ph.D.,
    Supply 1920-1922
Licentiate William C. Shaw,
    Supply 1922-1923
Mr. William H. Groff,
    Student Supply 1924-
Mr. Hoy L. Fesperman,
    Student Supply—Summers 1925-1926
Rev. Harvey A. Fesperman, D.D.,
    Supply 1926-

Rev. Harvey A. Welker,
    Supply 1926-1927
Rev. Charles E. Hiatt 1927-1937
Rev. Aubrey W. Hedrick 1938-1941
Rev. Sterling W. Whitener 1942-1946
Rev. Arthur R. Detwiler 1946-1949
Mr. Richard A. Cheek,
    Student Supply 1949-1950
Mr. John Lackey,
    Student Supply 1949-1950
Rev. Hoy L. Fesperman,
    Supply 1949-1950
Rev. John C. Peeler, D.D.,
    Supply 1949-1950
Rev. John C. Chatlos 1950-1953
Rev. John C. Peeler, D. D.,
    Stated Supply 1953-1955
Mr. Bobby R. Bonds,
    Student Supply 1955-1956
Rev. J. Wayne Fouts, Supply 1955-1956
Rev. John W. Settlemyre,
    Supply 1955-1956
Rev. C. Donald Lyerly,
    Supply 1955-1956
Rev. Jacob A. Palmer, D.D.
    Supply 1955-1956
Rev. James R. Cress 1956-1962
Rev. Carroll E. Bartholomew 1963-1965
Rev. John G. Truitt,
    State Supply 1965-

1. *Whitsett*, W., Thornton. History of Brick Church and the Clapp Family, 1925, p. 1.
2. *Ibid.* p. 7.
3. *Clapp*, Jacob C., Editor. Historic Sketch of the Reformed Church in North Carolina, 1908, p. 119.
4. *Ibid.* p. 120.
5. *Morgan*, Jacob L., History of the Lutheran Church in North Carolina, 1953, p. 236.
6. *Clapp. Op. cit.*, p. 123.
7. *Ibid.* p. 124.
8. ————. Minutes. Classis of North Carolina, Vol. I. 1931 p. —.
9. ————. Minutes. *Op. cit.*, 1931, p. 21 ff.

Bibliography

Cress, James R., Manuscript. History of Brick United Church of Christ, Evangelical and Reformed Church, 1962.
Snider, Frank W., Graduate Thesis. Early Reformed Churches in North Carolina, 1954.

Brightwood Church, Guilford County

CONFERENCES WERE HELD in 1938 with Mr. and Mrs. Thomas F. Huffman and Perry Greeson by Dr. Banks J. Peeler in the interest of establishing a church of their faith in the Brightwood community. Mr. Greeson was a member of the First Evangelical and Reformed Church, Burlington, and Mr. and Mrs. Huffman were members of St. Mark's. A year later Rev. Aubrey W. Hedrick continued these conferences, making arrangements to hold services in the homes of interested people in anticipation of founding a church. The first service was held in the home of Mr. and Mrs. Huffman on October

1, 1939. At that time 24 people indicated that they were interested in becoming members of such an organization.[1]

A second service was held November 5, 1939, in the home of Mr. and Mrs. R. R. Barber, when the Brightwood Evangelical and Reformed Church was officially organized. Twenty-eight people signed the charter member roll, these being Mr. and Mrs. Thomas F. Huffman, Mr. and Mrs. R. R. Barber, Evelyn Andrews, Thelma Rice, Mr. and Mrs. Garland Barber, Mr. and Mrs. James Butler, Mr. and Mrs. Harvey Clapp, Mr. and Mrs. Perry Greeson, Mr. and Mrs. Robert Hinton, Mr. and Mrs. T. D. Craven, Ila Craven, Mr. and Mrs. Owen Hinton, Mr. and Mrs. D. A. Hinton, Mr. and Mrs. Ben Hinton, Mrs. Jack Hinton and Mr. and Mrs. Jack Howell. Thomas F. Huffman and R. R. Barber were elected elders; Maurice Walker, Robert D. Hinton, J. C. Howell, T. D. Craven and Owen Hinton, deacons.

At its winter meeting on February 13, 1940, the congregation was enrolled as a member of Southern Synod of the Evangelical and Reformed Church and placed under the pastoral care of Rev. Aubrey W. Hedrick with a subsidy of $30.[2] At the same meeting the Synod made an appropriation of $1,000 to aid in the erection of a house of worship and set April 7, 1940, as "Brightwood Day" when the Sunday Schools of the Synod were asked to receive a special offering for the Brightwood Mission Fund.[3]

A building committee composed of T. D. Craven, Thomas F. Huffman and Owen Hinton was requested to develop plans for a church building and suggest ways and means of financing it. Sketches providing for a chapel, a foyer and four classrooms were approved and construction was started on a frame structure, located on a lot two miles west of Gibsonville, North Carolina, contributed by Mr. and Mrs. Thomas F. Huffman. By early fall services were being held in the incompleted chapel. Soon thereafter the Sunday School was started.

On December 1, 1940, a large audience witnessed the cornerstone laying ceremony. Activities were in charge of the pastor, assisted by Dr. Jacob C. Leonard, Rev. Joshua L. Levens and Dr. George E. Dillinger. Noticeable expansion occurred in all church activities upon entering the new building. An effective series of evangelistic services was held beginning the week of May 31, 1941. Dr. John C. Peeler was the preacher. Formal dedication of the church building took place on July 6, 1941. Dr. James D. Andrew delivered the dedicatory address, and the pastor conducted the ritual of dedication.

A hut designed to meet social and educational needs was erected in 1944, and finished a number of years later. Most of the work done on it was free labor, and material used in it consisted of voluntary gifts from people who lived in the parish area.

In 1958, Rev. Homer F. Yearick, then supply pastor, considered with the congregation the possibility of arranging for the services of a full-time pastor. A petition was sent to the Board of National Missions, with approval of Southern Synod, asking for enrollment as a mission project with subsidy.[4] The congregation was enrolled by the board with subsidy up to one-half of the salary of the minister, plus rental allowance on a proposed new parsonage. Rent allowances by the board in those days were used by local congregations to retire indebtedness on the property, which policy was approved in this case.

The parsonage was built on a lot donated by Mr. and Mrs. Quint Tickle located two miles northwest of the church on the Bethel Church Road. Plans for the house were adopted by the congregation on February 7, 1954. Construction on it began immediately. Dedication occurred in July of the same year. Rev. J. Wayne Fouts was master of ceremonies. Rev. C. Donald Lyerly, who graduated from The Theological Seminary, Lancaster, Pennsylvania in May 1954, was called to be the first full-time pastor of the church, which was now operating as a mission project under supervision of the Board of National Missions. He was installed June 6, 1954, by Dr. John C. Peeler, Rev. J. Wayne Fouts and Dr. Harvey A. Fesperman.

On July 1, 1964, the congregation purchased for $7,000 the Baldwin property, consisting of six acres of land and a dwelling adjacent to church property on the west side. A changing community has, at times, stymied the physical and numerical expansion of this congregation; however, since no other denomination is represented in the immediate area, it serves a definite need. It is composed of small farms and homes of industrial workers with continuing promise of expanding into a residential area.

These facts explain the reason for brief pastorates and many ministerial supplies, most of which have been arranged with neighboring pastors. Dr. Jacob A. Palmer, who has been serving the congregation as Stated Supply since 1958, lives in retirement at Thomasville, North Carolina. The church is debt-free, and has an enrollment of 119 confirmed members.

ROSTER OF PASTORS

Rev. Aubrey W. Hedrick,
   Organizer and Supply 1939-1941
Rev. William H. Causey, D.D.,
   Supply 1942-
Rev. Sterling W. Whitener,
   Supply 1942-
Rev. John C. Peeler, D.D.,
   Supply 1944-1951
Mr. Keith Sink,
   Summer Student Supply 1951-
Rev. John C. Peeler, D.D.,
   Supply 1951-
Mr. Bobby R. Bonds,
   Summer Student Supply 1952-
Mr. C. Donald Lyerly,
   Summer Student Supply 1952-
Mr. C. Keith Sink,
   Summer Student Supply 1952-

Rev. John C. Chatlos,
   Supply 1952-1953
Rev. Homer F. Yearick,
   Supply 1953-
Mr. C. Donald Lyerly,
   Summer Student Supply 1953-
Rev. J. Wayne Fouts,
   Supply 1953-1954
Rev. C. Donald Lyerly 1954-1957
Rev. James R. Cress,
   Alternate Supply 1957-
Rev. Huitt R. Carpenter,
   Alternate Supply 1957-
Rev. Charles E. Hiatt 1957-1958
Rev. Jacob C. Palmer, D.D.,
   State Supply 1958-

1. *Palmer*, Jacob A., Manuscript. History of Brightwood Evangelical and Reformed Church, 1964, p. 1 ff.
2. ———. Minutes. Southern Synod of the Evangelical and Reformed Church, 1940, p. 42.
3. *Ibid.* p. 19.
4. ———. Minutes. *Op. cit.*, 1953, p. 34.

Calvary Church, Davidson County

CALVARY REFORMED CHURCH, Route 1, Thomasville, North Carolina had its beginning in Moffatt's Grove school house, where as early as 1883 a Mission was "placed under the direction of Rev. Thomas Long until the next meeting of the Classis."[1] In 1888 the Classis of North Carolina heard with pleasure about efforts being made to build a Reformed Church in the vicinity of Thomasville, and appointed the Rev. J. W. Cecil and Rev. Joseph L. Murphy to cooperate in the effort.[2] In 1889, a committee reported that a congregation had been organized at Thomasville, and preparations were being made to build a church there. The Classis appropriated $500 toward the erection of a house of worship, to be paid on a ratio of $100 for each $200 raised by the congregation; also appointed Elder P. J. Leonard and Rev. Lewis Reiter to cooperate in the project. Rev. P. M. Trexler was commissioned to preach at Thomasville once each month until the next meeting of the Classis.[3]

Evidently this plan made limited progress because in 1890, "Thomasville was placed under the care of Revs. J. C. Leonard and A. R. Holshouser, while Classis is ready to aid that congregation in any efforts it may make to carry out their purpose to complete their organization and build a house for worship."[4] In 1891 the Mission at Moffatt's Grove was committed to Rev. J. C. Leonard, who was authorized to organize a congregation at his discretion, and the Classis pledged $100 for each $200 raised by the mission for the erection of a church not to exceed $600.[5] The Historic Sketch of the Reformed Church in N.C. says:

> After several services were held the outlook seemed favorable, and accordingly Calvary Reformed Church was duly organized November 31, 1891, with the following charter members: D. A. Long, Mrs. D. A. Long, John A. Long, Mrs. Mary A. Clinard, R. C. Clinard, Margaret Kanoy, Cicero Kanoy, Minnie Belle Kanoy, Luella E. Kanoy, Martha Belle Kanoy, Lizzie Kanoy, Frances V. Kanoy, A. F. Kanoy, Louisa V. Kanoy, F. W. Kanoy, Mary Ann Kanoy, John Shuler, Natan Ward, Alice Ward, Lottie Kanoy, Eliza Kanoy, Sarah Kanoy.
>
> Immediately afterwards Bethlehem Black and Mrs. Bethlehem Black were received. The first officers were D. A. Long and F. W. Kanoy, elders, and A. F. Kanoy, deacon. All the services were held in the school house.
>
> During the winter and spring the work of building a neat frame church was pushed forward. The lot was donated by Mr. & Mrs. D. C. Moffatt. The members of the church and friends in the community did a great deal of work. The new house of worship was dedicated May 29, 1892. The sermon was preached by Rev. P. M. Trexler, D.D., and the service was conducted by Rev. J. C. Leonard. In 1892 Calvary Church was attached to the Upper Davidson Charge. It remained in that connection until 1896, when it became a part of the newly constituted Thomasville Charge.[6]

In the pastorate of Rev. Dugan C. Cox, 1915 to 1925, the church was rebuilt and enlarged. On September 7, 1908, several acres of land adjacent to church property became available. Exercising admirable foresight, Elder Bethlehem Black for $780 purchased and made it available to the congregation for a cemetery. The ground was surveyed and properly laid off, which in turn has been sold to interested people for burial plots. The cemetery is well-kept and managed through an endowment system, guaranteeing perpetual care.

Calvary Church observed its 50th Anniversary of Organization

November 2, 1941. Dr. Jacob C. Leonard, who had guided the congregation through its early struggling years, was invited to deliver the anniversary sermon. The spirit of the occasion was captured in the unanimous vote by the congregation on that day to make preparations for building a new house of worship. Thus, began activities to discover ways and means for realizing their hopes. A very large building committee was set up, consisting of Rev. William C. Lyerly and Walter Sledge, general chairmen, Curtis Bowers, secretary, Mrs. J. W. Boyles treasurer, R. L. Lopp, Carl Black, Clifton Black, Everett Black, Arthur Black, Lowell Bowers, Cletus Bowers, Earlie Sink, M. W. Jackson, Robert Russell, Ford McCrary, S. P. Ball, Ita Petree, Hite Lambeth, Clayton Alexander, Cromer Alexander, Theo Bowers, Allan Kanoy and J. A. L. Conrad.

First logs were cut on the farm of John A. L. Conrad. In late summer 1944, plans for the sanctuary, with full basement, were accepted. Groundbreaking ceremonies occurred in the spring of 1945. The first service in the new church was the funeral rites for Mrs. Bethlehem Black on May 12, 1947. The house was dedicated April 4, 1948, on Sunday before the Tenth Annual Sessions of the Southern Synod convened in it, beginning April 6. The secretary of the Synod wrote:

> The sessions of Synod met in the new Calvary Church, a beautiful rural Gothic Church that was built during the ministry of Rev. William C. Lyerly. The cost of the new building, furnishings, and work on the grounds was $58,842. The dedication was held Sunday, April 4, 1948, at 2:30. The Rev. W. Calvin Leonard was assisted by Revs. A. Odell Leonard and Lawrence Leonard. The sermon was preached by the Rev. William C. Lyerly. The new Calvary Church was dedicated debt free. The Classis met in Calvary Church in 1895. Calvary Church has given one son to the ministry, the late Rev. David E. Bowers. The church had published a beautiful forty-page brochure for the dedication and this session of the Southern Synod.[7]

Calvary and Zion Churches became a two-point charge January 1, 1946, and continued in this charge arrangement until January 1, 1956. In 1949, a parsonage was built on a lot across the highway in front of the church, involving an expenditure of $15,000. Construction was under the supervision of a committee chaired by Walter Sledge, and its debt was completely liquidated in 1951. In the same year, an additional piece of land adjoining parsonage property on the North was purchased for $800. A Hammond electric organ was installed in the sanctuary April 16, 1953.[8]

Parish activities and numerical growth kept pace with physical expansion. From 1950 to 1957, the confirmed membership increased from 129 to 202 and the Sunday School to an enrollment of 240 pupils. Parish organizations, at that time, included the Women's Guild, Churchmen's Brotherhood, Youth Fellowship, Boy and Girl Scouts. By overture from the congregation, the church was declared by the Southern Synod a self-supported charge January 1, 1956.[9] This new arrangement left the church vacant; therefore, a call was extended to Rev. Aubrey W. Hedrick, who had been serving the Calvary-Zion Charge, to become pastor of Calvary Church, effective January 1, 1956.

In anticipation of much needed educational equipment, a building fund was started on April 8, 1956. A planning committee was set up in 1959, to find ways and means for providing such equipment. A building committee was appointed in 1961, consisting of Cleveland Alexander, Mrs. Peggy Grimes, Mrs. Florence Alexander, Ottis Koontz, Everett Crotts, Walter Sledge and Robert Russell. As a part of the renovation and expansion program in 1962, new windows were installed in fellowship hall, the outside of the church was cleaned and the stone sand-blasted, and one hundred folding chairs were purchased for general use.

In the same year, the building committee was ready to submit plans and specifications for the proposed new educational building. The contract was awarded July 7, 1962, and construction on it began July 10. The facility was completed and occupied in 1963, total cost being $101,339.69.

When Rev. Huitt R. Carpenter came to the parish April 15, 1963, steps were taken to methodically liquidate the $50,000 obligation created in the erection of the new Sunday School building. Norton Chimes with amplifiers were installed free of debt March 1, 1964.

Roster of Pastors

Rev. Jacob C. Leonard, D.D.	1892-1896	Rev. Dugan C. Cox	1915-1925
Rev. Clarence Clapp	1896-1899	Rev. Sterling W. Whitener,	
Rev. Jacob N. Faust	1899-1902	States Supply	1927-1928
Rev. Walter W. Rowe, D.D.	1902-1903	Rev. Sidney C. Safrit	1929-1933
Rev. Fredrick Cromer	1904-1905	Rev. Kendall B. Shoffner	1933-1938
Rev. Lucian Showers	1905-1906	Rev. William C. Lyerly	1938-1946
Rev. Irvin S. Ditzler	1907-1908	Rev. W. Calvin Leonard	1946-1949
Rev. William H. McNairy,		Rev. Aubrey W. Hedrick	1949-1957
D.D.	1908-1909	Rev. Allan L. Rohrbaugh	1958-1962
Rev. Clarence Woods	1910-1913	Rev. Huitt R. Carpenter	1963-
Rev. John B. Swartz	1914-1915		

1. ———. Minutes. Classis of North Carolina, 1883, p. 19.
2. ———. Minutes. *Op. cit.*, 1888, p. 10.
3. ———. Minutes. *Op. cit.*, 1889, p. 7.
4. ———. Minutes. *Op. cit.*, 1890, p. 9.
5. ———. Minutes. *Op. cit.*, 1891, p. 8.
6. *Clapp,* Jacob C., Editor. Historic Sketch of the Reformed Church in North Carolina, 1908, p. 187
7. ———. Minutes. Southern Synod, Evangelical and Reformed Church, 1948, p. 5.
8. *Carpenter,* Huitt R., Manuscript. History of Calvary United Church of Christ, 1965, p. 2 ff.
9. ———. Minutes. Southern Synod, *Op cit.*, 1955, p. 51.

Christ Church, Lexington

Christ Evangelical and Reformed Church, Lexington, North Carolina is an answer to a parish problem that had gradually developed over the years at the downtown First Church. Some sixty members and their families of that congregation, living in an

area northwest of Erlanger Village, were not involved in the total parish program, except for pastoral ministrations. This situation was brought to the attention of the First Church consistory, and a committee of Elders was named with power to act in studying the area. The committee was composed of Irvin L. Sink, Holland E. Shoaf and Paul Hinkle.

A meeting was scheduled October 14, 1945 at the home of Mr. and Mrs. Elmer S. Plummer, Winston Highway and Biesecker Road to which interested people were invited. Eleven representative individuals appeared. Following a period of devotions, the assembly was invited to "explore the reasons" for the meeting. Two things became clear resulting from this discussion. A reasonably large group of people desired some kind of religious activities in that neighborhood under the supervision of the First Evangelical and Reformed Church; and, any effort in that direction should be inclusive, seeking to unify the sharply divided religious interests in that community between a number of "warring" small churches.

Sunday afternoon meetings continued to take place in the Plummer home, in the form of study sessions. The question of how to manage the situation occupied the attention of the group over a period of weeks. In those days, sister denominations had been successfully handling similar problems through a practical development known as "The Outpost." An Outpost is a section of a parish set up under supervision of authorized leaders for the purpose of stimulating interest in education, evangelism and fellowship. This plan appeared to fit the need. Two additional people were added to the committee of elders in the persons of Elmer S. Plummer and Lloyd A. Weaver.

From this point activities began to move in several directions.

Because the Sunday afternoon gatherings had increased in numbers, the Sunday School was organized March 3, 1946. Lloyd A. Weaver was elected superintendent, John Skipper, assistant superintendent, and Elmer S. Plummer, secretary-treasurer. The school was divided into three sections; children under the leadership of Mrs. Elmer S. Plummer, young people supervised by Mrs. Lloyd A. Weaver, and Adults to be taught by the pastor and Charles W. Parks, Irvin L. Sink and R. Leo Leonard, volunteer laymen from First Church.

Once the Sunday School was organized, interest developed in securing property on which could be erected a suitable building for meetings. Mr. and Mrs. Elmer S. Plummer donated a lot across the Winston Highway above their home. Because this lot was too small to meet the need, it was sold and proceeds invested in the present church site, which had been arranged through K. E. Surratt, local realtor. A number of interested friends, in addition to Mr. Surratt, among them Dr. J. A. Smith, I. L. Sink, H. E. Shoaf and Charles W. Parks, paid the balance and made the property available to the committee free of debt.

Plans were drawn for an all-purpose building to be located on the back side of the lot, which could be converted into a dwelling, a recreation hall or classrooms for educational purposes, in anticipation of a sanctuary to be built in front of it facing the Winston Highway. Those were World War II days, when building material was all but prohibitive, most of it rationed, and available only when construction in some way contributed to the National Defense effort. Most of the material had to be selected from surplus stock piles, often of inferior quality. However, through the cooperation of such firms as Griff W. Smith Lumber Company, A. G. Thomason Construction Company, The Coble Dairy, Inc., and the Cunningham Brick Company, construction on the building began in August 1946. Friends and neighbors contributed a great deal of free labor. By December 22nd the house was enclosed. The first scheduled meeting held in the unfinished building took place December 30, 1946, when the Sunday School presented its first Christmas program.

The Church was organized April 2, 1947 by the committee of Elders who had supervised the work from the beginning. Irvin L. Sink, chairman of the committee and the pastor, were in charge of proceedings. Forty one names were on the charter roll, petitioning for a church organization. Lloyd A. Weaver and Elmer S. Plummer were elected elders, and Fred Varner, John Skipper and Fred Biesecker were named deacons. By popular choice the new organization was named "Christ Evangelical and Reformed Church," and the officials were instructed to overture Southern Synod for enrollment. This was done, and Christ Church became a member of Southern Synod April 17, 1947.[1]

Since that time seven more lots in the neighborhood have been added to the property. In 1951 an annex designed for youth activities and educational purposes was added to the north end and west side of the building. Later a floor furnace, pulpit furniture and pews, and appropriate floor covering were installed, greatly improving the utility of the building.

Dr. Banks J. Peeler nurtured and ministered to the congregation from its inception, in addition to his duties as pastor of First Church, until December 1, 1955. The congregation is indebted to Charles W. Parks, R. Leo Leonard and Irvin L. Sink who gave generously of their time and talents during these years, the latter serving as congregational lay leader most of the time. At the end of this period there was a confirmed membership of 118 and a Sunday School enrollment of 168 pupils. There were no debts.

Christ Church began to operate as an unattached congregation upon its enrollment by Southern Synod. Since that time ministers have been appointed by the Synod from year to year as Stated Supply pastors. Rev. Billy Joe Leonard served as Supply pastor beginning 1955, until 1962. Since that time Rev. Roy C. Whisenhunt has been serving under appointment by the Synod. The Twentieth Anniversary of the beginning of Christ Church was observed October 4, 1964 when Dr. Banks J. Peeler was invited to conduct the service and make the anniversary address.

1. ———. Minutes of Southern Synod, Evangelical and Reformed Church. 1947. p. 66ff.

The Church of the Master

As a result of a survey in Northeast Hickory, The Church of the Master was founded. The survey was made by Macedonia and Faith congregations of which Rev. Bobby R. Bonds was pastor and under his supervision. With the approval of Southern Synod, a petition was submitted to the Board of National Missions to be enrolled with subsidy.[1] The petition was made in 1961, and the project was enrolled in 1962. An exploratory meeting was called by the committee on National Missions of Southern Synod for May 2, 1962 and was held in the St. Stephen's Demonstration Club House.

A second meeting was held June 24, 1962, when a sponsoring committee was set up, consisting of C. W. Bumgarner, Mrs. Rena Robinson and James Moir, Sr. Fifteen people were present, representing a potential of forty-five members of the proposed church. Three other committees were authorized at the same time. One to find a pastor, another to arrange for a place for him to live, and still another to provide a place for religious services.

Regular services were begun in St. Stephen's Club House, February 3, 1963. These ministerial functions were shared in turn by Revs. Bobby R. Bonds, Nevin H. Feather, George E. Dillinger, Nevin R. Frantz and Edwin M. Alcorn. Several weeks later a Sunday School was started, supervised by James Moir, Sr. The Sacrament of Holy Communion was first administered to the unorganized group April 14, 1963.

In consultation with Rev. J. Edmund Lippy, Eastern Field Secretary of the Board of National Missions, Rev. Donald P. Flick, Hagerstown, Maryland was recommended as the missionary pastor. He was commissioned by the Board of National Missions, and arrived on the field in October 1963. An intensive survey of the community was launched, followed by door-to-door visitation to determine the constituency of this new venture. Attendance at worship reached an average of eighty people within a few weeks and the Sunday School an enrollment of sixty five pupils. Organization Day was scheduled for February 2, 1964. A description of these activities was reported and published in The Standard.

> The newest congregation within the bounds of Synod is located in the Northeast section of Hickory, North Carolina, and has been christened "The Church of the Master." Rev. Donald P. Flick is the organizing Missionary, who will be installed pastor of the church March 18, 7:30 P.M.
>
> The act of organization took place February 2, at 10:45 A.M. Visiting ministers who assisted in the ceremonies were Secretary J. Edmund Lippy, representing the Board of Homeland Ministries and Dr. Banks J. Peeler, president of the Synod.
>
> A second service of the day took place during the evening, when Revs. Bobby R. Bonds and E. M. Alcorn, members of the organization committee, participated in the worship. It was Area Church Night.
>
> The new church has been carrying on activities in the St. Stephen's Club House. Property has been purchased on which to build the first unit of the church and a parsonage. Construction on the parsonage will probably get under way within a matter of weeks.
>
> The Charter Membership List contained seventy five names, which is expected to reach one hundred by Easter.[2]

C. W. Bumgarner, S. A. Isenhour and Richard H. Edwards were elected elders, and Mrs. Rena Robinson, Mrs. Dorothy Hedrick, Alvin L. Arrowood, Wilber G. Garawan, Steven C. Estes and James W. Moir, Sr., deacons. There were 90 names on the charter roll when it was officially closed on Pentecost, May 17, 1964. The name

of the congregation was "selected by the original group as a reminder to all who came into her fellowship that Christ alone is her
Master and the Director of her actions."[3]

In this venture from the beginning, Catawba County Area United
Churches of Christ manifested a keen interest and became involved.
Four acres of land, to which later five more were added, were purchased as a site for the proposed church building. The Catawba
County churches agreed to provide money with which to pay for
the first five acres. An additional acre of land across the street was
acquired a few months later, on which to erect a parsonage. Since
the pastor and his family were living in a rented house, with the
help of the board and friends, it was built without delay. Its dedication occurred the afternoon of October 4, 1964, when Rev. Frank
K. Bostian, chairman of the Committee on National Missions of
Southern Synod, made an appropriate address. Immediately following these exercises, "Open House" was observed.

Representing the Church Building and Finance Department of
the Board of National Missions, Secretary August Burchardt met
with the congregation October 13, 1964, for the purpose of inaugurating plans in anticipation of the new church building. On the
following November 15 the congregation took action to proceed
with a detailed study of their needs. A building committee was
set up naming an Executive Committee and seven study groups,
involving eighty six people. Virtually the entire congregation was
involved in the venture whose purpose was defined by its chairman.

> A building committee demands serious planning from the beginning
> stages through dedication, for a church is more than the wood and brick
> and mortar used in construction. . . . Walls will be constructed around
> a church program and not a program to fit into a building designed by
> a skilful architect. A building built by a "family of God" should reflect
> its faith and convey its concern for the future. Such buildings do not just
> happen, but demand the thoughts and study of an entire congregation.
> The program of study will be interesting, exciting and rewarding.[4]

The greater part of the year 1965 was spent in hammering out
ideas of the study groups and fashioning them into plans for the
new house of worship. This document which added up to sixty
eight printed pages was placed in the hands of the Architect, who
made drawings based on these findings and submitted them for
approval. Ground was broken November 14, 1965, when Dr. Banks
J. Peeler, president of Southern Synod, made a brief address. Construction on the building was begun January 11, 1966.[5] The Church
of the Master was designed to provide maximum space for a com-
munity-type church program. It includes Sunday School rooms
suited for all ages, week-day kindergarten equipment, an activity
center with a family atmosphere, small party and recreation areas.
The chapel will seat 180 people for worship, and when the same
space is used for table fellowship, 150 guests. The approximate
cost of the project to date is $121,000.

This facility was dedicated to the service of Almighty God the week of September 11, 1966 in a series of well planned activities. Among denominational leaders who appeared on these programs were: Rev. J. Edmund Lippy, Secretary, New Church Development, Board of Homeland Ministries, United Church of Christ; Dr. James H. Lightbourne, Jr., Conference Minister of the Southern Conference; and Rev. Edwin M. Alcorn, Western Area Minister of Southern Conference.

A kindergarten, enrolling thirty-two five-year-old children was started September 1966. Teachers were Mrs. William Rankin and Mrs. Edward Rockett. The Church of the Master has a present membership of 125 confirmed people, representing sixty two families.

1. ———. Minutes. The Southern Synod, 1961. p. 58.
2. ———. The Standard. Vol. LXXII, 1964. p. 4.
3. *Flick*, Donald P., Manuel on Faith and Order, 1963. p. 2.
4. *Estes*, Steve C., Planning to Build a Church, 1964. p. 1.
5. *Flick*, Donald P., A Brief History. Dedication Program, The Church of the Master, 1966. p. 8ff.

Corinth Church, Hickory

EIGHT MONTHS BEFORE Hickory Tavern Village became an incorporated municipality, Corinth German Reformed Church was born. "Hickory Tavern existed as a municipality as of the first Monday in January, 1870."[1] Upon invitation by Henry W. Link and A. L. Shuford, who settled in the community in the spring of 1860, Dr. Jeremiah Ingold, then pastor of the Grace Charge, consisting of Grace, St. Paul's and Bethel churches, conducted services in the village for interested families. These took place under a "brushed covered stand" in summer months, and in the home of Mr. and Mrs. Henry W. Link in winter time. In 1886 the stand burned and these activities were transferred to the "Free Academy" building, where the congregation was organized.

By authority of the Classis of North Carolina the congregation was organized May 22, 1869,[2] under the supervision of Dr. Ingold and attached to the Grace Charge of which he was pastor.[3] There were twenty two charter members: H. W. Link, Catherine Link, Amidus Link, Peter L. Rowe, Adolphus Rowe, Andrew N. Rowe, Martha C. Rowe, William L. Ramsour, Carolina L. Ramsour, Adolphus Shuford, Abel A. Shuford, Abel Whitener, Elisa Whitener, John Fry, Emaline Fry, Susan Whitener, Henry Fry, Isaiah Ingold, William P. Reinhardt, Mary L. Reinhardt, Lovinia Killian, and Etta Graham Ramsour.[4] Henry W. Link and Peter L. Rowe were elected elders, and Abel A. Shuford and Amidus C. Link, deacons. These newly elected officials were immediately ordained and installed in their respective offices.[5]

The congregation worshipped in the academy building until 1871, when H. W. Robinson gave a 100 foot front lot adjoining the academy property on which to erect a church. A. L. Shuford, H. W. Link and W. P. Reinhardt were named to a building committee, which began immediate action. The cornerstone was laid in the fall 1871, and the house, a wooden structure, was finished in the spring of 1874, except for painting.

Remembering that these were reconstruction days following the Civil War, when the economy of the South was at an extremely low ebb, it is understandable that measures for help had to be undertaken. Indeed, this was a common practice through out the Classis involving mission churches at that time. A subscription list which had been authorized by the planning committee met with limited success. Because of these conditions, the Classis of North Carolina in 1871 took action with reference to the church at Hickory Tavern.

> Whereas the prospects of the Reformed Church at Hickory Station are of unusual promise, and as the effort at that place deserves support,—
> Resolved:
> That the Classis approves of the effort to erect a house of worship at that place, and will do all it can to encourage this important work;
> That this enterprise be recommended to the churches and people under the care of Classis as worthy of the bestowment of their means upon it;
> That ministers of Classis be not unmindful of this claim and bring it to the notice of their people;
> That the appeal to our brethren abroad be endorsed by this Classis as an urgent one and a worthy object of liberality.[6]

It is a matter of record that an appeal to the church at large, through the Reformed Church Review was made in 1875 for the Reformed Church at Hickory Tavern. The appeal was signed by H. W. Link and Peter Rowe.[7] J. F. Murrill, secretary of the Consistory in 1877, wrote, "The town of Hickory is comparatively new and the church, recently organized under the care of Rev. Jeremiah Ingold on missionary grounds, became a part of Grace Charge. The congregation though weak in both a numerical and pecuniary way, by encouragement of small contributions from distant friends and their own unfaltering efforts, succeeded in building a house of worship, the second in the town."[8]

The first church building burned March 26, 1887. Services were held in the First Presbyterian Church until the brick building was finished later in the same year. Dedication services did not take place until June 28, 1890. The congregation became a self-supported, independent charge in 1903, breaking away from Grace and Bethel churches with which they had been associated for a long period of time. Dr. Joseph L. Murphy, who had been serving the three point charge, resigned the former and became the first full-time pastor of the fast-growing Corinth Church.

By 1905 the congregation had out-grown the "little brick church." On September 20 of that year, A. A. Shuford proposed that a new house of worship be built, thereupon action was taken to purchase the Thurston property. G. H. Geitner and J. L. Murphy were asked to devise plans for the proposed building, which plans were adopted March 13, 1907. Subsequently a building committee was appointed by the Consistory consisting of A. A. Shuford, J. C. Fry, G. H. Geitner, E. L. Shuford, C. H. Geitner, S. L. Whitener and R. L. Whitener.[9] The corner stone was laid October 19, 1909, and the first service was held in the new church November 6, 1910. Dedication took place December 10, 1911.

In 1940 this third church building was completely redecorated. On the occasion of its rededication, Dr. Paul S. Leinbach, editor of the Reformed Church Messenger, made the address. In observing the 75th Anniversary of the organization of the church, a series of significant services were prepared, and scheduled for the week beginning with May 17, 1944. Speakers on that occasion were: Dr. Walter W. Rowe, Dr. George T. Fitz, Dr. Robert V. Moss, Jr. and Dr. George W. Richards. In 1952 the Sunday School section of the church building was altered and completely renovated at a cost of $25,000.

Because of a pressing need for additional educational facilities June 12, 1955, the congregation accepted "an offer" from the Shuford Mills, Inc., of a ten acre tract of land located in the Northeast section of the city as a site on which to erect a proposed new church. A planning committee composed of John G. H. Geitner, Cecil T. Bost and Harley Shuford was authorized. From this preliminary planning grew a parish Building Committee involving a very large part of the church membership. Groundbreaking ceremonies for the new church took place November 4, 1956, and the cornerstone was laid November 16, 1958. Dr. Harvey A. Fesperman, president of Southern Synod, made the address on the latter date. Departure was taken from the old church August 23, 1959, when the pastor Dr. Harry D. Althouse, who had guided the people through these days of construction, spoke feelingly of "The Days of Old."

Dedication services were held in the new "temple of worship" Sunday morning September 6, 1959, when the minister spoke on the topic, "The Master Builder." Southern Synod Night was observed in the evening of the same day, when Dr. Harvey A. Fesperman, president of Southern Synod and Dr. William T. Scott, superintendent of the Southern Convention of the Congregational Christian Churches, delivered addresses. The Sacrament of the Holy Communion was administered September 13, and that same afternoon William Self, organist and choir master of St. Thomas Episcopal Church, New York City, presented a program of appropriate organ music. Dedication of memorials took place September 20, when the address was delivered by Dr. Robert V. Moss, Jr., president of Lancaster Theological Seminary, a son of the congregation and great grand-son of Dr. Jeremiah Ingold.

The fourth sanctuary of this strategically important and widely influential congregation is a "temple of beauty," symbolizing devotion to Almighty God and a sharing of minds and money in the Cause of Christ. The following description is apt.

> Corinth Church was designed to retain the solemn dignity of old European cathedrals. The exterior of the building is of gray Georgia granite with Indiana limestone trim. The spire is of extruded and structural aluminum rising 164 feet and six inches from the terrace floor at the entrance. The windows in the sanctuary are of English stained glass set in lead cames with the entire window assembly being set in limestone frames, with limestone mullions and limestone tracery. The altar is of white Italian marble. In addition to the magnificent sanctuary for worship and solemn meditation, the church building provides an ample educational plant together with recreational facilities for its membership.[10]

Corinth Church has been widely influential in the life of the denomination of which it is a part, first the German Reformed Church, then the Evangelical and Reformed Church, and more recently in the United Church of Christ. The Classis of North Carolina met here in 1873, 1903, 1919, 1934; the Synod of the Potomac in 1911; the General Synod of the Reformed Church in the United States in 1923.

The congregation has made good investments of kind in the missionary enterprise of the denomination. Beside accepting its full share of the benevolent program of the church, it has in large measure been influential in starting four mission projects in the Hickory area. In the spring of 1901 a Sunday School was begun in Brookford which has since grown into a congregation of considerable influence. In more recent years "West Hickory Mission" and "Macedonia Church" have been beneficiaries of Corinth benevolence. Due largely to shifting population these congregations have been either disbursed or merged into other more promising groups, such as the fast-growing Church of the Master. In each of these units Corinth people have investments of leadership and money.

Perhaps the major concern of this church has been education, in particular education for young women. Of interest in this connection is a statement which appears in the Historic Sketch of the Reformed Church in North Carolina on this subject.

> At a meeting of the Consistory held in the home of Mrs. Livinia Wilfong April 24, 1880, she stated that she had the promise from Mr. and Mrs. H. W. Robinson of a part of the "Old Hickory Tavern Lot" as a donation for the new church. This was accepted and a motion carried that a new church be built and that the present church be converted into a school building for girls. It was also moved that a competent lady teacher be employed to cooperate with Messrs. Blair and Ivey, who were then conducting a mixed school in part of the church building. This was the beginning of Claremont College, for on the 10th day of July, 1880, the Consistory met at the home of Mr. A. L. Shuford for the purpose of considering a proposition from Rev. A. S. Vaughn to return to North Carolina and build up a female school of high grade in the town of Hickory.
>
> At a meeting of the Consistory held in August of the same year Rev. Mr. Vaughn appeared. . . . At this meeting a committee of arrangements made a report. The committee consisted of the following persons: J. F. Murrill, A. L. Shuford, A. A. Shuford, A. C. Link, Rev. J. Ingold, W. P. Reinhardt, M. L. McCorkle, S. T. Wilfong and J. W. Robinson. Six others making fifteen in all were to be chosen from other denominations as provided in the charter.
>
> We note the fact that the conception of the school was in the Consistory, that it was the Consistory that invited Rev. Mr. Vaughn to North Carolina, that the plan of arrangement was reported to the Consistory and that three-fifths of the Trustees must be members of the Reformed Church. It is safe to say that Claremont College owes its existence to Corinth congregation.[11]

When it became necessary to merge the interests of Claremont College with Catawba College, seeking to meet strenuous demands laid upon church related schools by the State of North Carolina, this congregation continued its interests in the schools of the church, particularly in Catawba College.

Two sons of this congregation appear on the denomination's roll of ministers: Dr. Walter W. Rowe, a strong and convincing preacher, who also served as professor of New Testament Literature at Central Theological Seminary, Dayton, Ohio; and Dr. Robert V. Moss, Jr., president of The Theological Seminary, Lancaster, Pennsylvania.

Keeping pace with the demands for professional services created by a growing church and an expanding constituency, in recent years, the church staff has been enlarged to include a Director of Christian Education and an Assistant Minister. Miss Jeanne Ingold has been serving as Director of Christian Education since 1957. Rev. Edwin M. Neff began a ministry of two years as an assistant in 1964, and Rev. John E. Harrison followed him in 1966.

ROSTER OF PASTORS

Rev. Jeremiah Ingold, D.D. ..1860-1874
Rev. Julius H. Shuford 1874-1876
Rev. Jacob C. Clapp, D.D.,
  Supply 1876-
Rev. John A. Foil, Ph. D.,
  Supply 1877-
Rev. Jeremiah Ingold, D.D. ..1878-1881
Rev. A. S. Vaughn 1881-1883
Rev. A. P. Horn 1883-1884
Rev. G. D. Gurley, Supply 1884-1885

Rev. Lewis Reiter 1885-1890
Rev. Joseph L. Murphy, D.D. 1890-1917
Rev. Walter W. Rowe, D.D. 1918-1924
Rev. Goerge Longaker 1924-1929
Rev. Harry D. Althouse, D.D. 1930

Assistant Pastors
Rev. Edwin M. Neff 1964-1966
Rev. John E. Harrison 1966-1968

1. *Presler,* Charles J., Jr., Editor. A History of Catawba County, 1954, p. 344.
2. ———. Minutes. Classis of North Carolina, 1869, p. 60.
3. ———. Minutes. *Op. cit.,* 1870, p. 74.
4: *Rowe,* Mildred Miller, Historical Sketch, Corinth Evangelical and Reformed Church, United Church of Christ, 1959, p. 2 ff.
5. *Clapp,* Jacob C., Editor. Historic Sketch of the Reformed Church in North Carolina, 1908, p. 316.
6. ———. Minutes. *Op. cit.,* 1871, p. 97.
7. *Rowe. Op. cit.,* p. 2.
8. *Clapp. Op. cit.,* p. 317.
9. *Rowe. Op. cit.,* p. 3.
10. ———. Manuscript. Corinth Church, 1964, p. 5.
11. *Clapp. Op. cit.,* p. 319.

Daniel's Church, Lincoln County

DANIEL'S REFORMED CHURCH stands on the oldest piece of ground in Lincoln County, dedicated to the causes of religion and education. The site is located fives miles northwest of the city of Lincolnton, and was a gathering place for German settlers before Lincolnton was incorporated. Its origin can be traced to 1750, some think earlier, when German migrants came to North Carolina from Pennsylvania, and found their way through the Piedmont section of the State, crossed the Yadkin River and arrived in the South Fork basin. They were "trappers on-the-move;" but, looking for a place to establish homes, most of them found this area to be to their liking. Two groups of them stopped in the western part of Lincoln County, in what came later to be known as "The Warlick Settlement," and "Ramsour's Mill."

These settlements took their names from representative families; the former from John Daniel Warlick and the latter from Derrick and John Ramsour. All three of these gentlemen were large land-owners, and influential in community affairs, particularly the "School House Church" and school. Other pioneers who joined these settlements were, the Lantzs, Summerrows, Hochs (Hokes), Reinhardts, Kistlers (Canslers), Coulters, Heedricks, Housers, Carpenters, Anthonys, Bierds, Clays and others, creating quite a colony of Dutch folks.[1]

A Nixon, writing in 1898, describes those hardy people as follows.

> Your lots have indeed been cast in a goodly country, and the lines have fallen to you in pleasant places. It speaks well for the judgment and wisdom of your ancestors that they selected and secured much of the finest lands. It speaks well for you that the same lands are today maintained in high state of cultivation. A glance at your forests of hickory and oak with scarcely a pine to be seen indicates a strong fertile soil. A glance at your valleys black with growing corn and great fields swaying with golden harvests proves that you are good farmers.
>
> The people of this community belong to the great toiling masses of middle classes. They have been industrious, law-abiding, God-fearing people where labor has been dignified and honorable. Their wants were few, they bought little and sold much; they made no debts or contracts they did not expect to pay or execute, and as a consequence, they have been a gallant, brave, independent and public spirited community. No one has ever become very rich and the very poor is a rare exception. The young have been trained and skilled in every ordinary labor and handicraft, but farming has always been the principal occupation. This was the original and natural employment of our race and today it stands foremost among all pursuits of man. It is in fact the foundation of all others. In the expressive language of an old adage, "It makes all, pays all, supports all.[2]

This is the nature and quality of people who settled in the Old Dutch School House neighborhood. Here they worshipped under the title of the "Old School House Church," until 1833, when the congregation for good reasons changed the name to "Daniel's Church," It was an act designed to reflect, in some measure, the unselfish devotion of John Daniel Warlick and his family.

The land on which this school house had been erected consists of a fifty acre tract, evidently laid out earlier by farsighted churchmen to be used for religious and educational purposes. It was a grant from King George III to one Matthew Floyd, made October 26, 1767. The following year, July 15, Mr. Floyd sold that land to a group of public spirited citizens in the community, Nicholas Warlick, Frederick Wise, Urban Ashebanner, Peter Stotler, Peter Summey and Teter Hafner, for ten pounds sterling. These citizens in turn, on January 9, 1774, conveyed it to "the two united congregations of Lutherans and Calvinists" (Reformed). Additions to this property since that time bring land holdings of the two congregations together to sixty-seven acres.[3]

To settle certain questions that had been raised about who would be entitled to share in the use of the property, December 29, 1962, the grant was resubmitted to state authority for clearance. The document was cleared and attested January 20, 1863, and signed by Governor Z. B. Vance; then, July 25, 1863, conveyed to the "Trustees of Daniel's Evangelical Lutheran and Reformed Churches."[4]

These two Churches continued to worship together in the School House Church until 1844, when a frame structure was built. In order to avoid friction, May 27, 1844, articles of agreement were formulated by which the new church building was to be erected. One line in these provisions is of interest in this connection. It says, "There is not to be any formal dedication of said church during the time the said congregations shall both occupy it and worship therein, but it is to bear the name Daniel's Church." However, after 34 years, in August 1878, by agreement the house of worship was "solemnly consecrated to the Service of the Triune God and the Evangelical Lutheran and Reformed Churches."[5] The act of consecration was in charge of the pastors, Rev. J. R. Peterson, Lutheran, Rev. J. H. Shuford, Reformed, Dr. Jacob C. Clapp delivered the consecration address.

This frame church building served the two congregations together until 1888. Observing that decay had played a damaging role on the old house, and that it no longer satisfactorily served the needs of the people, they acted to separate and each build their own house of worship. The Lutheran congregation dedicated its new church building July 28, 1889. While the Reformed congregation took action July 6, 1889 to build a new church, which was finished and ready for dedication April 1, 1894. Dr. Joseph L. Murphy made the dedicatory address. Thus, amicably coming to the parting of ways, they were destined to serve and worship side by each through the years to come. For the two houses of worship were located on the same property, only three hundred feet apart.

Titus Rhodes, Henry D. Warlick, Eli D. Ramsour, A. C. Hottenstein and W. E. Miller formed the committee which planned and directed the erection of the building. It was a brick structure, smaller than the Lutheran church, with a tower and spire, which could be seen as far away as Lincolnton. This church building was used until July 10, 1936, when it was struck by lightening and burned.

The school house, erected on church land prior to 1767, testifies to the value placed upon education in the life of the Dutch Community. It is certain that the house served a dual purpose for them over a period of years, but in 1882 it had evidently completed its mission. For February 22, 1882 a lot adjoining church grounds was purchased from C. and W. H. Motz, and conveyed to a committee consisting of David A. Coon, Jacob H. Rhodes and David W. Ramsour, on which a brick school house was built. As late as 1898 it was referred to "as the best public school house in Lincoln County."[6]

The date when Daniel's Reformed Church was organized has not been established. It is known that, prior to 1786, Daniel's Church site was a favorite preaching place among available Reformed preachers. Rev. James Martin met appointments there from 1759 to 1764, perhaps earlier.[7] Some historians believe that the church may have been organized during his tenure. It is important to remember that, upon the arrival in 1765 of John Frederick Dubbert in the community, itinerate preaching engagements appear to have diminished, if not stopped all together for a time. When Mr. Dubbert moved from South Carolina, April 16, 1765, he was given a grant of land on Beaver Dam Creek, where he made his home until 1778. He was the first resident Reformed minister west of the Catawba River, and undoubtedly figured largely in the life of the Daniel's congregation,[8] and could very well have been instrumental in strengthening if not effecting the organization. Rev. Samuel Suther also living between the Catawba and Yadkin Rivers in upper South Carolina about that time, continued his periodic visits to communities where Reformed Churchmen resided, among them Daniel's.[9]

With the arrival of Rev. Andrew Loretz in 1786, began a new era for Daniel's Church. He came to the Parish at the youthful age of 25 years, built a house among the people, and served them for twenty-six years. A Colleague writes feelingly about him.

> Daniel's Church owes its existence today to Rev. Andrew Loretz, more than to any other man. In fact the same can be said of all the churches under the care of North Carolina Classis. With a zeal that shunned no labor or privation, he gave himself to the work of visiting and preserving the churches in this State and in South Carolina.[10]

A grateful people, in January 1905, placed a bronze tablet in the church on the wall immediately back of the pulpit desk in his memory, which is the gift of a granddaughter, Mrs. Catherine R. Cochran, Boston, Massachusetts. The inscription reads: "In memory of Rev. Andrew Loretz, Born in Church, Switzerland, 1761. Died in Lincoln County, North Carolina, March 31, 1812. 'I have fought a good fight, I have finished my course, I have kept the faith.'"[11]

The Classis of North Carolina authorized a committee composed of Revs. Hoy L. Fesperman, John A. Koons and Elders Henry D. Warlick and Kenneth A. Link, to raise funds and to erect a suitable monument in the Daniel's Church Cemetery in memory of Mr. Loretz. The marker was unveiled and dedicated, May 31, 1936. Exercises were in charge of Dr. O. Bain Michael, pastor of the church, and the address was made by Dr. Jacob C. Leonard.[12]

From 1812 to 1906, twenty four ministers and theological students served the Daniel's Parish as pastors and/or supply preachers. One of these vacancies stretched out over twelve years. The shortage of ordained ministers, required that pastors share their time with other less fortunate churches scattered throughout the two Carolinas. It was, therefore, not unusual for a pastor to be away from his parish weeks at the time, while satisfying the spiritual needs of his fellow Churchmen and their families. Synod also sent out missionaries to these Churches to help fill the gap created by long vacancies. Among these missionaries were, Revs. James Riley, Jacob Schull, John S. Ebaugh, John Rudy and W. C. Bennet, all of whom evidently visited Daniel's Church.[13]

The brick church with a spire, that had served the congregation for forty two years, on July 10, 1936, was struck by lightening and burned to the ground, including practically all of its furnishing. Reflecting a brotherly spirit, like which had motivated the community since its beginning in 1750, the Lutheran congregation made available to the Reformed people their sanctuary, which was used for religious activities until the new Daniel's Reformed Church was ready for dedication. Under the leadership of their pastor, Dr. O. Bain Michael, and supported by the building committee composed of Hugh Warlick, Hugh Holly, T. A. Warlick, J. D. Warlick, T. F. Abernethy, C. F. Lantz and Henry D. Warlick, plans were developed for a new house of worship to be erected on the old site. Construction began immediately, and proceeded without delay, so that on October 31, 1937, the beautiful new "temple" of Gothic design, fit for a shrine was completed and made ready for dedication.

Extensive preparations were made for the occasion. Activities included three major public meetings. Actual dedication took place at 11:00 A.M., in charge of the pastor. Dr. Walter W. Rowe delivered the dedicatory address. At 2 P.M. a Service of Fellowship and Praise, in charge of Elder J. W. Warlick, occurred. The address was made by Dr. H. D. Althouse. The Western District Young Peoples' Institute convened in the afternoon and evening beginning at 4:30. Twenty ministers and educators were present for these history-making activities, among them President Howard R. Omwake of Catawba College. There were letters of greeting from fifteen boards and agencies of the denomination, including a number of former pastors.

Never numerically strong, its membership ranging from 80 in 1889, when the congregation built its own house of worship, to 60 in 1965, Daniel's Church has been associate through the years with from one to three other Churches, forming a Charge. A major cause for this limited membership, explained by churchmen, is due in great measure to large landholdings in this section of Lincoln County, traced to the beginning of the settlement. Much of the property has been passed down, in unbroken succession, from one generation to the next. A growing number of recent generations of young people have followed industry, merchandising, and the professions into more thickly populated centers of the State, leaving the "good land" to be tilled for the most part by tenants. This situation has created problems for the area, socially, economically as well as religiously.

Seeking to do something about the situation, in 1955, at the suggestion of Rev. Roy E. Leinbach, Jr., the Board of National Missions of the Evangelical and Reformed Church, was overtured to make a study of the South Fork Charge. The Charge consisted of Bethel, St. Paul's Grace and Daniel's churches. This was done through the board's Department of Town and Country Life, resulting in a division of the Charge, creating a parish out of Daniel's and Grace Churches. This new Charge was enrolled by the Board of National Missions for a period of five years, with a decreasing subsidy, subject to certain parish program adjustments.[14] A modern parsonage was erected in 1957, and on June first of that year, Rev. Robert F. Godfrey moved in to undertake the new venture.

This adjustment helped the situation, but due chiefly to extended vacancies and short pastorates, results of the effort have not been conclusive. A more recent study of the whole area, involving churches in Catawba and Lincoln Counties, has been made by the same agency. A group of these churches, including Daniel's, is presently involved in discussions, seeking answers to the current situation. In the meantime, to sell old historic Daniel's short, would be both shortsighted and tragic. Out of this congregation has gone many of the influential Christian leaders of the Evangelical and Reformed Church, now active in congregations scattered throughout the State of North Carolina. Rev. Charles W. Warlick, D.D. is a son of this congregation.

ROSTER OF PASTORS

Rev. Andrew Loretz 1786-1812	Rev. Theodore Hesson 1897-1902
Revs. James Riley, Jacob Schull,	Rev. Calvin B. Heller 1902-1906
John S. Ebaugh, John Rudy, W.	Rev. Samuel W. Beck 1906-1909
C. Bennet, Supplies 1812-1828	Rev. Harvey G. Kopenhaver 1910-1915
Rev. John G. Fritchey 1828-1840	Mr. Harvey A. Fesperman,
Rev. G. A. Leopold 1840-1841	Supply 1915-1916
Rev. John H. Crawford,	Rev. Harvey A. Fesperman,
Supply 1841-1842	D.D. 1916-1921
Rev. Solomon S. Middlekauff 1842-1845	Mr. Banks J. Peeler,
Rev. David Crooks 1846-1859	Summer Student Supply 1921-
Rev. Jeremiah Ingold, D.D. 1859-1874	Rev. John B. Swartz 1921-1922
Rev. Juluus H. Shuford 1874-1876	Rev. Banks J. Peeler 1923-1924
Rev. Jacob C. Clapp, D.D., Rev.	Rev. Ezra Gunther 1926-1927
John A. Foil, Ph.D.,	Rev. William C. Lyerly 1928-1931
Supplies 1876-1878	Mr. Carl H. Clapp,
Rev. Julius H. Shuford 1878-1880	Summer Student Supply 1931-
Rev. A. S. Vaughn, Supply 1880-1883	Rev. Huitt R. Carpenter 1932-1935
Rev. A. P. Horn 1883-1884	Rev. O. Bain Michael,
Rev. G. Dickey Gurley 1884-1885	S.T.D. 1935-1941
Rev. Joseph L. Murphy,	Rev. John A. Koons, Supply 1941-1942
D.D. 1885-1890	Rev. Karl R. Flocken 1942-1945
Mr. C. A. Starr,	Vacant—Supplies ? 1945-1946
Summer Student Supply 1890-1891	Rev. William C. Lyerly 1946-1953
Rev. J. M. Luther Lyerly,	Rev. Roy E. Leinbach, Jr.
Ph.D. 1892-1893	Supply 1954-
Rev. Jacob C. Clapp, D.D. 1894-1897	Rev. Roy E. Leinbach, Jr. 1954-1957

Rev. Robert F. Godfrey 1957-1960
Rev. Terrell M. Shoffner,
  Supply 1961-
Mr. Lynn Finger,
  Summer Student Supply 1961-
Rev. G. Ermine Plott,
  Supply 1961-1962

Rev. Martin L. Bupp, II. 1962-1964
Rev. G. Ermine Plott,
  Supply 1964-1965
Mr. William J. Campbell,
  Summer Student Supply 1965-1966
Rev. Donald S. Selby, Ph.D.,
  Supply 1966-

1. *Clapp*, Jacob C., Editor, Historic Sketch of the Reformed Church in North Carolina, 1908, p. 250.
2. *Nixon*, A., History of Daniel's Evangelical Lutheran and Reformed Churches, 1998, p. 55ff.
3. *Clapp. Op. cit.*, p. 251.
4. *Nixon. Op. cit.*, p. 7.
5. *Clapp. Op. cit.*, p. 253.
6. *Nixon. Op. cit.*, p. 6.
7. *Leonard*, Jacob C., History of the Southern Synod, Evangelical and Reformed Church, 1940, p. 303.
8. *Leonard*, Philip L. Manuscript. History of Daniel's Reformed Church, —.
9. *Leonard. Op. cit.*, p. 303.
10. *Clapp. Op. cit.*, p. 225.
11. *Leonard. Op. cit.*, p. 307.
12. ————. Minutes. Classis of North Carolina, 1937, p. 37.
13. *Clapp. Op. cit.*, p. 262.
14. ————. Minutes. Southern Synod of the Evangelical and Reformed Church, 1956. p. 38.

Edgewood Church, Burlington

EDGEWOOD UNITED CHURCH OF CHRIST, Burlington, North Carolina, was the second missions established jointly by the Evangelical and Reformed Church and the Congregational Christian churches in North Carolina following the merger. In financially underwriting the project, matching funds were contributed by the respective national boards for church extension. Boards and agencies of the United Church of Christ had not been merged at that time, so this mission became one of two ventures in the area of cooperation, the other being St. Peter's Church, Greensboro.[1]

A committee on cooperation, representing the three elements of administration, was set up early in 1958. First Evangelical and Reformed Church of Burlington was represented by Dr. Lonnie A. Carpenter, Duncan C. Bryan and John Xanthos; First Congregational Christian Church of Burlington was represented by Rev. Robert M. Kimbell, Mrs. Robert Morton, Jr., Dr. John R. Kernodle, Jr., and Mrs. Jessie Strader. The boards and agencies were represented by Dr. Harvey A. Fesperman of Southern Synod, Dr. William T. Scott of the Southern Convention, Rev. Ira Black of the Congregational Christian Board of Home Missions and Rev. J. Edmund Lippy of the Board of National Missions of the Evangelical and Reformed Church.

Interested people gathered for a first meeting on November 2, 1958, in the home of Mrs. Jessie Strader, Alamance Acres, Burlington. Rev. G. Harold Myers, who had developed a mission in Raleigh, North Carolina, was approved by the boards and commissioned missionary-on-the-field. He moved with his family into the recently acquired parsonage, located at Edgewood Avenue Extension and Forestdale Drive. The property had been purchased through church extension agencies for the sum of $15,000 and financed by a local committee of trustees.

Services were held in the home of Mr. and Mrs. Everett Knight beginnig March 1, 1959. The Church School was started April 5, 1959, enrolling 55 pupils. Lacking space large enough to accommodate this enrollment, it was divided into four sections and met in the homes of W. A. Ray, Clinton Hester, Claude Ward and Robert Morton, Jr.[2]

The congregation was officially organized on June 7, 1959, in the back yard at the home of Mr. and Mrs. Everett Knight. Fifty-two people were received into the Fellowship on that date. By the time the charter member list was declared closed on June 5, 1960, 81 names were on the roll. President Harvey A. Fesperman of Southern Synod preached the sermon and presided over organization proceedings. Rev. G. Harold Myers, pastor of the church, Dr. William T. Scott, Superintendent of the Southern Convention, and Rev. Robert M. Kimbell, pastor of the First Congregational Christian Church, assisted in the act of organization.

Of interest in this connection is the Statement of Belief drawn up by the congregation and approved by them before the church was founded:

We believe:
—That the Lord Jesus Christ is the head of the Church.
—That the Sacraments of the Church, instituted by Christ, are Holy Baptism and the Lord's Supper.
—That the mission of the Church is to call men to a saving knowledge of Jesus Christ, and to labor for the promotion of justice, the reign of peace, and the realization of human brotherhood.
—That the right of private judgment and the liberty of conscience

is a privilege to be accorded to all, but in all cases the final norm is the Word of God.

—That the congregation is allowed freedom of worship and government, as long as they adhere to the principles of the United Church of Christ.[3]

Two weeks later, June 21, 1959, a "temporary" church council was elected by the congregation. Mrs. Jessie Strader was named president; Rector Hunt, vice president; Mrs. Everett Knight, secretary; and Marvin Bryan, treasurer. Marvin Bryan, Rector Hunt, Everett Knight, Mrs. Jessie Strader and Claude Ward were named deacons; Earl Holt, chairman, Clinton Hester, Duncan C. Bryan, Paul Ellis and Rector Hunt were chosen trustees. Installation services for the missionary pastor were conducted September 29, 1959, by Dr. Fesperman and Martin T. Garren, president of the Southern Convention of the Congregational Christian churches. Mr. Garren delivered the address.

The young congregation moved immediately to provide a church home. A tract of land, consisting of five acres, located at the corner of Edgewood Avenue and Turrentine Road, was purchased from Duncan C. Bryan and H. A. Miller for $28,000. Shortly thereafter plans were approved for an all-purpose building, containing 6,900 square feet, allowing for a chapel and suitable educational facilities.

Groundbreaking activities took place November 1, 1959. Construction on the building began eight days later. The structure was complete in April 1960 at a cost of $69,725 and immediately occupied. Vernon Lewis, a member of the congregation, served as architect. Dedication rites took place June 5, 1960, and was presided over by the pastor. He was assisted in the service by Dr. Harvey A. Fesperman and Dr. J. Earl Danieley.

The congregation is self-supporting and has a confirmed membership of 191 people. It is organized for parish activities covering such areas as church school, Women's Guild, Churchmen's Fellowship, youth ministry and scouts. A capacity kindergarten is conducted during the winter months.

ROSTER OF PASTORS

Rev. G. Harold Myers 1958-1965   Rev. Mark W. Andes 1965-

1. ———. Minutes. Southern Synod, 1958, p. 58; 1959, p. 63.
2. *Mebane*, Barbara S., Edgewood United Church of Christ, 1964, p. 1 ff.
3. ———. Church Directory. Edgewood United Church of Christ, 1965, p. 1.

Emanuel Church, Davidson County

THE SITE of Emanuel Reformed Church, Route 2, Thomasville, North Carolina, was a focal point before a congregation was organized at that place. An old grave stone in the church cemetery bears the date of 1808; some other stones were not marked at all in those

early years. No specific date marks the organization of the congregation; although, if the original deed for the land can be regarded as significant, it must have occurred sometime prior to or during the year 1813. The deed for the land upon which the church stands is dated February 20, 1813, and was made to Philip Kanoy, Jacob Myers, Sr., and John Bowers by John Myers and his wife Elizabeth. The original tract contained three acres and the price was five dollars. Philip Kanoy, Jacob Myers, Sr. and John Bowers in the deed were referred to as "Elders of the Presbyterian (Reformed) and Lutheran German Churches."[1] Jacob Myers, Sr. and John Bowers were of the Reformed faith; it is supposed that Philip Kanoy may have been a Lutheran. At any rate the property from the beginning was jointly owned by Reformed and Lutheran people and the congregation operated as a union church.

> The first house built on the grounds here was a log structure, preceded by a brush arbor under which services were held whenever a visiting minister could be secured. Services were also held in the homes of the people, whenever a minister or a school teacher could be pressed into service. Prayer meetings and even preaching services were often held by the elders of the church in the long intervals when no minister could be had. The log house was used for both school and church purposes. . . . . .
> The name by which the first church was known is "Bowers Meetinghouse," after the original Jacob Bowers whose daughter Elizabeth Myers (wife of John Myers) donated the three acres of land. The proper name for the church has always been Emanuel.[2]

Absolom Grimes, David Myers and Lewis Livengood were the first Elders named in the records. Principal Reformed families were the Grimes, Myers, Imlers, Shulers, Lohrs, Livengoods, Veitches, among others.[3]

The second house of worship was begun in 1813, and finished the following year. It was a frame two-story building. There were galleries on three sides; on the fourth side stood a high pulpit from which the minister delivered the sermon. In those days the sermon was the main concern of the service, and churches were constructed to emphasize it. There were no Sunday Schools, but pastors conducted catechetical schools in which members, and those anticipating the vows of church membership, were instructed in the fundamentals of the faith. This church building was destroyed by fire on Sunday afternoon January 12, 1901. But on the same site, another more handsome building was erected, and finished the following year, equipped with a tower in which hung a bell. Both Reformed and Lutheran people joined hands and hearts in its erection. The pastor was Rev. Clarence Clapp, son of Dr. Jacob C. Clapp, whose long ministry on the parish and in education was a benediction to the church in North Carolina.

After one hundred and eleven years of united work and worship, in 1925, the Lutheran congregation decided to disband. Their interest in the property was purchased by the Reformed congregation for $400, but the cemetery continued to be available to all who sought to use it as a burial ground.

In 1926 seven Sunday School rooms were added to the building, two of these opening as transcept rooms into the sanctuary; also, a portico was added to the front of the church. This work was done under the supervision of John W. Bowers, Jesse E. Myers and Charles H. Shuler. The enlarged and refinished church building was rededicated August 29, 1926. In 1938 new furniture, including pews, were installed in the sanctuary.[4]

Emanuel Church was associated, from its earliest days, with other Reformed congregations in Davidson County in the interest of pastoral services. When, therefore, the churches of the Classis of North Carolina were, in the interest of pastoral care, grouped into charges, Emanuel was considered a part of the Davidson Charge. Among itinerate ministers periodically serving the Bowers Meeting-house were Revs. Jacob Christman and Andrew Loretz. Pastors who served the Davidson Charge 1812 to 1827 were: Revs: George Boger, James R. Riley, William Weinel, H. B.Dieffenbach, Jacob Scholl, J. S. Ebaugh, George Leidy and John Rudy. Undoubtedly a number of these were itinerate preachers or missionaries sent out by the Synod.

The oldest list of members on record is one made in 1845 during the Ministry of Rev. David Crooks. Because of its historical value is given here: Absolom Grimes, Catherine Grimes, David Myers, Catherine Myers, Lewis Livengood, Phebe Livengood, Michael Myers, Susanna Myers, George Black, John Black, Elizabeth Black, Samuel Black, Molly Black, Daniel Lore, Sally Lore, Soloman Lore, Rachael Conrad, Mary Lore, Eve Curry, Diana Trotter, Elizabeth Bowers, Polly Fouts, Christiana Fouts, Elizabeth Fouts, Wm. Sullivan, Margaret Sullivan, Andrew Myers, Magdalena B. Fouts, Sarah Myers, Polly Ann Myers, Catherine Hayworth, David Curry, Esther Curry, Charlotte Lore.

In 1849 the church roll contained twenty-eight names. There were six additional names of colored people on it.

> It was the time of slavery. These members of the church who owned slaves, offered them the means of grace of their own church, admitted them to their membership and communion, and taught them the Christian faith. Thru all these years Emanuel has kept her doors open to the colored race. The oldest member on the roll is Harriott Johnson, commonly known as Aunt Harriott Grimes. She came to the home of Elder A. L. Grimes about the beginning of the Civil War, united with the church during the ministry of Rev. P. Allison Long, and has thru all these years, lived with members of the Grimes family.[5]

The Lower Davidson Charge was created in 1864, and Emanuel Church was made a part of it. Rev. P. Allison Long was its pastor.[6] In those days membership exercised a tremendous disciplinary influence over church people, which was administered by the Consistory. People were brought to account for their conduct. Some were considered to be "unworthy members of the church." Others were charged with "drunkeness." It is significant that the "accused plead guilty, manifested great repentence, and promised to amend." Some were suspended for cause, then reinstated to full membership. Before the Lord's Supper was administered, elders inquired if church members were worthy to "come to the Lord's Supper." Some were "cited to attend trial," others were "restored to full membership upon promise to live better."

In 1898 another charge arrangement was made. This time Emanuel was yoked with Calvary and Heidelberg churches, naming it the Thomasville Charge. Rev. Clarence Clapp was called to be the pastor. In 1913 the Centennial was fittingly observed in a series of services scheduled for August 16 and 17. Speakers for the occasion were: Dr. Walter W. Rowe, Dr. William H. McNairy, Dr. Joseph L. Murphy, Dr. Jacob C. Leonard, Dr. James D. Andrew and Rev. Clarence Woods; also Elders T. W. S. Grimes and John W. Bowers. Elder Grimes, in his historical address, remarked,

> This church has always stood for the old Reformed doctrines. Its ministers have never been accused of being unorthodox. It has emphasized the importance of the means of grace, Holy Baptism, the Holy Supper, the Catechism, the prayer meeting, the evangelistic, held up as of the greatest importance in saving souls and building Christian character.

Still another grouping of churches occurred May 1913, when the Emanuel, Calvary and Zion congregations were declared by the Classis to be the Emanuel Charge.[7] A new parsonage was erected in Thomasville, on Lexington Avenue, in 1916. The cost was $1,651 of which Emanuel paid $654.

The 125th Anniversary of this church was observed October 29, 1939, in activities which began during the morning and continued through the afternoon. It was a memorable day. Among visiting speakers for the occasion were: Dr. James D. Andrew, Dr. Jacob A. Palmer, Dr. Jacob C. Leonard, Rev. C. Columbus Wagoner, Dr. Banks J. Peeler and Rev. Joshua L. Levens.

Discussion began during the pastorate of Rev. William C. Lyerly in anticipation of Emanuel becoming an independent, self-supporting congregation. With considerable skepticism in the minds of some people, this became a reality May 15, 1946.[8] Upon the resignation of Mr. Lyerly on May 15, 1946, Dr. Jacob A. Palmer was named supply, shepherding the people until November 15, 1946, when Chaplain Lawrence A. Leonard accepted a call to be the first full-time pastor of the church. A parsonage was built in 1947, on land that had been deeded to the church by Charles F. Myers. The pastor and his family moved into the new debt-free parsonage December 26, 1947.

More adequate educational facilities were essential; hence, resulting from studies made by a number of committees, on February 21, 1950, the Consistory approved floor plans for a modern educational unit. Groundbreaking ceremonies were held November 5. This new building was occupied the last Sunday in September 1951, and dedicated debt free November 18. With this act building plans were half completed. Activities began almost immediately to erect the second half, involving additional Sunday School rooms and the sanctuary. The second unit was dedicated May 31, 1953, when Dr. A. Odell Leonard preached the dedicatory sermon. On that occasion the pastor reminded the congregation that:

> Our dreams have come true. God has answered our prayers, blessed our labors, and to His Glory we dedicate Emanuel Church. Our accomplishments are made possible by the power of God; our failures are covered by His mercy; and by the inspiration of His Holy Spirit we praise and serve Him. . . . . .
>
> This service today is not a concluding exercise, but a commencement exercise. We are prepared better than ever before. Let us serve better than ever before. God invites each of us to an even greater service in the work of His Kingdom. As we accept this invitation, dedicate and consecrate our lives to the Cause of Christ, we shall experience even greater joy in the Lord.[9]

This practically brought to an end six years of physical and material progress, marked by spiritual renewal perhaps unmatched by any period of similar length in the history of Emanuel Church. Mr. Leonard resigned, effective March 31, 1954.

During the next four years, under the pastoral leadership of Rev. C. Keith Sink, debts were paid, additional land was donated to the church and a playground was developed; also, extensive improvements were effected on the cemetery.

Rev. J. Wayne Fouts came to the parish June 15, 1960, whose efforts were rewarded by an effective program of education and evangelism. Keeping faith with dedication to the cause of Christian service, four sons have become ministers in the United Church of Christ: Dr. Harvey Wilson Black, Rev. Van Dolan Grimes, Rev. Chester Walter Byerly and Mr. Robert A. Rickard. A list of pastors, itinerate and supply preachers, as accurately as the record provides them, appears below.

ROSTER OF PASTORS

Rev. Jacob Christman		
Rev. Andrew Loretz		
Rev. George Boger	1812-1827	
Rev. James R. Riley	1812-1827	
Rev. William Weinel	1812-1827	
Rev. H. B. Dieffenbach	1812-1827	
Rev. Jacob Scholl	1812-1827	
Rev. J. S. Ebaugh	1812-1827	
Rev. George Leidy	1812-1827	
Rev. John Rudy	1812-1827	
Rev. James Riley	1828-1832	
Rev. William Hauck	1828-1832	
Rev. W. C. Bennet	1833-1837	
Rev. David Crooks	1838-1846	
Rev. ? Jones—Supply, probably from another church	1846-1848	
Rev. F. W. Plassman	1846-1848	
Rev. Thornton Butler	1848-1851	
Rev. William Sorber	1853-1856	
Rev. P. Allison Long	1858-1866	
Rev. Michael L. Hedrick	1873-1887	
Rev. Allan R. Holshouser	1889-1892	
Rev. William H. McNairy, D.D.	1894-1896	

Rev. Clarence Clapp	1896-1902
Rev. Walter W. Rowe, D.D.	1902-1903
Rev. Jacob N. Foust	1903-1904
Rev. Frederick Cromer	1904-1905
Rev. Lucian W. Showers	1905-1906
Rev. Irvin S. Ditzler	1907-1908
Rev. Clarence Woods	1910-1913
Rev. John B. Swartz	1914-1915
Rev. Dugan C. Cox	1916-1925
Rev. Sterling W. Whitener, Stated Supply	1927-1928
Rev. Sidney C. Safrit	1929-1933
Rev. Kendell B. Shoffner	1934-1938
Rev. William C. Lyerly	1938-1946
Rev. Jacob A. Palmer, D.D. Supply	1946-
Rev. Lawrence A. Leonard	1946-1954
Rev. A. Odell Leonard, DD. Supply	1954-
Rev. C. Keith Sink	1955-1959
Rev. Richard A. Cheek, Supply	1959-
Rev. J. Wayne Fouts	1960-1967
Rev. Aubrey W. Hedrick	1968-

1. *Leonard*, Jacob C., Centennial History of Davidson County, 1927, p. 464.
2. *Leonard*, Jacob C., History of Southern Synod, Evangelical and Reformed Church, 1940, p. 183.
3. *Clapp*, Jacob C., Editor. Historic Sketch of the Reformed Church in North Carolina, 1908, p. 179.
4. *Lyerly*, William C., A Century and a Quarter in a Rural Church, 1940, p. 4 ff.
5. *Ibid.* p. 6.
6. ———. Minutes. Classis of North Carolina, 1864, p. 315.
7. ———. Minutes. *Op. cit.*, 1913, p. 62.
8. ———. Minutes. Southern Synod, 1947, p. 13.
9. Leonard, Lawrence A., Emanuel Church, Evangelical and Reformed, Dedication. 1953, p. 6.

Emanuel Church, Lincolnton
I. The White Church

EMANUEL CHURCH, Lincolnton, North Carolina began as a community effort, promoted chiefly by people of the Reformed and Lutheran faiths. The site for the town of Lincolnton was laid out in 1784, and chartered two years later. In describing the habits and character of citizens who founded this frontier town, William L. Sherrill, a native of Lincoln County, writes:

> On the frontier neighbors learned the meaning of neighborliness. They had log rollings, house raisings, corn shuckings and quilting parties, and those who refused to help in neighborly deeds lost caste. They were industrious and possessed varied gifts which served them well in their new environment. They had learned to work with their hands. They

were blacksmiths, carpenters, cabinet makers, millwrights, tanners, shoe-makers, saddlers, tailors, hatters, skilled workers in iron. These all worked their farms and also worked at their trades when needed. So the people were not only farmers but manufacturers from the start, and supplied their neighbors with such as they could produce by hand. Necessity being the mother of invention, it was wonderful how they found substitutes for many things. They used honey or sorghum for sugar, parched rye for coffee, ashes and waste grease combined were converted into soap. Corn and wheat were ground by hand and the people never heard of appendicidis.[1]

In support of these admirable traits was a radiant faith. Symbols of their devotion were a generous use of the Bible, the Catechism and the Hymn Book. They lived from week to week in anticipation of gathering for Public Worship. Thus, among the first buildings usually erected in the community was a Meeting House. In order to secure the land upon which such a house had already been built, on January 10, 1788, a deed was made by Joseph Dickson, in consideration for ten shillings, to Christian Reinhardt agent for the 'Dutch Presbyterians' and Andrew Heedrick agent for the 'Dutch Lutherans,' involving two acres and sixteen poles of land located in the southeast section of the town.

The land was purchased "for the purpose of building thereon a Meeting House for Public Worship, School Houses, both Dutch and English, and for a place for the burial of the dead, and the said Societies have at their joint expense already built a house for Public Worship on the premises, and the said Societies not having been incorporated, are desirous that the land hereby intended to be conveyed shall be vested in fee simple in the said Trustees, Christian Reinhardt and Andrew Heedrick and their heirs and assigns forever in Trust for the uses in this deed declared, and the said Socie-

ties have signified the same to the said Joseph Dickson and requested him to convey accordingly the lands hereby intended to
be conveyed."[2]

The house which stood on the land was a one story building, constructed of logs, of colonial design, equipped with crude wooden
furniture. It stood thus until 1819 when a second story was built
on it, weatherboarded, ceiled and a new pulpit installed. The pulpit was high, and reached by a stairway from each side, overspread
with a sounding board. Pews were high-backed and there were
ample galleries. A bell was added in 1827. The church was painted
white in 1830, from which the structure was named "The White
Church."[3] The Dutch and English school houses were never built.

First available records of the Church are dated 1794. At that
time Rev. Andrew Loretz was pastor of the Reformed congregation, and the Rev. John Gottfried Arends was pastor of the
Lutheran congregation. These ministers being warm friends ministered to their people without incident as long as they lived.
Family names which appear on that first record include, Hoke,
Finger, Cansler, Botz, Summerow, Reinhardt, Ramsaur, all ancestors of the current population.[4]

After the death of Rev. Andrew Loretz, for sixteen years the Reformed Church had no pastor on the parish. Beginning about 1823,
under the leadership of Dr. Humphrey Hunter and his successor
Rev. Joseph E. Bell, representing the Concord Presbytery, the Presbyterians occupied the White Church along with the Lutherans.
Doubtless, taking advantage of existing confusion among the people resulting from the term "Dutch Presbyterians" which appears
in the text of the deed to that property, virtually the entire Reformed congregation was enrolled as Presbyterians. First records
of the Presbyterian Church in Lincolnton, dated February 14, 1823,
report Joseph E. Bell, Moderator, and John Hoke, David Ramsaur,
Peter Summey and Michael Reinhardt, Elders.[5] These are names
normally appearing on the roll of Reformed Churches in the area.

A marked change took place in the fortunes of the Reformed congregation, when in 1828, Rev. John G. Fritchey, came to Lincolnton. Through his effort the deed for the White Church property
was submitted to the court, with the request that a decision be
made with reference to the term "Dutch Presbyterians." The court
ruled that the term meant "Dutch Reformed;" thus putting an entirely different light on recent conduct of Presbyterian leadership.
The Reformed congregation was reorganized. Subsequently, a division occurred in the Presbyterian Church, and a majority of its
members enrolled in the Reformed Church, reclaiming in a measure losses sustained by the previous confusion. Mr. Fritchey continued to serve the congregation until 1839, when he returned to
Pennsylvania. From the fourth Sunday in June 1839, the Presbyterians held no more Services in the White Church.

The Reformed congregation continued its organization under

pastoral supervision of Revs. J. H. Crawford, 1840-1842; Solomon S. Middlekauff, 1842-1845; David Crooks, 1846-1859. The Classis of North Carolina met in this church in 1853. But the congregation could never regain its former strength, ceasing to hold regular weekly services after 1859. When the Classis met at Daniel's Church in 1866, in his report on the "State of Religion," Rev. P. Allison Long remarked, "It is to be regretted that the congregation at Lincolnton, one of the oldest and once one of the most flourishing in the bounds of the Classis, has become destitute of regular pastoral care."[6]

Visiting missionaries conducted occasional services and took care of sacramental functions from time to time for the dwindling flock. Dr. John A. Foil, on subsidy from the Board of Home Missions, supplied the congregation in 1882. From 1885 to 1890 pastoral care was provided by Dr. Joseph L. Murphy, then pastor of the Lincoln Charge, residing in Maiden, and ministers stationed west of the Catawba River continued their ministerial services to them as schedules permitted.

The Old White Church was consumed by fire the night of December 23, 1893. Thus, was "blotted out a building with which all the religious history of the vicinity was associated." For during its long period of service to the community, Reformed, Lutheran, Methodist, Episcopal and Baptist, perhaps others, worshipped there. Quite possibly, in each case, first meetings of their respective congregations were held in that historic house.

Since the property had been deeded to the Reformed and Lutheran people in the vicinity, involving specific restrictions, after a lapse of time, negotiations between the two parties began, seeking a satisfactory settlement. Because the Lutheran congregation had erected a church building on the lot, complications developed. However, the Classis of North Carolina of the Reformed Church in the United States, approved a "quit claim deed" settlement for the consideration of $75 as early as 1898,[7] and on April 19, 1900 the transaction was reported as having been completed.[8] The sum of $75 received from the sale of the Lincolnton church property was "turned over to the Joint Consistory of the Lincoln Charge to be held and invested by them as may seem best."

II. New Emanuel Church, Lincolnton

THE NEW EMANUEL REFORMED CHURCH, Lincolnton, North Carolina is in fact the old one in continuity. After a quarter of a century, a new generation appeared and directed the remaining elements of the old Church, now dissolved, into new channels. It is a mistake to conclude that from 1890 until 1910 nothing was done to serve the religious needs of the Reformed people living in that community. On the contrary, available ministers of the Church, living in the western section of the Classis of North Carolina, held services for them in the various churches and ministered to their necessities. In 1904, Rev. Calvin B. Heller was named by the Classis to "look after the interests" in Lincolnton,[9] and in 1906 a committee recommended enrollment by the Homes Missions Board and that a missionary be placed on the field.[10] In 1907 a committee reported as many as twenty five interested Reformed people living there, and urged that an organization be effected, the Home Missions Board be overtured to enroll it, and a regular schedule of services be arranged for them.[11]

In October 1910 Lincolnton was enrolled as a mission point by the Home Missions Board, with a loan of $500. At its April meeting in 1911, Rev. Samuel W. Beck was commissioned to take charge of this work, but he apparently declined the assignment.[12] At the semi-annual meeting of the Board, July 1911, Dr. William H. McNairy was commissioned, and began work on the parish the following September 1. The Sunday School was organized the second Sunday in September, and four weeks later, October 8, the church came into being. Twenty six people composed the charter membership roll.[13]

This roll is interesting, since it contains names of families who originally settled Lincoln County and environs. It follows: E. D. Fox, Mrs. Laura Fox, P. D. Hinson, Jacob Holbrooks, Ethel Holbrooks, Pearl Holbrooks, J. T. Keever, Mrs. M. C. Keever, Mrs. B. E. McNairy, Wyatt McNairy, Miss Minnie Michael, Mrs. Hattie Rudisill, Miss Marie Rudisill, R. J. Ramsaur, John J. Ramsaur, K. M. Ramsaur, Mrs. Katie Ramsaur, Daniel A. Seagle, Mrs. Catherine Seagle, Vera Seagle, Ruth Seagle, Craig Seagle, Mrs. E. C. Shuford, James A. Shuford, A. P. Willis, Mrs. Della Willis.

E. D. Fox and Daniel A. Seagle were elected elders, and James A. Shuford and K. M. Ramsaur, deacons. The new church was named "Heidelberg," but on April 12, 1913, by unanimous vote of the congregation, it was changed to "Emanuel" in the interest of continuity.[14]

Arrangements were made to occupy the first floor of the Odd Fellows Hall, then located on East Main Street, where congregational activities took place until the new sanctuary was ready for occupancy. A lot, "two doors" east of the Odd Fellows Hall, and site of the present church, was purchased from the Baptist congregation for $1,600. By action of the Church, January 12, 1913, a building committee composed of Mr. McNairy, Chairman, James A. Shuford, E. C. Shuford and Frank Ramsaur, was appointed, with instructions to develop plans for a house of worship and to supervise its erection. The first Service was held in the new building December 25, 1913. A parsonage was built along the east side of the church in 1919 and 1920. These two buildings and a healthy well organized church bear testimony to the very substantial work done by Dr. McNairy over a period of ten years. He resigned the pastorate September 1, 1921.[15]

Improvements on the property occurred as needed; however, in

1931 major educational facilities were added, providing for urgently needed classroom space and a ladies parlor. A modern heating system was installed at the same time.

The one hundred forty-fifth anniversary of the founding of Emanual Reformed Church, Lincolnton, North Carolina, was observed May 15, 1932. Activities were under the direction of the minister, Rev. Hoy Lee Fesperman. Dr. William H. McNairy, a former pastor, returned to address the Sunday School; Dr. Jacob C. Leonard, Classical Historian, delivered the anniversary sermon; and Elder James A. Shuford read an interesting historical sketch of the congregation. Dr. John H. Keller, preached the sermon at the Evening Service, thus bringing to its close a memorable day for Reformed Church folks living in Lincolnton and the vicinity.

A second parsonage of modern design was built on Victor Street during the pastorate of Rev. Carl R. Martin. The present pastor of this small but effective congregation is Rev. Frank W. Snider.

Against a rather static environment Emanuel Church has made several successful adjustments. After lying dormant for a generation, in 1910 it was restored to activity. Joining the larger Fellowship in 1934, it emerged as a unit of the Evangelical and Reformed denomination, and again in 1957, took its place with other Churches of Southern Synod to become a part of the United Church of Christ. Currently Emanuel, and other sister churches in Lincoln County, are engaged in discussions designed to point the way to a larger and more satisfactory Christian Mission to their respective constituencies.

ROSTER OF PASTORS

Rev. William H. McNairy, D.D. 1911-1921
Rev. John B. Swartz, Supply 1922-
Rev. Banks J. Peeler, D.D. 1922-1924
Mr. E. Warner Lentz, Student Supply 1924-
Mr. Harvey W. Black, Student Supply 1925-
Rev. Hugo C. Kellermeyer 1926-1929
Rev. Hoy L. Fesperman 1929-1935
Rev. Huitt R. Carpenter 1935-1937
Rev. John H. Keller, D.D. 1937-1939
Rev. Walter C. Beck 1939-1952
Rev. Lewis E. Everline 1952-1956
Rev. Donald C. Selby, Ph.D. Supply 1956-

Rev. C. Larry Fisher 1957-1960
Rev. Donald C. Selby, Supply 1960-
Mr. Chester C. Byerly, Student Supply 1960-
Mr. Larry Sink, Alternate Student Supply 1960-
Mr. James L. Peeler, Alternate Student Supply 1960-
Rev. G. Ermine Plott, Stated Supply 1960-1961
Mr. Chester C. Byerly, Student Supply 1961-
Rev. Carl R. Martin 1961-1964
Rev. Donald C. Selby, Supply 1964-
Rev. Frank W. Snider 1965-

1. *Sherrill*, William L., Annals of Lincoln County, North Carolina. 1937. p. 12.
2. ———. Register or Deeds Office, Book ,III Lincoln County, 1788, p. 362.
3. *Clapp*, Jacob C., Editor. Historic Sketch of the Reformed Church in North Carolina, 1908, p. 275 ff.
4. *Sherrill. Op. cit.*, p. 467.
5. *Ibid.* p. 470.
6. ———. Minutes. Classis of North Carolina, 1866, p. 23.
7. ———. Minutes. *Op. cit.*, 1898, p. 47, Item 2.
8. ———. Minutes. *Op. cit.*, 1900, p. 131, Item 2.
9. ———. Minutes. *Op. cit.*, 1904, p. 252.
10. ———. Minutes. *Op. cit.*, 1906, p. 11, Item 5.

11. ———. Minutes. *Op. cit.*, 1908, p. 5 ff.
12. ———. Minutes. *Op. cit.*, 1911, p. 18, Item 12.
13. *Shuford*, James A., Manuscript. Essay on Emanuel Church, 1934, p. 3.
14. *Ibid.* p. 3 ff.
15. *Ibid.* p. 4.
16. *Ibid*, p. 5 ff.

Faith Church, Brookford

Faith Church, Brookford, North Carolina was originally an Outpost of Corinth Church, Hickory for four years before the congregation was organized into a church. Work began in the village shortly after the beginning of the year 1901. First efforts met with encouraging results, so that, following the leadership of Dr. Joseph L. Murphy, pastor of Corinth Reformed Church, Hickory, N. C., a plot of land was donated by Mr. E. L. Shuford and a building was erected immediately by the sponsoring congregation.

The frame building was completed; and on May 12, 1901, Dr. Murphy led a large and an appreciative audience, composed of towns people and Hickory folk, in the first service. This spirit of accomplishment, however, was short lived. On May 16, four days later, the new sanctuary was struck by lightening and burned to the ground.

As disappointing as such misfortunes usually turn out to be, this event discouraged neither the villagers nor friends in Corinth Church. They immediately set to work, and by that fall, completed a new church building. Dedication ceremonies were held November 3, 1901. It is worthy of note that the Corinth people, remembering that they were once a "mission point" receiving help from others, bore the major part of the cost for both buildings. Accepting this as an opportunity to express gratitude for what friends and church agencies had done for them.

From this point the congregation showed slow but substantial growth. Regular services were conducted each Sunday, and the Sunday School in particular gave promise of a successful future. Faith Reformed Church with twenty-two confirmed members, was organized into a church March 5, 1905. The following May, at the Annual Sessions of the Classis of North Carolina, this church was officially enrolled as a member of that ecclesiastical body. Dr. Murphy continued to serve the congregation until his death in 1917. Dr. Walter W. Rowe served it until August 1921, at which time Faith Church was linked with a proposed West Hickory project.[1] The West Hickory project was discontinued in 1925, and Faith Church became a part of the Catawba Charge now consisting of Faith, Trinity and Smyrna churches.

The Catawba Charge was dissolved on June 1, 1944, and Faith Church was enrolled as a "Mission Point" by the Board of National Missions, and served full-time by Rev. A. Wilson Cheek. While rehearsing a Christmas play on the evening of December 22, 1944, fire broke out in the church completely destroying the building. Out of the ashes of this second fire disaster, grew the present beautiful and well appointed brick sanctuary and educational annex.

Macedonia Missions, located in Southeast Hickory, was established on February 24, 1926, which, with Faith Church, composed the Brookford Charge. This charge was dissolved in December 1962, and Faith Church became a self-supporting congregation.

This congregation is well organized to promote activities in Sunday School, Lay Life and Work and youth interests. Two of its sons are serving in the Christian Ministry: Rev. Carl T. Daye and Rev. Carroll E. Bartholomew. It owns a comfortable parsonage, located in the community. Rev. Chester W. Byerly is the current pastor.

ROSTER OF PASTORS

Rev. Joseph L. Murphy, D.D. 1901-1917	Rev. Harry D. Althouse, D.D., Supply 1938
Rev. Walter W. Rowe, D.D. 1918-1921	Rev. A. Wilson Cheek, D.D. 1939-1947
Mr. O. Bain Michael, Student Summer Supply 1919-	Rev. Shuford Peeler, D.D., Supply 1948-
Mr. Banks J. Peeler, Student Summer Supply 1920-	Rev. Richard Rubright 1948-1951
Mr. Felix B. Peck, Student Summer Supply 1921-	Rev. Roy E. Leinbach, Jr., Supply 1951-1953
Rev. William H. McNairy, D.D. 1921-1923	Rev. Banks D. Shepherd 1953-1958
Mr. Harvey W. Black, Student Summer Supply 1923-	Rev. Donald J. Selby, Ph.D., Supply 1958-
Mr. Dobbs F. Ehlman, Student Summer Supply 1924-1925	Rev. Bobby R. Bonds 1959-1963
Rev. William R. Shaffer, D.D. 1926-1929	Rev. Harvey A. Fesperman, D.D., Supply 1963-
Rev. C. Columbus Wagoner 1930-1938	Rev. Cedric L. Hepler 1964-1965
	Rev. Chester W. Byerly 1966-

References: Leonard, Jacob C., History of the Southern Synod, 1940, p. 364.
Helper, Cedric L., Manuscript. Faith United Church of Christ, 1964.

First Church, Asheboro

IN ANSWER TO an overture from the Eastern District Ministerial Association, the Classis of North Carolina, on May 31, 1938 took action to begin church extension operations in the city of Asheboro, North Carolina. In making provision for the work to begin, the Classis appointed Dr. A. Odell Leonard to supervise it and appropriated the sum of $300 for expenses.[1]

Theological student A. Gail Holt was asked to survey the area during the months of June, July and August of 1938, and to make preparations for religious services such as would be required. The first service was held in the Pugh Funeral Home, Worth Street, on June 12. Thirty-eight people were present. One hundred twenty five people assembled in the funeral home chapel July 3, 1938, when the First Evangelical and Reformed Church was born. Two weeks later the charter member list, which was presented for approval, contained 44 names of people who had committed themselves to become members of the new organization.[2]

At the organization meeting, R. C. Cope and Shuford Plott were elected elders; E. C. Swing and H. A. Essick, deacons. Other officers of the congregation were named as follows: H. A. Essick, vice president of the Consistory, the presiding pastor being its president by virtue of his office; C. E. Swing, secretary of the Consistory; Mrs. H. A. Essick, financial secretary; Mrs. V. W. Wilson, treasurer of the congregation; R. C. Cope, superintendent of the Sunday School. Having completed the church organization, the congregation set out to develop plans for a church home.

Undoubtedly the next major step in the life of the mission was its enrollment on October 1, 1938 by the Board of Home Missions which was presently to become the Board of National Missions of the Evangelical and Reformed Church, with an expense appropriation of $50 per month. At the same time Dr. A. Odell Leonard was commissioned missionary pastor, who proposed to carry this responsibility in addition to his duties as pastor of the Second Evangelical and Reformed Church, Lexington, North Carolina. During the summers of 1938 through 1941 he was assisted on the field by Student A. Gail Holt.[3]

The congregation was officially recognized as a member of the Classis of North Carolina, on October 4, 1938 at which time a grant of $2,000 was voted to be paid out of the current treasury of the Classis with which to begin its church building. Suitable land had been purchased for $800, located at the corner of Randolph Avenue and Cliff Road, as a site for the new structure. A building committee composed of L. A. Hughes, chairman; C. H. Swing, Ray Hull, W. V. Wilson and L. M. Galloway, moved swiftly to engage an architect and to develop plans for the sanctuary. By April 1939 the foundation for the new building had been "poured," and on August 9 of the same year the cornerstone was laid. Official occupation of the sanctuary occurred on May 19, 1940. Dedication ceremonies took place August 3, 1941. Total cost of the lot and first unit of the building added up to $14,005.57.

After a rather promising beginning, for a number of years, life in the congregation languished, resulting in loss of members and financial difficulties. However, new leadership restored interest and set the congregation on its way again. A parsonage, located at 702 Redding Road was purchased shortly thereafter at a cost of $24,000, financed through the Board of Home Missions. By 1957, the congregation had gained sufficient numerical strength and the Sunday School enrollment had expanded so much that new educational facilities were essential. The Educational Annex, constructed at that time, provided 6,000 square feet of space, adequate to serve a congregation of 300 people. Some additional land, adjacent to the church property along the west line, has since then been purchased by the Churchmen's Brotherhood and deeded to the congregation.

After 19 years of support from the Board of National Missions of the Evangelical and Reformed Church and the Southern Synod, the congregation went to self support in 1957. Note-burning ceremonies were conducted November 7, 1965, when debts on the church building and parsonage had been retired.

This is a growing, serving congregation located in a thriving industrial community. It is currently being served by Rev. Donald M. Leonard. Its confirmed membership is 275; the Sunday School has an enrollment of 286.

ROSTER OF PASTORS

Rev. A. Odell Leonard, D.D.,	Rev. Arthur R. Detwiler 1945-1946
Organizing Supply Pastor ..1938-1941	Rev. Harvey H. Koonts 1946-1953
Mr. A. Gail Holt,	Rev. A. O. Leonard, D.D.,
Student Summer Supply 1938-1942	Supply 1954-
Rev. A. Windell Snyder 1942-1944	Rev. Lawrence A. Leonard ...1954-1960
Rev. A. Odell Leonard, D.D.,	Rev. Donald M. Leonard 1960-
Stated Supply 1944-1945	

1. ———. Minutes. Classis of North Carolina, 1939, p. 2.
2. *Ibid.* p. 12.
3. *Leonard*, Lawrence A., Twentieth Anniversary, First Evangelical and Reformed Church, 1958, p. 4.ff.

First Church, Burlington

BURLINGTON, NORTH CAROLINA was first known as "Company Shops," an unincorporated settlement inhabited principally by Germans, Scotch-Irish and English Quakers. It dates back to as early as 1700. The name appears to have settled upon the community from habitual use, because the North Carolina Railroad Company shops were located there. In 1885 a municipal organization was formed, and the name was by popular vote changed to Burlington.

In this community stood a rather large frame building, known later as "The Old White Church," sometimes referred to as the "Union Church," so named because various religious bodies represented in the community used it for their meetings. It was here that the interests of the Reformed Church first were fostered in 1889. That year the Classis of North Carolina met at nearby Brick Church and created the Alamance Charge, composed of St. Mark's, Stiner's and a congregation to be organized in Burlington.[1] The Tri-synodic Board of Home Missions of the Reformed Church had already voted a grant of $300 during its meeting, which convened April 8, to be used in the Burlington effort. Rev. Jesse Richards of Lakeside, Ohio, was commissioned missionary pastor and reported for work immediately.

A congregation was organized sometime later in the year in the home of Zimri M. Foust, who lived on South Main Street. The charter membership list contained the following names: Z. M. Foust,

J. J. May, J. P. May, W. N. Mebane, W. M. Mebane, Mrs. Rachel May, Mrs. Z. M. Foust, Miss Lulu Foust, Mrs. J. P. May, Mrs. W. M. Mebane and Mrs. Jesse Richards. Elders elected were Z. M. Foust and J. J. May, and deacons, J. P. May and W. N. Mebane.[2]

Mr. Richards held services in the old white church, preaching to large congregations. During his pastorate, which lasted only two years, membership increased to 50 people. But the next pastor, Rev. David P. LeFevre, who assumed his duties on October 1, 1891, served during a period that witnessed numerical loss in the congregation, leading to a decision by the Board of Home Missions to withdraw financial support from the Alamance Charge as of October 1, 1893.[3]

Other than an occasional visit from Rev. James D. Andrew, pastor of the Guilford Charge in whose care this work had been committed, nothing significant was accomplished on the Burlington parish during the next five years. In 1896, in his report to the Classis, Mr. Andrew said:

> Immediately after the annual sessions of the Classis, I visited Burlington and called the congregation together. I preached to this unorganized congregation once a month until October 20, 1895, when by the blessing of God we organized with 24 members. Since that time there has been one accession to the membership by confirmation. It is now a zealous little band of worshippers. We need a house of our own in which to worship, and a minister to give his entire time to this field. . . . The outlook for the future is promising.[4]

On September 14, 1897, Burlington, St. Mark's and a newly-organized congregation at Whitsett known as Fairview, were by the Classis constituted the Burlington Charge. The Charge was then re-enrolled by the Board of Home Missions beginning in January 1898, with a subsidy of $350, $100 of which was contributed by Elder B. Wolf, Jr. of Pittsburgh, Pennsylvania.

Rev. James D. Andrew was commissioned pastor of the Charge on April 1, 1898, but did not begin his ministry there until the following September. With 19 of the earlier 24 members, he began work. From this point the future of the Burlington church has never been questioned. It has weathered many storms and survived several serious reverses.

The immediate need was a church home. An individual, not a member of the Reformed Church, appears to have provided the incentive by making the first gift to the new building project. Progress in preparing for and building the new church was steady. On February 13, 1900, a lot on which the present church building stands was purchased for the sum of $265. Plans for the sanctuary were approved, and construction began immediately. The first service was held in the unfinished building on January 6, 1901. The pastor administered the sacrament of Holy Communion, and admitted three people into membership with the church. The house was not actually finished until two years later, in April 1903, when the walls were papered and pews and wood work were painted. Total cost of the church building added up to $3,275.

Financing for these operations came through the Ladies Aid Society which contributed $50; the Classis $400; and a loan of $500 from the Board of Home Missions. Small gifts, ranging from a few pennies upward, constituted the remainder of the fund. Cash entries show a total of 1,260 contributors. There was no building committee, the pastor serving a multiple role of building supervisor, soliciting agent, treasurer and general promoter.

Attention now turned to expanding the congregation. The membership grew steadily, as did the Sunday School enrollment. A Home Department, the first in any denomination in North Carolina, was created, as well as a cradle roll for small babies. By May 6, 1906, all financial obligations were paid, and the church was dedicated. On October 2, 1909, the congregation borrowed $500 from the Board of Home Missions with which to construct some badly needed Sunday School rooms.

Mr. Andrew resigned June 13, 1913, to accept the presidency of Catawba College. From 1913 to 1924 good progress was made under the leadership of three ministers,—Revs. Dugan C. Cox, A. H. Zechiel and Samuel J. Kirk. The parsonage was purchased in 1913, the second parsonage was built immediately behind the church in 1917, and the congregation was made an independent though not a self-supporting Charge, in 1918. The name was changed to "First" Reformed Church in 1924.

By the time Rev. Harvey A. Welker arrived to serve the parish in 1923, there was urgent need for new educational and worship facilities. On February 1, 1925, at a congregational meeting, a building and finance committee was authorized and instructed to make preparation for the project. The building committee was composed of L. A. Sharpe, J. M. Fowler, D. E. Clapp, A. C. Neese and John R. Hoffman. The finance committee consisted of Dr. H. M. Montgomery, George W. Hoffman, Herbert W. Coble, Ernest M. Cheek and George H. Fowler. Plans for worship and education needs were drawn and approved. Because the entire structure would entail too much of a financial burden for the congregation, it was agreed to build first the educational unit. Contract price for that unit was $37,800. Construction began on it May 1, 1928. Formal occupation occurred on May 12, 1932.

After a vacancy of six months, Rev. Banks J. Peeler became pastor on October 1, 1932. This period proved to be one of internal adjustment. The parsonage and chapel were repaired, and new furniture and equipment were installed in the new educational building. Debts were cleared on the building; the congregation went to self-support on January 1, 1934; church membership increased to 519; the Sunday School with an enrollment of 621 was completely departmentalized, and the adjoining Curtis property was acquired.

When Rev. George E. Dillinger began his pastorate in 1939, he concentrated on completing the building project that had been started in 1928. Observing the 50th Anniversary of the organization of the congregation on November 5, 1939, proved to be the incentive which set the movement in motion. On August 13, 1940, the Consistory was authorized to let a contract for the sanctuary, which was to cost approximately $50,000. This exceptionally beautiful and appropriate house of worship was dedicated in a Festival of Services beginning October 12, 1941.

The program of dedication carried out on succeeding evenings during the week included the following participants and themes: Rev. Harvey A. Welker spoke on dedication to church and church school; Dr. Banks J. Peeler, on dedication to young people; Professor Merton T. French, on dedication to Christian Education; Revs. A. Wilson Cheek, Terrell M. Shoffner and Carl H. Clapp on dedication to fathers, mothers and home; and Dr. Fred W. Paschall, on dedication to the community. The final service of the week was an organ recital held on Friday evening.

Dr. Harvey A. Fesperman began his ministry to the congregation December 1, 1945. The Wilson property adjacent to the church on the West side was purchased on April 11, 1948; the 10th Anniversary of the dedication of the new church structure was observed October 14, 1951; and in 1951 preparation began for the organization of St. John's Evangelical and Reformed Church in the Grove Park Community. The pastorate of Dr. Fesperman came to an end July 1, 1955, when he became president of Southern Synod.

Upon the arrival in Burlington on September 13, 1955 of Dr. Lonnie A. Carpenter, he found himself in the midst of influences which largely determined his services to the congregation. Air conditioning equipment was installed in the sanctuary; general repairs were made on school facilities; parking space was prepared on newly-acquired property; and Edgewood United Church of Christ, the first united venture in church extension undertaken by Southern Synod and the Southern Conference, was sponsored by the First Christian and the First Evangelical and Reformed churches.

The act of merger already had been taken by General Synod in 1957, forming the United Church of Christ, when Southern Synod held its annual sessions in the First Evangelical and Reformed Church beginning April 26, 1960, while a similar gathering of the Southern Convention of the Congregational Christian churches was taking place in the First Christian Church of Burlington. On the evening of the 26th, these two groups of Christians came together for worship in the First Evangelical and Reformed Church. It was a high moment and a blessed experience when more than 600 people representing the spirit of the New Church were served the Sacrament of Holy Communion.

The pastorate of Rev. Robert W. Roschy, which began on February 15, 1961 was marked by serious struggles within the congregation. These differences have been at least partially resolved, and the congregation is moving forward again under the imaginative leadership of Rev. Hiram E. Davis, whose ministry began September 1, 1965.

First Church has given to the Christian ministry the following sons: Rev. Carl H. Clapp, Dr. A. Wilson Cheek, Rev. Carl R. Martin, Rev. Bobby R. Bonds, Rev. George A. Fidler and Rev. Richard A. Cheek.

ROSTER OF PASTORS

Rev. Jesse Richards	1889-1891	Rev. George E. Dillinger,	
Rev. David P. LeFevre	1891-1893	S.T.D.	1939-1945
Rev. James D. Andrew, D.D.	1898-1913	Rev. Harvey A. Fesperman,	
Rev. Dugan C. Cox	1914-1915	D.D.	1945-1955
Rev. Albert H. Zechiel	1916-1918	Rev. Lonnie A. Carpenter,	
Rev. Samuel J. Kirk	1918-1922	D.D.	1955-1960
Rev. Harvey A. Welker	1923-1932	Rev. Robert W. Roschy	1961-1965
Rev. Banks J. Peeler, D.D.	1932-1939	Rev. Hiram E. Davis	1965-

1. ———. Minutes. Classis of North Carolina, Reformed Church in the United States, 1889, p. 7.
2. *Peeler*, Banks J., First Reformed Church, 44th Anniversary, 1933, p. 6.
3. ———. Minutes. *Op. cit.*, 1893, p. 9.
4. ———. Minutes. *Op. cit.*, 1896, p. 7.

Reference Material

Nance, H. L., History, First Reformed Church, 1962.
White, A. Howard, Editor. Burlington Daily Times-News, October 10, 1941.

First Church, Charlotte

THE CITY OF CHARLOTTE, NORTH CAROLINA is perhaps, the major commercial distributing center in the two Carolinas. For this reason, among others, it is a fast-growing community, attracting Reformed Church families to make their homes there. Members of the Classis of North Carolina discussed the possibility of beginning work in Charlotte three years before it was actually begun.[1]

In 1914, giving unsettled conditions in the Classis as a reason, a committee reported that nothing had been done during that year. But in 1915 the following action was taken:

> Resolved that the Board of Missions be earnestly requested to establish a mission in the city of Charlotte, North Carolina. . . . That this interest be committed to the care of Rev. Shuford Peeler, with instructions to urge the Board of Missions to enroll Charlotte as a mission point at the earliest possible date.[2]

From that point activities in the Charlotte area began to take form. By August 5, the project had been enrolled by the Board of Missions, and Rev. Shuford Peeler had been authorized by the Classis to organize a congregation.[3] The board also provided a first-year subsidy of $1,200.[4]

Rev. and Mrs. Shuford Peeler moved to Charlotte January 1, 1916. At a special meeting of the Classis held on February 2, 1916, the missionary pastor reported as follows:

> The organization of the Reformed Church in Charlotte, under the instruction of the Classis, was effected January 16, 1916, with eighteen charter members. M. C. Barnhardt and J. C. M. Rymer were elected elders; and J. C. Peck and J. W. Fulbright, deacons. The name chosen is the "First Reformed Church of Charlotte."

This report was accorded enthusiastic approval. A call from the new church to Mr. Peeler was confirmed, and an installation committee composed of Revs. John H. Keller, Paul Barringer and William H. McNairy was named.[5] Installation Services were held February 27, 1916.

Early activities, including worship and Sunday School, were conducted in the Y. W. C. A. building located on East Trade Street. Here the Sunday School was organized on May 1, 1916, with an enrollment of 23 pupils.

A lot at the corner of East Trade and Myers Streets was purchased the following July 17, on which to erect a house of worship. Money was a major problem from the beginning. The Classis of North Carolina contributed $3,000 from its contingent fund with which to meet immediate needs.[6] Later the Classis also contributed, from the sale of the Albemarle Mission property the sum of $1,620.[7] Reformed Churches in the state received the missionary kindly and responded generously to his appeal, as did many personal friends. By April 1917 the foundation of the church building was started. On the first Sunday in May 1918, after using the Y. W. C. A. two years and five months, the congregation occupied the sanctuary section of their new church.

Entering the pulpit for that first service with a sense of thankfulness to God for progress thus far made, the pastor reminded the people of their manifold blessings received from Divine Providence. Fifteen people were received into fellowship with the church that morning. At a popular service during the afternoon, Dr. John H. Keller spoke, and at 8 p.m. Mr. Joseph S. Wise, Treasurer of the Board of Home Missions addressed the congregation.

Dedication of the sanctuary was held July 14, 1918. Dr. Walter W. Rowe preached the sermon at 11 a.m.; Dr. Jacob C. Leonard delivered the dedicatory address during the afternoon. The pastor led the congregation in a consecration ritual. Dr. Ernest N. Orr, pastor of the neighboring Tabernacle A. R. P. Church, participated in the activities. Treasurer Joseph S. Wise of the Board of Home Missions made an address at 8 p.m. It was a full day, and refreshingly rewarding for the young church, providing initiative for further progress. By 1921 the Sunday School section of the church building had been completed, a $3,000 pipe organ installed in the sanctuary, and the parsonage, next door to the church on the west, had been erected.

The end of an unusually productive and highly satisfactory pastorate of nine years ended, when Mr. Peeler reigned on April 14, 1925 to become Field Secretary of the recently relocated Catawba College, Salisbury, North Carolina. Dr. Peeler returned to this parish in 1937, for a second pastorate of almost ten years.

By this time "downtown" Charlotte had drastically changed. Immediately in front of the church appeared a whole city block of municipal buildings; on the west side, within inches of the property line, was erected a large commercial building; and to the north within blocks of the church and increasingly economically depressed area had developed. For the next 28 years, pastors and supply ministers came and went at short intervals. Six pastors and three supply ministers served there during that time.

It was during the administration of Dr. Felix B. Peck that the congregation inaugurated a self-study, the results of which pointed conclusively in the direction of relocation. Property was purchased at the corner of Anderson and Byrnes Streets in the Plaza Section of the city in anticipation of such a move. The old church property was sold for $75,000 to the Ebenezer Baptist Church, the congregation worshipping last in the old church on March 1, 1953. Services were held in the Plaza School house beginning March 8, 1953, until June 27, 1954, when the new educational facility on Anderson Street was ready for occupancy.

A finance committee composed of J. Byron Davis, chairman, H. T. Radermacher, treasurer, A. L. Charles, Mrs. Carl Evans, and Mrs. T. F. Hart, and a building committee consisting of D. L. Drum, Sr., chairman, E. T. Moose, Ray P. Reichert and Mrs. R. A. Robinson were named. These committees moved swiftly in making preparations to begin construction on their new church home. Plans were approved for the new church August 9, and a contract involving approximately $103,000 was authorized for the educational unit. Groundbreaking ceremonies took place August 23. Dr. Aaron R. Tosh, president of Southern Synod, made appropriate remarks.

Others participating in the exercises were: The pastor, Dr. Joseph B. Hennessey; Dewey L. Drum, Sr., chairman of the building committee; M. M. McIver, chairman of the consistory; Mrs. R. A. Robinson, representing the women of the church; and Miss Glenda Watson, representing the children of the congregation.

Of interest in this connection is an expression of Christian cooperation by the Ebenezer Baptist Church, to which the old church property was sold. This congregation received a free-will offering to be contributed to the First Church Building Fund. Said the pastor, Rev. A. Jackson Ryan, "This is going to be a free-will offering at the conclusion of the Sunday morning service. We want to show good fellowship, do a bit to better race relations, and show our appreciation to those good people for the fine way they have dealt with us." Mr. J. Bryan Davis, chairman of the Building Fund, responded by saying, "We understand that their Board of Deacons and the entire membership concurred in the idea. This will be among the most appreciated of all our gifts."

The new facility was ready for use June 27, 1954, when the pastor anticipating the future, spoke to a happy congregation on the theme, "Greater Works Shall Ye Do." Dedication occurred October 3, 1954, when Dr. Felix B. Peck, who led the congregation in making a decision to relocate, spoke on the theme, "Stability of the Church." The congregation is currently free of debt, reaching that coveted position in 1965 under the leadership of Rev. Frank K. Bostian. A new program looking toward the erection of the sanctuary is now under way.

In spite of struggles within the congregation to maintain an effective Christian program of service in a changing community, in 1949, the First Church sponsored the organization of St. Matthew's Chapel located on Bancroft Street in the Northwest section of the city. At that time, the pastor, Rev. Huitt R. Carpenter envisaged a series of well located Evangelical and Reformed Churches in Charlotte and environs. A beginning was made in the founding of St. Matthew's Chapel. While these lines are being written, another congregation not yet organized is being developed in Southeast Charlotte.

Ministerial sons of the congregation serving in the United Church of Christ are: Rev. Claude W. Kelly and Rev. David G. Kelly, Jr.

ROSTER OF PASTORS

Rev. Shuford Peeler, D.D., Organizer 1916-1925	Rev. Huitt R. Carpenter 1946-1949
Rev. John W. Myers, S.T.D. 1925-1928	Rev. Felix B. Peck, Th.D. 1949-1952
Rev. Frank S. Bromer 1928-1932	Rev. Joseph B. Hennessey, D.D. 1953-1962
Rev. A. V. Vondersmith 1934-1936	Rev. Frank K. Bostian 1962-
Rev. Shuford Peeler, D.D. 1937-1946	

SUPPLY MINISTERS

Mr. Thomas R. Safrit, Student Supply 1925-	Rev. W. P. Parker, Supply 1933-
Mr. Kendall B. Shoffner, Student Supply 1932-	Rev. Wayne D. Witte, Supply 1952-1953
	Rev. G. Ermine Plott, Supply 1962-

1. ———. Minutes. Classis of North Carolina, 1912, p. 41.
2. ———. *Op. cit.,* 1915, p. 24.
3. ———. *Op. cit.,* 1916, p. 6.
4. ———. Ibid. p. 28.
5. ———. Ibid. p. 9.
6. ———. Ibid, p. 39.
7. ———. *Op. cit.,* 1919, p. 36.

References:

Bostian, Frank K., Manuscript. First United Church of Christ, 1965.
Bostian, Frank K., Directory. First United Church of Christ, 1965.

First Church, High Point

IN APRIL 1900, when the Classis of North Carolina of the Reformed Church in the United States convened at Beulah Church, Davidson County, favorable action was taken on resolutions submitted by its committee on missions as indicated below.

> In view of the interests of the Reformed Church in Lexington and High Point, we recommend the adoption of the following:
>
> Whereas, there is urgent necessity for the establishment of Reformed churches in the towns of High Point and Lexington, and
>
> Whereas, the Board of Missions has already under contemplation the enrollment of High Point as a Mission under its care. . . .
>
> Resolved, that the Board be urged to take up these two points as one mission and place a man over them by the first of July, if possible, or as soon thereafter as practicable.
>
> Resolved, that because of the urgency in the case, the interests at these two points be committed to the care of Revs. J. C. Leonard and H. A. M. Holshouser until the action of the Board may open the way for future action. . . . .

> Resolved, that in case the Mission Board places a missionary in charge of these points, the Classis pledge the sum of $400 toward building of a church in each town, and that the Treasurer of Classis be instructed to borrow the amount, giving his note for the same.[1]

Both projects were enrolled by the Board of Missions at its July meeting, and Rev. J. C. Leonard was appointed supervisory missionary over the High Point interest.

During the months of June, July and August, theological student Charles W. Warlick was appointed by the Sunday School Board of the Reformed Church to set up a Sunday School and to do preliminary survey work. Missionary Leonard became actively involved in parish activities October first. A lot located at the corner of South Main and Russell Streets was acquired during the summer for the sum of $450. A deed for it was made November 16, 1900. The first religious service took place March 1, 1901 in the home of Walter E. Conrad, East Green Street. Three weeks later, March 24, at the same place, the congregation was organized and named First Reformed Church of High Point.

The charter member list contained nineteen names: Emery T. Hedrick, Mrs. Emery T. Hedrick, Henry H. Hedrick, Mrs. Henry H. Hedrick, Ivey T. Hedrick, Mrs. Ivey T. Hedrick, Miss Dasie Millington, Walter E. Conrad, Joseph B. Wagner, Samuel R. Wagner, Jesse F. Bowers, James Sanes, Mrs. James Sanes, Mrs. Elizabeth Clark, Mrs. Minnie Hedrick Beck, Lewis S. Livengood, Jacob Livengood, Mrs. Jacob Livengood, Miss Augusta R. Livengood. Emery T. Hedrick, Lewis S. Livengood and Jesse F. Bowers were elected elders; Joseph B. Wagner and Ivey T. Hedrick, deacons.[2]

Plans were drawn and approved for a church building of frame material, consisting of a sanctuary, a lecture room, a pulpit recess and a tower. The seating capacity was 300 people. Its outside dimensions measured 40 by 53 feet. When finished it was a neat, well appointed church designed to meet the needs of a growing congregation. Total cost of the enterprise, including the lot, church and furniture added up to $2,650. The debt was promptly liquidated by means of a loan from the Board of Missions, gifts from friends and the Woman's Missionary Society of the North Carolina Classical. The builder was Elder Emery T. Hedrick, who was also for many years Sunday School Superintendent and choir director.

Construction on the building began May 31, 1901, and was completed in August of the same year. First services were conducted in it, though unfinished, on August 18, 1901. Dedicatory rites were held the following October 20. Dr. J. M. L. Lyerly preached the sermon. During the summer of 1901, theological student William Henry Causey, by appointment of the Sunday School Board, served the parish. Rev. David E. Bowers, licensed and ordained to the Christian ministry by the Classis of North Carolina in May 1902, was commissioned associate missionary to Dr. Jacob C.

Leonard, with responsibilities on the High Point parish.[3] This relationship continued until January 1, 1903, when Mr. Bowers was
commissioned missionary pastor by the board and by the Classis
installed minister of the church.

In 1911, expanding activities required additional floor space.
This need resulted in the erection of Sunday School classrooms on
Russell Street along side of the first parsonage. Supported with a
loan of $3,500 from the Board of Home Missions, the sanctuary
was erected and made ready for dedication May 3, 1914. Dr.
Charles E. Schaeffer, Secretary of the Board of Home Missions,
preached the sermon at 11 A.M., stating that "This beautiful house
has been built in vain unless Christ abide here." Dedication rites
were read by the pastor, Dr. Lee A. Peeler. During the afternoon
and evening, representatives of the Reformed Church and the community addressed large congregations. Bringing a full day to its
end was an appropriate sermon delivered at 8 P.M., by Rev. David
E. Bowers, first pastor of the congregation.

At that time the church had a confirmed membership of 89
people, and a Sunday School enrollment of 300 pupils. Six years
later the congregation numbered 155 confirmed members, and there
were 264 names on the Sunday School roll.

Depression years which occurred during the pastorates of Rev.
Milton Whitener and Dr. William R. Shaffer, were not kind to the
First Church people, and was economically reflected in the life of
the congregation. These were years of struggle, matched by similar
experiences in other congregations throughout the Classis. However, with economic conditions adjusting favorably and under the
leadership of Rev. Hoy L. Fesperman who arrived on the parish
April 1, 1935, the church began to move ahead. A large number of
people were admitted to membership in the church. The Wrenn
Street property, which had been used as a parsonage, was sold in
1945, and a new residence for the minister located on Woodrow
Avenue was purchased. The Emery T. Hedrick Bible Class, under
the driving leadership of S. E. Tucker, became especially effective
in envangelism and in promoting the interests of Nazareth Orphans'
Home; and in anticipation of new equipment, a building fund was
started.

Long-range planning also began during the pastorate of Mr.
Fesperman, which carried over into the administration of Rev.
Carl A. Grimm. Property at 901 English Street was purchased in
anticipation of relocation of the church. This happy thought became a reality when on August 19, 1952, ground was broken for
the educational unit of their new equipment. Mr. Grimm made appropriate remarks, and President Aubrey W. Hedrick of Southern
Synod brought greetings and good wishes.

When Rev. Lloyd E. Sechriest arrived in the community on May
15, 1953. Building operations were in progress. Church property
at the corner of South Main and Russell Streets, including two rent

houses, was sold at auction for $23,500 in June of 1953. The new educational building, which the congregation was to use during the next seven years as an all-purpose building, was dedicated September 6, 1953. The pastor preached an appropriate sermon and read the ritual of dedication. These building operations represented a total financial outlay of $126,000, all of which was paid by the end of 1954.

The next six years confronted the congregation with two major concerns. The building fund was the chief item of business, tapping financial resources wherever possible, therefore by 1958 it showed a cash balance of $61,000, plus $35,000 in pledges. The Ayers property was annexed in 1958. Plans for erecting the sanctuary also required study and deliberate consideration. To get this part of the program started a building committee was elected composed of Glenn A. Brown, L. Freeman Hill, Clifton A. Koontz, Paul W. Clapp and C. R. Myers. In order to expedite required preliminary studies, the following sub-committees were appointed, naming a chairman in each case. Worship and Religious Art studies were led by Clarence Wagner; Plans and Construction by C. R. Myers; Finance and Promotion by Clarence Wagner; Furnishings and Equipment by Roy Clapp; Heating and Air-conditioning by Thurmon Fox; Musical Appointments by George Gibhardt; Lighting and Color by Bruce Weavil; Exterior Planning by M. F. Crooks and Tom Wood.

Three architectual designs were presented to the congregation, which voted in favor of the parabolic arch design.[4] Plans were subsequently approved, and groundbreaking ceremonies took place September 13, 1959. Dr. Harvey A. Fesperman, president of Southern Synod, delivered an appropriate address. Construction on the building began the following November. The cornerstone was laid June 26, 1960 when the president of Synod made an address.

Dedication services were spread out over four successive Sundays, beginning September 18, 1960. On the 18th occurred the dedication of the sanctuary, when ceremonies were in charge of the pastor; President Harvey A. Fesperman of Southern Synod and Vice President Banks J. Peeler participating in the activities. The dedicatory sermon was delivered by Dr. Peeler. Open house was observed during the afternoon, when Dr. A. Odell Leonard addressed the assembly. Rev. Allan L. Rohrbaugh was the featured speaker at a youth banquet held the evening of September 25. Addressing his people on that unusual occasion, Rev. Richard A. Mensendiek, remarked,

> We rejoice in having been called to the pastorate to share in the building program of your new sanctuary. This has privileged us to serve you in the most significant venture of your congregation. What has been achieved is a most appropriate and beautiful edifice among the churches of your city. It remained for you to favor something new in church architecture, and yet not lose what has always been considered essential in such buildings; a structure in which the worshipful aspect has not been overlooked.

Through worship in this fine church, our people will be brought closer to God, and thus find themselves drawn closer to one another. Here we shall find that grand solemnity that comes from worshipping God. Here, people of all ages, drawn from all climes and walks of life will be drawn ever closer to their Lord and Master, in a consecrated life.[5]

Mr. Mensendiek retired from the active pastorate June 24, 1962, and was succeeded as pastor of First Church by Rev. John W. Settlemyre on September 3, 1962.

This congregation has been fortunate in its choice of leadership. Among laymen whose records are worthy of note, three elders should be mentioned in this connection. Emery T. Hedrick, who "literally ran our church in its infancy;" John W. Hedrick, Mayor of the City of High Point and for many years the church treasurer; and Dr. Edgar Whitener, president of the consistory and counselor to the congregation over a period of years, and for nineteen years a member of the Board of Trustees of Catawba College, the greater part of that time its trusted and highly efficient chairman.

ROSTER OF PASTORS

Rev. Jacob C. Leonard, D.D.,
  Organizing Missionary 1900-1902
Mr. Charles W. Warlick,
  Student Summer Supply 1900-
Mr. William H. Causey,
  Student Summer Supply 1901-
Rev. David E. Bowers 1903-1907
Rev. Lee A. Peeler, D.D. 1908-1917
Mr. Robert Thena,
  Summer Student Supply 1917-
Rev. Roy E. Leinbach, Sr. 1917-1921

Rev. Dallas R. Krebs,
  Two months 1921-
Rev. Milton Whitener 1921-1928
Rev. William R. Shaffer,
  D.D. 1929-1935
Rev. Hoy L. Fesperman 1935-1946
Rev. Carl A. Grimm 1947-1953
Rev. Lloyd E. Sechriest 1953-1956
Mr. Allan L. Rohrbaugh,
  Student Summer Supply 1956-
Rev. Richard Mensendiek 1956-1962
Rev. John W. Settlemyre 1962-

1. ———. Minutes. Classis of North Carolina, 1900, p. 144.
2. ———. Manuscript. History of First Church, United Church of Christ, 1965, p. 2 ff.
3. ———. Minutes. *Op. cit.*, pp. 225, 228.
4. *Mensendiek*, Richard A., Dedication Service. First Evangelical and Reformed Church, 1960, p. 10.
5. *Ibid.* p. 7.

First Church, Landis

THE TOWN OF LANDIS, NORTH CAROLINA developed around Linn-Corriher Mills, chiefly under the influence of C. A. Linn and L. A. Corriher, both of whom were members of Mt. Zion Reformed Church. Since Landis is located within the original Mt. Zion Parish, it is understandable that many of its members would locate in that immediate community. To provide religious services for these people, as early as 1904, Rev. Joshua L. Bowers preached occasionally in the local school house.[1]

In 1908 the Classis of North Carolina committed the interests of the Reformed Church at Landis to Rev. M. M. Noacker, who was then serving as pastor of the Mt. Zion Church. He conducted services regularly there each fourth Sunday in the Methodist Church with encouraging results.[2]

In 1912 the committee on missions of the Classis recommended that a canvass be made for $1,000 with which to support a general field secretary appointed by that body who would "give the first year of his time chiefly to the development of the Reformed Church interests in China Grove, Landis and Kannapolis."[3] This plan did not materialize, but these prospective fields were committed to the oversight of Rev. William H. Causey, Dr. William B. Duttera and Dr. Peter M. Trexler.

In 1915 the Classis took specific action with reference to a new congregation in the town of Landis.

> Whereas information comes to us to the effect that the town of Landis offers to us an inviting field for the founding of a Reformed Church, there being in the town and adjacent community fully seventy-five members of our denomination,
> Resolved, that a committee, consisting of Rev. J. H. Keller and Messrs. C. A. Linn and D. L. Correll, be appointed to take charge of the interests of the Reformed Church in the town of Landis, with authority and instructions to organize a congregation as soon as possible within the coming classical year.[4]

In 1918 a request from Reformed people living in Landis was laid before the Classis, "To make Landis a mission point, and that it be a part of the West Rowan Charge; that Classis donate $2,000 toward the erection of a church in Landis."[5] In answering this request, Dr. John H. Keller was authorized to organize the congregation, and the Classis appropriated $1,000 toward the erection of a church building.[6] The following year, Dr. Keller reported to this same body:

> Your committee appointed to organize a congregation at Landis North Carolina, begs leave to report that duty attended to Sunday, April 27,

> 1919. The First Reformed Church of Landis was organized in the new house of worship with eighty-five members. A consistory of four elders and four deacons was elected and installed.[7]

The new congregation was temporarily made a part of the West Rowan Charge, and Dr. Keller who had resigned that charge, became the pastor of the newly constituted Mt. Zion-Landis Charge.

An interesting development had occurred at Mt. Zion. On April 7, 1918 Mt. Zion church building was destroyed by fire. This proved to be an opportune time to build two churches instead of one; therefore, Reformed people living in and near Landis were invited to cooperate in erecting a church in that community. Under the wise guidance of Dr. Keller a building committee was named, consisting of C. A. Linn, chairman, G. H. Corriher, J. P. Linn, L. A. Corriher, J. Wilson Deal, Walter Honeycutt, J. U. Alexander, J. W. Correll, W. T. Adams, E. L. Fleming, O. L. Linn and activities began.

Plans for the church building were developed and agreed upon, which was erected on land given by C. A. Linn. Construction on it began and proceeded rapidly until finished. Cornerstone ceremonies were conducted on the fifth Sunday in September 1908, when the address was delivered by Dr. Jacob C. Leonard. The church is a modern brick structure, equipped for worship and educational purposes. Total cost including furnishings, amounted to $25,073. Dedication services took place June 29, 1919. Dr. Walter W. Rowe preached the sermon, and the pastor read the ritual of dedication. When the charter membership list was closed, it numbered 94 people.

Further organizations appearing in the congregation immediately following its founding, were A Woman's Missionary Society, a Girls' Guild and Mission Band and other appropriate youth groups; also, in time, a unit of the Churchmen's Brotherhood. O. L. Linn was named Superintendent of the Sunday School.[8]

First Church became an independent, self-supporting congregation January 1937, upon the retirement of Dr. John H. Keller. This development required the erection of a parsonage. L. A. Corriher was asked to supervise its construction, which was located along the south side of the church building. It was completed June 1, 1941 at an approximate cost of $12,000.

Appropriately planned memorials have been installed in the church through the years, such as art glass windows, an altar centered chancel, altar cloths and vases, candle holders, collection plates and tower chimes. The organ was placed in the sanctuary in the fall of 1946, and dedicated on October 13.

Realizing the need for increased educational facilities, a building fund was started, and in November 1956 the congregation acted to purchase additional land adjacent to church property along the east line. Expenditure was $11,500. Dr. Aaron R. Tosh, who had served the congregation faithfully and well over a period of twelve years, retired December 31, 1956.

The fortieth anniversary of the organization of the congregation was observed September 27-28, 1958. The pastor, Rev. Hiram E. Davis and his committees had detailed an appropriate series of activities for the occasion. Rev. Roy E. Leinbach, Jr. addressed a Fellowship Banquet on Saturday evening. At the Anniversary on Sunday morning Dr. John H. Keller led the prayer, and Dr. Aaron R. Tosh preached the sermon. For evening vespers ministerial students, sons of the congregation, Doyce F. Wise and Joseph W. Wise participated in the service, while Rev. Lawrence A. Leonard delivered the mediation.

The Anniversary Booklet was dedicated to the ministers of First Church.

> With deepest appreciation we gratefully dedicate this 40th Anniversary Booklet to the five ministers who have served the church from its founding to the present day. These five dedicated men have unselfishly given of their time and God-given talent to the spiritual as well as the physical building of our church.
>
> Their consecration, love and devotion have inspired, comforted, encouraged and strengthened us through the years.
>
> We shall forever be grateful to them for all they have contributed to the spiritual life of our church and indeed to the lives of each and every member of the congregation.[9]

Plans for the new educational building were presented to the congregation and approved February 17, 1959. Groundbreaking ceremonies took place October 18, 1959. Dr. Harvey A. Fesperman, president of Southern Synod, made the address when the building was dedicated November 27, 1960. The building is constructed of brick, stone and wood and is of contemporary design. It is fully equipped and cost approximately $150,000.[10]

To date the congregation has been fortunate in experiencing no long vancancies. When vacancies have occurred, well prepared ministers of the church and pre-theological students have ministered satisfactorily to the congregation. Two sons of the congregation are serving as parish ministers in the United Church of Christ: Rev. Doyce F. Wise and Rev. Joseph W. Wise. The current pastor, since January 1966 is Rev. Nevin H. Feather.

ROSTER OF PASTORS

Rev. John H. Keller, D.D.,	Rev. Aaron R. Tosh, D.D. 1944-1956
Organizer 1919-1936	Rev. Hiram E. Davis 1956-1965
Rev. Roy E. Leinbach, Jr. 1937-1940	Rev. Nevin H. Feather 1966-
Rev. Lawrence A. Leonard 1941-1944	

1. ———. Minutes. Classis of North Carolina, 1905. p. 406. *Correll*, James E., Manuscript. Mt. Zion Reformed Church, 1939, p. 2.
2. ———. Minutes. Classis of North Carolina, 1910, p. 19.
3. ———. Minutes. *Op. cit.*, 1912, p. 41.
4. ———. Minutes. *Op. cit.*, 1915, p. 66.
5. ———. Minutes. *Op. cit.*, 1918, p. 39.

6. ———. Ibid. p. 47.
7. ———. Minutes. *Op. cit.*, 1919, p. 38.
8. *Linn,* Carl P., History of First Evangelical and Reformed Church, 1965, p. 1ff.
9. *Corriher,* Frederick, Jr., Fortieth Anniversary, First Evangelical and Reformed Church, 1958, p. 1.
10. *Davis,* Hiram E., Religious Education Building, First Evangelical and Reformed Church, 1960, p. 5.

First Church, Lexington

THE FIRST REFORMED CHURCH, Lexington, North Carolina, was organized January 20, 1901. In May 1900 the Classis of North Carolina, named a committee composed of Rev. Jacob C. Leonard and Rev. Harvey A. M. Holshouser to look after the interests of the Reformed Church in High Point and Lexington, pending action by the Board of Missions, and appropriated $400 toward building a church at each place. Since the Board of Missions already had under consideration the enrollment of High Point, the Classis asked that the two be considered as one mission and a man be placed in charge of them if possible by July first.[1] The board acted favorably on this request and commissioned Rev. Jacob C. Leonard as missionary, whose services to the charge were to begin October 1 of that year.[2]

Because the situation required immediate attention, the missionary began activities in Lexington in July. A lot at the corner of East Center and North Salisbury Streets was purchased for $900. Encouraged by a loan of $1,000 from the Board of Mission, and cooperation of interested people living in the community and friends, plans were drawn for a church building to be erected on the lot immediately. The first brick was laid October 4, 1900, and work proceeded so well from that date that the building was practically finished before the congregation was invited to assemble for the first service.[3]

The first church building was constructed of brick and wood material, and the roof was covered with slate. Outside dimensions were 40 by 51 feet, containing a sanctuary, a lecture room, pulpit recess and bell tower. Seating capacity was approximately 300 people. Interior walls were plastered, and the overhead ceiling was of panelled yellow pine under hard oil, the wainscoting being finished in like manner. Pews were of pine; the chancel and aisles were covered with carpet. Total cost of the building added up to $3,600. It was dedicated February 17, 1901, when Dr. Joseph L. Murphy preached the sermon.

Thus, the house was finished and made ready, then began the gathering of a congregation. The first service in the new sanctuary was held January 20, 1901. The sanctuary was filled with worshippers, both morning and evening. Letters of transfer for seventeen persons were in the hands of the pastor, in addition to the names of five others who were ready to become a part of the organization. At the end of the first service that day, the First Reformed Church of Lexington, North Carolina, was organized. Twenty-two names were on the charter member list at the close of the day. These were: Mr. and Mrs. C. Columbus Burkhart, Mr. and Mrs. Charles H. Burkhart, Dupree Clodfelter, Earl Clodfelter, Charles L. Everhart, Mrs. Robert Heitman, Mrs. Devid Hinkle, Mrs. Earl H. Holmes, Mrs. J. F. L. Tussey, Mr. and Mrs. J. Tilden Hedrick, Mr. and Mrs. P. James Leonard, Mr. and Mrs. Edwin A. Rothrock, Mrs. Charles Rhodes, Miss Ada Rothrock, Mrs. Samuel Rothrock, Mrs. Amanda Sowers and Mrs. Joseph H. Sowers. P. James Leonard, Edwin A. Rothrock and C. Columbus Burkhart were elected elders; J. Tilden Hedrick, Charles L. Everhart and Dupree Clodfelter, deacons. The Sunday School was set up the following Sunday, when fifty five people were present. C. Columbus Burkhart was named superintendent.[4]

The first parsonage was built on the lot along side the church on the west, facing East Center Street, in the fall of 1901. Dr. and Mrs. Jacob C. Leonard moved into it January 29, 1902 and lived there until January 1, 1926, when the family moved to the second parsonage at 214 West Center Street.

In 1907 the church building was enlarged, under the supervision of Edwin A. Rothrock, D. H. Hinkle and J. Tilden Hedrick. This improvement consisted of adding a section to the rear, which provided for about one third additional seating capacity in the sanctuary. The congregation went to self support July 1, 1910, a little less than ten years from the date of its enrollment by the Board of Missions.

Another vital step forward occurred January 2, 1912. Elder J. Tilden Hedrick superintendent of the Sunday School who served in that office for eighteen consecutive years, proposed to the congregation that if the church would purchase and equip the building, he would erect a Sunday School facility on the lot opposite the church on the east side of North Salisbury Street, facing East Center Street. His proposition was gratefully and unanimously accepted. Operations began immediately to prepare for and to erect it. The cornerstone was laid August 9, 1912. Dedication took place July 13, 1913. Dr. Walter W. Rowe delivered an appropriate address.

The parish program was further enriched in 1920, when a lot immediately behind the school building, on the corner of North Salisbury and East First Streets was purchased and that space converted into an out-of-doors recreation area, suitable for children and young people.[5]

In 1922, perhaps the most significant step in the life of the church, since its organization, was taken. Having outgrown the first sanctuary, plans were made to provide more adequate worship facilities. A decision was reached by the congregation to erect a church on the site occupied by the first church building and the parsonage. This decision required tremendous adjustments on the part of the congregation in thought and habit, setting up a train of events destined to sharply alter the life and the program of First Church. A new house for the minister was erected at 214 West Center Street in 1925; the old parsonage was moved to the northeast corner of North Salisbury and East First Streets in 1926; the Sunday School annex appeared in 1927; and the beautiful and spacious new sanctuary was dedicated April 8, 1928. Dr. Paul S. Leinbach, editor of the Reformed Church Messenger, preached the sermon.

On that occasion the church bulletin explained:

> The church was built in 1927-1928 on lots formerly occupied by the old church and parsonage, the total cost being $97,988.82. There were many special gifts not counted in this sum, such as hymn boards, baptismal font, pastor's study furniture, pulpit rug, pulpit Bible, pulpit lamp, communion trays, piano for social rooms, balcony screen, kneeling cushions, communion table, communion table linen, several hymn books, cornerstone, palms, potted plants, metal stands, wall tablet.[6]

Financial obligations created by the erection of the new place of worship were promptly met, but the people were lost in the "strange bigness" and rigid orderliness of the magnificent new sanctuary. They remembered the precious intimacy and satisfying warmth, the wholehearted singing and the compelling evangelistic appeal so easily possible in the "little church." These values were none-the-less real in the new house, but their effectiveness was so largely swallowed up in space and neutralized by an atmosphere of ecclesiastical formality, that the worshippers often went away wondering. But time is a gracious benefactor. These same devoted people came to see in their new church home what its creators intended—the majesty, the beauty, the orderliness of the Eternal God—and love it.

After a continuous and an exceptionally fruitful ministry of thirty-eight years to this congregation, Dr. Leonard retired. His retirement was effective January 31, 1939. Devoted people bestowed upon him the title of Pastor Emeritus. The occasion of his retirement was fittingly observed January 29, 1939, in a series of services scheduled for morning and afternoon, entitled, "Thirty-Eighth Anniversary, First Evangelical and Reformed Church, Lexington, North Carolina, and its pastor, Dr. Jacob C. Leonard." The bulletin for the day carried the following statement:

> With the month of January A. D. 1939, the pastorate of Dr. J. C. Leonard in this church comes to a close, after a ministry of 38 years.
> The morning service is to be conducted by the minister in which he preaches his final sermon as pastor, but it is fondly hoped by him and his loyal people, not his last sermon in this church so dear to him and them.
> The afternoon service will be in charge of the Ministers' Association of Lexington, honoring their brother who is closing a ministry of 38 years in the First Church and a full half-century in the Gospel ministry.[7]

In 1940, accepting a suggestion from the new minister of the church, the consistory authorized that the Sunday nearest to each January 20 be observed as Anniversary Day, commemorating the founding of the church and honoring its Pastor Emeritus. Each year after that until his death March 15, 1943, Dr. Leonard detailed and conducted this important service to the delight of everyone. Official statistics in his ministerial career appear below: Infant baptisms 560; adult baptisms 1,025; received into the fellowship of the church by letter 551, by confirmation 1,515, renewal of faith 279; dismissals from the church by letter 335, erasure 353; losses by death 253; funerals conducted 1,035; marriage ceremonies performed 398; sermons, not including an infinite number of lectures and addresses, 6,852.[8]

> The record which he leaves is one which portrays energetic faithfulness. It covers more than a half century of active service to Church and State. The central theme of his life's work was, "The Kingdom of God." Practically every interest on the scale of his chosen profession claimed his attention. He was educator, administrator, author, pastor, preacher of the Word of God, and a friend of the people. If it would have been necessary to recognize him by only one of these titles, those who know him best, feel that he would have chosen the title, "A Preacher of the Word of God." . . . .
> Dr. Leonard was a "keeper of the records" for his denomination in North Carolina. For more than fifty years his study was the repository for the records of the North Carolina Classis and more recently the Southern Synod. This fact alone placed him in a position to be chief counselor in creating and directing policies of the church in North Carolina. During this period twenty-four of the fifty nine congregations in the state were organized; Nazareth Orphans' Home was founded; the Summer Missionary Conference was born; the Youth Movement was begun; summer youth camps were started; and the educational interests of the denomination were

repeatedly reorganized and adjusted to current needs, the latest being the reorganization of Catawba College at Salisbury, North Carolina. In all of this external and internal expansion his influence was keenly felt. . . . . .

Someone has said that with his departure "an era in our Church in North Carolina has come to an end." This statement surely contains truth; how much truth the next few years will reveal. Whether an era has ended and a new one has begun is, perhaps, not so important, but more lasting and far reaching is the fact that Dr. Leonard's work and influence will continue to be felt in Southern Synod for years to come.[9]

The second pastorate began March 1, 1939, when Rev. Banks J. Peeler came to the parish. Because, by earlier agreement, the second parsonage was deeded by the church to the Pastor Emeritus, the new minister and his family occupied a house at 141 West First Avenue, known as the "Ed Layden House," which was later purchased for $7,750. To underwrite certain anticipated property improvements, including extensive sanctuary repairs and redecoration plus the cost of the new parsonage, a campaign was launched in 1940 for $20,000.

The new pastorate had scarcely begun when war-drums began to beat in Europe; followed by Pearl Harbor December 7, 1941. This development required the up-rooting of a whole generation of young people, of which First Church had many. On the Service Roll, which hung during those days in the foyer of the church building, were one hundred forty-one names. Most of them were sons, but a few of them had married daughters of the congregation. While these young people, without exception, wore the uniform of their country with honor, it is appropriate to record here that seven of them were wounded in the line of duty, and four others made the supreme sacrifice. Lawrence A. Everhart died in training; R. Wade Biesecker of the Air Force, Arland A. Hudson a Paratrooper and Bobby Smith Lookabill an Infantryman, all died in action over Germany.

A sixteen bell Deagan Carillon was installed in the church tower, and dedicated March 29, 1942. The carillon was the gift of Mrs. Jones Tilden Hedrick, in memory of her husband, who for eighteen years was superintendent of the Sunday School and from the founding of First Church until his death either a deacon or an elder; and, also, a widely influential layman in the councils of Southern Synod, its boards and agencies.

Resulting from a fire which occurred on the evening of January 20, 1945, the Sunday School building was extensively repaired, reconditioned and decorated. In 1949 preparations were made for an observance of the 50th Anniversary of the Church. During that summer two oil burning furnaces were installed in an excavated chamber under the pastor's study of the sanctuary. Roof, walls, windows were repaired in the sanctuary and the interior completely redecorated. The parsonage was also reconditioned, involving a new furnace, outside painting and interior decoration. As a phase of this property expansion, in 1954, the G. F. Hankins property along the east side of the Sunday School building, facing East Center Street, was acquired.

The 50th Anniversary of the congregation was appropriately observed in a series of services and complimentary activities beginning January 14, 1951. Dr. A. Odell Leonard, a son of the congregation, preached the Founders' Day sermon on the 14th; Dr. Lonnie A. Carpenter, president of Southern Synod, spoke on denominational affairs the evening of the 17th; the five ministerial sons of the congregation appeared on the evening of the 18th, emphasizing life commitment. Open house was observed the evening of the 19th, when the congregation was at home to its friends and wellwishers.

Anniversary Sunday, observed on the 21st, presented Dr. Allan S. Meck, president of The Theological Seminary, Lancaster, Pennsylvania, at 11 A.M.; and Dr. Alvin R. Keppel, president of Catawba College, in a service for young people at 6:30 P.M. Sunday School anniversary and recognitions occurred on the morning of January 28.

After serving the parish sixteen years and nine months, Dr. Banks J. Peeler resigned, effective December 1, 1955. During this extremely difficult period of transition, beside material improvements and property additions recorded above, the staff was enlarged to include a director of Christian Education and the budget was boosted from approximately $8,000 to $24,000, and a total of 567 people were admitted to full membership in the church.

The church was vacant until May 1956, when Rev. Marlin T. Schaeffer became its pastor. Extensive repairs were made on the parsonage before his arrival. Shortly thereafter two committees were appointed, vested with authority to study equipment needs and to recommend ways and means of providing them. The building committee was composed of Giles Crowell, chairman, E. O. Hinkle, Dr. J. C. Leonard, Jr., Theodore Leonard, John F. Raker, Hoyt Sink, J. Frank Smith and G. Arthur Thomason; finance, Roby Leonard, chairman, James Mashburn, Simeon A. DeLapp, Moyer Smith, Robert Grubb, Henry Beck, Vernon G. Price, Jr., Clifford Lopp, James Swicegood, Foyle Wagner and Dr. Foyell Smith.

From studies which followed, the present well appointed educational building was erected. Old properties which stood on the lots involved were razed, and in their place was erected a $330,000 educational facility. It contains a fully equipped chapel, a fellowship hall, a modern kitchen and kitchenette, a ladies' parlor, offices for the pastor and secretary, a library, a recreation room and twenty seven class rooms arranged in departments. The house was dedicated January 19, 1964 by the pastor. Dr. Banks J. Peeler, president of Southern Synod, delivered the dedicatory address.[10]

The First Church has been at its best during periods of missionary outreach. In 1904, the Second Church of Lexington was founded, and with the help of summer supplies, Dr. Leonard served that congregation over a period of eighteen years. In 1930, serving as chaplain of the National Orphans' Home, Jr. O. U. A. M., located in South Lexington, he organized a non-denominational church among the children and leaders of that institution, and ministered to it until his retirement. Christ Church, Lexington, was begun in 1945 and organized March 2, 1947, being nurtured by devoted churchmen of First Church in the persons of I. L. Sink, Charles W. Parks, Holland E. Shoaf and Paul Hinkle, perhaps others. Dr. Banks J. Peeler, then serving as pastor of First Church, ministered to that congregation over a period of ten years.

The outreach of this congregation is further reflected in its support of the Forward Movement of the Reformed Church in the United States launched in 1919, underwriting it to the extent of $33,483; a chapel in Shiroishi, Japan; two dormitories at Nazareth Childrens' Home; the Hedrick Administration Building on the campus at Catawba College, and a cabin at Johns River Valley Camp.

This congregation has sent five sons into the Christian ministry: Rev. A. Odell Leonard, D.D., Rev. Lawrence A. Leonard, Rev. Harvey H. Koonts, Jr., and Rev. C. Keith Sink in the United Church of Christ; and Rev. W. Calvin Leonard in the Methodist Church.

ROSTER OF PASTORS

Rev. Jacob C. Leonard, D.D. 1901-1939   Rev. Marlin T. Schaeffer 1956-
Rev. Banks J. Peeler, D.D. 1939-1955

1. ———. Minutes. Classis of North Carolina, 1900, p. 144.
2. ———. Minutes. *Op. cit.*, 1901, p. 180.
3. *Leonard,* Jacob C., Anniversary Brochure, First Reformed Church, 1921, p. 7 ff.
4. *Leonard,* Jacob C., History of Southern Synod, Evangelical and Reformed Church, 1940, p. 203.
5. *Peeler,* Banks J., 50th Anniversary, First Evangelical and Reformed Church, 1951, p. 15.
6. *Leonard,* Jacob C., Bulletin. Thirty-Eighth Anniversary, First Evangelical and Reformed Church, 1939, p. 3.
7. *Ibid.* p. 2.
8. *Leonard. Op. cit.,* Southern Synod, p. 206.
9. *Peeler, Banks J.,* The Standard, Southern Synod, Evangelical and Reformed Church, Volume 51, Number 3, 1943, p. 4.
10. *Leonard,* Theodore, Dedication Brochure. First United Church of Christ, 1964, p. 2 ff.

First Church, Raleigh

OVER A PERIOD OF YEARS Reformed Church people, for professional and business reasons, established homes in the Capitol City of Raleigh, North Carolina. These church folk found their places in the community and eventually affiliated with churches of their choice. This situation stimulated discussion among church leaders of Southern Synod, resulting in investigation of possibilities for founding an Evangelical and Reformed Church there.

Among those who had not affiliated at the time with a church

in the Capitol City was W. Clifton Pickett, Jr. of Lexington, North Carolina, whose membership was in the First Evangelical and Reformed Church there. In 1953, encouraged by his pastor, Dr. Banks J. Peeler, he interviewed a number of Reformed people who were also hoping that someday Southern Synod would establish a church in Raleigh.

He found sufficient interest among them to justify a series of informal discussion meetings and some correspondence with officials of the Board of National Missions of the Evangelical and Reformed Church. At its annual meeting in November of 1953, the board listed Raleigh as a mission project. Developing it depended upon finding a suitable missionary to direct the effort.

On the evening of March 11, 1954, 19 persons met at the Raleigh Women's Club, when Rev. G. Harold Myers, prospective missionary for the field, was present. The meeting had been called by Rev. Lawrence A. Leonard, chairman of the committee on National Missions of Southern Synod, who presided. Dr. Ralph S. Weiler, Eastern Field Secretary of the Board of National Missions and Dr. Banks J. Peeler, its president, also were present. Growing out of this gathering, a steering committee was appointed to manage affairs on the field, which consisted of W. Clifton Pickett, Jr., chairman, Mrs. George Bailey, secretary, Edsel Cook, treasurer, Helen Peeler, Perry E. Moose and Max Warlick.

Mr. Myers agreed to undertake the work, and plans were made for his arrival June 1, 1954. A four-room apartment located at 1424 Park Drive became a temporary residence for the minister and his family. Later a suitable house in the northwest section of the city was rented for a parsonage. The missionary spent all of his time from June until September making contacts and developing plans incident to religious services scheduled to begin early in the fall.

The first service for the mission was held September 19, 1954, at the Sherewood Bates Elementary School on Oberlin Road, with an attendance of 55 people. The sacrament of Holy Communion was administered October 3, 1954. The Sunday School also was organized on October 3, enrolling 32 pupils, divided into five classes. Thirty one people signed the charter member list when it was presented October 31.

On November 7, First Evangelical and Reformed Church was selected as the name of the prospective organization, which was officially effected November 14, 1954. A Consistory also was elected on organization day, composed of W. Clifton Pickett, Jr. and W. B. Cope, elders; and Perry E. Moose, Edsel Cook, Helen Peeler and Parley King, Jr., deacons. These officers were ordained and installed in their respective offices on December 12, 1954. By the end of the year, official membership had climbed to 41; and, in June of 1955, when the charter member roll was closed, there were 55 names on it.[1]

During the fall and winter months, events rapidly succeeded each other, so that by the beginning of 1955, the young congregation felt itself reasonably well established. Various gifts of equipment and denominational cooperation contributed greatly to this confidence. Trinity Church, Conover, gave four offering plates; First Church, Lexington, sent 100 song books; Ursinus Church, Rockwell, and St. Matthew's Church, Maiden, provided money with which to purchase church hymnals; First Church, Winston Salem, gave 21 choir robes; and the Eastern Section Ministerium presented a Communion service set. The Women's Guild of Southern Synodical, in session during the fall months, had acted to raise $10,000 over a period of two years to be applied on the cost of a lot on which to erect a church building. The Board of National Missions, on December 29, 1954, purchased the lot on which the church stands at the corner of Wade Avenue and Dixie Trail in the name of the church, holding title to it until the congregation became financially able to take it over. A loan of $2,500 from the Churchmen's Brotherhood of Southern Synod completed the financial underwriting of $12,500 paid for the church lot.

A call was extended to Rev. G. Harold Myers January 9, 1955 to become pastor of the church. The call was accepted, approved by Southern Synod which also installed him February 6, 1955, as its first pastor. Rites were conducted by Dr. Harvey A. Fesperman, Dr. Banks J. Peeler, Rev. Lawrence A. Leonard and W. Clifton Pickett, Jr. Reporting to Southern Synod in April 1955, its committee on National Missions said:

> June 1, 1954, the Rev. G. Harold Myers having received the challenge and call of the Board of National Missions, began his pastorate in Raleigh. November 14, 1954, First Church, Raleigh was officially organized. January 9, 1955, First Church, Raleigh called Mr. Myers as their first pastor. He accepted and was installed February 6, 1955.[2]

Believing that church meetings should be held in the vicinity of the permanent church site, Sunday School sessions and worship services, beginning June 12, 1955, were held in the Fred Olds School on Dixie Trail. Looking ahead toward the erection of a suitable church building, two committees were elected: a building committee composed of Parley King, Jr., chairman, Perry E. Moose, Albert Banadyga, Daniel Van Mater and Helen Peeler; finance committee consisting of W. B. Cope, chairman, Mrs. George Bailey, Edsel Cook, Robert Klatt and John Herman. Ex-officio members of all church committees were the president of the consistory and the pastor of the church.

These committees acted immediately in developing church building sketches and a plan for financing the proposed sanctuary. Building plans were approved by the congregation early in September of 1955, but only the educational unit was authorized to be erected. This section of plans contained 5,705 square feet of space, including a chapel to seat 250 people, seven classrooms, church offices and a kitchen. Proposed expenditures involving lot, as well as building and furnishings, were budgeted at $85,000. This church plan, among 200 entries in the Church Architectual Guild of America Contest on the basis of utility and beauty, was awarded second place.[3]

Groundbreaking ceremonies were held on September 25, 1955, directed by the pastor. Associated with him in these activities were members of the consistory and members of other church organizations. Dr. Banks J. Peeler, representing the Board of National Missions, delivered an appropriate address.

Construction on the building began immediately. It was completed and ready for dedication on May 20, 1956. Dr. Harvey A. Fesperman, president of Southern Synod, preached the sermon. Dedication rites were read by the pastor, Rev. G. Harold Myers. Building operations were financed by a gift of $10,000 from the Board of National Missions, and a loan of $40,000 from the same source, plus pledges and cash from members and friends of the congregation.

The Opening Service Bulletin for the Christian Education building carried the following lines which significantly describe the spirit current in the congregation:

> Love built this shrine; these hallowed walls uprose
> To give seclusion from hurrying throngs,
> From rivalry and strife, from taunt of foes—
> If foes thou hast. On silent feet come in,
> Bow low in penitence. Who'er thou art
> Thou, too, hast sinned. Uplift in prayer thy heart.
> Thy Father's blessing waiteth. . . .[4]
>
> — *John Davidson*

Parish activities are, in some measure, reflected in the following church organizations: The Churchmen's Brotherhood was begun

January 23, 1955, the Women's Guild was organized January 27, 1955, and youth groups to serve young people of the parish and Evangelical and Reformed students on the campus of State College of the University of North Carolina have been effective since the church began. An under-shepherd plan of parish evangelism was inaugurated in January of 1955, dividing the parish area into four groups.

Furniture in the chapel was given in memory of Raymond Pethel, and the church organ in memory of John Herman, both charter members. During the 10 years of its history, congregational records yield the following revealing information: 206 people have been received into membership with the church—170 by transfer, eight by renewal of vows and 28 by the rite of confirmation. Losses occurring mostly by removal from the community, 74; deaths, 10; and erasures, 25. Membership as of February 25, 1965 was 97.

ROSTER OF PASTORS

Rev. G. Harold Myers,	Rev. John J. Carey, Ph.D.,
Organizing Missionary 1954-	Stated Supply 1959-
Rev. G. Harold Myers 1954-1958	Rev. Frank K. Bostian 1959-1963
	Rev. Merle F. Sollinger 1963-1966

1. *Peeler*, Helen E., Manuscript. History of the United Church of Christ—First Evangelical and Reformed Church, 1965, p. 2 ff.
2. ———. Minutes. Southern Synod, 1955, p. 42.
3. *Myers*, G. Harold, Our History, The Opening Service Bulletin, 1956, p. 5.
4. *Ibid.* p. 1.

First Church, Salisbury

IN 1768 JOHN L. BEARD, a devout Lutheran layman, deeded a plot of land to the Lutheran Church in the village of Salisbury, North Carolina, and provided in it that "the Reformed Calvin ministers at such times as the Lutheran minister doth not want to perform divine services therein" should have the use of it.[1] This reference implies that members of the Reformed faith were living in Salisbury at that time. This was the year when Rev. Samuel Suther, a Reformed Church minister, arrived in North Carolina, and began preaching to German settlers in various parts of the state. Five years after that Rev. Adolph Nussman, the first Lutheran pastor to preach in this section, arrived in North Carolina.[2] One hundred twenty-eight years later, a small group of Reformed people overtured the Classis of North Carolina to establish a church of their faith in Salisbury.[3] There are acceptable reasons for such neglect, but this case affords a good illustration of how hesitant were German settlers to break through the barriers of culture and language and become a part of the larger world around them.

Dr. J. M. L. Lyerly, Rev. Anthony Shulenberger, Dr. Jacob C. Leonard and Dr. Paul Barringer were "appointed to organize a congregation and take charge of the interest" in Salisbury.[4] Dr. Lyerly and Dr. Leonard organized the congregation June 28, 1896,[5]

in the home of Mr. and Mrs. F. M. Holshouser located in South-east Salisbury, naming it "Faith Reformed Church." There were eight charter members: Mr. and Mrs. F. M. Holshouser, Mrs. John Odell, Mrs. Cora Earnhardt and Dorsett Holshouser, members of Old Shiloh; M. D. Lefler of Bethel, Bear Creek; and Mr. and Mrs. Henry C. Corriher of Mt. Zion churches. M.D. Lefler was elected elder, and Henry C. Corriher, deacon. Both officers were ordained and installed in their respective positions at that first meeting.

This young congregation was correctly named. They were few in numbers and very limited in economic resources; indeed, they needed faith for the task which lay ahead of them. First meetings were held in the local Y.M.C.A. building, but this did not prove to be advisable. Working through the committee appointed by Classis, a conference was arranged with Superintendent A. C. Whitmer of the denominational Board of Missions, resulting in the enrollment of the Salisbury project with subsidy, and through that board also purchased a lot on the Northeast corner of South Church and West Horah Streets. The Classis pledged $500 toward a church building, and in order to encourage the congregation in its undertaking, authorized the treasurer of Classis to borrow the money and arrange a note for it.[6]

Rev. William H. Stubblebine was commissioned missionary pastor. He began his work November 1, 1896. A temporary chapel of wood construction was erected along the east line of the lot, where activities were carried on during the winter months. Erection of a church building of brick and wood material began early in 1897. The cornerstone was laid September 2 of that year. Services were held in the unfinished building in the fall of 1898. Mr.

Stubblebine resigned March 1, 1899, after serving on the parish only two years and four months.

Rev. Gerney Weber came to the parish in October 1899, making an impressive beginning, but when stricken with Typhoid fever in July 1900 he died in November of that year. The death of their new minister and a burdensome debt discouraged the small congregation; therefore, an appeal was made to the Board of Missions for financial aid and counsel. But the board was in no position to provide further financial assistance and suggested that the Classis undertake to raise the amount of the debt. Dr. Paul Barringer was asked to be an agent to promote the Salisbury Mission among the churches of the Classis, hoping to provide sufficient money to cover that obligation. A large part of the debt was liquidated by contributions from the churches and friends in Salisbury outside of the congregation.[7]

Licentiate William B. Duttera, Ph.D., became pastor of this church June 1, 1901. The Classis of North Carolina ordained him to the Christian ministry and installed him pastor of the church.[8] He was endowed with qualities of leadership required in this parish. He took firm hold of the situation, liquidating debts, finishing the church building, erecting a rent house along the east line of the church lot in 1906, and installing an organ in the sanctuary. The Potomac Synod met in Faith Church in October 1903.

Over a period of fourteen years the congregation thrived; then developed serious internal problems. Twenty three members of Faith congregation overtured the Classis to organize a second Reformed church in Salisbury.[9] Before the problem could be resolved, approximately one half of the confirmed membership withdrew from the church and the pastor resigned.[10]

A committee appointed by the Classis acted quickly in requesting the Board of Missions to reenroll the church with subsidy.[11] The church was enrolled by the board and Rev. C. Columbus Wagoner was commissioned pastor, arriving in Salisbury January 1, 1916. Mr. Wagoner conducted a healing ministry, counselling the confused, arbitrating differences and reorganizing the parish. Property was improved, including the construction of a basement under the church building to be used for educational and social purposes. Because of confusion concerning its name, that was changed to "First Reformed Church" and approved by the Classis May 4, 1919. When Mr. Wagoner resigned, August 1, 1922, the congregation had regained its equilibrium and was steadily moving ahead again, having more than doubled its confirmed membership and Sunday School enrollment.[12]

Dr. William H. Causey served the congregation for a brief period of eight months, before Dr. Banks J. Peeler began his ministry, May 1, 1924. Considerable property improvement took place on the parsonage and in the church building. Catawba College was in the process of being transferred from Newton, North Carolina to Salisbury, where it began operations in September 1925. Nervousness prevailed in the congregation in anticipation of this important event. However, loyal leadership cooperated in the venture so that "town and gown" moved remarkably well together, in spite of crowded conditions and inadequate equipment.

These conditions continued to remind the people of the urgent need for better facilities. So concerned became some of the more conscientious, forward-looking folks, that adventures were made from time to time hoping to discover a way to remedy it. A great deal of discussion prevailed with reference to locating the church on West Innis Street. With this in view, for a brief time, option was taken on a lot at the Northeast corner of West Innis and North Ellis Streets. Two small but highly important money gifts were made to a building fund in the late 1920s, which serve to illustrate how well aware a growing number of people in the congregation were of their unusual opportunity to effectively represent the Reformed denomination in the local community. Dr. W. Augusta Lantz, dean of women at Catawba College, contributed a check of $30 which represented rent money on certain property; Mrs. Freda Gardner Holshouser, a tither, made a contribution of $25, both of them ear-marked for that purpose. These ladies, and other interested friends, were looking ahead; indeed, they were looking ahead thirty years. Folks like these are responsible for the very beautiful and well appointed church edifice which now graces the elevation overlooking West Horah Street.

First Church went to self support October 1, 1928. The Miller property was acquired in 1929. Thereafter the Sunday School was divided into three sections; adults, occupying the sanctuary and annex; children, the basement area; and young people, the Miller house. The church grew in those years to a confirmed membership of a few more than 300.

Dr. George Taylor Fitz came to the community March 1, 1933. His administration continued, in effect, policies that had been established. By involving himself in community and inter-church affairs, he greatly extended the influence of the congregation in the city of Salisbury. Therefore, by the time of his resignation, March 31, 1937, the congregation numbered 393 members, and they were ready to take some very important steps forward.

The pastorate of Rev. Joshua L. Levens is marked by physical and material expansion. He came to the parish September 15, 1945. A new parsonage was purchased from Dr. and Mrs. Shuford Peeler, located on West Bank Street, and the old one was converted into an educational facility. In 1946 three important committees were appoined: Building, composed of Dr. Donald C. Dearborn, chairman, Hubert W. Lyerly, Manlius C. Barnhardt, Sr., Albert Willard, John J. Gminder, Alvin R. Keppel, B. D. Arey, William R. Bostian,

Sr., and Nathan O. Ribelin; Building Fund: Harold D. Isenberg, chairman, Albert Willard, Mrs. Raymond Jenkins, Mrs. J. Gerney Holshouser, Henry P. A. Trexler, John P. Robinson, Sr., and R. Paul Propst; Special Gifts and Memorials; Harry R. Peeler, chairman, Mrs. Nathan O. Ribelin, Marie Barringer, Mrs. James Bostian, Mrs. Keiffer A. Kluttz, Ralph A. Bostian, William M. Barringer and Elmer Lagg.

In 1947 the building fund balance had grown to $40,000. The B. V. Hedrick property, running through the 200 block on West Horah Street, on which were two houses, one of them facing Monroe Street, was purchased in 1950 for $25,000. This property was acquired in anticipation of a site for the new church building and a temporary parsonage. The house on Bank Street was sold in 1951 for $15,050, and the house on Monroe Street was reconditioned for a residence of the pastor. In October of the same year, the Murdock property at the Southwest corner of West Horah and South Church Streets became available and was purchased for the sum of $15,000. This property was converted into two rental apartments. The old church building was sold to the Knights of Pythias for $18,000 on September 22, 1954. Action authorizing the sale of the two houses on Horah Street for $12,000 was taken May 23, 1954.

Groundbreaking ceremonies for the new church building took place January 4, 1953, and construction on it began in the spring of that year. Unveiling of the cornerstone occurred October 3, 1954, when the pastor, Dr. Donald C. Dearborn and Manlius C. Barnhardt, Sr., participated in the ceremonies; after which, led by the pastor, the congregation occupied its long hoped-for sanctuary. The occasion was emphasized by a series of services which continued through the week, when Dr. Banks J. Peeler was the preacher.[13] At that time only the sanctuary was completed, with the education section framed in and sub-floored.

Mr. Levens resigned March 31, 1957, leaving a church membership of 454 people and property valued at near $400,000.

Rev. Porter Seiwell began a short but fruitful pastorate of three years, in June 1957. Sections of the unfinished educational building were finished, largely by free labor. This was a time of adjusting to the heavy financial load occasioned by building operations. Commendable progress was also made in an enriched and an extended parish program.

Perhaps the single outstanding occasion of this pastorate was dedication of the finished church building, which took place September 27, 1959. Former pastors, and the president of Southern Synod, expressed greetings. Rev. G. Harold Myers, chairman of the Synodical Committee on Christian Education, delivered a meditation. The pastor greeted his congregation with the following statement.

The words of the great hymn "Now Thank We All Our God" are most fitting here. We express our thankfulness to Him, for, with the exception of a few minor changes and additions, our physical plant is completed. It is beautiful; it is practical. Yet, the work has only begun. Every member of the parish must labor diligently in study, prayer and devotion to his high calling in order that the spiritual quality of our church surpass its physical beauty.[14]

Dr. Lonnie A. Carpenter has served the congregation since August 28, 1960. This pastorate has made a definite contribution to the total life of the parish. Debts have been methodically paid, and gradually other important additions to property and equipment have been realized such as: concrete pavements in 1962; the Deweese property along the west line of the church lot in 1963, involving $5,500; chandeliers in and redecoration of the sanctuary in 1965; and altar paraments and chancel equipment, also a new parsonage in 1966. The new parsonage is located on South Jackson Street, and represents a financial investment of $31,100.

Three sons of the congregation are serving in the Christian Ministry: Rev. Samuel J. Kirk, Rev. Charles L. Fisher and Rev. Frank K. Bostian; also, two daughters grace the homes of ministers of the church: Mrs. Eulene Fisher Shepherd and Mrs. Junia Keppel Moss.

ROSTER OF PASTORS

Rev. William H. Stlbblebine 1896-1899	Rev. Banks J. Peeler, D.D. ..1924-1932
Rev. Gerney Weber 1899-1900	Rev. George T. Fitz, D.D. ..1933-1945
Rev. William B. Duttera,	Rev. Joshua L. Levens 1945-1957
Ph.D. 1901-1915	Rev. Porter Seiwell 1957-1960
Rev. C. Columbus Wagoner ..1915-1922	Rev. Lonnie A. Carpenter,
Rev. William H. Causey,	D.D. 1960-
D.D. 1922-1923	

1. *Clapp*, Jacob C., Editor. Historic Sketch of the Reformed Church in North Carolina, 1908, p. 237.
2. *Ibid.* p. 29.
3. ———. Minutes. Classis of North Carolina, 1896, p. 11.
4. *Ibid.* p. 13.
5. ———. Minutes. *Op. cit.*, 1897, p. 7.
6. *Ibid.* p. 16.
7.. ———. Minutes. *Op. cit.*, 1902, pp. 211, 221.
8. *Ibid.* p. 219.
9. ———. Minutes. *Op cit.*, 1915, p. 36.
10. ———. Minutes. *Op. cit.*, 1916 pp. 4, 5.
11. *Ibid.* p. 20.
12. *Fisher*, Mrs. Hoy Lee, A History of the First United Church of Christ, 1965, p. 5 ff.
13. *Levens*, Joshua L., Opening Service of the New Church, First Evangelical and Reformed Church, 1954, p. 3 ff.
14. *Seiwell*, Porter, Dedication Service, First United Church of Christ, 1959, p. 10.

First Church, Winston Salem

A NUMBER OF YEARS before an attempt was made to establish a Reformed Church in Winston Salem, North Carolina, people were concerned about it. In 1902, an overture appeared on the agenda

of the Classis of North Carolina, from a group of people living in the area, asking that counsel and financial aid be provided in organizing a church in the Waughtown section of the city. That body responded as follows.

> We recommend that the Rev. H. A. M. Holshouser be instructed to organize a congregation at Waughtown at his discretion, and to take it under his pastoral care, if so organized; and that we regret our inability to grant $500 at this time towards the building of a church.[1]

In 1903 Dr. Holshouser reported on his stewardship.

> Having cossulted with our people at Waughtown in regard to the organization at that place, in accord with the instruction of Classis, we decided that inasmuch as there is at present no available place of worship and inasmuch as they are unable to erect a house without outside help, they think best not to organize.
>
> They ask Classis to remember their needs and consider the opening at their place for building up a congregation.[2]

Nothing further appears to have been done about it until 1905, except perhaps some pastoral visitation. At that time Rev. William H. Causey was appointed by the Classis to look after the interests of the Reformed Church at Waughtown. Mr. Causey reported on his activities in the spring of 1906.

> On September 8, 1905, we organized a congregation at Waughtown, North Carolina, with a membership of fourteen.
>
> We have not taken any active steps towards building, because we have been waiting for the action of the Board of Home Missions with reference to this place.
>
> Since the organization was effected, we have been preaching in the Baptist church at Waughtown, as much as we could, for our people.
>
> The congregation as such has no contribution for the Classis since practically all of the members contributed their moneys through Hebron congregation up until this time.
>
> Our members at Waughtown are excellent people, loyal to the Reformed Church, in high esteem by people of the town and very anxious for a church of their own in which to worship God.[3]

A congregation was organized in the home of Mr. and Mrs. John S. Wear, and named Zion Reformed Church. Due to a combination of factors, among them, difficult travel, lack of ministerial supervision and encouragement, perhaps the absence of financial aid, this young congregation languished and almost disappeared. In 1908, Rev. David E. Bowers, then pastor of Bethel Mission, High Point, was instructed by the Classis to reorganize the congregation and build a house of worship. To encourage him in the effort, $500 was appropriated toward his support.[4]

The reorganization meeting took place June 6, 1908 in the home of Mr. and Mrs. John S. Wear, when the name of the church was changed to First Reformed Church of Winston Salem. Names appearing on the charter member list were: John S. Wear, Andrew C. Wear, George A. Wear, Samuel A. Wear, James A. Wear, F. E. Wear, L. M. Wear, Mary A. Swaim, Albert A. Long, Lewis P. Long, David I. Long, J. Roscoe Long, E. E. Long and Mary Long. Since a suitable building in the community was unavailable, religious services were held during the summer months under a brush arbor located on Leight Street, erected for that purpose. The first service held there was on June 7, 1908, and thereafter the remainder of the classical year, each first and third Sundays in the month.

In the meantime, a lot on the corner of Art and Waughtown Streets was purchased from Lee Phillips, costing $500. On it was erected a temporary chapel, 20 feet by 30 feet in size, constructed of rough undressed lumber, and equipped with plain board seats with matching pulpit furniture. Plans were immediately evolved for a church building, Mr. and Mrs. John S. Wear laying the first brick September 28, 1909. On May 29, 1910 the building was ready to be used, and was dedicated March 19, 1911. Dr. Jacob C. Leonard preached the dedication sermon. These operations involved a financial outlay of $4,000, $500 of which was a contribution of the Classis of North Carolina.[5]

First Church, Winston Salem was detached from Bethel Church, High Point, December 14, 1909. Hebron congregation of the Upper Davidson Charge was then yoked with First Church, creating the Waughtown Charge.[6] First Church, Winston-Salem, was enrolled by the Board of Home Missions in October 1909, and Rev. A. Samuel Peeler was commissioned its pastor and installed the first regular minister of the charge on March 17, 1910. He served the parish until October 1911.[7]

Remembering his benefactions to the missions during organization and church building days, Rev. David E. Bowers was called to be the second pastor of the charge. This call was confirmed by Classis December 17, 1911, and he began his ministry there January 1, 1912. This pastorate continued until October 28, 1921, when Mr. Bowers died, leaving a personally devoted people and a congregation well established. A colleague wrote concerning him, "He was greatly loved by all who knew him, both in the church and those of other denominations."[8]

Certain historically important events took place during the pastorate of Mr. Bowers of First Church, Winston Salem. Bethlehem church was organized by him in 1912, and added to the charge. The house and lot adjoining church property along the west side was purchased December 28, 1917 for $1,200. This house was used for a parsonage until 1955, when remodeling made it into an acceptable youth center, serving this purpose until 1964, when it was demolished to provide space for the present youth activities building.

Prospects for an exceptionally effective ministry were cut short March 17, 1923, when Dr. J. M. L. Lyerly was stricken by death. Dr. Lyerly had begun his ministry to the charge May 1, 1922.

Encouraged by a physically expanding community and a numerically growing congregation, Rev. Augustus C. Peeler became pastor of the charge October 1, 1923. A need for more adequate facilities soon became evident. Thus, on May 17, 1925, the congregation took an important step forward, voting "in favor of a new and much larger house of worship." With considerable financial help and architectural counsel from the Board of Home Missions of the Reformed Church, the present commodious sanctuary was erected, requiring an investment of $75,000. It was dedicated June 10, 1927, ceremonies being in charge of the pastor. Dr. Charles E. Schaeffer, General Secretary of the Board of Home Missions, delivered the address.

A bulletin published by the congregation at that time tells an interesting story of those building operations.

> On June 7, 1925, the last services were held in the old church. This was a very sad and solemn service to the older members as they looked back to the days of struggles and small beginnings, but hopes brightened to look into the future to see a more beautiful temple to worship God in . . . . In two weeks time the work of razing the old church was complete. On June 29, at the close of the evening service, the entire congregation, old and young, took part in the groundbreaking service for the new church. This was a time of rejoicing and high hopes.
>
> August 17, 1925, after prayer of the pastor asking God's blessings upon the undertaking the act of building was begun. Under the direction of E. M. Ballard, brick contractor, Mrs. J. S. Wear and her husband laid the first brick. They also laid the first brick in the former building. Following these, the pastor and more than thirty of the members, each laid a brick. From June 7 to January 1, 1926, the congregation was without a house of worship, but regular services were conducted in a tent on the back of the lot.
>
> It was a day of rejoicing on the first Sunday in January 1926, when the homesick congregation went into the basement of the new building not yet completed to hold their first service, celebrating the Holy Communion of their Lord and Savior Jesus Christ. During this time the work of completion went steadily forward with the hope of being able to dedicate soon.[9]

When Hebron Church withdrew from the Waughtown Charge July 23, 1927, First Church purchased its interest in the parsonage for $1,000. These being depression days, the church experienced serious struggle in meeting current obligations. A burdensome debt, created by the erection of the new sanctuary, added to problems of finance. However, by the time Rev. Roy C. Whisenhunt arrived on the parish, March 1, 1938, national economy had improved so much that the congregation was able to take important first steps toward paying off its debt; also, the church was numerically strengthened during his pastorate.

A number of significant material advances mark the pastorate of Rev. Hiram E. Davis. Among these were: liquidation of the church debt in 1945; became an independent, self-supporting church January 1, 1946; installed an Estey pipe organ in the sanctuary in 1951; finished the new parsonage located in the 2500 block on Waughtown Street in 1955; and during the latter year observed the 50th Anniversary of organization of the church. Featured speakers during this series of anniversary events were: Dr. Allan S. Meck, president of The Theological Seminary of the Reformed Church, Lancaster, Pennsylvania, who spoke twice on anniversary Sunday, at 11 a.m. and at 7:30 p.m. Dr. Harvey A. Fesperman, president of Southern Synod and Rev. Lawrence N. Strunk, delivered addresses at the anniversary dinner.

Rev. Aubrey W. Hedrick, who came to the parish June 1, 1957, found the congregation undergoing fundamental adjustments. The withdrawal of a considerable number of its members who lived on the west side of Winston Salem to unite with St. Thomas Mission currently being organized, required budgetary considerations. Church equipment, while spacious, left much to be desired in providing adequately for effective parish activities, especially in the range of youth. These factors called for study. Committees were, therefore, created with instructions to survey the needs and report. A building committee composed of Marcus B. Crotts, chairman, H. B. Self and J. Marvin Furches was elected. Boyd J. Delp was made chairman of the furnishings committee; Roy C. Jordan of yard and parking; David E. Bowers of finance; Norman M. Hyatt of special services and brochure; and Ray Stafford of demolition of the old parsonage. Resulting from these studies a decision was reached to provide facilities, harmonizing in architecture with the present church building and allowing space for an assembly hall, library and office rooms, a kitchenette, a conference room and supporting class space for grades one through twelve.

Contract for the building was awarded April 4, 1964. Budgeted cost, including furnishings and paved parking areas, amounted to $90,000. It was dedicated January 24, 1965, five years after action was taken to undertake the project. Ceremonies were in charge of the pastor, Rev. Aubrey W. Hedrick. Dr. Banks J. Peeler, president of Southern Synod, preached the dedicatory sermon. An appropriate brochure took note of the 60th Anniversary of the congregation. The message of the pastor to the congregation on that occasion reflects the spirit and confidence current among members of First Church.

> It has been a great privilege to work with you in the construction of our new educational building. I am profoundly grateful for the unity and support of all the members and friends of First Church. A special word of appreciation is due the building committee for its tireless effort, the various other committees for doing their work well, and the consistory and trustees for their faith and diligence. . . . . . .
>
> Yet, we need to remember that the task is not complete. We have not built for the sake of having a building. The building will not be complete until it fills its purpose of fostering and strengthening the Christian way of life for whom it should serve. This challenges each of us to be true to our calling as God's children, and to give of our best in carrying out the total program of the church.
>
> In 1965 we observe the 60th Anniversary of First Church. We pay tribute to the fourteen charter members, and to all others through the years who have given of their devotion, their time and their money for the on-going work of God's Church.[10]

Two sons of the congregation are ordained ministers serving in the Christian Church: Rev. Frank W. Snider in the United Church of Christ, and Rev. Edward Heath, a member of First Church in boyhood, in the Methodist denomination.

In 1965, the congregation is well organized, and actively supporting all phases of Christian effort as defined by the United Church of Christ. It has a confirmed membership of 320 people, and an annual budget of $28,000.

ROSTER OF PASTORS

Rev. William H. Causey, D.D.,
Organizer 1905-1907
Rev. David E. Bowers,
Supply 1908-1909
Rev. A. Samuel Peeler 1909-1911
Rev. David E. Bowers 1912-1921

Rev. J. M. L. Lyerly, Ph.D. ..1922-1923
Rev. Augustus C. Peeler 1923-1937
Rev. Roy C. Whisenhunt 1937-1942
Rev. Hiram E. Davis 1942-1957
Rev. Aubrey W. Hedrick 1957-1966
Rev. J. Wayne Fouts 1967-

1. ———. Minutes. Classis of North Carolina, 1902, p. 232.
2. ———. Minutes. *Op. cit.*, 1903, p. 279.
3. ———. Minutes. *Op. cit.*, 1906, p. 10.
4. ———. Minutes. *Op. cit.*, 1908, p. 39.
5. *Hedrick,* Aubrey W., History of First United Church of Christ, 1965, p. 1 ff.
6. ———. Minutes. *Op. cit.*, 1910, p. 10.
7. *Ibid.* p. 10.
8. *Davis,* Hiram E., History of First Evangelical and Reformed Church, 1955, p. 2.
9. *Hedrick. Op. cit.*, p. 2.
10. *Hedrick,* Aubrey W., Dedication Brochure. First United Church of Christ, 1965, p. 1.

Grace Church, Catawba County

GRACE CHURCH, Catawba County, was a union venture, like most religious effort among German settlers in early North Carolina. Gatherings of a religious nature, prior to the establishment of a congregation took place in a large neighborhood barn in the summer time, and in private homes during the winter months.[1] These meetings were more than likely presided over by Rev. Andrew Loretz, Reformed, and his good friend, Rev. John S. Arndt, Lutheran. The record relates that, "In the year 1796 a meeting was held in the neighborhood to consider the propriety of building a house for worship." On "January 11, 1797, a deed for a tract of land containing a fraction over three acres of land was executed by Samuel Jarrett to John Yoder and John Huffman for the purpose of building a house of worship thereon."[2] The building erected on that piece of property was 25 by 30 feet, two-stories high, with galleries on three sides. The material was of logs. This being the architectural design used by German people for church buildings in those days.

No authentic records are available, containing names of charter members, and church officers. But it is certain that the congregation operated as a union effort from its beginning, composed of German Reformed and Lutheran families. Among them were such names as Conrad, Reinhardt, Wilfong, Whitener, Ramsaur, Coulter, Warlick, Finger, Carpenter, Ikard, Cline, Little, Hoyle, Herman, Reep, Seagle and Shuford. Mr. Loretz, whose home was five miles south near Daniel's Church, organized the congregation about the year 1797.[3]

Of significance is the type and quality of people elected elders and deacons of the congregation. A partial list of those who served through the years include John Coulter, Daniel Conrad, David Ramsaur, Philip Shuford, Henry Reinhardt, Peter Finger, E. P. Coulter, Elkanah Ramsaur, P. W. Whitener, S. T. Wilfong, Q. A. Wilfong, W. P. Dellinger, D. F. McGill, John Reinhardt, J. M. Clampitt, R. L. Shuford, H. C. Shuford, R. L. Whitener, G. S. Wilfong and Walter Reinhardt.[4]

That the office of elder in the church was highly regarded is reflected in the following action by the Consistory with reference to religious services. It says, "Resolved that we will hold public worship on the fourth Sabbath of each month, and when no minister can be secured, the elders shall conduct the service, and that it will be the duty of Brothers George P. Shuford and H. F. Ramsaur and John Coulter to superintend the meetings."[5]

Among Reformed people whose influence reached out into the life of Catawba and Lincoln counties and the state are: Conrad Yoder, County Surveyor and Militia Captain; Daniel Conrad, a member of the State Legislature from Lincoln County; George P. Shuford, Magistrate and chairman of the Catawba County Court; and E. P. Coulter, first Register of Deeds of Catawba County.[6]

After the death of Rev. Andrew Loretz, in 1812, Grace Church had no regular pastor for sixteen years. These were frustrating times for Reformed churches in the two Carolinas, especially for those in South Carolina, which for lack of pastoral attention eventually disappeared. The church did not have a sufficient number of pastors to cope with the need. In those days there was no organization, similar to the synod, to supervise the churches and to manage leadership. Each church managed for itself. Available pastors shared as much of their time as administratively feasible, but this sort of service could not make up for the shepherding care provided by the resident minister. Missionary James Riley visited Grace Church briefly in 1813, providing functional pastoral services, as undoubtedly did other itinerate ministers of the Reformed faith. From 1820 to 1825, Rev. J. E. Bell, a Presbyterian minister, evidently served the congregation as resident pastor.[7]

The appearance of Rev. John G. Fritchey in 1828, signalled the beginning of a significant period in the history of Grace Church, indirectly effecting all of the churches west of the Catawba River. He was young, vigorous, bold and very aggressive, appearing at time lacking in judgment, but sincere. He stated his convictions on public issues, and defended them in face to face combat. During his pastorate internal trouble developed in the congregation over the race problem. It became a lively issue among friends, sharply dividing the church. A record of consistory proceedings dated February 10, 1838 will tell the story:

> After prayer by Rev. J. G. Fritchey, the object of the meeting was made known by the chairman. A communication from John Coulter, one of the elders of the congregation, was received and read. After

which the Discipline of the German Reformed Church was read in the audience of the meeting. A communication from Elias Jarrett, Lutheran, one of the Trustees of the church, was received and read.

"Resolved, that the vote of the meeting be taken upon the question, whether people of color should be admittted into the church at times of public worship, when the German Reformed congregation meets for that purpose, or not."

The vote was taken as follows: Those voted in favor of admitting were: Barbara Coulter, Ann Shuford, Sarah E. Shuford, Hariet Ramsaur, Philip Shuford, Jesse Whitener, Henry F. Ramsaur, Daniel Conrad and David Ramsaur. Those opposing were: Solomon Shepherd, Levina Yoder, John A. Yoder, John Yoder and David Yoder, Sr.

After the vote was taken, the following resolution was adopted, viz.: That the blacks be allowed to occupy the two back seats in the gallery fronting the pulpit, whenever they are admitted, and that they shall not be allowed to go in until the whites are all seated, and then if there is sufficient room, they are to be invited in by one of the officers, and to remain there in their place until the whites have gone out of the church.[8]

This was a crisis in the life of Grace Church, and it sounds as modern as a church meeting reported in the 1966 morning newspaper. Our world in this generation continues to agonize over the race issue and to discuss matters concerned with human dignity.

The "Sunday School Society" was organized May 8, 1831. Officers named were: David Conrad, president; John Yoder, senior vice president; David Ramsaur, junior vice president; John Coulter, secretary; Solomon Ramsaur, treasurer; and David Shepherd, librarian. In addition to these officers, there were five managers. Elkhanah P. Coulter was made superintendent, and the teachers were George Shuford, Ephriam Shuford, Eli Shuford and his wife Maria.[9]

Mr. Fritchey's departure from the parish is reflected in the order used for the church service Sunday morning, April 14, 1840. It follows: "Sunday School opened with singing and prayer by the superintendent; closed with singing. Number present, 22. Remarks: This is a pleasant morning. Preaching by the Rev. John G. Fritchey. His farewell sermon from Hebrews, 13th chapter, 20th and 21st verses. A great collection of people assembled here, and much feeling on the part of the pastor and the congregation. May the Lord go with him who is going, and stay with us who stay, and bless us all."[10]

Rev. John H. Crawford, who had been serving churches in Orange, Alamance and Guilford counties, came to the parish in 1840, and served there until 1853. He was an able preached and well liked by citizens of the community. This was a period of prosperity for Grace Church. It grew in numbers, and extended its influence throughout Lincoln and Catawba counties, by virtue of a number of leading laymen who were members of the congregation at that time. Revs. Andrew Loretz, John G. Fritchey and John H. Crawford, whose combined ministry to the congregation covers a span of fifty years, almost the whole usefulness of that first log church, were leaders and great preachers in their day.

Following Mr. Fritchey, Grace Church was vacant for three years. During that time religious services were provided by available supply preachers. Rev. Jeremiah H. Ingold served the church from 1856 until 1873, the longest pastorate in its history of 150 years. On August 8, 1956, shortly after his arrival on the field, the two congregations, Reformed and Lutheran, adopted the following resolution:

> Resolved, that we build a new church edifice, and it shall be a union church, between the Lutheran and German Reformed congregations, provided each party pays one half of the cost and that we raise the sum of $1,200 by subscription and donations.[11]

Good progress was made in the undertaking because on June 13, 1847, the new Grace church building which stands today, was dedicated. Dedication ceremonies were arranged by the pastors, Rev. Jeremiah H. Ingold, D.D., Reformed, and Rev. Alfred J. Fox, Lutheran. Speakers for the occasion were: Rev. Polycarp C. Hinkle, D.D., Lutheran, and Rev. George W. Welker, D.D., Reformed.

In connection with this very satisfactory pastorate, Dr. Ingold organized, nurtured and developed Corinth congregation in the town of Hickory. Following his ministry, were a number of short pastorates and extended vacancies.

Rev. Joseph L. Murphy, in 1890, then a young minister, became pastor the charge consisting of Grace, Bethel and the new congregation at Hickory. These churches he served thirteen years. On October 13, 1897 the Reformed and Lutheran congregation united in observing the centennial of the organization of Grace Church. It was an impressive occasion. Rev. Peter M. Trexler, D.D., discussed the Swiss Reformation; Professor W. P. Cline explained the German Reformation. The two pastors also delivered appropriate addresses. Rev. Joseph L. Murphy discussed the Classis of North Carolina, and Rev. R. A. Yoder the Tennessee Synod.[12]

An historic event occurred in 1940, when the Lutheran congregation withdrew and erected a brick sanctuary across the road immediately in front of the old Grace Church. The agreement in disposing of the property which the two congregations had owned together for 145 years, is described below:

> In this new division Grace Reformed Church became owner of the tract of land on which the brick church was located, and that part of the driveway and circle in front of the church and all land south and west of the church. The cemetery and section of land between the cemetery and the highway is still the property of the two congregations.[13]

This separation was an incentive for greatly improving the old church that had served the people 1856. The two front doors were converted into two windows, and the central front window into double doors. The interior was remodeled, making an arch at the chancel. Overhead ceiling and floors were refinished. Pulpit furniture and new pews were installed, and two rooms were added to the west end of the building for educational purposes. A heating system was placed in a newly excavated furnace-room under the sanctuary.

Under the leadership of Rev. William C. Lyerly, the congregation observed its Sesqui-Centennial on October 26, 1947. As a part of these festivities, a brochure containing the order of the service and a reliable short history of the congregation was published. Speakers for the occasion were: Rev. Harvey A. Fesperman, D.D., a former pastor, and Rev. Walter W. Rowe, D.D.

Grace Church has given so generously of herself to other churches. Many of her sons and daughters have left the soil, and made their homes in more thickly populated centers of the country. Its actual confirmed membership at the present time is 46 people, and the Sunday School enrollment is 30 pupils. The congregation is presently yoked in a charge with Daniel's Church, and together they own a modern parsonage built in 1957, located in the Daniel's community.

Two sons who are brothers have served in the Christian ministry: Rev. M. L. Shuford, Reformed, and Rev. I. L. Shuford, Methodist.

ROSTER OF PASTORS

Rev. Andrew Loretz 1797-1812
Rev. James R. Riley,
  Visiting Missionary 1813-
Rev. Mr. Bell,
  Presbyterian Minister 1820-1825
Rev. John G. Fritchey 1828-1840
Rev. G. A. Leopold 1841-
Rev. John H. Crawford 1841-1853
Rev. Solomon S. Middlekauff,
  Assistant 1842-1845
Rev. David Crooks 1846-1849
Rev. Jeremiah H. Ingold,
  D.D. 1856-1873
Rev. Julius H. Shuford 1874-1876
Rev. Jacob C. Clapp, D.D.,
  Alternate Supply 1876-1877
Rev. John A. Foil, Ph.D.,
  Alternate Supply 1876-1877
Rev. Julius H. Shuford 1878-1879
Rev. A. S. Vaughn, Supply 1881-1883
Rev. A. P. Horn 1883-1884
Rev. G. Dickey Gurley 1884-1885
Rev. Lewis Reiter 1885-1890
Rev. Joseph L. Murphy, D.D. 1890-1903
Rev. Jacob C. Clapp, D.D.,
  Supply 1903-1915
Rev. Joseph L. Murphy, D.D.,
  Supply 1905-
Rev. Samuel W. Beck 1906-1909
Rev. Harvey G. Kopenhaver 1910-1915
Mr. Harvey A. Fesperman,
  Student Supply 1915-
Rev. Harvey A. Fesperman,
  D.D. 1916-1921

Rev. John B. Swartz 1922-1925
Rev. Ezra H. Gunther 1926-1927
Rev. William C. Lyerly 1927-1931
Mr. Carl H. Clapp,
  Student Supply 1931-
Rev. Huitt R. Carpenter 1932-1935
Rev. O. Bain Michael, S.T.D. 1935-1940
Rev. John A. Koons, Supply 1941-1942
Rev. Karl R. Flocken 1942-1945
Rev. W. A. Kerr,
  Supply, Methodist 1945-1946
Rev. William C. Lyerly 1946-1953
Rev. Roy E. Leinbach, Jr.,
  Supply 1954-
Rev. Roy E. Leinbach, Jr. ..1954-1956
Rev. Roy E. Leinbach, Jr.,
  Supply, Charge Divided 1957-
Rev. Robert F. Godfrey 1957-1960
Rev. Terrell M. Shoffner,
  Alternate Supply 1961-
Rev. Edwin M. Alcorn,
  Alternate Supply 1961-
Mr. H. Linn Finger,
  Student Supply, Summer 1961-
Rev. G. Ermine Plott,
  Stated Supply 1961-1962
Rev. Martin L. Bupp, II 1962-1964
Rev. G. Ermine Plott,
  Stated Supply 1964-
Mr. William Campbell,
  Student Summer Supply 1965-1966
Rev. Donald S. Selby, Ph.D.,
  Supply 1966-

1. *Clapp,* Jacob C., Editor, Historic Sketch of the Reformed Church in North Carolina, 1908, p. 265.
2. *Lyerly,* William C., Semi-Centennial, Grace Church, Evangelical and Reformed, 1947, p. 3.
3. *Leonard,* Jacob C., History of the Southern Synod, Evangelical and Reformed Church, 1940, p. 310.

4. *Clapp. Op. cit.*, p. 272.
5. *Ibid.* p. 272..
6. *Lyerly. Op. cit.*, p. 4.
7. *Leonard. Op. cit.*, p. 311.
8. *Ibid.* p. 312.
9. *Lyerly, Op. cit.*, p. 4.
10. *Ibid.* p. 4.
11. *Ibid.* p. 5.
12. *Leonard, Op. cit.*, p. 314.
13. *Lyerly, Op. cit.*, p. 9.

Grace Church, Newton

IN 1851 JOHN H. WHEELER wrote, "Catawba County was formed in 1842 from Lincoln County, and derives its name from the river which forms its northern and eastern boundaries. Its county seat is Newton, that sprung up only as yesterday, and has a commodious Court House, and other Public Buildings; many stores and many private residences. . . . Its inhabitants are distinguished for their industry and integrity."[1] In this flourishing town Grace Reformed Church, the first church of any denomination in the community, was founded.

Its origin is ecclesiastically irregular. Tradition says that religious services were held in the home of Reuben Setzer as early as 1842, conducted by Rev. John H. Crawford, who was then pastor of nearby Grace, St. Paul's and St. John's Churches. Evidently this interest increased, stimulated by the transfer of residence of a number of Reformed families from the county to the newly created County Seat. And with this growing interest came the desire for a church of their own faith in that community.

Acting without the support of a locally organized congregation, a group of laymen arranged for the land upon which a church could be erected. On August 10, 1846 a deed was conveyed from

Reuben Setzer to Joseph A. Reinhardt and Daniel Rowe, "Trustees of the German Reformed Church, Newton, North Carolina, and their successors in office . . . for the purposes and convenience of Publick and Divine Worship of God." The lot was 70 by 80 feet "lying at the south end of the west row of lots in the town of Newton," and was purchased for a consideration of $25.[2] Construction of the church building was begun shortly thereafter, and occupied unfinished in 1847.

This house was the focal point for a variety of community gatherings over a period of years.

> The church in its early history was not only used as a house of worship, but also was a home for Catawba College. In this old church Rev. J. C. Clapp, D. D., Rev. John Smith, Rev. Mr. Stirewalt, Major S. M. Finger and a host of other well known men gained their first knowledge of Latin. In this building the first commencement of the College was held, and here was aroused the impulse to educate in Catawba and adjoining counties. Here Stephen White delivered his great temperance lectures which shook the country and was the means of beginning the great temperance reformation in this part of the State.[3]

No exact date can be fixed when the congregation was organized. Before an audience of interested people who had gathered at St. Paul's Church, located two miles west of town, in August 1847, Rev. John H. Crawford ordained Abel Ikerd and Daniel Rowe elders of the proposed Newton Church. No deacons are mentioned. The Classis of North Carolina met at Newton in the recently finished "White Church" in the spring of 1849. Apparently no congregation had been organized at the time, for no statistics, not even a name for the congregation at Newton appears in the record for that year. But the statistical record of 1850 does report the newly constituted Newton Charge consisting of four congregations,[4] one of which was Grace Reformed Church, Newon, North Carolina.[5]

No charter membership list is available, but the type and character of people who composed the congregation are reflected in the officers of Grace Church who succeeded elders Ikerd and Rowe. Among these respected gentlemen were: elders: Reuben Setzer, A. D. Shuford, J. C. Clapp, W. H. Williams, D. F. Moose, F. D. Reinhardt, Joseph Reinhardt, M. L. McCorkle, S. M. Finger, H. A. Forney, Daniel Rowe, Clarence Clapp, Russell W. Whitener, Berry F. Waggoner; deacons: Moses Fry, J. F. Smyre, George McCorkle, C. M. Rowe, J. Lewis Schrum, Lee A. Sherrill, J. W. Hardister, H. A. Carpenter and others.

Grace Church was destined to play a key role in the life of the Reformed Church in North Carolina. Men of professional, business and political eminence, with their families, gravitated to this thriving Catawba County capital. While the congregation was in the throes of being born, preparations were under way for the establishment of a Reformed church-related school in that community. The Minutes of the Classis of North Carolina, February 25, 1852, records the following report of a committee that had been appointed in 1851, composed of Rev. J. H. Crawford, Rev. David Crooks and F. Reinhardt, Esq., M. L. McCorkle, Esq., and John Wilfong Esq. "to take care of the opening of the school" to be located in Newton.

> The committee appointed to put the school in operation . . . met soon after their appointment to determine, if possible, to commence the school on the first Monday of December 1851 and to give Mr. C. H. Albert a call to take charge of the school, as principal during the first session. . . .
>
> Mr. Albert accepted the offer and engaged Mr. H. H. Smith as assistant teacher, and opened the school on Wednesday the 3rd of December. The school is now in successful operation numbering thirty-two pupils, with encouraging prospects for the future.[6]

This is the initialing act of what later became Catawba College, into which Grace Church through the years invested so much of its life.

Licentiate C. H. Albert had been extended a call to become pastor of the newly created Newton Charge. In May 1852 he was, by the Classis, examined, ordained and installed pastor of the charge, which included Grace Church.[7]

It is interesting to note that the first Sunday School in the community was set up and conducted by Professor Charles W. Smythe, a teacher on the faculty of Catawba College. The school was begun in 1854, and conducted in the home of Professor Smythe as a union effort, until its enrollment became too large for accommodation. Then it was tranferred to Grace Church. Here it was fostered and continued to operate as a union school until about 1880. Beginning under the influence of Catawba College, this Sunday School has been in continuous operation for more than one hundred years.[8]

Under these circumstances the congregation continued to prosper, growing in numbers and influence. The Synod of the Potomac of the Reformed met here in 1883, greatly boosting denominational interest in this section of the State. Pastorates were usually of short duration, interspersed by ministerial supplies, until Licentiate Jacob C. Clapp came in 1886, who supplied the congregation the following year, when he was by the Classis ordained to the Christian Ministry and installed pastor of the charge. This happy relationship continued until 1890, when Dr. Clapp resigned to devote his entire energies to the presidency of Catawba College. During these years he had the able pulpit assistance of members of the college faculty, among them Dr. John A. Foil, Rev. G. D. Gurley and Rev. J. F. Hartzell.

By 1886 the "Old White Church" had served its day, and the congregation took action to erect a new one. A building committee, composed of the pastor, W. H. Williams and D. F. Moose was appointed. A deed for the lot on which to erect the church building was conveyed October 10, 1890 by J. C. Clapp and his wife, Emma, and W. H. Williams and his wife Mattie Williams, to H. A. Forney,

J. F. Smyre, M. L. McCorkle, Lafayette Rowe and J. W. Hardister, "Trustees of the Reformed Church of Newton and the Consistory thereof." The deed was registered July 15, 1893.[9]

The conerstone of the new building was laid in 1887; dedication ceremonies occurred in 1889. Dr. Jacob C. Clapp made the dedicatory address. This was his last major undertaking as a parish minister, for the following year he resigned to devote himself entirely to education. Thus, closed a ministry of twenty two years to this congregation which had been fruitful and satisfying to the hundreds who came within the sphere of his influence.

The healthy outlook of Grace Church at this time is reflected in the fact that, even though the congregation was without the services of a regular pastor for two years, they overtured the Classis to be constituted a self-supporting, independent charge.[10] Licentiate A. H. Smith was ordained to the Christian Ministry and installed pastor of the church October 9, 1892. During the next five years a parsonage was built on the lot adjoining the church building on the south side and a "deep-toned" bell was installed in the church tower. Extensive improvements and repairs on the property, primarily the sanctuary, were made during the following twelve years. These improvements included art glass windows, carpeted floors, redecorated walls, electric chandeliers and a central heating system.[11] Grace probably reached its peak of influence to date during these good years.

In 1922 the parsonage was enlarged and renovated. Rev. C. Columbus Wagoner, the pastor, led the congregation in erecting a hut of wood material, designed to take care of current educational and social requirements. This facility was located on the northeast corner of the church lot. In 1927, the hut having served its purpose, was razed and a three-story modern brick building was constructed, designed for educational and recreational purposes. It was occupied the second Sunday in February 1928. Dr. Charles E. Wehler, a former pastor, preached the dedicatory sermon on the following May 28. Mr. Wagoner read the dedicatory rites.

After seventeen years sentiment began to crystalize in favor of a completely new and modern church structure. On September 10, 1945 Julius W. Abrnethy made an intial gift of $1,000. to a building fund, with a promise that, for every dollar given to the fund by members of the congregation, he would match it. The first step in this new equipment program was the erection of a modern parsonage located on South Brady Avenue. The house was begun in 1950 and occupied by Rev. Terrell M. Shoffner and his family in 1951.

A building and finance committee was authorized, of which Attorney Russell W. Whitener was named chairman. A lot in the southeast section of the city, on Brady Avenue, was purchased in 1953 from Mr. and Mrs. D. C. Bost on November 10, 1954, by action of the Consistory, a building committee was appointed, of which

Fred L. Barkley was made chairman. These two committees began immediate action. The old church building and parsonage were sold to Calvary Baptist Church for $35,000. Architect A. Hensel Frick was employed in 1955, and was instructed to create suitable plans for the proposed church. Groundbreaking ceremonies took place Sunday afternoon October 6, 1957, and construction on the building began the 30th. The cornerstone was laid October 5, 1958, when Dr. Harvey A. Fesperman, president of Southern Synod, Evangelical and Reformed Church, delivered the address. Elder Clarence Clapp, Jr., a grandson of Dr. Jacob C. Clapp, placed sixteen articles in a box before it was sealed into the cornerstone.[12]

The morning of May 10, 1959 began a "day of fulfilment," when the new church building was formerly occupied by the congregation. Leading the service was the Rev. Terrell M. Shoffner, pastor, who had so wisely guided the congregation in the erection of this "architectual gem." Others participating in the activities were: Mackie Hedrick, Herman-Sipe Construction foreman; Berry Wagoner, president of the Consistory; Fred L. Barkley, chairman of the Building Committee; Attorney Russell W. Whitener, chairman of the Building and Finance Committee; and president Harvey A. Fesperman of Southern Synod.[13]

The church was dedicated May 8, 1960. Cooperating in these ceremonies were: Dr. Harvey A. Fesperman, who preached the dedicatory sermon, and Rev. Roy E. Leinbach, Jr., former pastor, who spoke at the Community Service at 7:30 in the evening. The house was appropriately dedicated to God with the following statement.

> Unto Him who through these years has so wonderously blessed us; to the only wise God, be honor and praise for all His loving-kindness and tender mercies toward us, world without end. Amen!
>
> To Him we dedicate this house, in the name of the Father, and the Son, and the Holy Spirit. Amen![14]

Roster of Pastors

Rev. J. H. Crawford 1845-1852	Rev. Charles E. Wehler, D.D. 1904-1909
Rev. C. H. Albert 1852-1853	Rev. Walter W. Rowe, D.D. 1909-1918
Rev. John Lantz, Supply 1853-1854	Rev. Lee A. Peeler, D.D. 1918-1919
Rev. John Lantz 1855-1860	Rev. Abram D. Wolfinger, D.D.,
Rev. A. S. Vaughn 1860-1861	Supply 1919-1920
Rev. John Lantz 1861-1868	Rev. Harvey G. Kopenhaver,
Licentiate Jacob C. Clapp,	Supply 1919-1920
Supply 1868-1869	Mr. Felix B. Peck,
Rev. Jacob C. Clapp, D.D. ..1869-1890	Student Supply 1920-
Associated with Dr. Clapp in	Rev. John A. Ditzler 1921-1922
pulpit supply during this period	Rev. C. Columbus Wagoner 1922-1930
were Dr. John A. Foil, 1875-	Rev. Clarence E. Whetstone 1931-1932
1876; Rev. G. D. Gurley, 1882-	Rev. Carl H. Clapp 1933-1940
1883; Rev. J. F. Hartzell, 1884-	Rev. Roy E. Leinbach, Jr., ...1940-1949
1885.	Rev. Terrell M. Shoffner 1949-1962
Rev. A. H. Smith 1892-1897	Rev. David E. Faust, Ph.D., Rev.
Rev. W. A. Long, Ph.D. 1897-1901	Porter Seiwell, Rev. Edwin Al-
Rev. W. H. Stubblebine,	corn, supply ministers, January
Ph.D. 1901-1903	to August 1962
	Rev. Nevin R. Frantz 1962-1967

1. *Wheeler,* John H., Historical Sketches of North Carolina, 1851. Reprinted 1925. p. 82.
2. ———. Book of Deeds, Catawba County, 1847, p. 168.
3. *Clapp,* Jacob C., Editor. Historic Sketch of the Reformed Church in North Carolina, 1908. p. 304.
4. ———. Minutes of the Classis of North Carolina, 1850, p. 115.
5. *Leonard,* Jacob C., History of the Southern Synod, Evangelical and Reformed Church, 1940, p. 339.
6. ———. Minutes. *Op. cit.,* 1852, p. 143.
7. *Ibid.* p. 142.
8. *Clapp,* Frank L., Manuscript. Historic Sketch of Grace Church, 1960, p. 3.
9. ———. Book of Deeds, Catawba County, 1893. No. 47, p. 149.
10. ———. Minutes. *Op. cit.,* 1891, p. 10; 1892, p. 8.
11. *Clapp. Op. cit.,* Historic Sketch of Grace Church, p. 5.
12. *Ibid.* p. 5.
13. *Shoffner,* Terrell M., Opening Service. Grace United Church of Christ, 1959, p. 2.
14. *Shoffner,* Terrell M., Dedication Brochure. Grace Evangelical and Reformed Church, 1960, p. 16.

Grace (Lower Stone) Church, Rowan County

GRACE, COMMONLY KNOWN AS LOWER STONE, is one of the oldest churches in central North Carolina. It is of the German Reformed tradition, whose date of organization is unknown, but generally accepted as having occurred sometime in the year 1745. It was founded by German settlers who came into this area from Pennsylvania during the period of 1739 to 1760. Only a few familes arrived at first, but their numbers increased as the tide of migration progressed, until a large part of Eastern Rowan County was settled by them.

They were a pious, God-fearing people who made much of the

Bible, the hymn book and the catechism. Most of them were of
the Reformed and Lutheran faiths. Assembling for Christian worship for them was a normal experience. First accounts of such
assemblies, either in a community meeting house or homes of
interested people, have been verbally handed down from generation to generation, and begins with a settlement in the vicinity of
St. Peter's Lutheran Church. Here, marked by a monument, the
first house of worship was erected about the year 1740. Since no
ordained ministers are known to have lived among them in the
earlier years, it is quite possible that religious services were conducted by chosen laymen, sometimes a school teacher.

Dr. G. D. Bernheim writes as follows about the religious activities of those early settlers.

> The first house of worship was located about seven miles from where
> Organ Church now stands, near where is now St. Peters Church. It was
> constructed of hickory logs, hence was called "Hickory Church," and was
> erected, owned and used jointly by Lutheran and Reformed people. Just
> when the house was built, we have no positive information, nor do we
> know how many years they occupied it. The ground upon which it stood
> was never deeded to either Church, and, hence, when it became necessary
> to make a change, they both abandoned it, and it was used no more by
> either.
>
> The house stood until it finally went to decay, the last crumbling re-
> mains being remembered by persons who are still alive.[1]

Just when the transfer was made to the Lower Stone community
can not be determined; however the inference is that it was grad-
ual, primarily to accomodate the larger number of German families locating on the Little Buffalo, Bear, Cold Water, and Dutch
Second Creeks. If this is true, the log church on Beattie's Ford
Road was erected about the year 1755, and stood on government
property.[2] For it was not until 1761 that the Earl of Granville
made a grant of 572 acres of land to Lorentz Lingle, which included the porperty on which this first log church stood.[3] These
proceedings appear to have been reliably described by Elder
Casper Holshouser who was born 1785 and died 1870 at the age
of 85 years.

The earliest documentary evidence of the location of a "meeting house" in the Beattie's Ford Road vicinity, is a deed on record
in the Rowan County Court House, dated February 1774 by which
Lorentz Lingle conveyed sixteen acres of land to Andrew Holshouser and John Lippard for "the use of the 'Calvin Congregation' adjacent or belonging to the meeting house on the following
land." The land described is that on which the present Lower
Stone Church is located, and the deed distinctly indicates that a
"meeting House" had been erected on that land prior to 1774.[4]
This could very well be the meeting house which served the Reformed and Lutheran people, organized into their respective
churches, until the separation occurred.

The Rev. C. A. G. Storch, who served Organ Lutheran Church

1788 until 1823, notes that, "Adolph Nussman and Gottfried Arndt arrived 1773. At that time there was only a union church for the Reformed and Lutherans together, the so-called Hickory church. Nussman preached in this church one year after his arrival. Then, arose some disagreement. The Lutherans resolved to build a church of their own, and so arose the so called Organ Church.[5]

The Lower Stone Church had, by this time, grown strong in numbers and within reason economically secure. Sentiment began to develop in favor of erecting a new house of worship; however, nothing was done until about 1795. At that time, on June 8, a second deed for the Lower Stone property was issued, evidently to satisfy a legal technicality, by Andrew Holshouser and John Lippard, who were named in the first deed drawn in 1774, to Jacob Fisher, Sr. and John Casper, "Elders in the German Presbyterian (Reformed) congregation on Second Creek in the Dutch Settlement, in behalf of the congregation, and their successors in office." This was the year in which construction on the stone house of worship was begun.[6]

Of interest is a decription of the stone church, which at that time, was under construction. By acutal measurement, checked in recent years by realiable Reformed and Lutheran Churchmen, the Lower Stone Reformed Church and the Organ Lutheran Church are within inches of being the same size. They are constructed out of similar material and on the same architectual plan.[7] Lower Stone church is 51 feet long, 40 feet 9 inches wide. The walls are 27 feet high, measuring at ground level 32 inches thick, at floor level 27 inches and at gallary height 21 inches. The floor was originally covered with smooth stones, but was in 1871 changed as it presently appears. The pulpit was originally of the wine-glass design, so generally used in European churches, with an over-head sounding board. This arrangement continued until 1876, when new pulpit and altar pieces were made by members of the congregation. Galleries were built on three sides of the house, providing additional seating space, and remained so until 1937, when these were transformed into Sunday School rooms. First pews were wooden slabs, fashioned without backs.

An inscription chiseled in stone appearing on the outside over each of the three doors, reflects something of their regard for moral and spiritual values.

Over the North door is the statement,

> We go into the House of God with heartfelt joy. In and out God permits us still to find the precious treasure, the Word of Life. Here He shows us heaven's gate, the forgiveness of our sins. Grace Church.

Over the West door appears,

> Let Thy Word in Zion resound. Go with each one out and in. And when in throngs we tread, where the Service of God is held, O, do Thou bless us, Lord. Grant also faithful ministers, who Thy Word pure with profit teach, and the world to Thee convert. Grace Church.

Over the South door the message is,

> To the glory of God has been built, the church which you here behold, by a people who God confess, and name themselves after Jesus Christ; who also are incorporated in Him; and they call themselves Reformed. 1795. Grace Church. The End.

A document written in German, but since translated into the English, evidently in 1798, while the stone church was under construction, gives further testimony to their faith; also, implies something of the difficulties with which they were confronted in managing building affairs. It is appropriately titled, "Immanuel," meaning "God with us."

> With the help of the triune God, have those who are herewith connected succeeded thus far that the building was commenced and completed. We herewith announce to our posterity who those were who undertook and brought it to completion, and upon what grounds the church was built, and who at this time were in control.
>
> 1. The church was built on the principal ground and corner-stone Jesus Christ, who has revealed His holy teachings and mysteries to His believing ones, and Drs. Calvin and Zwingli who have made us acquainted with the valuable understanding of Jesus Christ, and according to their doctrine we call ourselves Evangelical Reformed.
>
> 2. The house was built in the state of North Carolina, Rowan County, which is called Salzburger district, over which Governor William Davie now reigns. But unfortunately our government of the whole fourteen states is not founded on our faith in Jesus Christ. But anyone who believes in one God, and not in the Holy Trinity, can get so far as to be President, be he Jew, heathen or Christian, it is all the same.
>
> 3. This house shall be called Grace Church, because the eternal life and the means of grace for the same, are gifts from God the Father, through our Lord Jesus Christ.
>
> 4. This house shall, if God gives grace, be dedicated to our beloved pastor who has served us already six years—namely, Rev. Pastor Andrew Loretz, who was born a brother in the House of God, as a member of the Canton of Zurich, a Swiss from Europe.
>
> 5. For this edifice a building committee was elected, who were members of the congregation—namely, Sir George Henry Berger and John Sifford. They considered the burden too great and they, therefore, declined, and it was not undertaken. Finally the Consistory undertook the work—namely, Elders Jacob Fisher and John Casper and Deacons Franz Lingle and John Fisher, who with the aid of the congregation, were their own building masters, until the church was completed.[7]

The church was ready for dedication in November 1811. This should not imply that the house was not in use from 1795 until 1811; on the contrary, it does reflect the fact that during those years the congregation struggled to find ways and means of finishing it. It is known that at least one appeal was made to the Synod for financial help, to which the Synod did not respond. It appears that Divine Services were held in the sanctuary while finishing operations were in progress. When the happy day of dedication did arrive, the Rev. George Boger, then pastor of the church, was asked to invite the beloved Andrew Loretz to preach the sermon. This he did to the satisfaction of an admiring congregation.

Among major anniversary occasions observed by the congregation two should be noted. In 1923, a quadruple anniversary was announced:

> This event is in celebration of the one hundred sixty-eighth anniversary of the founding of Lower Stone Reformed Church; the one hundred forty-fourth anniversary of the title deed to the land on which the house of worship stands; the one hundred twenty-eighth anniversary of the completion of the walls of the present church building; it is also the one hundred anniversary of the dedication of this historic temple to the worship of the Triune God. These facts make the event a most interesting occasion.[8]

Dr. Charles W. Warlick was supplying the congregation at that time. Dr. Jacob C. Leonard, president of the General Synod of the Reformed Church in the United States, delivered the anniversary address. Others who spoke during the afternoon were: James L. Fisher of Salisbury and W. A. Foil of Concord.

The 200th Anniversary of the Congregation and 150th Anniversary of the church building were observed in a series of interesting services September 27-30, 1945. Climaxing this series with Homecoming Day on the 30th, Dr. Walter W. Rowe, delivered the anniversary address. Rev. Milton Whitener, pastor of the church, remarked:

> When we review the long history of this church, we are reminded that "others have labored and we have entered into their labors." Truly, we have a rich heritage, in which we rejoice and for which we are sincerely grateful.
>
> But we do not live in the past, glorious though it may be. We live in the present for the future. As we pause in this celebration, let us catch something of the spirit of the fathers of this church, that we may serve as devotedly, as daringly, and as hopefully in our day as they did in theirs.[9]

In the one hundred fifty years intervening since its dedication, quite a catalogue of changes, most of them improvements, have occurred. As an example, only a few of them can be recited in this connection. The first parsonage was built during the pastorate of Rev. Thornton Butler, between 1853 and 1869. The pulpit was changed and new furniture installed in 1876. The belfry and bell were added in 1901. The galleries were converted into Sunday School classrooms in 1937. A hut for educational and social purposes was erected in 1940. Following, in close succession, were the installation of an electric power plant, rebuilding the cemetery walls, provision for parking space and walks, and the appearance of a pipe organ. In 1950 action was taken to build the second parsonage, located across the road to the east of the church, involving an expenditure of approximately $20,000. Shortly thereafter a movement was launched looking toward a new educational facility, culminating in an educational unit which cost $100,000. It was completed and dedicated in 1964.

Lower Stone Church has been the source of many facets, effecting the Reformed churches throughout the state of North Carolina, particularly in Rowan and adjacent counties. Not least among them are sons who have served the church as ministers of the Christian Gospel. On this roll are: Revs. Peter M. Trexler, D.D., Paul Barringer, D.D., Allan R. Holshouser, James Lippard, J. M. L. Lyerly, Ph.D. and Harvey A. M. Holshouser, Ph.D.

It is difficult to determine who, among the Reformed ministers of that era served this congregation, prior to 1768. Those were days when a few dedicated souls did yoeman's service in looking after the spiritual needs of German settlements in North and South Carolina. Rev. Christian Theus, who resided just over the line in South Carolina, was serving in this manner in 1755, and made "occasional visits to the German settlements in North Carolina." Rev. James Martin also preached for the disbursed Germans in 1759, and in subsequent years." Rev. Richard Dupent appeared in 1764.[10]

ROSTER OF PASTORS

Rev. Samuel Suther	1768-1771	Rev. Walter W. Rowe, D.D.	1904-1908
Rev. Samuel Suther	1782-1786	Rev. J. Leidy Yearick	1909-1910
Rev. Andrew Loretz	1789-1795	Rev. William H. Causey,	
Rev. Samuel Weyberg	1795-1803	D.D.	1912-1913
Rev. George Boger	1803-1830	Rev. Harvey A. Welker	1915-1924
Rev. Daniel B. Lerch	1830-1834	Rev. James D. Andrew,	
Rev. John Lantz	1837-1853	D.D.	1925-1931
Rev. Thornton Butler	1853-1869	Rev. Roy C. Whisenhunt	1931-1938
Rev. John C. Denny	1869-1874	Rev. Lonnie A. Carpenter,	
Rev. Robert F. Crooks	1876-1881	D.D.	1938-1944
Rev. G. Dickie Gurley,		Rev. Milton Whitener	1944-1948
Supply	1882-1884	Rev. Milton Whitener,	
Rev. Calvin B. Heller	1884-1891	Supply	1948-1951
Rev. Paul Barringer, D.D.	1894-1896	Rev. Lloyd E. Sechriest	1951-1953
Rev. William H. McNairy,		Rev. John C. Chatlos	1953-1960
D.D.	1897-1900	Rev. George Hempshire	1960-1962
Rev. C. H. Riedesel	1900-1903	Rev. John D. Bonebreak	1963-

Periods of vacancy occurred between pastorates, sometimes as many as ten years. On these occasions, appropriate supplies were provided by the Classis and/or the Synod.

1. *Bernheim*, G. D., History of the Evangelical Lutheran Synod and Ministerium of North Carolina, 1902, p. 119.
2. *Clapp*, Jacob C., Editor. Historic Sketch of the Reformed Church in North Carolina, 1908, p. 193.
3. *Ibid.* p. 194.
4. *Ibid.* p. 194 ff.
5. *Whitener*, Milton, Historical Sketch, Grace (Lower Stone) Church, Anniversary Booklet, 1945, p. 6.
6. *Ibid.* p. 7.
7. *Clapp. op. cit.*, p. 197 ff.
8. *Leonard*, Jacob C., History of Southern Synod of the Evangelical and Reformed Church, 1940, p. 235.
9. *Whitener. Op. cit.*, p. 5.
10. *Leonard. Op. cit.*, p. 233.
    General Reference
    Bonebreak, John D., Manuscript. Digested Record of the Minutes of Consistory Meetings of Lower Stone Church, 1966.

Hebron Church, Davidson County

HEBRON REFORMED CHURCH, Route 5, Winston Salem, North Carolina, was organized in 1856. However interest in an established church in that community dates back as far as the summer of 1854, when William Scarboro conducted what appears to have been a series of revival services under a brush arbor. When Mr. Scarboro left the state, no regular services were conducted there for more than a year. Then, concerned people, among them Rev. Joseph Miller, a Methodist minister, Thomas Long and others explored the possibility of organizing a church. Two sites were available: "One on the land of Michael Miller and the other on the land of Thomas Long. To vote in the civil election at that time it was necessary for a man to own fifty acres of land. Mr. Miller owned just fifty acres, and to give a lot for the church would disfranchise him. Thomas Long owned more than the required amount, and he suggested that they select a lot on his land for the reason that he could give it and still be eligible to the right of voting."[1]

The present site was selected, and Rev. Thornton Butler, who was pastor of the Reformed Churches in Davidson County, supervised the organization and founding of Pleasant Retreat, later known as Hebron Reformed Church. Thomas Long and A. S. Long were elected elders; Jacob M. Thomas and Ephraim Rothrock, deacons. When the Classis of North Carolina convened in May 1856, that body heard a report on these proceedings and took appropriate action.

The Rev. Mr. Butler reported that he had organized a German Reformed Church at Pleasant Retreat, Davidson County, North Carolina. It was resolved that they be received under the care of Classis.[2]

This report was adopted and the new congregation added to the
pastoral care of Mr. Butler, whose charge already involved six
congregations.[3]

Members of the church met August 13, 1856, taking action to
erect a house of worship. It was to be constructed of brick and
wood, operations beginning on it the following August 30, when
Pleas Nifong, Andrew Charles, Sr. and Alfonzo Livengood cut
the first tree, which was converted into lumber and used in the
building. The church was completed within a few months and
formally dedicated.

From its beginning Thomas Long was the leading elder in the
congregation, often serving as Lay Preacher. His leadership in the
congregation in this fashion continued until 1863, when he was
by the Classis of North Carolina, licensed to preach the Gospel
and ordained to the Christian ministry. The committee on Ordination and Installation that year reported:

> The committee appointed to ordain and install Mr. Thomas Long in
> the event of his acceptance of a call from the Davidson Charge, attended
> to this duty at Sauer's Church on the first Sabbath in May 1863. The
> committee found the call in order and Brother Long signified his willing-
> ness to accept it. The committee confirmed the call, ordained and in-
> stalled him as associate pastor.[4]

A brief statement of this dedicated man's service to his church
deserves a place in the record. Thomas Long was one of the charter members, and an elder when the first church building was
erected at Pleasant Retreat.

> He was born in Davidson County near Bethany Reformed Church. . . .
> His brother Allison Long was a minister of the Reformed Church. Thomas
> Long received no education but that of the free schools of his day; but he
> was evidently a man of considerable natural ability. He applied himself
> to a diligent study of the Bible, exercised a true and abiding faith in God,
> lived out the great truths of the Gospel, and thus by his own wise per-
> severing efforts, he prepared himself to render the church in his day good
> service. . . . .
> During the Civil War there was a scarcity of Reformed ministers in North
> Carolina; so on the third day of May 1863, he was licensed to preach the
> Gospel. When the Reformed Church in Davidson County was divided
> and made to constitute the Upper Davidson Charge and the Lower David-
> son Charge, he became pastor of the Upper Davidson Charge. This was
> his first and only charge. Here he labored until 1886, when age and bodily
> afflction disqualified him for the duties of the ministry.
> Though he was without a college education, yet, by purchasing good
> books and consulting Dr. George W. Welker, he acquired a clear concep-
> tion of the principal theological doctrines then held by the churches. A
> doctrinal sermon preached by him is remembered in which he defended
> the Reformed view over against some other then being propagated, and
> his arguments were unanswerable. In some things he may not have held
> strictly to the Reformed customs. He always knelt in prayer. He was a
> farmer and worked on his farm and raised fine crops. In the pulpit he
> was awkward, making few gestures and seldom changing his position. He
> preached without notes, but his sermons had power. It is not known that

he ever received a salary. He served four congregations and often preached at school houses and "stands" in different parts of the county.

He later organized Mt. Tabor at the "Poor House," and when he resigned the charge he still retained the congregation for years; and when he became too feeble to stand and preach, these people so devoted to him, made a chair and he would sit and talk to them. He often travelled in a two-wheeled gig drawn by a little black mule, and with his long locks of hair flowing from beneath his broad-brimmed hat made a striking appearance. He advocated the neighborhood prayer meeting in the community, and great was the spiritual uplift received from these meetings. Father Long had a strong physical constitution, but by exposure and overexertion, he became a great sufferer from rheumatism in his old age, and was practically helpless for many years before his death. He was in great demand in his community. He was sought by many for advice in the adjustment of difficulties and disputes.[5]

The first church building was used as a house for worship until 1902, when during the pastorate of Dr. H. A. M. Holshouser, it was displaced by a new white frame building. Dedication ceremonies were conducted by the pastor October 13, 1902. Dr. James D. Andrew preached the sermon. Hebron Church became a part of the Waughtown Charge December 14, 1909. During the pastorate of Rev. David E. Bowers, in August 1913, Bethlehem Church was organized and added to the charge. This relationship continued until 1927, when Hebron became an independent self-supporting congregation, and Dr. A. Odell Leonard was assigned by the Classis of North Carolina to serve it as Stated Supply, which he continued to do until 1948.[6]

By unanimous action on July 28, 1929 the congregation decided to turn the church building around facing the highway, remodel it and add an educational annex. The whole structure was brick veneered. This work was done under the supervision of T. H. Livengood, R. F. Long and D. N. Smith. Dedication occurred November 10, 1929; the sacrament of Holy Communion was administered by the pastor at 11 a.m., and during the afternoon Dr. Jacob C. Leonard, a former pastor, delivered a reconsecration address. In 1940 the basement was enlarged and refinished. September 30, 1946, the consistory took action asking to be joined with Bethlehem and Bethany churches, forming the North Davidson Charge. On November 7 of the same year, the joint consistory asked Hebron Church to build a parsonage. Under the supervision of B. B. Kinlaw, Roby Nifong, Andrew Sink, Walter Sink, Carl Everhart, Francis Long and Fred Livengood, located on a lot facing the highway southwest of the church, the parsonage was built and promptly paid for.

Rev. John W. Settlemyre was called to be the first regular pastor of the North Davidson Charge, and installed in that office September 18, 1949. Rev. Thomas Hoffman followed him in May 1953. In 1956 Dr. A. Odell Leonard was again appointed temporary supply. An observance of significance occurred August 19, 1956, when the congregation celebrated its One Hundredth Anniversary. Dr.

Harvey A. Fesperman, president of Southern Synod, preached the anniversary sermon at 11 a.m., and Rev. Charles E. Hiatt, a son of the congregation, delivered an address at 2 p.m. A committee composed of the pastor, Fred Livengood, Lucy Miller, Kathryn Nifong, Mrs. T. A. Sink and Mrs. R. H. Livengood published an interesting anniversary brochure, in which they comment:

> We here at Hebron, under God, have made great strides, but there remains much to be accomplished. The challenge is impressive. More than three hundred are enrolled in the church and church school. The average attendance is more than 220.[7]

A tract of fourteen acres of land adjoining church property along the north line was acquired January 16, 1956, for the sum of $8,-401.50. The old parsonage was sold. On the newly acquired land a new parsonage was erected, being dedicated August 25, 1961.

When Rev. Charles Donald Lyerly came to the parish February 4, 1957, the church was equipped materially and spiritually to undertake effective Christian work in that community. For a time activities on the parish did flourish; then, internal difficulties developed. Disaffection between pastor and people occurred, resulting in the minister's resignation; also his withdrawal from the Evangelical and Reformed Church. Due to his influence, approximately one half of the congregation withdrew from the church.

A period of reorganization followed; first under the leadership of Dr. A. Odell Leonard and Rev. Donald M. Leonard, and after a few months, led by Rev. Aubrey W. Hedrick. The Rev. Rex O. Dobey began his ministry to the congregation June 25, 1961. Since that time the church has made steady progress, enjoying harmony within the fellowship, and blessed with program and material advances in all departments of parish life. Rev. William M. Everhart is the current pastor, beginning his ministry in 1967.

Rev. Thomas Long was a son of the congregation, as is the Rev. Charles E. Hiatt, both of them ministers in the United Church of Christ.

ROSTER OF PASTORS

Rev. Thornton Butler, Organizing Pastor 1856-1857	Rev. A. Odell Leonard, D.D., Stated Supply 1927-1948
Mr. Thomas Long, Lay Minister 1856-1863	Mr. John W. Settlemyre, Summer Student Supply 1948-
Rev. Thomas Long 1863-1886	Rev. Shuford Peeler, D.D., Supply 1948-1949
Rev. G. Dickie Gurley, Supply 1886-1887	Rev. John W. Settlemyre 1949-1953
Rev. J. H. Shuford 1887-1888	Rev. Thomas Hoffman 1953-1955
Rev. Jacob C. Leonard, D.D. 1889-1891	Rev. A. Odell Leonard, D.D., Supply 1956-
Rev. H. A. M. Holshouser, Ph.D. 1897-1903	Rev. Charles Donald Lyerly 1957-1959
Rev. William H. Causey, D.D. 1904-1907	Rev. A. Odell Leonard, D.D., Alternate Supply 1959-1960
Rev. John A. Ditzler, Supply 1908-	Rev. Donald M. Leonard, Alternate Supply 1959-1960
Rev. W. A. Long, Supply 1909-	Rev. Aubrey W. Hedrick, Supply 1960-1961
Rev. A. Samuel Peeler 1910-1911	Rev. Rex O. Dobey 1961-1967
Rev. David E. Bowers 1912-1921	Rev. William M. Everhart 1967-
Rev. J. M. L. Lyerly, Ph.D. ..1922-1923	
Rev. Augustus C. Peeler 1923-1927	

1. *Clapp*, Jacob C., Editor, Historic Sketch of the Reformed Church in North Carolina, 1908, p. 179.
2. ————. Minutes. Classis of North Carolina, 1856, p. 222.
3. *Ibid.* p. 223.
4. ————. Minutes. *Op. cit.*, 1863, p. 294.
5. *Clapp. Op. cit.*, p. 180 ff.
6. *Leonard*, A. Odell, One Hundreth Anniversary of Organization, Hebron Evangelical and Reformed Church, 1956, p. 4. ff.
7. *Ibid.*, p. 38.

Hedrick's Grove Church, Davidson County

In 1892 Dr. George W. Welker, Stated Clerk of the Classis of North Carolina, wrote.

The Classis of North Carolina met with the congregation of Hedrick's Grove Chapel, in Davidson County, North Carolina, to hold its Sixty-Second Annual Session.

This is a newly organized Reformed congregation, having completed a comfortable house of worship. The building is a two story frame structure, designed to be used on the first story as an academy with three classrooms, while on the second story is the audience room and place of worship. The whole structure and its purpose are quite creditable to the community and carries the old Reformed church idea of the parochial school and the house of God. Here is a fine farming country, and this well-to-do people welcomed the Classis of North Carolina with cheerful and bounteous hospitality.

. . . . . Only one drawback was felt,—the congregation has no pastor. This great need was all that marred the occasion. Here is a field that opens an inviting opportunity for an energetic man, who would do good and see the work of the Lord prosper in his hands. The membership is composed of young people who are looking up, active and ready to take hold and work. They only need a discreet and Godly leader to follow— in whom they can confide. The youth and children assure a population that for years will crowd the school and furnish material for the growth of the congregation.

The Lower Davidson Charge is a country charge, and Hedrick's Grove is about six miles from Lexington, the shire town of Davidson County.[1]

In the spring of 1889 a Sunday School was organized at Hedrick's Grove, in an old building formerly used as a store house. Daniel R. Hedrick was named superintendent. Since no church existed nearer than Beck's, Emanuel, Pilgrim, Mt. Tabor and Jerusalem congregations, Reformed people desired to have a church more conveniently located. Hedrick's Grove being a converging point, was chosen as the site. Seeking to provide a facility which would satisfy their needs in education as well as religion, it was decided to build a church and school together. Money and building material were collected in the summer of 1889, in preparation for such a structure, erection of which began that fall. The cornerstone was laid Thanksgiving Day. The building was enclosed and the floors laid during the winter, but the auditorium was not completed until the fall and winter of 1891 and 1892. Dedication services occurred July 31, 1892, when Dr. Jacob C. Leonard preached the sermon. In deference to the settlement, the church was named Hedrick's Grove in a joint consistory meeting of the Lower Davidson Charge held March 21, 1891, and the congregation was officially organized the following May 3.

Forty-one names were on the charter member list, assembled in the following manner. Transferred from Beck's church were: Emily Regan, Jacob Younts, Mrs. Alexander Smith, Mrs. Washington Smith, Alexander Beck, Laura Young, Isaac Rhodes, Crissie Leonard, Lamuel Allred, Allen Hedrick, Mrs. Neta C. Hedrick, Elizabeth Hedrick, Philip E. Hedrick, Wiley C. Hedrick, A. Eli Hedrick, Henry E. Hedrick, Jacob Hedrick, George W. Hedrick, Mrs. Jane Hedrick, Thornton Hedrick, Adeline Hedrick, Joseph Hedrick, Minnie E. Swing, R. Eli Hedrick, Mary E. Hedrick, G. Mathias Hedrick, Rachael Hedrick and Bettie Hedrick.

Those transferred from Emanuel were: David Grubb, Susanna Grubb, John L. Black and Frances Black; also, a group was received by confirmation. These were: Ida Regan, Laura Regan, Robert L. Beck, Samuel W. Beck, Jones Tilden Hedrick, Sara J. Hedrick, H. Frank Hedrick, Henry H. Hedrick and S. Adnet Hedrick. Allen Hedrick, John L. Black and R. Eli Hedrick were elected elders; and H. Frank Hedrick, Harvey H. Hedrick and R. L. Beck, deacons.

Land for the church and parsonage was donated by John Long, Philip Hedrick and George W. Hedrick. In those early days the congregation had no instrument with which to lead music; however, R. Eli Hedrick brought his melodion and Miss Sara J. Hedrick played it for church and Sunday School services.[2]

A week-day school was conducted in the new building in 1892 and 1893, by R. E. Leonard and Crawford Clapp. Dr. William H. McNairy also taught there several months during his ministry to the congregation. The public school of the district was taught in that building until 1924.[3]

Natural resources—fertile soil, good grazing land and virgin forests—account for the rapid development of this section of Davidson County over a period of years. Hedrick's Grove Church, therefore, became an immediate beneficiary of these material advantages, and arose to meet the religious needs of the community, serving a growing church constituency.

Realizing the need for more adequate facilities, a congregational meeting was called for the first Sunday in September 1920. At that time the decision was made to build a new church, authorizing the appointment of two committees. The building committee consisted of E. A. Hedrick, George L. Hedrick, J. W. Younts, Ed. F. Hedrick and R. L. Beck. On the finance committee were named Grover Hedrick, George W. Hedrick, John H. Beck, Henry Regan and Ed. F. Hedrick. Plans were developed, and submitted to the congregation for approval of a brick building providing space for a sanctuary and a number of Sunday School class-rooms. Brick was made by the people near the site of the church, and the lumber was cut from the ample forests of members of the congregation.

Construction on the building began August 21, 1921, when the pastor, Dr. John C. Peeler, laid the first brick. By late fall the structure was under roof. When the cornerstone was laid December 16, work was suspended until the spring of 1922. At that time operations were resumed. The church was finished and occupied during the summer months. Eight years later, June 29, 1930, Dr. Peeler, who had inspired its erection, preached the dedicatory sermon. Rev. A. Samuel Peeler, pastor of the congregation, performed the act of dedication. During the afternoon Dr. Jacob C. Leonard delivered an historical address.

Hedrick's Grove Church was enrolled by the Classis of North Carolina and yoked with Emanuel, Beck's, Mt. Carmel and Jerusalem congregations in 1891.[4] In 1896 Mt. Tabor was added to the charge.[5] The church continued to operate as a part of the Lower Davidson Charge, with varied congregational connections, until March 19, 1963. At that time a financial settlement was reached with other involved congregations with reference to the old parsonage property, and by Southern Synod declared a self-supporting church.[6]

The 50th Anniversary of its organization was observed by the congregation May 4, 1941. A program, directed by the pastor, Rev. Charles E. Hiatt, featured an historical address by the veteran educator, Robert L. Beck, an anniversary sermon by Rev. Roy C. Whisenhunt and an afternoon program of music rendered by the choir and a men's quartet. The quartet was composed of Robert L. Hedrick, Ed. F. Hedrick, Grover Hedrick and Odell Fouts. Other ministers present were: Revs. Terrell M. Shoffner, William H.

Causey, John C. Peeler, James D. Andrew, Jacob A. Palmer and Banks J. Peeler.

Numerical growth of Hedrick's Grove Church has been steadily upward. Thus, by 1955, educational facilities were again outgrown. Additional land was acquired. Building plans were formulated and approved by the congregation. On February 12, 1961 groundbreaking ceremonies were held. Construction of a modern educational building began shortly thereafter. The new building is located immediately back of the sanctuary. It is architecturally of modern design, containing 12,000 square feet of space. The structure was occupied unfinished, November 11, 1962. Dedication occurred Easter Sunday morning, March 29, 1964. It was debt free. Dr. Banks J. Peeler, president of Southern Synod, preached the sermon. Rev. Raymond C. Craven, the pastor, performed the act of dedication. Among other things he said:

> The building which we dedicate has been erected because "the people had a mind to work." This was evident as the people worked with their hands to shape this building with loving care. Yet, the building itself is not complete. Someday more partitions will be added to provide more classrooms. This is symbolic of something deper. The building will not be complete until it has fulfilled its purpose of fostering and strengthening the Christian Way of Life in all who meet here.[7]

The 75th Anniversary of the organization of the church was observed May 1, 1966. Ample preparation had been made by an anniversary committee consisting of Foy Harvey, Herman McNeely, Mrs. Paul E. A. Beck, Mrs. Emory M. Crotts and Odell Fouts. Rev. Charles E. Hiatt, who served the congregation from 1937 to 1950, preached the anniversary sermon. Rev. Aubrey W. Hedrick and Rev. J. Wayne Fouts, sons of the congregation, conducted the evening worship.[8]

The story of the parsonage is interesting. Lower Davidson Charge built a modest one-story residence for the minister at Hedrick's Grove, finishing it February 15, 1889.[9] In 1896 this house was rebuilt into a two story residence. Renovated and improved a number of times, it served the purpose until 1921. At that time a second parsonage, a frame house, was erected immediately behind the old one. This building served the charge until March 9, 1953, when Hedrick's Grove went to self-support and purchased the interests of other congregations involved. It then became the residence of Rev. and Mrs. Raymond C. Craven, the first full-time minister of the congregation.

The present commodious and modern parsonage was erected over a period of three years, largely by members of the congregation. It stands immediately in front of the old one, which has since been sold and razed, and represents an actual financial investment of $16,972.57. Dedication ceremonies took place Sunday afternoon, August 20, 1967.

Hedrick's Grove congregation has invested generously in the wider concerns of the Kingdom of God. As partial evidence of such stewardship, three of her sons have been ordained to the Christian Ministry in the United Church of Christ. Rev. Samuel W. Beck was ordained in 1903; Rev. Aubrey W. Hedrick in 1938; and Rev. J. Wayne Fouts in 1953.

ROSTER OF PASTORS

Rev. Allen R. Holshouser 1891-1893	Rev. John C. Peeler, D.D. 1918-1923
Rev. William H. McNairy, D.D. 1894-1896	Rev. A. Samuel Peeler 1923-1928
Rev. Lewis M. Kerschner 1897-1899	Mr. Roy C. Whisenhunt, Summer Student Supply 1929-1930
Mr. Irwin S. Ditzler, Student Summer Supply 1900-	Rev. James D. Andrew, D.D. 1931-1937
Rev. H. E. Sechler 1901-1902	Rev. Charles E. Hiatt 1937-1950
Rev. Paul Barriner, Stated Supply 1902-1903	Rev. Roy E. Leinbach, Jr., Supply 1950-
Mr. William H. Causey, Student Summer Supply 1902-	Rev. C. Nevin Stamm 1950-1952
Rev. William H. Causey, D.D. 1903-1904	Rev. Lionel A. Whiston, Ph.D., Supply 1952
Rev. Peter M. Trexler, D.D., Supply 1908-1909	Rev. Lawrence A. Leonard, Supply 1953-
Rev. J. M. L. Lyerly, Ph.D., Stated Supply 1909-1918	Rev. A. Odell Leonard, D.D., Supply 1953-1954
	Rev. Raymond C. Craven 1955-1967

1. *Welker,* George W., Minutes, North Carolina Classis, 1892, p. 3.
2. *Beck,* Robert L., Hedrick's Grove Church, The Standard, May 15, 1941, p. 1.
3. *Leonard,* Jacob C., Centennial History of Davidson County, 1927, p. 475.
4. ———. Minutes. Classis of North Carolina, 1891, p. 7.
5. ———. Minutes. *Op. cit.,* 1896, p. 32.
6. ———. Minutes. *Op. cit.,* 1963, p. 14.
7. *Craven,* Raymond C., Dedication, Religious Education Building, Hedrick's Grove United Church of Christ, 1964, p. 6.
8. *Craven,* Raymond C., Seventy-Fifth Anniversary, Hedrick's Grove United Church of Christ, 1966, p. 1 ff.
9. *Beck. Op. cit.,* p. 1.

Heidelberg Church, Thomasville

AT A MEETING of the joint consistory of the Upper Davidson Charge, called March 10, 1894, an overture was authorized to be presented to the Classis of North Carolina, asking "Classis to recognize Thomasville as a mission point and commit the interest to a minister with instructions to organize a congregation."[1] The request was granted, and the project placed under the care of Dr. Jacob C. Leonard.

The missionary proceeded to prepare for and to conduct a first service in the town of Thomasville, North Carolina, on the evening of June 3, 1894, at the home of Mr. and Mrs. Thomas A. Livengood, Main Street, located across the railroad from the site later selected for the first parsonage and church. Two weeks later, June 17, at the same place, Heidelberg Reformed Church was organized. There were sixteen charter members: John A. Long, Mrs. John A. Long, Daisy L. Long, Joseph P. Long, E. Cora Long, W. Lindsay Myers, Mrs. W. Lindsay Myers, Randall P. Murphy, J. Theodore Long,

Mrs. J. Theodore Long, Thomas A. Livengood, Mrs. Thomas A. Livengood, J. Lee Briles, Mrs. J. Lee Briles, Edward B. Clodfelter and Robert T. Cecil. W. Lindsay Myers and J. Theodore Long were elected elders; Thomas A. Livengood and Randall P. Murphy, deacons.

Most of the services during the remainder of the year were conducted in the same private home. However, at least one each was held in the Methodist Episcopal Church and a chapel at Baptist Orphanage.

In 1895, Dr. Leonard made his report to the Classis.

> Immediately after the adjournment of Classis, I went to Thomasville and sought out all members of the Reformed Church that I could find. These were ready and willing to enter into an organization. Meanwhile I corresponded with the Superintendent of Missions and through him succeeded in having Thomasville enrolled by the board as a Mission under its care.
>
> In the month of June, a congregation with sixteen members was organized under the name of Heidelberg Reformed Church. Services were at first held in a private house. Later, Elder W. L. Myers has given the congregation the use of his hall in which the services are at present held. A desirable lot has been secured, and the erection of a church undertaken. The new enterprise is in an encouraging condition.
>
> I hereby hand over to the Classis this new congregation, and ask that Heidelberg Church of Thomasville be recognized as a charge belonging to the Classis of North Carolina.[2]

The congregation was enrolled as a member of Classis, Elder J. T. Long was recognized as its official representative, as was the commissioning of Dr. Leonard by the Board of Missions as missionary-in-charge.

The erection of a house of worship went forward during the year, being occupied unfinished July 21, 1895. On the same day the Sunday School was organized, with an enrollment of thirty five pupils. The church was finished in the fall, and dedicated December 15, 1895, involving an expenditure of $2,330. A local newspaper described dedication activities in detail:

> The day of dedication was beautiful. The auditorium and lecture room together could not accommodate all who wished to enter; but seats were provided for at least four hundred people. Rev. J. L. Murphy, pastor of the Reformed Church of Hickory, North Carolina and president of Claremont College, preached the sermon on the "Glory of a United Church." The effort was grand and the congregation was pleased and delighted.
>
> The act of dedication was performed by the pastor, Rev. J. C. Leonard. In the afternoon an informal service was held, when brief addresses were made by several visiting ministers, Divine services were held at night also. The offering of the day amounted to $50. The following ministers were present at the dedication: Revs. J. L. Murphy, J. W. Cecil, W. H. McNairy and J. C. Leonard of the Reformed Church; Revs. Boone, Morton, Newton and Hall of the Baptist Church; and Rev. Irvin of the Methodist Church.[3]

Although Heidelberg Church was a mission under the care of the Board of Missions, until 1896, it was considered a part of the Upper Davidson group of churches. At that time the congregation was yoked with Emanuel and Calvary churches in the Thomasville Charge. From 1896 until 1910 seven different pastors served this mission. Sixteen years were required to assemble a confirmed membership of ninety-five people. Then, Rev. Clarence Woods, a young and energetic minister, came to the parish. In 1911, the church and parsonage were rolled back eighty feet on the lot and remodeled. A basement for social and educational purposes was constructed under the church building, and the comfort and beauty of the sanctuary were greatly enhanced by the installation of electric lights, carpet on the floor and new heating equipment. On July 1, 1913, realizing that the parish justified the services of a full-time pastor, it was declared by the Classis of North Carolina an independent congregation, receiving subsidy from the Board of Home Missions.[4]

By 1920 sentiment had developed in the congregation favorable to relocating the church, due largely to its proximity to the railroad. A lot on Fisher Ferry Street was purchased with that intention; however, sentiment shifted and the Paylor property on Salem Street was acquired April 27, 1927 and a year later the corner lot next to it along the west line was bought. In 1928 the Fisher Ferry Street property was sold. The church became a self-supporting congregation January 3, 1937, having had support from the Board of Home Missions since its enrollment by that body in 1894. This step was taken with some misgivings; however, the pastor, Dr. Jacob A. Palmer remarked later: "Nothing better could have happened to the congregation. Indeed, it should have happened before it did. Last year, 1944, was the first time for many years that the congregation paid its apportionment in full. All this in addition to raising a considerable sum for the building fund."[5]

On Easter Sunday, April 13, 1941, the note on the Salem Street property was publicly burned. This act cleared the church of debt, except an obligation of $900 to the Solliday Church Building Fund. This indebtedness was cleared up a year later. Falling short of a hope to observe the 50th Anniversary of its Organization in the new sanctuary, the congregation, however, rejoiced on that occasion in the fact that so much progress had been made in that direction; indeed, they stood on the threshold of its realization. For in late summer 1946, the erection of the new church building was begun. Elder W. Ernest Fouts served as contractor and builder until his death in 1951. Meanwhile the old church building had burned, and neighboring Calvary Reformed congregation made their facilities available until 1949, when the basement assembly room in the new church was usable for congregational activities.

In 1953 action was taken by the congregation to finish the interior of the sanctuary. Cornerstone laying ceremonies took place March 20, 1955. Dr. Palmer was in charge of the service, and assisting him were J. D. Stonesifer and Hobert Lee Fouts, co-chairmen of the building committee. On Palm Sunday March 27, 1955, dedication services began in the vestibule, when Hobert Lee Fouts presented to the congregation the key to the new church. The pastor preached the sermon and conducted the ritual of dedication. Dr. Donald C. Dearborn, Treasurer of Southern Synod and Dean of Catawba College, spoke for the Evangelical and Reformed Church.

> The interior of Heidelberg Church shows the pure form of the American Gothic Cathedral type church. The windows, made in Germany, contain medallions that tell the primary incidents in the life of Jesus Christ. The large rose window over the balcony is called the Good Shepherd window. From the vestibule entrance in the east to the altar in west, the central aisle symbolizes the way of Christian life—the way to God.
>
> The Schantz Pipe Organ, valued at more than $20,000, was the first of its kind in the state and was given by Dr. Jacob A. Palmer, his brothers and grandchildren, in loving memory of Daniel and Camilla Fisher Palmer. It was dedicated on April 10, 1955, with William Fisher Palmer, presenting the concert on the instrument.[6]

After serving the congregation thirty seven and a half years, in 1955, Dr. Palmer retired from the active pastorate. During his ministry the church was relocated, and the new church was erected and dedicated. He became a recognized and trusted leader in the Thomasville Community, serving on the welfare and public school boards. On June 14, 1959, by a devoted congregation, he was declared Pastor Emeritus of Heidelberg Church, and in 1963 the church celebrated his 50th Anniversary of Ordination to the Christian Ministry.

Rev. Richard A. Cheek began his work on the parish November 15, 1955. The old parsonage was razed in 1956 to provide a site on which to erect a new house, which was completed February 1957 at a cost of $30,000. The Sixty-Fifth Anniversary of Organization of Heidelberg Church was fittingly observed in a week of activities which began June 14, 1959. Anniversary Services occurred on Sunday at 11 a.m., the Pastor Emeritus, preached the sermon; at 7:30 p.m. Dr. Harvey A. Fesperman, president of Southern Synod, delivered the sermon. Other ministers of the denomination present for the occasion were: Rev. G. Ermine Plott, a former pastor; Revs. Lloyd E. Sechriest and Robert E. Myers, both sons of the congregation. On Christmas Sunday, December 25, 1960, the mortgage papers on the new parsonage were burned. Participating in this meaningful ceremony were: the pastor, the Pastor Emeritus, R. L. Pope, Thad Hedrick, Harold Hinkle and Harrison Black.

The last part of the new church structure to be erected was the bell tower, which was dedicated September 27, 1964. This tower houses the bell which hung for many years in the tower of the old church.

Rev. G. Harold Myers was called, and became pastor of Heidelberg Church, February 15, 1965. In 1966 a history room, which contains many important articles, books and records of an historical nature, was dedicated in memory of Mr. and Mrs. William Grimes Hinkle, life long members of the congregation. The address on that occasion was delivered by Rev. Frank W. Snider, chairman of the Historical Committee of Southern Synod. This church maintains a program of activities covering the field of Christian service as conceived by the United Church of Christ. The current confirmed membership is 264 people, and the Sunday School has an enrollment of 211 pupils.

ROSTER OF PASTORS

Rev. Jacob C. Leonard, D.D., Organizer 1894-1896	Rev. William H. McNairy, D.D. 1908-1909
Rev. Clarence Clapp 1896-1899	Rev. Clarence Woods 1910-1914
Rev. Jacob N. Faust 1899-1902	Rev. G. Ermine Plott 1915-1917
Rev. Walter W. Rowe, D.D. 1902-1904	Rev. Jacob A. Palmer, D.D. 1918-1955
Rev. Frederick Cromer 1904-1905	Rev. Richard A. Cheek 1955-1964
Rev. Lucian W. Showers 1905-1906	Rev. G. Harold Myers 1965-
Rev. Irvin S. Ditzler 1907-1908	

1. ———. Minutes. Classis of North Carolina, 1894, p. 8.
2. ———. Minutes. Op. cit., 1895, p. 8.
3. Palmer, Jacob A., Fiftieth Anniversary. Heidelberg Evangelical and Reformed Church, 1944, p. 2.
4. ———. Minutes. Op. cit., 1913, p. 62.
5. Palmer, Op. cit., p. 5.
6. Myers, G. Harold, Manuscript. History of Heidelberg Evangelical and Reformed Church, 1967, p. 3.

Keller Church, Cabarrus County

KELLER REFORMED CHURCH, Kannapolis, North Carolina, Route 1, was authorized by the Classis of North Carolina, August 13, 1903, when that body commissioned Dr. John H. Keller to organize a church in that community. After this a series of steps followed in anticipation of its founding.[1] A report made by Mr. Keller to the Classis in May 1904 tells the story.

> Your committee has made arrangements to erect a church and organize a new congregation within the bounds of the New Gilead Charge, to be known as Keller Reformed Church. We have elected officers, but have not ordained them as yet; are erecting a church and hold services at that point twice a month.[2]

Officers referred to in this report were: elders, John W. Cline and John M. O. Rymer; deacons, Harris A. Cook and John E. Brantley. These men were elected July 1, 1904, and ordained and installed in their respective offices August 18 of the same year. The charter membership list, recognized on the latter date, contained thirty names, and imply that the congregation was completely organized at that time. Charter member names were:

> Mr. & Mrs. J. W. Cline, Mr. & Mrs. W. E. Brantley, J. A. Brantley, Mr. & Mrs. B. C. Yost, Alexander Yost, Margaret Yost, Joicie Yost Ludwig, John P. Yost, Mary Yost, Florence Yost Allman, Ester Yost Stirewalt, Alexander Cook, Roscan Cook, Charles Cook, Mary A. Shank, James Yost, Ester Yost Troutman, H. A. Cook, Ida M. Edison, W. M. Edison, J. M. O. Rymer, E. S. Rymer, John D. Rymer, Ammom M. Rymer, Olive Cline, C. J. Rymer and A. J. Rymer.[3]

At a congregational meeting held November 28, 1904 action was taken "to proceed at once to build a church." J. W. Cline, H. A.

Cook and W. E. Brantley were named to the building committee and instructed to develop plans for and supervise its construction. A plain frame structure was agreed upon. Contract for the building was awarded in April 1905 to J. M. Blackwelder for the sum of $145. It was finished and ready to be occupied June 15, and dedicated to the service of Almighty God August 20, 1905. Dr. Paul Barringer preached the sermon, and the pastor read the ritual of dedication.

J. W. Cline was asked to raise money with which to finance the erection of the church. His report to the congregation lists 143 separate cash gifts, ranging from 30 cents to $136.[4] The house was dedicated free of debt. Land on which the old church stood and upon which the new church stands, was donated by John W. Cline and Wade Brantley. Some years later, four Sunday School rooms were attached to the west side of the building, and still later a combination recreational-educational hut was erected near the southwest corner of the church. In it were housed primary and junior groups of the Sunday School; also youth activities. This structure was enlarged in 1966 and equipped with modern conveniences at a cost of $9,000.

The Sunday School was organized August 20, 1905. Dr. Keller continued to minister to the congregation in whose honor it was named, until 1908. In 1906 Keller and New Gilead churches were constituted the Gilead Charge. In due time women of the congregation were organized into the Woman's Missionary Society and the men into the Churchmen's Brotherhood. A Youth Fellowship was created for young folks. These titles have all changed in the process of two denominational mergers, but purposes and objectives have remained practically the same through the years, namely, to promote the Christian faith at home and abroad. Keller congregation has never grown into a numerically large church, in fact at one time about thirty-five years ago, some doubts were current about its future. But men like Elder Aaron S. Cook refused to admit that the church had served its day, and made plans for the years ahead. Events have more than justified their faith.

At a congregational meeting held May 30, 1954, Vance Patterson raised the question of building a new house for worship; whereupon it was voted to build a new church. The vote was almost unanimous. This action opened the door to a new era in the life of Keller Church. A combined Finance and Building committee, later separated, was authorized. Its personnel consisted of Hilda Patterson, chairman, Vance Patterson, Johnny Cook, Ray Hurlocker, A. B. Patterson, A. B. Patterson, Jr., Ernest Haynes, Carl Cline, Frank Hendrix and the pastor. These people were asked to recommend ways and means of collecting money for the building fund and to develop plans for a church building suited to their needs.

On June 27, 1954, inspired by their young minister the Rev. Carl R. Martin, the 50th Anniversary of the Organization of Keller

Church was observed. Ministers appearing on that program were, Dr. John H. Keller, who had organized the church, delivered an address at 9:45 A.M.; Rev. Charles R. Patterson, who was confirmed in the Christian faith at Keller Church when a boy, preached the sermon at 11 o'clock. The anniversary bulletin commented as follows:

> Within the fifty years many have held membership in our church. Others have come and gone, but all have found within the walls of this little white country church peace, quiet, the spirit of true worship and the fellowship and friendship of a common folk whose true religion is worshipping God in truth and spirit and helping his fellow neighbor when in need.

This occasion appears to have generated in the congregation a new outlook concerning its mission to the local community as well as its involvment in general denominational causes. Plans proceeded in orderly fashion to accomplish their immediate aim. They needed new equipment to meet their new vision. The old church was moved back to provide space for the new one, and later sold to a neighbor for domestic purposes. Groundbreaking ceremonies took place May 29, 1955. Construction of the new building got under way in the fall of that year. The cornerstone was laid January 15, 1956, and the church equipped and ready for use was occupied July 15, of the same year. Rev. Carl R. Martin spoke at 11 A.M. on the "Conquering Church." A Service of Dedication took place at 2:30 in the afternoon, when Dr. Joseph B. Hennessey, pastor of First Church, Charlotte, North Carolina, preached the sermon. Reading the dedicatory ritual was the pastor. Since that time debts have been paid, so that the church now stands debt-free and adequately equipped to provide a highly satisfactory program of religious activities for the area.

Presently yoked with St. Paul's Church, Enochville, North Carolina, the charge is being served by Rev. G. Ermine Plott. An appropriate and well kept cemetery owned by the congregation lies adjacent to church property along the north and west lines.

Two sons of the congregation have committed themselves to the Christian Ministry: Rev. J. Keller Brantley in the United Church of Christ, and Rev. Charles R. Patterson in the United Lutheran Church.

ROSTER OF PASTORS

Rev. John H. Keller, D.D. 1903-1908	Rev. Roy E. Leinbach, Jr.,
Rev. Peter M. Trexler, D.D. 1909-1910	Supply 1939-1940
Rev. Dugan C. Cox 1911-1912	Rev. John H. Keller, D.D.,
Rev. Border L. Stanley 1913-1917	Supply 1940-1944
Rev. William C. Lyerly,	Rev. Huitt R. Carpenter,
Supply 1918-1923	Supply 1945-
Rev. J. Dudley Maeder 1923-1925	Rev. Carl T. Daye 1946-1948
Rev. Lee A. Peeler, D.D.,	Rev. Lewis E. Everline 1948-1952
Supply 1925-1927	Rev. Carl R. Martin 1953-1956
Mr. George A. Creitz,	Rev. Jacob A. Palmer, D.D.,
Student Summer Supply 1927-	Supply 1956-1958
Rev. Lee A. Peeler, D.D. 1927-1938	Rev. George R. Johnson 1958-1962
Rev. Charles W. Warlick, D.D.,	Rev. Harold H. Holtom 1962-1965
Supply 1939-	Rev. G. Ermine Plott, Supply 1965-1968
	Rev. Collie P. Seymour 1968-

1. ———. Minutes. Classis of North Carolina, 1904, p. 383.
2. ———. Ibid. p. 337.
3. ———. Church Register, 1904, pp. 4, 8, 16.
4. ———. Church Records, 1906, ff.

Lyerly Memorial Church, Rowan County

BETHANY, THE ORIGINAL NAME of Lyerly Memorial Evangelical and Reformed Church, Rowan County, was organized August 23, 1891. In 1890 a number of Reformed families, members of Lower Stone Church, petitioned the Classis of North Carolina to establish a church of their faith in that community. Dr. J. M. L. Lyerly, a leader in the movement and serving his first pastorate on the Central Rowan Charge, and Rev. Calvin B. Heller, pastor of the East Rowan Charge, were commissioned to organize it.[1]

A charter member list contained twenty four names: Dr. and Mrs. J. M. L. Lyerly, Mrs. Camilla Lyerly, Mr. and Mrs. Tobias Holshouser, Mr. and Mrs. James McCombs, Sr., Mr. and Mrs. William McCombs, Sr., Mr. and Mrs. Maxwell Holshouser, Mr. and Mrs. Crawford Peeler, Mr. and Mrs. Alexander Holshouser, Mr. and Mrs. Boyden A. Fesperman, Joseph McCombs, Mollie McCombs, Alice McCombs, William M. McCombs, Jr., James McCombs, Jr., Mattie Holshouser and Charles McCombs. William McCombs, Sr., and Maxwell Holshouser were elected elders, and William McCombs, Jr., and Boyden A. Fesperman, deacons.[2]

The new congregation was made a part of the Central Rowan Charge and placed under the supervision of Dr. Lyerly, who served that church seventeen years. Maxwell Holshouser donated three acres of land and Alexander Lyerly one acre, on which to erect a church and establish a cemetery. Deeds for the land are dated September 26, 1891. Plans ensued to build a modest frame church building, which was dedicated October 4, 1896. Dr. Jacob C. Clapp, president of Catawba College, preached the sermon. The pastor performed the act of dedication. A number of years later, four class-rooms were added to the front of the church, also a tower, which served the congregation until the present brick structure was erected in 1954.

From its beginning, Lyerly Memorial Church has been yoked with one or more neighboring churches in a pastoral charge. Its first alignment was with the Central Rowan group. In 1906 Lyerly Memorial and Mt. Hope churches were constituted the Crescent Charge. Lyerly Memorial and Shiloh churches were put together in 1909. In 1912 Lyerly Memorial became a part of the Rockwell Charge, with St. Luke's and Ursinus churches. In 1948 Lyerly Memorial and St. Luke's were detached from Ursinus, Rockwell and became the Crescent Charge, which alignment continues.

While the confirmed membership of Lyerly Memorial Church has never been numerically large, through the years, it has been the spiritual home of many people temporarily living in the community. When the Crescent Academy and Business College operated at Crescent, students of that institution looked to that church for worship and Chrisian fellowship, as have the staff and children of Nazareth Childrens' Home since 1906. It is, therefore, understandable that pressure for more adequate equipment than ordinarily required by the congregation would be felt almost from the day of its founding.

A study committee was named February 28, 1949 composed of Mrs. Robert Patterson, Mrs. Adam Lyerly, Thomas L. Moose, Lewis Sides and supply pastor, C. Columbus Wagoner, to determine this need and to recommend procedures. After a thorough survey, the committee recommended the erection of a new sanctuary on land along the line west of the old church building. Ill health removed Mr. Wagoner as supply pastor, and for a time building operations were at a standstill, until the arrival in 1951 of Rev. Carl T. Daye. A new committee was appointed consisting of Thomas L. Moose, chairman, Mrs. Robert Patterson, Mrs. Murray Penninger, Charles Ramsaur, Thomas O. Sinclair and Lewis Sides.[3]

When, in 1948, St. Luke's and Lyerly Memorial churches were aligned in a charge, this arrangement required the erection of a parsonage. Land on which it stands was donated for that purpose by the Board of Managers of Nazareth Childrens' Home, and it was completed, and occupied by Mr. Daye and his family in 1951.

Plans were drawn for the new church building and approved in 1952. Groundbreaking ceremonies were held December 20, 1953. Appropriately, among others, Mrs. J. M. L. Lyerly, wife of the founder of the church and its first pastor, participated. The cornerstone was laid and dedicatory services held October 31, 1954. Dr. Aaron R. Tosh, president of Southern Synod, and Rev. C. Donald

Lyerly, a son of the congregation, officiated. Mr. Lyerly preached the sermon. At the same time twenty-five memorials and a number of valuable gifts to the church were announced. This occasion was made possible by an accumulation of factors, involving contributions from the denomination and interested individuals. A particular cash gift of approximately $25,000 from Mrs. Maye Lyerly Coble, a daughter, and Carl Lyerly, a son, of Dr. and Mrs. Lyerly was announced.[4]

The Sixtieth Anniversary of the organization of the congregation was observed in an appropriately arranged series of activities beginning with the week of August 19, 1957. Featured in the series, in the order named, were: Dr. Aaron R. Tosh, former pastor; Rev. William C. Lyerly and Dr. Henderson L. V. Shinn, sons of the congregation. Fellowship evening was held Thursday, beginning with a picnic supper. Elder Ray P. Lyerly was master of ceremonies. Rev. Elmer Boggs preached the sermon Friday evening. Mr. Daye, pastor of the church, closed the eventful series on Sunday morning with an appropriate service of worship and sermon. St. Luke's congregation joined in observing the happy occasion.

On April 27, 1954, by request of the congregation, Southern Synod approved a change of its name to "Lyerly Memorial Evangelical and Reformed Church," honoring its founder.[5]

The purpose of these congregational stories is to relate the history of the churches of Synod, rather than to present biographic sketches. However, the history of this congregation would be incomplete without a brief appraisal of the life of its founder, who was also the leading spirit in developing the "Crescent Community."

Jacob Martin Luther Lyerly was born November 18, 1862. He was baptized at Organ Lutheran Church, but catechized and confirmed a member of Lower Stone Reformed Church. He graduated from Catawba College in the class of 1889, and was licensed to preach the Gospel by the Classis of North Carolina in May of the same year, being ordained to the Christian ministry the following October 10. He was married to Mary Virginia Peeler, and to them were born eleven children. Dr. Lyerly left his mark upon the Crescent Community, the Reformed Church throughout the state of North Carolina, and in particular upon several thousand young people who were the beneficiaries of his benevolent concerns.

In 1891 he successfully promoted the organization of Lyerly Memorial Reformed Church located in his native community. In 1896 he founded Crescent Academy and Business College, enrolling seventeen students the first year, which in 1909 served as many as 250 students. The school was related to the Reformed Church only through the devoted and unselfish leadership of its founder. It did quality work over a period of eighteen years, until the state education system provided adequately for learning on the high school and academy levels, closing in 1913.

Among the large number of young people prepared in that institution to take their places in society were: 13 Reformed ministers, 8 Lutheran, 2 Baptist, 4 Episcopal and 1 Presbyterian.[6] He owned and edited at different times, The Concord Chronicle, The Albemarle Chronicle; and, the Reformed Church Standard.[7] Dr. Lyerly was instrumental in establishing Nazareth Childrens' Home, and in 1903 was named chairman of its newly created Board of Managers. In that office he served with distinction until his death.

In 1909 and 1910 he was a member of the Catawba College faculty, and in 1915 and 1916 he directed the affairs of Claremont College, Hickory, North Carolina. His pastoral services to the Reformed Church include: the Central Rowan Charge, Lincoln, Lower Davidson, Guilford, St. Paul's at Enochville, and Waughtown, Winston Salem. He was effectively serving on the latter charge when on March 17, 1923, death took him. His body was laid to rest in the Lyerly Memorial Church Cemetery, close to the scene of the major part of his productive years as an educator, a wise administrator and a Christian minister.

A colleague has written impressively about him:

> Dr. Lyerly began to teach a private school near his home to supplement his salary, as many other pastors in the Classis of North Carolina have done . . . But Dr. Lyerly also had a higher motive than receiving the additional money that would come to him through teaching; he wished to help young people to secure a better education than the neighborhood school at the time provided. . . . .
>
> He built his private school into Crescent Academy and Business College. Only eternity can reveal the immense value of this school in the lives of scores of young men and women who received through it the blessings of a liberal education. . . . So outstanding an educator did Dr. Lyerly become, that a few years later one of the state parties nominated him for the office of State Superintendent of Public Instruction.
>
> Nazareth Orphans' Home, which is located in this village, owes its inception more largely to this same outstanding educator and philanthropist than to any other person. Dr. Lyerly's heart went out to orphaned children. Long before we had an orphans' home at Crescent, Dr. Lyerly had taken several orphaned children into his own home. . . .[8]

An event in the life of Lyerly Memorial Church was the note-burning ceremony which took place October 27, 1963. The service was in charge of the pastor, Rev. Robert E. Myers. Associated with him were: Thomas L. Moore, Mrs. Daisy Fisher Patterson and Thomas O. Sinclair, members of the building committee. This congregation, still handicapped in numbers, is equipped to minister effectively to the community in which it is located.

In keeping with its concern for young people, Lyerly Memorial Church has supported and sent six sons into the Christian ministry: Revs. Henderson L. V. Shinn, D.D., William C. Lyerly, Jacob N. Lyerly, Sidney C. Safrit, Thomas R. Safrit and C. Donald Lyerly.

ROSTER OF PASTORS

Rev. J. M. L. Lyerly, Ph.D.,
Founder 1891-1908
Rev. A. Samuel Peeler 1908-1909
Rev. Calvin B. Heller 1909-1912
Rev. John A. Koons 1912-1918
Rev. Samuel A. Troxell 1919-1921
Rev. Harvey A. M. Holshouser,
Ph.D. 1922-1929
Rev. Lee O. Carbaugh 1930-1939
Rev. Aaron R. Tosh, D.D. 1939-1944
Rev. Milton Whitener,
Supply 1944-1945
Rev. Carl R. Flocken 1945-1948
Rev. C. Columbus Wagoner,
Supply 1948-1949

Rev. David E. Faust, Ph.D.,
Supply 1949-1950
Mr. Thomas Hoffman,
Summer Student Supply 1949-
Mr. Robert W. Delp,
Summer Student Supply 1950-
Rev. Lionel A. Whiston, Ph.D.,
Supply 1950-1951
Rev. Carl T. Daye 1951-1954
Mr. Kenneth Heffley,
Summer Student Supply 1954-
Rev. Melvin T. Hamm 1955-1956
Rev. Roy C. Whisenhunt,
Supply 1957-
Rev. Robert E. Myers 1957-1967
Rev. Edwin C. Nagle 1967-

1.———. Minutes. Classis of North Carolina, 1890, p. 6.
2. *Daye*, Carl T., Sixteenth Anniversary, Bethany Evangelical and Reformed Church, 1951, p. 3 ff.
3. *Myers*, Robert E., Lyerly Memorial United Church of Christ, 1965, p. 5.
4. *Moose*, Thomas L., Dedication of the Lyerly Memorial Evangelical and Reformed Church, 1954, p. 2 ff.
5. ———. Minutes. Southern Synod, 1940, p. 9.
6. *Myers, Op. cit.*, p. 17.
7. ———. Minutes. Classis of North Carolina, 1923, p. 42.
8. *Leonard*, Jacob C., History of Southern Synod, Evangelical and Reformed Church, 1940, p. 267 ff.

Macedonia Church, Hickory

MACEDONIA EVANGELICAL AND REFORMED CHURCH, located at 408 Eighth Street, Hickory, North Carolina, is the response to a prolonged concern to meet the need for a third church in that community, expressed by ministers of the Western Section of Southern Synod and a number of representative Hickory citizens. In 1944, when Trinity Church, Conover was declared an independent, self-supporting congregation, and Faith Church, Brookford was enrolled with subsidy by the Board of National Missions, the way appeared clear for such a venture.[1] Rev. A. Wilson Cheek was commissioned missionary to Faith Church, including a Mission to be established in the environs of Hickory.

Acting upon results of a survey, first meetings were held in a vacant house at 916 Ninth Avenue, November 12 and 19, 1944, respectively. Sunday School classes were taught by teachers from Faith Church, Brookford. This property, owned by the Lang Chevrolet Garage, being rented, was no longer available. After a considerable search for a suitable place to meet, property including a house, at 408 Eighth Street became available and was purchased by the Board of National Missions, from W. H. Little for $3,300. The house was remodeled into a chapel and several classrooms, costing $2,000.

Here, on October 7, 1945, the Mission was officially begun. Sunday School, which met at 2:30 P.M., recorded an attendance of forty six pupils, and the worship which followed, noted sixty eight people present. J. Paul Hunt, superintendent of Faith Church Sunday School and teachers staffed the Mission School until leadership within the new fellowship could be arranged.

An area committee composed of Henry M. Moose, Faith Church, Brookford; Mrs. D. L. Miller, Corinth, Hickory; Mrs. Rena Robinson, Memorial, Maiden; and John M. Tate, South Fork Charge, were asked to receive suggestions for a name for the proposed church. Recommended by this committee, the name of "Macedonia Evangelical and Reformed Church" was adopted October 14, 1945. A temporary organization was effected October 21, and people who had signed the charter membership list, petitioned Southern Synod to be officially approved and enrolled by that body. On the same date a Consistory was elected, composed of D. C. Taylor, elder, and Earl Phelps and J. C. Willis, deacons. The Consistory was organized in a meeting held at the home of Earl Phelps, November 27, 1945, when Rev. A. Wilson Cheek was named president; D. C. Taylor, vice president; and Earl Phelps, secretary-treasurer. Later the office of secretary-treasurer was separated, and Robert C. Burns was named secretary, while Earl Phelps continued as treasurer.

A recognition service was held February 24, 1946, when the enrollment by Southern Synod was officially announced.[2] On the charter membership list presented at that time were the following names: Mrs. Lucille Willis, J. C. Willis, Virgie Willis, Wayburn Willis, Mrs. Cora Sparks, Thelma Sparks, Paul E. Raby, Mrs. Paul E. Raby, Janette Hines, Irene G. Hines, Mrs. Ruel B. Hines, David C. Taylor, Mrs. David C. Taylor, Earl Phelps, Mrs. Earl Phelps, Paul B. Burns, Mrs. Paul B. Burns, Virginia Peile, Robert C. Burns, Mrs. Robert C. Burns, James E. Tate, Mrs. James E. Tate and Mrs. Rena Robinson.[3]

Following the founding and the official enrollment of the church, it was properly organized to do acceptable work, after the pattern of the Evangelical and Reformed Church. The Sunday School was established but with the following officers: R. C. Burns, Sr., superintendent; James E. Tate, assistant; Miss Virginia Peile, secretary-treasurer. On April 5, the Women's Guild was launched, enrolling fifteen members. Officers named were: Mrs. D. L. Miller, president; Mrs. J. N. Johnston, vice president; Mrs. Rena Robinson, secretary-treasurer; Mrs. R. C. Burns, reporter.

During the first few years Macedonia Church made reasonable numerical and program progress. Then, the community began to change from a resident to a commercially zoned area, thus decidedly limiting its possibilities for effective service and growth in that particular community. Under the supervision of the Board of National Missions and with the approval of Southern Synod and the congregation, studies were made of the area. These studies led to the conclusion that the church should either be relocated or "phased out." This report was made to the congregation September 11, 1960, and approved:

> As a result of the self-study conducted by Dr. John H. Shope of the Board of National Missions and Rev. Van D. Grimes, who was associated with him in the study, the congregation of Macedonia Church respectfully requests:
>
> 1) That the Board of National Missions (and the Synodical Committee) approve the relocation of the congregation into another section of the Hickory area.
>
> 2) That the Board of National Missions give serious consideration as to the possibility of relocating the Congregation in the Forest Hills development, but that the final decision be made by the board.
>
> 3) That the Board of National Missions look upon the relocation as a new mission; thereby, granting full aid and subsidy.
>
> 4) That all assets of the present congregation be transferred to the relocated church.
>
> 5) The Congregation of Macedonia Church wishes to express its thanks and appreciation to the Board of National Missions and Dr. John H. Shope for the self-study conducted in our parish.[4]

The life of the congregation, and the community in which it is located, has been greatly enriched by gifts of service and money from many people. Among them are: The Board of National Missions; National Women's Guild, which contributed $1,500; Corinth Church, Hickory; Trinity, Conover; Faith, Brookford; Zion, Lenoir; Grace Newton; and the Youth Fellowship of Southern Synod. In response to such Christian liberality the congregation has supported in kind the benevolent causes of the denomination, including payment of the full apportionment each year.

A special committee appointed by Southern Synod to manage the affairs of Macedonia Church, consisting of Revs. Nevin H. Feather, Bobby R. Bonds, Edwin M. Alcorn, and LeRoy Davis and Marvin Hollar, reported as follows to the Synod May 1, 1963:

> The congregation of Macedonia Church, Hickory, voted on November 11, 1962 to disband as of December 31, 1962. . . .
>
> Before disbanding, the Macedonia congregation made requests pertaining to the disposal of its assets:
>
> 1) The indebtedness to the Board of National Missions of the former Evangelical and Reformed Church be paid in full (said indebtedness was $3,300.).
>
> 2) Any outstanding indebtedness of the congregation be paid in full,—insurance, lights etc.
>
> 3) Expenses involved in the disposal of the property to be paid in full.
>
> 4) The appointment and World Service challenge for 1963 be paid in full.
>
> 5) The remaining assets to be divided, giving 65% to Nazareth Children's Home, for the proposed Girl's Dormitory, and 35% to the kitchen fund at Johns River Camp, to apply to our obligation to them.
>
> 6) The organ, altar, altar ware, communion service, bell, hymnals and other items found in the church building be given to the new mission in N. E. Hickory. . . .
>
> The committee voted to put the sale of land and building into the

hands of real estate agent, Carroll Burns . . . Mr. Burns was able to complete the sale for a total of $5,500. . .

All of the members of Macedonia Church were notified by mail that they were to transfer their membership to another church of their own choice. They would be given until December 1, 1963 to do this; after this date, if any had not transferred their membership, their names would be erased.

All records of the congregation will be turned over to the proper authorities at Catawba College library.[5]

This report was adopted, and the requests of same were faithfully executed. In effect the dissolution of Macedonia Church marked the beginning of the Church of the Master, located in Northeast Hickory, with which quite a number of its members affiliated.

ROSTER OF PASTORS

Rev. A. Wilson Cheek, D.D. 1944-1947
Rev. Roy E. Leinbach, Jr.,
  Supply 1947-1948
Rev. Richard Rubright 1948-1951
Rev. Roy E. Leinbach, Jr.,

Supply 1951-1952
Mr. Banks D. Shepherd,
  Summer Student Supply 1952-
Rev. Banks D. Shepherd 1953-1958
Rev. Bobby R. Bonds 1959-1963

1. ———. Minutes. Southern Synod, Evangelical and Reformed Church, 1944. p. 32.
2. ———. Minutes. *Op. cit.*, 1946. p. 15.
3. *Shepherd,* Banks D., Tenth Anniversary Service, Macedonia Evangelical and Reformed Church, 1956. p. 6ff.
4. *Shope,* John H., *Grimes,* Van D., Self-Study. Macedonia Church, Hickory, North Carolina, 1960. p. 8.
5. ———. Minutes. *Op. cit.*, 1963. p. 44.

Memorial Church, Maiden

MEMORIAL REFORMED CHURCH, Maiden, North Carolina has a rich history. Its beginning dates back almost to the founding of the village in 1883.

Henry Franklin Carpenter, whose large farm lay near St. James Lutheran Church, southeast of Newton, had much experience in manufacturing ventures, and for many years had been a very successful operator of a flower mill and general custom grinding business, a wool carding plant, a cotton gin and an immense tan-yard. His three sons, D. A., D. M., and Perry A. Carpenter, had been associated with him, working for and with him in these enterprises from early boyhood.

In 1880, D. M. Carpenter, then only 22 years of age, went to South Carolina to work in the Clifton and Converse Mills, the former just having been built. For about six months he was employed at various departments in those cotton mills, performing almost every operation from erecting machinery to running spinning frames. This entirely new field so appealed to him that he decided to make it his life work, and he returned to his home.

With his father and brothers, a partnership was formed, H. F. Carpenter, Sons and Company. The concern also consisted of George W. Rabb, a well known confederate veteran. The purpose of the partnership was the building of a small cotton mill.[1]

Around this mill and other lesser business establishments the village was developed. The Carpenters and the Rabbs were of the

Reformed faith. By 1885 interest was manifested in founding a church of their faith in the village. This concern came to the attention of Rev. Joseph L. Murphy, pastor of the Lincoln Charge, who held occasional religious services for them. In 1886 these activities were brought to the attention of the Classis of North Carolina. Dr. Jacob C. Clapp and Mr. Murphy were "appointed a committee to look after the interests of the Reformed Church in the village of Maiden, and, if deemed advisable, to organize a Reformed congregation there."[2] The following year this matter was marked, "attended to."[3]

On Thursday evening, September 23, 1886, following a series of religious services, that had begun on the Sunday evening previously, Rev. Joseph L. Murphy, assisted by Dr. Jacob C. Clapp, organized the congregation with twenty nine members. Twelve of these were received into the church by the rite of confirmation; and seventeen others were transferred from St. Matthew's Church. H. F. Carpnter, J. P. Rabb, D. M. Carpenter, were elected elders;. L. A. Carpenter, J. F. Keener and D. M. Boyd, deacons. These first services were held in a store building owned by the Franklin Carpenter, Sons and Company, located at the intersection of Newton and Main Streets.[4]

Being the only church in the community, the congregation enjoyed a remarkable beginning, its membership in 1890 being 112 souls. Dr. George W. Welker, Stated Clerk of the Classis of North Carolina, which met in Memorial Church that year, prefaced the minutes of those sessions with the following remarks.

Maiden is a new manufacturing village on the Chester and Lenoir Narrow Gauge Railroad, seven miles south of Newton, in the county of Catawba. It is a growing place in the midst of a fine agricultural region.

It has grown up about the cotton manufactory of H. F. Carpenter, Sons and Company. The charter of incorporation forbids the presence of the saloon—or better, the grogshop—and this is the best security, if honestly adhered to, for its morals and thrift.

The sessions of the Classis were held in Memorial Reformed Church, erected by the family and friends of the young and devoted Perry Carpenter. The Carpenters are members of the Reformed Church, and are deeply interested in the prosperity of their church, of which the Rev. J. L. Murphy is pastor. He has been doing good and faithful work of the Master, the fruits of which do appear in the growth and activity of Memorial Church. It is a beacon in the village, and its Sabbath school does much to insure a safe future for the community. No doubt the increase in membership and its liberality will, as soon as proper men be found to meet the demand for ministers, have the Memorial Church made a separate charge, for even now it could fairly well utilize all the labors of a pastor.[5]

The church building was begun July 25, 1887 and occupied April 8, 1888. The Lord's Supper was observed May 13, 1888, and the house was dedicated September 16 in the same year, when Dr. George W. Welker preached the sermon. The congrgation was named "Memorial Church" in memory of Perry Albert Carpenter, a promising young churchman and junior member of the firm of Franklin Carpenter, Sons, and Company, who died July 9, 1886, shortly after the congregation was organized. For the erection of the church D. M. Carpenter gave the brick; Dr. P. J. Kluttz paid for their delivery on the grounds; L. A. Carpenter bore the expense of putting up the walls; J. P. Rabb contributed $25. The balance on building expenses, which amounted to approximately $600 was paid by Franklin Carpenter.[6]

The parsonage was erected prior to the building of the church. The land on which both church and parsonage stood consisted of two acres, parsonage and land on which it stood, being owned equally by the four churches in the Lincoln Charge—Grace, Daniel's, Salem and Memorial.

This church property through the years has been kept in good repair and expanded as needs have required. In 1914, during the supply pastorate of Dr. Charles W. Warlick, a belfry was erected. Extensive improvements on the sanctuary were made in 1926, consisting of a new ceiling, floor, windows, pews and redecorated walls. This was done under the supervision of John F. Carpenter, Sidney M. Finger, and J. Clarence Ikard. Pews, choir chairs and communion table were placed in the church in memory of Miss Maude Carpenter by her parents, Mr. and Mrs. D. M. Carpenter; the pulpit by Dr. A. Flint Kluttz in memory of his parents, Dr. and Mrs. P. J. Kluttz. The Seeburg organ was installed in 1930.

In 1936, as partial observance of the 50th Anniversary of the congregation, action was taken to build a much needed Sunday School annex. The building committee was composed of John F. Carpenter, Sidney M. Finger, J. Clarence Ikard, Thomas L. Finger, Robert S. Sigmon, Mrs. T. D. Finger, Miss Nellie Ikard. Ground was broken for it April 7; the cornerstone was laid November 15, and the building was occupied August 28, 1937. Extensive preparation was made for its dedication, which occurred May 22, 1938. A former pastor, Rev. Theodore C. Hesson, made the dedicatory address. During the afternoon appropriate addresses were delivered by Hon. Loomis F. Kluttz, a son of the congregation; Rev. C. Columbus Wagoner, a former pastor; and Hon. Joseph L. Murphy, whose father organized the congregation. Dr. O. Bain Michael led the afternoon devotions.

It is interesting to note that in 1950 the Consistory was constituted as follows: Pastor: Rev. John A. Koons; Life members: J. Clarence Ikard, Frank G. Boyd; Elders: Sidney M. Finger, Albert M. Ikard, Ivey F. Willis, Abel R. Ikard; Deacons: John F. Carpenter, George E. Hunsucker, T. Dodd Finger, Jack W. Moose. The congregation had a well organized Sunday School, and Women's Guild, the latter operating in two circles. There were seventy-four confirmed members on the church roll.

With the exception of a possible occasional pulpit supply, until 1965, pastors of Memorial Church have been the same as those for the Lincoln Charge. Currently the congregation is engaged, with other United Churches in the area, seeking guidelines by which to develop an effective and workable program for the future.

1. *Preslar,* Charles J., Jr., Editor, A History of Catawba County, 1954. p. 356.
2. ———. Minutes, The Classis of North Carolina, 1886. p. 9.
3. ———. *Op. cit.,* 1887. p. 7.
4. *Clapp,* Jacob C., Editor. Historic Sketch of the Reformed Church in North Carolina, 1908. p. 323.
5. ———. Minutes, *Op. cit.,* 1890. p. 2.
6. *Leonard,* Jacob C., History of the Southern Synod of the Evangelical and Reformed Church, 1940. p. 358ff.

Memorial Church, Davidson County

MEMORIAL EVANGELICAL AND REFORMED CHURCH, Davidson County, dates from September 6, 1953, when 95 people gathered in a garage on Highway 64 East of Lexington, North Carolina for a meeting. The assembly took action overturing Southern Synod of the Evangelical and Reformed Church to authorize its organization into a church. On the following Tuesday, the Council of Southern Synod met and made the following record:

> September 8, a petition signed by 60 members of Hedrick's Grove Church requested a new congregation be organized in the area of the Hedrick Grove Church and Lexington. They had already been dismissed by the Consistory and the supply pastor, Rev. L. A. Leonard. They were already worshipping in a building in that area. Rev. L. A. Leonard was given the responsibility for the nurture and the establishment of this new congregation.
>
> October 12, Rev. L. A. Leonard reported: "A lot of about five acres of land on U.S. Route 64, between Hedrick's Grove and Beck's Lutheran Church . . . . . could be obtained. There were sixty four former members of Hedrick's Grove that were petitioning the Synod to organize

them into a congregation named Memorial Church. Upon receipt of this
petition by President Tosh 'such congregation shall be duly organized;'
and the deed to the property be to the Evangelical and Reformed
Church.

December 20. Report to the Council was that said congregation was
organized, and requested to be received into the Synod was granted.[1]

The Sunday School was established September 13, 1953, naming
Robert Hedrick, Jr., superintendent. "Memorial" was chosen as a
name of the new church on September 25, but the congregation
was not organized until November 8, 1953. D. Ottis Hedrick, Carlie F. Beck, W. Deaton Young, Hoyle F. Foust, James N. Greer and
Robert G. Hedrick, Sr. were elected elders; and Harold F. Hedrick,
G. Woodrow Beck, Henry I. James, Mrs. Denese G. Davis, Alonzon
Kennedy and William G. Hartley, deacons. Carlie F. Beck was
named president of the Consistory. When the charter roll was
closed on Easter Monday 1954, 92 names were on it.[2]

An immediate need of the new church was a place to meet. A
first step in that direction was taken when Mr. and Mrs. Charlie
Fritts and Mr. and Mrs. Doctor Webb McCulloch donated four
acres of land on the South side of Highway 64, four miles East of
Lexington, North Carolina for a church site. A decision was made to
erect an all-purpose first unit of a total church facility. The building was to be constructed of brick, blocks and wood, 36 by 40 feet
with a basement 36 by 40 feet. In it were to be four classrooms and
an assembly room large enough to accommodate one hundred fifty
people. Construction on it began immediately, being used by the
Sunday School first on December 6, 1963. The structure was valued
at $25,000, and dedicated free of debt December 12, 1964. Expand-
ing parish activities and steady numerical growth of the Sunday
School required additional classroom space, which was attached
to the East end of the building in 1957. That annex was dedicated
free of debt February 23, 1958.

In 1958, a tract of land along the West line of church property

was purchased from Mr. and Mrs. Charlie Fritts on which to erect
a parsonage. That house was completed in the spring of 1958, and
dedicated free of debt the following September 14. It represented
an investment of $20,000. On the occasion of its dedication, in pre-
senting the keys of the parsonage to the pastor, the chairman of the
Consistory remarked:

> In token of our faith in the Church of Jesus Christ and deep interest
> in its spiritual maintenance and upbuilding, in token of our appreciation
> of the service and standing of God's minister in the community, in token
> of our community pride and of our purpose to exalt the worthfulness
> of things related to the Kingdom of God among us, on behalf of the
> Consistory, and in the name of the church and community, I gladly
> present to you the keys that unlock and guard the privileges and bless-
> ings of this new parsonage home.[3]

Rev. Lawrence A. Leonard continued to serve the congregation as
supply pastor and organizer until the spring of 1958, when Rev. Van
D. Grimes became its first full-time pastor. Having been previously
ordained to the Christian Ministry by Southern Synod of the Evangelical and Reformed Church, Mr. Grimes was installed on Sunday
afternoon, June 22, 1958. The confirmed membership of the church
at that time was 103 people, and the Sunday School enrollment 163
pupils.

Mr. Grimes served the parish until 1962, continuing its march of
progress. Rev. Roy C. Whisenhunt began his ministry to the congregation in March 1962, being installed pastor of the church on
the 11th day of that month.

Honoring their grandchildren David, Sheila, Mark and Julie Ann
Hedrick, Mr. and Mrs. George A. Peacock presented a Hammond
organ to the church for use in the sanctuary. The instrument was
installed May 17, 1964.

In anticipation of the proposed sanctuary, a number of committees were authorized in 1964 and their personnel named by the
chairman of the Consistory. Among these committees were: Exploratory, consisting of Harold F. Hedrick, D. W. McCulloch, William G. Hartley and Joseph E. Hedrick; Sanctuary: Carlie F. Beck,
Robert G. Hedrick, Jr., Harold F. Hedrick, Robert G. Hedrick, Sr.,
Alonzo Kennedy and Joseph E. Hedrick; Finance: William G. Hartley, D. Ottis Hedrick, Hortense Hedrick, Calvin Bean, Mrs. Donese
G. Davis and Mrs. Ruth B. Hedrick; Interior Furnishings and Dec-
orating: Mrs. Ruth Foust, Mrs. Effie F. McCulloch, Mrs. Virginia
R. Beck, Dale Hedrick and Henry Ijames; Grading and Grounds:
Jack R. McCarn, Charlie Hedrick, Dwight Hedrick, Sr., John Fritts
and Woodrow Beck.

Proposed plans for the sanctuary were developed, and on June
13, 1965 presented to the congregation for approval. First bids submitted on its construction on September 19, 1965 were declared un-
satisfactory. They were resubmitted for further study. The contract for the erection of the sanctuary was awarded February 27,
1966, involving an expenditure of $105,000. Groundbreaking cere-

monies took place at the close of worship Sunday morning, March 13, 1966. Formal opening of the new house of worship occurred on Sunday evening, February 19, 1967 at 7:30. Services were under the direction of the pastor. Rev. Lawrence A. Leonard, who organized the congregation, preached the sermon. Among other church representatives present who made congratulatory remarks were: Rev. Van D. Grimes, first full-time pastor; Dr. Donald C. Dearborn, president of Catawba College; Rev. J. Wayne Fouts, representing local United Church of Christ ministers; and Rev. Raymond C. Craven, representing the Davidson County Ministerial Association. The house was finished and equipped, with an outstanding indebtedness of only $16,000.

ROSTER OF PASTORS

Rev. Lawrence A. Leonard,	Rev. Van D. Grimes 1958-1962
Organizer and Supply 1953-1958	Rev. Roy C. Whisenhunt 1962-

1. ———. Minutes. Southern Synod, 1954, p. 16.
2. *Whisenhunt*, R. C., Memorial United Church of Christ Sanctuary, 1967, p. 2 ff.
3. *Grimes*, Van D., Parsonage Dedication Bulletin, Memorial Evangelical and Reformed Church, 1958, p. 3.
4. ———. Minutes. *Op. cit.*, 1959, p. 22.

Memorial Church, Winston Salem

IN MAY 1913, Rev. David E. Bowers, already involved in mission projects at First Reformed Church, Winston Salem, North Carolina and the Gum Tree Section of upper Davidson County, was asked by the Classis of North Carolina to investigate Reformed Church interests in South Winston Salem.[1] In 1914, based on his report, the Classis took further action.

Resolved, That the interests of the Reformed Church in Winston Salem be continued under the care of Rev. D. E. Bowers, with authority to organize a congregation.

Resolved, That a committee consisting of Revs. J. C. Leonard, D. E. Bowers and J. D. Andrew, be appointed with instructions to urge upon the Board of Missions, through the Superintendent, Rev. C. E. Schaeffer, D.D., the importance of Winston Salem as a mission point and to ask the enrollment of the same.[2]

An overture appeared on the agenda of Classis that year from Reformed people living in South Winston Salem, asking for an appropriation of $850 to be applied on the purchase of a lot located at the corner of Banner Avenue and Hollyrood Street. The request was granted and the lot on which the parsonage and church now stand was acquired for the sum of $1,700. The Sunday School was organized January 24, 1915 in a store building owned by C. D. Crouch located at the corner of Arcadia Avenue and Hollyrood Street. The congregation was organized there in May of the same year, numbering nine charter members, who were: Mr. and Mrs. E. A. Sink, Mr. and Mrs. P. M. McGraw, Mrs. M. D. West, Mrs. H. A. M. Holshouser, Hoy Holshouser and Mrs. Robert Conrad.[3] When the classis met in May 1915, Mr. Bowers reported,

With reference to the new work in Winston Salem committed to our care, we beg leave to report that we organized a Sunday School January 24, 1915, and looked after the interest of the Reformed Church until a pastor was secured, April 1, 1915, in the person of Brother H. A. M. Holshouser. Sunday, May 2, 1915, at 3:30 p.m., an organization was effected by the pastor with nine charter members, in my presence, in the hall over the store building where the services were being held. The pastor of this new field is here with a report, and an elder delegate who has not yet been recognized.[4]

Elder Everett A. Sink was recognized and seated as a member of the Classis, which body then took action to "Create two Gift Church Building Funds, the same, through the Board of Missions, to be presented to Schlatter Memorial Reformed Church of Winston Salem, the same to be known as the North Carolina Classis Church Building Fund."[5] The missionary pastor was also granted permission to present the cause of this Mission to congregations of Classis, contributions to be credited by the Board of Home Missions to the Classis as payments on additional building funds.[6]

Construction on the church building began in the fall of 1915. In order to provide a temporary meeting place for the congregation, a roof was built over the basement, where services were held until other parts of the building could be used. The cornerstone was laid October 16, 1916, and on Sunday, April 29, 1917, the usable section of the church was dedicated by the pastor. Treasurer J. S. Wise of the Board of Home Missions, spoke at 11 a.m. also at 7:30 p.m.; Dr. Jacob C. Leonard made an appropriate address at 3:30 in the afternoon. The church building was finished during the pastorate of Rev. G. Ermine Plott, which began October 1,

1917. On the third Sunday in March 1920 it was dedicated. Dr. Charles E. Schaeffer, General Secretary of the Board of Home Missions, preached the sermon. The parsonage was built in 1920, involving an expenditure of $4,000, on the lot adjoining church property facing Hollyrood Street.

Because of constant confusion with a similar name of a church of another Communion located in the Winston Salem area, with consent of Classis, in 1926 the name "Schlatter" was dropped and the congregation became officially known as Memorial Reformed Church.[7]

In 1938, Dr. George E. Dillinger led the congregation in effecting extensive improvements on the church building, involving sanctuary changes in the ceiling and the choir loft; also, window and wall repairs and interior decoration. Dr. William F. DeLong, treasurer of the Board of Home Missions, made an appropriate address at services of rededication. Other speakers for the occasion were former pastors, Rev. G. Ermine Plott and Dr. O. Bain Michael. During the pastorate of Rev. Terrell M. Shoffner, the Sunday School annex was rearranged into a two-story educational facility.

Resulting from a debt-reduction program, spear-headed by the pastor Rev. Homer F. Yearick, an obligation with which the church had been struggling over a period of thirty two years, was paid in full. The victory was appropriately celebrated in a series of services climaxed in a combination Thirty-Second Anniversary-Homecoming-Note-Burning ceremony which occurred October 17, 1947. Dr. George E. Dillinger preached the sermon. Other former pastors who addressed the congregation during the day were, Rev. G. Ermine Plott, Dr. O. Bain Michael and Rev. Terrell M. Shoffner.

During the week of preliminary Gospel services neighboring ministers appeared on succeeding evenings to preach the sermon. From Winston Salem were: Dr. George Mauze, First Presbyterian Church; Dr. Gordon Spaugh, Home Moravian; Rev. Sinclair Tebo, from the Veterans Administration; Dr. Mark Depp, Centenary Methodist; and from the Evangelical and Reformed Church: Dr. Harry D. Althouse, Rev. Huitt R. Carpenter, and Dr. A. Odell Leonard.

Because of the financial support provided this congregation by the building department of the Board of Home Missions, an itemized statement of church debt repayments appears below.

1915-1921	Congregation paid	$ 208.00
1927	Received from the Forward Movement	3,500.00
1939	Received from the Women's Guild	500.00
1944	Received from the Women's Guild	500.00
1944	Gift from the Board of Home Missions	5,982.00
1944	Paid by the congregation	500.00
1945	Paid by the congregation	1,000.00
1947	Gift from the Board of National Missions	500.00
1947	Paid by the congregation	6,000.00
		$18,690.00

The minister of the church sums up this situation in the life of the congregation in the following words:

> Today this church has taken a long step forward. It is now free of all debt. A clear title to all church property passes today from the Board of National Missions into the hands of the officers of the local church. Today we achieve the goal we set fifteen months ago, and three months ahead of schedule. . . . . . .
>
> The fruit of the labors of many people is realized here today. Praise is due the loyal people of this church through the years—the former pastors of the past thirty two years— the Missions Board—the Women's Guild of the North Carolina Classis—the present 175 members for their fine achievement of the past fifteen months—and last, the consistory of this year and last year who worked so faithfully and so cooperatively to reach the goal we set for our church.[8]

Through the years Memorial Church, often against extreme difficulty, has maintained a healthy outlook toward others, as expressed specifically in and through the boards and agencies of the denomination. Its confirmed membership in 1965 is 140 people, and there is a Sunday School enrollment of 110 pupils. Rev. Donald B. Orander, a son of the congregation, is an ordained minister of the United Church of Christ. Rev. Willard L. Stevens is the effective minister, serving the parish since 1963.

ROSTER OF PASTORS

Rev. H. A. M. Holshouser, Ph.D. 1915-1917	Rev. Terrell M. Shoffner 1940-1945
Rev. G. Ermine Plott 1917-1923	Rev. Homer F. Yearick 1946-1948
Rev. O. Bain Michael, S.T.D. 1923-1929	Rev. William A. Jones 1948-1950
Rev. William H. Causey, D.D. 1929-1936	Rev. Roy Coulter 1950-1960
Rev. George E. Dillinger, S.T.D. 1937-1939	Rev. Donald Burtt 1960-1963
	Rev. Willard L. Stevens 1963-

1. ———. Minutes. Classis of North Carolina, 1913, p. 63.
2. ———. Minutes. *Op. cit.,* 1914, p. 23.
3. *Yearick,* Homer F., Historical Sketch, Memorial Evangelical and Reformed Church, 37th Anniversary, 1947, p. 4 ff.
4. ———. Minutes. *Op. cit.,* 1915, p. 23.
5. *Ibid.* p. 43.
6. *Ibid.* p. 43.
7. ———. Minutes. *Op. cit.,* 1926, p. 32.
8. Yearick. *Op. cit.,* pp. 3, 8.

Mt. Bethel Church, Blowing Rock

MT. BETHEL REFORMED CHURCH, Blowing Rock, North Carolina, disappeared in 1921 as a congregation from the statistical roll of the Classis of North Carolina, but the Classis retained its property rights. At that time only four members were reported, and the Trustees of Classis recommended that "Mt. Bethel be erased from the roll of Classis and that the matter be left for future development."[1] This church had been in existence since 1886 as a Mission point, irregularly supplied by ministers living in Catawba and Caldwell counties; hence, for lack of consistent shepherding, had deteriorated.

A deed for the land on which the church building stands was issued by Jacob Kluttz and his wife, Mary L. Kluttz, on April 29, 1893, and registered May 1 of the same year. It was conveyed to Jacob Kluttz, S. L. Bollinger, D. F. Trexler and R. Ingle, making provisions as follows:

> One acre the same more or less. Also the right to use the spring of water near said lot, on the northeast side.
>
> To have and to hold, the aforesaid tract or parcel of land in trust and with privileges and appurtenance thereto belonging to the said Kluttz, Bolinger, Trexler, Ingle and their successors in office so long as said property is used by said Mount Bethel Reformed Church to their only use and behoof.[2]

In 1944, Dr. Walter W. Rowe, on the eve of the Assembly Grounds property acquisition, proposed to Southern Synod of the Evangelical and Reformed Church, successor to the Classis of North Carolina, that, since the Blowing Rock community had changed from an isolate mountain village to a thriving summer resort, Mt. Bethel Church property be conditioned for religious services during the summer months. Dr. Rowe was authorized to proceed with plans as he had described them. In 1946 his report to the Synod reads as follows:

> Regular services were held at Mt. Bethel during July and August, and also two weeks in June. The services were in charge of Rev. Roy E. Leinbach, Jr., Rev. W. A. Kerr, Jr., Rev. Aubrey W. Hedrick, Rev. Frank K. Bostian, Dr. David E. Faust, Dr. Shuford Peeler and Rev. Jacob A. Palmer, and the Chairman of the Committee. The interest manifested on the part of visitors to Blowing Rock convinces us that this work is very useful in giving publicity to our denomination in this famous summer resort . . . We appreciate the services so well rendered by the different ministers.[3]

Harland M. Deal, who acted as treasurer for the Blowing Rock project, at the same time, submitted an interesting financial report.

Receipts: Balance on hand April 1, 1945 ....$144.00
        Offerings 168.62

        Total receipts $312.62
Disbursements: 170.38

        Cash balance April 29, 1946 ....$142.24

These reports presented quite a contrasting picture to that which had been given through the years, of the Reformed Church interests in that community. It does credit to a group of pioneering Rhein-landers who were among the first settlers and founders of the Blow-ing Rock village.[4] Concerning early activities of the Reformed Church in that village, Dr. Jacob C. Clapp, in 1908, wrote:

> As early as 1882 and 1883 several families of Reformed people moved from Rowan County and elsewhere to the mountains of Watauga County and located in the vicinity of Blowing Rock. This section has since be-come a famous resort, visited annually by hundreds of people. Rev. John Ingle visited this settlement in December 1882, and while there preached at the residence of Mr. Jacob Kluttz. In April of the following year, Mr. Ingle moved his family to Blowing Rock and made the place his permanent home. He at once began to hold services in a schoolhouse at the location of the present village and organized a Sunday School.
>
> At the meeting of Classis in 1884, the Rev. Mr. Ingle called the atten-tion of Classis to this mountain section as a desirable mission field. He was authorized to organize a congregation to be called "Watauga Mis-sion." At the same time he was instructed to secure the assistance of one of the nearest ministers. The church was organized the fourth Sunday in July, 1886, by Revs. J. C. Clapp and John Ingle in a build-ing called the "Estes schoolhouse." The officers were Jacob Kluttz and George Thomason, elders, and S. E. Bollinger, D. F. Trexler, deacons. The following names were enrolled: James Holshouser, Mrs. Eliza Jane Holshouser, Mrs. Sallie Holshouser, Jacob Kluttz, Mrs. Mary L. Lentz, Mrs. S. R. Lentz, Mrs. Mary A. Ingle, Thornton Ingle, Minnie E. Kluttz, George Thomason, S. L. Bollinger, Crawford A. L. Holshouser, David F. Trexler, Mrs. Mary Trexler, W. C. Lentz, and Mrs. Martha J. Bollinger.
>
> The church was dedicated the first Sunday in November 1894. The sermon was preached by Rev. J. L. Murphy.[5]

An organized congregation is still in the future; however, in the light of recent developments at the Assembly Grounds, adjacent to and northeast of the church property, seeking to serve the entire Southern Conference of the United Church of Christ, an established congregation is much more than an idealistic dream.

1. ————. Minutes. Classis of North Carolina, 1921, p. 18.
2. ————. Book of Deeds, R., Watauga County, p. 26.
3. ————. Minutes. Southern Synod of the Evangelical and Reformed Church, 1946, p. 41 ff.
4. *Whitener*, Daniel J., History of Watauga County, 1949, p. 61.
5. *Clapp*, Jacob C., Editor. Historic Sketch of the Reformed Church in North Carolina, 1908, p. 321.

Mt. Hope Church, Guilford County

Mt. Hope Reformed Church in Guilford County grew out of missionary operations of Mt. Zion Union Reformed and Lutheran Church. This congregation was in existence as early as 1812 and bore the name Coble's Church in defference to the large number of the Coble clan which worshipped there.[1]

The Reformed element in it was organized by Rev. John Rudy shortly after 1821 during his pastorate at Brick Church. In those days travel was difficult and distances were extensive. Brick, Alamance and Coble's were the only churches in Southeast Guilford providing religious instruction; therefore, to a large part of the population living in the area, religious services were not easily available. For these reasons, Zion Sunday School, evidently a part of Coble's church parish, was started and given the original church name. The school was organized in 1832 in schoolhouse number thirty two. Textbooks were the Holy Bible and the church hymnal.[2]

Under these circumstances, Dr. George W. Welker conducted Sunday evening services at that place beginning May 10, 1844, then known as Neece's schoolhouse. It was located across the road from the present site of Mt. Hope United Church of Christ. The congregation was organized by Dr. Welker and named Mt. Hope Reformed Church in 1847, composed largely of people of the Reformed faith who withdrew from Coble's Union Church. Representative family names on the original church roll included Foust, Neece, Corsbie and Phipps. John Foust, Christian Foust, John Corsbie and John W. Phipps were elected elders, Dr. A. A. Phipps led the singing and taught the first Bible class.[3]

A brush arbor was erected, later enclosed by boards, which served as a place for worship until 1851 when the first church building was ready for use. The church, a brick structure, was built across the road from the schoolhouse on land donated by David

Reece. It stood in the corner of the present cemetery and was a one-story building 30 by 60 feet in size. Dr. Welker preached the first sermon in the new church on May 10, 1851, who also dedicated it the following day, holding services which continued through the afternoon. This house served the congregation until 1875 when the brick church, no longer large enough to accommodate the congregation, was replaced by a larger wooden structure. This building, with additions as required through the years, continues to serve the congregation as a sanctuary.

Each fall, until the beginning of the Civil War, camp meetings continuing for a week or more were held, bringing to the community such leading Gospel preachers as Rev. Samuel J. Fetzer, Rev. Thornton Butler and Dr. Jeremiah Ingold.

The church prospered in those days, adding to its membership large numbers of "middle-aged men and heads of families," resulting in marked moral and social effect on the area. This type of evangelism continued after the war, but in somewhat different pattern described as "protracted meetings." One of the more numerically effective of those meetings occurred in 1878, approximately two years after the new church had been erected. Rev. and Mrs. J. W. Cecil, working as a team, directed the services. Sixty-four persons, mostly young people, united with the church.

Dr. Welker continued to serve the Guilford Charge, including Mt. Hope Church, until ill health forced his retirement in 1893. At that time he had ministered to the Guilford Charge for 50 years; and was completing 47 years of service to the Classis of North Carolina as its Stated Clerk. In 1891, seeking to appropriately observe his long and faithful ministry to the church, the Classis authorized a committee "to confer with the Guilford Charge as to some proper recognition of the approaching semi-centennial of the ministry of their pastor."[4] This recognition took place at Brick Church on March 27, 1892, when Dr. Jacob C. Leonard and Dr. Jacob C. Clapp, two friends and colleagues, delivered appropriate addresses before a throng of people who had assembled to show their esteem for this veteran of the Cross. Two years later, on July 9, 1894, he died and his body was laid to rest near his home in the Mt. Hope cemetery.

Dr. Welker was born November 3, 1817, near Greencastle, Pennsylvania. He was prepared for the Christian ministry at Marshall and Ursinus colleges, graduating with honors in 1841. Coming to North Carolina in the fall of that year, he served various churches as visiting preacher until March 1842 when he accepted a call to the Guilford Charge. Here he spent the entire span of his parish ministry, but his influence was by no means confined to that frontier rural parish.

Dr. Joseph L. Murphy, a colleague and a warm friend, wrote:

The Reformed people of North Carolina have been true to their church, and the religion of their fathers.

Separated from the church, often without ministers, and surrounded by other denominations aggressive and inclined to proselyte, the Classis of North Carolina has held together and made progress.

Sometimes amid hardships and discouragements the action of Classis may have been such as to provoke criticism and censure of Synod; yet, if the true spirit which actuated the Classis could fully be understood, a more loyal and devoted people could nowhere be found. For their church, they have endured hardships and borne burdens. Among those who have labored for the church in North Carolina, none have shown truer devotion than the late George William Welker, D.D. Born in Pennsylvania, of high attainments and brilliant prospects, he came South and wholly and truly consecrated himself to the work in North Carolina.

He preferred to labor with the people of his adopted state, in a quiet country pastorate, to enjoying the honor of being pastor of a wealthy and influential church. He loved the poor. From a human standpoint it seems, if there had been no Dr. Welker there would be no Classis of North Carolina today. He was a man of great firmness and also of great tenderness. In the storms of life he was a rock and oak, in the sunshine of life he was vine and flower. In him were combined the boldness of Peter and the tenderness of John.[5]

Dr. Welker served as pastor, preacher, author, scribe, counsellor and friend in the Classis of North Carolina, a body which he helped to create, over a period of more than a half century. In appreciation for such leadership, a grateful people have appropriately marked his last resting place, and spread on its minutes a remarkable resolution:

Resolved that the Classis of North Carolina spread on her minutes a grateful sense of his eminent virtues, sterling worth, veteran services in the church and state, heroic championship of truth and human rights, incorruptible integrity, supreme loyalty to Jesus Christ, unwavering faith in God and humanity, answering courage in the performance of duty, power in the pulpit, superiority of intellect and nobility of heart; and that we mingle our tears, sympathies and veneration with those of his family and wide circle of sorrowing friends.[6]

In 1947, when Mt. Hope Evangelical and Reformed Church observed its One-Hundredth Anniversary, a marble plaque was installed on the wall in the foyer which bears the following inscription:

In Memory of George William Welker, D.D.
Born November 3, 1817, in Franklin County, Pennsylvania.
Graduated from Marshall and Ursinus Colleges, accepting pastorate of Guilford Charge 1842 and was licensed and ordained in 1812 at Brick Church. Thru his guidance the original Mt. Hope Church was built in 1850. As a member of the General Assembly, he introduced a bill creating Charitable Institutions in North Carolina.
The degree of Doctor of Divinity was conferred upon him by the University of North Carolina in 1870, by Heidelberg University of Ohio in 1871.
Was one of the founders of Catawba College.
He was one of the Great Spiritual Advisors and Statesmen of his time.
He died July 9, 1894, having served this Charge Fifty Years.
Age: 76 years, 8 months and 6 days.[7]

The death of Dr. Welker ended an era in the life of Mt. Hope Church. A son of the congregation, Dr. James D. Andrew, was chosen as his successor. That pastorate of five years, 1893 to 1898, was short but effective. A parsonage was built on land located one-fourth of a mile south of the church, and other essential property improvements were made during those years. It is significant that the Sixty-Seventh Annual Sessions of the Classis of North Carolina, Reformed Church in the United States, met at Mt. Hope Church May 5-8, 1897, when the Woman's Classical Missionary Society was organized. The record relates that, "By invitation of Rev. J. D. Andrew of the Guilford Charge, and in response to a stirring appeal sent out by Mrs. B. F. Davis of the Concord Church, a number of earnest women assembled in the schoolroom of Mt. Hope Church, at 1 o'clock p.m. Thursday, May 6, 1897. . . . Miss Fetzer explained the object of the meeting, and, on motion, proceeded to organize the Woman's Classical Missionary Society of North Carolina Classis.[8]

In effecting the organization, Miss Ida Hedrick was elected president; Mrs. J. L. Murphy, vice president; Mrs. Alice Ingold Murrill, recording secretary; Miss Mamie Clapp, treasurer; Mrs. B. F. Davis, corresponding secretary. During this historic gathering, the following communication was addressed to the Classis of North Carolina, in session in another section of the church building:

> Resolved, that we, the members of the Woman's Missionary Society of the Classis of North Carolina, thank you, the Classis of North Carolina, for the kindly greeting and cordial endorsement extended to us this afternoon. We respectfully ask your reverend body to cooperate with us in organizing Missionary Societies and Mission Bands in charges where they do not exist. Also, we ask you for your prayers that God will enable us to serve Him in such a way as to bring honor to His name and souls to His Kingdom.[9]

Thus, began one of the most potent forces for good in the long and useful career of the church in North Carolina.

The next 24 years marked a period of short pastorates and ministerial supplies. Surprisingly, however, the church continued to prosper. In 1913 the church building was greatly improved, with a foyer attached to the east end of the sanctuary. Rev. Charles E. Hiatt, a recent graduate of Central Theological Seminary, became pastor of the charge in 1927, serving until 1937. By steady, sympathetic and faithful pastoral oversight, the three congregations of the charge, St. Mark's, Brick and Mt. Hope, were unified in spirit and worked together in harmonious goodwill. Reflecting this spirit, the second largest group in its history united with Mt. Hope Church in 1932, when 37 people were admitted to membership.

Rev. Aubrey W. Hedrick, who graduated from the theological seminary in May 1938, began at that time to serve the charge. During the first year of his ministry 95 applicants were admitted to membership in the three churches. On March 26, 1939, an educational annex containing eight classrooms was dedicated. These rooms were attached to the west end of the sanctuary.

In preparation for the next pastor, a parsonage was built and equipped with modern conveniences. In 1942, during World War II, Rev. and Mrs. Sterling W. Whitener began serving on the parish, continuing until 1946. St. Mark's was detached from the Guilford Charge in 1945. Brick and Mt. Hope churches were then constituted the Guilford Charge. When, therefore, Rev. and Mrs. Whitener returned to the mission field, Rev. Arthur R. Detwiler was asked to supply the charge, and six months later on July 1, 1946, he accepted a call to become its pastor.

Mt. Hope congregation observed its One-Hundredth Anniversary April 13-20, 1947. As a part of this celebration, the church was host to the Ninth Annual Sessions of Southern Synod of the Evangelical and Reformed Church.[10] A week of special services commemorating this important event began on Sunday morning, April 13, and ended Sunday morning April 20. Ministers appearing on the program during the week were Dr. Shuford Peeler, Dr. Harvey A. Fesperman, Rev. Milton Whitener, Rev. Charles E. Hiatt, and Rev. C. Columbus Wagoner.

The Council of Southern Synod, responding to overtures from Brick and Mt. Hope churches took action on February 24, 1949 "That the Guilford Charge be dissolved, and that Mt. Hope congregation and the Brick congregation each be constituted a pastoral charge."[11] Rev. Homer L. Yearick supplied Mt. Hope Church beginning in the summer of 1949, and, receiving a call, became pastor of the congregation beginning September 24, 1950. In anticipation of adequate educational facilities, a building fund was started during his ministry. Also, a building committee was authorized, consisting of Howard Whitesell, chairman, George Neece, Joe Stanley, Cecil Reece and Robert Reece. These were requested to study needs of the congregation and report.

A new and modern educational building was erected in 1957 during the pastorate of Rev. John W. Settlemyre. Under the leadership of Rev. Billy Joe Leonard, financial obligations were liquidated. The new facility was dedicated on April 5, 1964. Rev. Homer F. Yearick and Rev. John W. Settlemyre delivered appropriate addresses, and the pastor read the ritual of dedication. The dedicatory bulletin carried the following message from the minister:

> I would like to take this opportunity to commend the congregation of Mt. Hope United Church of Christ for its outstanding accomplishment. Due to your untiring effort and able leadership of former pastors, you have built a fine building and paid off the note years in advance. Truly, this is a day of rejoicing and gratefulness! May we use this as an incentive to thank God for his blessings as truly "Our cup runneth over." I am personally grateful for the privilege of being your pastor during the period of "the harvest."[12]

Mt. Hope Church is honored by her sons and daughters. Among them are Rev. Frank Starr, Licentiate Charles A. Starr, who died before his ordination, Dr. William H. McNairy, Rev. Clarence Woods, Rev. Joshua L. Levens, Rev. Roy L. Frazier, Licentiate William C. Shaw, Rev. Banks D. Shepherd; Dr. James D. Andrew, president of Catawba College; Professor Charles H. Mebane, State Superintendent of Public Instruction and President of Catawba College; Dr. Caroline McNairy and Dr. C. Banks McNairy, widely known and influential physicians; and Miss Jean Ingold, authorized Director of Christian Education in the United Church of Christ.

ROSTER OF PASTORS

Rev. George W. Welker,
D.D. 1847-1893
Rev. James D. Andrew, D.D. 1893-1898
Rev. George A. Stauffer 1899-1902
Vacant: Supplies: Rev. Paul Barringer, D.D., Rev. Samuel W. Beck; Student supplies: Mr. William S. Clapp, Mr. C. Columbus Wagoner.
Rev. Joshua L. Bowers 1908-1911
Rev. Dugan C. Cox 1912-1914
Rev. Shuford Peeler, D.D.,
Supply 1914-1915
Rev. Albert Klinger 1915-1919
Rev. J. M. L. Lyerly, Ph.D.,
Supply Students: 1920-1922

Vacant: Supplies: Licentiate William C. Shaw; Mr. William Groff, Mr. Hoy L. Fesperman; Rev. Milton Whitener, Rev. Harvey A. Fesperman,
D.D. 1922-1927
Rev. Charles E. Hiatt 1927-1937
Rev. Aubrey W. Hedrick 1938-1942
Rev. Sterling W. Whitener ..1942-1946
Rev. Arthur R. Detwiler,
Supply 1946-
Rev. Arthur R. Detwiler 1946-1949
Rev. Homer F. Yearick,
Supply 1949-1950
Rev. Homer F. Yearick 1950-1953
Rev. John W. Settlemyre ...1953-1962
Rev. Billy Joe Leonard 1962-1967

1. *Morgan*, Jacob L., Editor. History of the Lutheran Church in North Carolina, 1953, p. 184.
2. *Detwiler*, Arthur R., One-Hundredth Anniversary of Mt. Home Evangelical and Reformed Church, 1947, p. 19.
3. *Clapp*, Jacob C., Editor. Historic Sketch of the Reformed Church in North Carolina, 1908, p. 136 ff.
4. ————. Minutes. Classis of North Carolina, 1891, p. 16.
5. *Welker*, George W., A Historical Sketch of the Classis of North Carolina, 1895, p. 3.
6. ————. Minutes. *Op. cit.*, 1895, p. 34.
7. *Detwiler*, *Op. cit.*, p. 9.
8. ————. Minutes. *Op. cit.*, 1897, p. 36.
9. *Ibid.* p. 19.
10. ————. Minutes. Southern Synod of the Evangelical and Reformed Church, 1947, p. 3 ff.
11. *Ibid.* Minutes. 1949, p. 13.
12. *Leonard*, Billy Joe, Service of Dedication, Mt. Hope United Church of Christ, 1964, p. 4.

Mt. Tabor Church, Davidson County

MT. TABOR REFORMED CHURCH, Route 1, Lexington, North Carolina began as a "preaching point" to accommodate members of Pilgrim Reformed Church living in the "Crotts Community." Occasional services were held in homes of interested people, particularly that of Mrs. Katie Crotts, by Rev. Thomas Long who was at the time pastor of the Upper Davidson Charge. A tent-like brush arbor was erected with a recess at one end constructed of lumber in the form

of a platform and chancel. From this structure the minister conducted services by appointment during the summer and early fall
of 1883.

At its meeting in May 1883, the Classis of North Carolina, granted
authority to "Rev. Thomas Long to organize a Reformed congre-
gation near the Davidson County Alma House."[1] Evidently the
congregation was organized within a few weeks after these sessions
of the Classis, enrolling Sallie Crotts, Katie Crotts, Bettie Crotts,
Andrew Crotts, John H. Crotts, David Crotts, Sr., David Crotts, Jr.,
Elizabeth Crotts, Rachael E. Crotts, Lemuel L. Burkhart, Sarah E.
Burkhart, Martha J. Smith, Mary Malinda Lohr, Amanda Crotts,
John Fritts, Isabel Fritts, Jeanette Beck, G. O. Musgrave, Martha
Musgrave, Mary Fritts, D. H. Tysinger and Isadora Musgrave.
David H. Tysinger, David Crotts, Jr., Alexander Burkhart and John
H. Crotts were elected consistorymen.

Land across the road from the brush arbor was donated to the
church, the deed of which states,

> April 11, 1884 by Robert Crotts and Rachael E. Crotts, his wife and
> M. A. Crotts and Catherine Crotts, of Davidson County and the state of
> North Carolina of the first part and David H. Tysinger, David Crotts, Jr.,
> Alexander Burkhart and John H. Crotts, Elders and Deacons of the Mt.
> Tabor Reformed congregation of the Reformed Church in the United
> States of America, of the second part. . . . . containing about one and one
> fourth acres, more or less . . . . in consideration of the sum of one dol-
> lar. . . . . conveyed . . . . to them and their successors in office, while the
> above named congregation remains as such, but as soon as it ceases, will
> go back to the party of the first part.[2]

On this property the first church building was erected, finished and
occupied in 1884.

Rev. Thomas Long continued to serve the congregation until
1888, when ill health required that he withdraw from the active
pastorate. The congregation was then regarded as an independent

mission and supplied by the Rev. A. R. Holshouser, Dr. Jacob C. Leonard, Rev. M. L. Hedrick and Dr. William H. McNairy. In 1895 statistical records of the Classis of North Carolina list Mt. Tabor as a mission supplied by Rev. M. L. Hedrick.[3] In 1896 it was incorporated with the Lower Davidson Charge, beginning May 5.[4] Dr. McNairy evidently served Mt. Tabor as alternate supply during the years 1894 to 1896, while ministering to the Lower Davidson Charge, and as pastor after its incorporation in 1896.

The first church building which had served the community for twenty-five years, was displaced by a new one in 1909 and 1910. The new frame church building was occupied February 22 of the same year. These building operations were under the supervision of Dr. J. M. L. Lyerly, stated supply for the Lower Davidson Charge, at that time. In 1935 an expanding Sunday School required more room; therefore, plans were developed to rebuild the sanctuary and add classroom space for graded and departmentalized instruction. This work was completed in 1937, in the ministry of Dr. James D. Andrew. In 1939 church property was squared with Holly Grove Road through the purchase of strips of land from Mart Everhart lying along the North and West lines. A building which stood on the Northwest corner was rolled to the rear of the lot and converted into a social and recreation hall.

An important turn occurred in the life of Mt. Tabor Church when, on February 27, 1947, a request was presented to The Council of Southern Synod to be detached from the Lower Davidson Charge and constituted an independent church as of June 1, 1947. The council acted as follows, "That Mt. Tabor be constituted a charge, upon enrollment by the Board of National Missions of the Evangelical and Reformed Church."[5] The congregation was enrolled by the board for a period of five years, with subsidy, under the supervision of the Department of Town and Country. This new development required the erection of a house for the proposed new minister. Construction on it began in July 1947, completed and made ready for use March 24, 1948. It was dedicated free of debt. Dr. Banks J. Peeler, a member of the Board of National Missions, performed the act of dedication. It is a nine-room frame building, two rooms on second floor being unfinished, and located on the Northwest corner of the church property.

These were good days for Mt. Tabor Church. In the summer of 1947, the church building was improved, redecorated, carpeted, equipped with a new forced air heating system, new pews and pulpit furniture. To meet a growing need for social and recreational facilities in the community, Fellowship Hall replaced the old social building in 1954. This new equipment was dedicated free of debt November 7, 1954 by the supply pastor, Rev. G. Melvin Palmer.

An occasion of note was the observance by the congregation of its 75th Anniversary of organization. Activities began August 17,

1958, continuing through the 24th. The program was supervised by the pastor, Rev. George A. Fidler, featuring addresses by church representatives and former pastors. Among these were: Dr. Harvey A. Fesperman, president of Southern Synod; Rev. Charles E. Hiatt, Rev. Roy C. Whisenhunt, Rev. Lawrence A. Leonard, Dr. Jacob A. Palmer, Rev. Henry J. Meier, Dr. A. Odell Leonard and Rev. G. Melvin Palmer. The 80th Anniversary was appropriately observed in August 1963, climaxing a series of revival services, commemorating the Sacrament of Holy Communion on Sunday morning, and ending with a picnic dinner at noon.

Mt. Tabor has a beautiful and well kept cemetery. Provision was first made for it May 24, 1889, when Mr. and Mrs. Robert Crotts for a consideration of five dollars deeded to Mt. Tabor Church one acre of land adjoining church property along the East line.[6] In 1948 "God's Acre" was completely renovated. Old shrubs and trees were removed, ground was graded and reseeded and grave markers were aligned and straightened. Most of this improvement was accomplished by volunteer labor.

Interest in providing adequate church equipment has been present in the congregation since its establishment, but especially intensified in the early 1950s. There was an accumulation of funds and material for this purpose. Then, confusion appeared in the congregation, and a sizeable number of members withdrew from Mt. Tabor Church in 1953 to establish New Friendship Evangelical and Reformed Church located in the Holly Grove community. Confusion having been dissolved, the congregation began moving ahead again. On January 13, 1956, by consistory action, a building fund was established. During the next ten years a number of important steps forward were made. A building committee was elected, consisting of Bruce Crotts, Robert Varner, William C. Layman, Artis Smith, Larry Pugh, Alfred Scarlett and Baxter Smith; a successful campaign for funds was inaugurated, bringing the cash balance in the building fund to approximately $50,000; and an architect was employed. Plans for the sanctuary and educational building were approved by the congregation March 17, 1965. In a postal message to his people, in preparation for making financial pledges to the new church building fund, Rev. George K. Ludwig remarked:

> Building is a spiritual experience, because a church building is a representation of the stweardship of the people. Giving for such a cause says to everyone who passes by that here is a people who hold the work of the Lord high in its importance. The building stands for many hours of toil dedicated to God and His kingdom. In a special way a building always represents the sacrifice which Jesus said must be a part of Christian discipleship.
>
> We come, now, to an important step in the spiritual experience of building here at Mt. Tabor Church. Years have been spent in dreaming, talking and planning. Serious and informed thought has been given to drawing up plans to fill the needs for facilities here. The time has come to move forward in commitment to a specific plan for church building. It rests with us to express our faith now that God is able to use our efforts to bring about His Holy will as we take this step.[7]

Events took place at regular intervals after the approval of church plans. The contract for the building was awarded August 15, 1965; groundbreaking ceremonies occurred fourteen days later on August 29; and construction began in October. The cornerstone was laid May 22, 1966. Partial occupation of the new sanctuary occurred July 10, when the last service in the old church building was held. However, formal occupation of the new church took place July 17, 1966, when two children were baptized and eight young people were received by confirmation.

Significant dedication activities began August 14, 1966, with a series of revival services. Former pastor, Rev. A. G. Sandrock, was the preacher. Dr. James H. Lightbourne, Jr., Minister of Southern Conference, United Church of Christ, preached the dedicatory sermon Sunday morning, August 21. Dedication rites were in charge of the pastor, Rev. George K. Ludwig. This building represents a complete church facility, admirably planned to fit the needs of that community. It contains a sanctuary fully equipped to accommodate three hundred people; an educational building with fifteen classrooms and department assembly space; an adequate parking area donated by Olen Crotts; and represents an investment in excess of $125,000.

Rev. Elmo Davis Beck, a son of the congregation, is an ordained minister in the United Church of Christ. The church has a confirmed membership of 236 people, and a Sunday School enrollment of 242 pupils. Rev. Earl T. Farrell is the current pastor.

ROSTER OF PASTORS

Rev. Thomas Long 1883-1888	Rev. John C. Peeler, D.D. 1918-1923
Rev. A. R. Holshouser,	Rev. A. Samuel Peeler 1924-1929
Supply 1888-1896	Rev. James D. Andrew, D.D. 1931-1937
Rev. Jacob C. Leonard, D.D.,	Rev. Charles E. Hiatt 1937-1947
Supply 1888-1896	Rev. A. G. Sandrock 1947-1951
Rev. Jacob C. Leonard, D.D.,	Rev. Lawrence A. Leonard,
Supply 1888-1896	Supply 1951-1952
Rev. M. L. Hedrick, Supply 1888-1896	Rev. Henry J. Meier 1952-1953
Rev. William H. McNairy, D.D.,	Rev. G. Melvin Palmer,
Supply 1888-1896	Supply 1953-1954
Rev. William H. McNairy,	Mr. George A. Fidler,
D.D. 1896-1897	Student Supply 1954-1958
Rev. M. L. Kerschner 1897-1899	Rev. George A. Fidler 1958-1959
Rev. H. E. Sechler 1900-1901	Rev. Donald J. Selby, Ph.D.,
Rev. William H. Causey,	Supply 1959-1960
D.D. 1903-1904	Rev. G. Melvin Palmer,
Rev. Paul Barringer, D.D.,	Supply 1960-
Supply 1905-1906	Rev. Van D. Grimes,
Rev. Peter M. Trexler, D.D.,	Supply 1960-1961
Supply 1907-1908	Rev. George K. Ludwig 1961-1966
Rev. J. M. L. Lyerly, Ph.D.,	Rev. Earl T. Farrell 1967-
Stated Supply 1909-1918	

1. ———. Minutes. Classis of North Carolina, 1883, p. 19.
2. *Deeds Record*, Davidson County, Book 30, p. 329, 1884.
3. ———. Minutes. *Op. cit.*, 1895, p. 39.
4. ———. Minutes. *Op. cit.*, 1896, p. 32.
5. ———. Minutes. Southern Synod, 1947, p. 13.
6. *Deeds Record.* Davidson County, Book 40, 1889, p. 417.
7. *Ludwig*, George K., Mt. Tabor United Church of Christ, 1965, Brochure. p. 2.

Mt. Zion Church, China Grove

THE ORIGIN OF MT. ZION REFORMED CHURCH, China Grove, North Carolina, is hidden in delightful folk-lore. According to this source, German settlers in southwest Rowan County developed a plan for erecting a church to fit their needs two and one-half miles west of the present site, but when a serious quarrel developed between participants, the project was dropped. However, two apostles of peace, traveling east on their way home from that disappointing experience, sat down at a pleasant place to eat their lunch. Discovering a refreshing spring nearby, it was agreed that this would be a good location for a church. Here, sometime later, a small church building was erected.[1] The historical accuracy of this story is rightfully in question, but its truth lingers. The fact that the church was not built on the originally selected parcel of ground two and one-half miles west instead of on the present site perhaps makes little difference, but that Mt. Zion church was born in peace does make a difference. It is important to posterity to know that two men of character had the courage to have nothing to do with the "erection of a house to Almighty God that has been born in bitter strife."

However, this is only part of the story. Having to deal with unbridaled passions of men is one thing, but the orderly struggle to overcome the emotional and physical difficulties involved in developing a peaceful community is quite another. The latter can be relied upon to produce enduring worth. This is the story of Mt. Zion Church, which at one time housed two factions of Lutheranism and one Reformed congregation. If the facts are to be relied upon, these citizens differing in faith, but lived together in reasonable harmony, and parted in peace.[2]

The date when this church was established is not known; however, there are reasons to believe that it came into being sometime before 1780.[3] German settlers had migrated to southeast Rowan County as early as 1740. Within reason they did not reach the southwest section of the county in numerical strength until about 1755,[4] most of the Reformed element being members of the Lower Stone and Cold Water churches. For a time this congregation was known as "Savitz's Church" quite probably named for a family of influence by that name, and later corrupted to "Savage's Church." From the beginning, however, its real name appears to have been Mt. Zion.

The first church building was a crude log structure, replaced some years later by a larger one painted red. Remembering that these were times when people believed in spirits, good and bad ones; responding to the benevolent care of the good ones but using every conceivable device to foil and destroy the bad ones, something akin to the modern concern for germs, it is understandable that an over-emotional person associating red with the Evil Spirit, burned down the church to get rid of the Devil. It was fantasy, of course, but the incident mirrors the times.

Another church building was erected shortly thereafter. This venture involved both Reformed and Lutheran congregations, who used it until 1836. In that year the Lutheran congregation withdrew and built a church of their own a few hundred yards east. The Reformed folks continued to use the old building until about 1844, when they purchased four acres of land from Catherine Partee for the sum of forty dollars, and built a brick church on it.[5] It is interesting to note the Consistorymen at that time: elders, Andrew Shuping, David Correll, Solomon Sechler and John Hileman, the latter in later years figuring so greatly in the affairs of Mt. Gilead, now New Gilead Church. Deacons were, Jacob Shuping, Jacob Shulemberger, Daniel Corriher and Levi Correll.

Two years later, in 1846, David Correll gave eighty five acres of land to the "Elders of the congregation in trust for parsonage purposes." Elders at that time were Henry Sechler, Solomon Sechler, Peter Deal and Jacob Shuping. On June 1, 1799 John Litaker deeded four acres of land to the "Elders and Trustees for the united German Congregations of the Presbyterians (Reformed) and Lutherians." Reformed and Lutheran congregations held this acreage jointly until 1898, when by mutual agreement, a division was made of the property. The share of Mt. Zion was four and a half acres adjoining their individually owned land referred to above.

In 1886 the old brick building was demolished, and in 1889 a new brick structure was begun. Low wages, scarce money and generally hard times combined to prolong operations, forcing the congregation to sacrifice its parsonage acreage in order to meet building obligations. Brick was made by hand at a number of places in the parish by members and friends. J. L. Hedrick supervised the brick-laying; and Jacob Correll and Jacob Bowman, the latter a native of Switzerland, finished the interior, making the pews and the pulpit furniture. Finally the new church with a steeple, giving it a "touch of old world atmosphere," was finished. It was made ready for use about the year 1881, perhaps as late as 1882.

In 1881, Dr. Paul Barringer began a richly rewarding ministry. The congregation grew in spiritual grace and numbers. But this happy pastorate came to an end December 31, 1891. At that time Mt. Zion and St. Paul's Church, Enochville, were constituted a charge, and the Board of Missions appropriated $100 for one year in support of the pastor. Dr. Peter M. Trexler became pastor of the new West Rowan Charge in 1892; Rev. Anthony Shulenberger in 1895. After a vacancy of one year, Rev. Joshua L. Bowers began to serve the charge in 1901. Because of this vacancy, the people scattered; however, faithful work on the part of the minister rallied the people, so that attendance at worship increased, Sunday School expanded and finances improved. Mr. Bowers also began holding occasional religious services in the schoolhouse in the village of Landis.

In the spring of 1908 Rev. M. M. Noacker was called to the parish, who held services regularly at Chian Grove and Landis. At Mt. Zion the sanctuary was improved and renovated, a Woman's Missionary Society was organized and Teacher Training classes were begun.

During the pastorate of Dr. John H. Keller, on April 7, 1918, a few hours after the Sacrament of Holy Communion had been administered to the congregation, the church building burned to the ground. Only the pulpit, a few chairs, the organ and some pews were rescued. If a catastrophe breeds new, fresh life, this is a case in question. A few days after the fire, James N. Fleming, a venturesome deacon volunteered to canvas the congregation for funds with which to rebuild the church. His effort resulted in pledges totalling $10,000. Encouraged by this ready response, the congregation elected a building committee, and gave it power to act. The personnel of that important group was: C. C. Deal, J. E. Corriher, Jr., J. P. Deal, B. S. Shuford, Ed. L. Deal, J. E. Correll, Dr. G. A. Ramsaur, D. L. Correll, James N. Fleming and C. B. Sechler.

The first world war was in progress at the time, and the price of material had begun to skyrocket; hence, the decision to move forward with all possible speed seemed advisable. Plans and specifications for the church building were developed and approved. Construction began immediately, laying the cornerstone on the fifth Sunday in September 1918, which was presided over by the pastor. Dr. Jacob C. Leonard made the address. The church building was occupied by the Sunday School June 22, 1919. Formal opening of the Sanctuary occurred June 29, 1919, and dedication took place May 30, 1920, in a two-days series of appropriately arranged activities. Rev. C. Columbus Wagoner spoke at the gathering on Saturday afternoon. Dr. Peter M. Trexler delivered the dedicatory sermon on Sunday morning, and the dedicatory rites were read by Dr.

Keller. Other dignitaries present for the occasion were: Revs. John A. Koons, Harvey A. Welker, S. Arthur Troxell, Walter W. Rowe, Paul Barringer, William C. Lyerly, Anthony Shulenberger and J. S. Wessinger of the Lutheran Church. It was a memorable occasion.

The church is a large brick structure, housing an expansive sanctuary, beautified by art glass windows, and the educational section contains twelve classrooms and a ladies' parlor. The total cost of these building operations amounted to $25,000. This is the equipment provided by the congregation to take care of the needs of 500 Sunday School pupils and a confirmed membership of well over four hundred people.

An important step of missionary interest took place during this unusual period. Over a number of years religious services had been conducted by ministers of the church for Reformed people living in Landis, North Carolina. On April 20, 1919, sixty-five people were dismissed from Mt. Zion church for the purpose of founding the First Reformed Church of that growing community, which act was accomplished April 27.[6] On May 4, 1919 a petition was sent to the Classis of North Carolina requesting that a new charge be created consisting of Mt. Zion and First Church, Landis. This request was approved, and Dr. John H. Keller was elected pastor of the charge, which he continued to serve until December 31, 1936.

Mt. Zion Church was declared an independent, one-church charge effective January 1, 1937.[7] Rev. Huitt R. Carpenter was called to be its first full-time pastor, beginning his services to the congregation the following May. A new brick veneer parsonage was erected in 1937 along side the old frame structure built in 1889, on land that had been donated for that purpose by Dr. C. W. Corriher. The One Hundred Seventy-First Anniversary and Twentieth Birthday of the Present Church Building was observed the week of September 13, 1939, climaxing in Homecoming Day activities on the 17th.[8] Attorney Loomis F. Kluttz delivered the major address during the morning.

In the summer of 1946, student G. Harold Myers, then a senior at The Theological Seminary, Lancaster, Pennsylvania, did student supply work on the parish. Upon graduation he was called to be pastor and installed January 4, 1958. Under his vigorous leadership, Mt. Zion again asserted its missionary concern in sponsoring the Rodger's Park Mission, beginning February 18, 1951.[9]

A new educational building, for which the congregation had long worked and hoped, was occupied December 22, 1957. Dedication services were held January 12, 1958. Preparations for this building were begun during the pastorate of Mr. Myers, who made the dedicatory address, but completed in the administration of Rev. Elden M. Spangler. Dr. Harvey A. Fesperman, president of Southern Synod, read the dedicatory ritual. All debts were liquidated after Rev. C. Larry Fisher came to the parish, and the note-burning ceremony took place September 17, 1961, when Mr. Spangler made the address. Total cost of this new facility was $120,000.

A step forward was made when, in November 1961, a part-time director of Christian Education was added to the staff. Three ministerial sons grace the church roll: Dr. Shuford Peeler, Rev. H. E. Sechler and Rev. James R. Cress. The Church is governed by a consistory composed of twenty people, half of whom are elders and half deacons, through a system of fourteen committees involving one hundred fourteen people.

ROSTER OF PASTORS

Rev. Samuel Suther	1768-1786	Rev. Peter M. Trexler, D.D.	1892-1894
Rev. Andrew Loretz	1789-1792	Rev. Anthony Shulenberger	1895-1900
Rev. Samuel Weyberg	1793-1802	Rev. Joshua L. Bowers	1901-1907
Rev. George Boger	1802-1830	Rev. M. M. Noacker	1908-1912
Rev. Daniel B. Lerch	1830-1834	Rev. John H. Keller, D.D.	1912-1936
Rev. John Lantz	1837-1845	Rev. Huitt R. Carpenter	1937-1946
Rev. Jeremiah Ingold, D.D.	1845-1856	Mr. G. Harold Myers,	
Rev. Samuel J. Fetzer	1858-1863	Summer Student Supply	1946-
Rev. Jesse W. Cecil	1863-1866	Rev. G. Harold Myers	1948-1954
Rev. John Ingle	1866-1874	Rev. David E. Faust, Ph.D.,	
Rev. Jesse W. Cecil	1874-1875	Supply	1954-
Rev. H. F. Long, Supply	1875-1876	Rev. Elden M. Spangler	1955-1959
Rev. Julius H. Shuford	1876-1877	Rev. John J. Carey, Supply	1959-
Rev. Peter M. Trexler, D.D.	1877-1881	Rev. C. Larry Fisher	1960-1967
Rev. Paul Barringer, D.D.	1881-1891		

1. *Clapp,* Jacob C., Editor. Historic Sketch of the Reformed Church in North Carolina, 1908. p. 211.
2. *Morgan,* Jacob L., Editor. History of the Lutheran Church in North Carolina, 1953. p. 237.
3. *Ibid.* p. 237.
4. *Clapp.* Op. cit., p. 210.
5. *Correll,* James E., Manuscript. Mt. Zion Reformed Church 1939. p. 1ff.
6. ———. Minutes. Classis of North Carolina, 1919. p. 38.
7. ———. *Op. cit.,* 1937. p. 20.
8. *Carpenter,* Huitt R., One Hundred Seventy-First Anniversary and Twentieth Birthday of the Present Church Building, 1939. p. 6.
9. ———. Minutes. Southern Synod of the Evangelical and Reformed Church, 1951. p. 34.

Mt. Hope Church, Rowan County

I. St. Paul's Church

ST. PAUL'S CONGREGATION, located four and one-half miles south of Salisbury, North Carolina, on the Old Concord Road, began as a union church. Prior to 1830, supposedly German settlers who lived in the area convened themselves as desired to consider matters of common interest, among them being the worship of Almighty God. Deciding to erect a church, perhaps in tradition of the meeting house, the first site selection appears to have been near the old Heilig Mill. But when Andrew Holshouser, Jr., a member of Lower Stone Reformed Church, made available for a nominal sum, five acres of land on which to erect a church building that could be

Mt. Hope Church

used by all denominations, his proposition was accepted. A frame church building was soon thereafter built on the site where St. Paul's Lutheran Church now stands.[1]

This property was deeded August 14, 1832 to Enoch Phillips and Michael L. Brown, "Trustees of the Presbyterians and Lutheran Church in common and their successors in office," for the sum of $25.[2] In deeds of this sort recorded in Cabarrus, Lincoln and Catawba counties the term "Presbyterians" is understood to mean "Reformed." Undoubtedly this is what the donor meant in this case; although the picture is clouded somewhat by the fact that Presbyterians did use the building for a time. The building is referred to as "Holshouser's Church," in something of the same connotation as when one refers to Holshouser's Mill, and used by all Christian denominations represented in the area who had cause to do so.

> The Lutheran, Reformed and Presbyterians held services regularly once a month, each having regular pastors, while the Methodists, and some say the Baptists held services occasionally, just as some minister of their denomination was passing through or when they were able to secure one to hold service. The Methodists often held protracted meetings which lasted for two weeks or more.[3]

Tradition relates that the congregation was organized March 30, 1830. By whom it is not known; although it has been suggested that the organizer was Rev. John Lantz. Rev. Samuel Rothrock, the first regular minister to the Lutheran element in the community, who served there beginning 1835, relates in his diary that he held services regularly once a month at Holshouser's Church, and that he attended the wedding there of Rev. John Lantz to Miss Nancy Fraley April 23, 1845. The ceremony was performed by Rev. David Crooks.[4] When the congregation was named St. Paul's is unknown, although it appears to have been referred to by that name after 1830.

II. St. Paul's - Mt. Hope Reformed Church

St. Paul's German Reformed Church was organized March 1850 by John Lantz. Seventeen people constitute the original roll of members: Jacob Lingle, John Lippard, Sr., John Lippard, Jr., Daniel Peeler, David Kluttz, Solomon Kluttz, Peter A. Fisher, David Fisher, John Yost, Michael Shuping, Margaret Kluttz, Barbara Kluttz, Anna Weaver, Mary C. Trexler, Sarah Peeler, Christiana Peeler and Eliza Rendelman. Jacob Lingle and Daniel Peeler were elected elders, John Yost and Solomon Kluttz, deacons.[5]

The congregation was officially received "under the care of Classis" in 1851, and continued under the supervision of Rev. John Lantz as a part of the East Rowan Charge, which consisted of Lower Stone, Bear Creek and now St. Paul's churches.[6] A meeting of the Classis of North Carolina was held at St. Paul's Church February 25, 1852, and again April 25, 1862. During these years St. Paul's was served by Revs. John Lantz, Thornton Butler and an associate in 1856 by the name of Gilbert Lane. Mr. Lane had transferred from the Dutch Reformed Church to the Classis, but returned to the Dutch church in 1857.[7]

The new church continued to operate at the old site until November 1865, when the Classis took the following action. "Voted, that three fourths of the members of St. Paul's Church, Rowan County concuring, that congregation be dissolved in order to reorganize at Mt. Hope in said county to form a new church, and that all the members be advised to connect themselves with the church at that place.[8] The new organization was effected, and the pastor Rev. Thornton Butler, reported same to Classis in 1866.

> In accordance with the resolution of the Classis, I organized a new German Reformed congregation at Mt. Hope, Rowan County on the 14th of January 1866 numbering thirty six members. The members of St. Paul's congregation, with very few exceptions, connected themselves with the new congregation.[9]

Officers elected at this first meeting were: elders, David Roseman and Solomon Kluttz; deacons, John W. Fisher, J. H. A. Lippard, E. S. P. Lippard and Martin Yost. Immediately these people began working on plans for a new church building. The house was to be 60 feet by 40 feet in size, constructed of brick and wood. Bricks were made on the parish by members of the congregation, and lumber was cut from timber on church property. Until these operations could materialize the congregation worshipped, during the winter months in a frame house which stood immediately back of the present church, and during summer months under a brush arbor. Finished about the year 1869, Mr. Butler led his people in an appropriate dedicatory service.

This transition period was marked by the exceptional leadership, among others of Elder Jacob Lingle. At the formal organization of the congregation, land was promised by Mr. Lingle and his brother, John on which to erect the church. On February 2, 1866, the former deeded four acres of land to Mt. Hope Church, and eight days later, February 10, the latter deeded six acres to the same cause.

The church made good progress during the next eighteen years, often against odds, chiefly because of alignment of the churches in the area into workable charges, which led at times to unrest. The first parsonage was built during that time. In 1878 Elder Jacob Lingle gave seventy acres of land for parsonage purposes, and $120 with which to start the project. The deed for this land was made February 25, 1879.[10] Thereafter money accumulated in the parsonage fund, so when on August 20, 1879 the one fourth interest in the old Lower Stone parsonage, owned by the Central Rowan Charge was sold, Mt. Hope was ready to proceed in building their own house. It was ostensibly erected in 1886.

Beginning in 1887 the church encountered its first serious internal trouble. It was caused by a lack of understanding between pastor and people, involving all of the churches in the Central Rowan Charge. In 1888 the report of the committee on vacancies of the Classis of North Carolina stated.

> There are within the bounds of the North Carolina Classis two vacant charges, Lower Davidson and Central Rowan, of the latter charge one congregation has been supplied by Rev. Mr. Heller, with the approval of the committee. Shiloh has been without preaching since January 1888, while Mt. Hope is still supplied by Rev. Mr. Crooks. . . . . We learn that Rev. Crooks refuses to accept a call and has asserted his intention to supply Mt. Hope independent of the authority of Classis, provided a majority of the members of the congregation sustain him and the Classis did not lock the doors against him.[11]

The Stated Clerk of the Classis, Dr. George W. Welker, summed up the situation in the following statement.

> It was apparent from all the facts that could be reached, that the real source of the trouble in each case was the presence of the retired ministers who still had their adherents that refused to unite with their brethren in a call for a pastor so long as they could have their old minister.[12]

Disposition of the case was made when the Classis acted to "Notify Rev. Robert F. Crooks to vacate the Central Rowan Charge at once and recall all his appointments."[13] Mr. Crooks did resign as pastor of the charge, but in sympathy for him, a number of people left the church. The usual happened in this case. The chief loss to the congregation was not the removal of a few people, but the damage done to the spirit and outlook of the congregation. Mr. Crooks continued to live in the parsonage for a time and to worship at Mt. Hope Church among friends. Being an excellent blacksmith and wood workman, he continued to serve the people in that manner, moving later to live at China Grove, North Carolina.

Ministerial Student J. M. L. Lyerly was asked to supply the Central Rowan Charge in 1889. Toward his support that year,

Classis appropriated $100. Mr. Lyerly became pastor of the charge in 1890 and served it until 1892, when for one year he ministered to the Lincoln Charge. Returning to the Central Rowan Charge in 1893, he served there until 1908. Counting his student supply year, this was the longest of the Mt. Hope pastorates to-date, being 18 years.

In a move to satisfy certain financial obligations, on July 1, 1906, the congregation took action to sell the parsonage property for the sum of $1,000 to Dr. Lyerly. This ended a period of struggle for the church; however, statistics reflect that good progress had been made. For in 1906 there were sixty communicant members on the roll, sixty eight people had communed at least once during the year, baptized children and young people in the congregation numbered sixty and the Sunday School had an enrollment of 140 pupils.

The period beginning with 1915 to the present time could be dubbed years of progress. Rev. Harvey A. Welker and Dr. James D. Andrew did much to dispel the atmosphere of defeat, and to inject the spirit of goodwill and well being. Both of those ministers were popular with the people, attracting visitors in large numbers to various church activities. During the pastorate of Dr. Andrew, for instance, fifty people were added to the membership. Other signs of progress were the organization of the Woman's Missionary Society on January 24, 1937; installation of pulpit furniture and pews in September 1841; and the erection of the educational annex and the organization of the Women's Guild in 1947. The educational annex was dedicated in 1948 to the memory of Pvt. Harold Brown Weaver and Mrs. Maggie Weaver. Dr. Lonnie A. Carpenter preached the sermon, and Rev. Milton Whitener read the service of dedication. During the afternoon of the same day the altar, a pulpit bible, a church bell and a piano were dedicated by the supply pastor, Rev. Terrell M. Shoffner.

In 1951 action was taken to erect a building for educational and recreational purposes. Edison Rhymer was made chairman of the building committee. The structure was to be of brick and wood, 28 feet by 60 feet in size. It was completed in 1953, and dedicated September 13 on Homecoming Day. Dr. Aaron R. Tosh, president of Southern Synod and Dr. A. Odell Leonard were guest speakers. The sanctuary was remodeled and the chancel made altar-centered in 1955.

By this time the congregation had begun to awaken to its strength, anticipating the day when it would be a self-supported, independent charge. The first step in this direction was taken January 27, 1957, when by vote of the congregation it was agreed to erect a parsonage along the south line of the church property. Ray A. Mault, Claude Woodie, Mr. and Mrs. Ralph Vanderford, Mrs. Lois Holt and Carl L. Deal Jr., were named to a building committee, and instructed to present plans for the house. Groundbreaking took place May 12, 1957; dedication September 1960. By request of the congregation self-support was approved by Southern Synod to be effective July 1, 1959.[14]

Rev. Elmo D. Beck became the first full-time pastor, beginning his work on the parish July 1, 1960. This was not a very happy pastorate, since internal difficulties developed, resulting in some losses in membership. It ended October 1962, when Mr. Beck resigned to accept a parish in Pennsylvania.

Rev. Carl C. Kreps began his ministry to the congregation January 1, 1963. Almost immediately interest developed in observing the Centennial Anniversary of the organization of Mt. Hope Church. Ivan Funderburk, Mr. and Mrs. Hubert Davis, Mr. and Mrs. Edgar Holt, Mrs. Russell Eagle, Mrs. Jack Eagle, Mrs. Ralph Horton and Rev. and Mrs. Carl C. Kreps were named to a committee responsible for detailing ways and means for its proper observance. Two major projects were undertaken: A History of Mt. Hope Evangelical and Reformed Church, and a series of appropriate activities for the occasion.

Among Anniversary Day speakers were: Rev. John C. Chatlos, who delivered the anniversary sermon; Rev. Roy C. Whisenhunt, who spoke during the afternoon and Dr. Banks J. Peeler, president of Southern Synod, who spoke in behalf of the Evangelical and Reformed Church and the recently created United Church of Christ. Dr. Lonnie A. Carpenter presented the sermon at 7:30 p.m. in the "Old Fashioned Lamp Light Service." The centennial bulletin carried the following statement, which accurately reflects the spirit of this important occasion.

> It is with a deep sense of gratitude to Almighty God that we as a church celebrate our centennial. As we survey the history of a hundred years, we see the hand of God in the midst of all the activities that have taken place in Mt. Hope Church. . . . We hope, therefore, that each one in our church might feel a deeper commitment to our church and our God as a result of this anniversary.

ROSTER OF PASTORS
I. St. Paul's German Reformed Church

Rev. John Lantz 1850-1852
Rev. Thornton Butler 1853-1865

Rev. Gilbert Lane,
Associate Pastor 1856-

II. Mt. Hope Church

Rev. Thornton Butler 1865-1869
Rev. J. C. Denny 1869-1871
Rev. Peter M. Trexler, D.D. 1871-1877
Rev. John Ingle 1878-1883
Rev. Peter M. Trexler, D.D.,
Supply 1883-1885
Rev. R. F. Crooks 1885-1888
Mr. J. M. L. Lyerly,
Supply 1889-
Rev. J. M. L. Lyerly, Ph.D. ..1890-1892
Rev. Paul Barringer, D.D.,
Alternate Supply 1892-1893
Rev. Peter M. Trexler, D.D.,
Alternate Supply 1892-1893
Rev. J. M. L. Lyerly, Ph.D. ..1893-1908
Rev. A. Samuel Peeler 1909-1910

Rev. Peter M. Trexler, Ph.D.,
Supply 1910-
Rev. Dugan C. Cox 1911-
Rev. Calvin B. Heller,
Supply 1912-1914
Rev. William H. Causey, D.D.,
Supply 1912-1914
Rev. Harvey A. Welker 1915-1923
Mr. Sidney Safrit,
Student Supply, Summer 1923-
Mr. Thomas Safrit,
Student Supply, Summer 1924-
Rev. James D. Andrew, D.D. 1925-1931
Rev. Roy C. Whisenhunt 1931-1938
Rev. Lonnie A. Carpenter,
D.D. 1938-1944

Rev. Milton Whitener 1945-1946
Rev. Terrell M. Shoffner,
    Supply 1948-1949
Rev. Huitt R. Carpenter,
    Supply 1949-
Rev. Joshua L. Levens,
    Supply 1950-1951
Mr. Frank W. Snider,
    Student Supply 1949-1951
Rev. Lloyd E. Sechriest 1951-1953

Mr. Frank W. Snider,
    Student Supply 1953-
Rev. John C. Chatlos 1953-1959
Rev. Samuel A. Troxell,
    Supply 1959-
Mr. Joseph Wise,
    Student Supply 1960-
Rev. Elmo D. Beck 1960-1962
Rev. Porter Seiwell, Supply 1962-
Rev. Carl C. Kreps 1963-1968

1. *Canup*, Maggie Julian, History of St. Paul's Evangelical Lutheran Church, 1964. p. 4.
2. ———. Rowan County, Book of Deeds, No. 31, p. 628.
3. Canup. *Op. cit.*, p. 4.
4. *Kreps*, Carl C., A History of Mt. Hope Evangelical and Reformed Church, 1965. p. p.
5. *Clapp*, Jacob C., Editor. Historic Sketch of the Reformed Church in North Carolina, 1908. p. 226.
6. ———. Minutes. Classis of North Carolina, 1851, p. 127.
7. *Creps. Op. cit.*, p. 10ff.
8. ———. Minutes. *Op. cit.*, 1865, p. 7.
9. ———. Minutes. *Op. cit.*, 1866, p. 19.
10. ———. Rowan County, Book of Deeds, No. 55, p. 468.
11. ———. Minutes. *Op. cit.*, 1888, p. 8.
12. *Ibid.* p. 9.
13. *Ibid.* p. 9.
14. ———. Minutes. Southern Synod of the Evangelical and Reformed Church, 1959, p. 37.

New Jerusalem Church, Davidson County

TEN MILES EAST of Lexington, North Carolina, off to the south of the Asheboro Road or old 64, stands the New Jerusalem Evangelical and Reformed Church. It is a symbol of Protestant cooperation for more than a century. This place became a preaching point as early as 1852, when Rev. Thornton Butler, a German Reformed Church minister, held services in the community under an apple tree. Being a German settlement, devoutly religious and home-loving, and battling problems of transportation, they welcomed these out-of-doors meetings as an answer to their social and religious needs.

Thus, it is not surprising that on "August 28, 1856, Levi Beck deeded a tract of land in that vicinity to Daniel Foust, A. J. Ward, David Beck and David Swing, trustees, to be used by the Lutheran, Reformed, Methodist and Baptist congregations, as a location for a church."[1] A Lutheran Church was organized in 1856, and it appears that in the latter part of 1857, a Reformed Church was established, Rev. Thornton Butler being the organizer. Sometime later, both Baptist and Methodist churches appeared. An old Reformed congregational record penned by M. L. and P. Hedrick in 1876, nineteen years after the congregation had been organized, will be of interest in this connection.

> This congregation was organized as a German Reformed Church, about the year 1857 A. D. This church was made up with members formally belonging to Beck's Church. Under the pastorate of P. A. Long, who labored about fourteen years in this congregation, a part of the time with great success. The church numbered between seventy five and one hundred members. But the war came on, and political strife came into the church. Many died in the army, others left the congregation and moved back to Beck's. . . . The pastor went North, and left the charge without a pastor for one year.
>
> Rev. M. L. Hedrick was called in the charge in the year 1872. . . . The congregation is weak, but has some faithful members and harmony prevails.
>
> Elders at this time are: Philip Hedrick and Obediah Swing; deacons, J. W. Hedrick and O. C. Hedrick.

In the same book is recorded the Constitution of Jerusalem Church adopted November 3, 1894. The first building, a frame, one-story structure, was erected shortly after the Reformed and Lutheran congregations had been organized. It was located in front of the cemetery, size, approximately that of the present sanctuary.

> The pulpit was located against the south side wall of the building in the center, with rows of wooden benches with straight backs arranged on each side so that the worshippers faced toward the center of the building and the minister. The male members sat on the left rows of benches, while the female members sat on the opposite side of the church. Other benches were placed against the walls, somewhat removed from the regular seating arrangements and were used by the Negroes of the community. This building served its holy purpose a full half-century.[2]

The second church building was erected in 1909, and stands about where the apple tree stood, during the pastorates of Dr. J. M. L. Lyerly, Reformed, and the Rev. A. L. Boleik, Lutheran, and was dedicated May 30th of that year. On that occasion, the Rev. T. A. Plyler, a Methodist Protestant minister, performed the act of dedication.

The Sunday School was union in every respect. All current obligations were met from the same treasury; the superintendent was altered from year to year between the participating denominations, as was the literature and other educational supplies. Teachers were elected without respect to denominational affiliation.

By 1938 the Union Church was strong enough to add four Sunday School rooms. These were attached to the rear of the sanctuary, and dedicated May 29, 1938. Rev. Charles E. Hiatt delivered the dedicatory sermon, and the dedication ritual was read by Rev. R. L. Fisher. The sanctuary was remodeled in 1950, involving new furniture, the construction of a vestibule, cement steps and walks leading to the building. An air heating furnace and an additional Sunday School rooms were provided in 1953. The all-purpose hut containing two classrooms, a recreation hall, a kitchen and toilet facilities was erected in 1960.

Four denominations owned and used the property. The Baptist congregation disbanded many years ago. Shortly after 1923, the Methodist Protestant Church ceased to operate, being disbursed among other churches in the area.[3] The Lutheran congregation moved east several miles to Silver Valley, where they built a new church, and the Reformed congregation, by legal agreement, purchased the old site and remained there. Church membership now number 130 confirmed people; while the Sunday School enrollment is 120 pupils.

From its founding Jerusalem Church has been associated with neighboring churches in the interest of pastoral services. In 1864, the Reformed churches in Davidson County were divided into what was then referred to as the "upper and lower Davidson group of churches." The upper group was served by the newly ordained Rev. Thomas Long, and the lower group by the Rev. P. Allison Long. These groups were subsequently recognized by the Classis of North Carolina and named the Upper Davidson Charge and the Lower Davidson Charge. In the Lower Davidson Charge, one by one these churches either became strong enough to support their own minister or were regrouped for practical reasons, and thus detached from the charge. The last one to be detached from the Lower Davidson Charge was Beck's Church, which went to self-support June 30, 1964. By unanimous action the joint consistory of the two congregations requested approval of the Classis, and New Jerusalem became a single church charge the first time in its history.[4] Economically unable to fully support a minister on full-time, the congregation has been served since 1964 by supply ministers under appointment by Southern Synod and more recently by Southern Conference.

During its one hundred ten years of existence, Jerusalem Reformed Church has changed names twice. First, in 1934, when the Reformed Church in the United States merged with the Evangelical Synod of North America to form the Evangelical and Reformed

Church; and again, in 1957, when the Evangelical and Reformed Church merged with Congregational Christian churches to form the United Church of Christ. It is interesting to observe that each of these adjustments has been made with ease and grace, characteristic of the catholic spirit inherent in the German Reformed Church.

ROSTER OF PASTORS

Rev. Thornton Butler,
Organizer 1852-1857
Rev. P. Allison Long 1858-1864
Rev. M. L. Hedrick, Rev. A. R.
  Holshouser, Rev. William H.
  McNairy, D.D., Rev. L. M.
  Kerschner, Rev. H. E. Sechler,
  Rev. William H. Causey, D.D.,
  Rev. Paul Barringer, D.D., Rev.
  Peter M. Trexler, D.D. 1865-1909
Rev J. M. L. Lyerly, Ph.D. ..1909-1918
Rev. John C. Peeler, D.D. 1918-1923
Rev. A. Samuel Peeler 1923-1929
Mr. Roy C. Whisenhunt,
  Student Summer Supply,
  2 summers 1929-1930
Rev. James D. Andrew, D.D. 1931-1937

Rev. Charles E. Hiatt 1937-1950
Rev. Roy E. Leinbach, Jr.,
  Supply 1950-1951
Rev. C. Nevin Stamm 1951-1952
Rev. Lionel A. Whisten, Ph.D.,
  Supply 1952-1953
Rev. Horace S. Sills 1953-1959
Mr. Wade H. Curran, Jr.,
  Summer Student Supply 1961-
Rev. Donald J. Selby, Ph.D.,
  Supply 1961-1962
Rev. Wade H. Curran, Jr. 1962-1965
Rev. George K. Ludwig,
  Stated Supply 1965-1966
Rev. Banks J. Peeler, D.D.,
  Stated Supply 1966-

1. *Morgan,* Jacob L., Editor, History of the Lutheran Church in North Carolina, 1953, p. 258.
2. *Sills,* Horace S., *Roof,* L. O., New Jerusalem Union Church, 1956, p. 13.
3. *Ibid.* p. 14.
4. ————. Minutes. Southern Synod, 1964, p. 64.

New Friendship Church, Davidson County

NEW FRIENDSHIP EVANGELICAL AND REFORMED CHURCH, Route 2, Lexington, North Carolina, began in a gathering of thirty five people which took place in the home of Mr. and Mrs. Cletus R. Swing, September 30, 1953. The purpose of the meeting was to discuss the possibility of establishing a church of their faith in the Holly Grove Community. Rev. Harvey H. Koonts, Jr. was present by request. Action was taken overturing Southern Synod for authority to organize said church, and a committee was instructed to present the document in person to The Council of Southern Synod at its next meeting.

The Council met October 12, 1953, heard the report and made the following record:

> Thirty-four members of Mt. Tabor congregation appeared before the Synodical Council with a petition signed by forty-seven people, members of Mt. Tabor, to be organized into a congregation and permission to locate to the rear of Davis-Towsend High School, 1.2 miles from Mt. Tabor.
>
> The Council adopted: "That the petition from the group of Mt. Tabor congregation be granted, giving them the right to organize a new congregation, and proceed with the purchase of property indicated, and the acquisition of certain materials now at Mt. Tabor on which they said there was common agreement."
>
> Rev. A. W. Hedrick was appointed advisor for the group.[1]

The Sunday School was established November 1, 1953, and the church was organized the following November 11. There were seventy-four charter members. This new congregation was enrolled by Southern Synod as a member of the Evangelical and Reformed Church on December 30, 1953.[2] Regular services were conducted in the old home of W. Andrew Beck, beginning October 12, 1953. On that date Synodical Counselor, Rev. A. W. Hedrick was present and participated in the service. "New Friendship" was adopted as the name for the new church. A request was made to the Synod for the services of Rev. Harvey H. Koonts, Jr. as supply pastor. The request was granted.

Lewis Everhart, Alfred Gurley, Johnny Younts, John Whitlock and Franklin Swing were elected elders; and James Grubb, Charlie Morgan, Blake Crotts, Brantley Beck and E. L. Myers, deacons. Deaconesses were also named in the persons of Mrs. C. R. Cook, Mrs. Vernon Beck, Mrs. R. G. Everhart and Mrs. Brantley Beck.[3]

On December 1, 1953, Mr. and Mrs. Grant Everhart presented to the congregation a deed to their "Indian Hill" property located on Turner Road in the center of Holly Grove Community.[4] On December 16, 1953, Cletus R. Swing submitted to the congregation a set of plans proposing and all-purpose, first unit, building. Those plans were approved. Groundbreaking ceremonies took place Christmas day, December 25, 1953, and construction on the edifice began immediately. Within a few months the incompleted structure was occupied.

When the charter member list was closed November 6, 1955, on it were 129 names of confirmed people. Such satisfactory progress had been made that on November 13, 1955, Rev. Harvey H. Koonts, Jr., who had supplied the congregation since its founding, was called to be its first regular pastor. Mr. Koonts was installed pastor of the church January 1, 1956, the service being in charge of President Harvey A. Fesperman of Southern Synod. Associated with him in these activities were Dr. Banks J. Peeler, Rev. Hiram E. Davis and Elder Cletus R. Swing.

Anticipating the erection of a parsonage, a lot was purchased from Cletus R. Swing containing two acres of land located on Highway 64. Upon receipt of a check of $700 covering the price of the lot, Mr. Swing endorsed the check which was then added to the church building fund.

New Friendship Church has established itself as being concerned about community welfare. As evidence, on July 10, 1955, the congregation voted unanimously to provide space in their church to operate the retarded children's program supported by Davidson County. Church facilities were used for this purpose week days until February 1959, when the county provided its own building. Also the congregation has established an effective program of parish activities, involving Sunday School, men's and women's work, youth training and a very strong Boy Scout Troup.

Debt free the church building was dedicated October 11, 1959. Rev. Alfred G. Sandrock preached the dedicatory sermon. Rev. Joshua L. Levens, secretary of Southern Synod, participated in the ceremonies, and the pastor performed the act of dedication. The persent church is the first unit of a proposed complete facility. It is a two-story structure, 120 by 40 feet in size, containing nine classrooms, a pastor's study, a children's assembly, dining room and kitchen space. On second floor is a large room equipped and used as a sanctuary.

Mr. Koonts has served the church since its founding. First as supply minister, and since 1955 as regular pastor. Miss June Grubb, a commissioned Director of Christian Education in the United Church of Christ, is a daughter of this congregation.

ROSTER OF PASTORS

Rev. A. W. Hedrick,	Rev. Harvey H. Koonts, Jr.,
Advisor and Organizer 1953-	Supply 1953-1955
	Rev. Harvey H. Koonts, Jr. 1955-

1. ———. Minutes. Southern Synod, 1954, p. 16.
2. *Ibid.* p. 16.
3. ———. The Standard, Official Organ of Southern Synod, June 15, 1954, p. 2.
4. *Koonts*, Harvey H., Jr., New Friendship Evangelical and Reformed Church, United Church of Christ, 1959, p. 3 ff.

New Gilead Church, Cabarrus County

NEW GILEAD REFORMED CHURCH, Cabarrus County, traces its beginning to a settlement of German immigrants who arrived in the area about the year 1758, and located on Cold Water Creek northeast of Concord, North Carolina. Colonial Governor Arthur Dobbs, on August 24, 1755, in reporting on an exploratory trip made by him through the western part of the Province, describes the Cold Water land and its people in the following language:

There were twenty two families of German or Swiss who are all industrious people, they raise horses, cows and hogs with a few sheep. They raise Indian Corn, wheat, barley, rye, and oats, make good butter and tolerable cheese, and they have gone into indigo with good success which they sell at Charles Town having a waggon road to it, though a 200 miles distance over roads not yet shortened and properly laid out. . . . The air is fine, water good, running springs from each hill and the country is so healthy that few or none have died since their settlement seven or eight years ago. They sow flax for their own use and cotton, and what hemp they have sown is tall and good.[1]

The date when the church was organized can not be established, however, it is certain that it is one of the oldest churches of the Reformed faith in that section of the state, and from the beginning operated as a Reformed congregation. Knowing the religious habits of early German settlements, it is reasonable to conclude that upon arrival in the Cold Water Creek section, religious services were conducted in their midst with reasonable regularity. These ecclesiastical functions were conducted either by especially appointed laymen or itinerate preachers, among them being Rev. John Nicholas Martin, Rev. Richard Dupert and Rev. Christian Theus.[2] "Silas Shinn married Elinor Overcash at the German Reform Church on Cold Water" in 1766. An incomplete list of Cold Water Church members in 1766 contains the names of twenty seven heads of families, which means that the church was sizable and very probably organized.[3]

It has been suggested that the church was organized sometime during the early part of the pastorate of Rev. Samuel Suther. Since Mr. Suther was an aggressive man, and instrumental in organizing a number of Reformed Churches in the Province of North Carolina, this suggestion is much more than an educated guess. Governor Tryon attended services at the Cold Water Church August 22, 1768 when he heard, "Mr. Luther (Suther) . . a Dutch minister recommend with warmth and due obedience to the laws of the country and a union of mind and heart to support the peace and tranquility of the Province."[4] Since Mr. Suther was the first known resident

German speaking minister of the Gospel in the area, he undoubtedly nurtured the young Cold Water congregation during its earlier struggling years to reasonable strength and influence.

It is a truism that when the leader falters, the followers scatter. Something of this nature is evidently what happened to the Cold Water Church. For when Mr. Suther resigned from the church in 1786, and returned to the Orangeburg District of South Carolina, this congregation prospered for a time, but faltered under the sporadic pastoral care available to it over a period of more than thirty years. Evidently the Reformed and Lutheran people in the area during that time were cooperating in religious matters, for in 1814 it became a union church.[5] When in 1843 those of the Lutheran persuasion withdrew to organize St. James Lutheran Church, Concord, North Carolina,[6] that exodus all but eclipsed the congregation, and for a number of years it was dormant.

The church building was old, dilapidated and uninviting, so that efforts of Rev. John Lantz to revive the congregation proved futile. In 1851 Dr. Jeremiah Ingold, then pastor of the West Rowan Charge, negotiated a property settlement with the Lutheran Church and with what was left of the congregation, relocated the church at the present site on the Old Salisbury-Concord Road, three miles north of the city of Concord. In making the transfer, Dr. Ingold had the unqualified support of such men and their families as John Hileman and Joseph Cook, among others. Rev. Banks D. Shepherd comments as follows concerning the transition.

> In April, 1854 a deed was granted to Mount Gilead Reformed Church, with John Hileman and Joseph Cook listed as elders. It conveyed a tract of 1 and ¾ acres of land to the German Reformed Church adjoining "Peter Fink, James Cline and others." This is the site of the present New Gilead. There are some interesting features about the deed, in addition to the new location of the church. First, the name of the church is now Mount Gilead. The name Cold Water was left behind at the former location. Second, the deed conveys land "whereon Mount Gilead Church now stands." This means that there was a church built there prior to the date of this deed.[7]

On the property described above a neat brick building had been erected and completed in 1857, which served the congregation for thirty five years. Here Elder John Hileman demolished an old building "approximately where the church now stands, . . . proceeded almost singlehandedly to build a brick building, in 1847, which would be called Mt. Gilead. Being a skilled workman in wood and iron he made, hauled and lay brick with his own hands."[8] In this house the descendents of the Cold Water Reformed fathers, after the manner of their ancestors, continued to worship Almighty God. On the current church roll could be found family names such as the Foils (Pyles), Hilemans, Clines (Kleins), Meisenheimers, Shinns, Cooks, Suthers etc.

In 1888 a new sanctuary was erected, which was dedicated in the fall of the same year. About the time the building was dedicated the name of the church was changed from Mount Gilead to "New Gilead Reformed Church." The reason for this change is not clear, but one suspects that it resulted from common use in making the transition from the old church building to the new one. When the new house was occupied, the old one continued in use as a Sunday School room until 1900, when on June 9 the old brick building known as "Mt. Gilead Church" was sold at auction to C. P. Cline for the sum of $51.27.

New Gilead faced the Twentieth Century at what appears to be a "low ebb" in the life of the congregation. A condition due largely to short pastorates, ministerial supplies, and very limited pastoral oversight. In 1918 the Consistory asked the pastor of Trinity Church, Concord, to serve the congregation as stated supply. This arrangement was approved by the Classis of North Carolina, and the Rev. William C. Lyerly continued to serve in that capacity until 1923. The short pastorate of Rev. J. Dudley Maedor was followed by miscellaneous supplies until 1929, when Rev. Hugo C. Keller-meyer became pastor of the charge composed of New Gilead and Trinity, Concord congregations. This relationship continued until 1942. Mr. Kellermeyer was followed by Rev. Roy C. Whisenhunt, who began serving the charge April 1 of that year, continuing to do so until 1949.

The sturdy old brick building that had served the congregation for fifty years, was still structurally sound, but the need for space required attention. In 1937 rooms for Sunday School purposes were attached to the rear of the sanctuary, and the narthex was extended on the front. Total cost of these operations was in excess of $6,000. During these fruitful years, the church was redecorated, the chancel made altar centered and an electric organ and chimes were installed. Plans were developed in anticipation of a new parsonage to be erected on land given to the church by Miss Mary Neisler and Miss Nell Neisler, located one half mile south of the church, on the Concord Road.

An event in this period of historical interest, was the unveiling of a bronze tablet commemorating the founding of Cold Water Church and honoring its founder, Rev. Samuel Suther. The occasion was scheduled for anniversary week, marking the one hundred seven-tieth anniversary of New Gilead congregation and took place Thursday, October 21, 1937 at 2:30 p.m. The presentation was made by Mrs. J. Walter Williamson, Wilmington, North Carolina, president of the Society of Colonial Dames, and unveiled by Miss Ruby Lee Suther and Mr. Fred W. Suther, descendents of the honoree. Dr. Walter W. Rowe, Lenoir, North Carolina, delivered an appropriate address on the "Life of Rev. Samuel Suther."

The tablet, which has been permanently placed on the Southwest corner of the outside wall of New Gilead Church, is inscribed as follows:

Commemorating the Cold Water Reformed Church,
Cabarrus County formerly Mecklenburg,
1766 Earliest known Date.
Governor Tryon attended this Church August 24, 1768.
Rev. Samuel Suther was then Pastor.
New Gilead is a successor to the above and about three Miles from the
Old Site.
Erected by the North Carolina Society of Colonial Dames of America
under the Auspices of the Cabarrus County Committee 1957.

Perhaps the most venturesome step forward in recent years was that taken in 1950, when the congregation asked Southern Synod to be constituted an independent, self-supporting charge,[9] and called the Rev. Charles E. Hiatt to be its first full-time pastor.[10] During his pastorate plans were created for a new educational facility, which was built and largely paid for during the pastorate of Rev. Merle F. Sollinger.

Operations which produced the new educational building were managed by two committees: one on finances composed of Mrs. Bayless Ridenhour, Mrs. Ralph Bonds, Lewis Patterson, Chester Misenheimer, Frank Earnhardt, Mrs. Fred Suther, Mrs. M. L. Walter and Kennethy McAnulty; and another on building consisting of Bernard Hileman, Clyde Cook, Ross Scott, Haynes Patterson, Mrs. Kenneth McAnulty and Mrs. Richard Benefield. The building was completed in March 1960 at a cost of $37,418, which obligation was liquidated in September 1963.

On the roll of ministers in the denomination are the following ministerial sons and one adopted son: Rev. George Boger, 1782-1865; Dr. John A. Foil, 1847-1911; Dr. William Henry Causey, 1872-1943. Dr. Causey was born and reared in Davidson County, but considered the New Gilead community his adopted home. His body lies in the nearby church cemetery.[11]

Out of the New Gilead environment have grown at least in part three neighboring churches: Trinity, Concord, 1881; St. James, Mt. Pleasant, 1894; Keller, Cabarrus County, 1904.

Two major events in the later life of New Gilead Church merit mention in this connection. They concurrently bring to a close the very meaningful pastorate of Rev. Banks D. Shepherd which began January 1963. The reference is to the celebration of The Bicentennial of New Gilead Church, scheduled for the week of August 21, 1966, and the release of a new publication entitled, "New Gilead Church, A History of the German Reformed People on Coldwater," whose author is Rev. Banks D. Shepherd.

The occasion brought to the community and to the congregation numerous leaders of the United Church of Christ, who spoke during the well planned week of religious activities. Among them were: Dr. Jack Yates, Assistant to the President of the United Church of Christ; Rev. Hugo C. Kellermeyer, former beloved pastor; Dr. James H. Lightbourne, Jr., Minister of the Southern Conference; and Rev. Edwin M. Alcorn, Western Area Minister of the Southern Conference.

In dedicating certain equipment of the church, installed as a prelude to the bicentennial celebration, an appreciative congregation published the following statement:

> In honor of our beloved pastor, Rev. Banks D. Shepherd and his wife, Eulene Fisher Shepherd, by the New Gilead Church . . . through their interest, devotion and hard work the members and friends of New Gilead Church are able to jubilantly celebrate the 200th Anniversary of its founding. The congregation wishes for them long years of fruitful service for our Master and His Church.

The current minister of New Gilead Church is Rev. H. Linn Finger.

ROSTER OF PASTORS

Rev. Christian		Rev. John H. Keller, D.D.,	
Theus ....Itinerate before 1786		Supply 1906-1909	
Rev. John Nicholas		Rev. Peter M. Trexler, D.D.,	
Martin ....Itinerate before 1786		Supply 1909-1910	
Rev. Richard		Rev. Dugan C. Cox,	
Dupert ....Itinerate before 1786		Supply 1911-	
Rev. Samuel		Mr. John M. Peck,	
Suther 1768-1771, 1782-1786		Summer Student Supply 1912-	
Rev. Andrew Loretz 1789-1795		Rev. Border L. Stanley,	
Rev. Samuel Weyberg 1796-1803		Supply 1913-1917	
Rev. George Boger 1803-1830		Rev. William C. Lyerly,	
Rev. Daniel B. Lerch,		Supply 1918-1923	
Supply 1830-1834		Rev. J. Dudley Maedor 1923-1925	
Rev. John Lantz, Supply 1837-1845		Rev. Hugo C. Kellermeyer 1929-1942	
Rev. Jeremiah Ingold, D.D. 1845-1855		Rev. Roy C. Whisenhunt 1942-1949	
Rev. Samuel Fetzer 1858-1861		Rev. Charles E. Hiatt 1950-1957	
Rev. J. W. Cecil 1864-1866		Mr. Van D. Grimes,	
Rev. John Ingle 1867-1873		Student Summer Supply 1957-	
Rev. Julius H. Shuford 1876-1877		Rev. Merle F. Sollinger 1958-1962	
Rev. Peter M. Trexler, D.D. 1877-1881		Rev. Felix B. Peck, S.T.D.,	
Rev. Paul Barringer, D.D. 1881-1894		Supply 1962-1963	
Rev. B. F. Davis 1894-1896		Rev. Banks D. Shepherd 1963-1966	
Rev. Paul Barringer, D.D. 1896-1900		Rev. H. Linn Finger 1966-	
Rev. John H. Keller, D.D. 1901-1906			

1. *Colonial Records*, North Carolina, Vol. V., 1752-1759, p. 256.
2. *Shepherd*, Banks D., New Gilead Church, 1966, p. 10.
3. *Ibid.* p. 10.
4. *Colonial Records*, North Carolina, Vol. 22, 1752-1759, p. 821.
5. *Clapp*, Jacob C., Editor, Historic Sketch of the Reformed Church in North Carolina, 1908, p. 203.
6. *Morgan*, Jacob L., Editor, History of the Lutheran Church in North Carolina, 1953, p. 186.
7. *Shepherd*, Op. cit., p. 24.
8. *Ibid.* p. 26ff.
9. ————. Minutes. Southern Synod of the Evangelical and Reformed Church, 1950, p. 12.
10. *Ibid.* p. 11.
11. *Shepherd. Op. cit.*, p. 42.

Paul's Chapel, Lexington

JAKESVILLE COMMUNITY is a settlement three miles West of Lexington, North Carolina, on the West Center Street Extension. Until 1946 no church had been established in that vicinity. In the spring of that year, a group of interested citizens consulted with Dr. A.

Odell Leonard, pastor of Second Evangelical and Reformed Church of Lexington, requesting that a church be established there. The request was referred to the consistory of Second Church, which body decided to sponsor the project and appointed a committee composed of Willie F. Everhart, David Briggs and Thad Hedrick to manage preliminary affairs concerning it.[1]

Ira Rea Michael granted permission to hold meetings in a tobacco pack house on his land near the present site of the church building, and on the afternoon of April 7, 1946, one hundred four persons assembled in the grove near the pack house for their initial meeting. The Sunday School was organized that afternoon, naming Cleveland Michael superintendent. Plans were also made to organize the congregation. On June 16, 1946, by popular vote, the assembly acted to affiliate with the Evangelical and Reformed Denomination. The congregation was formally organized Sunday afternoon July 21, 1946, with ninety-nine charter members, fifteen of whose letters of transfer had not yet been received.

Ernest Michael, Oliver Koontz, Paul Shoaf and W. M. Pickett were elected elders; and Virgil Leonard, Ray Roberson, William Leatherman and Clarence Coppley, deacons. Rev. Joshua L. Levens, president of Southern Synod, officially welcomed the congregation into membership with the Evangelical and Reformed Church. Dr. Ralph S. Weiler, Eastern Field Secretary of the Board of National Missions, expressed greetings and good wishes. Other members of the clergy present were: Rev. C. Columbus Wagoner and Rev. Hiram E. Davis. Dr. A. Odell Leonard, who had supervised operations to this point, was by the Council of Southern Synod appointed stated supply of the newly formed church.[2] The congregation was enrolled by the Board of National Missions with subsidy as of September 1, 1946.

Dr. O. Bain Michael donated the tract of land on which the church stands. Curtis Koontz gave an additional piece of land fronting on the hard surface road, and later, another tract of sixteen acres was acquired. This acreage "will give ample room for the proposed church building, cemetery, playground and community center, and other projects definitely in the future."[3] The building committee which had been named earlier, elected W. M. Pickett as its chairman; and the finance committee elected Conrad Koontz as its chairman. Building plans were developed to meet current needs, and these were approved. On Saturday afternoon, November 23, groundbreaking ceremonies were conducted.

Paul's Chapel is the subject of an interesting article under the caption of "The Church of the Week," which appeared in the Reformed Church Messenger January 21, 1947. It reflects something of the detailed activities in the early days of this unusual mission congregation.

Shortages on building materials were not going to keep this enterprising young congregation from getting the church building it so desperately needs. All last summer the people were holding services in a grove because the old tobacco shed where they were originally scheduled to meet could not accommodate the crowds who came—and never once was a service interrupted by rain. For evening services an electric line was extended and drop cords used to provide illumination. Since October they have been meeting in a little vacant house near by.

But the congregation proposes to have a church building without too much delay. After someone gave a tract of land, the people bought an additional sixteen acres for $1,900, and here they are assembling building materials from whatever source they can discover. Bricks have come from discarded tobacco barns, old chimneys, underpinnings of old houses, and even some removed in remodeling an old creamery have been brought in. When recently they dismantled the furnace of a blockade steam distillery, which county and federal officers had raided several weeks before, and added these new bricks to the stockpile at the church site, the pastor chuckled, "We really gave the old devil one right between the eyes that time."

. . . . . . Regular meetings were begun on the first Sunday in April of last year and have been held ever since. When three months later a congregation was organized, there were 104 charter members, with 140 children, young people and adults enrolled in the Sunday School. Members have been received by letter from the Lutheran, Baptist, Methodist, Dunkard and Evangelical and Reformed denominations, and others by adult baptism and confirmation.

. . . . . . Paul's Chapel congregation itself has contributed $3,842 and has raised and received from other sources a total of $11,000, all for the new church. A friend of the congregation, living over fifty miles away, seeing the possibilities a new church in this community would offer, wrote a check for $3,000 to furnish the interior when the church is completed.

And now work on the new building has actually been started. On Saturday afternoons the people will be digging the basement, using four of five tractors, and about twenty men. The excavating is practically complete and most of the materials necessary to enclose the building are on the grounds.

Paul's Chapel . . . has been so named in honor of Lindsay Paul Leonard, son of Rev. and Mrs. A. Odell Leonard, who lost his life in the war. The people in the neighborhood are working hard to develop a vital community center that will provide the necessary facilities for worship and education, a playground, and equipment for the varied activities that minister to the rural needs. Sponsored by the Board of National Missions, the congregation hopes to be free from any support by the board not more than five years after the date of organization.[4]

Regardless of available free labor and materials, large amounts of money had to be raised. The Women's Guild of the Evangelical and Reformed Church contributed $1,000; Southern Synod churches and friends added several thousand dollars more, and a loan was arranged from the Building Fund of the Churchmen's Brotherhood of Southern Synod. These favors helped, but the bulk of ready cash, always needed in building operations, came from members of the local congregation.

Cornerstone ceremonies for the new building took place Sunday afternoon, October 19, 1947, presided over by the pastor. Rev. C. Columbus Wagoner participated in the activities. Dedication occurred Sunday afternoon, November 19, 1949. Because the pastor was confined, recuperating from an attack of pneumonia, the officiating minister was Dr. Banks J. Peeler, a member of the Board of National Missions. Ceremonies began at the front doors, when Elder W. M. Pickett delivered the keys of the church to Treasurer Oliver Koontz. Following a responsive prayer, the congregation entered the sanctuary to complete the service. The dedicatory sermon was delivered by Dr. Lonnie A. Carpenter, president of Southern Synod. Other participating ministers were: Dr. Jacob A. Palmer, Rev. Lawrence A. Leonard and Rev. Charles E. Hiatt. Notes were burned as evidence that the building was free of debt.

Rev. Billy Joe Leonard was called to be the first full-time pastor of the congregation, being installed June 7, 1953. Rev. and Mrs. Leonard moved into the recently completed new parsonage located east of the church building, facing the hard surfaced road, December 12, 1953. During the next nine years, parish organizations were strengthened and the church program was greatly extended.

Rev. Homer L. Yearick began serving the church February 1963, and resigned in September 1964. Rev. James L. Peeler is the current minister of the congregation, which has a confirmed membership of 239 people, and a Sunday School enrollment of 234 pupils.

ROSTER OF PASTORS

Rev. A. Odell Leonard, D.D., Organizer and Stated Supply 1946-1953	Rev. Homer L. Yearick 1963-1964
Rev. Billy Joe Leonard 1953-1962	Rev. Harvey A. Fesperman, D.D., Supply 1964-1965
	Rev. James L. Peeler 1965-

1. *Leonard,* Billy Joe, Paul's Chapel, 10th Anniversary of Organization, 1956, p. 5 ff.
2. ————. Minutes. Southern Synod, 1947, p. 35.
3. ————. The Standard, No. 17, November 1, 1946, p. 2.
4. *Ibid.* No. 24, February 15, 1947, p. 1.

Peace Church, Greensboro

Greensboro, like other population centers in North Carolina, was neglected by missionary-minded leaders of the Reformed faith until the turn of the century. In March of 1901, an editorial by Dr. Joseph L. Murphy, appearing in the Reformed Church Corinthian, provoked discussion on this matter, reflecting specifically upon the Greensboro situation. The editorial, in part, commented, "The Rev. J. C. Leonard spent a day in Greensboro recently and took occasion to call upon some of the Reformed people living in that town. He finds a good number in the city who are standing aloof from other churches with the hope that sometime a congregation of their own faith will be organized."[1]

Evidently these loyal people had not only hoped that a church would be organized by the Classis of North Carolina, but had appealed to that body for assistance in founding one in Greensboro. In 1902 the Classis acted favorably on a resolution that had been presented for consideration. It reads:

> Whereas, the Reformed people living in Greensboro are earnest and persistent in their overtures for a Reformed Church in that city,
> Resolved, That the interests of our church in Greensboro be referred to Revs. J. C. Leonard and J. D. Andrew with instructions to minister to the people as time may permit and to canvass the whole matter with a view of organizing a congregation.[2]

Acting upon this authority, these two ministers preached alternately every two weeks in the homes of interested people and canvassed the area in anticipation of an organization. A first service was held in the home of George W. Clapp on Bragg Street, brother of Dr. Jacob C. Clapp.[3] Their report to Classis in 1903 follows:

> Soon after the adjournment of Classis, we made partial canvas of the city and found a number of Reformed people who were anxious for an organization. We held occasional services as time would permit, up to

March first of this year, when we organized a congregation with 17 charter members, under the name of First Reformed Church of Greensboro. John H. Lowe and D. E. Clapp were elected elders; and John F. Troxler and J. T. Plott, deacons, and were inducted into office.

In the meantime, we overtured the Board of Missions to enroll Greensboro as a mission, and our request was granted. Student H. S. T. Peeler will be commissioned to take charge July first next.[4]

Revs. J. C. Leonard and J. D. Andrew were appointed by the Classis to supply the mission until Student Peeler could finish his theological studies, be licensed to preach the Gospel and be ordained to the Christian ministry.[5]

Interested people were convened in the Friends Meeting House by these supply ministers on March 1, 1903 when the congregation was organized. Charter members included D. Ed Clapp, Mrs. D. Ed Clapp, Minnie Clapp, Mrs. James Clark, Emmitt H. Everhart, W. A. Greeson, Mrs. Mattie Lewis, John H. Low, Mrs. John H. Low, Thomas G. Lowe, Mrs. Thomas G. Lowe, Mrs. Callie Lowe McKeithan, John T. Plott, Mrs. John T. Plott, John F. Troxler, Mrs. John F. Troxler and Mrs. Nancy Clapp.[6]

Enrollment by the Board of Missions occurred in April of 1903. Arrangements were made with officials of the Christian Church, and services were held there during the first three months. Theological Student Shuford Peeler was commissioned by the Board of Missions as minister to the congregation, licensed to preach the Gospel by the Classis of North Carolina on May 20, 1903, and two months later, July 12, was ordained to the Christian ministry.

An imperative primary move was to find a place within the parish where the congregation could meet for worship. Property at the corner of West Lee and Spring Streets was acquired for the sum of $1,500. A brick dwelling which stood on the lot was immediately converted into a suitable chapel, and first meetings were held there on the first Sunday in October of 1903. On the same day, a Sunday School was established, enrolling 35 pupils. This arrangement met the immediate needs of the congregation but was soon outgrown.

In September 1904, a foundation for the first unit of the new church building was laid. This unit was constructed with a chapel and a number of classrooms and was architecturally designed to fit a larger plan, including the proposed sanctuary. First services were held in the new structure in April 1905.

Erection of the sanctuary began early in 1906 and it was occupied and dedicated November 18, 1906, in a series of services which began on Sunday morning and continued through the afternoon and evening. Dr. Jacob C. Leonard presented the Communion meditation at 11 a.m.; Dr. Jacob C. Clapp delivered the dedicatory address at 3 p.m.; and Dr. James D. Andrew and Dr. George A. Snyder addressed the congregation at the evening meeting. Activities of the day were under the supervision of the pastor.

This new house of worship, now complete, provided a sanctuary to seat 400 people and a Sunday School assembly room separated from the sanctuary by rolling partitions and certain classroom space. Expenditures to date amounted to slightly more than $11,000. This equipment met needs of the congregation during the next 16 years when in 1922, in order to provide for increased Sunday School enrollment, a hut was erected on a lot at the rear of the church building.

Stimulated by a fast expanding Sunday School enrollment and crowded conditions, ideas of relocation sifted through the congregation. For these reasons, during the pastorate of Dr. Harvey A. Fesperman, a lot on Mendenhall Street was acquired. Consensus in the congregation did not support the move to relocate at that time. Later, when it was considered inadvisable to build a church on it, the lot was sold. Instead of making further plans to relocate in the foreseeable future a three-story brick annex was erected on Spring Street, during the pastorate of Rev. William C. Lyerly, providing space for additional Sunday School and youth activities. This structure was dedicated November 15, 1931, and served the purpose until 1937.

Congregational interests continued to expand, and the influence of the parish spread over the larger Greensboro community. With this extended horizon appeared, again thoughts of relocation. Therefore, in 1951 a beautiful and ideally located property, covering approximately three acres of land, located at West Market Street and Lindell Road, was purchased for $14,000. By this time the confirmed membership of First Church had reached 546, large enough to undertake a sizable building program. Thus began one of the most demanding, and at the same time, rewarding periods in the life of the congregation. This undertaking involved relocation and the erection of appropriate buildings adequate for a modern church program in a growing city; also, including broad outlines for an effective program of Christian service on the parish, an undertaking always fraught with tremendous problems. Rev. Hoy L. Fesperman, a quiet, even-tempered gracious Christian minister, was destined to spearhead the venture.

A planning committee composed of Mr. Fesperman, Mrs. LeRoy Leftwich, Otis Walker, J. R. Holshouser, Raymond C. Keck, Robert H. W. Jones, Jr. and John W. Starr was named, under whose leadership plans for a multi-purpose church facility was developed, and in time, approved by the congregation. The decision was reached to erect first the educational unit, including a chapel, classrooms and office space; also a social hall with appropriate equipment, leaving the sanctuary for a later date when it could be adequately financed. Groundbreaking ceermonies occurred June 17, 1956, and construction began the following day. The cornerstone was laid October 28, 1956, when Dr. Harvey A. Fesperman, president of Southern Synod and former pastor of the church, delivered the address. First services were held in the new building on February 24, 1957, at which time expenditures thus far amounted to approximately $250,000. On that date the practice of two services each Sunday morning was begun, one scheduled for 9 a.m. and the other at 11 o'clock. Sunday School convened between the two worship periods. This plan met with such satisfaction that it has been continued. Dedication rites for the chapel and educational unit took place on June 16, 1957.

The story is interrupted at this point with a bit of healthy nostalgia. On Monday, February 25, 1957, following the first service in the new building, razing of the old building on West Lee Street began, the cornerstone being the first part to be removed. The dedicatory brochure commented as follows concerning it:

> It is with a deep sense of sadness we see the lovely old church on West Lee Street torn down; but we feel that it has accomplished a great purpose and we tell it goodbye with reverence. It was there we saw and felt much joy and some sorrow. However, time passes on, and we look to the future with much faith and hope that within a few more months we can worship in the new and complete church sanctuary, even as we now worship in the educational building and chapel.[7]

The West Lee Street property was sold in two parts. That part fronting on West Lee Street containing the old church building was sold in May of 1957 to the Sun Oil Company, and the back portion, fronting on Spring Street, was purchased in February 1960 by the Frank Hockett Supply Company. The old organ was sold to a Negro congregation in Graham, North Carolina.

The first parsonage was acquired March 16, 1916, when a house next door to the church on West Lee Street was purchased from Nathan S. Hunter for $4,750, reconditioned and made a home for the second pastor of the church, Dr. and Mrs. Abram D. Wolfinger. This house continued to be used as a parsonage until 1946, when the property located at 118 East Fisher Circle was purchased, which was later sold. Rev. and Mrs. Joshua L. Levens were the last people to live in the West Lee Street house. Sale of the Fisher Circle property left the church without a parsonage until in 1961, when a new modern house was erected as a home for the minister on Lindell Street, next door to the church. This structure involved an expenditure of $23,250.

Rev. Hoy L. Fesperman died June 16, 1960, after completing the first unit of a building program and measurably developing a plan of parish activities in which he had invested so much of himself. In March of 1961 an Interdenominational Outdoor Altar and Worship Center was dedicated to his memory. This dedication took place in conjunction with the 58th anniversary observation of the congregation. The center was his idea but unfinished when he died. It was fashioned by stone and shrubs, material assembled from many sources at home and abroad, and finished by a grateful people. It is a suggestive, relaxing spot located at the southwest corner of the church school building.

On October 5, 1958, St. Peter's United Church of Christ located on Phillips Avenue was organized with a charter list of 62 members. This was a project jointly sponsored by the First Evangelical and Reformed and the First Congregational Christian Churches. After the merger had been officially effected of the Evangelical and Reformed and the Congregational Christian Churches, forming the United Church of Christ, two "First" churches of the same communion in the same community created confusion, therefore, to adjust to the new picture, by action of the congregation, First Evangelical and Reformed Church became Peace United Church of Christ.

Since 1960 Rev. G. Melvin Palmer has been pastor of Peace Church. In completing the first unit of its modern church facility, the congregation moved to liquidate all debts on the property, and on June 5, 1966, observed the occasion with a noteburning ritual, conducted at the doors of the chapel. The ceremony was directed by the pastor. Dr. Banks J. Peeler, president of Southern Synod, Acting Association of Southern Conference, delivered the address.

Three sons of the congregation have been ordained to the Christian ministry, Rev. G. Ermine Plott, Rev. H. Grady Shoffner, D.D., and Rev. A. Gail Holt.

ROSTER OF PASTORS

Rev. Shuford Peeler, D.D. 1903-1915	D.D. 1921-1930
Rev. Abram D. Wolfinger,	Rev. William C. Lyerly 1931-1937
D.D. 1916-1918	Rev. Joshua L. Levens 1938-1946
Rev. Frank R. LeFevre 1918-1920	Rev. Hoy L. Fesperman 1946-1960
Rev. Harvey A. Fesperman,	Rev. G. Melvin Palmer 1960-

1. *Murphy*, Joseph L., The Reformed Church Corinthian, 1901, Vol. 8, p. 4.
2. ———. Minutes. Classis of North Carolina, 1902, p. 249.
3. *Levens*, Joshua L., The Fortieth Anniversary of the First Evangelical and Reformed Church, 1943, p. 4 ff.
4. ———. Minutes. *Op. cit.*, 1903, p. 280.
5. ———. Minutes. *Op. cit.*, 1904, p. 335.
6. *Jones*, Mrs. R. H. W., Sr., History of Peace United Church of Christ, 1965, p. 2.
7. *Jones*, Mrs. R. H. W., Sr., History of the Evangelical and Reformed Church, 1957, p. 18. Dedication Brochure.

Pilgrim Church, Davidson County

GERMAN MIGRANTS, originally from the Palatinate region around the Rhine River, came to Forsyth, Davidson and Rowan Counties from Pennsylvania in great numbers, beginning in 1740. The movement reached high tide about mid 1750. Among those reaching the "South Fork of Abbott's Creek," later known as "Leonard's Creek," were the following "heads of house" and their families: Jacob Berrier, Phillip Sowers, Jacob Hege, Henry Shoaf, Valentine Leonard, Christopher Sprecher, John George Sprecher, Adam Hedrick, Peter Meyers, Sr., Adam Conrad, Jacob Byerly and Peter Spengler.[1] These people were of the Reformed, Lutheran and Moravian faiths, and

thoroughly committed to the practice of religion as they understood it.

Among these were three men who established themselves as leaders and were widely influential in the affairs of the settlement in their generation. Jacob Berrier, who with neighbors established the site of the "Church of the Pilgrims"; Valentine Leonard, whose family was so largely a part of and active in the Pilgrim Congregation, that by common practice it came to be referred to as "Leonard's Church;" and Phillip Sowers, who acted to reserve the 50 acre piece of land which was later deeded to the congregation, and who became a charter member of Beulah (Sowers) Church when it was organized in 1787.

Pilgrim Church is located four miles North of Lexington, North Carolina, one half mile West of the Old Greensboro Highway. It stands on an elevation, in a grove of sugar-maple trees, overlooking "Leonard's Creek." There, in 1753 or perhaps 1754, Pioneer Jacob Berrier and his neighbors decided should be erected a "meeting house." So they moved to have the 50 acres of land lying between holdings of Phillip Sowers and Valentine Leonard reserved for that purpose.[2] The meeting house did not immediately appear, but following the practices of other migrants who had come to North Carolina, a brush arbor was erected under which religious gatherings took place. For as many as six years this temporary shelter met the needs of German settlers East of the Yadkin River. Thus, this place became the focal point for German Protestants in the area for a period of approximately thirty years.

The date when the Church was organized is in question. Some claim that it occurred as early as 1754,[3] certainly not later than 1757. The earliest known church book of Pilgrim Reformed Church, dated 1757, is in the State Department of History and Archives, Raleigh, North Carolina. In it are listed 145 baptisms, before the year 1787, of them 33 were recorded before 1772. Thirty six paternal heads of families, sometimes referred to as "baptismal sponsors" or "godparents," are listed. These are: Adam Hedrick, William

Younts (Janss), Henry Happes, George Hege (Heeke), Jacob Leonard, Phillip Leonard, Valentine Leonard, John Henry Darr, Michael Zink, Phillip Sowers (Sauer), John Zink, Phillip Zink, Michael Dag (Day), John Peter Spenger, Jacob Crotts (Kratz), Michael Leonard, John George Berrier, Peter Kiehn, Jr., Henry Hege, John Jacob Wagner, John George Clodfelter, Peter Meyer (Myres), Adam Conrad, John Henry Shoaf (Schaff), Henry Shoaf, Sr., Ludolph Younts, John Martin Berrier, David Berrier, Michael Myers, David Myers, Peter Myers, George Sprecher, Peter Everhart, Henry Conrad, Christian Grimes (Krime), Peter Lopp (Lapp).[4]

It is reasonable, therefore, to conclude that this historic act took place under the supervision of Rev. Christian Theus, who made seasonal visits to this parish over a period of years, prior to 1759. Pilgrim German Reformed Church could very well have been organized as early as 1754. It is difficult to believe that deeply religious business men such as Jacob Berrier, Valentine Leonard and Phillip Sowers would be satisfied to postpone an act so fundamentally important in the religious life of the settlement.

The first house of worship was built during the pastorate of Rev. James Martin, which began in 1759. It was erected on the 50 acres of land which had been previously reserved for church purposes, when North Carolina was a Province and the land belonged to Lord Granville, whose agent was one Henry McCulloch. Before North Carolina became a Sovereign State it was considered necessary to secure "Letters Patent," which act was attended to October 8, 1783. The document was signed by Governor Alexander Martin, and the land was conveyed to "Philip Sours (Sauer), P. Karn and M. Shiddles, Elders in the Dutch Congregation in trust for the aforesaid Congregation fifty acres of land lying and being in our county of Rowan on the waters of Abbott's Creek."[5] Four years later, in 1787, "Lutherans came in as co-tenants, and from that time on had the use of the church and the lands. There is no record as to the terms on which they were admitted."[6]

Later additions to the property, and legal actions involved, have been described as follows:

> December 1, 1792, a second tract of land consisting of eighty-six acres, was granted to "John Lopp, George Hege, George Clodfelter and Valentine Day, as Trustees of the Dutch Congregation and their successors."
>
> A third grant was made by the State of North Carolina, under the date of November 24, 1869, to Henry Darr, Wm. Sink, and Jesse Leonard, Trustees of Pilgrim Church. The plot surveyed by P. F. Zink, County Surveyor, calls for twenty-seven acres. There seems to have been some doubt about the second patent in 1792 concerning the land, and to make certain that this is church land, the above named trustees secured the patent signed by Governor W. W. Holden.[7]

With these transactions, titles appear to be clear on all land-holdings by the congregation, totaling 136 acres.

The first church building was constructed of logs, and fashioned after the common pattern of the day. It had a gallery at each end and on one side. At the other side stood the wine-glass pulpit. After using the old church for fifty years, in 1807, the Reformed and Lutheran congregations united to build a more suitable house of worship designed to more nearly meet the needs of the day. It was patterned after the old log church, but a frame two-story building. Extensively repaired in 1834, the house continued to serve the two constituencies until 1882, when the third and present sanctuary was erected. Dedication Services were in charge of Revs. Thomas Long, C. H. Bernheim and W. A. Julian. Dr. Jacob C. Clapp, president of Catawba College, made the dedicatory address.

Reformed and Lutheran brethren lived peaceably together until 1821, when an unfortunate rupture occurred in the Lutheran section of the Dutch Congregation. The Lutheran Church was divided. Two congregations resulted; one affiliating with the North Carolina Synod of the Lutheran denomination, and the other with the Tennessee Synod. All three groups then operated in the same building until 1903, when in the interest of peace and goodwill, an arbitrating committee was appointed to recommend an acceptable plan for the dissolution of the property, assets of which aggregated $5,800. "By the terms of the agreement, the land was sold in three tracts, over two acres being reserved for the cemetery, and the church building was sold separately. . . . The Reformed congregation purchased the largest tract of land, also the house of worship."[8] Since that time Pilgrim Reformed Congregation has been operating on the original site of the Dutch Congregation, and making commendable progress.

Pilgrim Church has established itself as a friend of education. This is authenticated by two effective schools created and largely supported by the congregation. The Pilgrim Schoolhouse stood for more than thirty years, Southwest of the sanctuary on church property. Upon his return from the Civil War, Adam Hedrick served for a number of years as headmaster of that school.[9]

Before the State School System established High Schools in order to fill the gap between the grades and college requirements, public-spirited citizens created private academies on the high school level, in order to meet the need. Pilgrim Academy was one of those schools. It was founded by Rev. Jacob C. Leonard in 1890, when he was pastor of Pilgrim Church, and supported by the congregation. The building as well as the ground upon which it stood were property of Pilgrim Reformed Church. The Public District School, which had been located near the original church site, was for a time conducted in connection with the Academy. When the Academy could no longer serve a purpose in the State School System, it was used by the county for school purposes, free of charge. In 1929 old Pilgrim Academy became a "Kiddy Kamp," sponsored by the Lexington Kiwanis Club as a part of its program for indigent children. This service continued until 1945, when the property was sold. Since then it has been privately owned.[10]

Pilgrim Church had no parsonage until 1888. Until then there was no actual need for one. Pastors either lived in other communities, or in their own homes. Then, a large two-story frame house was built on the Greensboro Highway four miles North of Lexington, near the church. The new pastor, Rev. Jacob C. Leonard, a bachelor and a son of the congregation, moved into the house, which was already occupied by Sheriff A. T. DeLapp and his family, who made a home for him, and a number of boys who were attending the nearby Pilgrim Academy. This house was used as a parsonage for the Upper Davidson Charge until 1934. During the pastorate of Rev. Joshua L. Levens, a new house was built for the Charge near Beulah Church.

When, in 1951, the Upper Davidson Charge was dissolved, and Pilgrim Church became a one-point Charge, a new seven-roomed frame house was built on church property. It was completed and ready for occupancy by December 1951. In April 1952, after 195 years of operating in a charge with one or more congregations, the Rev. Gerald R. Cobb moved into the parsonage as their first full-time pastor.

Two other units of material expansion during this period should be mentioned in this connection. In 1927, supported by the Woman's Missionary Society, a hut designed to meet increasing social and recreational needs was erected on the east side near the sanctuary. This building was expanded and improved in 1956, and again in 1957. In 1934 educational facilities, consisting of eight classrooms and a large basement room were attached to the North end of the church building. Additional classrooms, and a choir loft in the sanctuary, were constructed in 1960.

Following a well designed plan for program enrichment, begun in 1935, the congregation moved steadily in the direction of its 200th Birthday. The occasion was appropriately observed in a series of well planned religious services scheduled for August 13 to 18, 1957. Among former pastors who addressed the congregation during that important week were: Rev. Hoy L. Fesperman, Dr. Jacob A. Palmer, Rev. Gerald R. Cobb, Rev. Joshua L. Levens, Rev. Huitt R. Carpenter, Dr. A. Odell Leonard and Rev. Carl T. Daye. Dr. David Dunn, Professor of History, Lancaster Theological Seminary, delivered the anniversary address. A history of the congregation, entitled "First Church, Davidson County," edited by the pastor Rev. Frank W. Snider was released.

These activities added momentum to a movement begun August 11, 1957, when the consistory voted to begin a Building Fund, in anticipation of adequate educational and worship facilities. By 1959 a Building and Planning Committee was authorized. On August 7, 1960, the committee asked approval for the following proposal, and got it.

The Building and Planning Committee recommends, that an educational building approximately 90 feet by 40 feet be constructed on the West side of the present building, with classrooms in the basement (first floor) and a Fellowship Hall on the second floor. To be of brick and block construction, and to be constructed so that a sanctuary can be added later.

Under the leadership of Rev. Robert F. Godfrey, who began his ministry to the congregation January 1, 1961, preliminary plans for the building were ready for approval in November 1963. Bids totaling $112,000 were accepted in June 1964, and the building was completed and ready for use in 1965.

Pilgrim, the oldest Reformed United Church of Christ in Davidson County, has kept abreast of the time in equipment, program and leadership. Its equipment combines to a delightful degree the old and the new. Its program is inclusive, emphasizing most of the major interests of the denomination of which it is a part. Each generation has produced typically reliable leadership. For instance, Mrs. Ida Hedrick Conrad became the first president of the Woman's Missionary Society of the North Carolina Classical, when it was organized in June 1897. Mrs. Jesse Leonard Kepley is a commissioned Director of Christian Education in the United Church of Christ and a leading teacher in the public schools of Davidson County. Sons of the congregation who have served the Church as ministers of the Gospel are: Revs. H. F. Long, D.D., W. A. Long, Ph.D., J. C. Leonard, D.D., J. L. Bowers and Chaplain Lt. Col. Joseph D. Andrew.

ROSTER OF PASTORS

Rev. Christian Theus, Visiting
   Minister before .... -1759
Rev. James Martin 1759-1764
Rev. Richard Dupert 1764-1768
Rev. Samuel Suther 1768-1786
Rev. Jacob Schneider 1787-1792
Rev. Samuel Weyberg 1793-1798
Rev. Jacob Christman 1798-1803
Rev. George Roger 1803-1812
Rev. Andrew Loretz 1803-1812
Rev. William Weinel 1803-1812
Rev. H. B. Diefenbach 1803-1812
Rev. Jacob Schell 1803-1812
Rev. J. S. Ebaugh 1812-1827
Rev. George Leidy 1812-1827
Rev. John Rudy 1812-1827
Rev. William Houck 1828-1832
Rev. W. C. Bennet 1832-1838
Rev. David Crooks 1838-1846
Rev. F. W. Blassman 1846-1848
Rev. Thornton Butler 1848-1851
Rev. William Sorber 1853-1856
Rev. Thornton Butler 1856-1857
Rev. P. A. Long 1858-1864
Rev. Thomas Long 1864-1887
Rev. G. Dickie Gurley,
   Assistant 1885-1886
Rev. J. H. Shuford 1887-1888
Rev. Jacob C. Leonard, D.D. 1889-1897
Rev. H. A. M. Holshouser,
   Ph.D. 1897-1903
Rev. William H. Causey,
   D.D. 1903-1907

Rev. W. A. Long, Ph.D.,
   Supply 1907-1910
Rev. John A. Ditzler, Supply 1907-1910
Rev. William H. McNairy,
   D.D. 1910-1911
Rev. Jacob A. Palmer, D.D. 1912-1918
Rev. James D. Andrew, D.D. 1918-1924
Rev. A. Odell Leonard, D.D.,
   Supply 1925-1927
Mr. Charles E. Hiatt, Student
   Summer Supply, 2 summers 1925-1926
Rev. Hoy L. Fesperman 1927-1929
Rev. A. Odell Leonard, D.D.,
   Stated Supply 1929-1934
Mr. Huitt R. Carpenter,
   Student Summer Supply 1929-1934
Mr. Carl H. Clapp,
   Student Summer Supply......1929-1934
Mr. Joshua L. Levens,
   Student Summer Supply 1929-1934
Rev. Joshua L. Levens 1934-1937
Rev. C. Columbus Wagoner 1938-1946
Rev. Carl T. Daye 1947-1950
Rev. Alfred Sandrock,
   Supply 1950-1951
Rev. Gerald R. Grubb 1952-1956
Rev. G. Melvin Palmer,
   Supply 1956-
Rev. Frank Snider 1956-1961
Rev. Robert F. Godfrey 1961-1968
Rev. James E. Neese 1968-

1. *Snider,* Frank W., Editor. First Church, Davidson County, 1957, p. 8.
2. *Clapp,* Jacob C., Editor. Historic Sketch of the Reformed Church in North Carolina, 1908, p. 157.
3. *Morgan,* Jacob L., Editor. History of the Lutheran Church in North Carolina, 1953, p. 268.
4. *Leonard,* Jacob C., History of the Southern Synod, Evangelical and Reformed Church, 1940, p. 164.
5. *Ibid.* p. 165.
6. *Clapp. Op. cit.,* p. 164.
7. *Leonard. Op. cit.,* p. 166.
8. *Ibid.* p. 167.
9. *Godfrey,* Robert F., An Historical Sketch of Pilgrim United Church of Christ, 1964, p. 4.
10. *Leonard,* Jacob C., Centennial History of Davidson County, North Carolina, 1927, p. 228.

Rodger's Park Church, Kannapolis

RODGER'S PARK EVANGELICAL AND REFORMED CHURCH, Kannapolis, North Carolina, is the result of a suggestion made to his pastor, Rev. G. Harold Myers, by Benjamin Sechlar, that the Rodger's Park Area should be served by an organized church. With this thought in mind the two men visited the community, and subsequently founded an Evangelical and Reformed church there. The community was new and a considerable number of new homes had been erected. Mr. Myers began holding religious services in available homes among interested people. Interest in these activities grew. Mt. Zion Evangelical and Reformed Church sponsored them, which were supervised from the beginning by its pastor, until the congregation was organized and a missionary appeared on the field.

On February 1, 1951 twenty people presented a petition to the Synodical Council, asking that a church be organized and admitted into the Southern Synod. The petition was approved, and two weeks later, February 18, the congregation was officially organized, and reported to the Synod at its spring meeting.[1] The report follows:

> At the authorization of the Synod, Mt. Zion Evangelical and Reformed Consistory and Pastor organized Rodger's Park Evangelical and Reformed Church on February 18th at the home of Mr. & Mrs. Jesse Carter, Route 2, China Grove, North Carolina. Twenty-one charter members constitute the membership at the present time. Two elders: James Deal and Benjamine Sechler, and two deacons: Jesse Ritchie and Glenn Smith compose the consistory.
>
> We, the charter members of Roger's Park Church, desire to be received on the roster of churches of Southern Synod, with all rights and privileges of a duly organized congregation. Sincerely.

(Signed by)

> Mr. & Mrs. James Deal, Mr. & Mrs. Richard Correll, Mr. & Mrs. Glenn Smith, Mr. & Mrs. Jesse Ritchie, Mr. & Mrs. Talbert Howell, Miss Dorothy Carter, Mr. & Mrs. Benjamin Sechler, Mr. & Mrs. Floyd Deal, Mr. & Mrs. Ernie Carter, Mr. & Mrs. Jesse Carter, Raymond Sechler, Rev. G. Harold Myers, Pastor on the Mission Field, Mt. Zion Consistory, China Grove.[2]

Shortly thereafter the Mission was enrolled by the Board of National Missions with subsidy, and served during the summer of 1951 by ministerial student Earl Koehler. Fellowship Hall, a frame structure, was erected on previously acquired land, located on Route 1, Kannapolis, North Carolina, and dedicated June 10, 1951. The building was used for all purposes by the congregation until the new church was ready for occupancy. Fellowship Hall, and the parsonage located about a quarter of a mile east of the church, were constructed of material donated by the sponsoring congregation.

Rev. Walter Rauh was commissioned by the Board of National Missions as Missionary Pastor, and reported for duty beginning September 13, 1953. His installation as pastor of the church took place the following November 1. Through loans and a money grant from the Board of National Missions, and help from the sponsoring congregation and friends, a two-story brick church building was erected. Groundbreaking exercises occurred in June 1954. Because of limited funds, only the ground floor was finished and equipped for use.

From September 23, 1956 until 1959 the parish was served by ministerial students, studying at Catawba College and the Theological Seminary, Lancaster, Pennsylvania. Ordained ministers of the church living in the area took care of sacramental functions and rites such as confirmation, baptisms, weddings, funerals and administering the Holy Communion.

Theological Student Max L. Tussey, who had supplied the church during the previous summer, upon graduation from Theological School, became the second pastor, on June 21, 1959. He was installed pastor of the church July 12, and served there until December 1, 1962. His ministry was substantial, chiefly defined as consistent pastoral oversight and administrative intelligence.[3]

Another period of ministerial student supplies is recorded which began in 1959 and continued through 1963. This supply work was supported by neighboring pastors who filled in as required, chiefly Dr. Lonnie A. Carpenter, Rev. Huitt R. Carpenter and Rev. C. Larry Fisher. During this time financial obligation accumulated, resulting from loans and commitments previously made because of building operations; however, the outlook of the congregation continued positive and highly optimistic.

Rev. N. Ellis Vandegrift, with privilege of call, was invited to serve the congregation beginning November 1, 1963. Mr. Vandegrift was a transfer minister from the Southern Baptist Church. Serving with distinction during his apprentice year, upon that record was called by the Rodger's Park Church to become its pastor. The call was aproved by the Council of Southern Synod. Installation Services were conducted by Dr. Banks J. Peeler, president of the Synod, on October 25, 1964. Soon thereafter difficulties developed on the parish, and he resigned both the Rodger's Park Church and the Southern Synod, effective May 15, 1965.[4] During this short pastorate debts were paid, members were added to the church roll, and in April 1965, the sanctuary was finished, fully equipped and occupied at a cost of $20,000.

An arrangement was made with ministerial student David Gene Peeler, who was studying at Catawba College, to supply the congregation beginning June 1, 1965. This relationship continued until September 1966, when Mr. Peeler enrolled at the Theological Seminary, Lancaster, Pennsylvania for further study. Licentiate Donald D. Sledge began serving on the parish June 1, 1966. He was ordained to the Christian Ministry June 4, 1967 at the Rodger's Park Church, and at the same time installed its pastor. Officiating clergymen were Dr. Clyde L. Fields, who preached the sermon; Dr. Banks J .Peeler, who heard the ordination vows; and Rev. Edwin M. Alcorn, who conducted the installation rites.

This parish is set up for acceptable Christian service to the community. The Sunday School, Women's Guild, Churchmen's Brotherhood and youth activities were all begun in 1954. The congregation has a confirmed membership of 141 people, and a Sunday School enrollment of 160 pupils.

ROSTER OF PASTORS AND SUPPLIES

Rev. G. Harold Meyers,
    Supervisory 1950-1953
Mr. Earl Koehler,
    Summer Student Supply 1951-
Mr. James R. Cress,
    Student Supply 1951-
Mr. Frank W. Snider,
    Student Supply 1952-
Mr. Carl C. Kreps,
    Student Supply 1952-1953
Mr. Jack Kasten,
    Summer Student Supply 1953-

Rev. Walter Rauh 1953-1956
Rev. Lee A. Peeler, D.D.,
    Supply 1956-
Mr. Elmo D. Beck,
    Student Supply 1956-1957
Rev. John J. Carey, Ph.D.,
    Supply 1956-1957
Mr. Max L. Tussey,
    Summer Student Supply 1958-
Mr. Doyce Wise,
    Student Supply 1958-1959
Rev. Max L. Tussey 1959-1962

Rev. Lonnie A. Carpenter, D.D.,
Alternate Supply 1962-1963
Rev. Huitt R. Carpenter,
Alternate Supply 1962-1963
Rev. C. Larry Fisher
Alternate Supply 1962-1963
Mr. James L. Peeler,
Summer Student Supply 1963-

Rev. N. Ellis Vandegrift, Privilege
of Call, Supply 1963-1964
Rev. N. Ellis Vandegrift 1964-1965
Mr. David Gene Peeler,
Student Supply 1965-1966
Mr. Donald D. Sledge,
Student Supply 1966-1967
Rev. Donald D. Sledge 1967-

1. ———. Minutes. Southern Synod of the Evangelical and Reformed Church, 1951, p. 11.
2. *Ibid.* p. 34.
3. *Tussey*, Max L., Anniversary Parish Newsletter, 1961, p. 2.
4. ———. Southern Synod Records, the file, 1965.

Shiloh Church, Faith

THE SITE OF THE ORIGINAL "Shiloh German Reformed Church" is approximately three miles south of Salisbury, near the junction of what is currently known as the Faith and Old Granite Quarry roads. A tract of land consisting of two and one-half acres, located southwest from this point on a beautifully elevated wooded spot, was deeded by J. W. Fisher and T. W. Haynes to Dewalt Kluttz, F. M. Holshouser and Michael Beaver, deacons of the German Reformed Church for this purpose. The transaction took place January 1, 1873, and involved the sum of $5.00.[1]

Religious Services were conducted in the community log school house prior to 1871 by the Rev. J. C. Denny and ministerial student,

Peter M. Trexler, for the convenience of people who lived in the area. Resulting from these activities, sentiment began to develop in favor of organizing a church there. A church building was erected during the winter of 1870-1871. About two miles southwest of this location, stood an old frame church building which had fallen into disuse because of a defunct Methodist congregation. This structure was purchased for a small sum of money from the Methodist Conference, and usable material worked into the house of worship. When, on March 19, 1871, the congregation was born, because of its connection with this former Shiloh Methodist Church from which a few of the members of the new congregation had come, the new church was named Shiloh Reformed Church.

The congregation was organized by the Rev. J. C. Denny, who was then serving as pastor of the East Rowan Charge, with seventeen charter members. No record is available giving the names of this charter list, but it is known that J. W. Fisher and T. H. Webb were elected elders, and W. E. Dunham and Dewalt Kluttz were elected deacons. Peter M. Trexler, who had been licensed by the North Carolina Classis, and Mr. Denny cooperatively served the congregation until September 17, 1871, when Licentiate Trexler was ordained to the Christian Ministry and installed pastor of the newly created Central Rowan Charge, consisting of Mt. Hope and Shiloh congregations.[2]

The next twenty-five years tell a story of devoted churchmanship, struggle, and sickening intrigue. The first part of it reflects excellent churchmanship, and met with good results. On Saturday, September 16, 1871, following the Preparatory Service for the Holy Communion which was to be administered the next morning in connection with the ordination and installation of Licentiate Trexler, the Joint Consistories of the Rowan Charges convened at Shiloh Church. On this occasion the "famous Shiloh Resolutions" were presented, adopted and signed. These same resolutions evidently were later favorably acted upon by the Shiloh, Lower Stone and Bear Creek congregations, and in December of that year brought to the attention of the North Carolina Classis.[3] Because they reflect something of the unsettled conditions current among these involved churches as well as throughout the Classis, these resolutions are included in "The Shiloh Story."[4]

SHILOH RESOLUTIONS

At a special meeting of the Joint Consistories of the Rowan Charges, of the North Carolina Classis, called for the purpose, at Shiloh on the 16th day of September 1871, the following Preamble and Resolutions were unanimously adopted:

Whereas, The Rev. Dr. S. R. Fisher, Editor of the Reformed Church Messenger, whilst on a visit to his relatives residing within the bounds of these Charges, was by special solicitation induced to preach repeatedly in our several churches, we deem it due to him and to ourselves, that some written expression of our views and feelings in regard to his labors of love amongst us should be given, therefore,—

Resolved, that we and the people whom we represent, unitedly and individually, have been highly gratified and much edified by his purely evangelical, earnest and impressive sermons preached in our churches; and that we can not but regard his visit amongst us at this time as providential and believe that extensive beneficial results will flow from it.

Resolved, that we sincerely believe, that the true interests of the Reformed Church in North Carolina, will, and only can be successfully promoted by continuing our connection with the Mother Churches in the north, and by cultivating and preserving proper relations with them, and that, therefore, we not only cannot and will not entertain or cherish the least sympathy with movements from whatever quarter they may proceed, which look either directly or indirectly to the Secession or alienation of the Southern from the Northern Reformed Churches, but, also, most sincerely depreciate, and unqualifiedly denounce anything of its kind.

Resolved, that in accordance with the expression of sentiment given in a lengthy and able document by the Synod of the Reformed Church in the United States, in 1820, we hold that it is inconsistent in a minister of the Gospel, and prejudicial to his usefulness, to accept of, and fill a secular office under the temporal government, in any circumstance, and must therefore, disapprove of the conduct of such ministers of the Gospel as not only accept of such secular office, but also seek it in the use of the usual appliances incident to political electioneering campaigns—sad examples of which we have in the North Carolina Classis.

Resolved, that we highly approve of the Reformed Church Messenger, published by the Synod of the Reformed Church in the United States, as an excellent and well conducted religious paper, and that we will use every proper effort to have it placed, if possible, in every family within the bounds of the congregation belonging to the pastoral charges we represent.

Resolved, that we deem the "Child's Treasury," published by the Reformed Church Publication Board at Philadelphia, a most excellent paper, well adapted to the wants and interests of Sunday Schools, and, that we most cordially recommend it to our superintendents and teachers, and will endeavor to introduce it more fully into the several families within our bounds.

Resolved, that a copy of the above Preamble and Resolutions, signed by the President and Secretary of this meeting, be furnished the Reformed Church Messenger, and the Christian World for their publication in their respective columns.

T. H. Webb, President

F. Monroe Holshouser, Secretary

The second part of the Shiloh Story begins in the latter part of Mr. Denny's pastorate. In 1883 Mr. Denny was cited by the Classis for what appears to have been a series of bad administrative decisions on the local parish. An invitation issued by the congregation to the Methodist Conference in session at the time in Salisbury, to send to them suitable ministers to conduct a series of revival services, was promptly accepted. They did their work so well that, under the fever of revival excitement, an unauthorized congregational meeting was called to test sentiment for transferring the church into the Methodist Conference. The maneuver split the church; and, as a result, almost one half of the congregation was lost to the Methodist Church.

This experience greatly compromised the Christian Fellowship, and damaged the influence of the congregation in the community.

Undoubtedly, if it had not been for the sound judgment of John W. Fisher, Daniel M. Kluttz, F. Monroe Holshouser and Crawford Peeler, who refused to surrender the property, the entire congregation would have been lost to the denomination. Mr. Denny steadfastly refused to make an official report and/or to appear before the Classis for an explanation concerning these matters. Thus, after a series of attempts to resolve the problem without success, his name was erased from the roll of ministers. Later, after re-baptism, he was accepted into the Baptist Church as a minister of that faith.[5]

In the meantime, three miles further south on the Faith road a new community bearing that name, was beginning to form, numbering approximately two hundred citizens, mainly of the Reformed and Lutheran faiths. For a time the religious needs of that community were served by an active Y.M.C.A., which organization promoted a union Sunday School. However, this plan did not last long. For Reformed people desired a church of their own. A petition was placed in the hands of John A. Peeler, who circulated it in the community. On September 14, 1898, an interested group of Reformed people came together to consider their common religious needs, and took action to build a church, which was completed the following year. A one-room sanctuary was erected on a lot 60 by 100 feet donated by the Peeler Brothers,—John A., L. Monroe and P. Alexander. Total cost of the undertaking, including bell, furniture and an ornamental iron fence around the property, totaled $1,625.

The new church was a continuation of the old one, thus inheriting the property of the old as well as the name, Shiloh. The old church structure erected in 1870-1871, was sold in 1899 to Wesley Brown for $75, who moved it to Granite Quarry where it was converted into a merchandising store. Otherwise the property is still held by the church at Faith, including the cemetery.

What remained of a once prosperous congregation, now cast their lot with the new organization. These were: J. W. Gardner, Mary E. Gardner, W. S. Brown, Martha Brown, Robert Brown, Agnes Brown, Ivey Brown, Adam Fulk, Mary Fulk, William Bringle, Lorenza Walton, Mrs. L. Walton, Mamie Byrd, Thomas Byrd and Jane L. Byrd. In July 1899, the following members of St. Luke's Reformed Church, transferred their certificates of membership to Shiloh: John Franklin Wilhelm, Mrs. Mary Wilhelm, David D. Peeler, Mrs. Martha J. Peeler, John A. Peeler, Mrs. Clara A. Peeler, L. Monroe Peeler, Mrs. Mary E. Peeler, P. Alexander Peeler, Mrs. Mary L. R. Peeler, George H. Peeler, Mrs. Lottie E. Peeler, Jane C. A. Peeler, Mary Agnes Peeler and John Andrew Murray Peeler.

Dr. J. M. L. Lyerly, president of Crescent Academy and Business College, who had guided transfer and building operations, continued to supply the congregation until October 1, 1906, when

Rev. Calvin Boyd Heller became pastor. At its annual sessions in may of 1906, the Classis detached Shiloh Church from the Central Rowan Charge, and for the second time in its history declared the church an independent charge.

Although located in a somewhat static community, Shiloh Church has kept pace with progress in the denomination of which it is a part, promoting causes and supporting its institutions. Numerical growth has been steady. In 1906, by special arrangement with Mr. Heller, a house for the minister was built, which eventually became his property. The second parsonage was erected in 1915, and made ready for occupancy on March 1, when Rev. Harvey A. Welker arrived to serve the parish. By unanimous vote of the congregation the following June action was taken to erect a new house of worship to be located on a different site. Two committees were authorized. P. A. Peeler, J. L. Peeler, T. M. Byrd, J. A. Peeler and C. J. Shive composed the building committee, and L. M. Peeler, L. A. Holshouser, J. D. A. Fisher, George H. Peeler and Rev. H. A. Welker, the board of finance. To these people was delegated the responsibility for finding ways and means to realize their hopes.

A lot at the intersection of Main Street and Granite Quarry Road was acquired from W. C. Coughenhour on May 1, 1918. The old property was sold to T. M. Byrd on March 16, 1924. Of interest is the fact that the land on which the first two parsonages and the church building were erected, as well as the church cemetery established, was originally owned by the Peeler Brothers.

The first unit of the present native granite equipment was begun in 1919, and the sanctuary was completed for an actual cost of $34,411, not including an unrecorded amount of free labor and material. Classis contributed $1,500 on the project. Services were first held in the sanctuary May 18, 1924. Rev. Harvey A. Welker, who had resigned in 1923, returned to preach the sermon.

Then, followed a series of exceptionally productive pastorates. These included those of Dr. James D. Andrew, Rev. Roy C. Whisenhunt, Dr. Lonnie A. Carpenter, Rev. Terrell M. Shoffner, Rev. Huitt R. Carpenter, Rev. Carl R. Martin and Rev. Van D. Grimes. During this period debts were paid, the church basement was completed, and needed equipment was added. The congregation once again went to self-support on June 1, 1945. Also, begun and completed were two major building projects—the third parsonage, located at the corner of Main and Battle Streets, and the educational annex. The latter is also constructed of native stone and is of contemporary architectual design, and involves an expenditure of $147,869.

The congregation is free of debt, the same having been observed in a note-burning service held on Pentecost Sunday, June 1, 1964. Shiloh Church has a confirmed membership of 380 people, who support an annual budget of $25,000. Its program is fully coordinated with Christian activity as conceived by the United Church of Christ. Two ministerial sons have and continue to serve the church: Rev. A. Samuel Peeler and Dr. Banks J. Peeler.

Roster of Pastors

Rev. J. C. Denny 1871-	Rev. Harvey A. Welker 1915-1923
Rev. Peter M. Trexler, D.D. 1871-1876	Rev. James D. Andrew, D.D. 1923-1931
Rev. J. C. Denny 1876-1878	Rev. Roy C. Whisenhunt 1931-1938
Rev. John Ingle 1878-1883	Rev. Lonnie A. Carpenter,
Rev. R. F. Crooks 1883-1888	D.D. 1938-1944
Rev. J. M. L. Lyerly, Ph.D. 1889-1906	Rev. Terrell M. Shoffner 1945-1949
Rev. J. M. L. Lyerly, Ph.D,	Rev. Huitt R. Carpenter..........1949-1956
Supply 1906-	Rev. Carl R. Martin 1956-1961
Rev Calvin B. Heller 1906-1912	Rev. Van D. Grimes 1962-1966
Rev. William H. Causey,	Rev. Max L. Tussey 1967-
D.D. 1912-1914	

1. *Clapp,* Jacob C., Editor. Historic Sketch of the Reformed Church in North Carolina, 1908, p. 220.
2. *Ibid.* p. 221.
3. ——. Minutes. Classis of North Carolina, 1878, p. 222 ff.
4. *Grimes,* Van D., Manuscript. Shiloh Church, Faith, Rowan County, 1965.
5. ——. Minutes. *Op. cit.,* p. 224.

Salem Church, Lincoln County

As far as is known no Reformed Church minister preached regularly at Salem before 1849. During his pastorate at St. Matthew's Church, Rev. David Crooks preached there occasionally, and it is quite probable that, prior to that time, ministers who served Grace and Daniel's Churches conducted services there. The Reformed congregation was organized in 1874, with twenty one members, who were transferred from St. Matthew's Church. From that time until the present, ministers who served St. Matthew's in general have also served the Salem people.

Confirmed membership of Salem Church is fifty five, and the Sunday School has an enrollment of fifty. On its roll are the following family names: Abernathy, Angle, Arrowood, Carpenter, Crooks, Davis, Finger, Frye, Goodnight, Hoover, Ramsaur, Schronce, Sigmon, Smith, Thomasson, Turbyfill, Warlick and Whitener. Since this is the one remaining union church on the roll of the Southern Synod of the Evangelical and Reformed Church, the story which lies back of it, is worthy of relating in this connection.

Salem Church was founded by John Ramsaur, Henry Ramsaur and Daniel Carpenter, Reformed; and Joseph Killian, Anthony Hallman, Henry Cressamore, Jonas Rudisill, Henry Gross, Jonas Heedrick and John Cline, Lutheran. It is located in Lincoln County, on an eminence about two miles west of Clark's Creek on the public road leading from Lincolnton to Newton. The date of organization has not been established; however, on the head marker of Antione Hes, a school teacher, whose body lies in the Salem cemetery are these lines, "Died December 25, 1792." Dr. L. L. Lohr states that "an organization was effected in 1796."[1]

Nor can the date when the original log structure was erected be fixed. This building evidently was a multi-service meeting place and commonly referred to as the "Meeting House." It was old enough in 1814 to be in a dilapidated state, not "a pleasant meeting place." These facts imply that the house, as was usually the case among German pioneers, among the first public buildings erected in the settlement. If this supposition is correct, it could have been built as early as 1750 or thereabout.

That the meeting house was intended for use by people of all faiths, is supported by the following statement which appears on the title page of the Minutes of Salem Citizens dated August 29, 1814.

> Whereas it is proposed to repair the old meeting house known by the name of Salem, so as to render it commodious for the place of Divine Worship—to be free to all Christian denominations whatever, who may be properly authorized by and in good fellowship with the religious society to which he may belong, who may from time to time appoint to preach in said house, we subscribers do hereby promise to pay to Col. John Reinhardt, Captain Henry Ramsaur or Mr. Joshua Wilson (who are to act as commissioners to superintend the work) the several sums annexed to our names to aid and assist in preparing the aforesaid house for the aforesaid purpose. The money to be paid whenever the commissioners may call for it.[2]

The total cost of repair operations was $338.94. Of that amount the Reformed people living in the area contributed no less than $100. At that time the land on which the house stood, comprising two acres and thirty-two poles, was the property of Jacob Killian. It was by him deeded to the Commissioners July 19, 1815, "for the purpose of encouraging schools and a place for public worship." In 1863 Henry Killian of "York District, State of South Carolina, for the sum of one dollar, deeded three roods and twenty-five perches to John Coulter, Absalom Brown and Jacob Ramsaur, Trustees of Salem, for the purpose of encouraging Christianity and increasing the area of the cemetery."[3]

Another tract was added to this property October 22, 1903, containing 148 poles, when A. M. Lutz and his wife deeded it to Ambrose Costner, H. F. McCaslin and Charles Ramsaur, Trustees of Salem Church, for the consideration of five dollars.[4]

These additions seem to have settled the land problem, but the expanding population had begun to tax facilities of the meeting house, requiring better physical accommodations. On September 26, 1835, at a meeting of the citizens of Salem, a decision was reached to erect an addition to the house "to accommodate the people of color on days of public worship."[5] The committee named to assume responsibility for these activities was composed of John Killian, John Carpenter, Jacob Killian, Phillip Rudisill and James Summerow. Their report to the congregations follows:
Total cost of these operations was $69.85 and born about equally by the two denominations.

> The addition to be put to the pulpit end of the Meeting House, thirteen feet wide, with a shed roof, one-story high; to have twelve-light windows, one outside door, and from the body of the house into the addition to be finished off in plain manner, and that three logs behind the pulpit are to be cut out as far as the opening in the gallery.[6]

Thirteen years later, April 15, 1848, a consultation concerning repairs on the old meeting house was held. Since it was the first house built and designed for religious groups who found need for it, and the land was community property, Lutheran leaders considered the advisability of erecting a church for their own specific use. This, however, did not materialize. John Coulter, secretary of the Commissioners and of the Reformed faith, stated that the "Reformed had no congregation, and might not have, but on account of funerals, as some Reformed families buried their dead at Salem, he would like their interest to be continued." Jacob Killian, a Lutheran, expressed himself in favor of a union church, as did Jacob Heedrick and Ambrose Costner, resulting in action to continue Salem as a union church.

The committee authorized to develop plans and to supervise operations was composed of John Killian, John Carpenter, Jacob Killian, Phillip Rudisill, and James Summerow. They met April 29, 1848, in the home of John Coulter, and agreed to recommend the erection of a brick building, which was to be the property of the Reformed and Lutheran denominations. The recommendation was approved. Considering that the Reformed people had no organized congregation at Salem, and would not have for another twenty five years, this was an unusual procedure. The size of the building was to be "35 feet by 45 feet and 13 feet high in the clear; two doors and eight windows eighteen lights to be not less than 10 to 12 inches, and covered with good heart pine shingles.

Jacob Ramsaur, William McCaslin and David Heedrick were appointed to supervise the construction. The sanctuary was completed in 1849, total cost being $628.39, and dedicated "to the use of the Lutheran and German Reformed Churches."[7]

An occasion of historic significance was the observance of the One Hundredth Anniversary of the erection of the original building, which had been built, re-built and again re-built as a union church. The service took place July 18, 1896, when the Reformed and Lutheran people mingled as one, giving proof of cordial fraternalism which had existed among them since pioneer days. Something of the religious and cultural quality of these Services is reflected in the list of speakers who graced the program. Rev. R. A. Yoder was pastor of the Lutheran congregation; Dr. Jacob C. Clapp of the Reformed people. Dr. John A. Foil, Dr. Joseph L. Murphy, Reformed, and Professors J. C. Moser and W. P. Cline, Lutheran. All of them spoke on appropriate subjects. Ambrose Costner, Esq., related the story of Salem Church. Climaxing activities of the day, a bountiful picnic dinner was served in the grove.

On August 14, 1914 action was taken by the two congregations to effect some much needed improvements on the property. A committee was set up, consisting of Dr. C. W. Warlick, T. L. Finger, Jacob Ramsaur, J. S. Warlick and C. E. Ramsaur of the Reformed faith, and Rev. F. M. Speagle, S. A. Turbyfill, H. F. McCaslin, F. E. Bost and E. R. Rhodes for the Lutherans. This committee submitted the following working agreements, which were approved: "1) That steps be taken to renovate the building; 2) the Lutheran congregation assume three fourths of the cost and the Reformed congregation one fourth; 3) the Lutheran congregation be given three fourths interest in the property and the Reformed congregation one fourth interest."[8] Repairs included new ceiling, floor, pews, windows, belfrey and bell, pulpit annex and pulpit furniture. The cornerstone was laid Saturday, May 29, 1915 by Dr. Charles W. Warlick. Hon. A. Nixon, Clerk of Court of Lincoln County, delivered an historical address on Salem Church. The sanctuary was dedicated the following day by Rev. F. M. Speagle. Dr. L. L. Lohr made the dedicatory address. Dr. Warlick preached the sermon in the Service held during the afternoon.

Over a number of years there had been expressed interest in the congregations to provide much needed educational facilities. First steps toward meeting that need were taken July 15, 1935, when pastors John A. Koons and J. L. Norris met on the grounds with an architect to discuss plans for a building. Plans were drawn by the architect, and approved by the congregations. A building committee was authorized consisting of Odis C. Carpenter, Chairman, Raymond Ramsaur, Jacob Ramsaur, Evangelical and Reformed, and Garrett Chandler, secretary, J. P. Finger, and Iron Hall, Lutheran.

Erection of the building begain in the summer of 1936, and was occupied September 19, 1937. Dedication took place October 2, 1938, activities being in charge of the pastors, Rev. Mr. Koons and

Rev. A. W. Lippard. Dr. J. L. Morgan, president of the North Carolina Lutheran Synod, preached the sermon at 11 A.M., and Dr. Howard R. Omwake, president of Catawba College, delivered the dedicatory address during the afternoon.[9]

The Reformed congregation has made two major ecclesiastical and cultural adjustments in its history. In 1934, it took what appears to be its first long step, when the Reformed Church in the United States merged with the Evangelical Synod of North America, creating the Evangelical and Reformed Church; then, again, in 1957, the congregation was asked to adopt a strange new name foreign to its Reformation culture and become a part of the United Church of Christ. While these steps were of a major nature, Salem Reformed Church by experience was prepared to act first as Christians, then as denominationalists, for such had been their life since 1750 when the Salem Community began. This congregation is currently engaged in discussions with other United Churches in the area, and with their Lutheran brethren, seeking answers to the most effective stewardship of their resources in the days ahead.

ROSTER OF PASTORS, INCOMPLETE

Irregular Supplies	1874-1885	Rev. John A. Koons	1919-1944
Rev. Joseph L. Murphy, D.D.	1885-1891	Supplies	1944-1945
Rev. J. M. L. Lyerly, Ph.D.	1892-1893	Rev. William A. Jones	1946-1947
Rev. Jacob C. Clapp, D.D.	1893-1897	Rev. Shuford Peeler, D.D.,	
Rev. Theodore C. Hesson	1898-1902	Supply	1948-
Rev. C. B. Heller	1903-1906	Rev. John A. Koons	1948-1953
Rev. J. Leidy Yearick	1907-1908	Supplies	1953-1954
Rev. Jacob C. Clapp, D.D.,		Rev. Frank W. Snider	1954-1956
Supply	1909-1910	Rev. Terrell M. Shoffner,	
Rev. John A. Foil, Ph.D.,		Alternate Supply	1956-1957
Supply	1909-1910	Rev. Edwin M. Alcorn	
Rev. C. Columbus Wagoner	1910-1912	Alternate Supply	1956-1957
Vacant	1913-1914	Mr. Thomas Hamilton,	
Rev. Charles W. Warlick, D.D.,		Summer Student Supply	1957-
Supply	1915-1917	Rev. James D. Rumley, Jr.	1958-1965
Rev. James D. Andrew, D.D.,		Rev. Frank W. Snider,	
Supply	1917-1918	Supply	1965-
Rev. Harvey G. Kopenhaver,			
Supply	1918-1919		

1. *Morgan*, Jacob L., History of the Lutheran Church in North Carolina. 1953, p. 275.
2. *Clapp*, Jacob C., Editor. Historic Sketch of the Reformed Church in North Carolina, 1908, p. 279.
3. *Ibid.* p. 280.
4. *Ibid.* p. 281.
5. ———. Dedication Bulletin. Historical Sketch, 1938, p. 2.
6. *Clapp. Op. cit.*, p. 281 ff.
7. *Ibid.* p. 283.
8. ———. Bulletin. *Op. cit.*, p. 3.
9. *Leonard*, Jacob C., History of the Southern Synod, Evangelical and Reformed Church, 1940, p. 324.

Second Church, Lexington

IN 1904, Dr. Jacob C. Leonard, who had organized the First Reformed Church, Lexington, North Carolina, asked the Classis of North Carolina for approval to establish a church in East Lexington, in the vicinity of the Nokomis Cotton Mill Company.[1] In an-

ticipation of such an organization, the Nokomis Mill donated a lot near the Raleigh Road and Railroad bridge. On it began the erection of an adequate frame building, the first brick being laid in the foundation November 23, 1903. The church was opened for service March 13, 1904, and dedicated the following May 22, when Dr. Jacob C. Clapp preached the sermon.

At the annual meeting of the Classis in May 1905, the missionary submitted his report.

> I beg leave to report that the Second Reformed Church of Lexington was organized June 5, 1904. Thirteen persons presented certificates, and nine others were received on that date, making a total of twenty-two. A successful Sunday School has been conducted during the year, and preaching services have been held every two weeks in the afternoon. The new congregation gives promise of healthy growth.[2]

The congregation was committed to the care of the organizer, who proceeded to set up a schedule of parish activities.

R. H. Grimes and Stephen L. Thomason were elected elders; and T. A. Swing and W. B. Koontz, deacons. The Sunday School was organized May 29, 1904, enrolling eighty-eight pupils. R. Walter Koontz was elected superintendent. With the help of the following ministerial students, during summer months, this work made commendable progress: A. Samuel Peeler, J. Leidy Yearick, Lee A. Peeler, Clarence Woods, C. Columbus Wagoner, Jacob A. Palmer and William C. Lyerly; Rev. Samuel W. Beck also supplied for a time.[3]

On July 1, 1913, Rev. Macon A. Huffman became the first full-time pastor of the church. The Board of Home Missions enrolled Second Church as a missionary responsibility in October of that year, with an annual subsidy of $300. When on July 1, 1916, Mr.

Huffman resigned, Dr. Leonard was asked to again serve as Stated Supply. By 1917, the congregation requiring additional space, enlarged the church building. Reconsecration rites were in charge of Student Supply, Frank L. Fesperman, Dr. Abram D. Wolfinger preached the sermon. Other students who did summer work on this field were: Felix B. Peck, 1918; J. Wade Huffman, 1919; A. Odell Leonard, 1920 and 1921.

The church building was enlarged a second time in the spring of 1921, under the supervision of Dr. Leonard, G. W. Leonard, A. R. Williams and T. A. Swing, and reopened June 5. Dr. James M. Mullan, Field Representative of the Board of Home Missions, preached the sermon. Second Church was enrolled by the Board of Home Missions in the fall of 1921, with subsidy. At a congregational meeting held April 9, 1922, Theological Student A. Odell Leonard was unanimously elected and called to the pastorate of the church. He was ordained by the Classis of North Carolina and installed pastor June 21, 1922.[4] Action ensued to build a parsonage on property adjacent to the church building on the North side June 4, 1922, and the pastor and his wife moved into it in December of that same year.

The parish showed great promise from the beginning. Increased attendance was noted in all departments of church life, adding ninety one people to the church membership roll in 1923 and 1924. Physical expansion was necessary. The idea of erecting a hut to satisfy educational and recreational needs was rejected in favor of building a new and larger house of worship. A building committee consisting of B. C. Nance, J. M. Crotts, A. L. Burkhart, S. L. Welch, M. P. Bain and G. W. Leonard, was appointed. Encouraging cooperation between the Board of Home Missions, friends and the congregation, found the new church building ready to be occupied Sunday morning, December 25, 1927. Dr. Jacob C. Leonard preached the dedication sermon. During the afternoon and evening, Dr. Harvey A. Fesperman, president of the Classis of North Carolina; Dr. Jacob A. Palmer, a former student supply; Mr. Joseph S. Wise, Treasurer of the Board of Home Missions; and Rev. W. S. Holmes, president of the Lexington Ministerial Association, also addressed the congregation.

Having paid their last indebtedness on loans from the Board of Home Missions, the congregation went to self-support in 1934. These were World War II days when, like in neighboring churches, young men went into military service of their country. In 1939, to provide for a fast expanding Sunday School enrollment, preparations got under way for erecting Fellowship Center, an all-purpose building to be located west of the church. This facility, however, did not materialize until 1944, when in July the local unit of the Churchmen's Brotherhood held its organizational meeting in it, the first official gathering of any kind to take place in the structure.

This project was supervised by Earl Black, W. A. Bruff and Mozelle Crotts.

An event reflecting genuine gratitude occurred Sunday evening, March 1, 1943, when Second Church honored its founder, Dr. Jacob C. Leonard, Pastor Emeritus of First Evangelical and Reformed Church of Lexington. It was an occasion fraught with emotion, occasioned by personal notes, flowers, gifts and plaudit expressions from a grateful people. The significance of the occasion was heightened, when early the following morning, Dr. Leonard was stricken and died within a few minutes.[5]

By the fall of 1945 it was evident that the congregation had outgrown its facilities. A series of planning committees was set up, instructed to study needs and report. The building committee was composed of Elmer P. Nance, Mrs. C. L. Kepley, Mrs. A. O. Leonard, Odell M. Burkhart, Willie Frazier, Marvin Burkhart, D. Earl Black, Sam Welch and Mrs. Herman Williams. This project began with remodeling the sanctuary, converting it into an altar centered chancel. Work began on a three-story Sunday School annex to be erected along the East end of the sanctuary, in October 1949. It was finished in 1950. By encouraging all organizations to funnel their contributions into the building fund, and supported by many hours of free labor, the building estimated to cost $103,000 was free of debt in 1951. On December 9 of that year, it was dedicated. Dr. Jacob A. Palmer made an appropriate address.

The 50th Anniversary of the organization of the church was observed Sunday, May 30, 1954. It was a crowning day. Sixty-eight people were received into fellowship with the church, and eleven children were dedicated to the Lord in the Sacrament of Holy Baptism. Taking part in the services of the day were Revs. Billy Joe Leonard, G. Melvin Palmer and Ministerial Student Donald M. Leonard, all sons of the congregation.

In 1956 the church was ready to take another significant step forward. In March of that year, Student Donald M. Leonard, upon graduation from Theological School, was called to be Associate Pastor. Two parsonages were then built across the street in front of the church building, on recently acquired property. John Fox, Paul Huffman, Elmer P. Nance, Willie F. Everhart and Willie G. Frazier supervised the construction. Those houses were dedicated July 7, 1957, when Dr. Harvey A. Fesperman, president of Southern Synod, made an appropriate address. These pastors worked together, expanding and intensifying the parish program. On November 1, 1960 Rev. Donald M. Leonard accepted a call to the pastorate of the First Church, Asheboro, thus bringing to an end a short but happy father and son pastoral relationship.

In 1959, in anticipation of providing further necessary equipment, the "Christian Character Development Fund" program was set up. Each member of the church was asked to make a three-year financial pledge to the fund. This effort expanded into a parish enrichment program. An exploratory committee composed of Willie F. Everhart, Mrs. Elmer P. Nance and Miss Loretta Leonard was appointed, followed by a permanent building committee consisting of Elmer P. Nance, Willie F. Everhart, John Fox, Marvin Burkhart and E. C. Young.

Drawings were made for remodeling sections of the old building, and for a proposed educational facility to be erected at the West end of the sanctuary, replacing the old parsonage. These plans were approved by the congregation, September 8, 1963, involving a total estimated expenditure of approximately $300,000. At the same time the Trustees were authorized "to take whatever steps necessary for the securing of needed funds to complete payment on the whole project."[6] This major undertaking moved along with reasonable dispatch and the building was occupied, incompletely furnished, in 1966. All together the church owns property in Lexington bounding on the North by the Raleigh Road, on the South by Bristol Street, on the West by the Southern railroad, and on the East by Erlanger holdings. On it are two dwellings, used as residences for ministers, recreation grounds, adequate parking areas and a church structure which actually is four buildings in one.

The story of this congregation as here related, appears to have been a continuous venture in material and physical expansion. However, during the sixty-three years of its life, spiritual, cultural and religious factors have not been neglected. In fact primary consideration for these values explains in large measure its prosperity. Every phase in the benevolent program of the United Church of Christ has been supported. Nazareth Children's Home, Catawba College, Johns River Valley Camp, The Assembly Grounds, the proposed United Church Retirement Home, the Seminary Fund and benevolent causes covered by the Apportionment have received generous support from its resources, in forms of money and dedicated leadership.

Missionary concerns defined as "Consideration for others," have reached out in the renewal of Hebron Church, Route 4, Winston Salem; the founding of First Church, Asheboro, Paul's Chapel, Route 4, Lexington; and St. Andrew's Mission located near Pickett School, in West Lexington.

In the area of life service, Revs. George Melvin Palmer, Billy Joe Leonard, Donald Mark Leonard and Rex Oren Doby, all ordained ministers serving in the United Church of Christ, were nurtured in this congregation. Personal evangelism has been the captivating spirit in all phases in the life of the church, reflected in a confirmed membership of 1,150 people and a Sunday School enrollment of 1,357 pupils.

The inspiration for all of this over a period of forty seven years, including two years of student supply work, has been Dr. A. Odell Leonard, a man short of stature, but blessed with a dedicated spirit and tremendous energy. It represents for him, in the main, a life-time of service to the Kingdom of God. He believes that re-generation begins with personal salvation, involving the whole man. During these years he has given freely of his time and energy to causes within the denomination, but his chief concern has been the parish ministry. The record reflects a set of interesting facts: preached 3,629 sermons, 2,242 at Second Church, 1,387 in other churches; officiated at 1,512 funerals and 1,218 weddings.

June 4, 1967 will long be remembered by the Second Church people. At that time three major events were recognized: the dedication of the new educational facility, the Sixty-Third Anniversary of the Organization of the Church, and the retirement of their pastor from the active parish ministry. To commemorate the occasion an attractive anniversary brochure, entitled Second United Church of Christ, Sixty-Third Anniversary of Organization was published by a committee composed of Dr. Leonard, Mrs. C. L. Kepley, Mrs. Herman Williams, Mrs. A. William Hedrick, Odell M. Burkart, Willie F. Everhart, Willie G. Frazier, Leonard Beck, John Kepley and Elmer P. Nance. Dr. Banks J. Peeler, president of Southern Synod Acting Association of the Southern Conference, United Church of Christ, addressed the congregation at 9:45 a.m.; Rev. Edwin M. Alcorn, Western Area Minister, delivered the sermon at 11:00 a.m.; and Dr. James H. Lightbourne, Jr., Conference Minister, made the dedicatory address at 7:30 p.m. The pastor read the ritual of dedication. His message to the congregation follows:

> Forty-four years of service with such a wonderful people in Second Lexington, makes one most grateful to God for all of His marvelous blessings. Because of your interest and labor, I feel a deep humility and appreciation to you for allowing me to remain with you.
>
> The great opportunities for each member of Second Church constitute a challenge of major proportions. In this day of revolution, change and doubt, God is not dead and faith can be found on earth.
>
> Should we be given tomorrow to love and serve Him and His children, we dare not fail. We may not know all that is out front, but we are convinced that there is no defeat for righteousness.

Rev. Billy Joe Leonard, a son of Dr. and Mrs. A. Odell Leonard, was called to succeed his father, and began work in July 1967.

ROSTER OF PASTORS

Rev. Jacob C. Leonard, D.D., Organizer and Supply 1904-1913	Rev. A. Odell Leonard, D.D. 1922-1967
Rev. J. Macon Huffman 1913-1916	Rev. Billy Joe Leonard 1967-
Rev. Jacob C. Leonard, D.D., Stated Supply 1916-1922	Rev. Donald M. Leonard, Associate 1956-1960

1. ————. Minutes. Classis of North Carolina, 1904, p. 342.
2. ————. Minutes. *Op. cit.*, 1905, p. 409.
3. *Leonard*, A. Odell, Second Evangelical and Reformed Church and Fortieth Anneversary of Organization, 1944, p. 1 ff.
4. ————. Minutes. *Op. cit.*, 1923, p. 3.
5. *Leonard*, A. Odell, Second Evangelical and Reformed Church and 50th Anniversary of Organization, 1954, p. 12 ff.
6. *Leonard*, A. Odell, Second United Church of Christ, Sixty-Third Anniversary of Organization, 1967, p. 17 ff.

St. Andrew's Church, Lexington

EARLY IN 1954, discussion prevailed favorable to establishing an
Evangelical and Reformed Church in West Lexington, in the vicinity of Pickett School. Mr. and Mrs. M. Glenn Pickett, Sr., proposed
to donate a tract of land along the west line of school property for
that purpose. Dr. A. Odell Leonard became interested in the project, and brought it to the attention of the committee on Naional
Missions of Southern Synod, which in turn referred it to the Board
of National Missions of the Evangelical and Reformed Church.
Being only eight-tenths of a mile West of Christ Evangelical and
Reformed Church, in consideration for overlapping parishes, the
board took the following action: "We look with favor upon the beginning of new work in West Lexington, provided Christ Church
be the nucleus, with a view of its relocation."[1]

It was the hope of the board that these two areas could be linked
into what was at the time thought of as "the larger parish," served
by one minister, anticipating the merger of these two interests into
one congregation adequately equipped with a building and a program to serve the community. The idea was not acceptable.

In the summer of 1956, with the support of the Board of National
Missions, Theological Student Robert E. Myers made a survey of
the Pickett School area. The results of this survey reflected reasonable prospects for a substantial church. Since a cooperative program between the two areas did not appear feasible, sponsored by
Pilgrim and Second Evangelical and Reformed Churches of Lexington, activities in the Pickett School area began in 1958. A joint
committee consisting of Jacob Clodfelter, J. A. Sowers and Edward
Clark from Pilgrim, and Willie F. Everhart, John Fox and Jasper
Morgan from Second Church, was created to manage parish detail.
Rev. Frank W. Snider and Rev. Donald M. Leonard respectively
began promoting the project, holding services each Sunday morning alternately.

Arrangements were made to hold meetings in a small four-room frame house on Willowbrook Circle. An account of the organization meeting follows:

> On Sunday, November 2, 1958, St. Andrew's Evangelical and Reformed Church was organized in Lexington, North Carolina, with sixty two charter members. The organizational service began at 9:45 a.m., with devotions conducted by Rev. Donald M. Leonard and Dr. A. Odell Leonard. Members were then received by confirmation, adult baptism and transfer of membership. Fourteen members transferred from Second Church, Lexington, nine from Pilgrim Church, four from Paul's Chapel, one from Hebron Church, one from Mt. Tabor Church, and one from First Church, Lexington. Nineteen transferred their memberships from churches of other denominations, and thirteen were received by confirmation and adult baptism.
>
> Rev. Frank W. Snider conducted the congregational meeting. The following elders were elected: Edward Clark, William Fine and Lloyd Sprinkle; The following deacons were elected: Paul Gobble, Donald Smith and William Trantham.[2]

The congregation was enrolled by Southern Synod November 17, 1958.[3] Revs. Frank W. Snider and Donald M. Leonard continued as temporary supply ministers until June 1959. Student Rex O. Doby served the parish during the summer, and Dr. A. Odell Leonard was appointed Stated Supply by the Council of Southern Synod, beginning September 1, 1959.[4] A deed for five acres of land was officially presented to the church February 21, 1960. At that time, Dr. Leonard remarked, "Mr. and Mrs. M. Glenn Pickett have encouraged the members all along, and in donating the land have shown their Christian spirit of selflessness. The congregation and pastors are most grateful, and expect to put forth every effort to justify the interest and the gift." Participaing in his formal historical act beside the minister were: Rev. J. Edmund Lippy, Eastern Field Secretary of the Board of National Missions; M. Glenn Pickett, the donor; William Fine, president of the consistory; and Rev. Donald M. Leonard, supply minister.[5]

The city of Lexington extended its corporate limits to include the Pickett School section, thus providing utilities for the property. Plans were developed and approved for the erection of a suitable all-purpose building on the land, construction on it beginning in the summer of 1960. The first service was held in the partly completed structure March 26, 1961. On that day twenty six people were received into the membership, and eight children were baptized; also, a gift of $3,500 was announced from the Church Builder's Club of Southern Synod. Approximately one year later, April 15, 1962 at 3 p.m., the cornerstone was placed, and the church building was formally occupied and dedicated. The supply pastor was assisted in these activities by Revs. Frank W. Snider, Donald M. Leonard, Rex O. Doby and Robert E. Myers. Dr. Harvey A. Fesperman, president of Southern Synod, preached the dedicatory sermon.

Theological Student Chester W. Byerly did parish work during the summer of 1962. Dr. Leonard continued, with the assistance of Ottis Leonard, to supervise the Mission until June 1963. Mr. Byerly, having been licensed to preach the Gospel and ordained to the Christian ministry by Southern Synod, was installed the first full-time pastor of the church August 18, 1963, and served it until 1965.[6] Rev. Rex O. Doby served as Stated Supply in 1966. On a similar basis Rev. Marlin T. Schaeffer began supplying the church, providing pastoral care and services of worship, in the fall of 1966. The congregation continues under the supervision of the Department of Church Extension of the Board of Homeland Ministries of the United Church of Christ, its annual budget being partially underwritten by that body.

ROSTER OF PASTORS

Rev. A. Odell Leonard, D.D., Promoter-Organizer 1954-1959	Mr. Ottis Leonard, Associate Supply 1962-1963
Rev. Frank W. Snider, Alternate Supply 1958-1959	Mr. Chester W. Byerly, Student Summer Supply 1962-
Rev. Donald M. Leonard, Alternate Supply 1958-1959	Rev. Chester W. Byerly 1963-1965
Mr. Rex O. Doby, Student Summer Supply 1959-	Rev. Rex O. Doby, Stated Supply 1965-1966
Rev. A. Odell Leonard, D.D., Stated Supply 1959-1963	Rev. Marlin T. Schaeffer, Stated Supply 1965-1967
	Rev. Terrell M. Shoffner 1967-

1. ———. Minutes. Southern Synod, 1955, p. 42.
2. ———. The Standard, No. 16, November 15, 1958, p. 1.
3. ———. Minutes. *Op. cit.*, 1958, p. 24.
4. ———. Minutes. *Op. cit.*, 1960, p. 9.
5. ———. The Standard, No. 2, March 15, 1960, p. 1.
6. ———. Minutes. *Op. cit.*, 1964, p. 11.

St. James Church, Mt. Pleasant

ST. JAMES REFORMED CHURCH, Mt. Pleasant, North Carolina, is located in a rich agricultural section of Southeast Cabarrus County. In 1890 Mt. Pleasant was a thriving village in which had been developed cotton mills, wood working plants, tan yards, a tin shop, a blacksmith shop and a variety of retail stores. The Lutheran Church had established two good educational institutions there; the North Carolina College for boys and the Mont Amoena Seminary for girls. A number of Reformed families from Lower Stone, Bear Creek and New Gilead churches had located in the town, and become active in its cultural, business and religious life.

Dr. Paul Barringer, being a missionary minded man, had preached in that community for a number of years, as often as occasion required, stimulating interest in establishing a Reformed church there. In 1894 a petition was presented to the Classis of North Carolina from "persons at Mt. Pleasant (asking) that a Reformed church be organized in that town." The request was granted and the interest was committed to the care of Dr. Barringer, with instructions to "organize a congregation at his discretion."[1]

The congregation was organized December 3, 1894 in the home of Mrs. C. L. Foil. Eight people signed the charter membership roll: Mrs. C. L. Foil, Mrs. M. R. Miller, L. J. Foil, W. J. Heilig, Dr. A. W. Moose, Dr. M. A. Foil, Mrs. A. F. Sides and W. D. Foil. Dr. A. W. Moose was made an elder, and Dr. M. A. Foil was chosen a deacon. Only two officers were at first named. The new congregation was named "St. James Reformed Church." Dr. Barringer continued to serve the church, in addition to his work as pastor of the East Rowan Charge. Subsequently the New Gilead Church was detached from Trinity Church, Concord, and realigned with St. James, creating the New Gilead Charge. The New Gilead Charge was then enrolled by the Board of Missions with subsidy, and Dr. Barringer was commissioned its pastor, beginning October 7, 1896. Religious services were conducted in Holy Trinity Lutheran Church prior to the erection of their own church building.[2]

The young congregation prospered under the wise counsel and positive leadership of Dr. Barringer. Numerically small, it was materially and influencially strong, having in its membership many of the leading business and professional men and women of the community. Among first actions of the new church was a move in the direction of a place for worship. A lot was donated by W. J. Heilig. A building committee was appointed, consisting of Dr. A. W. Moose, W. J. Heilig and L. J. Foil. Plans were developed and work began on the building in September 1895. It was completed and ready for occupancy in May 1896.

Over the signature of Dr. M. A. Foil, secretary, an appeal was made to the Classis of North Carolina for financial aid.[3] An amount of $266.67, the balance in the Beneficiary Education and Home Missions fund, was given to be used on the new church building.[4] Bear

Creek congregation made considerable contributions in lumber and labor, in addition to their constant encouraging moral support during these operations. When, therefore, the church was dedicated April 30, 1896, all outstanding obligations had been paid or otherwise provided. The completed church building cost approximately $1,400. Dr. Jacob C. Leonard preached the dedicatory sermon, and the pastor read the ritual of dedication.

An attendant at the dedication service has described the new church building as it appeared on that day.

> Many present for the dedication service described the new church as a beautiful structure, well planned, well built, with the joist, wainscoting and ceiling of natural yellow pine. The walls were plastered. The pulpit was oak and the oak chairs were upholstered with leather. The carpet and gothic styled stained windows blended beautifully with surroundings. The bell was hung in a tower on the northeast corner of the church. The seating capacity was three hundred.[5]

This sanctuary served the people until 1923. At a meeting held July 10, 1921, the congregation voted in favor of erecting a new church. A building committee was appointed, consisting of J. L. Peck, O. A. Barringer, E. L. Foil, S. C. Kluttz, J. L. C. Miller, Mrs. H. E. Foil and Mrs. L. E. Foil. This group was instructed to formulate plans to replace the old church with a new brick structure. These plans were approved August 14, 1921, provided as much as $10,000 could be promised in pledges. On September 4, in the same year, a committee reported total pledges of $12,000. J. L. C. Miller and S. C. Kluttz were named foremen, and asked to supervise construction on the new church. But because of a disastrous fire in the lumber plant of Mr. Miller, construction was postponed until July 1923. The building was completed in 1924, costing $26,-000 furnishings and a pipe organ included. Dedication rites occurred June 26, 1924, when a series of services ran through the day. Among those who delivered appropriate addresses on that occasion were, Dr. Jacob C. Leonard, who preached the sermon; Rev. William C. Lyerly and Dr. John H. Keller, who were heard during the afternoon. Dr. Charles W. Warlick, pastor of the church, read the ritual of dedication.

This church building has been repaired and redecorated twice since its erection. Interior of the sanctuary was remodeled in 1951 at which time both sanctuary and Sunday School annex were redecorated and carpeted. In 1964 the pipe organ was rebuilt, requiring additional pipes and a new console. That project cost $7,000.[6]

The parsonage was built during the pastorate of Rev. E. Garver Williams, on a lot adjoining the church property along the south line. This lot was purchased from George Heilig on February 9, 1903 by Dr. M. A. Foil and later by him deeded to the church. Currently the parsonage is being used as an educational unit for children.[7]

Land was purchased for a cemetery in May 1897, and deeded to the Trustees of St. James Church and their successors. The cemetery is located on Walnut Street, which was purchased from May Jackson for the sum of $25. A second lot, across the street, was deeded to the Trustees of St. James Church for cemetery purposes in July 1950 by Mr. and Mrs. Winfred Petrea. A provision in that deed says, "to set aside an area of not less than 500 square feet of said land for a burial plot for persons who are unable to purchase or otherwise acquire a burial place."

In January 1945 a cemetery trust fund was set up by L. H. Barringer, Hoy A. Moose and Mrs. G. L. Herrin.

In keeping with its tradition, this church maintains an active parish program involving a Sunday School, Church Women, Men's Fellowship and appropriate youth groups. It has a reputation for liberally supporting all benevolent causes conceived and approved by the denomination. In 1920, during the Great Forward Movement promoted by the Reformed Church in the United States, State Director, J. Tilden Hedrick, after a very happy and successful visit to Mt. Pleasant, remarked, "that he had no further doubts of the success of this great denominational enterprise in North Carolina.[8] Other impressive instances of undivided support in recent years could very easily be recounted. Never numerically strong, St. James nevertheless has wielded a tremendous influence for good through out the Classis of North Carolina and its successor The Southern Synod, and may be relied upon to continue in character in the Southern Conference of the United Church of Christ.

ROSTER OF PASTORS

Rev. Paul Barringer, D.D. 1894-1900
Rev. John H. Keller, D.D. 1901-1906
Rev. E. Garver Williams 1907-1909
Rev. Anthony Shulenberger ..1910-1911
Rev. Border L. Stanley 1911-1913
Rev. William C. Lyerly 1914-1918
Rev. Aaron R. Tosh, D.D. 1919-1921
Rev. Charles W. Warlick,
  D.D. 1921-1929
Rev. William S. Gerhardt 1930-1941
Rev. Aubrey W. Hedrick 1942-1949

Rev. Lionel A. Whiston, Ph.D.,
  Supply 1949-1950
Rev. Thomas E. Hoffman 1950-1953
Rev. Lionel A. Whiston, Ph.D.,
  Supply 1953-1954
Rev. Carl T. Daye 1954-1958
Rev. Donald J. Selby, Ph.D.,
  Supply 1958-
Rev. Banks D. Shepherd 1958-1962
Rev. Felix B. Peck, S.T.D.,
  Stated Supply 1963-

Dr. Felix B. Peck is currently serving the Mt. Pleasant Charge, composed of St. James and Boger churches, as Stated Supply. He is responsible for excellent progress in this parish since 1963.

1. ————. Minutes. Classis of North Carolina, 1894, p. 11, art. 17.
2. *Clapp,* Jacob C., Editor. Historic Sketch of the Reformed Church in North Carolina, 1908, p. 235.
3. ————. Minutes. *Op. cit.,* 1896, pp. 15 and 11.
4. ————. Minutes. *Op. cit.,* 1898, p. 58.
5. *Cress,* Frances *Moose,* W. Lee., St. James United Church of Christ, 1964, p. 3.
6. *Ibid.* pp. 4 and 5 ff.
7. *Moose,* W. Lee, St. James Reformed Church, Celebrating Fiftieth Anniversary of Organization, 1944, p. 9.
8. *Leonard,* Jacob C., History of the Southern Synod, Evangelical and Reformed Church, 1940, p. 271.

St. John's Church, Burlington

IN A VERY REAL SENSE, the First Reformed United Church of Christ, Burlington, North Carolina, is the parent of St. John's Evangelical and Reformed Church of that city. In 1951, realizing the need for a church in the Grove Park area of the community, Dr. Harvey A. Fesperman, then pastor of First Church, brought this matter to the attention of the consistory. A committee was authorized with instructions to study the proposed area and report, consisting of Herbert W. Coble, chairman, Benjamin Sharpe, M. Glenn Pickett, Sr., Duncan C. Bryan, Carlton K. Day and George H. Fowler. The project appeared promising; therefore, upon recommendation of the committee, the congregation purchased a two-acre tract of land in the area, with a three-room house on it, for $9,000.

Theological Student J. Wayne Fouts, serving the First Church as part-time assistant pastor in the summer of 1952, in anticipation of starting new work in the Grove Park neighborhood under the supervision of the Board of National Missions, surveyed the area. Based on the findings of the survey, First Church contributed the property for the project and agreed to supervise building operations until a congregation could be developed and organized.

In 1953, upon graduation from The Lancaster Theological Seminary, Mr. Fouts accepted an appointment by the Board of National Missions to be the missionary pastor of the new project. Picking up where he had left off the previous summer, this young minister began in earnest to visit in homes of the community and to develop parish programs. Forty-seven people gathered at the home of Mr. and Mrs. K. A. Mincey on July 12, 1953, for the first stated service of worship. Six additional similar services were conducted in homes of interested people on successive Sundays, each with increased attendance.

A congregational organization was effected September 13, 1953. A consistory was named at the same meeting. Harold Madden, Frank Phillips and Clifton Day were elected elders; and Earl King, J. G. Longest and Ervin Blanchard were made deacons. At the first consistory meeting on September 16, Joseph H. Peele, Jr. was elected secretary, and James Mahan, treasurer. These properly elected officials were ordained and installed in their respective offices on September 20. On the same date, 66 charter members were rceived into the Fellowship, and the congregation was officially named, "St. John's Evangelical and Reformed Church." Shortly thereafter, the church was officially enrolled as a member of Southern Synod of the Evangelical and Reformed Church.

Mr. Fouts was elected pastor of the newly-created church on November 15, 1953, and having been ordained to the Christian Ministry earlier, was installed by a committee under authority of Southern Synod. The committee was composed of Dr. Harvey A. Fesperman, Dr. John C. Peeler and Elder Harold Madden. By the end of that year, the membership roll of the congregation had increased to 102 people.

From this point, organized congregational activities began to appear. The Sunday School was established on September 27, 1953. A Daily Vacation Bible School appeared in the summer of 1954, as did the Women's Guild and the Churchmen's Brotherhood. After that, the parish program was expanded to include youth activities, Boy and Girl Scouts, choirs and a full program of parish evangelism.

Physical developments also reflect an interesting story. The minister and his family began housekeeping in the three-room frame building on the original site June 1, 1953, which was to be their home during the next seven years. Later, a second bedroom was added and a floor furnace installed. Contract for the first unit of an all-purpose church building was let in April 1953. Construction on it began in June of that year and was completed by the following October. To meet the needs of a growing church, a second unit was added to the building in 1955. It was occupied December 25 and dedicated May 6, 1956. This new unit provided space for a fellowship hall on the ground floor and a sanctuary on the second floor. Thus, space was released in the old section of the building for a number of much-needed classrooms.

The site on which the new parsonage stands was acquired March 6, 1955, for the sum of $3,000, and the financial obligation created by this transaction was assumed by the Women's Guild. In 1960, as a part of a long-range expansion program recommended by a study committee and approved by the congregation, a committee was appointed with instructions to develop plans for a parsonage. Groundbreaking ceremonies for the new parsonage occurred February 21, 1960, and the lovely colonial brick building was completed the following August. Rev. Frank W. Snider, the new pastor, and his family, occupied the house on August 22, 1960. The congregation acted to purchase an additional tract of land adjacent to the old parsonage on the North April 26, 1964 for $11,000. This acquisition provides sufficient land for reasonable future expansion in recreation and parking.

A major event in the life of the church was the observance of its 10th Anniversary. The pastor and his committee had developed an impressive and richly rewarding program. Activities began on Saturday evening, September 7, 1963, when Dr. Harvey A. Fesperman spoke at the anniversary dinner. An historical pageant, entitled "Ten Years in the Life of a Church," was presented by young people of the congregation on Sunday morning at 10 o'clock. Rev. G. Melvin Palmer was the revival preacher, conducting services each evening during the week through Thursday.

St. John's is a vital, self-supporting congregation of 285 confirmed members. Its life is geared to the denomination's program of Christian witness, and, for the most part, is led by volunteer workers. The Sunday School has an enrollment of 270 pupils.

Rev. Joshua L. Levens began his ministry to the congregation on November 1, 1965. Miss Gennie Lou Piercy is the church's first full-time Christian service volunteer. She was approved by Southern Synod on April 28, 1964, and commissioned in the field of Christian Education by authority of the Synod in a public service held at St. John's Church the evening of June 14, 1964. Rev. J. Wayne Fouts, a former pastor, preached the sermon, and Dr. Banks J. Peeler, president of Southern Synod, read the commissioning vows.

ROSTER OF PASTORS

Rev. J. Wayne Fouts 1953-1960	Rev. Joshua L. Levens 1965-	
Rev. Frank W. Snider 1960-1965		

Bibliography
> Snider, Frank W., St. John's United Church of Christ, 1963.
> Snider, Frank W., History of St. John's United Church of Christ, 1964.

St. John's Church, Kannapolis

As EARLY AS 1911 Reformed Church interests in Kannapolis came to the attention of the Classis of North Carolina.[1] In 1912 the committee on Missions recommended to that body that a General Field Secretary be appointed by the Classis who should give the major part of his time the first year to the Kannapolis, Landis and China Grove area.[2] That plan did not materialize, therefore, these interests were assigned to a committee consisting of Rev. William H. Causey, Dr. William B. Duttera and Dr. Peter M. Trexler.

In 1916 Dr. John H. Keller, Dr. Paul Barringer and the "pastor of Trinity Church, Concord," were asked to concern themselves with Kannapolis, and instructed, if expedient, to organize a congregation there.[3] Except for services at convenient times, held at the Y.M.C.A., by Dr. J. M. L. Lyerly and Dr. Keller, very little actual headway toward an organization was made until 1919. At

that time a petition was prepared and sent to the Classis, to which was attached thirty five names of Reformed people living in Kannapolis, asking that a church be organized at that place.

> We, whose names are hereunto affixed, desire to be organized as a congregation, that we may have better facilities for enjoying the holy ordinances of the Christian Church, do hereby petition the Classis of North Carolina to organize us under the name of ——————————— congregation in the town of Kannapolis, and the state of North Carolina, and do declare our readiness to be governed by the Constitution of the Reformed Church in the United States.[4]

Kannapolis was enrolled with subsidy of $700. Ministerial Student Banks J. Peeler was appointed by the Board of Home Missions with approval of the Classis, to survey the field and prepare to effect an organization.[5] Arrangements were made with school authorities to hold meetings in the Woodrow Wilson School located in North Kannapolis. The first gathering of interested people took place on the fourth Sunday in May 1919. It was a rainy day, but thirty-two people were in the audience. The Sunday School was set up on June 1, enrolling forty-eight pupils. R. Baxter McCombs was named superintendent; T. P. Moose secretary-treasurer. Four classes were formed, and the following teachers were appointed: Mrs. T. P. Moose, children; Loula Belle McCombs, juniors; John H. Suther, young people; and Banks J. Peeler, adults.[6]

Organization day was scheduled for July 27, 1919, and was in charge of Rev. William C. Lyerly and Dr. Paul Barringer, two members of the committee appointed by the Classis. This meeting took place in the Woodrow Wilson School. Dr. Barringer preached the sermon and assisted Mr. Lyerly in organization proceedings. Thirty-six names were on the incompleted charter member list; it was agreed, therefore that the list should remain "open" for six months. The presiding minister confirmed three people, baptized

and confirmed one, and baptized one baby. Travis P. Moore and
R. Baxter McCombs were elected elders; Curtis M. Linn and Phifer
E. Correll, deacons. These officers were ordained and installed in
their respective positions.[7]

On September 2, 1919 Mr. Lyerly reported to the Executive Committee of the Classis of North Carolina:

> Your committee on the Kannapolis interest was instructed to urge
> the Board of Home Missions to enroll Kannapolis as a permanent mission.
> The board enrolled the Kannapolis Mission at their July meeting with an
> appropriation. The committee organized the Kannapolis Reformed Church
> July 27, 1919, at their regular place of worship, in the North School
> Building. Thirty-six members who had signed the charter membership
> roll were enrolled. Two elders and two deacons were duly elected and
> installed. Two members of the committee were present. Your committee
> recommend that the Kannapolis Reformed Church be enrolled as a con-
> gregation in the Classis of North Carolina.[8]

The newly organized congregation was yoked with St. Paul's
Church, Enochville, and known as the St. Paul's-Kannapolis Charge.
Dr. Lee A. Peeler was commissioned by the Board of Home Missions to become pastor of the charge, and began work October 1,
1919. An immediate task confronted the new minister. The survey
work that had been done during the summer months needed to be
shored up, land on which to erect required facilities with which to
serve the community had to be acquired, plans for a parsonage and
a church building must be agreed upon and developed. These details were attended to during the fall and winter months. On January 20, 1920 action was taken to increase the consistory by four
members; therefore, J. V. Blackwelder and Dorsett M. McCombs
were elected elders, and W. C. Goodnight and F. M. Correll, deacons. Action was taken March 7, 1920 changing the temporary
name "Kannapolis Reformed Church" to "St. John's Reformed
Church."

When, therefore, on February 1, 1920, the charter member list
was officially closed, thirty-eight names were on it. These were:
R. B. McCombs, Mrs. R. B. McCombs, Leo McCombs, D. M. Mc-
Combs, Mrs. D. M. McCombs, Maude McCombs, Stokes Mc-
Combs, T. P. Moose, Mrs. T. P. Moose, Eddrie Moose, C. M. Linn,
Raymond Linn, P. E. Correll, F. M. Correll, Mrs. F. M. Correll,
J. W. Correll, J. A. Correll, W. C. Goodnight, Mrs. W. C. Goodnight,
W. P. Goodnight, J. V. Blackwelder, Mrs. J. V. Blackwelder, Lil-
lian Blackwelder, D. C. Cline, Mrs. D. C. Cline, Mrs. Lee A. Peeler,
H. O. Archie, Mrs. H. O. Archie, Hattie Archie, Nannie Archie,
Annie Archie, Mrs. Florence Brown, G. F. Rickard, Mrs. G. F.
Rickard, Clora McCombs, Bennie Artz, Charles Artz, and Mrs. C.
M. Linn.

Building operations obviously had to be done subject to the approval and support of the Board of Home Missions. Groundbreaking ceremonies for the church building occurred July 21, 1920, when

appropriate remarks were made by Dr. John H. Keller. The corner-stone was laid on January 20, 1921, remarks being made by Dr. Jacob C. Leonard. An opening service was conducted in rooms on the ground floor of the church July 10, 1921. The sanctuary and additional Sunday School rooms were formally opened January 1, 1922. Appropriate dedicatory services were held Sunday, April 30, 1922. Dr. Charles E. Schaeffer, General Secretary of the Board of Home Missions, preached the sermon. Joseph S. Wise, Superintendent of the Church Building Department of the Board of Home Missions, addressed the congregation during the afternoon and at the vespers.

The new parsonage was completed, and consecrated on the evening of February 22, 1921. These physical appointments represent a financial involvment of: the church $49,000, the parsonage $8,500 plus the land on which they stand, given by the Cannon Mills Company. Among primary organizations effected in the congregation as the need arrived were: The Woman's Missionary Society, Girls' Guild, Mission Band, Young Peoples' Society and Scouts.

After seventeen years of faithful stewardship on this parish Dr. Peeler resigned effective November 15, 1938. He made a major contribution in establishing a widely influential church in that community. Reflecting something of the type of lay leadership that had developed in St. John's Church, during the vacancy of seven months, plans were detailed by which to gradually liquidate the burdensome debt that had been throttling the congregation since its founding. Thus, during the short pastorate of Rev. Joseph D. Andrew, which ended March 15, 1942, the congregation experienced a period of transition, finding its strength, and laying a foundation for future development and numerical growth.[9]

Rev. Frank K. Bostian, who began serving the parish July 15, 1942, provided excellent leadership in these developments. The organ was installed in the fall of 1942; the quota of benevolent apportionment was paid in full first time in the history of the congregation in 1943. Nineteen forty six was a crowning year. The record speaks for itself. On May 1, the long-standing debt was liquidated; July 1, the congregation became an independent, self-supported charge; and resulting from extensive alterations, involving an altar-centered chancel, a public mortgage-burning ceremony took place at public worship September 29. The ritual significantly said,

> And, now, as the mortgage burns, we thank God for the blessings and successes of the past, and pray for His continued favor and guidance, and dedicate ourselves anew to the work and support of our beloved Church and the extension of the Kingdom of God throughout our community, our nation and our world.[10]

Rev. Lawrence N. Strunk, who began serving the congregation March 10, 1948, continued to expand its program and influence. In a booklet published by the congregation shortly after Mr. Strunk arrived on the field, appears the following terse definition of the current program. "The church and its ministry is set with the one and all-consuming purpose firmly established: To lead men, women, boys and girls to Christ; To give them guidance for right living; To assist in the relief of suffering, whether it be physical or spiritual; to help restore wounded and wrecked lives; To advance the Kingdom of God in the community it serves."[11]

As an expression of this redemptive program a scout hut was erected in 1950. The 34th Anniversary of the organization of the congregation was observed July 26, 1953. Speakers on that occasion were: Rev. Frank K. Bostian, Dr. Lee A. Peeler and Dr. Banks J. Peeler. Two effective preaching missions occurred during this pastorate. Dr. Harold H. Wilke, who had spent months serving in military hospitals on the war front, led the first one and Dr. Allen S. Meck, president of The Theological Seminary, Lancaster, Pennsylvania, was the preacher for the second.

In 1952 the sanctuary was completely remodeled at an approximate cost of $23,000; also in 1928 plans were approved for remodeling the existing educational equipment and the erection of a fellowship hall.

The church observed its 40th Anniversary August 2, 1959, when the services of the day were in charge of Pastor Ivan T. Morrin. Speakers for the occasion were: Dr. Harvey A. Fesperman, president of Southern Synod, Rev. Lawrence N. Strunk and Dr. Lee A. Peeler. The Anniversary Brochure expresses the sentiment and reflects the spirit of that occasion.

> To be part of a church which has been active in a community for forty years fills us with a mingled sense of pride and humility. We rejoice as we look upon our short history and realize that our church has been richly blessed of God. We stand in awe before our loving Heavenly Father, who has made this wonderful history possible.

Another mile stone was passed Sunday, December 31, 1961, when as a first step, ground was broken for the erection of Fellowship Hall. Nine months later, September 2, 1962, doors to the completed building were opened and the pastor, Rev. Huitt R. Carpenter, read a ritual of dedication. Varied kinds of stewardship had gone into the creation of this new facility, ranging from the Spring Festival to generous donations of money, time and talents.

Rev. Bobby R. Bonds is the current popular and effective minister of the church. His ministry began August 1, 1963. St. John's congregation is organized to meet the needs of a modern industrial parish. Since the Kannapolis population is mobile, large numbers of people are received into the church each year, and a considerable number is dismissed to other communities. Its present confirmed membership is 311; Sunday School enrollment is 260; the annual budget is in the range of $25,000.

Five sons of the congregation are serving in the Christian Ministry: Rev. Horace S. Sills, Rev. Charles L. Fisher, Rev. Wade H.

Curran, Jr. and Rev. Ingle O. Cook in the United Church of Christ, and Rev. John R. Sills in The Methodist Church.

ROSTER OF PASTORS

Rev. Lee A. Peeler, D.D........1919-1938
Rev. Joseph D. Andrew 1939-1942
Rev. Frank K. Bostian 1942-1947
Rev. Lawrence N. Strunk 1948-1955

Rev. Ivan R. Morrin 1956-1959
Rev. Huitt R. Carpenter 1960-1963
Rev. Bobby R. Bonds 1963-

1. ———. Minutes. Classis of North Carolina, 1911, p. 16.
2. ———. Minutes. *Op. cit.*, 1912, p. 41.
3. ———. *Ibid.* p. 40.
4. *Bostian*, Frank K., Historical Booklet and Directory, St. John's Evangelical and Reformed Church, 1946, p. 16 ff.
5. ———. Minutes. *Op. cit.*, 1920, p. 6.
6. *Lyerly*, William C., Personal Record, 1946.
7. ———. Minutes. *Op. cit.*, 1920, p. 6.
9. *Bostian*. Op. cit., p. 21 ff.
10. *Ibid*. p. 54.
11. *Bonds*, Bobby R., History of St. John's United Churih of Christ, Manuscript, 1964, p. 13 ff.
12. *Morrin*, Ivan R., 40th Anneversary, St. John's Evangelical and Reformed Church, 1959, p. 3.

St. Luke's Church, Rowan County

To ACCOMMODATE THE RELIGIOUS NEEDS of German Reformed families living in the Stokes Ferry Road section of Rowan County, a union Sunday School was organized in the home of Nathan Brown, located one mile Southeast of Granite Quarry. The Brown residence stood near the present site of Christiana Lutheran Church. Thirty-five people gathered there March 4, 1866, for their first meeting. Convening weekly for purposes of Bible study and fellowship, the assembly was occasionally favored with a sermon by an ordained minister, when such was available. Two names have been mentioned in the record—Revs. Lamberth and Redwine.

The Sunday School appears to have flourished over a period of five years, when a division occurred. As a result, Christiana Lutheran Church was organized January 23, 1871,[1] and the following December 31, St. Luke's Reformed Church was born, the former with seven charter members, and the latter with seventeen. The organization meeting took place in the home of Alexander Peeler, under the supervision of Rev. Peter M. Trexler, who was then serving the Central Rowan Charge, of which St. Luke's Church became a part.[2] David D. Peeler and Peter Trexler, Sr., were elected Elders, and Alexander Peeler and A. M. Holshouser, Deacons.

On the charter membership list were the following names: male— Peter Trexler, Sr., Rev. Peter M. Trexler, David D. Peeler, Jacob Trexler, David Peeler, Alexander Peeler, Henry C. Peeler, James Holshouser, Joseph Peeler, and A. M. Holshouser; female—Camilla Peeler, Jane Peeler, Charlotte Peeler, Sallie Holshouser, Mary Holshouser, Mary C. Peeler and Mary C. Trexler.

Three acres of land, upon which the church now stands, were donated to the congregation by Alexander Peeler, father of Dr. Lee A. Peeler. The cemetery land was a gift from Peter Trexler, Sr.; however, because of the untimely death of Mr. Trexler, a deed for the property was made some years later, when it was in possession of the Cope Mining Company.

Evidently, for economic reasons, the congregation worshipped for two years under a brush arbor located on church grounds. That regular services were held under the arbor, except during cold winter months, is supported by the record. The first Baptismal Service held after the congregation was organized, took place under the arbor May 12, 1872. At that time George Henry, infant son of Mr. and Mrs. David D. Peeler, was received into the church by the Sacrament of Holy Baptism. That baby boy is the father of Dr. Banks J. Peeler. On the same date, five sons and daughters, ranging in age from 6 to 12 years, of Mr. and Mrs. Charles Mesimore, were similarly made members of "the Body of Christ."

The main section of the white frame church building, was erected in 1872 and 1873 by the charter members. Lumber for the structure was hewed out by hand, as were logs for sleepers and joists. Framing was tied together with wooden pegs and or shop made nails and braces. Construction of this first house of worship, not including free labor, totalled $698.03, a debt which was completely liquidated by 1877, when Treasurer David D. Peeler made the final payment of $3.00 to Peter Trexler, Sr., from whom money to build it had been borrowed. Dedication Services occurred the fifth Sunday in June 1873.

St. Luke's Church, at no time in its history numerically large, has contributed heavily in members to a number of other Reformed Churches in the State of North Carolina. On June 4, 1899, David D. Peeler, who had served the congregation as treasurer for twenty eight years, and sixteen other prominent people of the congregation, were dismissed to Shiloh Church, Faith; also, when Bethel Church, Blowing Rock, was organized, a large number was transferred to that congregation. First Church, Salisbury has consistently benefitted from the same source.

In 1936, a wing was erected on the left side of the building. In 1946, in memory of Elder and Mrs. David T. Peeler, an art glass window depicting Christ in Gethsemane, was installed by the family in the pulpit recess. The hut appeared in 1951, and art glass windows took the place of old ones in the sanctuary in 1952. During the summer of 1954, a wing providing modern utilities and educational equipment, was attached to the right side of the church. Old pulpit furniture was replaced with new in 1957.

A completely new building and renovation program was begun in July 1957. These operations involved brick veneering the church, paneling the sanctuary on the inside, and the erection of a cross on the church tower. The cross is in memory of Dr. and Mrs. Peter M. Trexler and given by a daughter, Mrs. Mary Trexler Lyerly. Also, the old hut was torn away, and a new brick structure erected and named Fellowship Hall. This entire project involved an expenditure of $24,500. Dedication services were held January 28, 1968, when the pastor, Rev. Edwin C. Nagel led the ceremony. Rev. James L. Peeler preached the sermon.

The church is well organized, and is doing excellent work, judged by denominational program standards. The Classis of North Carolina convened at St. Luke's Church in 1886, and the 75th Anniversary of the birth of the congregation was appropriately observed in 1948. Ministerial sons are: Rev. Peter M. Trexler, D.D., Rev. Lee A. Peeler, D.D., Rev. John C. Peeler, D.D., Rev. Augustus C. Peeler, Rev. James L. Peeler.

ROSTER OF PASTORS

Rev. Peter M. Trexler, D.D. 1871-1876	Rev. Aaron R. Tosh, D.D. 1939-1944
Rev. Jacob C. Clapp, D.D.,	Rev. Carl R. Flocken 1944-1948
Supply 1876-1878	Rev. C. Columbus Wagoner,
Rev. John A. Foil, Supply 1876-1878	Supply 1948-
Rev. John Ingle 1878-1883	Rev. Milton Whitener,
Rev. Robert F. Crooks 1883-1887	Supply 1949-1950
Rev. Calvin B. Heller, Supply 1887-1889	Rev. Huitt R. Carpenter,
Rev. J. M. Luther Lyerly,	Supply 1950-1951
Ph.D. 1889-1896	Mr. Robert Delp,
The Church was vacant thirteen	Student Supply 1950-
months while Dr. Lyerly served	Rev. Carl T. Daye 1951-1954
the Lincoln Charge.	Mr. Kenneth Hefley,
Rev. Walter W. Rowe, D.D. 1906-1908	Student Supply 1954-
Rev. J. Leidy Yearick 1909-1912	Rev. Lionel A. Whiston, Ph.D.,
Rev. John A. Koons 1912-1918	Supply 1954-1955
Rev. Samuel A. Troxell 1919-1921	Rev. Melvin T. Hamm 1955-1956
Mr. O. Bain Michael,	Rev. Carl R. Martin,
Student Supply 1922-	Supply 1957-
Rev. Harvey A. M. Holshouser,	Rev. Robert E. Myers 1957-1967
Ph.D. 1922-1929	Rev. Edwin C. Nagel 1967-
Rev. L. O. Carbaugh 1930-1939	

1. *Morgan*, Jacob L., Editor. History of the Lutheran Church in North Carolina, 1953, p. 183.
2. ———. Minutes. Classis of North Carolina, 1872, pp. 118, 123.
3. *Myers*, Robert E., and Peeler, Carr, Manuscript. St. Luke's Church, 1965.

St. Mark's Church, Alamance County

As EARLY AS 1745, Rev. Christian Theus ministered to the Reformed and Lutheran people living in the Shoemaker neighborhood. Shoemaker was a German settlement located two miles northeast of Gibsonville, which got its name from a German family in whose home a school originated. This home became a focal point for the settlement and a common meeting place for social and religious gatherings. It was to serve the religious needs of these people that brought Mr. Theus to the community. A brush arbor was constructed nearby under which regular religious services were conducted. He was followed by Rev. James Martin, Rev. Richard Dupert and Rev. John W. Bithahn, all clergymen of the Reformed faith.

Rev. Samuel Suther appeared in North Carolina in 1768, ministering to the people of this community from 1771 to 1773, during which time the Reformed congregation appears to have been organized. The only identifiable charter member of this congregation is one George Hoffman, an Elder and Trustee, who, with his two brothers John and Hans, migrated from Burke County, Pennsylvania in 1749.

The congregation was known as "Shoemaker's" and operated peacefully as a union church with the Lutheran segment of that community for many years. To meet their religious needs, a spacious log church building was erected in the center of the cemetery, which served that purpose over a period of 80 years. By the time Rev. J. H. Crawford appeared in 1828, something of the spirit of the "new world" had gripped most German settlements in North Carolina. He, therefore, undertook to change, at least in part, the Service of Worship from the German to the English language. The effort met with decided opposition. Members ceased to attend worship; some of them never renewed their interest, some affiliated with the Lutheran congregation, while others transferred their membership to the Brick Church several miles away. From this point the congregation began to disintegrate. In 1834 it was dropped from the roll of Classis.

When Rev. George W. Welker became pastor of the Guilford Charge in November of 1842, he began to give attention to the Reformed people living in the Shoemaker, now Frieden's community. This pattern of ministry continued for a number of years.

On January 13, 1855, the congregation was reorganized as Frieden's Reformed Church, and continued to operate as a union church. The congregation was small, numbering only 31 confirmed members. However, because of the popularity of the young pastor and his reputation as a preacher, the church was usually crowded to its doors on "preaching days." Leaders of the Reformed Church soon learned that coopeartion from the Lutheran congregation was not forthcoming, so made preparations to relocate. By unanimous action the congregation voted to relocate the church in the Boone Station Community. A site was selected at the intersection of the Hillsboro-Salisbury and Fayetteville-High Rock stage roads. Here, on land owned by Adam Whitesell, Jr., known currently as the W. R. Whitt homeplace, an arbor was erected and for five years, during the summer months, meetings were held under it. In the winter, services were held in homes of members of the congregation and their friends. However, special services like weddings, Baptisms, and the Holy Communion continued to be held in the Frieden's church building until 1861.

In 1862 a church was built on land purchased from Duncan Troxler and located about one-half mile south of the arbor. It was a frame structure with dimensions of 40 by 60 feet. These were war days; hence, for economic reasons, construction was slow. The house was enclosed and made suitable for meetings and thus used for a number of years.

The first service was held in the new building in August 1863. About this time, sentiment developed among the members in favor of renaming the congregation. Elder Jacob Barnhardt suggested "St. Mark's," after the Gospel which bears that name. His suggestion was approved.

In 1916, after 53 years, this first church building was badly in need of repairs. A building committee was appointed consisting of C. V. Boone, chairman, D. E. Clapp, J. M. Cheek, W. B. Montgomery and Everett C. Rumley, which after investigation recommended a new house of worship. While building operations were in progress, the congregation worshipped in the old Highland School House. Remembering that World War I was in progress, and building material as well as labor were scarce, the congregation adopted the pay-as-you-go plan for financing the effort, which of necessity spread out construction over a period of six years. The cornerstone was laid on April 20, 1919, and the building was completed and paid for by April 20, 1922. Sunday School rooms were added in 1929. A hut, designed for educational and social purposes was erected in 1941.

During the pastorates of Revs. Charles E. Hiatt, Aubrey W. Hedrick and Sterling W. Whitener, covering a period of 17 years, St. Mark's made excellent progress in all phases of its life. It was during this period that Southern Synod was engaged in a study of large rural and semi-rural charges in North Carolina, with the hope that better pastoral oversight could be made available to these congregations. Recently a new congregation had been organized in the Brightwood community southwest of Gibsonville. Thus, St. Mark's was detached from the Guilford Charge and yoked with Brightwood, creating the Boone Station Charge.

To this new charge Rev. John C. Peeler was called, beginning his pastorate July 1, 1944. Almost immediately there was need of better facilities at St. Mark's. As a result, in June of 1946 the congregation unanimously voted to build a new church, and the matter was referred to a committee for study and report. Ground was broken on April 15, 1947, and from that point work moved steadily to completion. The first service was held in the new building on May 16, 1948. The old house of worship that had served the congregation for 30 years was sold to the Textile Sales Room, Inc., and moved to the intersection of the Burlington highway and the Elon Road, where it continues to be used as a textile outlet.

After the church building had been completed and the debt retired, sentiment developed in the congregation in favor of building a parsonage in the vicinity of the church. A lot adjacent to church property on the south was purchased from Mr. and Mrs. E. W. Ferrell, and an additional 35 feet was donated by Mr. and Mrs. J. F. Wagoner. Plans for the house were accepted January 14, 1951. Construction began in April and was completed by October 1, 1951, the minister occupying the $14,000 structure immediately.

In the spring of 1951, at the meeting of Southern Synod, the Boone Station Charge was dissolved. St. Mark's was declared an independent, one-point parish. Dr. Peeler continued to serve the congregation until in 1955 illness required his withdrawal.

Rev. Huitt R. Carpenter came to serve the parish in 1956 and was instrumental in leading the congregation in additional program activities, meriting a citation by the North Carolina State Grange as "The Rural Church of the Year" in 1957. During these days the incentive was created and some financial preparations were made looking toward further religious education equipment.

By 1961 the congregation was ready to move ahead in providing adequate Christian education facilities. A study committee was created with instructions to develop plans designed to meet current and future needs. On August 12, 1962, these plans were presented and approved by the congregation. Groundbreaking ceremonies were held on February 3, 1963. Dedication services occurred September 16, 1965. The facility had been in use since November 24,

1963. The building is of modern design, well equipped, and planned' to meet present-day educational requirements. Total expenditures were $136,598.93.

Rev. Lawrence A. Leonard began his pastorate of the church August 1, 1960.

On the church roll of ministerial sons are: Revs. Thomas E. Hoffman, James D. Rumley, Jr., and Lester I. Somers. In the congregation are 393 confirmed members, and the Sunday School has an enrollment of 382 pupils.

ROSTER OF PASTORS

Rev. Christian Theus,	Rev. John Rudy 1821-1825
Swiss Reformed Missionary 1745-1760	Rev. William Paisley,
Rev. James Martin,	Presbyterian, Supply 1826-1827
Swiss Reformed Missionary 1761-1764	Rev. John H. Crawford 1828-1842
Rev. Richard Dupert,	Rev. George W. Welker, D.D. 1842-1889
Hugonot 1765-1767	Rev. Jesse Richards 1889-1891
Rev. Samued Suther, Swiss ..1768-1786	Rev. D. P. LeFevre 1891-1893
Rev. William Bithahn 1787-1789	Rev. James D. Andrew, D.D. 1893-1913
Rev. Samuel Weyberg,	Rev. Dugan C. Cox 1914-1916
Evangelist 1790-1801	Rev. Albert H. Zechiel 1916-1918
Rev. Andrew Loretz,	Rev. Albert Klinger 1918-1921
Visiting Minister, periodic	Supplies 1921-1927
Rev. Henry Dieffenbach 1801-1807	Rev. Charles E. Hiatt 1927-1938
Vacant 1807-1812	Rev. Aubrey W. Hedrick 1938-1942
Rev. J. R. Rilley,	Rev. Sterling W. Whitener 1942-1944
Visiting Evangelist 1813-1814	Rev. John C. Peeler, D.D. ..1944-1955
Vacant 1815-1819	Rev. Huitt R. Carpenter 1956-1960
Rev. George Leidy 1819-1820	Rev. Lawrence A. Leonard 1960-

Bibliography
> *Clapp*, Jacob C., Editor. Historic Church of the Reformed Church in North Carolina, 1908.
> *Leonard*, Jacob C., History of the Southern Synod of the Evangelical and Reformed Church, 1940.
> *Rumley*, Everett C., Sr., History of St. Mark's United Church of Christ, 1961.
> *Rumley*, Everett C. Sr., One Hundredth Anniversary of St. Mark's Evangelical and Reformed Church, 1955.
> *Leonard*, Lawrence A., St. Mark's Reformed Church, United Church of Christ, 1965.

St. Matthew Church, Catawba County

FIFTEEN YEARS BEFORE a church was built, the St. Matthew's Community was a focal point. As early as 1820 citizens living in the area were active in providing school facilities for their children. Daniel Hallman, who lived within "speaking distance of the present church," was evidently one of these concerned people. For in 1822 he gave the land on which the "Hallman School" house was built. In part, the deed reads as follows:

> In consideration of the esteem I have for learning and in order to promote and encourage education, I have given and granted unto my good neighbors the privilege of building a school house on my land, which house is now built and nearly finished.[1]

This log school house stood about 200 yards south of the church building, and was used regularly until school areas were re-dis-

tricted and the location moved to Piney Grove. An old record of the school session taught in the winter of 1828 by Abel Ikerd contains the following family names, all of them prominent in that section of the county today: Finger, Schrum, Derr, Carpenter, Summerrow, Blackburn, Smith, Hallman, and Johnson. In this old building, in later years, camp-meeting preachers were housed during the St. Matthew's series of services.

Obviously quite a number of German Reformed Church families lived in the area, most of whom held their memberships in Emanuel (Old White) Church, Lincolnton. To accommodate these pious folks, Rev. John G. Fritchey, pastor of the Lincoln Charge, periodically held services for them, usually in private homes. One such service occurred May 22, 1836 in the home of Michael Finger. On this occasion the audience consulted on "the propriety of building a meeting house" in their midst. John Coulter was made chairman of the meeting, and Benjamin Norris was named secretary. John Ramsaur (Tanner) agreed to give land on the road leading from Lincolnton to Island Ford on which to build a "house for worship of Almighty God." John Ramsaur and John Coulter were appointed Trustees; Joseph Finger, John Blackburn and Jacob Summerrow were asked to manage finances. David R. Bennick was elected secretary of the congregation.[2]

A second meeting of interested people, perhaps only a building committee that had been named, took place July 23, 1836, in the home of Joseph Finger. Agreement was reached to erect a building one-story high and measuring 30 by 40 ft., and to award the contract for erecting it to the lowest bidder. The contract was awarded August 13, 1836 to Joseph Finger for the sum of $265. A deed was drawn by John Ramsaur June 3, 1836 in favor of the Trustees, involving 5 acres of land, for the nominal sum of fifty cents. On the following day, Mr. Ramsaur leased the spring located near the church, to the Trustees for 199 years. This spring was later purchased by David Finger and deeded to the church. Pledges and cash received to date on the building program totalled $232. Pledges ranged from fifty cents to ten dollars. Other gifts were received later, covering the entire expense.

The Church was organized May 3, 1837. John Carpenter, Jacob Ramsaur (M W), John Ramsaur and Daniel Finger were elected elders; no mention is made of deacons. When the Classis of North Carolina convened beginning the following May 10, the new congregation was enrolled as a member of that body.[3] The charter membership list, most of whom were transferred from Emanuel Church, Lincolnton, contained forty seven names: John Ramsaur (Tanner), John Carpenter, Daniel Finger (Tanner), Anthony Ikerd, David Summerrow, Jr., Daniel Schrum, Michael Finger, Peter Summerrow, Michael Summerrow, Nancy Finger, Rachel Finger, Susan Ramsaur, Mary Schrum, Susan Finger, Margaret Summerrow, Rebecca K. Summerrow, Sarah Finger (Hinson), Sarah Summerrow, Rebecca Bolick, David R. Bennick, Wiley Hallman, Jacob Summerrow, Joseph Finger, Henry Summerrow, James N. Summerrow, Jacob Ramsaur (M W), Ambrose Bolick, Elisha Saunders, Mary Ann Bennick, Elizabeth Carpenter, Mary Carpenter, Widow Elizabeth Finger, Catherine Schrum, Barbara Hallman, Ann Ikerd, Barbara Summerrow, Elizabeth Finger (Reinhardt), Elizabeth Carpenter, Elmira Summerrow, Mrs. Mary Rudisill, Mrs. Saunders, Mrs. Louisa Goodson, Mrs. Nancy Boyd, Mrs. Nancy Murphy, Rev. David Crooks, Mrs. Catherine Crooks, Solomon Rudisill.[4]

The new church building was dedicated May 21, 1837. The elders were ordained and installed the same day in what appears to be the closing service of a series of evangelistic meetings.

Camp-meetings were popular and effective in those days. Three years after the church was built, on August 15, 1839, a camp-meeting program was established at St. Matthew's Church. On the previous September 9, John Ramsaur, for a consideration of fifty dollars, conveyed a deed involving twenty five acres of land to the Trustees of St. Matthew's Church, the same to be used for cemetery and camp-meeting grounds purposes. Until 1845 these services were held under the spacious brush arbor, when it was replaced by a more substantial arbor of wood construction. This was one of the smaller camp-meeting grounds, involving at most not more than twenty two tents, but it was popular and widely influential, substantially undergirding the moral and spiritual temper of the times. The Historic Sketch of the Reformed Church in North Carolina, describes in detail the benefits of this institution to the community in which it was located and the denomination of which it was a part.

An institution of great interest to the community and surrounding country for many miles was the camp-meeting held annually at St. Matthew's for a period of thirty five years, now called "protracted meetings." These meetings were held under a brush arbor until 1845, when a large frame arbor with hiproof was constructed, James Summerrow and Joseph Finger doing the work of construction, and Henry Whitener being the architect. Every year there came great numbers of Reformed people from Catawba and Lincoln counties to this place. With these annual gatherings are associated many hallowed memories. There under the spacious arbor were heard the voices of God's faithful ministers preaching the acceptable year of the Lord. There, too, many were brought to a saving knowledge of Jesus Christ and made a profession of their faith. . . . .

Not only all the churches of this section closed their doors on the Sunday over which the camp meeting was held, but the faculty and students of Catawba College attended, and we have been told that the sainted F. D. Reinhardt used to take his four-horse wagon and convey the students to this place.

In 1840 the Classis of North Carolina passed this resolution: "That a camp meeting shall be held at St. Matthew's Church, commencing on Friday previous to the third Sabbath in August next, and it shall be the duty of all ministerial brethren to attend said camp meeting."[5] This arrangement served to develop an "esprit de corps" in ministers and people and bound them more closely together in love and service for the Master. The camp meeting services here held are remarkable for good order and religious devotion. When the signal was given for public services, everyone went to the arbor without stopping to enquire who was to preach.

Not only were the people who habitually worshipped in the church and the crowds that assembled under the orbor noted for their orderly worship and conduct during public services and while on the grounds, but the whole neighborhood was once celebrated for its obedience to civil law. . . . . It was at St. Matthew's camp meeting ground in 1850, in John Coulter's tent during a meeting of the Loretz Beneficiary Society that the establishment of a literary institution was suggested. . . . . It was not long after this that Catawba College was founded as a result of this meeting.[6]

In 1906, writing in similar vein, Dr. Joseph L. Murphy remarked:

It is always profitable to meet together and spend sometime in the worship of God and in fellowship. The denominational value of the St. Matthew's meetings lies in the opportunity it gives for our people to come together once a year and mingle with each other and to know of each other's work.

The stranger may wonder what it is that draws so many people to this place of worship. There is no tenting and camping on the grounds. There is no special excitement in the manner of conducting the meetings. There has been no effort to secure sensational preachers or noted evangelists to conduct the meetings. These services are usually conducted by neighboring pastors and yet the people gather by the hundreds and thousands. What is the drawing power? It must be in the fact that this place and these meetings find a warm place in the hearts of the people. For more than sixty years the people have been gathering here. Here our fathers and mothers worshipped and around this holy place the spiritual birth place of many is to be found. There were camp meetings in those days and the multitude came to find rest of body and soul. . . . . .

It was on this occasion that we met for the first time some of the saints, now gone to glory, who helped to make this place the goodly land. There was Solomon Rudisill, Henry Schrum, Milton Campbell, William Hinson, Daniel Finger, H. A. Forney, A. F. Carpenter, Levi Schrum and others who came from Salem, Daniels, Grace and other nearby congregations. Who will ever forget the good mothers? Mothers Crooks, Hinson, Finger and others. We think it is because of these sacred memories and hallowed associations that many love to go to St. Matthews.[7]

In those days the Reformed Church in North Carolina, along with sister churches, encountered the race problem, similar to that of the current generation, and dealt with it in harmony with the spirit of the times. In 1838 the Classis of North Carolina took the following action:

> Whereas there are still some churches in our bounds, without room for colored people in the sanctuary, and without provision for their reception into the communion of the church, therefore, resolved:
> That all churches be recommended to follow the example of their sister Reformed Churches, and of the churches of other denominations generally . . . . in providing room and pews for colored people, in the house of God, and in opening the doors for their reception into the communion of the Church, whenever their knowledge of Truth and Piety shall render them fit subjects for Christian communion.[8]

Evidently St. Matthew's Church had made provision to serve colored people, because they were admitted to membership, the number being unknown, and provision was made for them in the sanctuary and for camp meetings. A record on an old minutes book, dated June 24, 1837 reads, "Resolved that the colored people occupy the two back seats at the end of the house, one on each side of the entrance, as often and as long as the consistory may think proper." In similar fashion a small arbor was constructed along side of the large one for their use.[9] Thus, the life of this influential rural congregation continued to minister to the needs of the area and met each new situation with candor and faith.

In 1907 there was need for new equipment. At a meeting called that year, in the home of Thomas L. Finger, being the same place where plans were laid for the first "meeting house," ways and means for providing this new equipment were developed. Thomas L. Finger, Julius L. Schrum and Daniel F. Campbell were named to a building committee. H. Jacob Crooks was chosen treasurer of the Building Fund.

Early in 1908, work began in assembling material. Lumber was cut and sawed on the church grounds. Brick was made on Levi Schrum's farm. The cornerstone for the building was laid on ascension day that year, and by autumn religious services were being conducted in the new building. The old pews were used until 1911, when new furniture was installed in the sanctuary. The pulpit is in memory of Michael and Elizabeth Finger, given by their son W. M. D. Finger; a communion table was placed in the chancel in memory of Mr. and Mrs. Phillip E. Campbell by their children, Mrs. Thomas Phillips and Daniel F. Campbell. In the summer of 1920 the church was redecorated, but dedication did not occur until September 3, 1923. The spacious arbor, still used for special services prior to the first Sunday in September, was re-roofed in 1921. A bell was installed in the tower in 1926.

Centennial of the church organization and the 25th Anniversary of the ordination of the pastor, Rev. John A. Koons, were observed

May 30, 1937. It was a full and meaningful day for the congregation and friends. Among speakers for the occasion were: Rev. Harvey G. Kopenhaver, Rev. C. Columbus Wagoner, a former pastor, Rev. Carl H. Clapp, Hon. Loomis F. Kluttz, Dr. Walter W. Rowe and Elder John F. Carpenter.

At a congregational meeting held January 1950, Paul J. McRee was instructed to develop plans for an educational annex to meet prescribed needs of the parish. This action had its beginning in 1944, when Adrian L. Shuford, Sr., of Trinity Church, Conover, made a sizable contribution to the building fund, and for which the congregation since then has been accumulating assets. Plans for the annex were presented to the congregation February 5, 1950 and approved.

Two days later the people were called together again, when personnel for two committees were selected; building: J. Paul McRee, H. Albert Schrum, Aubrey H. Campbell, Paul M. Hartzoge; finance: T. B. Parker, Theodore Campbell, Frank Bumgardner, J. O. Carpenter, Woodrow Schrum, R. Glenn McRee, Everett Campbell and Miles Schrum. Action on assembling material began immediately. Timber was cut on the church grounds; groundbreaking ceremonies took place March 5; the cornerstone was laid August 20; and the facility was occupied October 1, 1950. It was dedicated June 29, 1952.

St. Matthew's Church, through the years, has been a source of membership recruiting by churches in both Catawba and Lincoln counties. Special beneficiaries in this respect have been Salem and Emanuel, Lincolnton; Memorial, Maiden; and Grace Church, Newton. St. Matthew's Church has been yoked with other congregations in the area over a period of 128 years, operating as the Lincoln Charge. In 1965, by request of the congregation, it was declared by Southern Synod an independent, self-supporting charge. Rev. Martin L. Parker, Jr., has been the successful pastor of the church since that time.

Roster of Pastors

Rev. John G. Fritchey 1837-1840	Rev. Jacob C. Clapp, D.D. ..1894-1897
Rev. G. A. Leopold, Supply 1840-	Rev. Theodore C. Hesson 1897-1902
Rev. John H. Crawford,	Rev. Calvin B. Heller 1902-1906
Supply 1840-1841	Rev. J. Leidy Yearick 1907-1908
Rev. Solomon S. Middlekauff 1842-1845	Rev. Jacob C. Clapp, D.D.,
Rev. David Crooks 1845-1859	Alternate Supply 1909-1910
Rev. John Lantz 1859-1868	Rev. John A. Foil, Ph.D.,
Rev. Jacob C. Clapp, D.D.,	Alternate Supply 1909-1910
Supply 1868-1873	Rev. C. Columbus Wagoner ..1910-1912
Rev. Jacob C. Clapp, D.D.,	Rev. Charles W. Warlick, D.D.,
Alternate Supply 1873-1881	Supply 1913-1915
Rev. John A. Foil, Ph.D.,	Rev. James D. Andrew, D.D.,
Alternate Supply 1873-1881	Supply 1915-1918
Rev. John A. Foil, Ph.D.,	Rev. Harvey G. Kopenhaver,
Supply 1881-1885	Supply 1918-1919
Rev. Joseph L. Murphy, D.D. 1885-1890	Rev. John A. Koons 1919-1944
Mr. C. A. Starr,	Rev. Lonnie A. Carpenter, D.D.,
Student Supply 1890-1891	Supply 1944-1945
Rev. J. M. Luther Lyerly,	Rev. William A. Jones 1946-1947
Ph.D. 1892-1893	Rev. Shuford Peeler, D.D.,
Rev. John A. Foil, Ph.D.,	Supply 1948-
Supply 1893-1894	Rev. John A. Koons 1948-1953

Rev. Lewis E. Everline,
Supply 1953-1954
Rev. Frank W. Snider 1954-1956
Rev. Terrell M. Shoffner,
Supply 1956-1957

Rev. Lonnie A. Carpenter, D.D.,
Supply 1957-
Mr. Thomas R. Hamilton,
Student Summer Supply 1957-
Rev. James D. Rumley, Jr. 1958-1965
Rev. Martin L. Parker, Jr. ..1965-

1. *Hodges*, J. E., Manuscript. St. Matthew's Church, Rich in History, p. 2.
2. *Koons*, John A., Centennial Bulletin. St. Matthew's Reformed Church, 1937, p. 3.
3. ———. Minutes. Classis of North Carolina, 1837, p. 44.
4. *Clapp*, Jacob C., Editor. Historic Sketch of the Reformed Church in North Carolina, 1908, p. 290 ff.
5. ———. Minutes. *Op. cit.*, 1840, p. 118.
6. *Clapp*, *Op. cit.*, p. 292 ff.
7. *Murphy*, Joseph L., The Reformed Church Standard, August 15, 1906, p. 4.
8. ———. Minutes. *Op. cit.*, 1838, p. 102.
9. *Clapp*, *Op. cit.*, p. 296.

St. Matthew Church, Charlotte

ST. MATTHEW'S COMMUNITY CHAPEL, Bancroft Street and Concordia Avenue, was conceived as being first in a series of new Evangelical and Reformed congregations in the environs of Charlotte, North Carolina. The series was to be named Matthew, Mark, Luke and John in deference to the four Gospels recorded in the New Testament. This idea was presented to the Consistory of First Church by Rev. Huitt R. Carpenter, then serving it as pastor, and enthusiastically endorsed.[1]

The project was brought to the attention of the Council of Southern Synod on May 29, 1948, and by that body referred to its committee on National Missions for study, and to the Board of National Missions of the Evangelical and Reformed Church for enrollment and financial assistance.[2] Acting as sponsor, the Consistory of First Church set up a house-to-house survey in the proposed area, providing favorable information. The congregation donated $2,000 to the venture, and from interested friends and organizations, collected an additional $1,800. The project was enrolled by the Board of National Missions, voting a grant of $5,000 and a loan of equal amount with which to begin operations.

The lot on which the church building now stands was purchased in January 1949, costing $3,000. Groundbreaking ceremonies were set for January 31. Synod-wide interest in the new development is reflected by representative persons who appeared on the program. Activities were directed by Mr. Carpenter. Other participating dignitaries from First Church were: Dr. Shuford Peeler, its organizing pastor; Dewey L. Drum, Sr., chairman of the Consistory; and J. Bryan Davis, chairman of the Mission Building Committee. Present also were: Dr. Lonnie A. Carpenter, president of Southern Synod; Mrs. John T. Fesperman, president of the Synodical Women's Guild; and Thomas L. Moose, president of the Synodical Churchmen's Brotherhood.

Erection of a mission-type chapel, constructed of unfinished boards and painted brown, was begun immediately and finished by March 1, 1949. Total cost of the chapel was $8,000. Its occupancy occurred Palm Sunday, April 3, 1949 at 7:30 p.m. One hundred ninety-two persons were in the audience.

By action of the Synodical Council, Mr. Carpenter became the supply pastor, and for the next six months supervised this new work. With the help of laymen of First Church, he began immediately to organize what had been until this time, an unorganized movement of interested people. The Sunday School was organized April 17, 1949, naming Dewey L. Drum, Sr. as temporary superintendent. William H. Newman and Malcolm McIver continued to supervise the school for a number of months thereafter. The Sacrament of the Holy Communion was first served in the chapel Sunday evening, July 10, 1949. Sacramental elements were donated by a Jewish friend of the pastor, a Mr. Schwartz, who also made a donation of $100 to the Mission.

Official organization day was scheduled for August 7, 1949.[3] Sixteen names were on the charter membership roll: Mr. and Mrs. Harold L. Gilliland, Sr., Miss Clara Helen Gilliland, Mr. and Mrs. R. J. Gettings, Miss Linda Gladden, Mr. and Mrs. Wallace Davis, Miss Helen Davis, Mr. and Mrs. John A. Davis, Mrs. J. D. Davis, Mr. and Mrs. Herbert Beam, Jr., and Mr. and Mrs. Mike Lari. R. J. Geddings, Harold L. Gilliland, Sr. and Mike Lari were elected elders; John A. Davis, Wallace R. Davis and Herbert Beam, Jr. were named deacons.

Budgetary arrangements were made with the congregation by the Board of National Missions in preparation to call a full-time pastor. On August 7, 1949 Rev. Claude Kelly, a son of the First Church, was elected pastor. In preparation for his arrival a four-room brick house, located on Concordia Avenue was purchased on September

1, 1949 for $8,000. Mr. Kelly was succeeded by Rev. Richard Rubright on April 16, 1951. Having volunteered for foreign missionary service in Japan, he was subject to call. His summons came within a few weeks after moving to the parish, and he reported for missionary duty May 20, 1951.

Dr. Shuford Peeler, who had made an enviable record serving mission churches was at that time, living in retirement in the city of Charlotte. He was recalled by the Synod and appointed Stated Supply of the St. Matthew's Mission on June 1, 1951. This appointment continued seven years, until June 30, 1958. During this time St. Matthew's membership grew from 59 to 124. Sunday School rooms were added. The Shuford Peeler Recreation Center was erected and a new seven room brick parsonage was built on Grimes Street. The new house cost approximately $16,000.

During the pastorate of Rev. Thomas R. Hamilton, which began July 15, 1958, a well defined parish organization appeared. Property was improved, and 50 new members were added to the fellowship.

Rev. Terrell M. Shoffner became pastor of the church June 17, 1962. His ministry reflects steady progress in all departments of the congregation's life. He remarked, "At times progress has seemed slow at St. Matthew's, but with a membership of 157 souls, and a budget that has grown from $650 in 1950 to $11,600 in 1965, the future looks hopeful and encouraging."

The story of this church records four major special occasions, worthy of note. A service observing the Golden Anniversary of Dr. Shuford Peeler was conducted July 5, 1953, sponsored by the Churchmen's Brotherhood. An address on that occasion was delivered by Rev. William C. Lyerly. The Tenth Anniversary of the organization of St. Matthew's Church was celebrated April 5, 1959. The sermon being delivered on that occasion by its organizing minister, Rev. Huitt R. Carpenter.

A surprise "This is Your Life Service" was held February 21, 1960 at 7:30 P.M., honoring Dr. Shuford Peeler for his ministry on behalf of church extension. The speaker for that occasion was Dr. Purd E. Deitz, Executive Secretary of the Board of National Missions of the Evangelical and Reformed Church.

The Twenty-Fifth Anniversary of the ordination of Rev. Terrell M. Shoffner to the Christian Ministry was observed at 11 A.M. on July 19, 1964. Representing Southern Synod by appointment was the Rev. Richard A. Cheek, vice president. Mr. Cheek, a close friend of the pastor, delivered the anniversary sermon. Also present and presenting greetings were representatives from churches served by Mr. Shoffner.

ROSTER OF PASTORS

Rev. Huitt R. Carpenter, Organizer 1948-1949	Rev. Richard Rubright 1951-
Rev. Claude W. Kelly 1949-1951	Rev. Shuford Peeler, D.D., Stated Supply 1951-1958
Rev. Felix B. Peck, Th.D., Supply 1951-	Rev. Thomas R. Hamilton 1958-1961
	Rev. Terrell M. Shoffner 1962-1967

1. ———. Minutes. Southern Synod of the Evangelical and Reformed
    Church, 1949, p. 16.
2. *Ibid.* p. 16.
3. ———. Minutes. *Op. cit.*, 1950, p. 12.
       Reference: Shoffner, Terrell M., Manuscript. A History of St. Mat-
    thews' United Church of Christ, 1965.

St. Paul's Church, Enochville

A NUMBER OF YEARS prior to 1886 there was interest among Reformed people in the area in organizing a church of their faith in
the Patterson School House community. The idea was suggested
to Dr. Paul Barringer, who was pastor of the West Rowan Charge,
consisting of Mt. Zion and Gilead churches.[1] This concern was
brought to the attention of the Classis of North Carolina at its spring
meeting in 1886, which body authorized certain action:

> Resolved that Revs. Barringer and Trexler be a committee to look
> after the Reformed members at and near Enochville, and other points
> in Rowan county who are not convenient to any Reformed Church, and
> that when they deem it advisable to organize congregations.[2]

At that time, other than Salisbury, the village of Enochville was
probably the most prominent place in Rowan county. Naturally,
the founding of a church there was imperative. Two meetings were
held in St. Enoch Lutheran Church located in the village. Another
preaching appointment was scheduled in August 1889 at the Deal
School House, with the view of assessing sentiment and support
favorable to establishing a Reformed Church there. Dr. Peter M.
Trexler conducted the service and presided over the business session which followed.

Another meeting was held October 9 in the home of L. B. Corriher. At that time action was taken to proceed with preparations in anticipation of an established church. W. C. Rose and L. B. Corriher were named elders, and J. Wilson Deal and C. L. Beaver, deacons. W. C. Rose, L. B. Corriher and J. W. Deal were made a committee to prepare a charter membership list.

Later in the same month a meeting took place in the "Old Cooper House" when the charter membership list was presented. Elected officials were ordained and installed in their respective positions. The new congregation was named St. Paul's Reformed Church, and David Deal, Lock Beaver and W. C. Rose were asked to recommend a building site for the proposed new house of worship.

On the membership list were: C. L. Beaver, Mrs. Betty Beaver, Gemima Beaver, W. B. Beaver, Jane Beaver, L. B. Corriher, Mrs. L. B. Corriher, S. J. Corriher, T. A. Corriher, Emma Corriher, Mrs. W. A. Deal, Sr., W. A. Deal, Sr., J. Wilson Deal, D. A. Deal, W. A. Deal, Jr., S. J. Deal, J. D. Foutz, Mrs. J. D. Foutz, J. A. Hombarrier, Mrs. J. A. Hombarrier, Mrs. Mary E. Poston, W. C. Rose, Mrs. W. C. Rose, Sarah E. Rose, Mary Louisa Rose, Mrs. Clarissa Stirewalt.

A number of locations were suggested by the committee, but the present site was selected by popular vote of the congregation. It involved one acre of land purchased from Aaron Yost for the sum of fifty-five dollars. Deed for it bears the date of November 5, 1886. W. A. Deal was elected Trustee. Preparations for erecting a house of worship went steadily ahead. A cornerstone laying service was held in August 1888, when Dr. George W. Welker, Stated Clerk of the Classis of North Carolina and president of the General Synod of the Reformed Church in the United States, made an appropriate address. The Classis contributed $150 to the building fund.[3] Debt free, the house of worship was dedicated to Almighty God August 31, 1890. Dr. Jacob C. Leonard preached the dedicatory sermon.

St. Paul's Church was officially recognized by the Classis at its spring meeting in 1887, when Elder W. C. Rose presented required credentials and was admitted to a seat in the sessions.[4] In the same year the Classis was so well pleased with progress made at Enochville that it approved an appropriate resolution.

Resolved that the Classis have such confidence in the judgment and prudence of the committee to whom was given the option of the organization of a Reformed Congregation at Enochville, Rowan county, that the entire disposition of the matter, as regards the location of the church etc. be committed to them.[5]

"St. Paul's Mission" appears first in the statistical report of Classis in 1889, when there were twenty eight confirmed and twenty unconfirmed members.[6] The Sunday School appeared on this record in 1891, enrolling fifty four pupils.[7] However, the Sunday School appears to have been organized in 1887. At that time William Fleming, a member of the Mt. Zion congregation, was the superintendent. Dr. Paul Barringer continued to minister to the congregation until 1892, when St. Paul's, in a reconstruction of charges, was aligned with Mt. Zion Church, China Grove, to be known as West Rowan Charge. This relationship continued until 1919, when St. Paul's was yoked with St. John's Mission located in North Kannapolis and known as the Kannapolis Charge. At the same time the charge became a beneficiary of the Board of National Missions, receiving an annual subsidy from that source until 1935, when it went to self-support. St. Paul's was yoked with Keller Church in 1946, which alignment continues to the present time.

The fortieth anniversary of the organization of the church was observed October 8 to 10, 1926. Dr. John H. Keller spoke to the congregation at 7 p.m. on the 8th; the pastor, Dr. Lee A. Peeler, conducted activities on the 9th, and was master of ceremonies during Anniversary Sunday on the 10th. Dr. Shuford Peeler and Rev. Anthony Shulenberger assisted in administering the sacrament of Holy Communion during the morning. After a sumptuous picnic dinner, the congregation returned to the sanctuary where Elder W. C. Rose read a paper on "The History of St. Paul's Church." Dr. Elmer R. Hoke, president of Catawba College, also delivered an appropriate address.

The present property includes the original building site and house of worship, attached Sunday School rooms, a cemetery, a farm and a parsonage built near the church in 1946. Fellowship hall, erected in 1954, stands by the southwest side of the church. Current parish organizations cover the Sunday School in operation since 1887, Woman's Missionary Society now the Women's Guild organized in 1919, and operating in two circles, youth groups begun in 1920, and Men's Fellowship started in 1949.[8]

Roster of Pastors

Rev. Paul Barringer, D.D.	1886-1891	Rev. David E. Faust, Ph.D., Supply	1948-
Rev. P. M. Trexler, D.D.	1892-1893	Mr. Richard A. Cheek, Summer Student Supply	1948-
Rev. Anthony Shulenberger	1894-1900	Rev. Lewis E. Everline	1948-1952
Rev. Joshua L. Bowers	1901-1907	Ministerial Student Supplies from Catawba College	1952-1953
Rev. M. M. Noacker	1908-1912	Rev. Carl R. Martin	1953-1956
Rev. John H. Keller, D.D.	1912-1918	Rev. Jacob A. Palmer, D.D., Supply	1956-1958
Rev. J. M. Luther Lyerly, Supply	1918-1919	Rev. George R. Johnson	1958-1962
Rev. Lee A. Peeler, D.D.	1919-1938	Rev. Harold H. Holtom	1962-1965
Rev. John C. Peeler, D.D., Supply	1938-1939	Rev. G. Ermine Plott, Suppy	1966-1968
Rev. Joseph D. Andrew	1939-1942	Rev. Collie Seymour	1968-
Rev. Frank K. Bostian	1942-1946		
Rev. Carl T. Daye	1946-1947		

1. ———. Manuscript. Information on St. Paul's Reformed Church, 1965. p. 1ff.

2. ———. Minutes. Classis of North Carolina, 1886, p. 10.

3. ———. Minutes. *Op. cit.*, 1890, p. 9.

4. ———. Minutes. *Op. cit.*, 1887, p. 6.

5. ———. *Ibid.* p. 7.

6. ———. Minutes. *Op. cit.*, 1887, p. 20.

7. ———. Minutes. *Op. cit.*, 1891, p. 22.

8. Johnson. George R., St. Paul's United Church of Christ, 75th Anniversary and Homecoming, 1961, p. 3.

St. Paul's Church, Catawba County

Old St. Paul's Church

ST. PAUL'S REFORMED CHURCH, Startown, North Carolina, is rooted in the Old St. Paul's Church located two miles west of Newton, in the South Fork section of Catawba County. The latter place appears to have been some sort of focal point in 1702, perhaps earlier. For in the church cemetery is a grave stone bearing that date, and on it is inscribed, "Here lies in peace our beloved Abraham Mauser. He was old."[1] The area around the church was sparsely settled in 1712. Tradition relates that, "As early as 1733 . . . there was a crude, one-story log cabin standing between two white pines that was used for worship."[2] The old log cabin was struck by lightning, and burned to the ground. Later, a new building was erected across the road in 1757.

The date when this church was organized is debatable. Undoubtedly religious services were conducted there by itinerate preachers and congregationally appointed laymen from its inception. The Rev. Christian Theus made occasional visit from South Carolina to German settlements in North Carolina beginning in 1739.[3] And, since it is known that a Swiss Reformed minister preached to an established congregation in the St. Paul's community in 1757, it is more than likely Mr. Theus was that person. It is also certain that the Old Dutch Meeting House, as it was known in those days, operated as a Union Church serving the Reformed and Lutheran settlers, perhaps as an unorganized congregation over a period of years. These Dutch brethren had earned a reputation of living together peaceably in domestic, economic and religious affairs. Since Rev. James Martin, another Swiss Reformed minister, is reliably reported to have been the first regular pastor of the Re-

formed congregation, beginning in 1759, it is reasonable to conclude that the church was organized sometime during the later
visits of Mr. Theus.

A pioneer in the South Fork settlement was Henry Weidner
(Whitener). The "patent" for his land in that vicinity is dated
1740, which afterwards was developed into quite an estate. Five
years before that date, he appeared at Sherrill's Ford on the
Catawba River, where, during winter months he trapped for furs
and traded with Indians. While the summer months were spent on
a farm in Pennsylvania raising a crop. This schedule continued
until about 1740, when he married Miss Mary Mull, a young woman
of sixteen years, and brought her from Pennsylvania to make their
home in the South Fork neighborhood. Their descendents are
numerous. Many of them were influential members and leaders in
the Old St. Paul's Church, and, later, in the various Reformed
churches throughout Catawba County and other parts of the state.

Mr. and Mrs. Whitener were followed by other migrants, beginning about 1745. Among these were the Conrads, Reinhardts, Bosts,
Wilfongs, Forneys, Summeys, Bollingers, Rauchs (Rowe), Ram-
saurs, Coulters, Fingers, Zimmermans (Carpenter), Ikards, Clines
(Klein, Little), Hoyles and Hermans.[5] These and their children,
greatly enlarged the membership of St. Paul's Church, until the
congregation became one of the more influential churches west of
the Catawba River.

The first building specifically designed for religious purposes was
erected in 1757. No doubt some sort of an agreement had been
reached concerning the ten acres of land on which it stood prior to
that time, but the actual deed was made a few years before North
Carolina became a Sovereign State. It was issued May 20, 1771 by
Paul Anthony, and his wife Fronty, in favor of the Christian
churches, "Lutarin" and "Presbetaren," and to their heirs forever,
to be used for religious purposes.[6] "Lutarin" of course referred to
those of the Lutheran faith, and "Presbetaren" to those of the Reformed persuasion.

The church building was constructed of hewn logs of tremendous
size. These were put together with hand-made nails and pegs. The
house was two-stories high, with doors on three sides. A wine-glass
pulpit stood against the fourth wall, and was approached from the
opposite corners by steep, winding steps. A communion table
occupied the space immediately in front of the pulpit. Straight-
backed wooden pews were arranged along three sides of the first
floor and in the balcony. In 1808, this log church having fallen into
decay, was demolished, and usable material built into the new
structure. The new building was sealed on the inside and weather
boarded on the outside. That house was so well constructed that it
stands today reasonably well preserved.[7] The name of the old
Meeting House was changed about 1800 to South Fork Church,
and later to St. Paul's.

An interesting description of the early struggles of St. Paul's Reformed Church appears in the Historic Sketch of the Reformed Church in North Carolina, edited by Dr. Jacob C. Clapp. It follows:

No records are to be found of the early ministers. But in 1764 Dupert* was recognized as pastor of St. Paul's. He lived near Paysower's Mill in what now is Gaston County. Near his home was a Reformed and Lutheran Church which was burned during the Revolutionary War. Schrum, Schneider and Bithahn also preached there before 1786, and Rev. Andrew Loretz, a young but scholarly, active and eloquent Swiss, came to this section from Hagerstown, Maryland. After the death of Loretz, St. Paul's was without a pastor for sixteen years. During these years Synod sent to the churches west of the Catawba, as to others in North Carolina, occasional missionaries, as Riley, Rudy and others, to look after this part of the scattered fold. In 1828, Rev. John G. Fritchey, just from the seminary at Carlisle, Pennsylvania, took charge of all the Reformed churches west of the Catawba River. He came just in time to strengthen the things that remained for grievous wolves had crept in and some of the folds were scattered. But during the twelve years of his pastorate he restored the old congregations to renewed life and activity and organized several new ones.

These were palmy days for old St. Paul's; members often came from Burke County, 30 miles, and regularly ten to fifteen miles. In 1840 Rev. John H. Crawford became pastor of St. Paul's. In 1845 Catawba County was formed from Lincoln County, and Newton, the county-seat, was located within one and one-half miles east of St. Paul's. The first church built in Newton was mainly by members of the Reformed congregation at St. Paul's. The new organization so depleted the old, that eventually it disintegrated. Rev. John Lantz preached to the remnant of the members who still clung to the sacred spot until he was called to Middlebrook, Virginia. Soon after this, Rev. J. C. Clapp, D.D., confirmed a class of thirty-two catecumens at St. Paul's camp-grounds. In this class were many capable and active young persons. They petitioned for the re-organization of the congregation. This was done, and soon about 80 members were enrolled with prospects bright and cheering. Could proper pastoral care have been bestowed a strong congregation should have perpetuated the name and fame of this venerable house of God.

Dr. John A. Foil, then a young minister just from Ursinus College and Seminary, 1872, and associated with Rev. J. C. Clapp as Professor in Catawba College, ministered to the new congregation for a few years. But they together on account of the dearth of ministers served all of the ten congregations west of the Catawba River, and served several in Rowan for a number of years, while putting in full time in the schoolroom five days in the week. Of course St. Paul's suffered for lack of attention. However the organization survived. It became a part of the Catawba Charge, and under a pastorate of Dr. Clapp for a number of years, and then under that of Revs. H. A. M. Holshouser, Riedesel, Henry Sechler and S. W. Beck, it has become the strongest in the Catawba Charge.[8]

In more recent years, the center of population shifted from the site of old St. Paul's Church to Startown, an enterprising community several miles South. To meet the opportunity created by this shift of population, in 1903, Rev. Samuel W. Beck led the con-

---

*Quite probably John Frederick Dubbert, referred to the Daniel's story.

gregation to erect a new church in Startown where it has since been located. The building was occupied in February 1904. A parsonage was erected in the grove across the road in front of the church in 1906. About the same time St. Paul's was yoked with Bethel, Grace and Daniel's churches and named the South Fork Charge, which combination of churches continued until 1955, when by action of Southern Synod, the South Fork Charge was divided and St. Paul's was yoked with Bethel Church forming the United Charge.

St. Paul's Church—Startown

During the first pastorate of Rev. William C. Lyerly, in order to provide social and recreational facilities. a hut was erected alongside of the sanctuary, and in 1947, during his second pastorate, the present brick parsonage was built. Other property acquisitions have been, an adjoining house used for educational purposes purchased in 1955 and a ten acre tract of land north of the church site in 1958. The latter in anticipation of totally new church equipment.

The Bi-Centennial of St. Paul's Church was observed the week of October 4, 1959. Appropriately this was a cooperative venture with their Lutheran neighbours, who had also transferred their congregation from the old St. Paul's site in 1904, and located in the Startown Community immediately across the road in front of the Reformed, now the United Church of Christ. It was a rewarding week. Rev. Roy E. Leinbach, Jr. and the Rev. Ernest W. Ridenhour, pastors of the Reformed and Lutheran churches respectively, with the support of appropriate committees, worked together in producing a series of Festival Services on the general theme of "Christ Lives in Me." Meetings were held alternately during the week, except on Sunday, when each conducted their own services of worship. Among guest speakers who graced the occasion, were:

Rev. Terrell M. Shoffner of Newton and Dr. Harvey A. Fesperman, president of Southern Synod, representing the United Church of Christ; Rev. Samuel Sox of Greensboro, Dr. Walter T. Nau of Hickory and Dr. F. L. Conrad, president of the North Carolina Lutheran Synod, representing the Lutheran Church.[9]

St. Paul's Church did not have a Sunday School of its own prior to the turn of the century. From the time the church was organized until 1910, the congregation participated in a community Sunday School with their Lutheran and Methodist neighbors. Since that time the school has been operating as a denominational organization, currently enrolling 115 pupils. The church has a confirmed membership of 107 persons. It carries a full program of denominationally oriented activities. The current pastor is Rev. Roy E. Leinbach, Jr. who has served the charge since 1954.

ROSTER OF PASTORS

Rev. James Martin 1757-1764
Rev. John Frederick Dubbert 1764-1768
Rev. Samuel Suther 1768-1786
Revs. ——— Schwam, J a c o b
Schneider, John W. Bithahn,
supplies during the pastorate of
Mr. Suther.
Rev. Andrew Loretz 1786-1812
Revs. J. S. Ebaugh, James Riley,
John Rudy, J a c o b Scholl,
Supplies 1812-1828
Rev. John G. Fritchey 1828-1840
Rev. John H. Crawford 1840-1852
Rev. John Lantz 1853-1858
Rev. Jacob C. Clapp, D.D.,
Supply 1868-1869
Rev. Jacob C. Clapp, D.D. 1869-1896
Rev. H. A. M. Holshouser,
Ph.D. 1896-1897
Rev. Charles H. Riedesel 1897-1900
Rev. Henry Sechler 1901-1902

Rev. Samuel W. Beck 1903-1909
Rev. Harvey G. Kopenhaver 1910-1915
Mr. Harvey A. Fesperman,
Supply 1915-
Rev. Harvey A. Fesperman,
D.D. 1916-1921
Mr. Banks J. Peeler,
Summer Student Supply 1921-
Rev. John B. Swartz 1921-1926
Rev. Ezra H. Gunther 1926-1927
Rev. William C. Lyerly 1928-1931
Rev. Carl H. Clapp, Supply 1931-1932
Rev. Huitt R. Carpenter 1932-1935
Rev. O. Bain Michael, S.T.D. 1935-1941
Rev. Roy E. Leinbach, Jr.,
Supply 1941-1942
Rev. Karl R. Flocken 1942-1945
Rev. Roy E. Leinbach, Jr.,
Supply 1946-
Rev. William C. Lyerly 1946-1953
Rev. Roy E. Leinbach, Jr. 1954-

1. *Boaz*, Doris, Faith of Our Fathers Living Still, ———, p. 1.
2. *Ibid.* p. 1.
3. *Leonard*, Jacob C., History of the Southern Synod, Evangelical and Reformed Church, 1940, p. 294.
4. *Ibid.* p. 294.
5. *Clapp*, Jacob C., Editor, Historic Sketch of the Reformed Church in North Carolina, 1908, p. 244.
6. *Books of Deeds*, Lincoln County, Book I., 1771, p. 532.
7. *Boaz*, Op. cit., p. 2.
8. *Clapp*, Op. cit., p. 245 ff.
9. *Leinbach*, Roy E., Jr., Ridenhour, Ernest W., Two Hundredth Anniversary, St. Paul's Church, 1959, p. 2 ff.
General Reference:
   Leinbach, Roy E., Jr., Manuscript. St. Paul's Church, Catawba County.

St. Peter's Church, Greensboro

PRELIMINARY MEETINGS for a proposed mission church in the Forest Hills section of Greensboro, North Carolina, were held during the late summer and early fall of 1957, in the Bessemer Elementary School building. Seventeen people came for the first meeting, which

was presided over by Rev. Hoy L. Fesperman, pastor of the First
Evangelical and Reformed Church of that city. Dr. W. E. Wisseman, pastor of First Congregational Christian Church also was
present and participated.

For a number of reasons it was thought wise to make this a joint
effort. Families representing the Evangelical and Reformed as well
as the Congregational Christian churches lived in that area of the
community. Also, a merger between the Evangelical and Reformed
Church and the Congregational Christian churches, creating the
United Church of Christ, had been effected in June 1957. It, therefore, was agreed to seek counsel through Southern Synod from the
Board of National Missions of the Evangelical and Reformed
Church.

A second meeting of interested people was held October 6, 1957,
when 26 people were present. A Steering Committee was named
at that time, consisting of Charles W. Starr, chairman, Charles C.
Kirkman, Julian Head, Robert Enochs and Mrs. Roger Hollifield to
manage affairs on the field. Southern Synod was asked to recommend enrollment for the project by the Board of National Missions,
which occurred at its annual meeting in November 1957.

The Sunday School was organized November 3 when 40 people
were present for the session. Julian Head was elected superintendent. Other officers named at that meeting were: statistical secretary,
Mildred Dunn; corresponding secretary, Charles C. Kirkman; and
treasurer, Harvey L. Starr. It was agreed to schedule services of
worship for the second and fourth Sundays in each month at
9 a.m. Dr. William E. Wisseman, pastor of First Congregational
Christian Church of Greensboro, who consented to serve as temporary supply preacher and pastor, provided the wise counsel and

sympathetic encouragement through which a group of concerned people began to emerge. Other ministers of the church in the area filled in as schedules permitted.[1]

In the meantime, resulting from the merger of the Evangelical and Reformed Church with the Congregational Christian churches, area church extension agencies were seeking ways and means for developing mission projects jointly. Thus, the committee on National Missions of Southern Synod, reporting to that body in April 1958, said:

> On May 9 (1957), a joint meeting of our committee with the Mission Board of the Southern Convention of Congregational Christian churches met in Memorial Church, Winston Salem. The committee met for conversational purposes, seeking to understand the thoughts of each other about church in areas where we serve. The meeting was non-legislative and was approved by both President Fesperman and Superintendent Scott. Your committee feels that it was a most helpful meeting, where helpful approaches to our work were discovered, aiding greatly in pooling our efforts, and avoiding waste of time and money. It was agreed that Dr. Banks J. Peeler, president of the Board of National Missions, be asked to served as moderator. A complimentary luncheon was served by the ladies of Memorial.
>
> On September 17, both committees met again at First Evangelical and Reformed Church, Greensboro. The purpose of the meeting was to consider the advisability of starting a new church in the Greensboro area and another in the Burlington area, both to be joint projects. Rev. Hoy L. Fesperman presented the report concerning the new church in Greensboro, and Rev. Lonnie A. Carpenter on the new church in the Burlington area.[2]

A year later the same committee reported:

> Since all mission work is now of interest to both the Congregational Christian and Evangelical and Reformed Church bodies of the United Church of Christ, a joint committee on strategy was formed. It will be the purpose of the committee to, 1) acquaint church leadership with plans now being developed for North Carolina, 2) plan church strategy for each area of the state in which we have a responsibility or concern, 3) combine the several strategies into a state strategy.[3]

Thus, it was agreed that the Southern Convention and/or the Congregational Christian Mission Board should supervise the development of Edgewood, Burlington, and that the Board of National Missions of the Evangelical and Reformed Church should have supervisory responsibility for the Forest Hills Mission in Greensboro. Dr. Banks J. Peeler, president of the Board of National Missions, met with the Steering Committee on January 5, 1958, to discuss plans for the future, involving a missionary for the parish and property on which to erect a church building.

Early in 1958, two acres of land on Phillips Avenue in Greensboro were purchased by the Board of National Mission as a site for the church. A few months later a house located immediately across the street at 4108 Phillips Avenue was acquired for a parsonage. Two rooms were added, making it reasonably adequate for a family of five people. A budget was agreed upon, supported by both

Evangelical and Reformed and Congregational Christian boards of missions, each underwriting it to the extent of $5,000.

Rev. Carl T. Daye was commissioned by the Board of National Missions and reported on the field for work June 1, 1958.[4] On July 8, 1958, by unanimous vote, the proposed church was named St. Peter's United Church of Christ. On the following Sunday, the church charter was first presented, when 29 people signed it. Left open until the church was organized, October 5, 1958, it contained 61 names. On that date, four elders and four deacons were elected, composing the consistory: Roy Shaw, Julian Head, Charles W. Starr and Charles C. Kirkman, elders; Douglas Foster, Harvey L. Starr, Marlin Wagner and Bernard Heath, deacons. Rev. Carl T. Daye was elected pastor of the newly-created church. Dr. Harvey A. Fesperman, president of Southern Synod, assisted the minister in administering the sacrament of Holy Communion. The morning was brought to a close with a picnic lunch at noon.[5]

The pastor-elect was installed Sunday evening, November 2, 1958. This service was in charge of Dr. Fesperman, Dr. Wisseman, Elder Charles W. Starr, and Dr. Peeler, the latter preaching the installation sermon.

Looking ahead to a church building, on August 2, 1959, the following committee was appointed: Charles W. Starr, chairman, Bernard Heath, Charles C. Kirkman, Mable Mitchell and Carl T. Daye. Plans to provide for a modern church program were developed and adopted, but only the educational unit was authorized to be erected. Groundbreaking ceremonies took place on Sunday afternoon, April 2, 1961. The service was divided into five parts, involving phases in the life of the local congregation, the denomination and the church universal.

Construction on the first unit began immediately, which was completed by September 24, 1961, when the cornerstone was laid, and the first service was held in the chapel. This unit was dedicated by the pastor October 1, 1961, beginning a week of special services. Rev. J. Edmund Lippy, Eastern Field Secretary of the Board of National Missions, delivered the dedicatory address at 11 a.m. Other representative people who appeared on the program of the week were: Dr. Clyde L. Fields, Superintendent of the Southern Convention; Dr. Harvey A. Fesperman; Rev. Norman Blythe, pastor of Bessemer Baptist Church, and Dr. William T. Scott, pastor of Oakland Christian Church and former Superintendent of the Southern Convention.

The building, which adequately served current needs, was so planned that it would meet a variety of program requirements. On the ground floor are eight classrooms, rest room facilities, storage and furnace space; the second floor contains a multi-purpose room which serves for worship, fellowship and recreation, as well as space for a kitchen and a pastor's study. Its cost was in excess of $65,000.

In 1963 the congregation assumed responsibility for the parsonage which, with the construction of the two additional rooms, represents an outlay of $14,000. The church debt was financed through the building department of the Board of National Missions.

St. Peter's Church is well organized for modern church activities, patterned after the United Church of Christ program of Christian service. It has a confirmed membership of 120 people, and carries a budget of $14,000. Since 1966, Rev. Carl F. Dunker has been its pastor.

ROSTER OF PASTORS

Rev. Carl T. Daye 1958-1965   Rev. Carl F. Dunker 1966-1967

1. *Starr*, Charles W., Manuscript. St. Peter's United Church of Christ, 1967.
2. ————. Minutes. Southern Synod of the Evangelical and Reformed Church, 1958, p. 58.
3. ————. Minutes. *Op. cit.*, 1959, p. 63.
4. ————. Minutes. *Op. cit.*, 1958, p. 23.
5. *Daye,* Carl T., Manuscript. St. Peter's United Church of Christ, 1965, p. 2 ff.

St. Thomas Church, Winston Salem

ST. THOMAS EVANGELICAL AND REFORMED CHURCH, Winston Salem, North Carolina is an outgrowth of the First Church of that rapidly expanding modern city. As early as 1956, interested people observed that a substantial number of Evangelical and Reformed church people were migrating in increasing proportions to the west side of the city, locating in the vicinity of Shoreland, Sherwood Forest and Robin Hood Trail developments. Alert to these shifts in populations, Rev. Hiram E. Davis, pastor of the First Church, invited those who were interested in establishing a church of their own faith near their homes to a conference to be held at the parsonage for the purpose of discussing it. Nineteen people were present at the meeting.

These developments were brought to the attention of the committee on National Missions of Southern Synod, which recommended to the Synod that in "Winston Salem, the new Wake Forest development shows great promise, and your committee looks with favor upon the new mission being established there, and that it be placed on the 1957 list for support from the National Mission Board."[1]

The board did list the project for financial support in 1957 and commissioned Rev. Joshua L. Levens to be the missionary-on-the-field. Mr. Levens began his work there April 1, 1957, moving into a temporary parsonage rented for that purpose, located on Crepe Myrtle Drive.[2] A steering committee composed of Bob Jones, chairman, Raymond Thrift and Ray Thornburg, was appointed to manage affairs on the local parish until the congregation could be officially brought together and organized. Arrangements were made to hold services in the Wall-Glade Funeral Home, where the first service was held April 28, 1957, with an attendance of fifty-two people.

There weekly services were held for approximately two years. The charter was presented at that first meeting, when thirteen people signed it. Anticipating the organization, it was named St. Thomas Evangelical and Reformed Church, by popular vote, on October 6, 1957. The consistory was named October 20, C. W. Ellis Sr., and J. W. Murphy, Sr., being elected elders; and Paul Moyer and Raymond Thrift, deacons.

The church was founded November 3, 1957. At the same time Missionary Levens was elected and officially called to be its first pastor. Dr. Harvey A. Fesperman, president of Southern Synod, conducted the election, and Dr. Joseph B. Hennessey, chairman of the committee on National Missions, assisted in the activities. On the official charter list were thirty-nine names, recorded below:

Mr. and Mrs. Robert Andrew, Richard Andrew and Robert Andrew; Mr. and Mrs. James Correll and Jimmy Correll; Mr. and Mrs. Peter Cradilis; Mr. and Mrs. Bob Jones; Mr. and Mrs. M. F. Jones and Steven Jones; Mr. and Mrs. W. C. Kirkman; Mrs. Joshua L. Levens; Mr. and Mrs. Paul Moyer and Wayne Moyer and Linda Moyer; Mr. and Mrs. J. W. Murphy, Sr.; Mr. and Mrs. J. W. Murphy, Jr.; Mr. and Mrs. Donald Myers; Mr. and Mrs. B. F. Swaim; Mr. and Mrs. Kellis Taylor; Mr. and Mrs. Robert Thomas; Mr. and Mrs. Ray Thornburg; Mr. and Mrs. Raymond Thrift; and Mr. and Mrs. R. D. Yokeley.[3]

The sacrament of Holy Communion was served to the new congregation November 10. The church was subsequently enrolled as a member of Southern Synod, its call to Mr. Levens approved, and by that body the pastor was installed minister of St. Thomas Church February 2, 1958.[4]

Confronted with the problem of finding a home for the church, in June 1957, property located on the corner of Robin Hood Road and Sherwood Street was purchased by the Board of National Missions for $16,000. Within a few weeks thereafter, a lot adjacent to church property along the west line and facing Robin Hood Road, was purchased on which to erect a parsonage. The parsonage was finished by January 15, 1958 and immediately occupied by Rev. and Mrs. Joshua L. Levens, involving an expenditure of $16,042.

Plans were subsequently developed for the church building, approving for erection only an all-purpose unit, which included a chapel. The contract price was $43,294. Groundbreaking ceremonies were held March 15, 1959, the President of Synod turning the first shovel of dirt. An entering-into and a dedication service for the new building took place December 13, 1959, when Dr. Harvey A. Fesperman preached the sermon, and the pastor read the dedicatory ritual. This building is two-stories high, containing an altar centered sanctuary, a pastor's study and a nursery on the first floor; and on ground floor, a fellowship hall, two class rooms and a kitchen.

The parish organization is traditional, but includes active Lay Life units, a Youth Fellowship and a troop of Boy Scouts. The annual budget is approximately $14,000, including missions support. Confirmed membership numbers ninety six people.

Originally stimulating pastoral leadership and counsel were provided by Rev. Hiram E. Davis, then serving as pastor of First Church, located on Waughtown Street. Rev. Joshua L. Levens served as organizing missionary until September 1, 1962; then Rev. Aubrey W. Hedrick effectively supplied as interim pastor until January 1, 1963. At that time Rev. Allan L. Rohrbaugh moved to the parish, and served the people until 1967. Rev. Charles Larry Fisher is currently in charge of the church.

ROSTER OF PASTORS

Rev. Joshua L. Levens 1957-1962	Rev. Allan L. Rohrbaugh 1963-1967
Rev. Aubrey W. Hedrick,	Rev. Charles Larry Fisher 1967-
Interim Pastor 1962-1963	

1. ———. Minutes. Southern Synod, Evangelical and Reformed Church, 1957, p. 43.
2. ———. Minutes. *Op. cit.,* 1958, p. 57.
3. *Thrift,* Raymond, St. Thomas United Church of Christ, 1965, p. 2 ff.
4. ———. Minutes. *Op. cit.,* 1958. p. 57.

Smyrna Church, Catawba County

THE REV. WILLIAM C. RANKIN prepared the people in the Smyrna Community for the establishment of a Reformed Church. He was under commission by the "Missionary Society of the Classis of North Carolina," operating as a missionary-at-large at the time. Having prepared for the meeting, which obviously took place in the area school house, Missionary Rankin discovering that he could not be present for it, asked the Rev. John G. Fritchey to effect the organization, which took place June 18, 1836.

On the charter list thirty three names were recorded. Elders

elected at that meeting were, Nathaniel Edwards, John H. Shuford and Jacob Lantz. If deacons were named, the record does not give them. The following family names appeared on the list, many of whom are still active in the congregation: Edwards, Shuford, Lantz, Litten, Robinson, Null, Rowe, Stine, Ward, Douglas, Wilkinson.

Since the school house and apparently the community were known by that name, the congregation adopted "Smyrna" as its name. An eleven acres tract of land was donated to the new congregation by Isaac Douglas, and immediately a substantial log church was built on it. This first building still stands; although it was sold in 1888 along with several acres of the original tract.

As is often the case, a very human act of generosity on April 4, 1886, started a movement which resulted in a new church building program. The story was related by Dr. Jacob C. Clapp, and it occurred during his pastorate. Mrs. Catherine Lantz Hartman, daughter of Jacob Lantz who was a charter member of the congregation and a sister of the Rev. John Lantz, placed $50.00 in gold upon the altar during the Service of Worship saying, "This is for a new church." That same day a building committee was appointed consisting of Quince Rowe, Miles Edwards and J. E. Raine, with instructions to proceed with preparations.

It is interesting to note that a neighboring Methodist congregation helped on the project with gifts of labor and money, so that by December 3, 1886, the church was completed, and used the first time for religious services. Dedication was postponed until April 3, 1887 because of cold weather during the winter months. Rev. Jeremiah H. Ingold made the dedicatory address, and the pastor Dr. Jacob C. Clapp, read the ritual of dedication. It was in serving this congregation that Dr. Clapp began his ministry in 1867, and here also it ended on June 12, 1910, preaching his last sermon two days before his death.

This building was remodeled in 1924. The congregation had no cemetery until 1935, when a parcel of ground East of the church was cleared of trees and laid off in lots for that purpose. During that same year, the church and grounds were made ready for centennial activities. These operations involved redecoration of the sanctuary and addition of some new equipment. On June 14 appropriate anniversary services were conducted during the morning and afternoon. Dr. John C. Peeler, a former pastor, delivered the sermon, and L. F. Kluttz, Esq. addressed a large assembly of people in the afternoon.

Throughout its history Smyrna Church has been numerically small, associated in one way or another with neighboring churches for pastoral ministrations. Smyrna and Bethany were by Southern Synod declared a Charge on September 10, 1945, and served by Rev. Claude W. Kelly. A new parsonage for the charge was built beside Bethany Church in 1946, being owned jointly by the two congregations.

Smyrna took another step forward on June 29, 1952, when it acted to begin preparations for the erection of a new sanctuary. A building committee was appointed composed of Preston Edwards, Norman Edwards, Winfred Sherrill, Hobson Edwards and John Edwards. The pastor, Rev. Nevin H. Feather, was named advisor. Plans were developed for the new church and approved by the congregation . Construction on it began in September 1952, and was finished in May 1953.

The first service, which included cornerstone laying ceremonies, was held in the new sanctuary May 10, 1953. Dedication occurred the following June 14. Rev. Hoy L. Fesperman, a former pastor, delivered the sermon, and the pastor read the ritual of dedication. On June 18, 1961 the One Hundred Twenty Fifth Anniversary of the organization of the Church was observed. President Harvey A. Fesperman of Southern Synod, Evangelical and Reformed Church, preached the sermon.

In 1945, when Bethany and Smyrna were constituted a Charge, it was enrolled by the Board of National Missions in the Department of Town and Country, receiving financial assistance from that source until January 1, 1957. At that time the Charge became self-supporting. Smyrna is an influential rural church, cooperating completely in Kingdom efforts as conceived by the denomination of which it is a part. Its present membership is 115 confirmed people, and now has under consideration the erection of some new educational facilities.

ROSTER OF PASTORS

Rev. John G. Fritchey 1836-1840	Rev. H. E. Sechler 1901-1902
Rev. John H. Crawford 1840-1852	Rev. S. W. Beck 1902-1905
Rev. C. H. Albert 1853-	Rev. John A. Foil, Ph.D.,
Rev. John Lantz 1854-1867	Supply 1905-1906
Rev. Jacob C. Clapp, D.D. 1867-1896	Rev. Milton Whitener 1906-1908
Rev. H. A. M. Holshouser,	Rev. John H. Keller, D.D. 1909-1912
Ph.D. 1896-1897	Rev. John C. Peeler, D.D. 1912-1918
Rev. C. H. Riedesel 1897-1900	

Mr. Banks J. Peeler,
    Student Supply 1918-
Rev. Oliver H. Sensenig 1919-1921
Mr. O. Bain Michael,
    Student Supply 1922-
Mr. Dobbs Ehlmann,
    Student Supply 1922-
Rev. Harvey G. Kopenhaver,
    Supply 1922-1925
Rev. William R. Shaffer,
    D.D. 1926-1929
Rev. Hoy L. Fesperman 1929-1935

Rev. Huitt R. Carpenter 1935-1938
Mr. Lonnie A. Carpenter,
    Student Supply 1938-
Rev. John H. Keller, D.D.,
    Supply 1938-1939
Rev. Carl H. Clapp 1939-
Rev. Walter C. Beck 1939-1945
Rev. Claude W. Kelly 1945-1949
Rev. Shuford Peeler, D.D.,
    Supply 1949-1951
Rev. Nevin H. Feather 1951-1956
Rev. Banks D. Shepherd 1966-

References:
> *Feather*, Nevin H., History of Smyrna United Church of Christ, 1964.
> *Clapp*, Jacob C., Editor, Historic Sketch of the Reformed Church in North Carolina, 1908.
> *Leonard*, Jacob C., History of the Southern Synod of the Evangelical and Reformed Church, 1940.

Trinity Church, Concord

As EARLY AS 1879 Dr. Peter M. Trexler was asked by the Classis of North Carolina to "look after the interests of the Reformed Church in the town of Concord."[1] This he did in addition to his duties as pastor of the West Rowan Charge. In 1880 the same body acted favorably on a petition laid before it by "a group of Concord laymen, asking for pastoral oversight and regular services."[2]

Negotiations were begun immediately with Dr. Theodore Appel, superintendent of the Board of Missions for supervisory oversight and financial help. The Board commissioned Rev. G. Dickey Gurley as missionary on the field and he reported for work late in the fall of 1880. Religious services, which had been held in the Cabarrus County Court House, were transferred to a hall in the Means

Building located on South Church Street, which had been reconditioned for that purpose. Here, January 1, 1881, a group of interested people met, drew up a Constitution, named the venture Trinity Reformed Church, and signed fourteen names to the charter list.

These fourteen names were: John W. Fetzer, Mrs. Eunice Foil, James Foil, Mrs. James Foil, Mrs. Mark Fink, Anthony Bost, Mrs. Martha Jane Bost, Mrs. Lou Hoover, Mrs. Hester Foil, Mrs. A. H. Fetzer, Nevin Fetzer, Willie Fetzer, Alexander Foil and Henry Cook. Evidently the organization was not completed at that first gathering, because a second meeting took place January 30, when the following officers were named: elder, Alexander Foil; deacons, J. W. Fetzer and J. W. Foil. These officers were ordained and installed March 20. Shortly thereafter nine more names were added to the list. These were H. A. Barrier, Mrs. M. E. Barrier, J. C. Lippard, Mrs. C. E. Lippard, Smith Shuping, Mrs. S. A. Shuping, R. T. Lippard, Mrs. C. E. Mitchell and Mrs. Jeremiah Foil.[3] The congregation first appeared on the statistical roll of the Classis in 1881.[3]

After a slow and rather disappointing start, the new congregation made good numerical and material progress under the supervision of Dr. Paul Barringer who served as supply pastor from 1881 to 1884, in addition to his duties as minister of the West Rowan Charge. During that time, because it had no regular pastor mission support was withdrawn, but restored in 1884 when Rev. Jesse W. Cecil was commissioned missionary on the field.

A lot at the Southeast corner of Church and Means Streets previously had been purchased, so that operations began immediately to erect a house of worship on it. Cornerstone ceremonies took place in May 1884, and the church was ready for use April 13, 1885. Dedication Services were held the following May, when Dr. George W. Welker, pastor of the Guilford Charge, preached the sermon.

It should be remembered that those were days of scattered population and "scarce dollars," when limited results represented great effort and exceptional progress. Dr. George W. Welker, Stated Clerk of the Classis of North Carolina, initialed the Minutes of the Classis in 1887 with the following statement:

> The Seventy Fifth Annual Meeting of the Classis of North Carolina, was in the year of Grace, 1887, held in the busy town of Concord, the Shire-town of Cabarrus County, North Carolina. The Reformed Church has congregations in but few of the towns of North Carolina, and it makes a pleasant diversion for the members of the Classis when appointed to meet in the neat place of worship recently built for the Reformed congregation in one of these villages.[4]

Near the close of those sessions a resolution of thanks to the congregation was unanimously adopted and made a part of the Minutes. It reads, "Resolved: that the thanks of the Classis be tendered to the families of the Reformed Church, and others, of Concord who have bestowed their generous hospitality on those attending its sessions, and invoke the blessings of the Great Head of the church for making our sojourn among them so pleasant."[5] Trinity Church was six years old at that time. Its statistical report for that year shows Dr. Peter M. Trexler to be the pastor, twenty-five confirmed members, thirty unconfirmed members, fifty pupils enrolled in the Sunday School, benevolent giving $27, and congregational expenses $360. Thus entertaining the official ecclesiastical body of the denomination for that congregation was no small undertaking.

In 1892 Trinity and New Gilead churches were constituted a charge, and Dr. Paul Barringer became its pastor. A new, modern parsonage was built on the lot adjoining the church along the south line, where Dr. Barringer lived during the two years of his pastorate. This charge arrangement continued until 1896, when Trinity Church was reenrolled by the Board of Missions and made an independent charge.

The pastorate of Rev. B. F. Davis, 1894-1898 is significant. Inspired by Rev. and Mrs. Davis the congregation developed a decided missionary compulsion, manifesting itself in a number of very practical ways.[6] In 1896, a group of zealous men and women purchased property on West Corban Street, in the village of Cannonville, near the Cabarrus Mill, and built a chapel on it. This was an effort to serve people who "would not come down town to church." This work served a growing number of people over a period of years, but as missionary zeal faded, that congregation dwindled, and the property was sold. It has since been developed into a strong congregation by The Church of God.

In the home of Mrs. Sarian Shuping, 35 West Corban Street, on January 18, 1897, ten people met to organize a Woman's Missionary Society. On that charter membership list were the following names: Mrs. B. F. Davis, Mrs. J. C. Lippard, Miss Mollie Fetzer, Mrs. R. T. Lippard, Miss Fannie Lippard, Mrs. Sarian Shuping, Mrs. G. T. Crowell, Mrs. M. E. Barrier, Mrs. L. P. Davis and Miss Addie Barrier. These women not only nurtured the flame of missionary zeal in the local church, but were prime movers in launching the North Carolina Classical of the Woman's Missionary Society of the Reformed Church, which is the antecedent of Southern Synodical Women's Guild.

The Mission Band, a program designed for children, eventually expanded into a phase of the Synodical Woman's Society work, was pioneered in Trinity Church, Concord by Mrs. A. W. George, nee, Fannie Lippard. Mrs. George had an abiding desire to serve as a missionary on "foreign soil." When this appeared to be impossible she directed her interests to missionary education among the children of the church. In Shogama, Japan stands a church building given to that community by Miss Mildred Suther, who in early life came under the missionary influence of this devoted woman.

From 1898 to 1918 there were six pastoral changes and a vacancy which lasted three years. During these years, especially the extended vacancy, the congregation scattered. On March 1, 1918 Rev. William C. Lyerly came to the parish, then composed of Trinity and New Gilead churches, a recently constituted charge, and served there until November 1927. The nine years that Mr. Lyerly labored on this parish were eventful. They involved the transplanting of the congregation, the erection of a new sanctuary and the development of a workable and effective parish program.

On March 18, 1923 the congregation took action to erect a new church building. Two weeks later the site on which the church now stands, on Church Street, was purchased. On March 16, 1924 permission was granted the Consistory to sell the old church property for the sum of $26,000. Plans for the new church were tentatively approved June 8, and groundbreaking ceremonies took place August 3, followed by the cornerstone laying on November 23 all in the same year. The new church was ready to be used and occupied March 7, 1926. All of it except Fellowship Hall had been finished. Dedication of the new church took place November 7, 1926, when Dr. Harvey A. Fesperman, pastor of First Church, Greensboro, preached the sermon.

In 1925, when the new owners of the old church property asked for possession, with permission of city school authorities, pews and some ecclesiastical furniture from the old church were installed in the auditorium of the Clara Harris School, East Corban Street, and the congregation moved into it. Here religious activities were carried on for almost ten months. On Easter Sunday, April 12, 1925, after administering the Sacrament of Holy Communion, the doors of the old church were closed and the people turned away from the sanctuary that had served them for approximately forty years.

The ground upon which it stands and the new church edifice represent an investment of $61,500. Of this amount $26,000 came from the sale of the old church property, $2,000 as a gift from the North Carolina Classis, and $18,000 in cash from members of the congregation. On the day of dedication, approximate indebtedness on the building stood at $16,000, the most of which was covered by building and loan shares.

These were days of fiulfilment. The congregation numbering 200 confirmed members and the Sunday School enrolling approximately the same number of pupils, settled down in their new quarters. There they sought to expand their services to the community, and to become more involved in promoting the Kingdom of our Lord at home and abroad.

Members of the consistory who bore the larger part of responsibilities during these building operations were: elders Rufus T. Lippard, Caleb P. Cline, Jacob O. Moose, Sr., Berry F. Wagoner, Gordia A. Fisher and John H. A. Holshouser; deacons Mack B. Moore, H. Smith Barrier, Charles B. Blackwelder, Eugene G. Martin, J. Albron Peck and Walter E. Swinson.

With the completion of the new house of worship ended an era in the life of this congregation; also began a new phase in its development. Necessary additions were made to the property, but the chief concern was and continued to be the organized activities, stewardship and numerical growth of the church. During the thirteen years which ensued "communicant membership increased 44%." Church School organization and curriculum were strengthened and organized parish activities were extended. A parsonage located at 87 Hillcrest Avenue was purchased February 26, 1949. About the same time Trinity Church became self-supporting, as an independent charge.

On January 1, 1957 the church was debt-free; although urgently needed material improvements created new obligation. In 1959 the chancel was made altar-centered and the sanctuary completely repaired and redecorated. Fellowship Hall was modernized in 1961. Air conditioning equipment was installed in the church in 1962. Confirmed membership of the church reached beyond 300; although an inactive group reduced the active roll to 286. Additional property was purchased in 1967, adjacent to and on the north side of the church in anticipation of erecting a modern activities facility.

Rev. George A. Fidler effectively served the congregation beginning January 1, 1964.

Through the years Trinity Church has given generously of her time, talents and resources in promoting the work of the Church through denominational channels and otherwise. Two of her sons are serving in the Gospel Ministry: Dr. Robert W. Delp as a minister in the United Church of Christ, and Rev. Boyce Blackwelder in the Church of God. Elder Thomas L. Moose served as superintendent of Nazareth Children's Home, beginning September 1, 1943. Three of her daughters have become wives of ministers: Mrs. Samuel W. Beck, Mrs. Homer L. Frye and Mrs. Billy Gene Trull.

Theologically conservative, the congregation has proven itself fraternal and ecclesiastically cooperative. Beginning as a German Reformed Church, an easy and complete transfer was made into the life and culture of the Evangelical and Reformed tradition after 1940, and since 1957 has been successfully making progress in adjusting to the new and larger United Church of Christ atmosphere.

ROSTER OF PASTORS

Rev. Peter M. Trexler, D.D., Exploratory Pastor 1879-1880	Rev. Samuel W. Beck 1905-1906
Rev. G. Dickey Gurley 1880-1881	Rev. William H. Causey, D.D. 1907-1912
Rev. Paul Barringer, D.D., Supply 1881-1884	Rev. W. B. Werner 1913-1915
Rev. Jesse W. Cecil 1884-1885	Rev. William C. Lyerly 1918-1927
Rev. Peter M. Trexler, D.D. 1885-1891	Rev. E. T. Rhodes 1928-
Rev. Paul Barringer, D.D. 1892-1894	Rev. Hugo C. Kellermeyer 1929-1941
Rev. B. F. Davis 1894-1898	Rev. Roy C. Whisenhunt 1912-1951
Rev. J. N. Faust 1898-1899	Rev. Joseph T. Hamomnd 1952-1955
Rev. William H. McNairy, D.D. 1900-1903	Mr. William L. Swing, Summer Student Supply 1955-
Rev. Harvey A. M. Holshouser, Ph.D. 1904-1905	Rev. Banks J. Peeler, D.D. ..1955-1963
	Rev. George A. Fidler 1964-1968

1. ———. Minutes. Classis of North Carolina, 1879, p. 238, 256.
2. *Suther*, Mildred, Manuscript. A Brief History of Trinity Evangelical and Reformed Church, 1964, p. 1.
3. *Ibid.* p. 1.
4. ———. Minutes. *Op. cit.*, 1887, p. 3.
5. *Ibid.* p. 16.
6. *Peeler*, Banks J., A Brief Story of Trinity Evangelical and Reformed Church, 1956, p. 6ff.

Trinity-St. John's Church, Conover

I. St. John's Church, Catawba County

EARLY RECORDS OF ST. JOHN'S CHURCH, Catawba County have been lost. Practically the only reliable early document that escaped the ravages of time, is the deed for the land upon which the church now stands. About that deed, Dr. Jacob C. Leonard writes:

> The original deed for six acres of land was made November 25, 1798, by Henry Pope of Lincoln, now Catawba, County to the "Elders of the united congregations of St. John's and their successors in office forever in trust for the said congregations consisting of Episcopalians, Lutherans and Presbyterians, where the regular ministers of the said denominations are to have full and free liberty to exercise the duties of their office when legally called thereto agreeable to an act of the General Assembly of this State (North Carolina) passed at the city of Raleigh A.L. 1796, entitled an act to secure property to religious societies or congregations." The instrument is recorded in book 19, page 200, in Lincolnton.
>
> Those called "Presbyterians" in the deed were "German Reformed," as in so many other deeds of church property. Neither Episcopalians or Presbyterians ever laid claim to any property rights at St. John's. From the first it was a union of Reformed and Lutherans. Henry Pope signed his name in German script, and it was witnessed by John Perkins and Jacob Fullbright. The tract of six acres was no doubt a donation by

Henry Pope, though the consideration is named as ten pounds. It was a small part of a tract of 350 acres conveyed to Henry Pope by a king's patent October 13, 1765, while Wm. Tryon was Governor.[1]

The deed implies that there was an organized congregation at that place before it was written, probably a union arrangement, since it was drawn in favor of the "Elders of the united congregations of St. John's."[2] Established also is the fact that "Pennsylvania Dutch" people were living in the area in 1760; and, in the nearby cemetery are grave markers bearing birth dates as early as 1741. Rev. Paul Henkel, an itinerate "missionary" in 1805 wrote about his travels as follows: "I drove through the hills for several miles to my old friend Peter Mack on the Great Catawba River, and spent the day there. I was visited there by his son-in-law and his wife. The son-in-law had been instructed with others and confirmed in St. John's Church last August (1804); the wife in the year 1789, as she was still at home with her parents."[3]

It is reasonable to conclude that these sturdy religious pioneers, in keeping with customary practices of their fathers, had erected a building in the area suitable for public gatherings and for religious services. Any such religious services depended upon available ministers of the Reformed and Lutheran faiths, which at best were periodic. These factors give credence to the claim that St. John's Church is one of the five first churches organized in Catawba County, with a strong possibility that it is the second.[4]

In 1812, when St. Paul's Church located three miles West of Newton, acted to erect a new sanctuary, Reformed and Lutheran members living in the "bend of Catawba River" two miles Northeast of Conover, withdrew from the mother church, in the interest of convenience, and erected one of their own in the St. John's Community. This log structure is described by Rev. C. O. Smith, a native of the area and a former pastor of St. John's Lutheran congregation.

Here, it is said, that this first church was erected about 1812. Whether this is correct I do not know, but I do know that this first church was built of logs. I was baptized in it, and confirmed in the brick church which was erected when the first church was torn down.

This log church was weatherboarded and ceiled; was two-stories high; had a gallery with floor space more than half the size of the first floor; had a 'goblet' pulpit, entered by a little stairway from the rear, and in it the minister was in a position to address the audience on both floors. Slaves sat in the gallery. The pulpit was a real work of art in workmanship. Every plank and every nail used in the church and in the pulpit was made by hand. A certain Mr. Sigmon made the nails in his blacksmith shop.[5]

The Reformed people of St. John's, at best, were provided with only occasional religious services through 1828. In 1812, when Rev. Andrew Loretz died, until 1828, a period of sixteen years, all of the churches west of the Catawba River were without regular pastoral care, suffering irreparable damage. Then came Rev. John G. Fritchey into the area, who became pastor of all these people, St. John's Church included. During his pastorate of twelve years St. John's became well established, resulting in considerable numerical expansion. It has been suggested that during his ministry the Reformed Church as a denominational entity in North Carolina was organized; if organized prior to that time, then so securely established that its future was unquestioned. Among the families more prominently represented in the congregation were the Hunsuckers, Hermans and Rowes; the latter, ancestors of Dr. Walter W. Rowe, an influential minister of the Reformed Church in North Carolina.

Then followed a period of successful pastorates and effective supplies. Dr. Jacob C. Clapp, for instance, supplied the congregation with others in the area for almost thirty years in conjunction with his duties as president of Catawba College.[6] Remarkable physical and numerical progress occurred in the whole area during these years.[7]

Circumstances, partially due to short pastorates and supply periods of limited ministerial and pastoral services, witnessed the general decline of this once effective congregation. So that, in 1913 the memberships of St. John's and Trinity Church, Conover were "combined" into "Trinity-St. John's." Property rights, however, were retained at St. John's, and a schedule of religious services was continued on the fourth Sunday in each month. This arrangement was still in effect July 12, 1931.[8]

A partial roster of pastors and supply preachers beginning with 1828 appears below.

Rev. John G. Fritchey 1828-1840
Rev. John H. Crawford 1840-1852
Rev. Charles H. Albert,
   Supply 1853-
Rev. John Lantz 1853-1866
Rev. Jacob C. Clapp, D.D.,
   Supply 1866-1894
During this period Dr. Clapp drew freely on members of the Catawba College faculty and ministerial students to fill supply appointments for him in event of conflicting engagements.
Rev. Harvey A. M. Holshouser,
   Ph.D. 1894-1897
Rev. Charles H. Riedesel 1897-1901
Rev. Henry Sechler 1901-1903
Rev. Samuel W. Beck 1903-1906
Rev. Milton Whitener 1906-1908

1. *Leonard,* Jacob C., History of the Southern Synod, Evangelical and Reformed Church, 1940, p. 325.
2. *Morgan,* Jacob L., Editor, History of the Lutheran Church in North Carolina, 1953, p. 298.
3. *Preslar,* Charles J., Jr., Editor, A History of Catawba County, 1954, p. 104.
4. *Ibid.* p. 104.
5. *Ibid.* p. 105.
6. *Cheek,* A. Wilson and *Warlick,* Farel W., Historical Record of Trinity Evangelical and Reformed Church, 50th Anniversary, 1942, p. 9ff.
7. *Leonard, Op. cit.,* p. 326.
8. *Cheek and Warlick, Op. cit.,* p. 10; Minutes, Trinity Evangelical and Reformed Church, July 12, 1931.

II. Trinity Church, Conover

TRINITY CHURCH, Conover, North Carolina is, in fact, the continuation of old St. John's Church, Catawba County. When Trinity Church was organized in 1892, fifteen of the seventeen charter members were transferred from St. John's, and in 1913 the two congregations were "combined" to form "Trinity-St. John's."

It should also be remembered that major factors which prepared the way for the founding of the Reformed Church in the village of Conover, were two small independent Sunday Schools operating in the vicinity. Sessions of one of these were held in "the old log school house, located near the site of the present depot." The other one was located north of the village "in the old home place of Pink Rowe." Both of these schools served mostly members of St. John's Church, being led by laymen, since no such activities were provided for them at that place.

Thus, sentiment was encouraged in favor of a church of their own faith in the immediate community. Led by Caleb Herman, J. P. Cline, James Propst, E. A. Hunsucker, T. L. Hunsucker and W. J. Hunsucker, property was acquired from Mr. and Mrs. Elcanah Ekard, December 5, 1891, for the sum of $75, and deeded to J. P. Cline, T. L. Hunsucker, and P. G. Herman designated trustees of the "German Reformed Church." Directed by a building committee composed of T. L. Hunsucker and J. P. Cline a neat brick sanctuary was erected on the lot. In the tower was placed a bell donated by Dr. Jacob C. Clapp, which had been used in the "Old White Church" of Newton.

The building was completed before a congregation was organized by Dr. Clapp August 20, 1892. Seventeen names were on the charter membership list. Caleb Herman, J. P. Cline, E. A. Herman, T. L. Hunsucker, W. J. Hunsucker, Frank Hoke (colored), Mrs. Amanda Hunsucker, Mrs. Elizabeth Herman, Mrs. Elizabeth Cline, Mrs. Sharah C. Hunsucker, Mrs. Bettie Rockett, Miss Carrie Cline, Miss Catherine Turner, Mrs. Dora Herman and Miss Eva Cline were transferred from St. John's Church, and Mr. and Mrs. James Propst from St. Paul's. T. L. Hunsucker and James Propst were elected elders, and E. A. Herman and J. P. Cline, deacons. The new congregation was named Trinity.[1]

In May 1893, these proceedings were reported to the Classis of North Carolina by Dr. Clapp, when the congregation was enrolled as a member of that body and made a part of the Catawba Charge, consisting of St. John's, St. Paul's and Smyrna churches.[2] A house located in Conover was purchased by the charge from W. P. Smith and J. Pierce Young and used for the parsonage.

Dr. Clapp continued to supply the charge until 1893, when Dr. H. A. M. Holshouser followed him, beginning his pastorate in 1894. All debts having been paid on the young congregation in March 1897, the original deed was transferred to James Propst, Alonzo

Herren, T. L. Hunsucker and Preston Cline, Trustees of Trinity Reformed Church. The first church building was formally dedicated April 4, 1897. Dr. Jacob C. Clapp, founder of the church, preached the sermon. Dedicatory rites were read by the pastor.

Slow growth is reported during the next fifteen years, occasioned in large measure by short pastorates and limited supply pastoral care. But in 1912, fortunes for the congregation made a turn for the better. Student John C. Peeler, serving as supply in addition to his studies at Catawba College, was ordained to the Christian ministry on June 1, 1913, beginning a pastorate which continued until April 30, 1918.

In 1913 an agreement was reached between people concerned to combine St. John's Church with Trinity Church, Conover. This transaction added 18 names to the Trinity Church roll, but not as members of Trinity Church. For the act appears merely to have combined the two congregations rather than merged them; thus the name Trinity-St. John's appears on the record. Evidently the St. John's Consistory continued in existence, perhaps as a segment of the local church governing body.

On July 12, 1931, the following document was addressed to "The pastor and Church Council of St. John's Lutheran Church, Missouri Synod" by "authority of St. John's Reformed congregation:"

> You are hereby officially notified that the contract between your congregation and the Reformed congregation of St. John's Church concerning the renting of the church building for one fourth of the time is cancelled.
>
> You are further notified that St. John's Reformed congregation intends to exercise her rights to use the church building one fourth of the time, including the fourth Sunday in each month.
>
> Please take due notice and govern yourselves accordingly.[3]

This situation existed until October 13, 1946. At that time the following report was made to the Consistory of Trinity Evangelical and Reformed Church, successor to the Consistory of Trinity Reformed Church:

> In a called meeting of the Consistory of Trinity Evangelical and Reformed Church following the morning service on Sunday, October 13, 1946, the announcement was made that the committee of the St. John's congregation, in settling the affairs of the church, propose to give the sum of $497.26 to the building fund of Trinity Church and that the additional sum of $200 be put in the treasury of the Trinity Church to be used for the upkeep of the St. John's cemetery, this fund to be replenished from time to time to be kept to the amount of $200.
>
> Motion was made, and passed with thanks, for the gift for the building fund and the other money, and the obligation of taking care of the cemetery was accepted by the Consistory.[4]

Since 1946, property interests have been settled, and the "Reformed interest" purchased by the Missouri Synod Lutheran congregation.[5] The hyphenated title, "Trinity-St. John's" has been dropped and the single name "Trinity" has been restored. The titled name, therefore, is "Trinity Evangelical and Reformed Church." Since the merger of the Evangelical and Reformed Church with the Congregational Christian churches in 1957, the congregation is known as Trinity United Church of Christ.

During the pastorate of Dr. William R. Shaffer, property interests in the parsonage of the Catawba Charge were purchased by Trinity Church, the old house torn away and replaced by a two-story brick dwelling.

The pastorate of eight years by Rev. C. Columbus Wagoner was eventful. The Fortieth Anniversary of the congregation was observed August 21, 1932; and action was taken by the church on December 31, 1933 to erect a new sanctuary. E. L. Hunsucker, A. L. Shuford, Sr., S. S. Rowe, M. H. Travis and W. P. Herman were asked to develop plans and to supervise construction of the new building. The Classis of North Carolina contributed $1,500 of the total cost which was in excess of $11,000.[6] The sanctuary was dedicated July 7, 1955. Dr. John H. Keller, a former pastor, preached the sermon and the pastor read the dedicatory ritual.

After receiving and giving financial and leadership assistance to sister Reformed churches in the area over a period of forty two years, on January 1, 1934, the congregation voted to go to self-support. Although continuing as a yoked church in the Catawba Charge, full responsibility for its share of financial obligations was assumed. By 1939 the church was free of debts.

Further plans for material expansion were developed in 1941; however, pressures of World War II forced their postponement until 1945. At that time the congregation voted to discard previous drawings designed to enlarge the old structure and "proceed with plans to build a new edifice and educational building." The present site of the church was purchased from heirs of Elcanah Eckard. Specifications for the new building were adopted in August 1950. Groundbreaking ceremonies were held December 3, 1951, the cornerstone was laid May 12, 1952, and the building was formally occupied August 2, 1953. Total indebtedness of this new equipment which involved expenditures of $413,000 was liquidated in September 1955.[7]

As a token of esteem for the man who had given liberally of himself in talents and resources over a period of a half century, almost 30 years of which as superintendent of the Sunday School, the educational section of the new church was named in honor of Adrian L. Shuford, Sr. Mr. Shuford tersely defined his philosophy of church management in a statement which appears in 50th Anniversary brochure of Trinity Church. He said, "The lesson that the years-gone-by have taught is that each time our school has made improvements in its program and equipment, new interest was manifested, and healthy growth experienced. Folks will work when they have something with which to work, and the public will become interested in things that present a challenge."[8]

Dr. Lonnie Carpenter was pastor of the church during these years of material expansion.

The old parsonage was sold in 1958, and on land immediately in front of the church a new ten-room house was erected as a residence for the minister. Rev. Edwin M. Alcorn, pastor of the church and his family moved into the house in the fall of 1958, when on December 14 it was presented to the congregation in "open house."

New equipment required additional professional leadership. For a number of summers, theological students and/or religious education trainees conducted a program of recreation and education, leading to an action by the Consistory to employ an Assistant Minister. Therefore, in 1965, after having served the congregation two summers as a student, Mr. Joseph William Wise, accepted a call to the position of Assistant Minister with responsibilities in the areas of youth and Christian Education. Mr. Wise was ordained to the Christian ministry by Southern Synod and installed in his position September 26, 1956. Rev. Van D. Grimes is the current pastor of the church, beginning his ministry in the fall of 1966.

Two sons of this influential congregation have been ordained to the Christian ministry: Rev. Carl F. Herman and Rev. John W. Settlemyre. Nineteen pastors have served the church, eleven of whom began their ministry among these devoted people. A roster of pastors and supply preachers appears below.

ROSTER OF PASTORS

Rev. Jacob C. Clapp, D.D.,
Supply 1892-1893
Rev. H. A. M. Holshouser,
Ph.D. 1894-1897
Rev. Charles H. Riedesel 1897-1900
Rev. Henry Sechler 1901-1902
Rev. Samuel W. Beck 1902-1905
Rev. John A. Foil, Ph.D.,
Supply 1905-1906
Rev. Milton Whitener 1906-1908
Rev. Jacob C. Clapp, D.D.,
Supply 1908-1909
Rev. John H. Keller, D.D. ..1909-1912
Rev. John C. Peeler, D.D. ..1912-1918

Mr. Banks J. Peeler,
Student Supply 1918-1919
Rev. Oliver H. Sensnig 1919-1921
Mr. O. Bain Michael,
Student Supply 1922-
Mr. Dobb F. Ehlmann,
Student Supply 1925-
Rev. William R. Shaffer,
D.D. 1926-1929
Rev. C. Columbus Wagoner ..1930-1938
Rev. A. Wilson Cheek, D.D. 1939-1944
Rev. Lonnie A. Carpenter,
D.D. 1944-1955
Rev. Edwin M. Alcorn 1956-1966
Rev. Van D. Grimes 1966-

ASSISTANT PASTOR

Rev. Joseph W. Wise 1965-1966

1. *Cheek*, A. Wilson and *Warlick*, Farel W., Historical Record of Trinity Evangelical and Reformed Church, 50th Anniversary, 1942, p. 9 ff.
2. ———. Minutes. Classis of North Carolina, 1893, pp. 5, 15.
3. ———. Minutes. The Consistory of Trinity Church, 1931, July 12.
4. ———. Minutes. *Op. cit.*, 1931, October 13.
5. *Morgan*, Jacob L., Editor. History of the Lutheran Church in North Carolina, 1953, p. 299.
6. ———. Minutes. Classis of North Carolina, 1934, p. 30.
7. *Alcorn*, Edwin M., Manuscript, History of Trinity Church in Conover, N.C., 1965, p. 5.
8 *Cheek and Warlick, Op. cit.*, p. 15.

Ursinus Church, Rockwell

THE TOWN OF ROCKWELL, NORTH CAROLINA was an important focal point as early as 1838,[1] and for two very good reasons. It is the site of the old "rock well," a favorite camping place on the old "Wagon Road" leading from Salisbury to Cheraw, South Carolina. It is also the area commonly known in earlier days as "Courthouse Hill," so named because at one time it was considered the location of Rowan County's court center.[2]

When, in 1890, the Yadkin Railroad was laid through Southeast Rowan County, only two houses stood in the neighborhood. One of them was owned by J. W. Peeler, and the other by Eli Holshouser. Shortly thereafter Mr. Peeler founded the Rockwell Furniture Company, which, by 1899 had become the Rockwell Casket Company. The Barringer Mill Company was started in 1907.[3] These two business ventures appear to have been the beginning of a progressive agriculture-industrial community.

It is understandable that people living in the vicinity were concerned about moral and religious training for their families. However, prior to 1900, no church existed in the immediate area. The Preamble to the Constitution of Ursinus Reformed Church reflects the situation.

> There was no church in Rockwell, and for some years there has been great need for a place of worship, and a place where Sunday School could be held.
>
> A few years ago, a meeting of surrounding neighbors and members of the Reformed and Lutheran Churches, was held, with a view of putting up a union chapel in which services could be held and Sunday School carried on, but the effort failed, and for several years the case seemed to be hopeless.
>
> The Methodist had previously secured a lot on which to build a church, but the field naturally belonged to the Reformed Church, and the Methodist Church decided to hold off, if the Reformed people would build.

The demand and necessity for a church in Rockwell was great. Families were not able to go to church, and their children did not go to Sunday School.

During the spring of 1899, a list for subscriptions was started, and the encouragement was sufficient to justify a beginning. So, during the month of August, work was begun, and during the following winter the church was enclosed and Services were held twice a month.

This work was under the care of the Rev. W. H. McNairy, pastor of East Rowan Charge. He canvassed part of the Reformed Church of the North Carolina Classis for funds, with good results.[4]

On January 9, 1900, at a Special Meeting of the Classis of North Carolina, the Mr. McNairy was authorized to organize a church at Rockwell.[5] This was accomplished April 5, 1900, and the new congregation was by the Classis incorporated in the East Rowan Charge, whose pastor was the Rev. C. H. Riedesel.

There were ten names on the charter member list—Mary L. Peeler, B. A. Fesperman, Lottie Fesperman, J. B. McCombs, G. H. Peeler, Ledora J. Peeler, Willie Cress, Lenora H. S. Peeler, J. W. Peeler and Lenora H. Peeler. J. W. Peeler was elected elder, and B. A. Fesperman, deacon. The new Church chose "Ursinus" for its name, honoring the author of the Heidelberg Catechism, the official handbook of the Reformed Church.

The lot on which the present church and parsonage stand was donated to the congregation for that purpose by J. W. Peeler. Although begun in the summer of 1899, before a congregation was organized, the church building was not completed until 1904, during the pastorate of Rev. Walter W. Rowe. The cornerstone laying took place May 28, 1904, and the following Sunday, May 29, the completed sanctuary was dedicated "to the Triune God."[6]

The pastor, who had been living in the old parsonage which was property of the East Rowan Charge and located near Lower Stone Church, moved into the new parsonage March 18, 1907. The new house was erected on a lot located on the West side of the church building. J. W. Peeler, H. W. Bost and H. W. Barnhardt supervised its construction.

Having provided adequate equipment with which to do its work, the young congregation turned its attention to a program of spiritual enrichment and missions at home and abroad. Elaborate Christmas and Easter programs were prepared; its organized life was active, and the causes of the denomination were a matter of primary concern to the people. This sort of emphasis continued through four pastorates.

When, therefore, Dr. Harvey A. M. Holshouser, became pastor on March 21, 1922, the church was ready to develop plans for more adequate equipment. H. W. Barnhardt and the pastor were authorized to canvas the people in the interest of a new church. By February 17, 1924, enough money had been raised to insure the project, so a committee was appointed with instructions "to secure plans, specifications etc. for the new building estimated to cost

$25,000." The committee was composed of J. M. Holshouser, H. W. Barnhardt, J. B. McCombs, G. T. Holshouser, H. W. Bost, G. W. Peeler and C. T. Misenheimer.

Since the new church was to be erected on the old site, different facilities had to be found for church activities in the interim. These requirements were found in the local High School building. Taking leave of the old church, on March 30, 1924, the Sacrament of Holy Communion was administered to the congregation. Marked progress was made in erecting the new church building, so that by August 18, 1924, the cornerstone was set in place. On November 2, 1924 the congregation began operating comfortably in the "basement." The church was completed and ready for dedication May 31, 1926. Rev. A. O. Leonard preached in a series of services each evening during the preceeding week; Dr. George Longaker delivered the dedicatory address on Sunday morning; and the pastor, Dr. Holshouser, read the ritual of dedication.

A new and modern church required an adequate parsonage. Upon examination, the old parsonage, which had housed pastors and their families for more than twenty years, was declared inadequate. Action was taken August 8, 1926 to erect a new brick house to harmonize with the church. To supervise this venture J. W. Peeler, C. A. Bost, J. L. Lentz and R. W. Brown were delegated. Within sixty days it was ready to be occupied.

A Möller Pipe Organ was installed in 1941; and complimenting the organ, a set of Schulmerich Tower Chimes was installed in 1949. The congregation was declared by Southern Synod a one-point charge as of June 29, 1948. Appropriate 50th Anniversary Services were conducted beginning the week of June 4, 1950. Among those addressing the congregation on this important occasion were: Dr. A. Wilson Cheek, Dr. Harvey A. Fesperman, Rev. Clifford P. Fisher, Jr., Dr. Aaron R. Tosh, Dr. Lonnie A. Carpenter and the Rev. Karl R. Flocken. Mr. Flocken preached the anniversary sermon. Rev. Richard A. Cheek, the pastor, dedicated hearing aids, new sanctuary light fixtures and the tower chimes.

That an increasing need be met, the congregation acted to erect a modern Christian Education building, attached to the north side of the sanctuary, authorizing C. A. Cozart, Wade H. Fisher, Marvin W. Hall, Hugh W. Bost and Lex E. Honeycutt, to develop plans and supervise construction of the same. Ground was broken for it March 13, 1955, when the pastor remarked—

> Almost fifty-six years ago a small group of devoted Christian men and women . . . organized Ursinus Church that they might have a place to worship God, where their children might learn about Jesus Christ. . . . . In order to meet the growing need . . ., they have from time to time rebuilt . . . . Today the congregation finds its facilities inadequate to meet the needs of the congregation.

This education building was dedicated April 12, 1959, and has been the inspiration for a greatly improved and purposeful parish program of Christian activities. The hope and purpose of leaders have been to enrich the life of the congregation, in harmony with the denomination's concept of Kingdom effort. These elements include meaningful experiences in worship and education, involving the new curriculum, the unified budget, the emphasis on evangelism, and the current approaches to activities for men, women, and young people as conceived in the Lay Life and Work Movement. This sort of effort is in keeping with its long established policy of Christian cooperation. To this end, laity of Ursinus Church have given freely of their time, talents and money in serving on boards and agencies of the denomination.

Four sons have gone from the congregation into the Christian Ministry: Dr. Harvey A. Fesperman, Dr. Franklin L. Fesperman, Rev. Hoy L. Fesperman and Rev. J. Yorke Peeler, Jr.

The Church has certain endowments totalling $29,266. It maintains a cemetery, with accumulated endowments of $6,880, which are included in the above total.

ROSTER OF PASTORS

Rev. William H. McNairy, D. D. 189911900	Rev. Harvey A. M. Holshouser, Ph.D. 1922-1929
Rev. C. H. Riedesel 1900-1903	Rev. Lee O. Carbaugh 1930-1939
Rev. Walter W. Rowe, D.D. 1904-1908	Rev. Aaron R. Tosh, D.D. 1939-1944
Rev. J. Leidy Yearick 1909-1912	Rev. Karl R. Flocken 1945-1949
Rev. John A. Koons 1912-1918	Rev. Richard A. Cheek 1950-1955
Rev. Samuel A. Troxell 1919-1921	Rev. Roy C. Whisenhunt 1956-1962
Student O. Bain Michael, Supply 1921-	Rev. James R. Cress 1962-

1. *Dedication Program.* Rockwell Municipal Building, 1954.
2. *Brawley*, James A., The Rowan Story, 1953, p. 299.
3. *Ibid.* p. 299.
4. ———. Minutes. Ursinus Reformed Church, 1900, Vol. 1., p. 3.
5. ———. Minutes. Classis of North Carolina of the Reformed Church, 1900, p. 133, Item 15.
6. ———. *Op. cit.,* Minutes of Ursinus Church, p. 13.

General Reference
> *Peeler,* J. Yorke, Manuscript, History of Ursinus Evangelical and Reformed Church, 1965.
> *Cheek,* Richard A., Anniversary Booklet, Ursinus Evangelical and Reformed Church, 1950.
> *Cress,* James R., The Ursinus Visitor, Vols. 1963, 1964, 1965.
> *Leonard,* Jacob C., History of the Southern Synod of the Evangelical and Reformed Church, 1940.

Zion Church, Davidson County

ZION METHODIST CHURCH two miles Northwest of Thomasville, North Carolina, divided in 1908. One group formed the Pine Woods Methodist Church, the other established Zion Reformed Church. Seeking the counsel of Dr. William H. McNairy, pastor of the Thomasville Charge, an initial meeting was held in the fall of 1908 in the home of J. T. Mendenhall. From that date services

were held regularly on Sunday afternoons in the Mendenhall and other homes of the community.

The congregation was organized February 7, 1909 in the Mendenhall home. A Constitution was adopted at that meeting, first lines of which state, "The name of this congregation shall be Zion Reformed Church of Thomasville, North Carolina. . . . And the object of this congregation shall be to provide its members with stated preaching of the Word, and the administration of the sacraments, the facilities of public worship and the exercise of Christian discipline and to adopt and prosecute from time to time such measures as are in harmony with the spirit, teaching and customs of the Reformed Church in the United States, and shall tend to promote the general interest of the Redeemer's Kingdom."[1]

J. T. Mendenhall and J. W. Veach were elected elders; Levi W. Johnson and E. W. Saintsing, deacons. It was decided to build a church near the site of the old Zion Methodist Church. George Saintsing gave a plot of ground across the road on which to erect the new church building. Two committees were appointed to manage building activities: building, which consisted of Levi W. Johnson, G. W. Saintsing and Robert Kennedy; finance, which was composed of J. T. Mendenhall, J. W. Veach and William A. Ensley. These committees proceeded to find ways and means to erect a one-room frame building which was occupied in the fall of 1909.

Five weeks after the initial meeting, March 14, 1909, the congregation convened again, at which time the charter member list was presented. On it were twenty nine names, with certificates of transfer or otherwise prepared to affiliate with the new organization. These were Phoebe Regan, Courtney Regan, Viola Burton, Eugenia Burton Jones, Vada Burton Royes, Vada Saintsing, Estelle Kennedy, Lille Kennedy, Lizzie Kennedy, J. T. Mendenhall, Stamey Mendenhall, M. J. Mendenhall, John T. Hilton, L. A. Hilton, J. Ad Kennedy, Mary J. Kennedy, D. R. Kennedy, N. E. Kennedy, L. W. Johnson, Annie J. Johnson, E. W. Saintsing, Lewis Kennedy, W. A. Ensley, J. W. Veach, H. V. Regan, Cromer Regan, W. Hamilton Kennedy, Bertha Cecil and Mary L. Kennedy. In less than three months fifty two people had been received into the membership, and the congregation was ready to affiliate with the Reformed Church in the United States.

Upon application, the Classis of North Carolina enrolled Zion Church May 1, 1909, seated Elder John W. Veach as an official member of that body and contributed the sum of $200 toward the erection of their new church building.[2] In the statistical report of the Classis for that year are two interesting items: Zion church had reported fifty two confirmed members and these had contributed a total of $1,200 for congregational purposes. The congregation was yoked with Bethel Mission, High Point, North Carolina with subsidy and temporarily placed under the pastoral care of Rev. David E. Bowers. The following year those two churches were made a charge, and Mr. Bowers became its authorized pastor.[3] By the end of 1909, under the leadership of the supply pastor, sixty-six people had been admitted to membership in Zion Church. Forty-two were received at one service on October 3 of that year. This happy pastoral relationship continued until December 12, 1911, when Mr. Bowers resigned.

Two short pastorates followed. Rev. C. Columbus Wagoner went to the Zion-Bethel Charge October 8, 1912, but resigned May 15, 1913; however he continued to supply it until Rev. John B. Swartz arrived March 2, 1914. He served there until May 21, 1915. In the meantime Zion Church had been placed in a newly formed Emanuel Charge composed of Emanuel, Calvary and Zion congregations, beginning May 1, 1913. Rev. Dugan C. Cox, a transfer minister from the Friends denomination, became pastor of the Emanuel Charge December 14, 1915, serving it until December 31, 1925.

The small one-room church became crowded; thus, in 1926, seven Sunday School rooms were added to the building. A portico was attached to the front end. Two of these rooms, on the right and left of the pulpit, were used as transcept areas to the sanctuary. In the same year, a warm air heating system was installed in the church building.

The pastorates of Rev. Sterling W. Whitener, missionary on leave from China, 1927-1928, Rev. Sidney C. Safrit, 1929-1933, were wholesome but uneventful. The Zion Church cemetery property acquired in 1902 through the effort of G. W. Saintsing, J. R. Stone and W. A. Ensley, was further promoted during the pastorate of Rev. Dugan C. Cox, and revived as the Memorial Association in the ministry of Rev. Sidney C. Safrit. This land was purchased from W. M. Saintsing.

A tower was erected on the church in 1935, and new pulpit furniture installed the same year. This work was sponsored by the Young Men's Bible Class of the Sunday School. Promoted by the Ladies Aid Society, in 1939, sanctuary walls and ceiling were re-plastered and decorated; also, new hardwood pews were installed.

In 1946, Rev. William C. Lyerly, who had served the Emanuel Charge since 1938, resigned. At that time Emanuel became a self-supporting church. Calvary and Zion were yoked in the Zion-Calvary Charge. Rev. W. Calvin Leonard served the charge until 1948. Rev. Aubrey W. Hedrick began ministering to the people December 1, 1948. A new communion table was placed in the sanctuary in 1950. A strip of land was added to the property in 1951; another lot fronting on the east side of Hasty Road and Highway 109 was purchased in 1952. Mr. and Mrs. J. Van Cashatt gave land for the parsonage in 1954. The new parsonage was erected in 1955, at a cost of $16,700. It was dedicated free of debt February 19, 1956 when Dr. Harvey A. Fesperman, president of Southern Synod, made an appropriate address.

Zion-Calvary Charge was dissolved April 1955 effective January 1, 1956, each church becoming a self-supporting congregation; however, Rev. Aubrey W. Hedrick continued to supply Zion Church until the new minister arrived.[4] Rev. Bobby R. Bonds was installed its first full-time pastor July 22, 1956.[5]

Events appear to have spurred an already live congregation to further activity. For in the spring of 1956, the congregation voted to proceed in making plans to erect a new church building. A planning committee was appointed consisting of Stamey Mendenhall, Mrs. Marshall Saintsing, Fonzo Sink, Wayland Hunt, J. Van Cashatt, Marshall Johnson and Mr. Bobby Bonds, pastor-elect. An additional strip of land was presented to the church by Willard Saintsig. Church plans were developed and approved in the fall of 1956. The building committee, appointed to supervise construction of the building, consisted of Stamey Mendenhall, Mrs. Blanche Frazier, Mrs. Arkless Saintsing, J. Van Cashatt, E. M. Johnson and Rev. Bobby R. Bonds. Groundbreaking ceremonies took place April 7, 1957. First service was held in the unfinished church Easter Sunday morning, April 6, 1958. At that time the sacrament of Holy Communion was administered to 223 communicants.

The old church building that had served the community almost fifty years, was sold at auction for the sum of $210 on March 29, 1958. The last regular service in it was conducted the following day, which was Palm Sunday. Dedication ceremonies for the new house of worship were held December 21, 1958. President Martin

T. Garren of the Southern Convention of Congregation Christian churches of the United Church of Christ, delivered the address. Dr. Harvey A. Fesperman, representing Southern Synod, read the ceremony of dedication. The service was in charge of the pastor, Mr. Bonds. This building represented an expenditure of approximately $100,000.[6]

The 50th Anniversary of its organization was observed by the congregation, in a week of special services beginning April 13, 1959 featuring former pastors and other invited guests.[7] Rev. George A. Fidler began serving on the parish October 1, 1959, continuing until December 20, 1962. During his pastorate unusual parish activities were apparent. For instance, Easter Sunday 1962, thirty one people were admitted to membership in the church, and a men's chorus composed of twenty-six voices sang at eleven different churches during that year.[8]

Signifying a debt-free church, a note-burning ritual took place June 20, 1965. Rev. Bobby R. Bonds, former pastor, delivered an appropriate sermon; Dr. Banks J. Peeler, president of Southern Synod, expressed good wishes and participated in the activities; and the pastor, Rev. Lynwood L. Hubbard, directed the service.[9]

This congregation is well organized for effective parish work. Besides a graded Sunday School, there is a Women's Guild, a Churchman's Brotherhood, a Junior and Senior Youth group, a Young Women's Fellowship and a troop of Boy Scouts. Confirmed membership now numbers 385 people. Rev. Lynwood L. Hubbard is the current pastor.

ROSTER OF PASTORS

Rev. William H. McNairy, D.D.,
  Organizer 1909-
Rev. David E. Bowers 1909-1911
Rev. C. Columbus Wagoner ..1912-1913
Rev. John B. Swartz 1914-1915
Rev. Dugan C. Cox 1915-1925
Rev. Jacob A. Palmer, D.D.
  Supply 1926-1927
Rev. Sterling W. Whitener 1927-1928

Rev. Sidney C. Safrit 1929-1933
Rev. Kendall B. Shoffner 1934-1938
Rev. William C. Lyerly 1938-1946
Rev. W. Calvin Leonard 1946-1948
Rev. Aubrey W. Hedrick 1948-1956
Rev. Bobby R. Bonds 1956-1959
Rev. George A. Fidler 1959-1964
Rev. Lynwood L. Hubbard 1965-

1. *Bonds*, Bobby R., Zion United Church of Christ, 1959, p. 16 ff.
2. ———. Minutes. Classis of North Carolina, 1909, pp. 40, 41.
3. ———. Minutes. *Op. cit.*, 1910, p. 10.
4. ———. Minutes. Southern Synod, 1955, p. 51.
5. ———. Minutes. *Op. cit.*, 1957, p. 15.
6. ———. The Standard, No. 19. January 1, 1959, p. 1.
7. ———. The Standard, No. 5. May 1, 1959, p. 2.
8. ———. The Standard, No. 6. May 15, 1962, p. 1.
9. ———. The Standard, No. 9. July 15, 1965, p. 4.

Zion Church, Lenoir

ZION REFORMED CHURCH, Lenoir, North Carolina is the result of an expressed concern by a group of laymen for a church of their own faith in that fast growing industrial community. The interest stemmed from the arrival of J.P. Rabb and his family in 1890 to

make their home there. He was followed, shortly thereafter, by
C. H. A. Rupp from Lehigh County, Pennsylvania. Other Reformed
people arriving later were G. R. Boyd, J. F. Bost and J. J. Gall.
These churchmen invited Dr. Joseph L. Murphy, then pastor of
Corinth Church, Hickory to visit with and conduct Religious Ser-
vices for them at irregular intervals. A beginning was made, No-
vember 30, 1896, when a small group of people made their way to
Mary's Grove Chapel, located approximately one mile and a half
South of Lenoir for the purpose of worship.

The following spring, in May 1897, a communication appeared
on the agenda of the Classis of North Carolina, supported by six
laymen from Lenoir, requesting Stated Services for their group.[1]
Their request was referred to a committee composed of Dr. Jacob
C. Clapp, Dr. A. H. Smith and Elder M. J. Rowe for investigation
and action. Dr. Murphy was asked to continue his ministry to them,
and in 1898 made the following report to the Classis.

> As missionary to whom the interests of the Reformed Church in and
> around Lenoir were committed for the past year, I beg leave to report:
> Services were conducted by members of the faculty of Catawba College,
> and chiefly by Rev. P. M. Trexler, D.D., have been held once a month in
> a chapel about one and a half miles south of the town of Lenoir. On
> Sunday, May 8, a congregation of nine members was organized. The con-
> gregation will ask to be received by your body at this meeting of Classis.[2]

The organization was effected by Dr. P. M. Trexler, enrolling
the following people: J. P. Rabb, Mrs. S. A. Rabb, I. G. Rabb, J. P.
Rabb, Jr., George F. Thomason, Mrs. George F. Thomason, G. R.
Boyd, C. H. A. Rupp, and John F. Bost. J. P. Rabb and George F.
Thomason were elected elders; C. H. A. Rupp and G. R. Boyd,
deacons.[3]

The congregation was enrolled as a member of the Classis that year, with an expense appropriation of $20, and placed under the care of Dr. Trexler.[4] Subsequently Mt. Bethel, Blowing Rock, and Zion Church, Lenoir were constituted a charge with an appropriation $200.[5] In 1901 Dr. Murphy was again asked to supervise the charge,[6] who arranged with Ministerial Student Walter W. Rowe to serve it during the summer months of 1901 and 1902.

At a congregational meeting held June 8, 1902, Zion Church decided to erect a house of worship in the town of Lenoir. A building committee was appointed, composed of J. P. Rabb, G. R. Boyd, Preston Rabb, John F. Bost and C. H. A. Rupp, with power to act. A lot on West College Avenue was purchased, on which a frame church building was erected, at a cost of $1,575, $300 of which was a gift from the Classis of North Carolina.[7] The house was occupied May 10, 1903. In the same year the congregation was enrolled by the Board of National Missions, and commissioned Dr. William H. McNairy missionary in charge of the parish. At that time the confirmed membership numbered fourteen people. A progress report was made to the Classis in 1904.

> Your committee to whom Lenoir and Blowing Rock were committed beg leave to report as follows:
> Lenoir was supplied until October 1, 1903 by Drs. Clapp and Trexler. On the 9th of August a new church at Lenoir was dedicated under the name of Zion Reformed Church. The sermon was preached by Dr. Clapp, and the building was dedicated by Rev. J. L. Murphy. Rev. W. H. McNairy was commissioned by the Board of Missions to take effect October 1, 1903, and since that time the work at Blowing Rock and Lenoir has been under his care.[8]

The next three pastors, Revs. William H. McNairy, J. W. Bell and A. Samuel Peeler, wrestled with problems typical to missionary parishes, involving finances, enrollment and a related program of activities. Numerical growth was steady, but not phenomenal. Families of the Reformed faith continued to migrate to the furniture center of Caldwell County, expanding the facilities and program of the church as required. The story of its physical development is especially interesting. While Rev. A. Samuel Peeler served the congregation, a house adjacent to the church on the North was purchased for a parsonage. By 1923, the frame church building had served its purpose, so on June 23, action was taken by the congregation to sell it to the South Lenoir Baptist congregation for the sum of $3,250, and to purchase the First Baptist Church propery located at West Harper Avenue and Church Street. The latter transaction involved $17,500. An extensive reconditioning program was immediately begun on the new property, which was occupied January 1924. Most of these property improvements were effected during the pastorate of Dr. John C. Peeler. The congregation also went to self-support under his leadership.[9]

Dr. Walter W. Rowe, who had served this congregation as a student, during the summers of 1901 and 1902, on August 1, 1935, was called to be the fifth pastor of Zion Church. With his arrival on the parish, began a period of progressive physical and spirtiual expansion. By congregational action, January 19, 1936, the old parsonage was sold and a new one erected at 101 Poplar Street. The building committee was composed of Macon M. Williams, Clyde R. Hedrick and C. Dennis Rabb.

December 29, 1941, the Consistory, acting for the congregation, purchased a lot at 221 West College Avenue, formerly a part of the Davenport College campus, as a site for a proposed new sanctuary. Consistorymen involved in this transaction were: Carroll E. Rabb, K. A. Link, Dr. Clyde R. Hedrick, Macon M. Williams, G. W. Kluttz, George W. Greer, C. Dennis Rabb, J. W. Self, George E. Rabb and Harland M. Deal. Thus, began a movement to accumulate a building fund with which to provide for a proposed new church facilities.

A pastorate so auspiciously begun was definitely crippled when, in 1948, Dr. Rowe suffered a cerebral stroke. Incapacitated, but by using supply ministers for Sacramental as well as Worship Services, he managed parish activities from his home until his successor arrived in February 1949. During his short pastorate Dr. Rowe was the recipient of two distinct honors bestowed by his devoted people. June 22 and 26, 1947, the forty-fifth anniversary of his ordination to the Christian Ministry was appropriately observed; and, upon his resignation from the Zion Church pastorate, he was named Pastor Emeritus, of the church that he had helped to nurture in its infancy.

Worthy of note in this connection are several synod-wide projects promoted during his Lenoir pastorate. Acting through Zion Church, and supported by laymen of the congregation, Dr. Rowe was instrumental in acquiring the Johns River Valley camp site for Southern Synod. In 1940, through his efforts, Mt. Bethel Church, Blowing Rock was restored and made usable. In 1943, with the support of such people as Mr. and Mrs. A. L. Shuford, Sr., Harland M. Deal, Oran S. Whitener and others, the Blowing Rock Assembly Grounds property, as a memorial to the late Abel A. Shuford, was made available to the Synod.

Rev. Arthur A. Detwiler began his ministry to the congregation in February 1949, greatly expanding the parish program, including adult and youth activities. Construction began on the educational unit of the proposed new church equipment in 1951. It was completed and occupied in 1952, Elder C. Dennis Rabb being chairman of the building committee. Dedication Services were held March 1952. President Aubrey W. Hedrick of Southern Synod, delivered the dedicatory address.[10]

Rev. Henry J. Meier served Zion Church from November 1, 1953 until May 1961. The major event of his ministry was the erection and dedication of the new sanctuary. Dedication Services occurred

November 1, 1956. President Harvey A. Fesperman of Southern Synod made the dedicatory address. The cornerstone was laid in an appropriate ceremony held during the afternoon, when Rev. Roy E. Leinbach, Jr., delivered an address.[11] Total cost of these new facilities to date, educational unit and sanctuary was $212,095. The erection of the sanctuary and the selection of its equipment were supervised by a committee consisting of Macon M. Williams, C. Dennis Rabb, Thomas C. Harville, John F. Bost, Dr. Clyde R. Hedrick, Dr. Verne H. Blackwelder, Earl O. Abernethy, Mrs. John F. Bost and Mrs. Clarence B. Hedrick.

Dr. George E. Dillinger moved to the community and began a ministry to the congregation on February 15, 1962, which ended September 15, 1966. In preparation for his arrival, the parsonage was completely remodeled, spending $6,000 on the project. His pastorate was marked by a note-burning ritual held February 3, 1963, signaling the complete liquidation of all outstanding indebtedness on the church property. The new denominational church school curriculum was adopted September 1, 1964. Two memorials were established in the Southern Synod Chapel on the campus at Catawba College, furnishing "The Pastor's Room" in memory of Dr. Walter W. Rowe, and "The Clergy Room" in memory of Dr. John C. Peeler.

Art glass windows were installed in the sanctuary in 1964, and dedicated on Palm Sunday, March 27, when Dr. Banks J. Peeler, president of Southern Synod, delivered the address. In anticipation of additional educational facilities, a committee has under consideration ways and means of providing them which will be erected on property adjacent to the church on the east.

Rev. Robert E. Myers began to serve the parish January 1, 1967.

In addition to carrying its full share of denominational benevolences, Zion Church has contributed liberally in leadership to the work of Southern Synod. Among those who have served on commissions, boards and committees are: C. Dennis Rabb, treasurer of Johns River Valley Camp and his successors Albert Carpenter and George E. Rabb; Harland M. Deal, associate in promoting the Blowing Rock Assembly Grounds; Dr. Caroline McNairy and Dr. Verne H. Blackwelder, Trustees of Catawba College; Thomas C. Harville, key man in National Churchmen's Brotherhood and similar synodical activities.

ROSTER OF PASTORS

Rev. Joseph L. Murphy, D.D.,
    Counselor and Supply 1896-1898
Rev. Peter M. Trexler, D.D.,
    Supply 1898-1900
Mr. Walter W. Rowe,
    Student Summer Supply 1901-1902
Rev. William H. McNairy,
    D.D. 1903-1908

Rev. J. W. Bell 1908-1911
Rev. A. Samuel Peeler 1911-1922
Rev. John C. Peeler, D.D. 1923-1935
Rev. Walter W. Rowe, D.D. 1935-1948
Rev. Arthur R. Detwiler 1949-1953
Rev. Henry J. Meier 1953-1961
Rev. George E. Dillinger,
    S.T.D. 1962-1966
Rev. Robert E. Myers 1967-

1. ———. Minutes. Classis of North Carolina, 1897, p. 15.
2. ———. Minutes. *Op. cit.*, 1898, p. 49.
3. *Rowe,* Walter W., Forty-Fifth Anniversary, 1935, p. 10.
4. ———. Minutes. *Op. cit.*, 1898, p. 7 and 64.
5. ———. Minutes. *Op. cit.*, 1899, p. 101.
6. ———. Minutes. *Op. cit.*, 1901, p. 185.
7. ———. Minutes. *Op. cit.*, 1902, p. 232.
8. ———. Minutes. *Op. cit.*, 1904, p. 334.
9. *Deal,* Harland M., History of Zion Church, 1965, p. 2 ff.
10. *Ibid.* p. 4.
11. *Meier,* Henry J., Zion Evangelical and Reformed Church, Dedication Services, 1956, p. 6 ff.

CHAPTER VII

Discontinued, Merged or Reorganized Churches in North Carolina

WHITTIER WROTE, "Of all the sad word of tongue or pen, the saddest are these: 'It might have been.'" It is even sadder to say of a church, it was but isn't. This brief portion of the History of Southern Synod is sad but true. It relates stories of churches that have been discontinued, merged or reorganized. Since these congregations no longer exist, some having been discontinued as long as 150 years. Information is of necessity very sketchy concerning some of them.

Brief resumes are given of all congregations on which we have been able to gather any information. Here we should mention others that existed but left only a name. Lyles Creek Church in Lincoln now Catawba County became a member of the Classis of North Carolina in 1839.[1] By 1895 this congregation had disappeared from the roll of the Classis.[2]

There are a number of inferences also references indicating that there was a union Reformed and Lutheran Church in Gaston County, near Paysewer's Mill.[3] This church reportedly was burned during the Revolutionary War.[4] On this church there are no records.

1. *Welker*, George W. Historical Sketch of the Classis of North Carolina, 1895, p. 18.
2. *Ibid.* p. 27.
3. *Clapp*, Jacob C., Historic Sketch of the Reformed Church in North Carolina, 1908, p. 245.
4. *Ibid.* p. 245.

Barton's (Richland's) Randolph County

BARTON's (RICHLAND's) CHURCH was located in the northeast corner of Randolph County, about one mile north of the town of Liberty. The church was started about 1776 or soon thereafter, by people of the Reformed and Lutheran faiths. It was first called Barton's Meeting House.[1]

After a few years, the Reformed and Lutherans separated. The Reformed congregation moved to a house of their own, nearer to the town of Liberty, on the road which led from Guilford Court House to Fayetteville. The site for the church was conveyed by John Collier to the "Calvanistic" congregation for ten pounds. The deed bears the date of April 28, 1791.[2]

This early congregation was composed of Browers, Keims, and other adherents of the Reformed faith. Through the ministry of Rev. John Rudy it was a living congregation. After that time, it was allowed to go down, finally disappearing from the roll of congregations. There are no records providing further details.

1. *Morgan*, Jacob L., Editor, History of the Lutheran Church in North Carolina, 1953, pp. 273-274.
2. *Clapp*, Jacob C., Editor, Historic Sketch of the Reformed Church in North Carolina, 1908, p. 134.
3. *Ibid.* p. 134.

Bethel, High Point

IN THE FALL OF 1903, the Sunday School Board of the Reformed Church in the United States provided for the purchase of a lot at the corner of Front and Second Streets in High Point, North Carolina for the beginning of a new congregation. On that site a chapel was erected, and made ready for a first service December 13, 1903.

Under the leadership of Rev. D. E. Bowers, pastor of the First Reformed Church of High Point, a Sunday School was organized enrolling fifty pupils. The work progressed and on October 24, 1905, Mr. Bowers led the congregation in organizing a church consisting of 28 members. J. H. Everhart, G. Y. Stone and Lewis Livengood were elected elders; and Percy O. Wall, Madison M. Martin and Jesse L. Barger were elected deacons.[1]

Bethel Church was served by the following ministers: Rev. D. E. Bowers, 1903-1912; Rev. C. Columbus Wagoner, 1912-1916; Rev. H. G. Kopenhaver, 1916-1917; Rev. J. Wade Huffman, 1917-1920. After seventeen years the church was dissolved. The church was sold for $4,000. The parsonage valued at $3,000 was donated to the First Church of High Point. The Board of Home Missions was reimbursed for its investment in the property; and $1,500 was contributed to the First Reformed Church (Waughtown), Winston Salem, North Carolina to aid that congregation in its building operations.[2]

1. *Leonard,* Jacob C., History of the Southern Synod, Evangelical and Reformed Church, 1940, p. 154.
2. ———. Minutes. Classis of North Carolina, 1922, p. 15.

Clanton Park, Charlotte

IN 1960 THE CHURCH EXTENSION DEPARTMENT of the Board of Homeland Ministries of the United Church of Christ, in cooperation with the committee on National Missions of Southern Synod and the First and St. Matthew's Churches of Charlotte, North Carolina, undertook to establish a third congregation in that city. Property consisting of a house, a three-car garage and several acres of land, located at 1200 Clanton Road, was purchased by the Church Extension Department, in anticipation of a suitable program to serve that community. Licentiate James Jackson, who was later ordained to the Christian Ministry by the Southern Convention, was commissioned to serve the parish. His work began September 15, 1960.[1]

The minister lived in the house, occupying several upstairs rooms, using other areas of it for worship, educational and recreational purposes. The garage was later converted into a comfortable chapel, first using it for worship on April 9, 1961.[2] At the end of 1961, on the charter roll were nineteen names. The congregation was officially organized in October of that year.

Mr. Jackson resigned in 1962, and for the next several months the Rev. Terrell M. Shoffner, pastor of St. Matthew's Church, directed the work of the parish. Under the impetus of the new minister, Rev. William T. Joyner, the membership of the mission increased to thirty one.[3] However, traces of discouragement crept into the thinking of the constituency, prompting a survey study of possible services and prospects for growth in that community. Results led the congregation to petition for dissolution. Therefore, early in 1963 the Church Extension Department of the Board of Homeland Ministries was notified of the action and requested to take over the property.

1. ———. Minutes. Southern Synod, 1961, p. 58.
2. ———. Minutes. *Op. cit.,* 1962, p. 8.
3. ———. Year Book of the United Church of Christ, 1963.
4. ———. Minutes. *Op. cit.,* 1963, p. 10.

Coble's, Guilford County

COBLE'S CHURCH was located in Guilford County about twelve miles southeast of Greensboro. It was organized about 1812, and became a member of the first meeting of the Classis of North Carolina. According to a Lutheran record,[1] the original name of the congregation was Zion. The deed for the land records it "Mt. Zion." Later, in deference to the Coble clan who attended the church in large numbers, the church became known as "Coble's."

The first building was constructed of logs, with galleries on three sides, and the pulpit on the fourth side.[2] It was a union church, used jointly by Reformed and Lutheran families until 1847. At that time the Reformed element withdrew and organized Mt. Hope Church in Guilford County. Early pastors of Coble's Church were the same as those who served Brick and Stoner's Churches.

1. *Morgan*, Jacob L., Editor, History of the Lutheran Church in North Carolina, 1953, p. 185.
2. *Ibid.* p. 185.

Fairview, Whitsett

FAIRVIEW CHURCH, Whitsett, North Carolina, was located three miles south of Gibsonville in Guilford County. It was organized by Dr. James D. Andrew. On a number of occasions Dr. Andrew had been invited to preach at the Whitsett Institute by Dr. W. T. Whitsett who had founded the school. A considerable community had grown up around it, but no denomination was represented in it. After a number of successful preaching engagements at the Institute, and at the suggestion of Dr. Whitsett, Fairview Church was organized in the summer of 1895.[1]

Reformed families living in the community were consulted and soon thereafter work was begun. Dr. Whitsett donated a lot on which to erect a church. Its erection was begun in the fall 1895, and completed by October 1896, the first service being conducted in the new structure May 2, 1897. The congregation was organized as Fairview Reformed Church, enrolling thirty members. D. Edward Clapp was elected elder and C. C. Barnhardt, deacon.

The congregation was served by pastors of the Burlington Charge, consisting of First, Burlington and St. Mark's. Later, and until its dissolution, the parish was a part of a four church charge including St. Mark's, Brick and Mt. Hope congregation.[2]

Because the school had been closed and the community had scattered, in 1926, the church was disbanded. Most of the twelve remaining members were transferred to Brick Church. The lot reverted to its donor. The building was sold, razed, and the money turned over to the Treasurer of the Classis of North Carolina.

1. *Leonard*, Jacob C., History of the Southern Synod, Evangelical and Reformed Church, 1940, p. 150.
2. ———. Minutes. Classis of North Carolina, 1911, 1916, 1921.

First, Albemarle

ALBEMARLE, NORTH CAROLINA is the capital city of Stanley County. It is located on the Eastern edge of the Reformed constituency in the Piedmont Section of the state. Ordinarily the Reformed Church should be in a position to serve that community, since large numbers of German people have migrated there.

As an expression of this sense of opportunity, an overture appeared on the agenda of the Classis of North Carolina in 1910 from interested people living in that city, asking that a Reformed Church be established.[1] The overture evoked immediate response from the Classis, appointing a sponsoring committee in the persons of Revs. C. B. Heller, and J. L. Yearick, and recommending the project to the Board of Mission for enrollment by them. Pending its enrollment, the Classis pledged $500 on the current budget.[2] The church was organized September 18, 1910, and named "First Reformed Church" enrolling eleven members.[3]

In 1911 the sponsoring committee was enlarged to include Rev. W. H. Causey. The young church was enrolled by the Board of Missions with subsidy as of January 1, 1912. At that time Rev. F. S. Zaugg was commissioned missionary pastor, and began a very successful but short ministry. The Lutheran Church of Albermarle having recently erected and occupied a new sanctuary at a different location, leaving the old one vacant, it was purchased by the Reformed congregation. The site was good and the building was adequate. Beginnings were very encouraging; however, in December 1912, after only one year of pastoral service, Mr. Zaugg resigned.

Eight months later, on August 10, 1913, Rev. M. M. Noacker became pastor. He served to the end of that year, and was succeeded by Rev. A. F. Nace on January 1, 1914. That pastorate lasted about two years, closing February 2, 1916. From that date until June 1917 the congregation was served by visiting supply ministers. Revs. John A. Koons, C. Columbus Wagoner, Paul Barringer and William C. Lyerly took turns in providing religious services and pastoral visitation, preaching twice each month.[4] In the meantime, First Church was removed from the Board's list of financially aided missions.[5]

However, when Rev. Lee A. Peeler was commissioned pastor of the church in June 1917, the financial subsidy was restored with the assurance of further help if and when needed. This pastorate lasted less than one year, ending in May 1918. Events had so completely discouraged the constituency, that the congregation petitioned Classis for dissolution of the Church. Therefore, Rev. Lee A. Peeler and elders J. W. Peeler and J. C. L. Miller were appointed by Classis as agents to dispose of the First Reformed Church of Albermarle. The report of that committee, submitted in May 1919, follows:

> Your committee appointed to give letters of dismission to the members of Albermarle Missions and to dispose of the property of said mission beg leave to make the following report:
> 1. The members of said mission were granted letters of dismission to the church of their choice.
> 2. The church property was placed in the hands of Attorney W. L. Mann and was disposed of by him, and the following is the financial statement:

Receipts:

Amount in treasury of the mission	$	6.76
Church furniture		115.00
Church building		115.00
Returned premium on insurance		3.24
Church lot		3.000.00

Total receipts	$	3,240.00

Disbursements:

Express, crating, postage etc.	$	6.24
Revenue stamps for deed		3.00
Cost of order from court		15.10
Lawyer's fee		75.00
Note and mortgage to J. S. Wise, Treasurer		1,100.00
Note to J. L. Fisher, Treasurer		100.00
Note and interest to J. B. Leonard, Treasurer		277.65
Check to D. E. Bowers, Treasurer		1,662.61

Total Disbursements	$	3,240.00

The hymn books, pulpit Bible and Baptismal bowl were donated to the Charlotte Mission; the Sunday School song books to the Kannapolis Mission.

The following supplementary action was taken:

Resolved, that from this fund now in the hands of the Treasurer the Board of Missions shall be reimbursed for the loss on the Spencer chapel, and that the remainder shall be donated to the Charlotte and Winston Salem Missions in equal sums.[6]

1. ———. Minutes. Classis of North Carolina, 1910, p. 17.
2. *Ibid.* p. 34.
3. ———. Minutes. *Op. cit.,* 1911, p. 19.
4. ———. Minutes. *Op. cit.,* 1916, p. 40.
5. ———. Minutes. *Op. cit.,* 1917, p. 24.
6. ———. Minutes. *Op. cit.,* 1919, p. 35.

Friendship, Alexander County

THE HISTORIC SKETCH of the Reformed Church in North Carolina, quotes Rev. A. L. Crouse, a Lutheran minister, in his Historical Sketches, as follows:

> A large portion, if not a majority, of the Germans who settled in Alexander County belonged to what was then the German Reformed Church. These were the Richards, Hermans, Rowes, Benfields, Kellers, Prices and some say the Wittenbergers.[1]

People of the Reformed persuasion established a congregation in Alexander County, then Caldwell, in 1844 at or near All Healing Springs, located about seven miles southwest of Taylorsville.[2] A record found among the personal papers of the late Dr. Jeremiah H. Ingold says:

> Commencing on the 3rd day of May, 1844. I was ordained on the 4th of April at the Brick Church, Guilford County. Preached my introductory sermon on the 3rd Sunday of May. The congregation had been organized about two months previous by Rev. J. H. Crawford. Mr. Plassman and myself were present.

Fourteenth of September, 1844, laid the cornerstone of a new church. Rev. J. H. Crawford preached. I resigned my congregation in Caldwell County on the 3rd Sabbath in October, 1845, and removed to Henry Sechler's Mineral Springs in Rowan County on October 23rd.[3]

That excellent progress had been made during the seventeen months of the Ingold pastorate, is supported by two current entries in the parish record:

Catechumens in the Caldwell Charge: John Price, Jonas Miller, Clement Head, Elizabeth Rauch, Margaret Price, Catherine Miller, Marcus Harmon, Wilson Price, West Bradburn, Rachael Bradburn, Susan Miller, Sarah Miller and Christina Keller.

Baptisms entered on April 5, 1845 at the "Caldwell County Stand:" John Dallas Alexander, son of Joseph and Malinda Rowe; Absalom Andrew, son of Absalom and Anna Price; Andrew Alexander, son of Charles and Jane Benfield; Sarah Jane, daughter of Conrad and Catherine Benfield.[4]

In keeping with practices of early German communities, Reformed and Lutheran brethren evidently worshipped together in a "Log Meeting House" which provided galleries for the use of slaves during worship.[5] On a piece of land located a short distance from the meeting house, and owned by a Mr. Price, the Reformed people began to erect their own church. Although the cornerstone was laid in September 1844, it was never completed. For this church, like so many other Reformed congregations in North Carolina and South Carolina, went by default. Lacking pastoral oversight and religious instruction in their chosen faith, a promising membership scattered. Mr. G. P. Rowan later purchased the farm, and since a deed had not been issued for the land on which the church stood, the house was razed and its timbers used in the construction of a barn. The only remaining visible signs that a large number of people once gathered there for Divine worship is a small cemetery which contains twenty-four unmarked grave headstones.

1. *Clapp*, Jacob C., Editor, Historic Sketch of the Reformed Church in North Carolina, 1908, p. 310.
2. *Morgan*, Jacob L., Editor, History of the Lutheran Church in North Carolina, 1953, p. 207.
3. *Clapp*, *Op. cit.*, p. 310.
4. *Ibid.* p. 310.
5. *Morgan.* Op. cit., p. 207.

Granite, Granite Quarry

AT ITS ANNUAL MEETING held in Corinth Church, Hickory, beginning April 29, 1903, the Classis of North Carolina committeed the interest of the Reformed Church at Granite Quarry to Dr. J. M. L. Lyerly with instructions to organize a congregation if advisable.[1] The next year Dr. Lyerly reported that, "Early this year we organized a congregation at Granite Quarry, North Carolina under the

name of "Granite Reformed Church" with 26 names on the roll."[2]
The new church was incorporated with Central Rowan Charge,
thus continuing it under the pastoral supervision of Dr. Lyerly.

Without property or a house in which to worship, the congregation scattered. In 1906 it was not listed with the Central Rowan
Charge consisting of Mt. Hope, Shiloh, St. Luke's and Bethany.[3] On
November 5, 1909 at a special meeting of the Classis which occurred
in Bethany Church, Crescent, N. C. Revs. C. B. Heller, W. B. Duttera and J. L. Yearick were "authorized to organize a Reformed
church at Granite Quarry.[4] These developments imply that the
congregation had met with reverses, and the organization had undoubtedly disintegrated.

In 1910 the committee made its report to the sessions of the Classis:

> Your committee appointed by your reverend body at a special meeting
> held at Crescent, North Carolina, to organize a Reformed Church at
> Granite Quarry, has performed its duty. Regular services were held on
> two Sundays of each month. An organization was effected on Sunday,
> the 8th of December, 1909, with eight members. A lot has been secured,
> and all paid for by receiving a loan of $100 from the Central Church
> Worker's District; the balance has been raised by various congregations
> of the Central District. What is now needed is a church building, or a
> Sunday School room. The significance of this needs no further argument
> in this fast-growing town.
>
> That the much needed building may be secured at a very early date,
> and for the encouragement of the few faithful members of the Granite
> Quarry congregation, we petition Classis to loan this congregation the
> sum of $500, the congregation to pay the interest, and the Classis to
> apportion $100 per year until the full amount be raised.[5]

The request for aid was not granted, and the work was continued
under the supervision of a supply committee. Obviously such services did not meet with the degree of success hoped for by the congregation.

> In 1911 the committee reported that services had been conducted reg-
> ularly for the Granite Quarry Church. It was placed under the care of
> Rev. J. L. Yearick for the coming Classical year. No report was submitted
> to the Classis in 1912. . . . Explanation was made by ministers and elders
> of the Granite Quarry community that not sufficient progress was being
> made by the congregation to warrant its continuance. The explanation
> was accepted by the Classis and the work was accordingly discontinued and
> the congregation dissolved. The "Central District" officials were instructed
> to dispose of the property and take charge of the proceeds; also to dismiss
> members to churches of their choice.[6]

Detail having been attended to, the Granite Reformed Church,
Granite Quarry, North Carolina was erased from the roll of the
Classis in 1912.[7]

1. ———. Minutes. Classis of North Carolina, 1903, p. 276.
2. ———. Minutes. *Op. cit.*, 1904, p. 332.
3. ———. Minutes. *Op. cit.*, 1906, p. 58.

4. ———. Minutes. *Op. cit.*, 1909, p. 9.
5. ———. Minutes. *Op. cit.*, 1910, p. 25.
6. *Leonard,* Jacob C., History of the Southern Synod, Evangelical and Reformed Church, 1940, p. 284.
7. ———. Minutes. *Op. cit.*, 1912, p. 23.

Haas', Catawba County

IN CATAWBA COUNTY, about three miles south of the present St.
James Lutheran Church, and about the same distance southeast of
Newton, North Carolina, is an old cemetery. It is overgrown with
bushes and weeds, but is a large burying place. Nearby once stood
a Union Reformed and Lutheran Church, commonly known as the
"Old Haas," or Hass Church.

A deed for the property, executed in Lincoln County in the name
of David Haas and George A. Ikard, is dated 1834.[1] Tradition relates that a log building stood on that site and was used jointly by
Lutheran and Reformed families. The History of Catawba County,
edited by Charles J. Preslar, Jr., states that "the church was used by
both Lutheran and Reformed members until 1845, when the Reformed members withdrew and built a church of their own in Newton."[2] The History of the Lutheran Church in North Carolina makes
the same assertion, giving the date of the Reformed withdrawal as
1852.

Lutherans used the "Old Haas Church" building until about 1867
when St. James Lutheran Church was founded about one mile
northwest of the original site.[3] Tradition has it that Reformed people continued to use the Old Haas Church until the organization
of Memorial Reformed Church in Maiden. There are no known
records of this early Reformed congregation.

1. *Morgan,* Jacob L., Editor, History of the Lutheran Church in North Carolina, 1953, p. 291.
2. *Preslar,* Charles J., Jr., A History of Catawba County, 1954, p. 111.
3. *Morgan. Op. cit.,* p. 291.

Heidelberg, Davie County

FOUR MILES FROM THE PRESENT CITY of Mocksville, North Carolina,
on Dutchman's Creek, stood very early a union church called the
"Dutch Meetinghouse."[1] It bore the name of Heidelberg. Church
records which date 1766 were still in existence in 1940, but are not
in possession of the Reformed Church. Those records were in German script and had been well preserved. This congregation had a
building which stood for many years, before it was abandoned, on
the site known as "The Dutch Meeting House Grounds."

George Soelle, Moravian "traveling preacher," paid several visits
to Dutchman's Creek. On one occasion he spent the night Heinrich
Bube. He preached again at this time (1772) near here. From the
Moravian records we find the following statement, "Pastor Wart-

mann is mentioned as living in the Dutchman's Creek neighborhood, having been born in Hanover and being an educated, ordained minister. Can Cleft, a Dutchman sixty years old, was a
leader in the group that gathered at the Dutchman's Creek meeting house."[2]

Rev. Richard Utley of the Moravian Church is recorded as having preached on Dutchman's Creek from time to time in 1775. In
January of that year he preached, and was invited to come again.
"Nearly all of the German settlers in the neighborhood were present."[3] "On the 21st of February he had a largely attended meeting
for the German settlers in John Henly's house; Jacob Bub was
touched with a sense of sin."[4] There are no more references to
Dutchman's Creek in the Moravian Records of that period, but
references are made to Mr. Utley's going and preaching at his
"usual" places. These references would imply that he regularly
preached at Dutchman's Creek during that time. These visits were
quite probably once a month.

Just how long the Heidelberg Reformed congregation at Dutchman's Creek existed or when it disbanded is not known. The Lutheran congregation continued until 1925. In 1815, the congregation possibly just Lutheran, relocated in the Jerusalem settlement,
a mile or so from the original site. In 1873 the congregation was
again relocated. The church was reorganized and named "Reformation," but came to be popularly known as Cherry Hill.[5]

1. *Leonard*, Jacob C., History of Southern Synod, Evangelical and Reformed
   Church, 1940, p. 166.
2. *Fries*, Adelaide L., Records of the Moravians in North Carolina, Vol. II,
   1922, p. 739.
3. *Ibid.* p. 863.
4. *Ibid.* p. 867.
5. *Morgan*, Jacob L., Editor, History of the Lutheran Church in North Carolina, 1953, p. 190.

Mt. Carmel, Davidson County

A SCHOOLHOUSE IN DISTRICT 26 of Davidson County located five
miles south of Lexington, North Carolina, became a preaching point
beginning January 1848. Rev. Thornton Butler, a recently ordained
minister of the German Reformed Church, conducted services there
to accommodate Pilgrim and Beulah Churches people living in that
vicinity, chiefly the Koontz and Hedrick families. Mr. Butler organized the church in August 1849, and they named it Mt. Carmel
Reformed Church. Andrew Koontz and John Hedrick were elected
elders; and Samuel Koontz and John L. Hedrick, deacons. It was
first listed in the statistical record of the Classis of North Carolina
in 1849, with Beck's, Pilgrim Emanuel, Sauer's (Beulah) and Fredericktown (Bethany) congregations of the Davidson Charge.[1]

Divine services were conducted in the schoolhouse until 1855.
At that time an arbor was erected nearby. After that, depending

upon the weather, both served the needs of the people until 1880. Then, a comfortable frame sanctuary was built.[2] In 1864, in order to more adequately serve the Davidson Charge which consisted of all Reformed churches in Davidson County, it was divided into the Upper Davidson Charge and the Lower Davidson Charge, Mt. Carmel being listed with the lower group.

The Classis of North Carolina convened its annual sessions at Mt. Carmel in May 1888. Introducing the minutes of those sessions, Dr. George W. Welker, Stated Clerk, remarked:

> The Classis of North Carolina held its fifty-eighth annual meeting at Mt. Carmel Church of the Lower Davidson Charge. The place of meeting is about five miles from Lexington, the shire-town of Davidson County, and in the midst of a fine farming country. The congregation is small in membership, but they have built themselves a neat and comfortable church and shows signs of activity and progress. . . . A most serious drawback is that they have no stated preaching as the Lower Davidson Charge is now vacant.[3]

The lack of pastoral oversight, incurred by long periods of vacancy and sporadic services, so characteristic among Reformed churches in North Carolina prior to the turn of the century, explains why Mt. Carmel did not grow into a numerically strong rural congregation. After more than fifty years, in 1906, its confirmed membership was only nineteen people. Under those circumstances, the Methodist Protestant constituency living in the immediate community, organized a congregation and established a Sunday School which met in the Mt. Carmel church building. Therefore, in an adjourned meeting of the Classis, held on September 20, 1907 a study committee composed of Dr. Peter M. Trexler, Dr. J. C. Leonard and H. D. Hinkle, recommended that the property be donated to the Methodist Protestant Church. Remaining members of the Reformed congregation were dismissed to churches of their choice.[4]

1. ————. Minutes. Classis of North Carolina, 1849, p. 115.
2. *Clapp*, Jacob C., Editor, Historic Sketch of the Reformed Church in North Carolina, 1908, p. 184.
3. ————. Minutes. *Op. cit.*, 1888, p. 3.
4. ————. Minutes. *Op. cit.*, 1908, p. 8.

Murphy Memorial, Hickory

DR. JOSEPH L. MURPHY, pastor of Corinth Church, Hickory, North Carolina, long an exponent of missions, was concerned to see a Reformed Church established in the Longview Section of the city. This occurred September 9, 1921, when a congregation enrolling eighteen people was effected. J. R. Boyd and M. E. Thornburg were elected elders; and J. C. DeRhodes and A. L. Huffman, deacons. The church was named Murphy Memorial Reformed Church, honoring Dr. Murphy.

Student Felix B. Peck did survey work and organized a Sunday School during the summer months of 1921, in addition to his supply services to Faith Church, Brookford. The Classis of North Carolina had committed this venture to the supervision of a committee composed of Revs. W. H. McNairy, W. W. Rowe and Elder J. F. Herman.

The Board of Home Missions enrolled the newly organized church, and it was by the Classis involved with Faith Church, Brookford in the West Hickory Charge. Mr. McNairy was commissioned pastor of the charge and began work on September 1, 1921.[1]

Property, on which was a house, located in the Longview Section of the community was purchased. The house was immediately reconditioned for general use as a parsonage and an activities center. Here Mr. McNairy lived with his family until May 1, 1923, when he resigned pastorate of the charge.[2]

For four years thereafter the mission was under supervision of a supply committee appointed by the Classis. The committee was chaired by Dr. George Longaker, pastor of Corinth Church. In his report to the Classis in 1927, he remarked:

> Your committee on the Murphy Memorial Reformed Church, West Hickory, would report that no Sunday School work nor preaching services were held during the past year. As was noted before, most of the members affiliated with Corinth congregation; others moved away and their whereabouts are unknown. The Bible School dwindled down until practically none were attending and the leaders felt that the school should be discontinued. . . .
>
> Consultation was had with representatives of the Board of Home Missions in regard to the disposition of the property. It is our judgment that the Classis would do well to dissolve the congregation. . . .

By action of the Classis Murphy Memorial Church was dissolved in 1927, and Mr. Longaker commissioned to attend matters of constitutional provision.[3]

1. ———. Minutes. Classis of North Carolina, 1922, p. 5.
2. *Leonard*, Jacob C., History of the Southern Synod, Evangelical and Reformed Church, 1940, p. 366.
3. ———. Minutes. *Op. cit.*, 1927, p. 18.

Shiloh, Forsyth County

SHILOH LUTHERAN CHURCH is located near the town of Lewisville, about ten miles west of Winston Salem, North Carolina. Bernheim's History of the German Settlements and the Lutheran Church in North and South Carolina, quotes the following from Martin's History of North Carolina. "About eight miles above the Hope Meeting House and ten miles from Salem, on the west side of Muddy Creek, a meetinghouse was built in 1782, by a German Lutheran and Reformed congregation, wherein, since the year 1797, divine service is held by some of the ministers of the Brethren's (Moravian) church, every fourth Sunday, in the German language."

In the records of the Moravians, published by the State Department of Archives and History, there is this entry in Volume V, page 23001: "October 17, 1790, Br. Kramsch preached by invitation in a church built by the Lutherans and Reformed, who have no pastor. It is ten miles from Salem, beyond Muddy Creek."

Dr. Douglas Rights, former Moravian historian, writes, "This church is located a short distance from Lewisville. It was taken over by the Lutherans, who still have charge. It is called Shiloh."

No early records of this church are available, and no records, traditions, or histories give us any indication as to the duration of the Reformed congregation or its discontinuance.

Stoner's, Alamance County

STONER'S (STEINER'S) CHURCH was one of seventeen congregations that cooperated in organizing the Classis of the German Reformed Church in North Carolina in 1831.[1] It was located Southwest of the town of Graham, near the village of Belmont off highway 49. The church cemetery is still in existence, but poorly kept.

Stoner's was first very probably a Union Reformed and Lutheran Church, with what is now St. Paul's Lutheran Church, Alamance County. It was founded not later than 1773.[2]

About the year 1800 the Reformed element in the congregation withdrew from the union church under the leadership of Rev. Samuel Weyberg and organized Stoner's Reformed Church on the site of the present cemetery.[3] Early church records are in the archives at Catawba College. However, pages of the book that may have recorded these first years are missing, as are numerous other pages. First records in the book are dated 1801, listing a burial.[4]

No pastor's name is recorded with the first entries in this book. As early as November 14, 1802, 43 persons received the Lord's Supper. In 1804, 39 persons were present for a similar service. Rev. John Rudy's name is first recorded as administering the sacrament of baptism on July 11, 1817. Mr. Rudy served an active, growing congregation from that date until at least 1824. In 1822, he administered the sacrament of Holy Communion to 75 persons and in 1823 on April 15 to 94 persons.

Rev. William Paisley, a Presbyterian minister, served this congregation as supply in 1825, Rev. J. G. Fritchey in 1829. Rev. J. H. Crawford was pastor from 1831 to 1835. Rev. Richard Crooks administered the sacrament of baptism in 1841.

After 1842, the only name of a pastor to appear in church records is that of Dr. George W. Welker. In 1844, soon after the arrival of Dr. Welker, 60 communicant members were reported. Of this number 13 were "African." He served the congregation for a number of years, during which time the membership sharply declined. For a number of years no active congregation is reported or were services held at Stoner's Church.

The church record then states "Steiner's Church was reorganized after a lapse of preaching regular for twenty two years. Preaching regular reoccurred in 1878 by Rev. George W. Welker and reorganized with regular officers in May 25, 1880 by organizing a meeting of members, Rev. George W. Welker taking the chair as president of the meeting." Thirteen members were listed and the officers elected were: Elders, Alfred Sharp, George K. Faust, and Cad C. Curtis; and Deacons, Emanuel R. Sharp and Isaac Sharp. A new building was erected soon thereafter, for the record book states, "Members confirmed at the new church, Steiner's, September 19, 1886, the first and only one, Robena Bell Faust."

This small group did not grow, and soon the congregation again disappeared from the roll of churches of the Classis of North Carolina. Family names appearing on the Steiner's Church record include: Albrecht, Basons, Faust, Friedel, Gambel, Gerrit, Gobel (Coble), Greson, Holt, Istland (Esland, Isley), Kanzelmand (Counselman), Lay (Loy), Nies (Neese), Noe (Noah), Reitzel, Ricach (Ritch, Rich), Rogers, Scherb (Sharp), Schastner, Steiner, Vogleman and Wolf.

1. *Leonard*, Jacob C., History of the Southern Synod, Evangelical and Reformed Church, 1940, p. 33.
2. *Morgan*, Jacob L., Editor, History of the Lutheran Church in North Carolina, 1953, p. 329.
3. *Clapp*, Jacob C., Historic Sketch of the Reformed Church in North Carolina, 1908, p. 134.
4. ———. Minutes. Steiner's Reformed Church, Alamance County.

The Chapel, Spencer

At the turn of the century, leaders of the Reformed Church in North Carolina were greatly concerned about church extension. In 1904 the committee on missions, in its report to Classis took note of the "open door for missionary work within her bounds" and called upon the people for liberal offerings to support it. Pastors in Greensboro, Burlington, Thomasville, Salisbury, High Point, Lexington, Concord Newton and Hickory were instructed to canvass new parts of their respective towns with a view of organizing new work. Where situations gave promise of establishing Reformed Churches, beginnings should be made through Sunday Schools.

As a result of this report, the following persons were appointed to investigate the places named: Gibsonville, Rev. J. D. Andrew; Waughtown, Rev. W. H. Causey; Spencer, Rev. W. B. Duttera; Granite Quarry, Rev. J. M. L. Lyerly; Landis, Rev. J. L. Bowers; Charlotte, Rev. H. A. M. Holshouser; Gastonia and Lincolnton, Rev. C. B. Heller.[1]

At that time Spencer, North Carolina was a budding industrial community, largely economically supported through operations of the Southern Railroad Repair Shops located there. A major portion of the working population was employed by that establishment, therefore of a transient nature. Even though the Reformed constituency was limited, a Sunday School was organized in 1907 which gave sufficient promise of an established church that the Classis appropriated $200 for its support.[2]

Also in 1907 Revs. W. B. Duttera, J. H. Keller and J. M. L. Lyerly were constituted a committee to supervise the "interest at Spencer." In 1908 that committee reported on its stewardship:

> Through the help of the Home Mission Board and a few friends a suitable building was erected on the lots given by the Southern Railway. Nothing has been given by the Reformed Church in North Carolina aside from the invaluable assistance both in cash and service of the Salisbury congregation and $10 from the Woman's Classical Missionary Society.
>
> A Sunday School was organized in November with a good enrollment which has been maintained each Lord's Day, supplemented by a brief service. It has been necessary for one of the members of the committee to exercise direct supervision of the work since no Reformed material is there to place in charge of it. There is but little prospect for the organization of a congregation at the present time and especially since the depletion in population has reduced Sunday School enrollment and attendance.
>
> The location etc., augers well for the future but its permanent status is now rather a remote probability.[3]

In 1909 Mr. Duttera reported that, through the assistance of lay leaders of First Church, Salisbury and the help of Student C. Columbus Wagoner during the summer months, regular services had been maintained.

> However, on account of the depression which caused the removal of many, and the existence of contagious disease, effort in this direction was abandoned and the school closed. Another severe blow to our prospects was the killing of our Assistant Superintendent in the explosion which occurred in the shops. He was in no sense connected with the Reformed Church, but had expected to become identified. In fact, it should be clearly understood that during the entire interval since the work was started, no local Reformed material has been identified with the work.
>
> Accordingly the outlook for the future is uncertain, even though we have the finest location, and equipped to do good missionary work.[4]

After this no active work was done on the field at the chapel, since the Reformed constituency did not require or recommend it. In the light of this information, and since the deed to the property was held by the Board of Home Missions, Treasurer Joseph S. Wise of the board, recommended that this work be discontinued. In 1918, Rev. C. Columbus Wagoner reported to the Classis of North Carolina:

> Your committee on the Spencer Mission begs leave to report that conditions did not require the holding of services this year. There being no Reformed Material out of which to form an organization, the Board of Home Missions has decided to dispose of the property.[5]

An organized church was never established in the Spencer Chapel; however for a time a thriving Sunday School did exist, reaching an enrollment of as many as sixty pupils.

1. ———. Minutes. Classis of North Carolina, 1904, p. 351.
2. ———. Minutes. *Op. cit.*, 1907, p. 44.
3. ———. Minutes. *Op. cit.*, 1908, p. 26.
4. ———. Minutes. *Op. cit.*, 1909, p. 25.
5. ———. Minutes. *Op. cit.*, 1918, p. 33.

CHAPTER VIII

Living Churches in Florida

Reception and Transfer of the Florida Churches

WHEN SOUTHERN SYNOD WAS ORGANIZED May 30, 1939, five churches outside of the State of North Carolina were on the roll. These were: St. John's, Atlanta, Georgia; and United, Lowell; Robertson Memorial, Miami; First, Jacksonville; and St. John's, Redlands, now First Church, Leisure City, all in the State of Florida. First Church, Jacksonville was never reported on the statistical roll of the Synod, for on November 21, 1939, Superintendent J. J. Braun of the Home Missions Board of the Evangelical Synod, notified the Southern Synod Council that it had been dissolved.[1] St. John's Church, Atlanta, Georgia continued an active congregation on the roll of Synod, under the care of Rev. H. A. DeWald, until its dismissal on August 22, 1945 to the United Lutheran Church.[2] *

Long distances and the resultant lack of fellowship with other congregations of the Synod made church work in Florida extremely difficult; however, three of the original churches continued their affiliation with the denomination and three other flourishing congregations were organized during the next twenty two years. During this time, the State of Florida, due to a shift in population involving many Evangelical and Reformed people, had become a field ripe for church extension activities, offering unusual opportunities for the establishment of "new mission starts," most of which could not be managed. After the merger had occurred in 1957 between the Evangelical and Reformed Church and the Congregational Christian Churches, areas within the denomination were redistricted and churches of the United Church of Christ in each area were advised to affiliate with their respective conferences. Accordingly, in January 1962 First Church, Leisure City; United, Lowell; Robertson Memorial, Miami; First Orlando; and Trinity, St. Petersburg were transferred to the Florida Conference of the United Church of Christ. Ministers transferred at the same time

---

* See Leonard, The History of the Southern Synod, p. 368.

were: Revs. Richard N. Davis, Robert Frey, Daniel Horn, Harland
Musser, John W. Myers, Theodore N. Tiemeyer, Frederick Andres,
Rudolph Blemker, Paul T. Bratzel, Walter C. Pugh, Carl A. Marich,
R. O. Chatlos, B. M. Fresenborg, John A. Borger and Aaron R.
Tosh. Rev. Carl H. Kluge was transferred to the Texas Synod.[3]
On the following pages are stories about these five churches trans-
ferred to the Florida Conference.

1. ———. Minutes. Southern Synod, 1939, p. 13.
2. ———. *Op. cit.,* 1946, p. 14.
3. ———. Minutes. *Op. cit.,* 1962, p. 14.

First Church, Leisure City

THE FIRST UNITED CHURCH OF CHRIST, Leisure City, Florida has its
roots in a mission project which began among a group of Volgar
German Evangelical families located two miles North of Homestead. The congregation was organized in 1920 as St. John's Evangelical Church by the Rev. Oscar Nussman, who made occasional
visits to the community, conducting religious services and administering to their sacramental needs. This work Mr. Nussman did in
addition to his pastoral responsibilities at Robertson Memorial
Church, Miami, Florida. The congregation was affiliated with the
Evangelical Synod of North America.[1]

The area was known as Redlands at the time. The congregation
being small, numbering only about sixteen confirmed members,
limited in constituency by language and culture, purchased an
abandoned Episcopal church building, where they worshipped for
about six years. In 1926, a hurricane severely damaged the church
building and many homes of its members. Discouraged, and probably somewhat undecided as to the future, no immediate effort was
made to rebuild the church located at the Northeast corner of Baur
Drive and Krome Avenue. Because of decreasing population in
that immediate area, the Home Missions Board of the Evangelical

Synod considered further investment of money and leadership in the project to be unwise. Therefore, the property was sold for the sum of $2,500 and another ten-acre plot on the Southeast corner of Baur Drive and Krome Avenue was purchased for $1,500 and held as a site for a future sanctuary.

From 1945, over a ten-year period, services were held once each month in homes of the members by visiting ministers, primarily for the purpose of retaining the church charter.

In 1954, the Homestead Air Force Base (SAC) was designated by the Federal Government as a permanent installment. An influx of people into the vicinity was immediate, doubling the population of South Dade County in approximately two years. It was at this time that the Board of National Missions of the Evangelical and Reformed Church commissioned Dr. John W. Myers as Missionary-on-the-Field. His work began September 1, 1955. A survey of the field strongly indicated that the original property located two miles North of Homestead in the Redlands neighborhood would not be the area of immediate growth. A resident sub-division was being developed Northeast of Homestead mid-way from the Air Force Base called Leisure City. This new community presented an opportunity for the establishment of a new church. Thus, the Board of National Missions purchased a four-acre plot of land at 29800 S. W., 153rd Court, Leisure City for $16,000 in anticipation of erecting an all-purpose building on it. The old property in the Redlands neighborhood was sold for $37,500 and invested in the new project. During this time, services were being held in the Leisure City public school building. A new parsonage was built immediately, and by leaving out certain partitions this house became the living quarters of the minister and a place of worship for the congregation, beginning March 1956. This arrangement continued until the first unit of the church building was ready for use.

The congregation was organized July 22, 1956 as the First Evangelical and Reformed Church, Leisure City, Florida, in the unfinished church structure. Services were in charge of the Missionary. Dr. Banks J. Peeler, president of the Board of National Missions, assisted in the ceremonies, effected the organization and installed Dr. John W. Myers pastor of the Church. Fellowship Hall was completed, and dedicated January 19, 1958, providing ample facilities for worship, educational activities and social functions. Thus equipped, the church grew in numbers and influence in the community, attaining a confirmed membership of 130 people and a Sunday School enrollment of well over 100 pupils. Because of the mobile nature of the citizens in that area, turnover in membership is rapid.

Enjoying a successful pastorate of eight years, Dr. Myers resigned August 15, 1963.[2] Rev. J. L. Phillips became pastor May 1, 1964.

Since 1966 the congregation has been without regular pastoral oversight, but served by interim preachers.

1. *Leonard,* Jacob C., History of the Southern Synod, 1940, p. 372.
2. *Myers,* John W., Manuscript. First United Church of Christ, 1967.

First Church, Orlando

THE FIRST UNITED CHURCH OF CHRIST, Orlando, Florida, is a product of cooperative missionary effort by the Board of Home Missions of the Congregational Christian churches and the Board of National Missions of the Evangelical and Reformed Church. Although these two denominations had merged in 1957 creating the United Church of Christ, boards and agencies were not yet consolidated. However, in church extension the mission boards had worked out a plan of cooperation on the parish level. The Orlando project was the first effort in Florida guided by that policy.

In June 1959, First Congregational Christian Church, Winter Park, Florida, created a sponsoring committee consisting of Billy G. Farmer, Dwight Lawrence, Paul Savage, Frederick Hahn, Robert Timson and Sidney Blaze, charged with responsibility for managing the affairs in preparation for establishing a church to be located in Southeast Orlando. Ten acres of land were purchased at 4600 Curry Ford Road in suburban Dover Shores for the sum of $57,750. A house at 1211 Vantage Drive to be used as a parsonage was also purchased for the sum of $21,500.[1]

In consultation with and approval of representatives of the two boards, the Rev. Horace S. Sills, Lexington, North Carolina, was called to provide leadership for the proposed church. He came to the parish June 15, 1959. With the help of personnel from First Congregational Christian Church, Winter Park, a survey was made of the Dover Shores area. Boone High School was engaged as a meeting place, where a first Service of Worship occurred July 12, 1959, attended by sixty-two people. Charter enrollment was begun on the following August 2. Forty signatures were affixed to the charter, indicating the intention of the owners to affiliate with the new enterprise. By December 20, 1959, one hundred eight people had signed the charter and those were received as members into the "First United Church of Christ, Orlando, Florida." The congregation was fully organized January 13, 1960, at which time officers were elected and the Constitution and By-Laws were adopted. First Church was officially enrolled by Southern Synod September 23, 1959,[2] and recognized by the Northeast Association of the Florida Conference February 28, 1960. Rev. Horace S. Sills was installed pastor of the mission February 28, 1960 at a service planned for that purpose in First Congregational Christian Church, Winter Park, which church had mothered the mission and given $4,673 toward purchasing its site.

A building committee consisting of Rudolph Jacobus, chairman, A. L. Kenney, Merl Sickler, Jesse Myers, Mary Matthews, Richard Morcom, Doris O'Connor, Guy Koontz, Harold Crosby, Dwight Lawrence, John Gundlach, Irvin Sailer, Eleanor Howen, Barbara Hoadley and the pastor was named. These people worked steadily in developing plans for suitable facilities, counselled by an architect who had been employed March 15, 1960. Specifications for the buildings were presented and adopted by the congregation on the following May 8, when approval was also given for a Capital Funds Campaign to cover a reasonable portion of the $80,000, estimated cost of construction. Groundbreaking ceremonies were held November 27, 1960 for Fellowship Hall and two church school units. These new buildings were ready to be occupied Palm Sunday, March 26, 1961, when the first formal Service of Worship took place in the sanctuary. At that time, applications for membership were received, and those persons admitted into full fellowship with the Church. These additions brought the confirmed membership of the mission to a few more than two hundred souls.

A series of "Opening Services," began with cornerstone laying ceremonies at 9:30 Palm Sunday morning, when at the doors of the church building the minister declared:

> Our help is in the name of the Lord, who made heaven and earth. Except the Lord build the house, they labor in vain that build it. Other foundation can no man lay that is laid, which is in Christ Jesus, Glory be to the Father, and to the Son, and to the Holy Spirit; as it was in the beginning, and ever shall be, world without end. Amen.

Taking part in this significant ritual, other than the minister, were: Preston Elliott, the contractor; Hill Stiggins, the architect;

Rudolph E. Jacobus, the president of the congregation, and Frederick Hahn. Dedication of the buildings occurred immediately following these ceremonies on the inside of the sanctuary. Participating were: Rev. J. Edmund Lippy, Eastern Field Secretary of the Board of National Missions; Rev. Robbins Ralph, Superintendent of the Florida Conference; John E. Morse, Secretary in the Department of Church Building of the Board of Home Missions, who delivered the address. The rite of confirmation was conducted for a group of young people by the pastor, and these and others were officially received into membership with the Church.

Holy Week Services which occurred each evening during the week at 7:30 presented to the congregation representative visiting ministers from neighboring churches. On Monday, Rev. H. Fikrett, pastor of Grace Covenant Presbyterian Church was the preacher; on Tuesday Rev. Elwood Rawls, pastor of Delaney Baptist Church brought the message; and on Wednesday Rev. Richard N. Davis, missionary pastor of Faith United Church of Christ, Clearwater, Florida, spoke to the congregation. The Sacrament of the Lord's Supper was administered Maundy Thursday evening, and on Friday, Rev. Rankin Shrewsbury, pastor of First Congregational Christian Church, Daytona Beach, delivered the concluding sermon.

Events occurred in quick succession on the parish in those days. Sunday School enrollment continued to expand, as did attendance at stated hours of worship. The young church appeared well on its way. However, it suffered a temporary jolt when in July 1961, Rev. Horace S. Sills resigned to accept a secretarial appointment with Town and Country Department of the Board of National Missions.[3] The vacancy was filled when, on April 1, 1962, Rev. H. Wayne Peck began his ministry to the congregation. Under the caption of "Our Church Today," Mr. Peck wrote shortly after his arrival on the parish:

> From its rather meagre beginnings three years ago, our church has grown in spirit and numbers to its present membership of 242. The expanding program in areas of fellowship, education, and service, is designed for the whole family. There is a Women's Fellowship, a Men's Fellowship, Junior and Senior High Fellowships, Boy Scouts and an excellent choir. The program also includes Summer Camp and Vacation Church School, both of which supplement the Sunday Church School. A Confirmation Class will begin an extended program of study in the early fall.[4]

The present pastor, Rev. James C. Tremble, arrived on the parish August 1, 1966. Laboring under an original debt of $155,901, the congregation has gradually reduced it to $80,000. It has an operating budget of $21,000, and a current confirmed membership of two hundred forty people.

1. *Sills*, Horace S., First United Church of Christ, 1961, p. 11.
2. ———. Minutes. Southern Synod, 1960, p. 13.
3. ———. Minutes. *Op. cit.*, 1962, p. 13.
4. *Peck*, H. Wayne, First United Church of Christ, 1962, p. 2.

Robertson Memorial Church, Miami

ROBERTSON MEMORIAL EVANGELICAL AND REFORMED CHURCH, Miami, Florida was founded March 1914, as a mission under the supervision of the Home Missions Board of the Evangelical Synod of North America. It was organized by Rev. Ernest Bratzel to serve German speaking families living in the area. He ministered to them until 1917, conducting services twice each month. The organization meeting took place in the Women's Club building of Miami, which housed the congregation until 1915, when a frame church building at N. E. First Avenue and 15th Street was purchased from a Baptist congregation.

Various supply ministers served the church until 1919. At that time the Rev. Oscar Nussman became the first full-time resident pastor. In 1920 a parsonage was erected; in 1922, the old church building gave way to a new one built on the same site. Upon occupying the new church building, two important steps forward were taken: Services were conducted in the English language, and the congregation was named the "First Evangelical Church." These adjustments to the environment in which the people lived, added incentive, and assured the numerical growth of the congregation as well as broadened its sphere of influence.

In 1925, Mrs. Frederick K. Robertson, in memory of her husband, donated to the congregation a valuable piece of property located at N. E. Second Court and 23rd Street. On it was a comfortable house, since then used as a parsonage. The bequest also included cash in the amount of approximately $10,000. Shortly thereafter the congregation moved to erect a beautiful modified Gothic church building involving an expenditure of $70,000 along side of the parsonage. It included a sanctuary with seating accommodations for three hundred people, and adequate Sunday School facilities. The sanctuary was equipped with an excellent pipe organ, ten art glass windows which portray the life of Christ, altar and pulpit appointments, and other features which add to its beauty and worshipful atmosphere. The building was dedicated in the fall of 1925, when the congregation went to self-support. The old church house was purchased by a Greek Catholic congregation in Miami.

It will be remembered that these were the days of the great "Florida Boom," when people from all sections of the country went to Florida; some to visit, but many to live permanently. Therefore, for the next six years, the congregation flourished financially and numerically. The hurricane of 1926 severely damaged the property; destroying the church tower, shattering the art glass windows, and completely drenching the interior of the church. Hurricanes in 1932 and 1935 also caused severe damage to church property. The financial crash of 1929, effecting the total economy of the nations, especially brought hardships to the people living in Florida. Many of the church families moved back North to their original homes, depleating the ranks of church membership. But time has a way of healing hurts. As nature is expert in removing scars by fresh vegetation; so, the congregation assessed its losses and made plans for the future. Renewed interest in the total program of the church and numerical expansion were the rewards.

Rev. Oscar Nussman continued to serve the congregation until 1930, when Rev. E. L. Weidenmann began a pastorate which ended in 1934. The Rev. George M. Poth administered to their spiritual needs until 1937. He found the congregation discouraged and disorganized, but, using his valuable ministerial experience and natural optimism, did much in restoring the life and hopeful outlook in the church.

Rev. Norman C. Zulauf began his ministry to the congregation in February 1937. In 1940, Dr. Jacob C. Leonard wrote:

> During recent years the congregation has grown in numbers and spirit, and both pastor and people are looking forward to fruitful years ahead. The congregation is privileged to worship in a very beautiful building, and it serves not only its own constituency of several hundred persons, but it ministers to a great many visitors during the winter tourist season.[1]

Rev. Norman C. Zulauf, after a successful pastorate of seven years, resigned April 18, 1944, to become missionary pastor on a new parish in St. Louis.[2]

Rev. Edward William Ullrich, Selinsgrove, Pennsylvania was called to the parish in May 1944. Convinced that the church should become active in community affairs, he took a vital interest in such matters as the Community Chest, Dade County "Blue Ribbon" Grand Jury system, and health and welfare education. By so doing extended the influence of Memorial Church beyond its parish. That was a transition period, in which the congregation followed with some reluctance. Mr. Ullrich died while serving the parish on January 7, 1957.[3]

The current minister of Robertson Memorial Church is the Rev. H. C. Musser, who was installed its pastor September 8, 1958.[4] From the establishment of this church in 1914 until 1957, the congregation served alone as a sort of frontier denominational outpost. Other than St. John's Church, thirty miles to the South at Leisure City, the nearest Evangelical and Reformed Church was several hundred miles away. But with gracious devotion and consistent cooperation, it was loyal to all phases of the denomination's program of work and Kingdom Service. Since 1962, when Southern Synod transferred Memorial Church, one of six others, to the Florida Conference of the United Church of Christ, its loyalty and fellowship have shifted to the neighboring churches of the denomination in the Miami Area. Its current confirmed membership is 211 people.

1. *Leonard*, Jacob C., History of the Southern Synod, 1940, p. 372.
2. ———. Minutes. Southern Synod, 1944, p. 10.
3. ———. Minutes. *Op. cit.* 1957, p. 74.
4. ———. Minutes. *Op. cit.*, 1958, p. 17.

Trinity Church, St. Petersburg

TRINITY EVANGELICAL AND REFORMED CHURCH, St. Petersburg, Florida, is a dramatic illustration of church extension at its best in the home land. It reflects the missionary zeal and churchmanship of Dr. Charles F. Freeman, a retired minister of the denomination, who was living in that community in 1952. He was asked by the Board of National Missions of the Evangelical and Reformed

Church to serve as temporary missionary-on-the-field, with instructions to survey the area and manage detail in anticipation of establishing a church. This, Dr. and Mrs. Freeman did from November 1952, until May 1953, using his seasoned judgment, zeal and energy in developing the project.[1]

On November 15, 1952 the Board of National Missions purchased a section of the Shelton Orange Grove on 49th Street North in a rapidly growing area of the city. The first service of worship was held December 21, 1952 in the Mt. Vernon Elementary School building. It was a Christmas Service presided over by Dr. Freeman, and attended by eighty people. Evidently a partial organization was effected, naming Clarence Kline, Claude Rupert, Wilmer Strock and Frederick Werner, elders; and Stewart Evert, Robert Hirsch, Gerald Johnson and William Nice, deacons. Thereafter weekly services of worship were conducted in the Mt. Vernon School building, until provision had been made to hold them in the first unit of the new church. The Charter was officially presented for signatures Easter Sunday morning 1953. By March of that year attendance at worship had grown to one hundred forty five persons.

At a dinner meeting on February 4, 1953, Dr. Ralph S. Weiler, Eastern Field Secretary of the Board of National Missions, presented Rev. Robert B. Frey, Sandusky, Ohio, who was available as Missionary Pastor and could begin work on the field shortly after Easter. Dr. Weiler assisted in the worship and preached the sermon on the following Sunday. Dr. Kenneth Kohler, Executive Secretary of the National Churchmen's Brotherhood spoke to the congregation at 11 a.m. March 22, and presented the newly organized local chapter of the Brotherhood with its charter. Through his influence the national organization adopted Trinity Church as its financial project for the year 1952-1953. From this source the congregation received a total of $17,000 which was used in its urgently needed building program.

Upon the arrival on the field of Rev. Robert B. Frey in May 1953, a new chapter in the life of the congregation began. Dr. and Mrs. Charles F. Freeman, who had served the mission well in its beginning months, greatly endearing themselves to this fast-growing congregation, continued to give generous support to its program. A house located at 20th Avenue North was rented and made available as a home for the new pastor, which could also be used as a meeting place for committees and small organized groups during week-days. Operations began to develop in two directions. First, a parsonage had to be provided at the earliest possible date, located on church property at 49th Street North. Groundbreaking ceremonies for this project occurred July 12, and upon its completion the house was dedicated Sunday, October 25, 1953.

Equally urgent was an all-purpose structure to serve as a first unit of the proposed church equipment. Groundbreaking ceremonies for this building were conducted on the same date of the parsonage dedication. Construction on it began immediately, and proceeded without interruption until finished shortly after the first of the year. In appreciation of the financial support given this project by Churchmen's Brotherhood chapters through out the denomination, the building was named Fellowship Hall, and dedicated February 7, 1954. Dr. Aaron R. Tosh, president of Southern Synod, preached the sermon.[2]

The acquirement of this facility provided space for further expansion of congregational activities, such as a fully organized Sunday School for all ages, the organization of the Women's Guild and Youth Activities. Until this time, Sunday School instruction had been provided only for children, which took place in a private home. Numerical growth was immediate, and facilities were soon crowded; therefore, on Sunday July 11, 1954, ground was broken for two additional buildings to meet the needs of children and teen age young people. On a wall of one of these units is a plaque bearing the inscription—

> To the Glory of God and in Honor of
> The Rev. Charles F. Freeman, D.D;
> Who, in 1952 Organized this Congregation;
> These Educational Buildings are Dedicated,
> 1955.[3]

In those days there was constant need for more space and equipment. Two houses adjoining the property on the West were purchased August 15, 1954; a new electric organ was acquired on the same date; seven lots North of 12th Avenue were added March 1, 1957, providing space for 200 off-street parked cars. The ability to meet these material needs and the evident numerical growth of the congregation, generated a magnificent spirit of wellbeing among the people. All of which prepared the congregation for its greatest challenge to date. At the Fifth Annual Congregational Meeting held January 21, 1958, approval was voted of sanctuary plans, the construction of which was estimated to cost $175,000. A fund raising campaign was immediately undertaken to raise $50,000 with which to begin the new enterprise. On Sunday, April 25, 1958, groundbreaking ceremonies were held and construction on the sanctuary began the following day. The first service was held in the new church building December 14, 1958; all Christmas services and programs were likewise held in it.

Dedication Services for the sanctuary were conducted January 4, 1959. Dr. Purd E. Deitz, General Secretary of the Board of National Missions of the Evangelical and Reformed Church, delivered an appropriate address, the services being in charge of the pastor. During the afternoon a program of organ music was provided by David Elwood. On January 11, the Holy Communion was administered to a very large audience of worshippers. Dr. Harvey A. Fesperman, president of Southern Synod, preached the sermon. Memorials were dedicated on the morning of January 18. The dedication brochure for the occasion states, "In all some $300,000 have been invested in the property, buildings and equipment. An indebtedness of $110,000 remains."

When the congregation observed its Tenth Anniversary that debt had been reduced to $60,000. In 1960, when the congregation went to self-support, the pastor remarked:

> Nineteen Sixty was the year in which Trinity became a self-supporting congregation. The association with the Board of National Missions has been pleasant and they have been most helpful. When we think of the fact that the Evangelical and Reformed Church at large through the Churchmen's Brotherhood and the Board of National Missions gave us a total of $42,000 in outright grants that do not have to be repaid, in addition to sums loaned at low interest rates, we are indeed most grateful for the support and confidence shown in this project, and in us.
>
> At this moment of growing maturity as a congregation, I feel it would be very fitting for us to send to the Board, Brotherhood and the Church, an expression of appreciation for this support from the whole Church. These gifts are from our Christian brothers, and our heart-felt thanks are due them.[4]

This thriving congregation has continued to grow in numbers and in effective service at home and abroad. The chapel, church school unit and church office were dedicated February 23, 1964. In honor of its first pastor, the congregation named this sanctuary the "Robert B. Frey Chapel." Mr. Frey resigned, effective January 30, 1966. The Rev. Donald W. Hafner became the second pastor of Trinity Church, beginning July 17, 1966.

A Fifteenth Anniversary Service was held December 31, 1967, when the Mr. Frey preached the anniversary sermon. The congregation is a thriving church of 818 confirmed members, with facilities worth in excess of $500,000. Its program provides for Christian Worship, adult, youth and children's activities to meet the needs of a growing community. These are administered by the enterprising minister of the church, Rev. Donald W. Hafner.

1. *Frey*, Robert B., Trinity United Church of Christ, Tenth Anniversary, 1963, p. 2 ff.
2. *Hafner*, Donald W., Trinity United Church of Christ, Fifteenth Anniversary, 1967, p. 4.
3. *Frey, Op. cit.*, p. 5.
4. *Ibid.* p. 8.

United Church, Lowell

In 1914 a number of German families moved from central Illinois to Marion County near Lowell, Florida. Being farmers, mostly first generation Americans, they purchased land and settled in a community which came to be known as Germantown, later changed to Lowell. Among them were Rev. Henry Neidernhoefer a retired Evangelical minister and his family. Under his influence religious

services were held in neighboring homes, eventually stimulating enough interest to organize a church on November 1, 1914.[1] It affiliated with the Evangelical Synod of North America, and through its missionary agencies received limited financial aid and valuable supervisory counsel for a time.

Twenty eight people composed the charter membership roll. These were: Mr. and Mrs. Carl Gutschlag, Louis T., Marguerite; Mr. and Mrs. Fred Ziegler, Oscar, Albert, Ida, Laura, Emma; Mr. and Mrs. Matthew Reiff, Anna, Erich; Mr. and Mrs. John Reiff, Florence, Clarice; Mr. and Mrs. Justus Pfeil, Martha, Amelia, John, Annetta; Mr. and Mrs. Louis Justus Pfeil, Martha, Amelia, John,

Realtors Howell and Chambliss, from whom most of the German families living in the community had purchased their land, donated five acres of land on which to erect a church and one for cemetery purposes. With the added assistance of the Evangelical Synod Board of Missions and free labor from citizens of the community, a modest but adequate church house was erected and dedicated Palm Sunday April 16, 1916. Two services were held during the day. Mr. Neidernhoefer preached the sermon in the German language, conducted a brief ritual of dedication and confirmed a class of six young women in the forenoon. Rev. E. Shultz, who had been a missionary to India, addressed a large audience in English during the afternoon.

Erecting the house of God was a cooperative undertaking. Most of the material was donated by members and friends, who also did a large part of the labor involved. Carl Gutschlag, president of the church and chairman of the building committee, managed operations. Total cost of the building in cash was only $240.32. A parsonage was erected in 1926.

Membership in this church always has been limited, quite possibly reaching no more than fifty confirmed members at any one time. This has been conditioned largely by two factors: culture, meaning the German language barrier, and sporadic ministerial leadership. Pastoral services usually have been supplied by neighboring ministers or students, living in Tampa and Jacksonville, a number of whom have been retired from active service in the denomination. Dr. Paul D. Yoder, for instance, lived in retirement at Gainesville.[3]

ROSTER OF PASTORS

Rev. Henry Neidernhoefer,		Rev. William P. Jenkins	1938-1939
Organizer	1914-1918	Rev. John Gatermann	1940-1945
Rev. Theodore N. Hauck	1919-1920	Rev. ? Wilkins	1947-1948
Rev. Albert Butenmueller	1921-1925	Vacant	1948-1954
Rev. Erick Genther, D.D.	1926-1927	Rev. Paul D. Yoder, D.D.	1954-1962
Rev. A. Janke	1927-1928	Rev. Walter Pugh	1963-
Rev. Roland Mernitz	1929-1930	Rev. Frederick Murphy	1963-1965
Mr. Frederick J. Sager,		Rev. John Touchberry	1965-1966
Student Supply	1931-1932	Mr. Charles McCormac,	
Rev. Herman Ritter	1932-1934	Student Supply	1967-
Rev. William Bretz	1935-	Mr. George Hildebrand,	
Rev. Fridolin Tschudy	1935-1938	Student Supply	1967-

1. *Yoder*, Paul D., Fortieth Anniversary of the Dedication of the United Evangelical Church, 1956, p. 3 ff.
2. *Gutschlag*, Clarice, Manuscript. History of the United Evangelical, United Church of Christ, 1968, p. 1 ff.
3. *Leonard*, Jacob C., History of Southern Synod, 1940, p. 369 ff.

CHAPTER IX

Statistics

Statistics have been compiled from available sources, many of which are fragmentary. The purpose is to provide, as far as possible, reliable pertinent information about each minister on the roll since 1740, official annual meetings of the Classis and Synod, their presidents, stated clerks, secretaries and treasurers.

Research and tabulation have been done by Rev. Frank W. Snider.

ABBREVIATIONS

b., born; c. or col., college; chg., charge; cl., classis; d., deceased; f. & m., Franklin & Marshall College; Lan., Lancaster; lic., licensed; miss., missionary; ord., ordination; p., pastor; sem., seminary; so., Southern; sup., supply; syn., synod; theo., theological; u., university; wc., without charge.

Annual Meetings of the Classis of North Carolina and The Southern Synod, also the Presidents

Date	Place	President
1831	Brick Church, Guilford County, William Hauck.	
1832	Pilgrim Church, Davidson County, J. H. Crawford.	
1833	Savitz's Church, Mt. Zion, Rowan County, J. G. Fritchey.	
1834	Grace Church, Lincoln County, J. H. Crawford.	
1835	Brick Church, Alamance County, J. G. Fritchey.	
1836	Pilgrim Church, Davidson County, W. C. Bennet.	
1837	Grace Church, Lower Stone, Rowan County, W. C. Rankin.	
1838	St. Paul's Church, Catawba County, J. G. Fritchey.	
1839	Coble's Church, Guilford County, G. A. Leopold.	
1840	St. Matthew's Church, Lincoln County, John Lantz.	
1841	Emanuel Church, Davidson County, John Lantz.	
1842	Savitz's Church, Mt. Zion, Rowan County, David Crooks.	
1843	Beck's Church, Davidson County, G. W. Welker.	
1844	Brick Church, Alamance County, David Crooks.	
1845	St. Matthew's Church, Lincoln County, Jeremiah Ingold.	
1846	Grace Church, Lower Stone, Rowan County, John Lantz.	
1847	Emanuel Church, Davidson County, J. H. Crawford.	
1848	Brick Church, Alamance County, Jeremiah Ingold.	
1849	White Church, Newton, J. H. Crawford.	
1850	Savitz's Church, Mt. Zion, Rowan County, Thornton Butler.	
1851	Beck's Church, Davidson County, Jeremiah Ingold.	
1852	Brick Church, Alamance County, Thornton Butler.	
1853	White Church, Lincolnton, Jeremiah Ingold.	
1854	Mt. Gilead Church, Cabarrus County, John Lantz.	
1855	Bethany Church, Davidson County, William Sorber.	
1856	Brick Church, Alamance County, J. H. Crawford.	
1857	Grace Church, Newton, John Lantz.	
1858	Grace Church, Lower Stone, Rowan County, David Crooks.	
1859	Pilgrim Church, Davidson County, Jeremiah Ingold.	
1860	Brick Church, Alamance County, S. J. Fetzer.	
1861	Grace Church, Catawba County, A. S. Vaughn.	
1862	St. Paul's Church, Rowan County, Jeremiah Ingold.	
1863	New Jerusalem Church, Davidson County, Thornton Butler.	
1864	Mt. Hope Church, Guilford County, P. A. Long.	
1865	Grace Church, Lower Stone, Rowan County, Jeremiah Ingold.	
1866	Daniel's Church, Lincoln County, J. W. Cecil.	
1867	Bethany Church, Davidson County, Thomas Long.	

Date	Place	President

1868   St. Mark's Church, Alamance County, John Ingle.
1869   Grace Church, Newton, Jeremiah Ingold.
1870   Mt. Zion Church, Rowan County, J. C. Denny.
1871   Emanuel Church, Davidson County, J. C. Clapp.
1872   Brick Church, Alamance County, Jeremiah Ingold.
1873   Corinth Church, Hickory, J. W. Cecil.
1874   Grace Church, Lower Stone, Rowan County, J. C. Clapp.
1875   Hebron Church, Davidson County, Jeremiah Ingold.
1876   Brick Church, Alamance County, J. A. Foil.
1877   Grace Church, Newton, P. M. Trexler.
1878   Mt. Zion Church, Rowan County, John Ingle.
1879   Emanuel Church, Davidson County, J. H. Shuford.
1880   Brick Church, Alamance County, Jeremiah Ingold.
1881   Salem Church, Lincoln County, M. L. Hedrick.
1882   Mt. Zion Church, Rowan County, Jeremiah Ingold.
1883   Pilgrim Church, Davidson County, G. D. Gurley.
1884   Mt. Hope Church, Guilford County, G. D. Gurley.
1885   St. John's Church, Catawba County, P. M. Trexler.
1886   St. Luke's Church, Rowan County, J. C. Clapp.
1887   Trinity Church, Concord, Paul Barringer.
1888   Mt. Carmel Church, Davidson County, Thomas Long.
1889   Brick Church, Alamance County, C. B. Heller.
1890   Memorial Church, Maiden, P. M. Trexler.
1891   Bethel Church, Bear Creek, Stanley County, J. L. Murphy
1892   Hedrick's Grove Church, Davidson County, J. C. Clapp.
1893   Bethel Church, Catawba County, J. M. L. Lyerly.
1894   New Gilead Church, Cabarrus County, P. M. Trexler.
1895   Calvary Church, Davidson County, J. A. Foil.
1896   Trinity Church, Conover, A. H. Smith.
1897   Mt. Hope Church, Guilford County, J. L. Murphy.
1898   Grace Church, Newton, Paul Barringer.
1899   Grace Church, Lower Stone, Rowan County, W. A. Long.
1900   Beulah Church, Davidson County, Anthony Shulemberger.
1901   Shiloh Church, Faith, J. D. Andrew.
1902   Daniel's Church, Lincoln County, W. H. McNairy.
1903   Corinth Church, Hickory, H. A. M. Holshouser.
1904   First Church, High Point, J. C. Clapp.
1905   First Church, Lexington, J. L. Bowers.
1906   Bethel Church, Bear Creek, Stanley County, C. B. Heller.
1907   First Church, Burlington, D. E. Bowers.
1908   Trinity Church, Concord, C. E. Wehler.
1909   First Church, Greensboro, S. W. Beck.
1910   Zion Church, Lenoir, W. W. Rowe.
1911   Heidelberg Church, Thomasville, J. A. Foil.
1912   St. Matthew's Church, Lincoln County, W. B. Duttera.
1913   Mt. Zion Church, Rowan County, J. D. Andrew.
1914   Ursinus Church, Shuford Peeler.
1915   Grace Church, Newton, J. L. Murphy.
1916   First Church, Winston Salem, L. A. Peeler.
1917   First Church, Salisbury, D. C. Cox.
1918   St. Paul's Church, Catawba County, J. H. Keller.
1914   Ursinus Church, Rockwell, Shuford Peeler.
1920   First Church, High Point, C. C. Wagoner.
1921   Trinity Church, Conover, J. C. Peeler.
1922   St. James Church, Mt. Pleasant, J. A. Palmer.
1923   First Church, Charlotte, J. A. Koons.
1924   St Mark's Church, Alamance County, W. C. Lyerly.
1925   Grace Church, Lower Stone, Rowan County, H. A. Welker.
1926   Hedrick's Grove Church, Davidson County, S. W. Whitener.
1927   St. Matthew's Church, Lincoln County, H. A. Fesperman.
1928   Zion Church, Lenoir, H. A. M. Holshouser.
1929   First Church, Lexington, C. W. Warlick.
1930   Bethel Church, Bear Creek, Stanley County, Banks J. Peeler.
1931   Brick Church, Alamance County, Centennial Meeting, W. C. Lyerly.
1932   Memorial Church, Maiden, A. O. Leonard.
1933   Trinity Church, Concord, F. L. Fesperman.
1934   First Church, Winston Salem, A. C. Peeler.
1935   Emanuel Church, Davidson County, H. C. Kellermeyer.
1936   First Church, Greensboro, C. E. Hiatt.
1937   Grace Church, Newton, H. L. Fesperman.
1938   First Church, Salisbury, R. C. Whisenhunt.
1939   First Church, Charlotte, H. D. Althouse. Final meeting of the Classis.

Date	Place	President

1939 First Church, Salisbury, H. D. Althouse. Organization Meeting of Southern Synod.
1940 Zion Church, Davidson County, H. D. Althouse.
1941 Ursinus Church, Rockwell, H. D. Althouse.
1942 Grace Church, Lower Stone, Rowan County, H. R. Carpenter.
1943 First Church, Greensboro, H. R. Carpenter.
1944 First Church, High Point, G. T. Fitz.
1945 Trinity Church, Conover, G. T. Fitz.
1946 First Church, Landis, J. L. Levens.
1947 Mt. Hope Church, Guilford County, J. L. Levens.
1948 Calvary Church, Davidson County, L. A. Carpenter.
1949 Paul's Chapel, Davidson County, L. A. Carpenter.
1950 Hebron Church, Davidson County, L. A. Carpenter.
1951 First Church, Lexington, L. A. Carpenter.
1952 Second Church, Lexington, A. W. Hedrick.
1953 First Church, Salisbury, A. W. Hedrick.
1954 Trinity Church, Conover, A. R. Tosh.
1955 First Church, Winston Salem, A. R. Tosh.
1956 Bethel Church, Bear Creek, Stanley County. H. A. Fesperman served as full-time president.
1957 Heidelberg Church, Thomasville, H. A. Fesperman.
1958 Zion Church, Lenoir, .I. A. Fesperman.
1959 Trinity Church, Concord, H. A. Fesperman.
1960 First Church, Burlington, H. A. Fesperman.
1961 Grace Church, Newton, H. A. Fesperman.
1962 First Church, High Point, H. A. Fesperman.
1963 First Church, Greensboro, H. A. Fesperman.
1964 Peace Church, Greensboro, Banks J. Peeler.
1965 First Church, Lexington, Banks J. Peeler.
1966 Catawba College Chapel, Salisbury, Banks J. Peeler.
1967 Southern Synod as an Acting Association of Southern Conference of the United Church of Christ being phased out, Banks J. Peeler.
1968 The Council of Southern Synod, in session at the Synod House, January 31, dissolved the organization, referring certain matters to the Trustees for attention.

SECRETARIES AND STATED CLERKS OF THE CLASSIS AND SECRETARIES OF SOUTHERN SYNOD

Date	Name	Date	Name
1831-	J. H. Crawford, Secretary	1838-1847	J. H. Crawford, Stated Clerk
1832-	D. B. Lerch, Secretary	1847-1892	G. W. Welker, Stated Clerk
1833-	W. C. Bennet, Secretary	1892-1939	J. C. Leonard, Stated Clerk
1834-	Elder John Coulter, Secretary	1940-1942	J. C. Leonard, Secretary
1835-	J. H. Crawford, Secretary	1943-1952	W. C. Lyerly, Secretary
1836-	J. G. Fritchey, Secretary	1953-1968	J. L. Levens, Secretary
1837-	J. H. Crawford, Secretary		

TREASURERS OF THE CLASSIS AND OF SOUTHERN SYNOD

Date	Name	Date	Name
1831-	D. B. Lerch	1897-	Col. H. A. Forney
1832-1835	George Boger	1898-1904	M. J. Rowe
1836-	Henry Sechler	1905-	P. J. Leonard
1837-1844	Jacob Lantz	1906-1912	William H. McNairy
1845-1846	Daniel Finger	1913-1921	D. E. Bowers
1847-1855	G. W. Welker	1922-	G. E. Plott
1856-1866	Col. George Barnhardt	1923-1939	Milton Whitener
1867-1868	J. W. Cecil	1940-1952	Milton Whitener
1869-1887	Thomas Long	1953-1962	D. C. Dearborn
1888-1895	Col. H. A. Forney	1963-1968	W. W. Greenland
1896-	Abel A. Shuford		

Ministers of the Southern Synod

ALBERT, CHARLES HARMONY
b. Allentown. Pa. 8-25-1824, d. in Ark. 7-17-1868. AB. Marshall C. 1848, Lan. Sem. 1848b-1849b; Lic. Leb. Cl. 1850, Ord. NC Cl 1852. P. Newton. NC 1852. Pres. Catawba C. 1852; prin. Young Ladies Seminary, Lincolnton, N.C., 1853, Mt. Pleasant Sem., Boyertown, Pa. 1853-54; took deacon's orders, Prot. Epis. Church, 1854; p. San Augustine, Texas, 1854; moved to New Orleans, La. and took Priest's orders, 1856; served various parishes in Southwest; p. St John's, Camden, N.J. 1860, Peru and Kankakee, Ill. 1861-1866; miss., Batesville, and Jacksonport, Ark. 1866-68.

ALCORN, EDWIN MYERS
b. Manchester, Md. 11-24-1924. AB F. & M. 1944, Lan Sem. 1947 BD; Yale Divinity School; Lic. and Ord. Potomac Synod, 1947; P. Timberville, Va., 1947-52; Middletown, Md. 1952-56; Trinity, Conover, N.C. 1956-65; Western Area Associate Minister, Southern Conference, UCC, 1966-.

ALTHOUSE, HARRY DANIEL
b. Womelsdorf, Pa. 5-27-1898. A.B. F. & M. 1919; B.D. Lancaster, Sem. 1922; D.D Catawba College 1941 Lic Leb Cl. 1922, Ord. Wyo. Cl. 1922; p. Berwick, Pa. 1922-27; Shippensburg, Pa. 1927-30; Corinth, Hickory, N.C. 1930-. Member, General Council, Evangelical and Reformed Church 12 years. Last President N.C. Cl. 1939; First Pres. Southern Synod, 1940-41.

ANDES, MARK WINSTON
b. 6-3-1923, Rockingham Co., Va. Elon College, A.B., 1944; Duke Divinity School, B.D. 1948. Lic. Va. Central Conf. C.C. 1942; Ord. Va. Central Conf. C.C. 1943, p. Berea, Elon College, N.C. 1943-46; Virgilina, Va. 1946-54; Center, South Boston, Va. 1954-59; Congregational, Winchester, Va., 1959-65; Edgewood, Burlington, N.C. 1965-.

ANDREW, JAMES D.
b. 9-27-1864, Guilford Co., N.C. d. 1-3-1949, Lexington, N.C. Catawba Co. 1893, D.D. Catawba College. Lic. 5-6-1893, N.C. Cl.; Ord. N.C. Cl. 5-30-1893, p. Guilford chg., 1893-1898; Burlington Chg. 1898-1913; President Catawba College 1913-1918; p. Upper Davidson Chg. 1918-24; Faith Chg. 1925-31; Lower Davidson Chg. 1931-37; Retired. Lexington, N.C. 1937. President, N.C. Cl. 1901 and 1913.

ANDREW, JOSEPH D.
b. 2-10-1913; Burlington, N. C. A.B. Catawba Col., 1936; B.D. Eden Theo. Sem., 1939; Air War C., Maxwell A.F. Base, Montgomery, Ala., 1949, Lic. N.C. Cl. 6-27-1939; Ord. June 1939, Southern Syn., p. St. John's, Kannapolis, 1939-42; Chaplain, U.S. Air Force, 1942-66; Retired, Asheville, N.C. 1966.

BARTHOLOMEW, CARROLL E.
b. 2-10-1935, Hickory, N.C. B.S. Lenier Rhyne C., 1960; B.D. Lancaster Theo. Sem. 1963. Lic, So Synd 5-1-1963; Ord So. Synd. 6-23-63, p. Brick Church, Whitsett, N.C., 1963-65; Chaplain, U. S. Navy, 1965-.

BARNHARDT, WILLIAM
b. 2-7-1903, Saegerstown, Pa. A.B. John's Hopkins U., 1923; Union Theo. Sem. 1927; A.M. Columbia U., 1924; Ph.D. Columbia U. and Union Theo. Sem. 1927., D.D. Pacific University, 1938 Lic Baltimore-Washington Classis, May 1926; Ord. Oregon Cong. Conf. May 1930, p. Professor of Religion, Pacific Univ. Oregon, 1927-30; Head of Dept. of Religion Hood College, Frederick, Md., 1930-1958; Exec. Secretary of Federation of Churches, Washington, D.C., 1940-1941; Pastor of Circular Congregational Church, Charleston, S.C., 1958-.

BARRINGER, PAUL
b. 9-16-1850, Mt. Pleasant, N.C., d. 2-10-1925, Mt. Pleasant, N.C. N.C. Lutheran C., Mt Pleasant; Catawba C, Heidelberg C and Sem., Tiffin, Ohio, Lic. N.C. Cl., 6-25-1881; Ord., 1st Sun. Sept., 1881 p. Mt. Zion-Gilead, Rowan Co., 1881-91; Concord Chg., 1891-94; East Rowan Chg., 1894-97; Mt. Pleasant Chg., 1897-1900.

BECK, ELMO DAVIS
b. 12-15-1922, Lexington, N.C., Catawba C., 1955-57; Certificate, Lancaster Theo. Sem., 1960, Ordained So. Syn. 6-26-1960, p. Mt. Hope, Salisbury, 1960-62; Jerusalem-St. Peter's Chg., Glen Rock, Pa., 1962-.

BECK, SAMUEL W.
b. 5-13-1872, Lexington, N.C. d. 9-4-1958, Littlestown, Pa., Catawba C., Ursinus Theo. Sem., Lic. 5-17-1902; Ord. 3-22-1903. Served in N.C., Pa., Va. Dismissed to Philadelphia Cl., Eastern Syn. 4-20-1913.

BECK, WALTER C.
b. 1-13-1885, Hazelton, Pa., d. 8-25-1960, Lincolnton, N. C. B.S., Schuykill Col. 1904; Schuykill Sem. 1908, Graduate Study, Buckell Univ. Lic. Evangelical Assn. 2-14-1908; Ord. 1912. p. Evangelical Churches in Pa., for 13 years; received by E. Susquehanna Classis of Reformed Ch., 1917; p. Nescopeck Chg. Pa. 1917-1939; Emanuel, Lincolnton, N.C. 11-15-29 to 9-5-1952.

BELL, JOSEPH W.
p. Zion, Lenior 1908-1911, Supt., Nazareth Children's Home, 1911-1917. Received from Zion Cl., Potomac Synod, 10-16-1908. Dismissed to Abingdon Presbytery, Presbyterian Ch. USA 5-24-1921.

BENNET, WILLIAM CROSBY
b. 4-14-1804, Long Island, N.Y. d. Boiling Springs, Pa. 4-12-1870. Ord. Exec. Com. Syn. as miss. to N.C. & S.C. 1832. p. in S.C. 1933; Pilgrim, Beck's and Sour's, Davidson Co., N.C. 1834-36; Shippensburg, Pa. 1837-39; Newville, 1840-44; East Berlin & New Oxford, 1845-46; Miss. & Sup. Res. Carlisle, 1847-48; Liverpool, 1849; Newburg 1850-52; agt. Pub. Bd. 1854-70.

BLACK, HARVEY W.
b. 1-17-1896, Thomasville, N.C. A.B. Catawba Col. 1922; B.D. Central Theo. Sem. 1925; M.A. Northwestern Univ. 1927; D.D. Catawba Col. 1954; Lic. 7-20-1925, N.C. Cl.; Ord. Westmoreland Cl. Pittsburgh Syn. 3-18-1928; p. Director of Ch. Ed. Second Ch., Greensburg, Pa. 1927-28; p. St. Paul's, Derry, Pa. 1928-31, Christ Ch., Latroba, Pa., 1931-52; Fulltime Pres. Pittsburgh Syn. 1952-62; Retired Greensbourg, Pa., 1962, Thomasville, N.C. 1968.

BOGER, GEORGE
b. 12-15-1782, Cabarrus Co., N. C., d. 6-19-1865. Studied under Rev. Samuel Weyberg, Rev. Mr. Storch (Lutheran) and Rev. Andrew Loretz. Ord. 3-6-1803, Mt. Zion, China Grove by Rev. Andrew Loretz, p. Rowan County Chs. 1803-1847.

BONDS, BOBBY RAY
b. 5-12-1931, Cabarrus Co., N.C. A.B. Catawba Col. 1953; B.D. Yale Univ. Divinity School, 1956, Lic. Sou. Syn. 1956, Ord. Sou. Syn. 1956, p. Zion, Thomasville, N.C. 1956-59; Brookford Chg., 1959-62, Faith Ch. Brookford, 1963; St. John's Kannapolis, N.C. 1963-.

BONEBREAK, JOHN DIEHL
b. 4-4-1936 Martinsburg, Pa. A.B. F. & M., 1959; B.D. Lancaster Theo. Sem. 1963, Lic. West Penn. Conf. Juniata Assn. 1963, Ord. 7-21-1963, W. Penn. Conf. Juniata Assn.; P. Grace (Lower Stone), Rockwell, N.C. 1963-.

BOSTIAN, FRANK KELLER
b. 4-30-1912, China Grove, N.C. A.B. Catawba Cl. 1932; B.D. Lancaster Theo. Sem. 1934; Lic. N.C. Cl. 5-28-1934; Ord. Carlisle Cl. Potomac Syn. 9-2-1934; p. Zion Chg., Blain, Pa. 8-1-1934-37; St. John's, Chambersburg, Pa. 1937-42; St. John's Kannapolis, 1942-47; Messiah, Baltimore, Md., 1947-59; First, Raleigh, N.C. 1959-62; First Church, Charlotte, N.C. 1962-.

BOWERS, DAVID ELI
b. 4-9-1873, Thomasville, N.C., d. 10-28-1921, Winston Salem, N.C. Catawba C., 1899; Ursinus School of Theo., 1902. Lic. 5-17-1902; Ord. 5-17-1902, p. Asst. Lexington and High Point, N.C., 1902-03; First, High Point, N.C., 1903-07; Bethel, High Point, N.C., 1905-09; Bethel-Zion Chg., 1909-11; Waughtown, 1911-21 Treasurer of Cl., 1913-21.

BOWERS, JOSHUA L.
b. 7-24-1874, Thomasville, N.C., d.   A.B. Catawba Col. 1898, Lancaster Sem. 1893-01. Lic., 5-21-1901, Ord. 7-14-1901, p. West Rowan Chg. China Grove, N.C. 1901-08; Guilford Chg. Julian 1908-11; Dismissed to Orange Presbytery, Presbyterian Ch. U.S.A., 7-12-1911; p. Brim N.C. 1911-13; teacher Woodleaf 1913-21; retired 1921.

BRANTLEY, JOHN KELLER
b. 3-8-1906, Concord N.C. A.B. Catawba Col. 1931; B.D.; Lancaster Theo. Sem. 1934. Lic. N.C. Cl. 1934; Ord. Somerset Cl. 1934; p. Jennerstown, Pa. 1934-40; Glade Chg. Walkersville, Md. 1940-45; Carroll Chg. Westminster, Md. 1945-53, Thomasville, Pa., 1954-59, Mt. Crawford, Va., 1960-62; Newport, Pa., 1962-.

BROMER, FRANK S.
b. 5-4-1872, Schwenksville, Pa., d. Lititz, Pa. 4-19-63. Ursinus Theo. Scho., ord. Ref. Lebanon, Pa. 1904, p. St. Stephens Ref. ch. Lebanon Pa. 1904-05; 1st Ref. ch., Cedar Rapids, Iowa, 1905-23, Grace Ref. ch., Hanover, Pa., 1923-28; 1st Ref. ch., Charlotte, N.C., 1928-32; pod. 1932-55.

BROWN, JOHN
b. 7-21-1771, Bremen, Germany, d. 1-26-1850, Bridgewater, Va.   Came to America, 1797; studied under Rev. Philip Stoech, Chambersburg, Pa., 1798-99; Lic. Eastern Synod, 5-12-1800; Ord. Eastern Synod, 5-10-1803; p. Shennadoah Valley, Va., 1800-50. Was enrolled as a member of Classis in 1831. Never attended a meeting of Classis and his name was removed from the roll of Classis in 1837.

BUPP, MARTIN LUTHER II
b. 5-26-1937, York, Pa. A.B. Catawba Col. 1959, B.D. Yale, 1962, Ord. 6-21-1962, Mercersburg Syn. p. Grace-Daniels Chg., Lincolnton, N.C. 1962-64; Ass't. Pastor, St. John's, Lansdale, Pa. 10-1-64-.

BURTT, DONALD ROBERT
b. 11-20-1933, Chicago. Ill. A.B. Lakeland Col., Sheboygan, Wis., 1956; B.D. Eden Theo. Sem., 1961; Lic. Southern Syn. 1960; Ord. North Ill. Syn. 6-12-60; p. Memorial, Winston-Salem 1960-63; Salem, Winnipeg, Manitoba, Canada, 1963-65; teacher, Vancouver, British Columbia, Canada, 1965-.

BUTLER, THORNTON
b. 10-4-1820, Catawba Co., N.C., d. 11-2-1870. A.B. Marshall Col., Lancaster, Sem. 1864b-1847a; Lic. 1-26-1848, N.C. Classis; Ord. 3-11-1848, p., churches in Davidson Co. 1848-51, w.c. 1851-58, p., Gold Hill 1858-1868, Anna, Ill. 1869-1870, Dismissed to Illinois Cl. 1869.

BYERLY, CHESTER WALTER
b. 11-22-1933, Davidson Co., N.C. A.B. Catawba College, 1960, B.D. Lancaster Theo. Sem., 1963. Lic. Southern Syn. 5-31-1963; Ord. 6-23-1963, Southern Syn. p. St. Andrew's Lexington, N.C., 1963-65; Faith, Brookford, 1965-68; w.c. Claremont, N.C. 1968-.

CARBAUGH, LEE OTIS
b. 10-15-1889, Mummasburg, Pa., d. 7-24-1959, Harrisonburg, Va. A.B. Gettysburg C. 1913; Lancaster Sem., 1913-16; Lic. Gettysburg Cl. 1916; Ord. Clarion Cl. 1916, p. Dayton, Pa. 1916-21; Apollo, Pa. 1922-30; Rockwell, N.C., 1930-39; South Bend Chg. Pa. 1939-42; Rockingham chg. Va. 1942-59.

CAREY, JOHN JESSE
b. 10-13-31, Ft. Wayne, Ind. A.B. Duke University 1953; B.D. Yale Divinity Sch. 1956; Yale, S.T.M., 1957; Duke Univ. Ph.D. 1965. Lic. Mich.-Ind. Syn. 5-3-1956, Ord. Mich.-Ind. Syn. 1957 p. West Haven, Cong. Ch., West Haven, Conn. 1956-57 (Ass't. Pastor) Campus Minister, Catawba Co., 1957-60; Campus Minister, Fla. State Univ. Tallahassee, Fla. 1961-64., Duke U. 1965-1966, Tallahassee, Fla. 1966-.

CARPENTER, HUITT RUDISILL
b. 10-21-1907, Maiden, N. C. Catawba Col. 1929, Lancaster Theo. Sem., 1932, Lic. N.C. Cl. 5-23-1932, Ord. 7-5-1932, p. South Fork Chg., Newton, 1932-35; Emanuel, Lincolnton, N.C. 1935-37; Mt. Zion, China Grove, N.C. 1937-46; First, Charlotte, 1946-49, Organizing Pastor, St. Matthew's Charlotte, 1948-49; Shiloh, Faith, N.C. 1949-56; St. Mark's Burlington, N.C. 1956-60; St. John's, Kannapolis, 1960-63; Calvary, Thomasville, 1963-. President Sou. Syn. 1940-42.

CARPENTER, LONNIE ALFRED
b. 2-28-1914, Lincolnton, N.C. A.B. Catawba College, 1935; B.D. Lancaster Theo. Sem. 1938; D.D. Catawba College, Lic. N.C. Cl. 5-31-1938; Ord. 6-5-1938; p. Faith Chg. 1938-44; Trinity, Conover, N.C. 1944-55; First, Burlington, 1955-60; First, Salisbury, 1960-. President Sou. Syn. 1948-52.

CAUSEY, WILLIAM HENRY
b. 12-2-1872, Silver Hill, N.C., d. 12-15-1943. A.B. Cat. Col. 1900, Lancaster, 1900-03, D.D. Central Uni. 1933. Lic. N.C. Cl. 5-20-1903, Ord. 6-7-1903, p. Lower Davidson chg. Lexington, N.C. 1903-04; Upper Davidson chg., 1904-1906, Concord 1907-12; Faith chg. Salisbury, 1912-14; Mt. Crawford, Va. 1914-16; Woodstock Va. 1916-22; Rockingham Chg. Harrisonburg 1923-29; Memorial, Winston-Salem, N.C. 1929-37; Retired Winston-Salem, 1937.

CECIL, JESSE W.
b.   d. 3-5-1899. Received as Licentiate from M.E. Church, April 25-1862, Ord. 7-18-1863. p. Gilead Chg. 1864-66. Concord 1884-85.

CHATLOS, JOHN CALVIN
b. 5-5-1919, Cumberland, Md. A.B. Catawba Col. 1943; Lan. Theo. Sem. 1945. Lic Susquehanna Syn. 10-23-45; Ord. Susquehanna Syn. 12-16-1945; p. Wapwallopen Chg. Pa., 1946-50; Brick Ch. Burlington, N.C. 1950-53; Lower Stone chg., 1953-59; Incarnation-St. James chg. Myd., 1959-.

CHEEK, ARTHUR WILSON
b. 7-7-1914, Alamance Co., N. C. A.B. Cat. Col. 1936; B.D. Lan. Sem. 1939; D.D. Catawba Col. 1959. Lic. N.C. Cl. 5-30-1939; Ord. 6-7-1939; p. Catawba, N.C. Chg. 1939-45; Faith, Brookford; Macedonia, Hickory; 1945-47; Director, Youth Work, E. & R. Church, 1947-50; Director of Youth Work and Ex. Sec. of United St. Youth Work, N.C.C.; 1950-57; Dir. Youth Work, NCCCUSA 1957-59; Ass. Gen. Sec. World Council of Ch. Ed. 1959-65; Associate General Secretary; Religious Ed. Assn. 1965-.

CHEEK, RICHARD ALBRIGHT
b. 5-4-1927, Burlington, N.C. A.B. Catawba, 1947; B.D. Lancaster Theo. Sem. 1950; Lic. Sou. Syn. 5-29-1950; Ord. 6-2-1950, p. Ursinus Ch., Rockwell, N.C. 1950-55; Heidelberg, Thomasville, N.C. 1955-64; St. John's, Richmond, Va. 1964-.

CHRISTMAN, JACOB
b. Orange Co., N.C. 1745, d. 1810, Ohio. Studied under Moravians, Salem, N.C. Proposed for Ord. 1794, Ord. Synod of Pa. 1798, p. six congregations, Davidson Co., N.C., 1798-1803; Organized First Reformed Congregation in Ohio, near Springboro, in 1804.

CLAPP, CARL HOMER
b. 4-28-1903, Alamance Co., N.C. A.B. Elon College, 1929; B.D. Lan. Sem. 1933; Lic. N.C. Cl. 7-11-1933; Ord. 8-20-1933, p. Grace, Newton, N.C. 1933-40; First, Pitcairn, Pa., 1940-44; St. Mark's Cumberland, Md. 1944-1967. Retired 1967, Burlington, N.C.

CLAPP, CLARENCE
b. 2-7-1873, d. 1-1-1936, Newton, N.C. Catawba Col. 1893; Ursinus School of Theo. 1896, Baltimore School of Pharmacy, 1898-. Admitted to N.C. Bar in 1929. Lic. 5-9-1896, Ord. 5-31-1896, p. Thomasville chg. 1896-1898. Name disappeared from roll 5-12-1906.

CLAPP, JACOB C.
b. 9-5-1832, Guilford, d. 7-2-1910, Newton, N.C. Catawba Col., Amherst Col., 1857. Lic. 4-27-1867 N.C. Cl. Ord. 5-2-1869, p. Reformed Ch. Newton, N.C., Churches in Lincoln and Catawba Counties. Pres. Catawba Col. 1885-1900.

CLAPP, WILLIAM S.
Lic. N.C. Cl. 5-12-1906, Dismissed to Lehigh Cl., Eastern Syn. 5-18-1907.

COBB, GERALD ROBERT
b.   . Lic. 4-16-52, So. Syn. Ord. 4-12-53, So. Syn. Received from Presbyterian Church; p. Pilgrim, Lexington, N.C. 1952-56, Ben Arnold, Texas 1956-61, First Goshen, Ind., 1961-67; Salamanca, N.Y., 1967-.

COOK, INGLE OSCAR
b. 2-17-1935, Kannapolis, N.C. A.B. Cat. Col., 1957; B.D. Lan. Sem. 1964; Lic. April 1964- So. Syn.; Ord. 6-28-1964 So. Syn., p. Zion U.C.C. North Canton, Ohio, (Ass't) 1964-66 p. Beck's, Lexington 1966-.

COULTER, ROY D.
b. 12-26-1902, Riverview, Ala. B.A. Elon Col. 1931; B.D. Vanderbilt, 1934, M.A. Geo. Washington Univ. 1952. Lic. & Ord. Alabama Conf. Congregational Ch. Ch. 1932; p. Shenrock Parish, New Market, Va. (C.C.) 1936-44; Timber Ridge Cong. Ch., High View, W. Va. 1945-51; Memorial Church, Winston-Salem, N.C. 1951-59; Christ, Shepherdstown, W. Va., 1960-66. Retired Supply-Cana, Va. 1967-68.

COX, DOUGAN C.
b. 10-24-1854 Chatham Co., N.C., d. 12-27-1932, Thomasville, N.C. New Garden High School. Ord. July 1896, Society of Friends; Rec'd from Friends Ch. 12-2-1910; p. Gilead Ch. Concord, N.C. 1911-1912; Guilford Chg. 1912; Burlington 1912-15, Emmanuel Chg. Thomasville, 1915-25. President N.C. Classis 1918-19.

CRAWFORD, JOHN HENRY
b. 7-23-1801, Carroll Co., Md., d. 10-9-1864. Ord. Syn. 1828, Lancaster 1825-28a, p. Guilford and Orange Co. N.C. 1828-1840; Upper and Lower Chgs. Lincoln Co., 1840-1842, Grace, St. Paul etc. Catawba Co. 1843-57, Middlebrook, Va. 1858-1864. First Secretary of Classis, Host Pastor for First Classis; Dismissed to Classis of Va. in 1858.

CRAVEN, RAYMOND CLARENCE
b. 6-2-1923, Davidson Co., N.C. A.B. Cat. Col. 1952; B.D. Lancaster Theo. Sem. 1955; Lic. So. Syn. 5-27-1955; Ord. So. Syn. 5-29-1955; p. Hedrick's Grove, Lexington 1955-67; Mt. Hope, Whitsett, 1967-.

CRESS, JAMES REID
b. 7-7-1931, Rowan Co., N.C. A.B. Cat. Col. 1953, B.D. Lan. Theo. Sem. 1956. Lic. So. Syn. 3-5-1956, Ord. So. Syn. 6-10-1956; p. Brick Church, Whitsett, N.C. 1956-62; Ursinus, Rockwell, N.C. 1962-.

CROMER, FREDERICK
Rec'd from Eastern Ohio Cl. Ohio Syn. 10-29-1904; Dismissed to Ohio Syn. 11-20-1905.

CROOKS, DAVID
b. 3-12-1820 Pa., d. 1-24-1859, Lincoln County, N.C. Att. Lan Sem. 1837B, Lic. Zion's Classis, Ord. N.C. Cl. 1838, p. Lexington, N.C. 1838-1845, Lincolnton, N.C. 1846-1859.

CROOKS, ROBERT F.
Lic. 5-26-1877, Ord. 1st Sun. June, 1877. Name disappeared from role 7-17-1888. Rowan County, p. Lower Stone, 1876-81; Mt. Hope, 1885-88.

CURRAN, WADE HAMPTON, JR.
b. 3-7-1933, Asheville, N.C. A.B. Cat. Col. 1958, B.D. Yale, 1961; Lic. So. Syn. 4-28-1961; Ord. So. Syn. 6-18-1964, p. Lower Davidson Charge (Beck's, Jerusalem) 1961-65; Chaplain, U.S. A.F. 1965-.

DAVIS, B. FRANK
Rec'd from Miami Cl. 7-28-1894. Dismissed to Pres. Ch. 11-14-1901, p. Gilead Chg. Concord, N.C. 1894-96.

DAVIS, HIRAM ELLSWORTH
b. 12-8-1915, Fairplay, Md. Ashland Col., Ashland, Ohio, 1937; Ashland Theo. Sem. 1938-39, Lan. Theo. Sem. 1942, Lic. Potomac Synod, 4-15-1942; Ord. Potomac Syn. 5-22-1942; p. First Church, Winston-Salem, N.C. 1942-1957; First Church, Landis, 1957-65; First Church, Burlington, 1965-.

DAVIS, RICHARD NEVIN
b. 12-31-1920. Kent State Univ. 1952; Union Theo. Sem. 1956; Lic. 1956, Massillon, Ohio. S. E. Ohio Syn., Ord. 1956, Canton, Ohio, S. E. Ohio Syn., p. Kenilworth, Kenmore, 1956-59; Faith Ch. Clearwater, Fla. 1960-65; WC Hamilton, Ohio; Kalamazoo, Mich.

DAVIS, THOMAS RICHARD, JR.
b. 8-5-1934, Scranton, Pa. B.A. Dartmouth Co. 1956; B.D. Union Theo. Sem. N.Y. 1960; Ord. 7-10-1960; Trinity Ch. Scranton, Pa. Susquehanna Syn., p. Ass't Chaplain United Student Fellowship Ohio State U. 1958-59, University of N.C. Chapel Hill, 1960-65, Saratoga Springs, N.Y. 1966-.

DAYE, CARL THEODORE
b. 6-28-1921, Hickory, N. C. A.B. Catawba College, 1944, B.D. Lan. Theo. Sem. 1946, Grad. Study, Lutheran Sem. Columbia, S.C. Lic. So. Syn. 7-3-1946; Ord. 7-19-46 So. Syn., p. St. Paul's-Keller Chg. N.C. 1946-47; Upper Davidson Chg. 1948-51; Crescent Chg. 1951-54; Mt. Pleasant Chg. 1954-58; St. Peter's, Greensboro 1958-65; Pembroke Manor, Virginia Beach, Va. 1965-.

DELP, ROBERT WORLEY
b. 6-2-1925, La Grange, N.C. B.S. Davidson, 1947; B.D. Lan. Theo. Sem. 1951; M.A., Ph.D. George Wash. Univ. Lic. 5-25-1951, So. Syn.; Ord. 5-27-1951, Trinity, Concord, So. Syn., p. Zion Church, Hagerstown, Md. 1951-58; Supply, Protestant Community Ch. Baltimore 1958-62; Professor, Atlantic Christian College, Wilson, N.C. 1962-1968; Professor, Elon College, 1968-.

DENNY, J. C.
Received as Licentiate from Pres. Ch. 9-15-1866. Ord. 9-15-1866 by Classis as Committee. Name disappears from roll, 11-14-1878. P. Lower Stone Ch. 1869-74; Mt. Hope Ch. 1869-71; Shiloh Ch. 1876-78.

DERENDINGER, ERNST
b. 5-9-1378; Rheinfelden, Switzerland. Commercial and Secretarial Col. Basel, Switzerland, 1900; Theo. Sem. Bloomfield, N.J. 1908; Univ. of Berlin, Germany, 1911; Univ. of Erlangen, Germany, 1912, Ph.D. Lic. Presbytery U.S.A. Newark, N.J. 1908, (never ordained) Prof. of German and Greek, Catawba College, Newton, N.C. 1912-13; Head of Dept. of History, Hood College, Frederick, Md. 1913-18; Secretarial Work, 1918-25; Prof. Catawba College, 1925-42; Received from Newark Presbytery, Pres. Ch. U.S.A. 12-29-1912. Dismissed to Maryland Cl. 10-24-1913; Rec'd from Maryland Cl. 2-18-1926. Retired 1942, Coral Gables, Florida.

DETWILER, ARTHUR R.
b. 12-20-1920, Phoenixville, Pa. A.B. Catawba Co., 1942; B.D. Lancaster Theo. Sem., 1945. Lic. Philadelphia Synod, 2-1-1945; Ord. Philadelphia Synod, 2-18-45; p. First, Asheboro, N. C. 1945-46; Guilford chg. N.C. 1946-49; Zion, Lenoir, N.C. 1949-53; Emanuel, Sandusky, Ohio, 1953-54; St. John's Columbus Ohio, 1954-59; First, Houston, Texas, 1959-64; St. Luke's, Columbus, Nebraska, 1965-66; WC Charlotte, N.C., 1966-67; First, Raleigh N.C. 1967-1968.

DEWALD, HENRY ADAM
b. 4-13-1880, Lembach, Alsace, Lorrain, Germany, d. Tucker, Ga. 9-30-67. University, Edinborough Scotland; Basel Sem. Switzerland. Ordained, Lembach, Alsace, Germany, 1905. Missionary, Gold Coast, West Africa, 1906-18; Honduras, Central America, 1919-28; p. St. John's Evangelical and Reformed Church, Atlanta, Ga., (now Lutheran), 1930-45. Retired, 1945, after unsuccessful cataract eye operation.

DIEFFENBACH, HENRY
b.   , d. Ohio, 1839. Ordained, Eastern Synod, 5-18-1802, p. Guilford, Orange, and Randolph Counties N. C., 1802-1805; Ohio, 1838-39.

DILLINGER, GEORGE EDWARD
b. 5-28-1901, Lawrence, Mass. B.S., Ursinus College, 1930, B.D. Central Theo. Sem., 1933; M.A., Duke University, 1943; S.T.D. Temple University, 1954. Lic. Philadelphia Cl. 1933; Ord. 7-29-1933, Philadelphia Cl.,p. Hickory, Bottom chg., Penn., 1933-37; Memorial, Winston-Salem, N.C., 1937-39; First Burlington, N.C. 1939-45; Trinity, Philadelphia, Pa., 1945-62; Zion, Lenior, N.C. 1962-66; Executive Director, Blowing Rock Assembly Grounds., 1966-.

DITZLER, IRVIN S.
Rec'd from Zion Cl., Potomac Synod, 5-8-1907; Dismissed to Juniata Cl., Potomac Syn. 4-29-1908.

DITZLER, JOHN ALVIN
b. 7-8-1881, Hamilton twp Adams Co., Pa., d. 3-9-1924, Myersdale, Pa. A.B. F.&M. 1907, Lancaster, 1907-10, Lic. Gettysburg, Cl. 1910, Ord. W. Sq. Cl. 1910, p. Selinsgrove-Pa., 1910-14; Grace, Frederick, Md., 1914-20; Newton, N.C. 1921-22; Meyersdale, Pa., 1922-24.

DOBY, REX OREN
b. 11-17-32, Lexington, N.C. B.A. Catawba College, 1958; B.D. Lancaster, 1961. Lic. So. Syn.   Ord. So. Syn. 6-25-1961, p. Hebron, Winston-Salem, N.C. 1961-67; St. John's, Houston, Texas, 1967-.

DUBARD, WILLIAM (Du Pert)
Preached in N.C. in 1764, lived near Paysour's Mill, Gaston Co., N.C. Died of the small-pox in Charleston, S.C. near close of Revolutionary War.

DUTTERA, WILLIAM B.
b. 12-25-1865, Littlestown, Pa., d. 11-30-1938, Salisbury. Gettysburg, Pa., Col. 1890-94; Heidelburg Theo. Sem., Tiffin, Ohio, 1897. Received as Licentiate from Tiffin Cl., Ohio Syn. 6-26-1901; Ord. 6-26-1901. Dismissed to Cong. Assn. of N.C. 8-5-1915; Received from Wyo. Cl., Eastern Syn. 2-10-1932, p. First Salisbury, 1901-1915. Mill Creek, Va. 1924-27.

EHRGOOD, GEORGE ALBERT
b. Gibralter, Pa., 8-12-1892. A.B., Research University, B.D. Lancaster Theo. Sem. 1915; Atlanta Theo. Sem. L.L.B. and L.L.M. Cumberland University Law Dept., L.L.D. Atlanta Law School. Lic. Leb. Cl. 1915; Ord. Juniata Cl. 1915, p. Hollidaysburg, Pa., 1915-22; Chap. U.S. Army, France, 1918-19; Prof. Greek N.T. Atlanta Theo. Sem., Atlanta, Ga., Prof. Church History and World History, Oglethorpe University, Atlanta, Ga., lawyer, Atlanta, Ga., retired Gibralter, Pa.

EVERHART, WILLIAM M.
P. Asheboro C.C. Ch.,Hebron, Winston -Salem, 1966-.

EVERLINE, LEWIS, E., SR.
b. 1-26-1926, Cumberland, Md. A.B. Catawba Col. 1945; B.D. Lancaster 1948 M.S.W. Tulane Univ. 1964. Lic. & Ord. Pittsburgh Synod 1948, p. St. Paul-Keller, Kannapolis, N.C.; Emanuel, Lincolnton, N.C.; St. Mark, Gratna, La.; Social Work, Bethany Children's Home, Womelsdorf, Pa.

FARRELL, EARL THOMPSON
b. 10-11-21, Chatham Co., Pittsboro, N. C. ,A.B. 1945 Elon, B.D. Duke 1949. Lic. Western N.C. Conf. 1942; Ord. Western N.C. Conf. 1944, p. Pleasant Hill, Liberty and Haw River (Student Pastorate) Sunbury, N.C. and Cypress Chapel, Va. 1949-1955; Wake Chapel, Fuquay, Varina, N.C. 1955-1962; Bayside, Va. Beach, Va. 1962-1967; Mt. Tabor, Lexington, N.C. 1967-.

FAUST, ALLEN KLEIN
b. Bernville, Pa., 8-20-1869. A.B. F.&M. 1897, B.D. Lancaster, 1900; Ph.D. University of Pa. 1909. Lic. and Ord. Lancaster Cl. 1900; Missionary to Japan, 1900-1903; teacher, North Japan College, 1900-1913; Pres. Miyagi College, 1913-30; Prof. of Social Science, Catawba C., 1930-43. Retired 1943, Phoebe Home, Allentown, Pa., 1948-.

FAUST, DAVID EARL
b. 8-24-1897, Mercersburg, Pa. F. & M., A. B. 1919; B.D. Yale Divinity Sch., 1924, Ph.D., 1929. Lic. Mercersburg Cl., Potomac Synod, 1929. Ord. Southern Synod, 7-1-1945, Professor of Bible and History, Catawba College, 1929-1967. Retired Salisbury, N.C.

FAUST, J. N.
P. Trinity, Concord, N.C. 1898-99. Received as Licentiate from Goshenhoppen Cl. 6-11-1898. Ordained 6-11-1898. Dismissed to Philadelphia Cl. 5-16-1902.

FEATHER, NEVIN HOY
b. 12-8-1925, King, Pa. A. B. Franklin-Marshall, 1948; B.D. Lancaster, Theo. Sem., 1951. Lic. Central Pa. Synod, 5-25-1951; Ord. Central Pa. Synod, 6-3-1951, p. Smyrna-Bethany chg., Claremont, 1951-66; First, Landis, 1966-.

FESPERMAN, HARVEY A.
b. 10-11-1892, Rowan Co., N.C. B.A. Catawba College, 1914; Central Theo. Sem., 1915-16; D.D., Catawba, 1938. Lic. N.C. Cl. 2-21-1916, Ord. 4-23-1916, p. South Fork Chg., Newton, 1916-21; First, Greensboro, 1921-30; Christ's, Hagerstown, Md., 1930-45; First, Burlington, 1945-55. President, Southern Synod (Fulltime), 1955-63. Retired, Faith, N.C. 1963. Bd. Trustees, Catawba C., Lancaster Theo. Sem., Hood College, Homewood Ch. Home. FIRST FULLTIME PRESIDENT OF SOUTHERN SYNOD.

FESPERMAN, HOY LEE
b. 10-5-1901, Rockwell, N.C., d. 6-30-1960, Greensboro, N.C. Heidelberg College, 1925; Central Theo. Sem. 1927. Lic. N.C. Cl. 5-12-1927, Ord. 6-12-1927, p. Upper Davidson Chg., 1927-29; Emanuel, Lincolnton, 1929-35; First Church, High Point, 1935-46; First, Greensboro, 1946-60.

FESPERMAN, JAMES FRANKLIN LYERLY
b. Faith, N.C., 12-29-1894. Catawba Col. A. B. 1916; Central Theo. Sem. B.D. 1919, Columbia University, M.A. 1925. Lic. N.C. Cl. 5-7-1919; Ord. 5-7-1919. Missionary to Japan, 1919-43, Asst. Sec. Commission on World Service, St. Louis, Mo., 1946-50. p. First Japanese Ch., San Francisco, Calif., 1950-55; Mill Creek, Mt. Jackson, Va., 1955-61; Lovettsville-Brunswick, Potomac Synod, 1961-65; Asst. Pastor, Evangelical Reformed Ch., Frederick, Md. 1965-.

FETZER, SAMUEL J.
b. 9-14-1820, Woodstock, Va., d. 8-8-1861, Rowan Co., N.C. Marshall College, 1839; Lic. 1842, Va. Classis; p. Mill Creek Chg. Va. 1842-1846 Pendleton Co., Va. 1846-50, Augusta Chg. Va. 1850-1858; West Rowan Chg. N.C. 1858-1861.

FIDLER, GEORGE ARTHUR
b. 1-5-1931, High Point, N.C. A.B. Cat. Col. 6-1954; B.D. Duke Divinity Sch. 1958; Lic. So. Synod 6-24-1956; Ord. So. Synod. 2-2-1958, p. Mt. Tabor 1954-59, Zion, Thomasville, N.C. 1959-64, Trinity, Concord, N.C. 1964-1968; St. John's, Collman, Ala., 1968-.

FINGER, HOWARD LINN
b. 8-10-1938, Lincolnton, N.C. A.B. Cat. Col. 1960; B.D. Lan. Theo. Sem. 1964. Ord. 6-21-1964, Christ Ch. Lykens, Pa., p. Christ, Lykens, Pa. 1962-66; Zion, Marietta, Pa. 1966; New Gilead Concord, N.C. 1966-1968, Chap. U.S.A. 1968-.

FISHER CHARLES LARRY
b. 2-28-1932, Kannapolis. A.B. Catawba College, B.D. Lancaster Theo. Sem. Lic. Southern Syn. 5- -1957, Ord. Southern Syn. 6-23-57, p. Emanuel, Lincolnton, N.C. 1957-60; Mt. Zion, China Grove, N.C. 1960-67; St. Thomas, Winston-Salem, N.C. 1967-.

FITZ, GEORGE TAYLOR
b. 2-5-1897, Waynesboro, Pa. Shippensburg State College, Pa., 1916; A.B. Catawba
Col. 1935; Lancaster Theo. Sem. 1924, D.D. Catawba Col., 1955; Lic. Mercersburg, Cl.,
Potomac Synod, 5-14-1924; Ord. Maryland Cl., Potomac Synod, 6-1-1924; p. St. Paul's
Ridgely, Md., 1924-26; Bethany, Ephrata, Pa., 1926-33; First, Salisbury, N.C. 1933-45;
St. John's Johnstown, Pa., 1945-61; Brush Creek, Irwin, Pa., 1961-66. Retired 1-1-1967,
Irwin, Pa.; President, Sou. Syn. 1943-45.

FLICK, DONALD PAUL
b. 2-10-1930, Rinersburg, Pa. B.S. Grove City College, Grove City, Pa., B.D. Lancaster
Theo. Sem. 1956. Lic. Pittsburgh Synod 1956; Ord. Pittsburgh Synod 1956; p. Church
of Holy Trinity, Hagerstown, Md., 1956-63; Church of the Master, Hickory, N.C. 1963-.

FLOCKEN, KARL ROEBUCK
b. 10-29-1915, Lebanon, Pa. B.S. Lebanon Valley C., 1937, B.D. Lancaster Theo. Sem.
1942; M.S.W., U. Pa., School of Social Work, Phila., Pa., 1967. Lic. and Ord. Lancaster Synod, 1942. p. South Fork Chg., Newton, N.C., 1942-45; Rockwell Chg., Rockwell, N.C., 1945-49; Hummelstown, Pa., 1949-65. Other Work 1966-.

FOIL, JOHN A.
b. 12-12-1847, Cabarrus Co., d. 11-28-1912. Catawba C., Ursinus C., 1873, Lic. Philadelphia
Cl. 1873, Ord. 7-5-1874, Received N.C. Cl. 5-2-1874. Professor Catawba College, supplied
churches throughout Classis.

FOUTS, JOHN WAYNE
b. 6-8-1925, Lexington, N.C. N.C. State College, B.S. Engineering, 1948; Lancaster
Theo. Sem., B.D. 1953; Lic. 5-23-1953 Southern Synod; Ord. 6-7-1953, Southern Synod,
p. St. John's, Burlington, N.C., 1953-60; Emanuel, Thomasville, 1960-67; First, Winston-
Salem, N.C., 1967-.

FRANTZ, NEVIN RICHARDS
b. 4-23-1910, Telford, Pa. A.B. Catawba C. 1933; B.D. Lancaster Theo. Sem. 1936; Lic.
Lancaster Cl. 6-8-1939; Ord. Lancaster Cl. 6-28-1939, p. Cashtown Chg., 1939-42; Grace,
Northampton, Pa., 1942-44; Arendtsville Chg., 1944-62; Grace, Newton, N.C., 1962-67;
Shiloh, York, Pa. 1967-.

FRAZIER, ROY LEE
b. 1-27-1908, Colfax, N.C. A.B. Cat. Col. 1929; B.D. Lan. Theo. Sem. 1932; Lic. N.C.
Cl. 5-23-1932; Ord. Va. Cl. 1933, p. Mt. Crawford Chg., Weyers Cave, Va. 1933-34;
Warren, Pa. 1934-39; Rimersburg 1939-42; w.c. 1942-44; Beaver Chg., Monroe, Pa.
1944-52; St. Paul's Butler, Pa. 1952-.

FREY, ROBERT BARRICK
b. 9-20-1916, Tiffin, Ohio. Heidelberg Col. A.B. 1938; Union Theo. Sem., B.D. 1941;
Heidelberg Col. D.D. 1964, Lic. N.W. Ohio Synod, 7-6-1941; Ord. N.W. Ohio Synod
7-6-1941. p. Broadlands, Ill., 1941-43; Chaplain, U.S. Army, 1943-46; Emanuel, Valley
City, Ohio, 1946-48; Emanuel, Sandusky, Ohio 1948-53; Trinity, St. Petersburg, Fla.,
1953-66; First Congregational, Columbus, Ohio 1966-. President Fla. Council of Churches
1959.

FRITCHEY, JOHN G.
b. 2-7-1802, near Harrisborg, Pa., d. 3-12-1885, Lancaster. Lancaster Theo. Sem. 1825-
1828. First student in the seminary at its opening. Ord. Eastern Syn. 1828; p. Lincolnton, N.C. 1828-40; East Berlin, Pa., 1840-45; Mechnicsburg, Pa., 1845-50; w.c.
1851; Tanneytown, Md., 1852-64; w.c. Lancaster, Pa., sup Zwingli Harrisburg, 1880-
81. FIRST CORRESPONDENCE SECRETARY OF CL.—DISMISSED TO ZION'S CL.
IN 1841.

FROELICH, CARL FREDERICK
Reformed member of Corpus Evangelicum, South Carolina, 1787-89.

GARRISON, J. SILOR
b. 9-6-1867, Middlebrook, Va., d. 5-22-1951. A.B. Catawba C. 1891, Lancaster 1891-
94, D.D. Catawba C. 1938, Lic. Va. Cl. 1894; Ord. 1895., p. Harrisonburg, Va., 1895-
97; Edinburg, Va., 1897-98; first Pres. Massanutten Acad. Woodstock, 1898-1903; p.
Duquesne, Pa., 1903-04; Prof. English, Catawba C., 1904-08; p. Harrisonburg, Va.,
1908-43. Retired 1943; Author: History of Va. Cl., 1949.

GERHARD WILLIAM SEIBERT
b. 8-20-1881, New Holland, Pa., d. 11-26-1959, Allentown, Pa. A.B. F.&M. C., Lancaster Theo. Sem., 1906-09, Lic. Lancaster Cl., 1909; Ord. Wyo. Cl. 1909, p. Orange-
ville, Pa., 1909-14; Jefferson, Md., 1914-19; East Petersburg, Pa., 1920-23; Freeburg,
Pa., 1923-30; Mt. Pleasant N.C., 1930-41; Middlebrook, Va., 1941-51. Retired Lancaster,
Pa., 1951, Phoebe Home, Allentown, Pa. 1958.

GODFREY, ROBERT FRANKLIN
b. 2-1-1931, New Carlisle, Ohio. A.B. Catawba C., B.D. Lancaster Theo. Sem. 1957, Lic.
Southwest Ohio Synod 5-23-1957; Ord. Southwest Ohio Synod 6-9-1957, p. Grace-Daniels
Chg., Lincolnton, N.C., 1957-60; Pilgrim Ch., Lexington, N.C. 1961-68, Mt. Zion,
China Grove, 1968-.

GODLING, RICHARD ALBERT
b. 10-20-1924, Millersburg, Pa. A.B. Franklin and Marshall C. 1946; B.D. Theo. Sem.
of E. & R. Church, 1949; Ph.D. Pa. State Univ. 1954, Lic. Lancaster Synod May,
1949; Ord. Lancaster Synod, August, 1949. Minister to Students at Pa. State Univ.,
1949-52; Immanuel, Williamsport, Pa. 1953; Professor, Duke Divinity School, 1954-.

GRIMES, VAN DOLAN
b. 5-19-1925, Thomasville, N.C. A.B. Catawba C., 1963; Lancaster Theo. Sem., B.D.
1963 (Certificate of Graduation from Lancaster Theo. Sem. 1958), Lic. Southern Synod
1958; Ord. Southern Synod 1958, p. Memorial Ch., Lexington, N.C., 1958-62; Shiloh
Ch., Faith, N.C., 1962-66; Trinity Ch., Conover, N.C., 1966-.

GRIMM, CARL A.
p. First, High Point, 1949-53.

GUINTHER, EZRA HENRY
b. 3-4-1883, Winchester, Ohio, d. 10-22-1965, Chippewa Lake, Ohio. McCormick Theo.
Sem. Ordained 6-1913. Missionary, Sendai, Japan, 1913-25, p. Bucyrus, Ohio, 1925-
26; Newton, N.C., 1926-27; Canal Fulton, Ohio, 1927-30; Canton Ohio, 1930-38;
Alliance, Ohio, 1938-40; Warner Chg., Ohio, 1940-42; Walnut Creek Chg., Ohio, 1942-
44; Medaryville-Francesville-Beaver Twp. Chg. Ind., 1944-54.

GURLEY, GEORGE DICKIE
b. 9-22-1847, Armstrong Co., Pa., d. 10-4-1924, Thornton Home, Newburg, Ind. A.B.
F.&M. 1872, Lancaster 1873-76, Lic. Westmoreland Cl. 1876; Ord. E. Sq. Cl. 1876, p.
Bloomsburg, Pa., 1876-78; Latrobe, 1878-80; Concord, N.C., 1880-83; Hickory, 1883-85;
teacher, Catawba C., Newton and Asst. to Rev. Thomas Long Upper Davidson Chg.,
1885-87; p. Tipton, La., 1887-93; dis. Des. Moines Pby. 1889; p. Leon, 6 years, Dallas
Center 7 years, New Sharon 2 years.

HAMILTON, THOMAS RAY
b. 10-2-1933, Massillon, Ohio. Heidelberg, 1951-52; Catawba C. A.B. 1955; Eden Sem.
B.D. 1958, Lic. Southeast Ohio Synod, 1958; Ord. Southeast Ohio Synod, 1958, p. St.
Matthew's, Charlotte, N.C., 1958-61; Faith UCC, Englewood, Ohio, 1961-67; Elon
Community Ch. 1967-.

HAMM, MELVIN T.
b. 7-25-1923, Hanover, Pa. A.B. Catawba C., 1945; B.D. Lancaster Theo. Sem., 1948;
University N.C. MSW, 1962, Lic. Mercersburg Synod, 1947; Ord., 1-25-48, Mercersburg
Synod, p. Shepherdstown Chg., Shepherdstown, W. Va., 1947-54; Crescent Chg., Rockwell, N.C., 1955-57; Superintendent, Nazareth Children's Home, 1957-60; Hoffman Home
for Children, Littlestown, Pa., 1962-.

HAMMOND, JOSEPH T., JR.
b. 10-23-1922 Philadelphia, Pa. Catawba C., Lancaster 1946-49, Lic. & Ord. Philadelphia
Synod 1949, p. Messiah (Woodlawn), Baltimore, Md. 1949-52; Trinity, Concord, N.C.
1952-54. Dismissed to Shepherdstown, W. Va., Episcopal Church.

HAMPSHIRE, GEORGE JAY
b. 9-15-1932, Swissvale, Pa. B.A., Mt. Union College; B.D. Lancaster Theo. Sem.,
Ord., 6-12-1960, Pittsburgh Synod, p. Grace, Lowerstone, Rockwell, 1960-1962. Sept.
1, 1962, dismissed to Episcopal Church.

HARRISON, JOHN EVERETT
b. 4-12-1941, Lenoir, N.C. A.B. Catawba C., 1963, B.D. Lancaster Theo. Sem., 1966;
Ord Southern Synod, 6-12-1966, p. Assistant, Corinth, Hickory, N.C., 1966-68, U.C.C.
Southern Pines, 1968-.

HAUCK, WILLIAM
Native North Carolina. Examined by Eastern Synod, 1814, Ord. 1818 p., N.C., Prior
to 1814-1818; Wythe Co., Va., 1819-1830; Upper Davidson, Co., N.C. 1830-36. "He then
went to Missouri, where he died" (Letter of Rev. John G. Fritchey from Heisler).
FIRST PRESIDENT OF CLASSIS OF N.C.
Name disappeared from the roll in 1837.

HECKERT, PAUL C.
b. 5-30-1929, Lewistown, Pa. A.B. Catawba C., 1951; B.D. Lancaster, 1954; M.S.
Cornell U., 1959; Ph.D. Cornell U., 1964, Lic. Central Pa., Synod, 1954; Ord., Central
Pa. Synod, 5-30-54, p. Missionary, E. & R. Board of International Missions, Honduras
C.A., 1954-60; Methodist Church, Central N.Y. Conference, 1960-64; Professor, Catawba
C., 1964-.

HEDRICK, AUBREY WILSON
b. 3-18-1912, Davidson C., N.C. A.B. Catawba C., 1935; B.D. Lancaster Theo. Sem.,
1938, Lic. N.C. Cl. 5-31-1938; Ord. 6-5-1938, p. Guilford Chg., Whitsett, N.C., 1938-
41; Bear Creek Chg., 1942-50; Calvary-Zion Chg., 1951-56; First Winston-Salem, 1957-
1966 Superintendent, Nazareth Children's Home, 1967-68, Emmanuel, Thomasville, 1968-
President of Southern Synod, 1950-52.

HEDRICK, MICHAEL L.
b. 11-13-1837, d. 11-16-1929, Lic. 5-23-1864; Ord. 1-12-1873, p. Lower Davidson Ch.,
1-1873-1887.

HELLER, CALVIN BOYD
b. 12-12-1853, Madison twp., Columbia Co., Pa., d. 5-19-1935, A.B. F.&M. 81; Lancaster,
1884, Lic. Md. Cl., 1884; Ord. 6-30-1884 p. E. Rowan Chg., N.C., 1884-91; Mt. Crawford, Va., 1892-98; Everett, Pa., 1898-1902; Maiden N.C., 1902-06; Faith, N.C., 1906-
12; entered Presbyterian CH., U.S., 1912; Spencer, N.C., 1912-15; Second, Salisbury,
1912-23; Elizabethtown, 1923-29. Retired, Salisbury, N.C. 1929-1935.

HELPER, CEDRIC LAMBETH
b. 4-28-1933, Thomasville, N.C. B.A. Stetson University, 1957; B.D. Southeastern Theo. Sem., 1962; Th. M. Southeastern 1965, Lic. Gainesville, Fla. Baptist Church, 1953; Ord. Miami, Fla., 1956; p. Bedford Chg., Bedford, Va., 1962-63; Faith, Brookford, N.C., 1964-65; transferred to So. Syn. 1964, SunnyBrae, Arcata, Calif, 1965-67; N.B. Campus Minister, 9-1965, Humboldt State C., Arcata, Calif.

HENNESSEY JOSEPH BENJAMIN
b. 5-10-1905, Morgantown, W. Va. Burton C. and Seminary, B. Th., 1939; Temple C., formerly of Seattle, D. Th., 1941, D.D. Burton C. & Sem. 1952. Lic. N.E. Ohio C. 9-22-1934; Ord. N.E. Ohio Cl., 10-18-1934; p. Christian Community Ch., 1932-33; Miller Ave. E. & R., 1933-53; First, Charlotte, N.C., 1953-62; First, Apollo, Pa., 1962-.

HERMAN, CARL FRANKLIN
b. 5-19-1911, Conover, N.C. A.B. Catawba C., 1933; B.D. Lancaster Theo. Sem., 1936. Lic. N.C. Cl., 5-25-36; Ord., E. Sq. Cl., 1936; p. Zion, Ashland, Pa., 1936-43; transferred Episcopal Ch., 1943; p. St. Stephens Ch., Erwin, N.C., 1943-45; St. Andrew's Ch., Greensboro, N.C., 1945-.

HERZOG, FREDERICK
b. 11-29-1925, Ashley, North Dakota. University of Bonn, 1947, University of Basle, 1949; Th.M. Princeton, 1950; Th.D., Princeton Theo. Sem., 1953; Lic. 9-29-50, Eureka Classis, North Dakota Ord. 9-29-50, Eureka Classis, North Dakota; p. Ashley Reformed Ch., Ashley N.D., 1950-53; Professor of Theo., Mission House, Theo. Sem., 1953-1960; Associate Prof. Theo., Duke University, 1960-.

HESSON, THEODORE CALVIN
b. 4-23-1870, Littlestown, Pa., d. 4-30-1952, St. John's Pa. A.B. F.&M. 93, Lancaster, 1894-97; Teacher Schuykill Sem., Fredricksburg, Pa., 1893-94; Lic. Gettys C., 1897; Ord. N.C. Cl., 7-18-1897; p. Catawba-Maiden Chg., N.C., 1897-1902; Arendtsville, Pa., 1902-25; St. John's Pa., 1925-51.

HIATT, CHARLES EDWARD
b. 1-3-1897, Lexington N.C. Catawba C., Heidelberg C., 1924; B.D. Central Theo Sem., 1927; Lic. 5-12-1927 N.C. Cl.; Ord. 6-26-1927; p. Guilford Chg., 1927-37; Lower Davidson Chg., 1937-49; New Gilead Ch., Concord, N.C., 1950-57; Brightwood, Gibsonville, 1957-58; Bethel, Bear Creek, 1958-67. Retired 2-1-67, Concord, N.C., President of N.C. Classis, 1936.

HOFFMAN, THOMAS ERVIN
b. 3-3-1926. A.B. Elon, 1947; Lancaster, 1950; Lic. & Ord., S. Synod, 1950; p. Bear Creek Chg., 1950-53; Hebron, Winston-Salem, 1953-55; Bethlehem, Pa. 1953-.

HOKE, ELMER RHODES
b. 9-16-1892, Ada, Ohio, d. 3-25-1931, Salisbury N.C. A.B. F.&M. Co., 1913; B.D. Lancaster, 1917; Ph.D. Johns Hopkins University, 1922; Lic. W. Sq. Cl., 1917; Ord. Westld. Cl., 1917; p. Trafford, Pa., 1917-18; Trinity, Baltimore, Md., 1918-20; Prof. Education and Social, Hood C., Frederick, Md. 1920-22; Lebanon Valley C., Annville, Pa., 1922-24; Sup. Richland, 1924; President, Catawba C., 1924-31.

HOLSHOUSER, ALLEN R.
b. 3-9-1853, Rockwell, N.C., d. 2-26-1920. Catawba C., University of N.C.; Heidelberg Theo. Sem., Tiffin, Ohio, 1881; Ord. 8-1-1881; Lic. to practice medicine 5-29-1906; p. Lyons, Kansas, Lower Davidson Ch., N.C., 1889-1892; Pres. of Kansas Cl.

HOLSHOUSER, HARVEY A.M.
b. 6-2-1867, Rowan Co., N.C., d. 1-26-1934, Salisbury, N.C. Catawba C., 1894; A.M. Emporia C., Ph.D. University Chicago; Lic. 4-27-1894; N.C. Cl.; Ord. N.C. Cl; p. Catawba Chgs., 1894-97; Upper Davidson Chg., 1897-1903; Trinity, Concord, N.., 1903-05; Member of Emporia Presbytery, Presbyterian Ch., U.S.A., Dwight, Kansas, 1905-13; Liberal, Kansas, 1913-15; p. Memorial Reformed Winston-Salem 1915-17, Rockwell Chg., 1922-29; Retired, Salisbury, N.C., 1929.

HOLSTE, HAROLD WAYNE
b. 2-14-31 Rock City, Ill. A.B. Catawba Col., 1964; Master of Divinity, Eden Sem., 1967; Ord. 6-11-1967, Northern Association of Ill. Conference; p. Bethel, Bear Creek, Mt. Pleasant, N.C., 1967-.

HOLTOM, HAROLD H.
b. 2-16-1917, Akron, Ohio. B.S. Heidelberg C., 1940; Brite C. of the Bible, Texas Christian University, 1957-58; Lancaster Sem. 1958-62 Lic. Texas Synod, 1957-58; Lancaster Synod, 1958-59; Reading Synod, 1959-62; Ord. Southern Synod, 1962; p. St. Paul's Keller Chg., Kannapolis, N.C., 1962-65; W.C. Salisbury, N.C., 1965-.

HORN, ALFRED PIERCE
b. 12-26-1852, Lehighton, Pa., d. 8-7-1906, Lehighton, Pa. A.B. F.&M. 1880, Tutor id. 1881-83; Lancaster 1883; Lic. Leh. Cl., 1883; Ord. Potomac Synod, 1883; p. Grace Chg., Newton, N.C., 1883-84; Summit Hill, Pa., 1884-93; Springfield Ch., Hellertown, Pa., 1893-1906. Author: The Re-Union of Apple's Church of the Boehm Family, 1902.

HUBBARD, LYNWOOD L.
b. 11-28-1926, Langdale, Ala. Southern Union C., 1954, Elon C. B.A., 1961; Lic. East Ala. Assn. of C.C. Chs., 1951; Ord. East Ala. Assn. of C.C. Chs., 1954; p. Bethel Cong. Ch., Ala., 1956-57; Hunt Memorial C.C. Ch., 1956-57; Pleasant Ridge and Spoon's Chapel U.C.C. N.C., 1957-64; Zion U.C.C., N.C., 1964-.

HUFFMAN, J. WADE
p. Bethel, High Point, 1917-1920; Roanoke, Va., 1927-31; Received from Va. Cl., 5-6-1919 as Licentiate; Ord. 6-8-1919; Dismissed to Lancaster Cl., Ohio Synod, 5-5-1920.

HUFFMAN, MACON A.
Lic. 5-1-1913, N.C. Cl.; Ord. 9-24-1913; Dismissed to Winston-Salem Dist., Methodist E. Ch., South, 6-18-1917.

INGLE, GEORGE A.
Lic. 5-7-1919; N.C. Cl., Dismissed to Iowa Cl., Interior Synod 5-7-1919.

INGLE, JOHN
b. 9-7-1835, d. 6-23-1926. Lic. Cl. of N.C., 5-25-1863; Ord. 5-23-1864; p. Iredell Mission, 1864-66; West Rowan Chg., 1867-74; Asst. to Dr. Welker in Guilford Chg., 1874-78; Central Rowan Ch., 1878-83; Blowing Rock Mission, 1883-90.

INGOLD, JEREMIAH
b. 9-25-1816, Guilford Co., N.C., d. 2-12-1893, Hickory, N.C. A.B. Marshall C., 1841, Lancaster, 1842-43, D.D. F.&M. 1884; Lic. N.C. Cl. 4-27-1844; Ord. N.C. Cl. 4-27-1844; p. Friendship Chg., N.C., 1844-45; W. Rowan Chg., 1845-57; Lincolnton, 1858-73; w.c., Hickory, N.C., 1874-77; Hickory, 1878-85. Retired 1886.

JENKINS, WILLIAM P.

JOHNSON, GEORGE R.
b. 10-26-1898 near Clearfield, Northampton Co., Pa. Wheaton C., 1926-28; Cen. Theo. Sem. 1924-26; Lancaster Theo. Sem., 1930-31; Lic. E. Pa. Cl., 1931; Ord. W. Sq. Cl., 1931; p. Nittany Valley Chg., Howard, Pa. 1931-39; Jordan 1939-44; Chap. U.S. Army, 1944-46; Salem, Rohrerstown, Pa. 1946-51; Christ, Lower Saucon 1951-1953; Faith Chapel on Wheels, Aiken, S.C., 1953-55; Union Ch., Ardmore, Md., 1955-58; St. Paul's Keller's Chg., 1958-62; Calvary Hill Chg., Lebanon, Pa., 1962-64; Salem-Princetown Chg., Pa., 1964-67; Pfafftown, N.C. 1967-.

JONES, WILLIAM ANDREW
b. 8-8-1921, Norristown, Pa. A.B. Catawba C., 1943, B.D. Eden Theo. Sem., 1945; Lic. Philadelphia Synod, 12-28-1945; Ord. Philadelphia Synod, 12-30-1945; p. Lincoln Chg., Maiden, N.C., 1946-47; Memorial Ch., Winston-Salem, N.C., 1948-51; Fifth Ch., Cleveland, Ohio 1951-55, St. Matthew Ch., Lyonville, Indiana, 1955-56; Lamar Fulda Chg., Lamar, Ind., 1956-59; St. Paul's, Covington, Ky., 1959-.

KELLER, JOHN HENRY
b. 1-26-1874, Centre Hall, Pa., d. 11-21-1958. A.B. F.&M. 1898 Lancaster Sem., 1901; Lic. W. Sq. Cl., 1901; Ord., 6-30-1901; p. New Gilead, N.C., 1901-08; Conover, 1908-12; Zion, China Grove, N.C., 1912-36; Emanuel, Lincolnton, 1937-39; teacher N.C. College, Mt. Pleasant, N.C., 1901-02; Mt. Amoena Sem., 1902-08; Claremont College, 1908-12; Retired China Grove, N.C., 1940.

KELLERMEYER, HUGO C.
b. 1-28-1901, St. Mary's, Ohio, d. 5-23-1967, Canton, Ohio. B.A. Heidelberg C., 1923; B.D. Central Theo. Sem., Dayton, Ohio, 1926; Lic. 5-19-1926, West Ohio Cl.; Ord. 7-11-1926; N.C. Cl., p. Emanuel, Lincolnton, 1926-29; Trinity and New Gilead, Concord, N.C., 1929-42; Trinity, Upper Sandusky, Ohio, 1942-48; Calvary, Lima, Ohio, 1948-53; Second, Tiffin, Ohio, 1953-57; Grace, Canton, Ohio, 1957-67; Retired 4-30-1967, Canton, Ohio.

KELLEY, CLAUDE WILLIAM
b. 11-5-1918, Gastonia, N.C., A.B. Catawba C., 1943; B.D. Lancaster Theo. Sem., 1945; Lic. 10-27-1945, Southern Synod; Ord. 11-4-1945; p. Smyrna-Bethany Chg., 11-1945-9-1949; St. Matthew's Chapel, Charlotte, N.C., 9-1949-1-1951; First Ch., Rising Sun, Ind., 1-1941-10-1955; First Ch., Hamilton, Ohio, 10-1955-10-1966; St. Paul's Lansing, Mich., 10-1966-.

KELLY, DAVID GREY, JR.
b. 5-31-1942, Charlotte, N.C., A.B. Pfieffer C., 1965; B.D. Lancaster Theo. Sem., 1968; p. Minister of Christian Ed., Mt. Zion, China Grove, N.C. 1968-

KEPPEL, ALVIN ROBERT
b. 1896, Buffalo, N.Y. Ohio Wesleyan C., Delaware, Ohio, A.B. 1917; Ohio State Univ., Columbus, Ohio, 1921; Lic. 1930-42; Evan. Synod of N.A., Exec. Sec. Bd. of Christian Ed. & Pub., 1930-42; Pres. Catawba C., 1942-1962. Director Piedmont University Center, Winston-Salem, N.C., 1962-67. Retired, Blowing Rock, N.C., 1967.

KERSCHNER, L. M.
Received from East Pa. Cl., 12-30-1897; Dismissed to the Presbyterian Ch., 4-19-1900.

KIRK, SAMUEL JONES
b. 1-13-1889, Salisbury, N.C. A.B. Catawba C., 1912; Lancaster Theo. Sem., B.D. 1915; Lic. Va. Cl., 1915; Ord. 6-20-1915; p. Middlebrook, Va. Chg., 1915-18; First, Burlington, N.C., 1918-22; First, Royersford, Pa., 1922-25; St. John's, Riegelsville, Pa., 1925-58. Retired Riegelsville, Pa. 1958.

KLINGER, ALBERT
Received from Presbytery of Little Rock, Presbyterian Ch., U.S.A. 5-3-1916. Dismissed to Maryland Cl., 1-25-1922; p. Guilford Charge, 1916-20.

KOONS, JOHN A.
b. 1-30-1886, State Line, Pa., d. 5-31-1953, Newton, N.C. Ursinus C., 1908; Central Sem., 1912; p. Rockwell N.C. 1912-19; Lincoln Chg., Maiden, N.C., 1919-44; taught school, 1944-48; Lincoln Chg., 1948-53; Pres. of Classis, 1923.

KOONTZ, HARVEY H.
b.   Davidson Co., N.C. Catawba C.,   Lancaster Theo. Sem., Lic. Southern Synod, 7-3-1946; Ord. 7-21-1946, Southern Synod; p. First, Asheboro, 1946-1953; Bethany, Winston-Salem, N.C., 1954-1956; New Friendship, Lexington, N.C., 1956-.

KOPENHAVER, HARVEY GRANT
b. 3-20-1869, Dauphin Co., d. 8-12-41, Charlotte, N.C. p. Catawba Co. N.C., 1910-1915; Bethel, High Point 1916-17; Lincoln Chg. N.C.; 1918-19; Received from Lancaster Cl., Eastern Synod, 5-4-1910; Dismissed to Miami Cl., Ohio Synod, 7-6-1915; Received from same, 3-17-1916.

KREBS, DALLAS R.
b. 12-27-1874, Silver Run, Md., d. 2-2-59, Hanover, Pa. p. First, High Point, 8-1-1921—9-18-1921; Received from Philadelphia Cl., Eastern Synod, 8-29-1921; Dismissed to Schuylkill Cl., Eastern Synod, 10-7-1921.

KREPS, CARL CLAYTON
b. 2-26-1932, Mifflin Co., Pa. A.B. Catawba C., B.D. Lancaster Theo. Sem., Lic. Central Pa. Synod, 4-10-1956; Ord. 6-7-1956; p. North Davidson Chg., 7-1-1956—4-30-61; Bethany Ch., Winston-Salem, N.C., 5-1-1961—12-23-62; Mt. Hope, Rowan Co., 1-1-1963-.

LANE, GILBERT
Lic., Dutch Reformed Ch.; Ord. in 1856 by Cl. as a committee. Dismissed to Cl. of Schoharrie, Reformed Dutch Ch., 9-19-1857.

LANTZ, JOHN
b. 5-11-1811, Lincoln Co., N.C., d. 1-26-1873. Lic. by Synod, 9-1837; Ord. 8-5-1838; p. Rowan Co., N.C., 1838-51; Newton, N.C., 1858-68; Middlebrook, Va., 1868-72; Taneytown, Md., 1872-73.

LAROSE, JOHN JACOB
b. 2-1755, Lehigh Co., Pa., d. 11-17-1845, Miamisburg, Ohio. Revolutionary Army, 1776-77; Private study, Guilford Co., N.C., 1780-90; examined and Lic. by Presbyterian Ch., N.C., 1790; Ord. Synod of U.S., 5-22-1821; p. Guilford Co., N.C., 1790-1804; Miamisburg, Ohio, 1805-12; Highland Co., Ohio, 1812-16; Montgomery Co., Ohio, 1816-18; Eaton, 1818-23.

LEFEVER, FRANK R.
Received from Lebanon Cl., Eastern Synod, 6-22-1918; First Ch., Greensboro, 1918-1920; Dismissed to Lancaster Cl., Eastern Synod, 4-15-1921.

LEFEVRE, DAVID P.
b. 1-5-1839, near Gettysburg, Pa., d. 4-26-1917. A.B. Dickenson C., Lancaster, 1871-74; Lost an arm at battle of Spottsylvania; Lic. Zion's Cl., 1874; Ord. Ia. Cl., 1874; p. Boulder Chg., Central City, Ia., 1874-75; Blairstown 1875-76; Pleasant Valley Chg., 1876-85; Faith, Baltimore, Md., 1885-88; Ridgely, 1888-91; Burlington, N.C., 1891-93; Retired Chambersburg, Pa. 1893-95, Reading, 1895-1917.

LEIDY, GEORGE
b. 11-7-1793, Montgomery Co., Pa., d. 5-30-1879, Norristown, Pa. Studied under his uncle, Rev. Casper Wack, Germantown, Pa.; Lic. 1818, Ord. 1819; p. 1819; Traveling Missionary in N.C. and Va. Woodstock, Va. 1820-23; Westminister, Myd. 1823-31; Cumberland Valley, 1831-35; Shellsburg, Pa., 1835-1844.

LEINBACH, ROY EZRA, JR.
b. 7-13-1909, Landisburg, Pa. B.S. Catawba C., 1933; B.D. Lancaster Theo. Sem., 1936; Lic. Carlisle Cl. of Potomac Synod, 1936; Ord. N.C. Cl. of Potomac Synod, 5-23-1937; p. First, Landis, 1937-40; Grace, Newton, N.C., 1940-48; South Fork Chg., Newton, N.C., 1954-56; United Chg., Catawba Co. 1956- Member N.C. State House of Representatives, 1951-53. President Sou. Conf. 1967-.

LEINBACH, ROY E.
b. 12-29-1879, White Deer, Union Co., Pa.; d. 7-26-1943, Carlisle, Pa. Ursinus College, 1902; Ursinus College School of Theology, 1905; p. Landisburg Chg., 1905-1912; St. Mark's Wyndmoor, Pa., 1912-1917; First, High Point, N.C., 1917-1921; First Carlisle, Pa., 1921-1941; Lic. 1905; Ord. 1905

LEONARD, ALDRICH ODELL
b. 4-12-1899, Davidson Co., N.C. A.B. Catawba C., 1919; B.D. Central Theo. Sem., 1922; D.D. Catawba C., 1952; Lic. N.C. Cl., 5-12-1922; Ord. 6-21-1922; p. Second Ch., Lexington, N.C., 1922-67; Organized First Ch., Asheboro; Paul's Chapel, Lexington; Pres., N.C. Cl., 1932; Chairman, Commission on Evangelism, Evangelical and Reformed Ch.; Member, Board of Homeland Ministries, United Church of Christ.

LEONARD, BILLY JOE
b. 3-8-1926, Lexington, N.C. A.B. Catawba C., 1950; B.D. Lancaster Theo. Sem., 1953; Lic. Southern Synod, 5-23-1953; Ord. Southern Synod, 5-24-1953; p. Paul's Chapel, 1953-62; Mt. Hope, Guilford Co., 1962-67; Second Ch., Lexington, N.C., 1967-.

LEONARD, DONALD M.
b. 8-14-1931, Lexington, N.C. B.A. Catawba C., 1953; Lancaster Theo. Sem. B.D., 1956; Lic. Southern Synod, 4-12-1956; Ord. Southern Synod, 6-10-1956; p. Asst. Second Evan. and Reformed Ch., Lexington, 1956-60; First, Asheboro, N.C., 1960-.

LEONARD, JACOB C.
b. 2-13-1867, Davidson Co., N.C., d. 3-15-1943, Lexington, N.C. A.B. Catawba C., 1889; B.D. Ursinus School of Theo., Lic. N.C. Cl., 1889; Ord. N.C. Cl., 10-10-1889; p. Upper Davidson Chg., 1889-97; Field Secretary of Catawba C., 1897-98; Prof. History & English Catawba C., 1899-1900; p. Lexington and High Point, N.C., 1900-03; First Ch., Lexington, N.C., 1903-39; Organized: Calvary, Thomasville; Heidelberg, Thomasville; Frst, Lexington; Second, Lexington; First, High Point. Stated Clerk— N.C. Cl., 1892-1940; President, General Synod, Reformed Ch. in U.S., 1923-26.

LEONARD, LAWRENCE A.
b. 6-18-1914, Lexington, N.C. A.B. Catawba C., 1938; B.D. Lancaster, 1941; Lic. & Ord. Southern Synod, 1941; p. First, Landis 1941-43; Chaplain, U.S. Army 1944-46; Emanuel, Thomasville, 1946-54; First, Asheboro, 1954-60; St. Mark's Burlington, 1960-.

LEONARD, WARREN CALVIN
b. 1-9-1922, Lexington, N.C. A.B. Catawba C., 1944; B.D. Lancaster, 1946; Lic. Southern Synod, 1946; Ord. Southern Synod, 1946; p. Calvary-Zion Chg., Thomasville, N.C., 1946-49; Marshville, Methodist Ch., 1949-.

LEOPOLD, GEORGE A.
b. North Carolina,   d.   California. Lancaster Theo. Sem., 1829-32; Lic. 1832, again 1933; Ord. Md. Cl., 1833; p. Mill Creek Chg., Mt. Jackson, Va., 1833-37; Asst. Rev. John Brown, D.D., Harrisonburg, Va., 1837; w.c., Lincolnton, N.C., 1838-39; Winchester, Va., 1840; susp. N.C. Cl., 1842; dep. 1843; went to Calif. Received from Md. Cl., 1839; Disappeared from roll, 1843.

LERCH, DANIEL B.
b. 7-7-1808, Pa., d. 3-18-1834. Lancaster Theo. Sem., 1828-30; Ordained Synod, 1830, at Hagerstown, Md. p. Rowan, Cabarrus, Montg. Co., 1830-34. FIRST TREASURER OF CLASSIS.

LEVENGOOD, ALBERT JAY
b. 10-2-1886, near Bloomfield (now Clark), Ohio, d. 3-30-1956, Dayton, Tenn. Academy of the Mission House, 1906-16; Lighthouse Bible C., Ordained 1916; p. Walnut Creek, Ohio; Warren, Pa.; Indianapolis, Ind.; Louisville, Ky.; St. Louis, Mo.; New Bedford, Ohio; Founder of Tenn. Mtn. Misson, Inc., 1938; Founder of Cumberland Springs Bible Camp, 1945; Superintendent, Tenn. Mtn. Mission.

LEVENS, JOSHUA LEROY
b. 3-8-1908, Guilford Co., N.C. A.B. Catawba C., 1931; B.D. Lancaster Theo. Sem., 1934; Lic. N.C. Cl., 5-28-1934; Ord. N.C. Cl., 7-15-1934; p. Upper Davidson Chg., 1934-37; First, Grensboro, N.C., 1938-45; First, Salisbury, N.C., 1945-56; St. Thomas, Winston-Salem, N.C., 1956-62; Bethlehem, Winston-Salem, N.C., 1962-65; St. John's Burlington, N.C., 1965-. President, Southern Synod, 1944-46; Secretary, Southern Synod, 1953-.

LONG, P. ALLISON
p. Davidson, Co., N.C., 1858-1862; Lic. 2nd Sun. in June, 1858, N.C. Cl.; Ord. 12-14-1858 by Cl. as a committee. Dismissed to Tuscarawas Cl., 12-20-1871.

LONG, THOMAS
b. 11-18-1818, Davidson Co. N.C., d. 12-25-1898, Davidson Co. N.C. Lic. N.C. Cl., 4-28-1862; Ord. 1st Sun., 5-1863; p. Upper Davidson Chg., 1862-1887, Organized Mt. Tabor, 1883.

LONG, WILLIAM A.
p. Newton, N.C., 1897-1901; Received from Juniata Cl., 5-12-1898; Dismissed to Philadelphia Cl., 5-10-1902.

LONGAKER, GEORGE
p. Corinth, Hickory, 1924-1929; Received from Tuscarawas Cl., Ohio Synod, 3-29-1924; Dismissed to Southwest Ohio Cl., Ohio Synod, 9-27-1929.

LORETZ, ANDREW, JR.
b. Tschritschen, Canton of Grisons, Switzerland, Baptized 4-14-1726, d. 3-31-1812, buried in Daniel's Ch. Cemetery. Came to America with his father, Rev. Andrew Loretz, Sr., 1784; Married 1786 in Baltimore, Md., and came to N.C. p. Lincoln and Catawba Co. Churches, 1786-1812. Made missionary trips to all Reformed Churches in N.C. and S.C.

LUDWIG, GEORGE KENNETH
b. 6-15-1925, Lancaster Co., Pa. A.B. Lebanon Valley C., Annville, Pa. 6-1955; B.D. Lancaster Theo. Sem., 6-1958; Ordained Lehigh Synod, 6-8-1958; p. Hill-Jerusalem Chg. St. John-Hill, New Jerusalem Churches 1958-1961; Mt. Tabor Ch. 1961-1966; Zeltenreich Ch., New Holland, Pa. 1966-.

LYERLY, CHARLES DONALD
b. 8-23-1929. B.A. Catawba C., 1951; Lancaster Theo. Sem. B.D., 1954 Lic. and Ord. Southern Synod, 4-22-1954; p. Brightwood Ch., Gibsonville; Hebron Ch., Winston-Salem, Withdrew from E. & R Church, 1959.

LYERLY, JACOB MARTIN LUTHER
b. 11-18-1862, Rowan Co., N.C., d. 3-17-1923, Winston-Salem, N.C. Catawba College, 1889; Lic. 5-4-1889, N.C. Cl.; Ord. N.C. Cl., 10-10-1889; p. Central Rowan Chg., Lincoln Chg., Waughtown Chg., Winston-Salem, N.C., 1923; Founder and Operator of Crescent Academy & Business College 1896-1913; Founded and chairman of Board of Directors, Nazareth Children's Home, 1903-1923; Nazareth Orphan's Home, 1903-06.

LYERLY, WILLIAM CLARENCE
b. 11-8-1889, Rowan Co., N.C., d. 3-22-1954, Newton, N.C. Crescent Academy, Heidelberg C., 1910, Central Theo. Sem., 1914, grad. work, Northwestern University; Lic. Miami Cl. Ohio Synod 5-5-1914; Ord. N.C. Cl. 6-14-1914; p. Bear Creek Chg., 1914-18; Trinity, Concord, N.C., 1918-27; South Fork Chg., 1927-31; First, Greensboro, N.C., 1931-37; Emanuel Chg., Davidson Co., N.C., 1938-46; South Fork Chg., 1946-54; Sec. of Southern Synod, 1943-54.

McNAIRY, WILLIAM H.
b. 11-23-1868, Guilford Co., N.C., d. Chambersburg, Pa. 12-20-1941. Catawba College, 1894 D.D., 1937; Ursinus College, Collegeville, Pa., Lic. 4-27-1894; Ord. 7-29-1894; p. Lower Davidson Chg. 1894-97; East Rowan Chg., 1897-1900; Trinity, Concord, 1900-1903; Zion, Lenoir 1903-1908, Thomasville Chg.; Upper Davidson Chg.; Emanuel, Lincolnton, 1912-21; West Hickory Chg., 1921-23; Superintendent, Nazareth Children's Home, 1923-32.

MADREN, WELDON THOMAS
b. 1-19-1922, Alamance Co., N.C. A.B. Elon College, 1943; B.D. Duke Divinity Schl., 1947; Lic. 1941, Southern Convention; Ord. 1943, So. Convention; p. Halifax Co., Va. 1951-56; Happy Home, Ruffin, N.C., 1956-66; Bethlehem, Winston-Salem, N.C., 1967-.

MAEDER, J. DUDLEY
b. 6-17-1859, Mahone Bay, Nova Scotia, d. 11-5-1934, Salisbury, N.C. Graduate from Mt. Allison University Sem., Sackville, New Brunswick Drew Sem., Madison, N.J. Lic. and Ord. Nova Scotia Methodist Conf., 6-20-1898; p. Fort Lawrence; Shubenacadie, Louisburg, Mulgrave, River Herbert, and Selma. Missionary to the Bermuda Islands. p. in New York State; New Jersey, Vermont; Enrolled by East Pa. Cl., Eastern Synod, 1923; p. Gilead Chg., 1923-25; Retired, Salisbury, N.C., 1925.

MARTIN, CARL REED, SR.
b. 10-22-1920, Guilford Co., N.C. A.B. Elon C., 1942; B.D. Lancaster Theo. Sem., 1953; Lic. 5-23-1953, Southern Synod; Ord. Southern Synod; p. 5-30-1953; p. St. Paul's-Keller Chg., Kannapolis, N.C., 1953-56; Shiloh, Faith, 1956-61; Emanuel, Lincolnton, 1961-64, Bethany, Winston-Salem, 1964-67, Bayside Ch. Virginia Beach, Va., 1967-.

MARTIN, JAMES (JOHN NICHOLAS)
p. Western N.C. Churches from about 1759-1764.

MARTIN, WESLEY WILLIAM
b. 11-24-1913, St. Louis, Mo. B.A. McKendree C. 1939; Eden Theo. Sem., 1940-42; M.A. St. Louis University, 1947. Lic. 1936; Ord. 1939 St. Louis Conference, p. St. Paul's, Lemay, Mo., 1944-50; Methodist Chg., Bellflower, Mo., 1938-43; Leadwood, Mo., 1943-44; supplied at Norcross, Ga. 1950-.

MEIER, HENRY JOHN
b. 10-4-12, Africa. B.A. Mission House C., 1934; B.D. Mission House Theo. Sem., 1937. p. St. Paul's, Malone, Wisc., 1937-38; Peace Ch., Stevens Point, Wisc., 1938-43; Zion Ch., Dyer, Ind., 1943-51; Mt. Tabor, Lexington, N.C., 1951-53; Zion Ch., Lenoir, N.C., 1953-61; Beulah Ch. Lexington, N.C., 1961-68, St. Matthews, Charlotte, N.C., 1968-.

MENSENDIEK, RICHARD AUGUST
b. 1-25-1897, St. Louis, Mo., d. 4-18-1965, Buffalo, N. Y. Eden Theo. Sem., Ord. Evang., St. Louis, Mo., 5-4-1922, p. St. Paul Ch., Manly, Iowa, 1922-24; St. John's Ch., Ft. Madison, Iowa, 1924-29; St. Paul Ch. Waterloo, Ill., 1929-31; Salem Ch., Qunicy, Ill., 1931-45; St. John's Ch., Lorain, Ohio, 1945-56 & Pres. N.E. Ohio Synod, 1951-55; p. First Ch., High Point, N. C., 1956-62; Salem Ch., Buffalo, N.Y., Asst. 1962-64; Retired Tonowanda, N.Y.

MICHAEL, O. BAIN
b. 6-24-1895, d. 3-16-1966. p. Edinburg, Va. 1930-35; South Fork Chg. 1935-. Lic. 5-10-1923; Ord. 6-24-1923.

MIDDLEKAUFF, SOLOMON SAYLOR
b. 1818, Hagerstown, Md., d. 5-21-1845, Mineral Springs, N.C. A.B. Marshall C., 1839, Lancaster, 1841, Lic. Mercerburg Cl. 1842; Ord. 8-1-1842, p. Lower Chg., Lincoln Co., N.C., 1842-45.

MORRIN, IVAN RICHARD
b. 8-9-1924, Bird-In-Hand, Pa. B.A. Emory University; B.D. Lancaster Theo. Sem. Lic. Lancaster Synod 5-14-1952; Ord. Lancaster Synod 5-25-1952, p. Glen Rock Chg., Pa., 1952-56; St. John's Ch., Kannapolis, N.C., 1956-59; Olivet Ch., Norristown, Pa., 1959-62; Emmanuel Ch., York, Pa., 1962-.

MOSS, ROBERT VERELLE, JR.
b. 3-3-1922, Wilson, N.C. A.B. F & M 1943; B.D. Lancaster Theo. Sem., 1945; Ph.D.
Chicago University, 1952; D.D. Catawba C., Lic. Southern Synod, 1945; Ord. Southern
Synod, 1946(6-30). Student, Chicago University, 1945-46, 50-51; Ins. Dept. of Rel.
F & M, 1946-49; Asst. Prof., 1949-50; Prof. N.T. Science, Lancaster Theo. Sem., 1951-;
Pres., 1955-.

MURPHY, JOSEPH L.
b. 7-10-1858 Davidson Co., N.C., d. 10-11-1917 Hickory, N. C. Catawba College, Ursinus
College, 1885. Lic. 10-23-1885; Ord. 10-23-1885, p. Lincoln Chg., 1885-90, Hickory Chg.,
1890-1903, Corinth Hickory 1903-17. First Editor, "Reformed Church Standard."

MUSSER, HARLAN CLAYTON
b. 1-18-1920, Centre, Hall, Pa. B.A. Pa. State University, 1941; Lancaster Theo. Sem.,
1944; University of Pittsburgh, Western Theo. Sem., Pittsburgh Xenia Sem.; Lic.
Central Pa. Synod, 1944; Ord. Central Pa. Synod, 1944, p. First Ch., McKeesport, Pa.,
1944-57; Robertson Memorial, Miami, Fla., 1957-.

MYERS GEORGE HAROLD
b. 8-31-1923, Hagerstown, Md. A.B. Catawba C., 1945; B.D. Lancaster Theo. Sem.
1947. Lic. Potomac Synod, 12-28-1947; Ord. 12-28-1947, p. Mt. Zion, China Grove,
N.C., 1948-54; First, Raleigh, N.C., 1954-60; Edgewood U.C.C., 1960-65; Heidelberg,
Thomasville, N.C., 1965-. Organizing Pastor, Rodger's Park Ch., 1951.

MYERS, JOHN WILLIAM
b. 7-23-1896, New Oxford, Pa. A.B. Ursinus C., 1920; Central Theo. Sem., B.D. 1923;
M.R.E. Boston University, 1924; M.A. Columbia University, 1931; S.T.D. Temple,
1937. Lic. 5-15-1925. Gettysburg Cl., Potomac Synod; Ord. 9-13-1925, N.C. Cl., p. First
Ch., Charlotte, N.C., 1925-28; Milton Ave. Ch., Louisville, Ky., 1931-38, (taught, Ca-
tawba C., 1928-30); Christ Ch. Orville, 1938-41; St. John's, Fort Wayne, Ind., 1941-47;
Trinity, Tiffin, Ohio, 1947-55; First United, Homestead, Fla., 1955-63; Associate, First
Congregational, Winter Park, Fla., 1963-. Pres. of Synod of Mid-West, 1935.

MYERS, ROBERT E.
b. 11-4-1931, Thomasville, N. C. Pfeiffer C., Catawba C., B.D. Lancaster Theo. Sem.
Lic. Southern Synod, 5-1-1957; Ord. Southern Synod, 6-9-1957, p. Crescent Chg.,
6-1-1957—1-4-1967; Zion U.C.C., Lenoir, N.C., 1-4-1967-

NACE, ALBERT FRANKLIN
b. 7-26-1868, near Seitzland, Pa., d. 7-30-1954, Decatur, Ga. A.B. F & M, C., 1894;
Lancaster, 1894-95, 1899-1901. Lic. Zion's Cl., 1901; Ord. Juniata Cl., 1901, p. Oster-
burg, Pa., 1901-05; Juniata, 1905-13; Albemarle, N.C., 1913-16; Newspaper work,
Tenn., 1 yr.; Supt. schools, Jonesboro, Tenn., 3 yrs.; teacher Boys High School, Atlanta, Ga., 1920-32. Retired Decatur, Ga. 1933.

NAGLE, EDWIN CLINTON
b. 12-23-1909, Allentown, Pa. A.B. Wheaton College, 1936, B.D. Lancaster Sem., 1939.
Lic. 5-18-1939, Lehigh Cl., Ord. 5-28-1939, Lehigh Cl., p. Glenside, Pa., 1937-39; Spies-
Bern Chg., 1939-1953; Trubauersville-Ridge Valley Chg., 1953-67; Crescent Chg., Rockwell, N.C., 1967-.

NEFF, EDWIN MILLER
b. 4-21-1936, Canton, Ohio. Chemical Engineer Univ. of Cincinnati 1960; B.D. Lancaster 1964. Ord. 6-7-1964 E. Ohio Asso. Ohio Conference, p. Asst. Corinth, Hickory,
N.C. 1964-66; Charlotte Mission 1966-.

NOAKER, MILTON MONROE
b. 11-22-1860, Pallas, Snyder Co., Pa., d. 10-10-1930, Los Angeles, Calif. Selinsgrove
(Pa.) Inst. 1879; Lancaster, 1887-89. Lic. E. Sq. Cl., 1890; Ord. Lancaster Cl., 1890,
p. Maytown, Pa., 1890-93; Arendtsville, 1893-1901; Duquesne and Homestead, 1901-03;
Duncannon, 1903-07; Enola, 1907-08; W. Rowan Chg., N.C., 1908-12; Cheney, Kan.,
1912-13; Albemarle, N.C., 1913; Dismissed to Concord Presbytery, Presbyterian Ch.,
U.S., 1914; p. Fifth Creek, Statesville, N.C., 1914; Returned to Ref. Ch., 1914; Woodstock, Va., 1914-16; Dismissed to Los Angeles Presbytery, Presbyterian Ch., U.S.A.,
1916; p. Presbyterian Ch., Arcadia, Calif., 1917-19; Res. Los Angeles, Calif., 1919-30;
with Near East Relief, 1919-21; p. Trinity Ref. Ch., West Hollywood, California 1921-
1929. Retired 1929.

PALMER, GEORGE MELVIN
b. 4-15-1928, High Point, N.C. A.B. Catawba C., 1949, B.D. Lancaster, 1952. Lic.
5-24-1952, Southern Synod; Ord. 6-1-1952, p. Beulah, Lexington, N.C., 6-2-1952- 10-31-
1960; Peace, Greensboro, N.C., 11-1-1960-. FIRST PRES. OF THE SOUTHERN CON-
FERENCE U.C.C. Nov., 1964-66.

PALMER, JACOB ALEXANDER
b. 1-12-1885. B.S. Catawba C., Central Sem., 1913, D.D. Catawba C., Lic. 5-1-1913;
Ord. 6-1-1913, p. Upper Davidson Chg., 1913-18; Heidelberg, Thomasville, 1918-52.
Retired Thomasville, 1952; Supply, Brightwood, Gibsonville, 1958-.

PARKER, MARTIN LUTHER, JR.
b. 8-3-1916, Louisiana. Utica C., N.Y., 1953; Lakeland C., Plymouth, Wisc., 1959;
Mission House Sem., 1962. Ordained North Wisconsin Synod, p. St. John's, Buckskin,
Ind., 1962-65; St. Matthew's Maiden, N.C., 1965-.

PECK, FELIX BREVARD
b. 2-1-1897, Cabarrus Co., N.C. A.B. Catawba C., 1919; B.D. Central Theo. Sem., 1922; S.T.D. Westminster Theo. Sem., 1936. Lic. N.C. Cl., 5-12-1922; Ord. Md. Cl., 6-18-1922, p. Clear Springs Chg., Md., 1922-27; St. Mary's, Silver Run, Md., 1927-38; Milton Ave., Louisville, Ky., 1938-44; Sec. to Service Men of Ch. Federation of Greater Chicago, 1944-46; Director, Ch. Extension, Board of National Missions, So. Chicago area, 1946-49; p. First Ch., Charlotte, N.C., 1949-52; Minister of Defense Service Area of N.C.C. in Paducah, Ky., 1952-54; Executive Director, Council of Churches., Yonkers, N.Y., 1954-62. Retired 1962, Mt. Pleasant, N.C.

PECK, HOWARD WAYNE
b. 9-16-1926, Hagerstown, Md. A.B. Catawba C., 1947; B.D. Eden Theo. Sem., 1951. Lic. Southern Synod, 1951; Ord. Southern Synod, 7-1-1951, p. Associate Pastor, First Greensboro, N. C., 1951-52; Youth Associate, Dept. Youth Work, E & R Ch., 1952-53; St. John's, Michlyn, Allentown, Pa., 1953-56; Belfort E & R Belfort, Pa., 1956-62; First, Orlando, Fla., 1962-66; Administrator, Uplands Retirement Center, Pleasant Hill., Tenn., 1966-.

PEELER, AUGUSTUS CALVIN
b. 10-11-1892, Rowan Co., N.C. Catawba C., 1916; Central Sem., 1919; B.D. 1925. Lic. N.C. Cl. 5-7-1919; Ord. Va. Cl. 6-3-1919, p. Middlebrook Chg., Va., 1919-24; Waughtown Chg., 1924-37; Old Springfield, New Middletown, Ohio, 1941-44; Grace, Loyal Oak, Ohio, 1944-50; First U.C.C., Pittsburgh, Pa., 1950-.

PEELER, A. SAMUEL
b. 1878, Faith, N.C., d. 1-22-1942. Crescent Academy 1899, Catawba C., U.N.C., Northern Indiana U., 1903; Ursinus School of Theo. 1906. Lic. N.C. Cl. 5-12-1906, p. Waynesburg Chg., Ohio 1906-1909; Crescent Chg., N.C. 1909-10; Waughtown Chg., 1910-11; Zion Church, Lenoir, 1911-22; Superintendent, Nazareth Childrens Home, 1922-23, Lower Davidson Chg., 1923-28; Lovettsville Va., 1929-38; Trinity, McCutchenville, Ohio, 1938-42.

PEELER, BANKS J.
b. 2-11-1897 Faith, N.C. A.B. Catawba C. 1919; B.D. Central Theo., Eden 1922; M.A. Duke School of Religion 1936; D.D. Catawba C. 1943. Lic. & Ord. 5-28-1922 Emanuel Ch., Lincolnton, N.C., p. Emanuel Ch., Lincolnton, N.C. 1922-24; First Ch., Salisbury, N.C. 1924-32; First Church, Burlington, N.C. 1932-39; First Ch. Lexington, N.C. 1939-55; Trinity Ch., Concord, N.C. 1955-63; Organized Christ Church, Lexington, Pres., Southern Synod 1963-68; Bd. Nat'l Miss. E. & R. 1947-58; Homeland Min. U.C.C. 1958-68; Ch. Steering Comm., Org. So. Conf. U.C.C., 1962.

PEELER, JAMES L.
b. 4-1-1940. A.B. Catawba Col. 1962; B.D. Lancaster Theo. Sem. 1965; Lic. and Ord., So. Synod 1965, p. Paul's Chapel, 1965-.

PEELER, JOHN CALVIN
b. 10-11-1886, Rowan Co., N.C., d. 4-3-1957, Burlington, N.C. Catawba C., 1914; D.D. Catawba C. Lic. 5-15-1913; Ord. 7-6-1913, p. Catawba Chg., Conover, 1913-18; Lower Davidson Chg., 1918-23; Zion Ch., Lenior, N.C., 1923-35; Director, Public Relations, Catawba C., 1935-44 (Dean of Men, 1937-43); p. Boone Station Chg., Burlington, N.C. 1944-50; St. Mark's, Burlington, N.C. 1950-56.

PEELER, LEE A.
b. 9-8-1886, Rowan Co., N.C., d. 6-12-1966, Charlotte, N.C. Central University, D.D.: Catawba College A.B. 1905; Ursinus School of Theology B.D. 1908. Lic. N.C. Cl. 5-30-1908; Ord. N.C. Cl. 6-14-1908, p. First, High Point, N.C., 1908-17; First, Albermarle, N.C., 1917-18; Grace, Newton, N.C., 1918-19; Kannapolis, N.C., 1919-38; St. John's, Middlebrook, Va., 1938-41; Bethel, Arlington, Va., 1941-51; Gladeland Chg., Pa., 1951-56. Retired 1956, Salisbury, N.C.

PEELER, SHUFORD
b. 11-12-1875, Rockwell, N.C., d. 1-31-1967, Charlotte, N.C. Catawba C., 1900; Ursinus School of Theo., B.D. 1903 D.D. Catawba C. Lic. 5-20-1903 N.C. Cl.; Ord. 5-12-1903, p. First, Greensboro, 1903-16; First, Charlotte, N.C., 1916-25; Catawba Cl., 1925-30; Exec. Sec. N.C. Sunday School Association, 1930-36; First, Charlotte, N.C. 1937-47. Retired Charlotte, N.C. 1947.

PITHAN (PYTHAN), JOHN WILLIAM
b. 5-3-1740, Ober-Ingelheim, Palatinate, Germany, d. 1788, Guilford Co., N.C., buried in Brick Ch. Cemetery. University of Heidelberg, Germany, 1759. Ordained by Palatinate Consistory, came to America in 1769. Supplied Easton, Pa., 1769-70; Dryland, Pa., 1769-72, p. Catawba Co., N.C., 1772-86; Guilford Co., N.C., 1786-88.

PLASSMAN, F. W.
b. 1816, d. 9-30-1848, Floral College, N.C. Lic. 4-17-1844, N.C. Cl. Ord. 4-17-1844. miss., China Grove, U.C. 1844, p. Davidson Co., N.C. 1846-47

PLOTT, GEORGE ERMINE
b. 12-4-1888, Rockwell, N.C. Catawba C., 1912, Lancaster Theo., Sem., B.D. 1915. Lic. N.C. Cl. 5-23-1915; Ord. 6-13-1915, p. Heidelberg, Thomasville, N.C., 1915-17; Memorial, Winston-Salem, N.C., 1917-23; Jefferson, Md., 1923-26; Greencastle Chg., Pa., 1926-48; Jefferson, Md., 1948-58. Retired Davidson, N.C., 1958; Pres. of Mercerburg Cl. 3 terms.

RANKIN, WILLIAM C.
b. North Carolina, d. Jasper, Ind. 1839. Received from Tenn. Synod, Lutheran Ch., 1835, Missionary, Mountain Creek, N.C. 1835. In 1838 he went West as a missionary.

RAUH, WALTER FREDERICK
b. 7-7-1920, Louisville, Ky. B.A. Elmhurst C., 1942; B.D. Union Sem. 1951. Lic. 8-2-1951, South Indiana Synod; Ord. 8-26-1951, South Indiana Synod, p. Rodgers Park, Kannapolis, 1951-56. Transferred into Episcopal Church, 1956.

REITER, LEWIS
b. 9-24-1854, Kittaning, Pa., d. 6-1-1926. A.B. F & M 1881; Lancaster, 1882-85; teacher Spring Mills, Pa. Academy 1881-82. Lic. & Ord. N.C. Cl., 10-2-1885, p. Hickory, N.C., 1885-90; Roanoke, Va., 1891-98; Beaver Chg., Monroe, Pa., 1898-1900; Punxsutawney, 1900-03; Meadville 1903-05; Harmony, 1905-10; Shoop's Chg. near Harrisburg, 1910-19. Retired Harrisburg 1919.

RHODES, EDWIN TRACY
b. 4-7-1874, Manchester, Md., d. 6-2-1938. A.B. F & M 1899; Lancaster, 1899-1902. Lic. Lancaster Cl., 1902; Ord. W. Sq. Cl. 1902, p. Lewiston, Pa., 1902-17; St. Stephen's, York, 1917-26; wc. York, Pa., 1926-27; sup. p. Concord, N.C., 1928. Received from Zion Cl., Potomac Synod, 5-17-1928; Dismissed to same 5-20-1935.

RICHARDS, JESSE
p. First, Burlington, 1889-1891. Received from Tiffin Cl. 5-1-1890; Dismissed to Tiffin Cl. 12-12-1894.

RIEDESEL, CHARLES H.
Heidelberg Sem., 1896, Conover, N.C. 1897-1900. Received from Ursinus Cl. 12-30-1897; Dismissed to Heidelberg Cl. 11-30-1903.

ROHRBAUGH, ALLEN L.
b. 12-17-1932. York Junior C. 1953; Catawba C. 1955; B.D. Lancaster Theo. Sem. 1958, p. Sup. First Ch. High Point, N.C. 1956; Calvary Ch., Thomasville, N.C. 1958-1962; St. Thomas Ch., Winston-Salem, N.C. 1963-1965; wc. Winston-Salem 1966.

ROSCHY, ROBERT WINFIELD
b. 8-12-1910, Emlenton, Pa., d. 9-30-67, So. Pines, N.C. A.B. F & M 1931, B.D. Lancaster Theo. Sem. 1934. Lic Clarion Cl., Pittsburgh Synod 6-10-1934; Ord. Clarion Cl., 6-10-1934; p. St. Petersburg Chg., Pa., 1934-38; St. Vincent, Pa. Chg., 1938-45; St. Luke's Lancaster, Pa., 1945-50- Executive Sec., Associated Churches, Fort Wayne, Ind., 1950-53; First Ch., Carlisle, Pa., 1953-61; First, Burlington, N.C., 1961-65, Southern Pines, N.C., U.C.C., 1965-67.

ROWE, WALTER W.
b. 10-28-1879, Catawba Co., N.C., d. 6-27-1957, Lenior, N.C. A.B. Lenior Rhyne C., 1898, B.D. Ursinus School of Theo., 1902, A.M. Catawba C., D.D. Heidelberg C. Lic. N.C. Cl., 5-17-1902; Ord. 7-22-1902, p. Thomasville Chg., 1902-04; East Rowan Chg., 1904-08; Prof. Catawba C., 1908-09; p. Grace, Newton, N.C., 1909-18; Corinth Ch., Hickory, N.C., 1918-24; Prof. NT Lit., Central Theo. Sem., 1924-27; p. Central, Dayton, Ohio, 1927-35; Zion, Lenior, N.C., 1935-47. PRES., POTOMAC SYNOD, 1922-23; OHIO SYNOD, 1930-31.

RUBRIGHT, RICHARD WILLIAM
b. 6-3-1917, Cressona, Pa. A.B. F & M 1939, B.D. Lancaster Theo. Sem. 1946. Studied University of Pa., 1847-48. Lic. & Ord. Reading Synod 1946, p. Marysville, Pa., 1946-48; Brookford Chg., Hickory, N.C., 1948-51; Missionary to Japan, 1951-.

RUDY, JOHN
b. Switzerland, 1791; d. New York City, 2-2-1842. Lic. and ord., Syn. U.S., 1821, p. Guilford Co., N.C. 1821-24; Germantown, N.Y., 1825-35; Miss. to Germans, N.Y. City, 1835-38; Ger. Ev. Mission, N.Y. 1838-42. Entered Ref. D. Church, 1840.

SAFRIT, SIDNEY C.
Lic. 5-9-1929 N.C. Cl.; Ord. 6-23-1929. Name disappeared from roll 2-8-1933.

SANDROCK, ALFRED GEORGE
b. 2-10-1922, Hazelton, Pa. B.A. Catawba C., 1943; B.D. Lancaster Theo. Sem. 1945. Lic. Susquehanna Synod, 10-23-1945; Ord. Susquehanna Synod, 11-1945, p. Trinity Chg., New Bloomfield, Pa., 1945-1947; Mt. Tabor, Lexington, N.C., 1947-51, Weatherly Chg., Pa., 1951-61; Schaefferstown, Pa., 1961-.

SCHAEFFER, MARLIN THOMAS
b. 1-5-1918 Tamaqua, Pa. A.B. Franklin & Marshall C. 2-1943; B.D. Lancaster Theo. Sem.; S.T.M. Temple Univ. School of Theo. 1954; S.T.D. 1955. Lic. Schuylkill Cl. of Reading Synod 2-15-1945; Ord. 3-4-1945, p. Mt. Zion Chg., 3-1945—10-31-1947; St. John's, Schuylkill Haven, Pa. 11-1-1947—5-1-1956; First Lexington, N.C. 5-1-1956.

SCHIEMANN, RICHARD
b. 3-4-1923, Rochester, N.Y. B.A. Elmhurst Co. 1956; B.D. Eden Theo. Sem., 1959 Ph.D. Vanderbilt Univ. 1966, Ord 1959, Elmhurst, Ill., p. Asst. St. Peter's, Elmhurst, Ill., 1959-61 First U.C.C., Belvidere, Tenn., 1961-65 Professor, Catawba Co. 1966-.

SECHLER HENRY E.
Catawba College, 1896, p. Trinity Conover, 1901-02. Lic. 5-6-1899 Ord. 11-9-1899.
Dismissed to Los Angeles Conference M.E. Ch. South on 5-11-1922.

SCHNEIDER, JACOB
p. Davidson Co. N.C. 1787-1792.

SECHRIEST LLOYD EFRED
b. 6-13-1920, Thomasville, N.C. A.B. Catawba C.; B.D. Lancaster Theo. Sem. 1951.
Lic. Southern Synod, 5-25-1951; Ord. Southern Synod 5-27-1951, p. Lowerstone Chg.,
Rockwell, N.C., 1951-53; First, High Point, N.C., 1953-56; St. Paul, Roanoke, Va.,
1956-61; Carthage, Cincinnati, Ohio 1961-64; Timberville Chg., Timberville, Va., 1964-.

SELBY, DONALD JOSEPH
b. 2-7-1915, Kansas City, Mo. A.B. William Jewell C. 1946; B.D. Andover Newton
Theo. Sem., 1949; Ph.D. Univ., Boston, 1954. Lic. 1937, Linden, Missouri; Ord. 1938,
Linden, Missouri, p. First Baptist Ch. Garden City, Kansas 1943-45; Asst. Minister,
Philip's Memorial Ch., Cranston, R.I., 1946-48; Pilgrim Congregational Ch. Merrimac,
Mass. 1948-56. Prof. of Rel. Catawba Co. 1956-.

SENSENIG, OLIVER H.
b. 4-11-1880, Bird-in-Hand, Pa., d. 2-26-1955, Bethlehem, Pa. Ordained 6-29-1919.
Received from Lancaster Cl., Eastern Synod, 6-25-1919. Dismissed to Juniata Cl.,
Potomac Synod, 1-13-1922; p. Conover, N.C. 1919-1921.

SETTLEMYRE, JOHN WILLIAM
b. 10-23-1926, Conover, N.C. A.B.Catawba C. 1946; B.D. Lancaster Theo. Sem. 1949.
Lic. Southern Synod 1949; Ord. Southern Synod 1949, p. N. Davidson Chg. 1949-53;
Mt. Hope, Whitsett 1953-61; First High Point, 1961-.

SEYMOUR, COLLIE
b. 2-1-1918, Madison Co., Ga. B.A. Piedmont College, 1941, B.D. Vanderbilt Uni. Div.
School 1944. Lic. Ga. Conf. C.C. Churches, Sept. 1941; Ord. East Ala. Assn. C.C.
Churches 1944, p. Alabama, 1944-48; Valparaiso, Fla. Community Ch. 1948-53; Garden
City, Mtn. Grove Parish, Ala. 1956-57; Albemarle, N.C. First C.C. 1957-61; Gibsonville,
N.C. Apple's Chapel U.C.C. 1961-1964; Sanford, N. C. Shallow Well C.C. U.C.C.
1964-68; St. Paul's-Keller Charge, Kannapolis, N.C. 1968-.

SHAFFER, WILLIAM R.
b. 9-2-1900, Phil., Pa., d. 11-1-64. Central Sem., 1926, p. Conover, N.C. 1926-29; High
Point, N.C. 1929-35; Faith, Philadelphia, Pa., 1935-1964. Li. Philadelphia Cl., Eastern
Synod 6-28-1926; Ord. 7-8-1926. Dismissed to Philadelphia Cl. 1-31-1935.

SHAW, WILLIAM C.
Lic. 5-12-1922. Dismissed to Ft. Wayne Cl., Mid-West Synod, 10-10-1924.

SHEPHERD, BANKS DEROY
b. 10-28-1928, Guilford Co., N.C. A.B. Catawba C., 1950; B.D. Lancaster Theo. Sem.,
1953. Lic. Southern Synod, 5-23-1953; Ord. Southern Synod, 6-7-1953, p. Brookford
Chg., 1953-58; Mt. Pleasant Chg., 1958-63; New Gilead, Concord, N.C., 1963-66; Smyrna-
Bethany Chg., 1966-.

SHOFFNER, KENDALL BAXTER
b. 6-14-1904, Burlington, N.C. A.B. Catawba C., 1930; B.D. Lancaster Theo. Sem., 1933.
Lic. 7-11-1933; Ord. 3-4-1934, p. Emanuel Chg., Thomasville, N.C., 1934-38; Lovettsville-Brunswick, Md., 1938-42; Sharpsville, Pa., 1942-44; Robertsville, Ohio, 1945-49;
St. Paul's, Detroit, Mich., 1949-1966. WC, Williamsport, Md.

SHOFFNER, TERRELL MARTIN
b. 5-14-1909, Alamance Co., N.C. A.B. Catawba C. 1936, B.D. Lancaster Theo Sem.,
1939. Lic. 5-30-1939; N.C. Cl., Ord. N.C. Cl. 7-2-1939, p. Memorial, Winston-Salem, N.C.,
1939-45; Shiloh, Faith, N.C., 1945-49; Grace, Newton, N.C., 1949-62; St. Matthew's
Charlotte, N.C., 1962-68; St. Andrew's, Lexington, 1968-.

SHOWERS, LUCIAN W.
b. 10-8-1850 McAllisterville, Pa., d. 2-10-1912 Kittanning, Pa. Methodist Episcopal
Church, Received into Reformed Ch. Clarion Classis, Pittsburg Synod, 1892, p. Plum
Creek Chg., Armstrong, Co., Pa.; Fayette, N.Y. Received from Clarion Cl., Pittsburg
Synod, 11-20-1905. Dismissed to same 10-22-1906.

SHUFORD, JULIUS H.
b.   , d. 10-13-1924. Lic. 7-4-1874; Ord. 7-5-1874, p. Gilead Chg. Concord, N.C. 1876-
77; Upper Davidson 1887-88, Middlebrook, Va. 1890-92. Dismissed to Cl. of Shelby,
6-25-1881; Received from Cl. of Northern Ill., 5-9-1888. Dismissed Cl. of Va., 5-1-1889;
Received from Cl. of Va., 4-26-1894.

SHUFORD, MORTIMOR L.
b. 1-24-1818 Rutherford Co., N.C., d. 11-7-1883 Washington, D.C. A.B.Marshall C. 1843,
Lancaster Sem. 1841-43. Lic. Va. Cl. 1844; Ord. Va. Cl. 1844, p. Lovettsville, Va.
1844-49; Glade Chg., Myd; 1849-57; Sharpesburg Chg. Myd. 1857-63; Boonsboro, Myd.
1863-67; Winchester, Va. 1867-73; Burkittsville, Va. 1874-83.

SHULENBERGER, ANTHONY
b. 2-19-1848, near Newburg, Pa., d. 1-21-1928. F & M 1870-72, Lancaster Sem. 1872-1875, Lic. & Ord. Ia. Cl., 1875; p. Leighton and Oskaloosa, 1875-76; Mt. Pleasant, Md., 1876-94; wc. 1895; W. Rowan Chg., China Grove, N.C., 1896-1901; Edinburg, Va., 1901-06. Retired China Grove, N.C., 1906.

SIEWELL, PORTER
b. 8-18-1912 St. Clair, Pa. A.B. Catawba C. 1935; B.D. Lancaster Theo. Sem. 1938. Lic. Ord. Schuyl Cl. 1938, p. Minersville, Pa. 1938-42; Grace, Shippensburg 1942-57; First, Salisbury, N.C. 1957-63; Campus Minister Catawba C. 1960-.

SILLS, HORACE STEVENSON
b. 11-16-1922, Gaston Co., N.C. Catawba C., Lancaster Theo. Sem. 1953. Lic. Southern Synod, 5-23-1953; Ord. Southern Synod, 5-24-1953, p. Lower Davidson Chg., 1953-59; Organizing pastor, First, Orlando, Fla., 1959-61; Sec. Dept. of Town & County Ch., U.C.C. Board for Homeland Ministers, 1961-68; Conference Minister, Penn. West. Conference, 1968-.

SINK, CHARLES KEITH
b. 4-1-1928, Lexington, N.C. B.S.Davidson C., 1949; B.D. Lancaster Theo. Sem., 1952. Lic. Southern Synod, 6-19-1952; Ord. Southern Synod, 6- -1952, p. U.S. Army Chaplain, 1952-55; Emmanuel Ch., Thomasville, N.C., 1955-59; U.S. Army Chaplain, 1959-.

SLEDGE, DONALD
b. 7-28-1935, Norfolk, Va. A.B. Marion College, Marion, Ind., B.D. Southern Baptist Sem. 1967. Lic. 5-3-1966, Southern Synod, p. Long's Chapel U.C.C., Burlington, 1963-66; Rodger's Park, Kannapolis, 1966-.

SMITH, ANDREW HOFFA
b. 10-2-1865, Womelsdorf, Pa., d. 7-26-1930. Carroll Inst., Reading, Pa., 1887-89; Lancaster, 1889-92. Lic. Schuylkill Cl., 1892; Ord. N.C. Cl. 1892, p. Grace, Newton, N.C. 1892-97; McKeesport, Pa., 1897-1902; Toms Brook, Va., 1902-10; St. Stephen's, York, Pa., 1910-17; Supt. Hoffman Orphanage, 1917-26. Retired York, 1927.

SNIDER, FRANK WILLIAM
b. 7-5-1929, Forsyth Co., N.C. A.B. Catawba C., 1951; B.D. Lancaster Theo. Sem. 1954, p. Lincoln Chg., Maiden N.C., 1954-56; Pilgrim Ch., Lexington, N.C., 1956-60; St. John's, Burlington, N.C., 1960-65; Emanuel, Lincolnton, N.C., 1965-. Organizing Co-Pastor, St. Andrew's, Lexington, N.C., 1958.

SNYDER GEORGE ALBERT
b. 8-10-1863 Summitt Co., Ohio, d. 5-26-1942 Lancaster, Calif. A.B. Heidelburg Col. 1885; Heidelburg Sem. 1888; President, Catawba College, 1904-08., . Christ Ch. Hagerstown, Md. 1888-1904, Christ Ch. Middletown, Md. 1908. Received from Md. Cl., 10-3-1904; Dismissed to Md. Cl., 10-3-1908.

SNYDER, REUBEN WENDELL
b. 3-8-1916, Shamokin, Pa. A.B. Amherst C., 1937; B.D. Lancaster Theo. Sem., 1942. Lic. & Or. Sq. Cl. 1942, p. Asheboro, N.C., 1942-44; Trinity, Columbia, Pa., 1944-47; wc. 1947-. Sales Representative, Hamilton Watch Co.

SOLLINGER, MERLE FLOYD
b. 1-22-1909 Emlenton, Pa. A.B. Catawba C. 1932; Franklin & Marshall 1930-31; B.D. Lancaster 1935; Gettysburg Lutheran Sem., Pa.; School of Theology, Temple Univ.; Southern Lutheran Theo. Sem., Columbia, S.C. Lic. Pittsburgh Synod 1935; Ord. Potomac Synod 1945, p. Utica Chg., Frederock Co., Md. 1945-50; Greenscastle Chg., Pa. 1950-54; Bethel (Bear Creek) Mt. Pleasant, N.C. 1954-58; New Gilead, Concord, N.C. 1958-62; Raleigh, N.C. 1963-66; Waverly, Va. 1966-.

SOMMERS, LESTER ERVIN
b. 8-16-1920 Burlington, N.C. A.B. Elon Col. 1942; B.D. Lancaster Theo. Sem. 1942-45. Lic. & Ord. Southern Synod 1945. Chaplain U.S. Navy Reserve 1945-47; Studied Univ. of Calif. Pac. School Rel. 1947-49, p. Post St. E. & R. Ch., San Francisco, Calif. 1947-48; U.S.N.R. 1950-.

SORBER, WILLIAM
b. 10-4-1826, Montgomery Co., Pa., d. 12-7-1878. Chester Co., Pa. Lic. Philadelphia Cl.; Ord. 4-13-1853, N.C. Cl. as a committee. Dismissed to Philadelphia Cl., 1856. p. Davidson Charge, N.C. 1853-55.

SPANGLER, ELDEN M.
b. 1-21-1920, Reading, Pa. A.B. Albright C., 1947; B.D. Lancaster Theo. Sem., 1949. Lic. Reading Synod, 5-23-1949; Ord. Reading Synod, 5-29-1949, p. Willow St. E. & R. Willow St., Pa., 1949-55; Mt. Zion, China Grove, N.C., 1955-59; St. Stephen U.C.C., New Holland, Pa., 1959-.

STAMM, CHARLES NEVIN
b. 10-3-1904, Centre Co., Pa., d. 6-10-1961, Lancaster, Pa. Catawba C., Central Theo. Sem., Ord. 1935, p. Lower Davidson Chg. 1951-52, p. Muddy Creek Chg. 1952--61.

STANLEY, BORDER LEVI
b. 10-30-1883, Shenandoah Junction, W. Va., d. 6-25-1965. A.B. F. M. 1908; Lancaster Theo. Sem., 1908-11. Lic. Va. Cl., 1911; Ord. 10-15-1911, p. Mt. Pleasant, N.C., 1911-13; Gilead Chg. Near Concord, N.C., 1913-17; Prin. High School, Weyers Cave, Va., 1917-23; Harrisonburg, 1923-48. Retired Harrisonburg, Va., 1948.

STAUFFER, G. A.
Lic. from East Susquehanna Cl., 1-7-1899; Ord. 3-12-1899. Dismissed 9-11-1902 to Lancaster Cl. (Ohio Synod).

STEVENS, WILLARD LESLIE
b. 8-6-1917, Greenbackville, Va. B.S. State Teachers, Salisbury, Md.; Westminster Sem., 1948; Temple University, Philadelphia. Lic. Peninsula Conf. Methodist Chg., 1941; Ord. Peninsula Conf. Methodist Ch., 1948, p. Chance, Md., 1948-49; Sharystown, Md., 1949-52; Stockton, Md., 1952-54; Hayward, Mo., 1954-58; Jefferson, Md., 1958-63; Memorial, Winston-Salem, N.C., 1963-.

STRUNK, LAWRENCE NORMAN
b. 10-14-1917, Weatherly, Pa. B.A. Catawba C., 1940; B.D. Lancaster Theo. Sem. 1943. Lic. East Pa. Synod, 5-7-1943; Ord. E. Pa. Synod, 5-12-1943, p. St. Stephen's, Harrisonburg, Va., 1943-46; Supt., St. Lucas Deaconess Hospital, Fairbault, Minn., 1947-48; St. John's Ch., Kannapolis, N.C., 1948-55; Christ's, Hagerstown, Md., 1955-.

STUBBLEBINE, WILLIAM H., Ph.D.
p. First Salisbury, N.C., 1896-99, p. Newton, N.C. 1901-03. Received from Wyoming Cl. 1-28-1897; Dismissed to Miami Cl. 5-4-1898; Received from Miami Cl. 2-28-1902; Dismissed to Philadelphia Cl. 5-26-1904.

SUTHER, SAMUEL
b. 5-18-1722, Switzerland, d. 9-28-1788, S.C. Came to America, 1739, was schoolmaster in Philadelphia, 1749. Ordained in Philadelphia, p. Rowan Co., N.C. 1768-71; Guilford Co., 1771-82; Rowan Co., 1782-86; Orangeburg, S.C., 1786-88.

SWARTZ, JOHN B.
p. South Forks Chg., Catawba Co. 1922-25. Ordained 3-23-1914. Received from Tohickon Cl., Eastern Synod, 3-16-1914; Dismissed to Iowa Cl., Synod of Interior, 7-6-1915. Received from Tiffin Cl., Ohio Synod, 8-24-1922; Dismissed to Tohicken Cl., Eastern Synod, 9-5-1925.

THEUS, CHRISTIAN
b. Switzerland, d. after 1789. Examined, Lic., and Ord. by the "English Presbyterian Ministerium", Charleston, S.C. in 1739, p. St. John's Ch., Saxe-Gotha, on the Congaree River, S.C., and N.C. during 1740-80. Grave and marker in cemetery, Sandy Run Lutheran Ch., south of Columbia, S.C.

TOSH, AARON ROBERT
b. 6-21-1888, Eckly, Pa. A.B. Catawba C., 1915; Lancaster Theo. Sem. B.D. 1919; D.D. Catawba C. Lic. N.C. Cl., 5-23-1919; Ord. 6-1-1919, p. Bear Creek Chg., 1919-21; Roanoke, Va., 1921-26; Asst. to Pres. of Hood C., 1926-27; Christ Ch., Philadelphia, Pa., 1927-39; Rockwell Chg., 1939-44; First, Landis, N.C., 1944-1957. Retired 1957, Dunedin, Fla. National Roll Clerk, Evangelical & Reformed Merging Synod in 1934; Pres. of Southern Synod, 1952-54.

TREXLER, PETER M.
b. 5-18-1844, Rowan Co., N.C., d. 5-7-1923. A.B. F. & M. 1883; Lancaster, 1885; D.D. Catawba C., 1890; tutor F. & M. 1883-85. Lic. Ord. N.C. Cl. 6-2-1871, p. Central Rowan Chg., 1871-76; wc. Salisbury, 1876-78; W. Rowan Chg., 1878-80; Concord, N.C., 1885-92; W. Rowan Chg., 1892-95; Prin. schools, China Grove, N.C., 1895-96; Prof. Catawba C., 1897-1901; wc. Newton, N.C., 1901-03; Sup. Bethel Cong., 1902-03; Fin. Agt. Catawba C., 1903-04; teacher Crescent Acad., 1905-07; p. Lower Davidson Chg., 1907-09; teacher Public schools, 1909-23 (near Rockwell).

TROXELL, SAMUEL ARTHUR
b. 11-24-1892, Lorane, Pa. A.B. Catawba C., 1916; Lancaster, 1916-19; Lic. 5-23-1919; Ord., 5-25-1919; p. Rockwell, N.C., 1919-21; Ridgely, Md., 1921-23; Grace, Baltimore, 1923-37; W.C., 1937- Agt., Hancock Mutual Life Ins. Co.

TUSSEY, MAX LAFAYETTE
b. 5-19-1931, Davidson Co., N.C. B.A. Catawba C., 1954; Lancaster Theo. Sem., 1959; Lic. Southern Synod, 6-21-1959; Ord. Southern Synod, 6-21-1959; p. Rodger's Park, Kannapolis, N.C., 1959-62; Emanuel, Freysville, Pa., 1962-67; Shiloh, Faith, N.C., 1967-.

ULLRICH, EDWARD WILLIAM
b. 1-15-1905, Hazelton, Pa., d. 1-7-1957, Miami, Fla. Ursinus C., 1926; Lancaster Theo. Sem., 1929; Lic. Philadelphia Cl., 1929; Ord. E. Pa. Cl., 1929; p. Jacob's Ch., Weissport, Pa., 1929-31; Royersford, 1931-34; Selinsgrove, Pa., 1939-44; Robertson Memorial, Miami, Fla., 1944-57.

VANDERGRIFT, N. ELLIS
b. 4-10-33, Odennville, Ala. B.S. Ga. Southern Col., 1959; B.D. Southeastern Sem., 1962; Lic. Baptist 1954; Ord. Baptist Ch., Macon, Ga., 1956; p. Wades, Union Baptist Ch., Sylvania, Ga., 1956-59; Olive Branch Baptist Ch., South Hill, Va., 1960-62; Rodgers Park, Kannapolis, 1963-65; Dismissed from Southern Synod 1965.

VAUGHN, A. S.
Received 5-4-1860 from Goshenhoppen Cl. p. Newton, N.C. 1860-61. Name disappeared from roll in 1861. Received 6-14-1882 from Presbyterian Ch.; Dismissed to Presbyterian Ch., 3-24-1884. Pres. Claremont College, 1882-84.

VONDERSMITH, ALBERT V.
b. 1877, Balitimore, Md., d. 11-7-1936, Charlotte, N.C. Moody Bible Institute, Chicago, Ill.; Lic. and Ord. Ill. Conference, United Brethren Ch., 1903; Received by Allegheny Cl. Pitsburgh Synod, 11-8-1926; p. Hough Ave. Ch., Cleveland, Ohio, 1927-34; First Ch., Charlotte, N.C., 1934-36.

WAGONER, CHRISTOPHER COLUMBUS
b. 4-30-1884, Stanley Co., N.C., d. 6-16-1951, Rockwell, N.C. Mt. Pleasant C. & Inst., Catawba C., 1907; Central Theo. Sem., 1910; Lic. N.C. Cl., 1910; Ord. N.C. Cl., 7-17-1910; p. Lincoln Chg., N.C., 1910-12; Bethel-Zion Chg., High Point, N.C., Thomasville, N.C., 1912-16; First, Salisbury, N.C., 1916-23; Grace Ch., Newton, N.C., 1923-30; Trinity, Conover, N.C., 1930-38; Upper Davidson Chg., N.C., 1938-47; Retired Rockwell, N.C., 1947; Pres. of Cl. 1920.

WARLICK, CHARLES WHARTON
b. Lincoln Co., N.C., 10-11-1876, d. Salisbury, N.C., 5-10-1967. A.B. Catawba C., 1899; B.D. Lancaster 1900-03, D.D. Catawba C., 1956; Lic. N.C. Cl., 1903; Ord. Juaniata Cl., 1903; p. Friend's Cove Pa., 1903-04; Man's Choice Pa., 1904-08; Martinsburg, Pa., 1908-12; Lincoln Chg. N.C., 1913-16; Teacher Maiden 1916-21; p. Bear Creek Chg., 1921-29; Retired, Mt. Pleasant, N.C., 1930- Paterson's Rest Home, Spencer, N.C., 1966-.

WEHLER, CHARLES E.
b. 10-18-1864, New Oxford, Pa.. A.B. Ursinus Col., 1887; M.A. 1890, Ord. 1889, p. Newton, N.C., 1904-09; Pres. Ch. Ingleside, Ga., 1909-10; Prof. Hood. Col., 1911-23; p. Faith, Baltimore, Md., 1923-. Received from Philadelphia Cl. 10-3-1904; Dismissed to Atlanta Presbytery, Presbyterian Ch. 9-12-1910.

WELKER, GEORGE WILLIAM
b. 11-3-1817, near Greencastle, Pa., d. 7-9-1894, Lamont, N.C. A.B. Marshall C., 1839; Lancaster, 1840-41; D.D. U. N.C., 1870; D.D. Heidelberg C., 1871; Lic. 3-27-1842 N.C. Cl.; Ord. 3-27-1842; p. Guilford Chg., N.C., 1842-92; Retired 1893.

WELKER, HARVEY A.
b. 7-1-1869, Red Hill, Pa., d. 2-6-1952, Burlington, N.C. Ursinus C., Union Theo. Sem., Auburn Theo. Sem., 1896; p. Pottstown, Pa., 1896-99; Bluffton, Ind., 1899-1908; Royer's Ford, Pa., 1908-14; Faith Chg., N.C., 1914-23; First Ch., Burlington, N.C., 1923-32; Mt. Crawford, Va., -----46; Retired Burlington, N.C., 1946, Homewood Ch. Home, 1951-52.

WENTZ, BRUCE ALBION
b. 11-13-1893, near Glen Rock, Pa. A.B. F.&M., 1915; B.D. Lancaster, 1918; Ph.D. John Hopkins University, 1928; Lic. W. Sq. Cl., 1918; Ord. Juniata Cl., 1919; p. Loysburg, Pa., 1919-20; Teachers Boys' High School, Frederick, Md., 1921-22; Prof. History and Bible, Catawba C., 1922-23; student, John Hopkins University, 1923-1926; Prof. Education and Psychol. Catawba C., 1926-29; Prof. Phil. and Psychol. Catawba C., 1929-1965. Retired Salisbury, N.C.

WERNER, WILLIAM B.
b. 12-7-1861, Mountain Berks Co., Pa., d. 7-22-1931, Tuscarora, Md. A.B. F.&M. 1889; Lancaster, 1890-93; Lic. Leh. Cl.; Ord. Goshn Cl., 1893; p. Schwenksville, Pa., 1893-1908; W.C., Bernville, 1908-09; Hudson, Ind., 1900-12; Concord, N.C., 1912-15; Brunswick, Md., 1915-17; Supt. Nazareth Children's Home, N.C., 1917-22; p. Burkittsville, Md., 1922-31; Retired Tuscarora, Md., 1931.

WEST, JAMES KING
b. 9-13-1930, Keysville, Va. University of Richmond, Lynchburg Col., Southern Baptist Theo. Sem., Ph.D. Vanderbilt University, 1961; p. Crystal Hill Baptist, Va., 1957-58; Lancing-Wartburg Presbyterian Chg., Lancing, Tennessee, 1958-59; Professor, Catawba College, 1961-; Transferred So. Synod 1964-.

WEYBURG, SAMUEL
(son of Casper D. Weyburg, pastor of Race St. German Reformed Ch. Phil.)
b. 9-19-1773, Philadelphia, Pa., d. 6-18-1833, Mo. Studied Law; Then Theo. Ordained by Coetus of Pa., privately in 1793; p. Lincoln, Rowan, and Cabarrus Cos., N.C., 1793-98; First pastor in Ohio, 1799- also in Mo., Ind.

WHETSTONE, CLARENCE E.
p. Grace, Newton, 1931-32; Received from Md. Cl., Potomac Synod, 1-12-1931; Dismissed to E. Pa. Cl., Eastern Synod, 11-30-1932.

WHISENHUNT, ROY CHAST
b. 1-24-1904, Hickory, N.C. A.B. Lenior Rhyne C., 1927; Central Theo. Sem., 1930; Princeton Theo. Sem., Th.M., 1931; Lic. 5-7-1930; Ord. 6-28-1931; p. Faith, N.C. Chg., 1930-38; First, Winston-Salem, N.C., 1938-42; Trinity, Concord, N.C., 1942-52; St. John's, Hamilton, Ohio, 1952-56; Ursinus, Rockwell, N.C., 1956-62; Memorial, Lexington, N.C., 1962-; Pres. N.C. Cl. 1938.

WHISTON, LIONEL ABNEY, JR.
b. 5-30-1918, Luneburg, Mass. A.B. Bates C., 1939; B.D. Andover Newton Theo. Sem., 1942; Th.D., Harvard University, 1951; Lic. Suffolk South, Mass. Conf., C.C. Ch., 1940; Ord. Middlesex Association, Mass. Conf., 1942; p. Phillipston Cong. Ch., 1941-42; First Ch., Newbury, Mass., 1942-48; Prof. Religion, Catawba C., 1948-56; Prof. of Old Testament, Eden Theo. Sem., 1956-.

WHITENER, MILTON
b. 6-17-1881, Newton, N.C., d. 11-17-1952. A.B. Catawba C., 1903; Lancaster, 1906; Lic. 5-12-1906; Ord. 7-20-1906; p. Conover, N.C., 1906-08; Timberville, Va., 1908-12; Lovettsville, Va., 1912-15; Littlestown, Pa., 1915-21; High Point, N.C., 1921-28; Endowment Sec. Catawba C. and Treas. So. Synod, 1928-45; p. Lower Stone Chg., 1946-51; Retired 1952; Treas. of Cl. and Synod for 31 yrs.

WHITENER, STERLING H.
b. 6-27-1921, Kuling Ki, China; AB. Catawba C. 1945; M.A. Yale 1946; D.D. Catawba Col., 1967; Lic. 7-1-45 Southern Synod; Ord. 7-1-45, Salisbury, N.C. Southern Synod, China Missionary 1946-1967; Prof. Catawba and Livingstone College 1967-.

WHITENER, STERLING WILFONG
b. 8-14-1894, Catawba Co., N.C., d. 9-8-1950, Hickory, N.C. Catawba C., 1916; Central Theo. Sem., 1919; Cornell U., 1940-; Lic. 5-7-1919 N.C. Cl.; Ord. 5-7-1919; Missionary to China, 1919-; p. Emanuel Chg., Thomasville, N.C., Guilford Charge, N.C., 1941-1946.

WILLIAM, E. GARVER
b. 1845, Jefferson, York Co., Pa., d. 8-23-1920, Tabor, N.C. Ursinus C., 1875; Ursinus Theo. Sem., 1877; D.D. 1897; p. Mt. Pleasant, N.C.; Supt., Nazareth Orphan's Home, 1910-11. Received from Eastern Ohio Cl., Ohio Synod, 5-8-1907.

WISE, JOSEPH WILLIAM
b. 10-31-1940, Landis, N.C. A.B. Catawba C., 1962; B.D. Lancaster Theo. Sem., 1965; p. Asst. Trinity United Ch. of Christ, Conover, N.C., 1965-67; Hanover, Pa., 1967-.

WOLFINGER, ADAM D.
p. Rockingham, Va., 1895-1900; President, Catawba College, 1916-1923; Received from Philadelphia Cl., Eastern Synod, 3-17-1916; Dismissed to Eastern Ohio Cl., Ohio Synod, 11-28-1923.

WOODS, CLARENCE
b. 2-11-1882, Julian, N.C., d. 12-23-1941. A.B. Catawba C., 1907; Lancaster-special-1907-10; Lic. 5-20-1910 N.C. Cl.; Ord. 5-20-1910; p. Thomasville, N.C., 1910-14; Roanoke, Va., 1914-17; YMCA in U.S. and France, 1917-19; p. Winchester, Va., 1919-22; w.c., Roanoke, 1922-24; Middlebrook, 1924-25; Wilson Ave., Columbus, Ohio 1926-28; Asst. Grace, Akron, 1928-29; w.c., Greensboro, N.C. 1929-41.

YEARICK, HOMER FRAZIER
b. 5-8-1919, Jacksonville, Pa. A.B. Catawba C., 1940; B.D. Lancaster Theo. Sem., 1943; Lic. and Ord. Central Pa. Synod, 1943; Chaplain, U.S. Navy, 1943-46; p. Memorial, Winston-Salem, N.C., 1946-47; New Berlin Chg., Pa., 1948-49; w.c., Duke University, Durham, N.C., 1949-50; p. Mt. Hope Whitsett N.C., 1950-52; Missionary to Japan; Saxton, Pa.; Paul's Chapel, Lexington, N.C., 1963-64; w.c., Beaufort, N.C.

YEARICK, JONAS LEIDY
b. 7-21-1870, Hilltown, Bucks Co., Pa., d. 11-3-1936. Lancaster, 1904-07; Lic. Tohic. Cl.; Ord. N.C. Cl., 1907; p. Maiden, N.C., 1907-08; E. Rowan Chg., Rockwell, 1908-12; McConnellsburg, Pa., 1912-18; Boswell, 1918-20; Export, 1920-27; Ruffsdale, 1927-28; Harrison City, 1928-33; w.c., Souderton, 1933-35; p. Saegertown, 1935-36.

ZAUGG, FREDERICK SAMUEL
b. 6-9-1871 Salt Creek Twsp., Wayne Co., Chio, d. 10-17-1941, Wooster, Ohio. Received from Lincoln Cl., Synod of the Interior, 1-18-1912; Dismissed to Miami Cl., 12-29-1912.

ZECHIEL, ALBERT H.
p. Burlington, N.C., 1916-1918; Received from Tiffin Cl., Ohio Synod, 6-22-1916; Dismissed to Dayton Presbytery, Presbyterian Ch., U.S.A., 11-22-1918.

ZULAUF, NORMAN CHARLES
b. 6-3-1906, Baltimore, Md. John's Hopkins, 1924-26; A.B. Elmhurst, 1929; B.D. Eden Theo. Sem., 1932; D.D. Elmhurst C., 1957; Lic. Atlantic Dist., Evangelical Synod, N. America, 6-19-1932; p. Bethel Ch., Rockford, Ill., 1932-37; Robertson Memorial, Miami, Fla., 1937-44; Hope Ch., St. Louis, Mo., 1944-64; Hope U.C.C., Rockledge, Fla., 1964-66; Asst. Past., St. John's, Evansville, Ind., 1966-.

Bibliography

Bernheim, G. D., History of the Evangelical Lutheran Church, 1902.
Clapp, Jacob C., Editor, Historic Sketch of the Reformed Church in North Carolina, 1908.
Dunn, David and Others, A History of the Evangelical and Reformed Church, 1961.
Fries, Adelaide L., Records of the Moravians in North Carolina, Vol. 1-7, 1922.
Garrison, J. Silor, The History of the Reformed Church in Virginia, 1948.
Good, James I., History of the Reformed Church in the United States, 1725-1792, 1899.
Good, James I., History of the Reformed Church in the United States in the Nineteenth Century, 1911.
Hammer, Carl, Rhinelanders on the Yadkin; the Story of the Pennsylvania Germans in Rowan and Cabarrus Counties, 1943.
Harabaugh, Henry, Fathers of the Reformed Church, Vols. 1-3, 1857-1858.
Heisler, D. Y., Fathers of the Reformed Church, Vols. 4-6, 1831-1888.
Hinke, William J., Ministers of the Reformed Congregations in Pennsylvania and other Colonies in the Eighteenth Century, 1951.
Klein, H. M. J., The History of the Eastern Synod of the Reformed Church in the United States, 1943.
Lady, David B., The History of the Pittsburgh Synod of the Reformed Church in the United States, 1920.
Leonard, Jacob C., History of Catawba College, 1927.
Leonard, Jacob C., Centennial History of Davidson County, 1927.
Leonard, Jacob C., History of the Southern Synod, Evangelical and Reformed Church, 1940.
Lyerly, William C., Nazareth Orphans' Home, 1936.
Moose, Thomas L., Nazareth Orphans' Home, 1956.
Morgan, J. L., Editor, History of the Lutheran Church in North Carolina, 1953.
Nixon, A., Daniel's Evangelical Lutheran and Reformed Churches, 1898.
Patterson, Mrs. R. E., and Others, Facts, Faces, Memories, 1939.
Presler, Charles J., Jr., Editor, History of Catawba County, 1954.
Richards, George W., History of the Theological Seminary of the Reformed Church in the United States, 1825-1934; Evangelical and Reformed Church, 1934-1952, 1952.
Rights, Douglas L., Records of the Moravians in North Carolina, Vol. 8, 1954.
Rumley, E. C., Sr., History of St. Mark's United Church of Christ, 1961.
Shepherd, Banks D., New Gilead Church, a History of the German Reformed People on the Coldwater, 1966.
Sherrill, William L., Annals of Lincoln County, 1937.
Snider, Frank W., Early Reformed Churches in the Carolinas, 1954.
Snider, Frank W., Editor, The First Church, Davidson County, 1957.
Welker, George W., A Historical Sketch of the Classis of North Carolina, 1895.
Wheeler, John H., Historical Sketches of North Carolina, 1851.
Whitsett, W. Thornton, History of Brick Church and the Clapp Family, 1925.

DOCUMENTS

———. Constitution and By-Laws of the Evangelical and Reformed Church, 1940.
———. Constitution and By-Laws of the United Church of Christ, 1965.
———. Minutes. The Classis of North Carolina, Reformed Church in the United States, 1831-1940.
Keppel, Alvin R., Report Volumes, Board of Trustees Meetings of Catawba College, 1942-1962.
Dearborn, Donald C., Report Volumes, Board of Trustees Meetings of Catawba College, 1963-1968.
———. Minutes. Southern Synod of the Evangelical and Reformed Church, 1940-1965.
———. Minutes. Southern Synod, Acting Association of the United Church of Christ, 1966.
———. Minutes. Southern Conference of the United Church of Christ, 1966.
———. Minutes. Board of Trustees of Catawba College, 1951-1966
———. Minutes. Woman's Missionary Society of the Reformed Church, 1897-1939.
———. Minutes. Women's Guild of the Evangelical and Reformed Church, 1940-1964.
———. Manuscripts, Anniversary Brochures and Bulletins of the Churches on file in the Archives at Catawba College.
———. Year Books: The Reformed Church in the United States. The Evangelical and Reformed Church.

PERIODICALS

———. The College Visitor, 1887-1894.
———. The Reformed Church Corinthian, 1894-1896.
———. The Reformed Church Standard, 1903-1939.
———. The Evangelical and Reformed Church Standard, 1940-1966.
———. Evangelical and Reformed Church, a New Venture of Faith, 1935.

Index of Names

Names of congregational visitors, charter and committee members do not appear in this index. A roster of pastors appears at the end of each church story. Ministerial statistics appear on pages 474 thru 494.